If Only Walls Could Talk

By

Kim Gregory-Baney

Copyright ©2019 by Kim Gregory Baney

All rights reserved.
Published independently in the United States using KDP Publishing
ISBN: 978-17-9085-882-8

1st Edition: December 2019

All reproduced newspaper articles, unless
otherwise noted, are 3rd party articles taken from
The Times Union, P.O. Box 1448, Warsaw, IN 46581-1448.
Years and dates of publications are
listed throughout the book.

Photograph credits appear on pages 495-496.

All driver names are listed as they were
spelled in the race articles, unless a misspelling
was confirmed, then it was corrected.

1949-50, 1954-59 Newspaper microfilm research
conducted by Marjorie Priser

For additional photos not used in the book, check out the Warsaw Speedway Historical Website at: www.warsawspeedway.net

Historical Notes

1949 – A Dream is Born	Page 7
1951 - Joe Hamsher & Milo Clase Emerge	Page 28
1952 - A Year of Transition & Improvement	Page 40
1953 - The "Hoot" Gibson Era	Page 53
1960 - "Wings" & Things	Page 107
1970 - Speed & More Speed	Page 216
1978 - Time for a Change	Page 300
1981 - Grindle Gives it a Go	Page 341
1983 - Monty Miller & a Track to be Reckoned With	Page 368
1989 - Gaerte, Chapman, & Too Much of a Good Thing	Page 461
1990 – The Black Flag Falls	Page 476

"Articles of Interest"

July 13, 1949 - Warsaw Hot Rod Racer Injured
Fred Boggs Sustains Broken Collarbone

July 15, 1949 - Speedway Races Over WRSW Network

July 7, 1951 – 4,500 Race Fans See Bill Holland At Local Speedway

Aug. 28, 1953 – Stock Car Racers Speak at Rotary

Aug. 9, 1958 – Pit Mechanic Killed,
Race Track Death Mars Final Night of Fair

Aug. 20, 1960 – Race Driver Critcally Hurt in Crash at Warsaw Speedway

July 4, 1963 – Race Car Hits, Kills N. Manchester Mechanic At Local Speedway

July 23, 1966 – Crash At Local Speedway

Aug. 9, 1968 – Flagman Performs 'Under Fire' At Local Speedway

Oc.t 13, 1971 – Warsaw Champ Elliott Loses Sight of Eye

Aug. 14, 1972 – Towing Race Car, Auto Goes Out of Control on U.S. 30

May 31, 1977 – Tragedies Mar Holiday For Families of Three

July 8, 1978 – Drivers and Fans Boycott Warsaw Speedway

July 25, 1978 – Warsaw Drivers Buy Out Gibson, to Race Saturday

Aug. 25, 1978 – World of Outlaws Visit

Sept. 5, 1986 & May 21, 1988 – A Young Jeff Gordon Visits The Track

Late-Fall, 1988 - Warsaw Race Track Leases To 2 Private Individuals

June 28, 1989 - Fair Board Sued - Suit Seeks Speedway Closure, Plus $500,000

July 1, 1989 - Race Track Case Could Hinge On Precedent Case

Aug. 5, 1989 – Tony Stewart's Only Visit in a Midget

Aug. 28, 1989 – WASP's Request Swatted Away

June 12, 1990 – Speedway To Close

July 19, 1990 – Warsaw Speedway To Close
Fair Board Approves Out-Of-Court Pact; Racing Ends August 11

July 20, 1990 – Race Fans Frustrated By Decision

July 21, 1990 – Potpourri ~As The Dust Settles On Warsaw Speedway

Aug. 11, 1990 – Black Flag Falls On Warsaw Auto Racing

To Butch and Tony ~

*Thank you... Your continued encouragement and positive enthusiasm kept this dream alive.
I wish you were here to see this day finally happen.
Love and miss you both.*

"Good evening, racing fans, this is Milo Clase, WRSW Sports Director, speaking to you direct from the pagota at the Warsaw Speedway where in just a moment we will bring to you racing thrills, spills and chills, as we paint a word picture of racing at its best."

This we have said every Saturday and holiday night for the entire season and have enjoyed every lap, every exciting moment – these are the kind of thrills no other sport boasts.

If you are not a racing fan, stay away, beware! It is a disease, it seeps into the blood stream, and there is no cure – you get only temporary relief by going to every race.

The cooperation has been swell, the boys are good sports in a dangerous hobby. Sometimes tempers flare, but it is understandable. Next season don't start going to the races or you too, will get race fever. IT'S CONTAGIOUS!!

Good night,

Milo Clase

Taken from the Warsaw/New Paris 1951 Souvenir Edition Racing Program

Jeff Culp & Wheaties Smith ~ 1951
What racing's all about....

1949
A Dream is Born

Considered one of the most scenic speedways in the Midwest, the Warsaw Speedway opened its gates with much celebration on Saturday, June 11, 1949, in front of an estimated 4,000 spectators. The track, located on the north shores of Winona Lake at the Kosciusko County Fairgrounds, had been used for horse racing for several years, but in 1949, the fairgrounds decided to try this up-and-coming sport, auto racing. Phil Tyrrell was hired as the Warsaw Speedway Managing Director, who saw to it that the initial races were full of exciting thrills, variety, and great media coverage! Tyrrell was not just a local racetrack promotor, but had a history of over 25 years of managing actors and actresses and helping many famous stars get their start in the entertainment business. Besides several local newspaper articles, the news of the racetrack spread rapidly through word-of-mouth to many other states, and by July of '49, the Speedway was hosting its first live broadcast of midget races on the Hoosier Radio Network which was also broadcast on Warsaw's local WRSW radio station.

The Warsaw Speedway continued in its huge popularity drawing drivers from all over the Midwest on a regular basis for the midget races sanctioned initially by the United Automobile Racing Association of Chicago. Hot Rod races were added also within the first year of racing which added the excitement of many local drivers getting into the act, and more variety for the speedway. Both types of racing were highly supported and attended.

May 25, 1949
Warsaw Plans Midget Racing

Warsaw, Ind. – Auto races will begin here June 4 on a new quarter mile track now being constructed at the Kosciusko county fairgrounds, on the north shore of Winona Lake. A contract for use of the grounds was signed Monday by officers of the fair association and Phil Tyrrell, of Winamac, managing director of Hoosier Speedways. Eight races of midget cars will be held on opening night. Lights and extra seats are now being installed. Seats will be provided for approximately 3,000 spectators.

Help Wanted Ads, Thursday, June 9, 1949

> **WANTED**
> GIRLS & BOYS FOR SPEEDWAY CONCESSION STANDS
> We will use twenty boys and girls for each Saturday night 5:30 p. m. until 11:30 p. m., during the summer months at the Auto Races. Report to Mr. Phil Tyrrell, Warsaw Speedway Secretary's office (Fairgrounds) Thursday, between 3 and 4 o'clock.
> **WARSAW SPEEDWAY**

> ★ Help Wanted ★ Help Wanted
>
> ## WANTED
>
> MEN FOR PARKING CARS, AND GUARDS AT THE NEW WARSAW SPEEDWAY EACH SATURDAY NIGHT DURING SUMMER MONTHS OF AUTO RACES. REPORT TO MR. PHIL TYRRELL, SECRETARY'S OFFICE, (FAIRGOUNDS), THURSDAY BETWEEN 3 AND 4 O'CLOCK.
>
> ## WARSAW SPEEDWAY

Saturday, June 11, 1949
Midget Races Make Big Hit

Capacity Crowd At Opening Events. Warsaw's new speedway, on the north bank of Winona Lake, at the fairgrounds, opened to a capacity crowd of an estimated 4,000 persons Saturday night. They saw a thrill-packed program of powerful midget racers, fighting for lucrative shares of heavy prize money.

No one was seriously injured during the opening night's racing, although four of the tiny cars went into spins and slid through the inner walls of the track. One driver was treated by doctors after a chunk of packed dirt from the track was thrown into his face as he sped down the straight-of-way at 80 miles per hour. That was Chuck Brown, of Crown Point.

A fire truck, ambulance and doctor stood by throughout the program in case of major accidents. Officials of the racing circuit said that three of their steady drivers were now in hospitals and could not appear Saturday night due to injuries received during the past ten days. Still, there were some 40 drivers and cars there, all members of the United Auto Racing association of Chicago.

Fast time trials, preceding the actual races, were broadcast over WRSW by the Kaufman Motor Sales, of Warsaw. This program will be aired every Saturday night from 7:30 o'clock until 8 o'clock during the racing season.

City Officials There. The pace car for the first race was a new Buick convertible driven by Henry Schwierking, of Warsaw. City and county officials rode the first lap around the track. They were Mayor Charles H. Rice, Police Chief Roy Adams, Fire Chief Carl Latta, Prosecuting Attorney Gene B. Lee, and Sheriff Ray Henderson.

Track managers said that the drivers from Indiana, Illinois, and California were highly complementary when speaking of the new track, and said they would spread the word this week among other drivers, probably leading to a tripled field for next Saturday night's races. Track officials were planning to continue work on the track this week, repairing and improving soft spots disclosed in the opening night's program.

Petey Peterson, of Fort Wayne, won the time trials with his fastest time of 18.29 seconds around the quarter-mile track. The first race was won by Ferde Scholtes, of Hollywood,

Calif. His time for the 10 laps was 3:00.75. The second race, 10 laps, went to Ray Elliott, the third race to Petey Peterson, the fourth race to Paul Anderson, the fifth race to Ferde Scholtes.

The first feature race, a 15-lap Australian pursuit event, was won by Hank Nickaza, and the big event on the program, the 25-lap finale, was won by Ray Elliott. Pete Peterson was second and Tony Saylor was third.

Saturday, June 18, 1949
Ray Elliott Wins Feature Race At Warsaw Speedway

A large crowd witnessed the midget auto races Saturday night at the new Warsaw Speedway, located at the county fairgrounds. It was the second weekly race car show and attracted drivers from Illinois, Indiana, Florida, New Jersey and Minnesota.

Time trials preceded the seven races. In the race against time, Ray Elliott, of Lockport, Ill., turned in the fastest lap of 19.02 seconds. Elliott also won the featured 25-lap event and finished fourth in three of the other 10-lap races.

Due to heavy rains during the week, drivers could not get up as much speed as they did a week ago, but there nevertheless was plenty of excitement as they slipped and slid around the turns.

Joe Gersick, of Paterson, N.J., was winner of the first race, with Paul Ambrose, Chicago, second; Hank Mykaba, Chicago Heights, third, and Ray Elliott, Lockport, Ill., fourth. The second race was won by Tony Saylor, of Rockdale, Ill., with Red Basher, Wooddale, Ill., second, and Ferdie Scholte, third. Chuck Brown, of Crown Point, won the third race, followed by Larry Johnson, Minneapolis, Minn., and Jack Boucher, a former Warsaw boy, was third.

More Winners. Al Alpren, of Chicago, won the fourth race. Walter Johnson, of Chicago, was second, and Ham Dempsey, of Joliet, Ill., was third. Winner of the fifth race was Larry Johnson, of Minneapolis, with Tony Saylor of Rockdale, second, and Ferdie Sholte, third. The sixth race, a 15-lap feature, was won by Chris Willy, of Miami, Fla., with Ham Dempsey second, and Bill Weed, of Oak Park, third.

The seventh and feature race on the program was won by Ray Elliott. Red Basher, of Woodale, Ill., was second; Larry Johnson, Minneapolis, third; Walter Johnson, Chicago, fourth; Ferdie Scholte, fifth; Tony Saylor, sixth; Joe Gersick, seventh; Paul Ambrose, eight; Joe Bursa, of Joliet, ninth; and Hank Mykaza, tenth.

Phil Tyrrell, managing director of the new speedway, said there will be more thrill-packed races next Saturday night, and with some help from the weather man, the track should be in top condition.

Saturday, June 25, 1949
New Jersey Racer Wins Feature At Warsaw Speedway

The Warsaw Speedway track record for one lap was broken in the time trials Saturday night as Joe Gersich, of Paterson, J.J., sped around the oval in 17.91 seconds. It was one of the highlights of the third weekly midget auto races, held before a large crowd at the fairgrounds.

The 25-lap feature race, final event on the program, was won by Gersich, with Ray Elliott, of Joliet, Ill., finishing second; Larry Johnson, of Minnesota, third, Chuck Rodee, of Chicago, fourth; Pete Peterson, Chicago, fifth, and Ferdie Scholtes, of Los Angeles, sixth.

In that final race, Dick Cashmere, of Streator, Ill., collapsed on the track when struck by an exhaust stack. He fell from his racer and was unconscious for 10 minutes in the Bilby ambulance before being revived by Dr. George Haymond. Cashmere, who was hit in the head and arm, was removed to his home in Streator.

Races are scheduled again on Saturday night of this week. The track was in excellent shape last Saturday night, and with the addition of brick dust this week, it should be even faster.

Results of Races. In addition to the feature race, several other races provided thrills. The results of those races were as follows:

First Race – Joe Gersich, Paterson, N.J., 1st; Ham Dempsey, Joliet, Ill., second; Chuck Rodee, Chicago, third.

Second Race – Pete Peterson, Chicago, first; Ray Elliott, Joliet, second; Red Boscher, Wooddale, Ill., third.

Third Race – Larry Johnson, Minnesota, first; Sunny Bessett, Joliet, second; Cliff Adams, Elmhurst, Ill., third.

Fourth Race – Ferdie Scholtes, Los Angeles, first; Joe Bersa, Joliet, second; Al Linke, Michigan City, third.

Handicap Race – Ray Elliott, Joliet, first; Pete Peterson, Chicago, second; Larry Johnson, Minnesota, third.

Semi-Feature Race – Sunny Bessett, Joliet, first; Cliff Adams, Elmhurst, Ill., second; Norm Lignor, Joliet, third; Bud Johnson, Terre Haute, fourth; Chuck Brown, Crown Point, fifth; Bud Watts, Joliet, sixth.

Wednesday, July 6, 1949
AROUND OUR TOWN AND COUNTY

Some Like 'Em Better —Quite a few people, after sampling the "stock car" races here last week, decided they liked them better than the midget races. Stock cars are just ordinary automobiles. Racing rules prohibit the owners from fixing them up in any special way. In other words – no "souping" to increase their speed and power by means of mechanical alterations. But the drivers have their own ways of getting the most out of them. During the recent race, we got talking to a fellow who had just retired from the game. Had a broken arm and a beginner was working out his car in the race. This retired speedster told us how each of the tires is pumped up to a different pressure to take up the shock. He looked over the field at the start of one race and told just how he would go about winning it. The winner did it just that way too, running in second gear on the outside of the track until he reached the first turn, then cutting in to freeze out all but the leader and eventually squeezing the leader away from the inside and going on for first money.

Just for fun. Our racing friend said that stock car racing is an expensive hobby. The participants do it because they like it and for no other reason. Most of them, he said, own used car lots in the cities. After watching the way they hammer their vehicles around the track, you would suppose that the drivers would be afraid to use any tires but the best. However, they pick up second-hand ones for two bucks or so. Since they skid the cars, they don't want much tread. In fact, on an asphalt track, the tires have to be completely bald or they will cause the cars to upset. People might have noticed in the race the other night that the Buick kept riding the outer wall. Our friend said that Buicks always performed that way on clay tracks and seldom did much good. On asphalt tracks, they are hard to beat he told us. One stock racer, swinging a little too wide, grazed the fence in front of the grandstands and gave the spectators a chill before bringing his auto under control. Had he broken the rail, all racing would have been stopped until it was replaced, we were advised.

Wednesday, July 13, 1949
Warsaw Hot Rod Racer Injured
Fred Boggs Sustains Broken Collarbone

Fred Boggs, outstanding Warsaw hot-rod race driver, suffered a broken collarbone and fractured ribs Tuesday night when his hot-rod racer crashed into a fence on a South Bend track. Boggs, 28, married and the father of two children, is in the Memorial Hospital at South Bend. His condition is not serious. Boggs and his family live west of Warsaw, on State Road 25.

Freddie Boggs, Warsaw

Just last weekend, Boggs had broken track records in his hot-rod racer at the Sisters Lake and New Paris quarter-mile race tracks. Sisters Lake is located near Dowagiac, Mich. His luck appeared to be holding out for him Tuesday night at South Bend when he finished first in one heat (10 laps) and second in another 10-lap race which featured the 4 fastest cars in the field.

However, in the feature race, a 25-lap affair, his car and hot-rod went into a spin while rounding a curve with several other cars. Boggs' car hit the fence, bounced off and turned over. Boggs was not thrown from his racer. His car, No. 66, was badly damaged. Boggs and Perry Bunch, of Columbia City, had built the hot-rod racer, which is said to be a real speed demon. Boggs also has another hot-rod racer, No. 14.

Friday, July 15, 1949
Speedway Races Over Network
WRSW To Originate Feature Program

The Warsaw Speedway has been chosen as the scene for the week's top event by the Hoosier Network, which will broadcast Saturday's midget auto races direct from the speedway, located at the county fairgrounds in Warsaw. WRSW will be the originating station for the broadcast, which will feature a description of the race track festivities by Bill Mollenhour from 7:30 to 8:30pm, Daylight Saving Time.

The half-hour broadcast will include ten minutes of time trials, five minutes of interviews with some of the tip drivers and mechanics, and 15 minutes of a description of a race between the fastest qualifying cars of the season. Kaufman Motor Sales, of Warsaw, sponsors the broadcasts each Saturday night over WRSW.

The midget races, staged by the United Automobile Racing association of Chicago, were cancelled last week because of rain, but the stage is all set for a big night of race thrills this Saturday.

Expect 35 Cars – Right now the track is in good condition, and more than 35 cars and drivers are expected to be on hand when the time trials start at 7 o'clock. The first race will get underway at 8:30.

The feature race will set off the spark of feuding between Ray Elliott, Wally Johnson and perhaps Ham Dempsey, who was shaken up when he and Corky Singer tangled in a spill at Gill Stadium on Sunday. Singer is now resting in a Chicago hospital. These three have been battling it out for top honors at the Warsaw oval, with Elliott holding three wins in four races.

It has also been announced that the Hot Rods association of Chicago has been scheduled to provide a night of hot rod racing here on Saturday night, July 23. The stock cars, which made such a big hit with Warsaw Speedway fans a few weeks ago, will be the feature on Saturday night, July 30.

It is also planned by the American Motorcycle association to stage a six-star race here during the month of August. This event is slated to bring together 75 of the nation's champion motorcycle racing stars. The date for the motorcycle races will be announced later.

Saturday, July 16, 1949
Walter Johnson Cops Feature at Warsaw Speedway

Walter Johnson of Chicago didn't win one of the 10-lap heats at the Warsaw Speedway Saturday night, but he saved his speed for the 25-lap feature race, which he won over such fine competitors as Chuck Rodee, of Chicago, and Ray Elliott of Lockport, Ill who finished second and third respectively.

A large crowd was at the county fairgrounds to see the races, and countless people throughout the state heard a radio broadcast of part of the track action over WRSW and the entire Hoosier Network.

Honors for posting the fastest qualifying time in the time trials went to Paul Ambrose of Chicago who circled the quarter mile dirt track in 18.28 seconds. The semi-final race was won by Ferdie Scholtes of Los Angeles, Calif., with George Van of Oaklawn, second, Al Alpern, of Chicago, third, and Curt Carlson of Plano, Ill., fourth.

Winners of the other races were Elliott, who edged out Tony Saylor of Rockdale, Ill in the Handicap event; Bill Weed of Oak Park, Ill, who won the first heat; Elliott again was winner of the second heat; Ambrose, who beat out Scholtes in heat three; and Red Boscher, of Wooddale, who captured the fourth heat. On Saturday night of this week, the lightning fast hot rod racers are scheduled to be here for the first time.

Saturday, July 23, 1949
Dick Geyer Wins Hot-Rod Honors Saturday Night

Dick Geyer, of Goshen, was the star performer at the hot-rod auto races, held before a large crowd Saturday night at the Warsaw Speedway, located at the county fairgrounds in this city. Geyer, driving a car owned by the injured Fred Boggs, of Warsaw, won every race he was in, including the feature 25-lap event.

Boggs suffered a broken collarbone a few weeks ago when his car hit a wall during a race on a South Bend track. He is still wearing a cast. Driving in his place here Saturday night, Geyer won the first 10-lap race; the fourth race, which was a six-lap affair for the four fastest qualifying cars; the Australian pursuit race, and the feature race. Other races were won by Sonny Stegmann, of Aurora, Ill., Earl Walker, of Sandwich, Ill., and Reb Hart, of Berwyn, Ill.

Fred McKown, Jr., a local entry, placed third in the 10-lap race won by Walker, and Robert Miner, of Winona Lake, placed fourth in the same heat. Miner also placed third in the fifth race, won by Hart. Racing at the speedway will continue on Saturday night of this week.

Wednesday, August 3, 1949
Hot Rod Races Friday Night
Thirty Speedy Cars Will Compete Here

There will be hot rod racing this Friday night at the Warsaw Speedway. Phil Tyrrell, managing director of the speedway, announced Wednesday that the usual date of racing has been changed from Saturday night for this week only in order to present for the first time the Midway Hot Rod Association of Goshen.

The Goshen association is composed of a group of Hoosier drivers who have been making great progress at the South Bend, Sisters Lake and New Paris race tracks. There are thirty cars, including those driven by Fred Boggs of Warsaw, Ralph Weber, Columbia City; Dick Geyer, Goshen; Fred McKown, Jr., Warsaw; Ebe Yoder, Goshen; Bob Miner, Winona Lake; Baldy Metzger, Goshen; Melvin Miller, Claypool; Bud Rink, Millersburg; John Nisley, Goshen; and Dick Morley, of Kalamazoo. Boggs, however, suffered a broken collar bone three weeks ago while racing at South Bend and will not be inaction here this week. His No. 66 car was driven by Geyer in the first hot rod races held here a few weeks ago, and Geyer won every race he was in, including the feature.

Experiment With Date? Many fans in the Warsaw area have requested a Friday night race, and speedway officials are using Friday night of this week as an experiment to see whether future races will be run on Friday or the usual Saturday program.

A large crowd is expected to be on hand Friday night when the time trials start at 7 o'clock. The first race is scheduled for 8:30. The drive-in system of the speedway is getting a big play from the fans who enjoy the races from their own cars. It also works as an answer to the "babysitting" problem.

Saturday, August 5, 1949
Large Crowd Sees Midget Races at Warsaw Speedway

A large crowd attended the hot rod races held Friday night at the Warsaw Speedway. Fans enjoyed several fast, close races, in which there were some minor crashes, but no injuries.

Four Kosciusko drivers were among the participants. They were George Woodling, of Warsaw, Bob Miner, of Winona Lake, Gene Smith, of Syracuse and Melvin Miller, of Claypool. Dick Morley, of Kalamazoo, won the feature event, winning over Rut Ralston, Goshen, second; Ralph Weber, Columbia City, third; Chuck Grover, Goshen, fourth; Bob Miner, Winona Lake, fifth; John Nisley, Goshen, sixth; and Ebe Yoder, Goshen, seventh.

Morley also won the first heat over Ralph Kikes of Millersburg and Yoder, who were second and third respectively. Other heat winners were Ralston, Stan Shidecker of Sandwich, Ill; Weber twice and Yoder, who captured the semi-final event.

Saturday, August 13, 1949
Large Crowd Sees Midget Races at Warsaw Speedway

George Wilkins of Indianapolis captured the 25-lap feature and also won the third heat and placed second in the midget auto races held Saturday night before a large crowd at the Warsaw Speedway. Wilkins and 16 other members of the new Mid-State Racing Association competed in a total of seven races following the time trials with a mark of 18.32. Wilkins was close behind with his qualifying time of 18.37 seconds.

Wilkins Wins Feature. Wilkins finished ahead of Lefty Hirschman of Crown Point and Dick

Windsor of Gary, who finished second and third respectively in the feature race. The semi-final race was twenty laps and won by Bill Neighbor of Logansport. Carl Mills of Peru was second and Bill Vanderford of Fort Wayne was third.

In the shorter races, Dick Windsor won the first heat, Carl Mills the second heat, Dick Windsor the third heat, Red Layton of Peru the fourth heat, and Lefty Hirschman the fifth heat, which was a "dash" race.

Next Saturday night the Chicago Hot Rod Association will appear at the speedway with an all-star cast of professional drivers. However, there is an open invitation to local hot rod drivers and Fred Boggs, Fred McKown and Bob Miner have indicated that they will have cars entered.

Saturday, August 22, 1949
Midget Cars Here Wednesday; Stock Cars Saturday

On Wednesday night the Warsaw Speedway will be the scene of an added scheduled race of the midget cars. In this first season of auto racing in Warsaw, most of the events have been held on Saturday nights. However, the midgets will be here on Wednesday of this week and the regular Saturday night program will be set aside for stock car races.

Last Saturday night, a fairly large crowd saw hot rod races, featuring a field of professional drivers from the Hot Rod Association of Chicago. There were many thrills, and one driver luckily escaped injury when his car crashed.

Wednesday night's midget racing program will begin with time trials at 7 o'clock and the first race at 8:30. The same times will prevail Saturday when the stock cars make their second appearance here. So a full schedule of automobile racing of all types, plus the bathing beauty contest, is offered to race fans this week.

Wednesday, August 24, 1949
Fastest Field of Midget Cars
Track Record Broken Wednesday Night

The fastest field of the summer season thrilled a rather small crowd at the Warsaw Speedway Wednesday night in what everyone agreed were the best midget races held here. Previous track records went toppling as 27 champion drivers from the Kokomo, Muncie and Indianapolis area circuit competed for prizes.

Two drivers knocked more than a full second off the old record. Walt Geise, of Indianapolis, circled the quarter-mile in 16.92 seconds for a new mark, but this fell when George Wilkins, also of Indianapolis, got the checkered flag after going around in 16.84 seconds in the qualifying time trials. Wilkins showed that his time trial mark was no fluke by finishing first in the 25-lap feature race. Eddy Yeager, Indianapolis, was second, Geise was third and Ray Duckworth, of Anderson, was fourth.

Other Winners. The semi-feature race was won by Wally Hostettler, of Indianapolis. He finished ahead of Mark Henn of Elwood, and Johnny Hughes of Fort Wayne. In the short races, the first heat went to Johnny Remsnyder of Lafayette with Geise second, and Lefty

Hershman of Crown Point, third. Harold Wildhaver won the third heat, ahead of Junior DeShamp of Kokomo. Jimmy Thomas of Kansas City was winner of the third heat. Wally Hostettler was second. Heat number four went to Shorty Haskett of Indianapolis. Red Lucas of Monticello was second and Sil Hatcher of Kokomo third. Ray Duckworth, Anderson, won the handicap heat, ahead of Geise, Yeager and Wilkins.

These same cars and drivers will return on Saturday afternoon of the fair, Sept. 3 for special races that should attract a capacity crowd. This Saturday night the stock cars will return to the speedway with time trials starting at 7 o'clock and the final heats at 8:30.

Saturday, August 27, 1949
Bernie VanDron Wins Feature At Stock Car Races

Bernie VanDron, of Fort Wayne, was king of the stock car drivers Saturday night at the Warsaw Speedway. A fairly large crowd was on hand at the fairgrounds to see the stock cars race here for the second time this summer.

VanDron stole the show. He was the only one to break 20 in the qualifying trials. VanDron circled the track in his 1938 Ford in the excellent time of 19.47 seconds. In addition, he won the first heat, then came back to win the 25 lap feature race. There were several Warsaw and Kosciusko County drivers participating in the races. Mel Miller of Warsaw and Jim Lozier of Claypool were winners of heats.

Midgets Saturday. Next Saturday afternoon during the county fair there will be an outstanding attraction of races. The midget cars and drivers who turned in record times here on Wednesday night of last week will return for another performance. These are the speedsters from Lafayette, Kokomo, Muncie and Indianapolis area speedways.

Results of the stock car races were as follows:
First Heat--Bernie VanDron, Fort Wayne, first; Harold Bunnell, Peru, second; Oda Green, Dayton, O., third.
Second Heat--Bud Shlater, Churubusco, first; Johnnie McMahlon, Dayton, second; Jake Zimmerman, Fort Wayne, third.
Third Heat--Jim Lozier, Claypool, first; Dick Wilson, Fort Wayne, second; Rusty Hartman, Fort Wayne, third.
Fourth Heat--Bob Kellar, Waynedale, first; Ed Roy, Fort Wayne, second; Russ Brown, Fort Wayne, third.
First Semi-Final--Mel Miller, Warsaw, first; Possum Penn, North Webster, second; Dick Heeter, North Manchester, third.
Second Semi-Final--Olin Frier, Bluffton, first; Windy Cole, Fort Wayne, second; Don Nusbaum, third.
Feature Race--Bernie VonDron, Fort Wayne, first; Jake Zimmerman, Fort Wayne, second; Johnnie McMahlon, Dayton, third.

Saturday, September 3, 1949
Local Drivers Steal the Show in Stock Car Races

Local drivers stole the show Labor Day night at the Warsaw Speedway competing against a string of championship stock cars and race drivers. Miss Peggy Sumpter, 18, of Warsaw, was named "Queen of the Speedways" in competition with nine beautiful girls and two cars that overturned on the curves, making it a banner night for spectators.

"Pete" Peterson, Warsaw driver, won his first race at the fairgrounds speedway, taking the third race of the evening in a hotly contested grind and Dick Heeter of North Manchester took third position in the same race.

Jim Lozier of Warsaw captured top honors in the fourth race Monday night, beating out Bernie Vondron of Fort Wayne who has been winning feature races all across Indiana the past two weeks.

Bob Silveus of Etna Green driving his initial race, lost a heartbreaker. He was leading the field when his car was smashed broadside off the track in the final laps of the race. Peterson also placed fourth in the 50-lap feature race of the evening, a race that saw numerous spin outs and afforded spectators a long, hair-raising contest.

Queen Is Named. During the semi-final intermission, prominent local judges selected a beautiful girl, Peggy Sumpter, "Queen of the Speedway for 1949" winning for her an all-expense paid trip into Chicago. **Her court of honor**. The two runners-up in the contest were Marvis Long, 19, of Warsaw, and Ann Lou Edler, 16, of Warsaw. Other contestants, any one of whom could have easily been picked the winner were JoAnn Heagy, 19, Warsaw; Josephine Holloway, 20, Warsaw; Sharon Washburn, 19, Warsaw; who captured the fancy of the crowd and kept them chanting her number throughout the contest.; Mary Hedington, 16, of Mentone; Barbara Amos, 19, Warsaw; and Pat Ward, 16, Niles, Mich.

1950

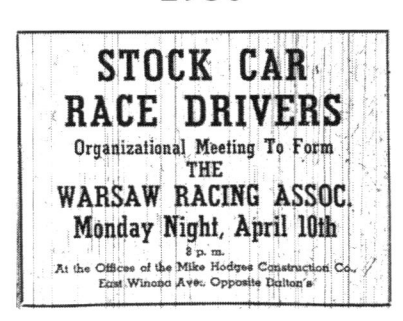

STOCK CAR RACE DRIVERS
Organizational Meeting To Form
THE
WARSAW RACING ASSOC.
Monday Night, April 10th
8 p.m.
At the Offices of the Mike Hodges Construction Co.,
East Winona Ave., Opposite Dalton's

Saturday, May 13, 1950
Local Speedway Offers Thrills

42 Cars Qualify for Big Program – A packed house at the Warsaw Speedway Saturday night saw an opening-night performance by the stock car drivers of the Fort Wayne Racing association that had them standing on their feet most of the time, with North Manchester drivers taking their share of the purses.

With the track in excellent, smooth condition at the fairgrounds, high speeds brought on an unusual number of accidents that had the crowd roaring. Olin Friar, a Bluffton, Ind., race jockey, was the star of the evening, winning his first heat race and the feature 25-lap event. All together the crowd witnessed 95 laps of racing opening night, due to a full field of 42 qualified cars.

Plenty of Excitement – Dick Heeter, of North Manchester, gave them an added thrill by easily walking off with the third race of the night. The second heat race was taken by Mickey Potter, of Fort Wayne, and the fourth by Don Nusbaum of Fort Wayne.

In the two semi-finals, each with a starting field of 16 cars, another North Manchester driver, Russ Brown, rammed his way to the lead and held it, winning the event. In the second semi – again it was a North Manchester driver taking the checkered flag, Rollin Smith.

The crowd shuddered at one point, when a fast-moving racer, out of control, slid into the infield and struck a flagman, throwing him violently into the air. Silence reigned over the track as the ambulance sped across the infield to his side, only to find the man brushing off the dust and insisting that he was alright, even though dazed and shaken by his narrow escape. Wednesday night, the Warsaw Speedway will feature hot rods.

Saturday, May 20, 1950
No. Manchester Drivers Feature Stock Car Races

Northern Indiana stock car drivers scored heavily again Saturday night on the fast Warsaw Speedway during the program of seven races. A large crowd was on hand for the action. The hot-rods will be back at the Speedway on Wednesday night.

Dick Heeter, of North Manchester, romped home the winner in the first race, well ahead of the field. Another North Manchester driver, Russell Tracy, caught the checkered flag in the second race, with Bob Silveus, of Etna Green, a close second.

Max Couch, of Fort Wayne, won the third race. Mickey Potter, of LaPorte, made up for his tough luck of overturning on the east turn in the previous week's racing, by winning the fourth race Saturday night.

The semi-final feature of 15 laps was won by Olin Friar, of Bluffton, who took both a heat race and the feature event on the previous Saturday.

The feature event was a close race all the way between five cars. Bob Kellar was the winner, followed by Hig Hillegas, of Huntington; Bob Silveus, of Etna Green; Dick Hire, of Fort Wayne; and Dick Heeter, of North Manchester.

A new wrinkle in stock car racing, a "Powder Puff Derby", featured women drivers. Mrs. Betty Smith, of North Manchester, copped the honors as the crowd cheered the girls each time they roared down the straight-of-way.

Tuesday, May 30, 1950
Dick Hire Wins Feature Race At Local Speedway

Dick Hire, of Fort Wayne, was top winner Tuesday night at the thrilling stock car races held at the Warsaw Speedway. Hire crossed the finish line ahead of all other drivers in the big feature race and in addition, got the checkered flag in the second race of the evening. It was one of the most exciting programs yet staged at the fairgrounds track. Although no one was injured, there were many spins and "bumps", and several of the races developed into close finishes.

In addition to Hire's double victory, other winners were Rusty Hartman, of Bluffton, in the first race, Bob Stonebraker, of Fort Wane, the third race; Norm Wiese, Fort Wayne, fourth race; Bob Silveus, Etna Green, the first semi-feature; and Ralph Malcolm, Fort Wayne, the second semi-feature. Betty Smith, of North Manchester, again proved to be the master of the fairer sex as far as race driving is concerned. Betty, for the second time, won the "powder puff" race.

Saturday, June 3, 1950
Four-Car Crash At Local Races

Stock Cars Provide Plenty of Thrills. A four-car crash in the feature event provided the highlight of thrills Saturday night at the stock car races held at the Warsaw Speedway, but fortunately the drivers escaped with only minor cuts and bruises.

Bernie Vondron, veteran Fort Wayne driver, came out on top in the feature, with Dick Hire running a close second. The yellow flag was out during a major portion of the event. The first crash came when Don Nusbaum, of Warsaw, went through the fence and struck the end of the concrete grandstand. Several laps later, and at almost the same spot on the track, a car driven by Boots Lee, of Huntington, struck a disabled car which in turn hit a car driven by Don Plummer. The impact caused Plummer's car to climb the fence and overturn.

At this point, Bob Malcolm attempted to avoid the wreckage caused by the other three vehicles and also struck the fence in front of the grandstand. All four cars were disabled.

Timer Takes Powder. During these hectic minutes, the crowd in the grandstand was on its feet screaming, racing cars were sliding in all directions to avoid the wreckage, and the official timer left the judges'' stand in considerable haste and did not return until the race was ended. The judges' stand had been nipped during three or four races by skidding cars.

While the feature race provided most of the fireworks, the other events, too, had their exciting moments. Winners of the other races during the evening were Dick Hire, Jake Simmerman, Bob Silveus, of Etna Green, and Jim Lozier, of Warsaw.

The "powder puff" derby was won by Mena Potter. These woman drivers put on an exciting show, and Laverne Smith, of Huntertown, wrecked her car trying to take the lead. The speedway will be the scene of hot-rod races on Wednesday night. (No race results found for a Wed., June 7 race)

Saturday, June 10, 1950
Record 50 Cars Thrill Fans At Local Speedway

A record field of 50 cars turned out at the Warsaw Speedway to give a near capacity crowd plenty of thrills in the stock car races Saturday night. The feature event, a 50-lap race, was won by Bob Kellar, high-point man in the Fort Wayne Racing association.

Kellar won his place in the feature event as the result of an unusual accident in the first race of the evening, which was won by Dick Heeter, of North Manchester. Kellar and Mickey Potter were fighting it out for third place, and as they came out of the northeast turn on the last lap, Kellar spun in front of Potter. The two cars hooked together and Potter pushed Kellar's car sideways the length of the stretch and over the finish line to third position. This qualified him for the feature event.

In the second race, Bernie Vondron, of Fort Wayne, got to within 50 feet of the finish line running in second and lost control of his car. The race was won by Kindle. Other winners during the evening were Wallace, Ruff and Russ Brown, all of Fort Wayne, and Jack Higley, of Laporte. The "powder puff" derby, featuring women drivers, had a record number of 12 entries. The winner was Marjorie Eitnear, of Antwerp, Ohio who was driving her first stock car race.

The highlight of excitement came during the fourth race of the evening when a car driven by Gallogy, of Fort Wayne, went straight out of the west turn, through the fence, and stopped with the front end resting bumper to bumper with an automobile parked on the outside of the wire fence. The driver was not injured, but the car was disabled for the remainder of the night.

Saturday, June 17, 1950
Bob Keller Wins Feature At Local Speedway

The Fort Wayne Racing association's high-point man proved his right to that title Saturday night at the Warsaw Speedway. Bob Kellar, of Fort Wayne, increased his point standing by winning the feature stock car race and also made himself the undisputed champion at the local speedway by taking his third feature event out of four starts this season.

Highlights of the night's excitement started in the very first race when the car driven by George Thompson, of Disco, climbed upon the guard rail and crashed through after riding the rail for several feet. Thompson escaped without injury. The thrill occurred on the back stretch during the first lap of the race.

In the first consolation race of the evening, a car driven by Bill Holle, of Silver Lake, also climbed the rail at the same spot. Holle was more fortunate as his car went about 20 feet on the rail and then came back down on the track so that he could finish the race.

Winners of the various races were Bob Silveus, of Etna Green, Rusty Hartman, of Fort Wayne, Dick Hire, of Fort Wayne, Dunkin, of Fort Wayne, Mike Holderman, of North Manchester, and Joe Cutler, of Warsaw. Edna Tracy won the "powder puff" race for girls. Edna received the checkered flag after Marjorie Eidnear, of Antwerp, Ohio spun out on the south turn near the end of the race. Marjorie, last week's winner, was leading when the mishap occurred. Betty Smith, of North Manchester, wound up in second place.

Saturday, July 1, 1950
Boat, Stock Car Races On Sports Program Tuesday

Sport fans spending the Fourth of July holiday at home are reminded of two big sporting events at the Kosciusko County fairgrounds in Warsaw. There will be something going on all day Tuesday, with boat races sponsored by the Lakeland Boat Club scheduled for the daylight hours, followed by stock car races at night.

Track Record Falls. A capacity crowd and record number of cars should be on hand Tuesday night, judging from the races here on Saturday night. The track record, held for more than a year by Bernie Vondron, fell to the talents of Russ Brown, of North Manchester, who went around the quarter-mile oval in 19.28 seconds. Then, to add to his laurels for the evening, Brown won the first heat race and the big 25-lap feature.

In the second race of the evening, only four cars out of a field of nine were able to finish due to several minor collisions. Bob Silveus, of Etna Green, finally won the race. The biggest thrill came in the second consolation race when a car driven by Lanyard Osborn, of Warsaw, rolled over in the middle of the track, in front of the grandstand. Osborn was not injured and continued in the race after his car was righted.

Other winners Saturday night were Norm Wiese and Zent, both of Fort Wayne, Olin Friar, of Bluffton, and Art Johnson, of Warsaw. The powder puff derby for women was again won by Marjorie Eidnear, of Antwerp, Ohio.

Tuesday, July 4, 1950
Speedway Track Record Broken By Russ Brown

Russ Brown, of North Manchester, took another 0.3 seconds off his track record during the stock car races at the Warsaw Speedway Tuesday night and walked away with top honors by winning the feature event, a 25-lap race. Dick Heeter, of North Manchester, was second. Brown got his chance to win when Rusty Hartman, who was leading, threw a wheel in front of the grandstand and had to come into the infield. Francis Ruff finished third.

Just last Saturday night, Brown had set a new track record with his lap of 19.28 seconds. Tuesday night he made it in 19.25 seconds.

Francis Ruff, of La Porte, won the first heat race, which lasted only seven of the scheduled 10 laps, due to the fact that several of the 11 cars entered had collisions. Bud Schlater won the second heat, with Don Plummer finishing second and Jake Zimmerman, of Warsaw, third. Mickey Potter won the third heat, ahead of Jack Higley and Joe Cutler. The fourth heat was won by Norm Wiese, with Rollin Smith second and Don Esterline third.

Rusty Hartman won the first consolation race, ahead of Bob Keller and Olin Friar. The second consolation was won by Art Smith. Dick Heeter was second and Clarence Rousch was third.

In the special "powder puff" race for women, the winner was Betty Smith, of North Manchester. Edna Tracy was second and Pat Fraley third. The stock cars will race again at the Speedway on Saturday night, with time trials starting at 7 o'clock and the first race at 8:30.

Saturday, July 8, 1950
Speedway Track Record IS Again Broken By Brown

Russ Brown, of North Manchester, again broke his own track record for one lap to feature Saturday night's activities at the Warsaw Speedway. Brown drove his stock car around the quarter-mile over in 19.09 seconds to better his mark of 19.25 set last week.

A large crowd saw Brown pull away from 15 other stock cars to win the feature 25-lap event. He also ran second in the first heat race of the evening. Rusty Hartman, of Fort Wayne, finished second in the feature race.

Hartman won the first consolation race, and had also received the checkered flag in the first heat race of the evening, only to be disqualified for not starting in the right position. Ollin Friar was moved up as the winner in that first race after Hartman's disqualification. Other winners during the night of thrilling races were Dick Hire, Mickey Potter, and Don Easterline, all from Fort Wayne, and Mike Holderman, of North Manchester.

The regular "powder puff" race for women drivers was won by Edna Tracy, of North Manchester, while Betty Smith was second. She is also from North Manchester. There will be more stock car racing on Tuesday night, with time trials starting at 7 o'clock, and the first race at 8:30.

Saturday, July 15, 1950
Plenty Of Spills In Stock Races Saturday Night

Sports fans who came to the Warsaw Speedway on Saturday night looking for thrills and spills went home with their appetites well satisfied, for the stock car drivers of the Fort Wayne Racing association provided an abundant crop of crashes and near collisions.

Art Johnson, of Warsaw, was leading in the first heat race of the evening when he had a smash-up. Bob Silveus, of Etna Green, went on to win the race. In the second heat, Baldy Himes, of Warsaw, brought fans to their feet as he hurdled the guard rail just east of the grandstand. The winner in this race was Olin Friar, of Bluffton. Jim Lozier, of Warsaw, came out victorious in the third race, and Mickey Potter, of Fort Wayne, won the fourth heat race of the evening.

Car Badly Damaged. The thrills of the consolation race were provided when several cars went into spins in front of the grandstand. A car driven by Junior Lee, of Huntington, was badly damaged. Archie Holle, of Barbee Lakes, won the consolation.

Bob Kellar, point leader in the Fort Wayne association, won the feature 25-lap race of the evening after leading all the way. Dick Heeter, of North Manchester, was a close second. A four-car crash in the early stages of the race provided the thrills in this feature event. Edna Tracy, of North Manchester, continued her winning ways by finishing first in the "powder puff race" for women drivers.

Saturday, July 22, 1950
Russ Brown Wins 50-Lap Feature And Gold Trophy

Russ Brown, of North Manchester, proved his recent successes on the Warsaw Speedway were not flukes by capturing the feature 50-lap race Saturday night before a large crowd at the local fairgrounds.

Brown, holder of the track record here and a consistent winner at Fort Wayne and other tracks during the past weeks, won the right to take home the beautiful mid-season championship gold trophy, which was awarded here Saturday night. He took the lead in the first lap and kept his stock car there the rest of the way.

Another North Manchester driver, Rollin Smith, proved fans with a thrill in the fourth race of the night. Smith was running third and was sure of a place in the feature when he blew a tire on the last lap and nearly rolled the car in front of the grandstand. Then in the second consolation race, Smith ran second until the last few laps, when he passed Mickey Potter, of Fort Wayne, to get the checkered flag in a fine exhibition of driving.

Russ Brown, N. Manchester

The highlight for excitement came early, as six cars collided on the first lap of the first race of the evening. Winners of the Saturday night races, in addition to Brown and Smith, were Ivan Ort, of Fort Wayne; Lucky Long, Fort Wayne; Bob Locks, Fort Wayne; Francis Ruff and Bud Shlater, Churubusco. Due to the 50-lap feature, there was no race for women drivers.

Saturday, July 29, 1950
Russ Brown Still Best Driver At Local Speedway

Russ Brown, of North Manchester, again weaved his driving magic over the rest of the field at the Warsaw Speedway last Saturday night by winning the feature stock car event, a 25-lap affair on the quarter-mile track. Brown took the lead in the first lap and held it the rest of the way, though pressed closely by Rusty Hartman, of Fort Wayne, who finished second.

There were many thrills during the evening. On the seventh lap of the feature race, Don Nusbaum rolled his car over on its top in front of the grandstand. The car came to rest on the starter's platform. Ed Bright, of Fort Wayne, the starter, jumped to safety just before the car hit the platform, and the flag was knocked out of his hand.

Warsaw Drivers Win. Warsaw drivers made a fine showing by winning three of the races. Art Smith, Archie Holle, and Art Johnson were the local winners. Other races were won by Bob Stonebraker, of Huntington; Jim Hoagland, of Fort Wayne; and Huttinger, of Fort Wayne. Jean Sheppard, of Goshen, proved her skill by romping home ahead of six other cars in the women's "powder puff" race.

There were many spin-outs and collisions during the night. The ambulance crew got its first call to duty by giving first aid for a scratch and putting a band-aid on the wrecker driver.

Saturday, August 5, 1950
Russ Brown Adds Another Feature Win At Speedway

The stock car drivers are still having trouble trying to catch Russ Brown, of North Manchester. It was Brown all the way in the 25-lap feature at the Warsaw Speedway Saturday night, as a large crowd saw 15 of the 16 starting cars finish the race, a record for the season. There were thrills galore, starting as early as the first race when a car driven by Ivan Ort, of Fort Wayne, rolled completely over in the backstretch.

Rusty Hartman, who had the third fastest time in the qualifying heats, was forced to the sidelines before the races began when his car broke an axle in the warm-up lap. He didn't get into the night's competition.

In addition to winning the feature, Brown also won one of the heat races. Other winners were Don Nusbaum, Norm Wiese, and Elmer Harpe, all of Fort Wayne; and Archie Holle, of Warsaw. Jean Sheppard won the women's "powder puff derby" for the second consecutive week.

Norm Wiese, Fort Wayne

Saturday, August 12, 1950
Warsaw Drivers Among Winners At Speedway

For the first time in several weeks, Russ Brown, of North Manchester, did not win the feature stock car race at the Warsaw Speedway last Saturday night. The reason? Brown wasn't here. A large crowd saw Don Plummer, of Huntertown, win the 25-lap event after losing the lead several times.

Warsaw drivers again gave a good account of themselves. Jim Lozier and Joe Cutler, both of Warsaw, won heat races. Other heat winners were Mickey Potter, of Fort Wayne, and Ike Holderman, of Huntington. Plummer came back to win the first consolation race, and a dead heat was declared in the second consolation race between Rollin Smith, of North Manchester, and Mike Klingerman, of Warsaw. In a three-lap runoff, Smith got the checkered flag.

Several crashes, spin-outs and lost wheels made the evening an exciting one for the fans. In the third race, cars driven by Maynard Osborne, of Warsaw, and Max Couch, of Fort Wayne, crashed through the fence on the south-east turn. Neither driver was injured.

Jean Sheppard again showed her dominance over other women drivers by winning the "powder puff" derby. The stock car races will be held again at the speedway next Saturday night.

Saturday, August 19, 1950 – Rainout

Saturday, August 26, 1950
Goshen Driver Wins Feature At Local Speedway

Gene Darr, of Goshen, won the 25-lap feature Saturday night as drivers of the Tri-State Racing association made their first appearance of the season at the Warsaw Speedway. A near-capacity crowd was on hand for the stock car races.

The gold trophy that will be awarded to the winner of the 100-lap championship race on Sept. 23 was on display at the track for the first time Saturday night. Gene Detchemendy, manager of the speedway, announced that there will be stock car races next Saturday night, the final night of the county fair.

Darr had to overtake Jim Lozier, a local driver, late in the feature race in order to cross the finish line first and get the checkered flag. Darr had also won the first heat race of the night. Lozier had won his way into the final race by copping two 'firsts' and finishing second in earlier races. Other winners during the night were Jake Birtfield, of Syracuse, Bob Silveus of Etna Green, Dick Raiza, of Hobart, and Art Johnson, of Warsaw.

Two Ambulance Runs. The Bilby ambulance made two runs to the McDonald Hospital during the night's exciting events. Lloyd Lyons, of Milford, crashed the fence on the southwest turn in the time trials and was knocked unconscious. Lyons was released from the hospital when no serious injuries were discovered and he was back at the track to race later during the night.

The other ambulance run was made following the feature event when Harold McVoy suffered a bad cut over his left eye as the result of his car going through the fence in the feature race. Two stitches were required to sew up the wound. The cars of Art Johnson and Ralph Alberts also finished the feature event on the spectator's side of the fence.

Lenny Juday, of Goshen, hit a light pole head-on in the third race and broke it off at the ground. He was not hurt.

Saturday, September 2 & Monday, September 4, 1950
Goshen Driver Wins Stock Car Feature Monday

A large Labor Day crowd braved chilly weather Monday night to witness the stock car races at the Warsaw Speedway. They saw several accidents, one of which sent Baldy Himes, of Warsaw, to the McDonald Hospital for emergency treatment after his car struck a fence. He was dismissed and returned later to the track.

The 50-lap feature race provided most of the thrills and a heartbreaking effort on the part of Art Smith, of Warsaw. Smith led the entire field for 49 laps. Then came the bad luck. On the 49th lap, a wheel came off his car, which went into the fence. Gene Darr took over the lead at this point and won the race, with Jim Lozier, of Warsaw, finishing second. Bob Silveus, of Etna Green, had the fastest time trial during the preliminary heats. During the night's entertainment, one car turned over in front of the grandstand, and the crowd roared as several other cars came close to hitting the upset speedster.

Dick Heeter, N. Manchester

Saturday Races. The stock cars also raced here on Saturday night as a feature of the final session of the Kosciusko County fair. The feature race was won by Dick Heeter, of North Manchester, who was a favorite of the capacity crowd jammed into the bleachers. As on Monday night, Art Smith led Saturday's feature before his car got involved in a tie-up on the east turn. He crashed into a light pole, but still managed to finish third.

Heeter also won a heat race Saturday night. Other Saturday night winners were Dick Raiza, of Hobart; Ralph Albert, Skid Lucas, and Mike Salay, of South Bend; Bob Whooton, of New Paris; and Jim Lozier and Art Smith, of Warsaw.

Saturday, September 9, 1950
Art Smith Wins Feature At Local Speedway

Art Smith, of Warsaw, broke his string of bad luck by winning the feature stock car race at the Warsaw Speedway Saturday night. Smith had led in the feature both on the previous Saturday night and on Labor Day, only to lose out in both events. This last Saturday night, he came from far back and took the lead early in the race. He held it the rest of the way to get the checkered flag.

The evening started out as though Smith would again be the victim of misfortune. In the very first race, his car crashed into the fence. However, he came back to finish first in the race of the four fastest qualifiers, then capped the evening by winning the feature.

Other winners were Vern Schrock and John Nisley, of Goshen, Ralph Likes, of Millersburg, Gene Bowers, of Columbia City, and Art Johnson and Joe Cutler, of Warsaw.

Sportsmanship Display. A fine display of sportsmanship on the part of Gene Darr, of Goshen, helped Johnson win his race. In the eighth lap was a three-car collision on the east turn. Johnson was leading at the time, but in the confusion he slowed down. Darr passed him and went on to win. However, the fans did not seem to understand the Tri-State ruling in regard to accidents on the track, the ruling being that the race continues unless there is personal injury. When Darr heard the dissatisfaction of the fans, who took it on themselves to be the judges, he drove to the judge's stand and willingly gave the race to Johnson. Darr received a great hand from the crowd when the announcement was made. Prior to the race, Darr had received a trophy from a Peru cub scout in tribute to his clean driving.

Saturday, September 16, 1950
Papenbrock, Of Churubusco, Tops Auto Card

Buck Papenbrock, of Churubusco, took the feature event of the Tri-State racing card at the fairgrounds here Saturday night although an error permitted Art Smith, of Warsaw, to pass him on an extra lap. The starter failed to get the signal for the white flag when Papenbrock went into the 25th and last lap out in front. In the 26th, Smith went around and got the checkered flag, but a check of the charts showed Papenbrock to be the winner.

Bob Kellar, of Fort Wayne, came from behind to take the semi-final race. He also won in the race featuring the four fastest qualifying cars. Junior Dear, of Columbia City, won the first consolation race and Buck Lotz, of Silver Lake, driving his first race, won the second consolation. In the latter event, Deere rolled his car in the backstretch, but was not injured.

100-Lap Feature Saturday. It was announced that the big 100-lap feature race for the gold trophy put up by the Fitch Jewelry store will be run next Saturday night. The racing card last Saturday got off to an exciting start when Bob Salesman, of Columbia City, flipped his car during the time trials, in which a record number of 54 stock cars were registered.

In the fourth race of the evening, Bob Malcolm, of Huntertown, rolled his car in the backstretch to avoid hitting two others who had tangled. Malcolm was rushed to the McDonald Hospital in the Paul M. Bilby ambulance. However, X-ray photographs failed to reveal more than leg and shoulder bruises and Malcolm was returned to the track before the evening was over. The fourth race went to Dick Heeter, of North Manchester.

The first three races of the evening were won by Papenbrock, of Churubusco, Art Smith, of Warsaw, and Bob Silveus, of Etna Green. In the semi-final race, won by Bob Kellar, of Fort Wayne, Mishler, of Goshen, rolled his car in front of the grandstand.

Saturday, September 23, 1950
Dick Raiza Wins 100-Lap Race At Warsaw Speedway

Dick Raiza, of Hobart, won the 100-lap championship stock car race Saturday night at the Warsaw Speedway before a capacity crowd of enthusiastic spectators who braved a cold wind to attend the season's most outstanding racing program.

Raiza took over the first place during the 15th lap from Gene Bowers, of Columbia City. The Hobart driver held the lead until the 47th lap when a spin caused him to give up the top position to Art Johnson, of Warsaw. However, two laps later, Raiza was back in first place and he remained there until he finally won the checkered flag, the beautiful Fitch gold trophy, and top prize money. Gene Darr, one of the Midwest's most successful stock car drivers, came up from near last place and was only about a half-car's length behind Raiza at the finish line. Johnson was a close third. The three leaders ran the entire 100 laps without a pit stop.

Art Smith, of Warsaw, had his hopes for winning the trophy dashed early in the first race of the evening when he rolled his car over in the backstretch and was unable to get repairs in time for the later races. Smith had the fastest qualifying time of the evening. Another local driver, Joe Cutler, had motor trouble in the time trials and was out for the remainder of the night.

Raiza's comment on winning the championship trophy, in an interview over WRSW, was "I go for my army physical the 28th of this month, and I wanted to take the trophy with me." In addition to the prize money, Raiza won the greater share of the lap prizes donated by local merchants and business men. Raiza won all of the lap money except for the 10th lap, which went to Gene Bowers.

In the earlier races, winners were Gene Darr, of Goshen; Raiza; Skid Lucas, of South Bend; Gene Bowers and Jim Salesman, of Columbia City; and K. Marman, of Warsaw. The Speedway management announced during the night that there will be races again next Saturday evening.

1951
Joe Hamsher & Milo Clase Emerge

Gene Detchemendy, from St. Louis, took over the management of the speedway in 1951 as part of the Tri-State Racing Association. The track was run in tandem with the New Paris Speedway with many drivers running both tracks. "Rollen" Joe Hamsher, who managed the New Paris Speedway for many years, was the flagman with Milo Clase and John Niccum as announcers. Hamsher was known for flagging from the track and then jumping over the guardrails to get away from the herd of stock cars headed towards him.

The two tracks shared an end of year Souvenir Edition 1951 Stock Car Racing program that included many officials' comments and listed several of the drivers, along with their car numbers and a paragraph about each of them personally. This was also the year WRSW AM & FM radio started airing 30 minutes of the racing action each Saturday night with Milo Clase behind the microphone.

Saturday, May 26, 1951
No Races Saturday Due To Showers

Rain forced cancellation of the first scheduled stock car racing program Saturday night at the Warsaw Speedway. Gene Detchemendy, track manager, said today that the races will be held Wednesday night, Memorial Day, with time trials at 7 o'clock and the first heat race at 8:30.

Several of the cars were on hand early Saturday evening, but the track was wet from an all morning rain, and when showers started to fall again at 6:30 it was decided to call off the program. An outstanding Memorial Day program is slated for Wednesday night, and a large crowd is anticipated to help give the racing season a rousing send-off in Warsaw.

Tuesday, May 29, 1951
Stock Car Races Sports Feature On Memorial Day

Sports activities in Warsaw on Memorial Day will be highlighted by the opening night of stock car racing at the Warsaw Speedway, located at the county fairgrounds. There will be no softball games here Wednesday night, so it appears as though the speedway will be the sole source of entertainment for sports-minded fans.

Plenty of action is assured, according to Gene Detechemendy, speedway manager. Outstanding drivers from the area, sanctioned by the Tri-State racing circuit, will be on hand when the time trials start at 7 o'clock around the quarter-mile oval. The first of a program of eight races is scheduled for 8:30.

WRSW will take its listeners to the speedway at 8:45 p.m. with Milo Clase on hand to broadcast a full 30 minutes of action through the sponsorship of Main Automotive, of Warsaw.

Saturday, June 2, 1951
Olin Friar Wins Feature Race at Warsaw Speedway

Olin Friar, veteran Fort Wayne stock car driver, had a big night Saturday at the Warsaw Speedway winning the 25-lap feature race, as well as the race for the six fastest cars and the first heat race.

A large crowd witnessed the racing program, which went off smoothly with no serious accidents or injuries. McNagney, of Columbia City, gave the fans a thrill in the first heat race, however, when his car failed to negotiate the first curve and ran through the fence.

Mike Lott, of Nappanee, won the second heat race, while Ralph "Cowboy" Likes, of Millersburg, captured the third heat. Winner of the fourth heat was Hick Hildegas, of Fort Wayne.

LOCAL DRIVERS WIN. A local favorite, Joe Cutler, of Warsaw, pleased the crowd by getting the checkered flag in the race for the six slowest cars. Another Warsaw driver, Mike Klingerman, breezed home first in the semi-feature race. Bob Wiles, of Nappanee, won the consolation event.

Several of the races were broadcast over WRSW by H O Kring Motors. The stock car races will be again next Saturday night with time trials at 7 o'clock and the first race at 8:30. WRSW will again be on the air with a description of the races between 8:45 and 9:15 with Woodie's Sinclair Service as the sponsor.

Saturday, June 9, 1951
5 Car Crash In Feature Race At Speedway; Gene Bowers Wins

The feature race of the evening Saturday at the Warsaw Speedway turned out to be the most thrilling as several of the faster stock car drivers were put out of the 25-lap race by crashes. Gene Bowers, of Columbia City, won the race but only after five cars were eliminated after being involved in one accident. The drivers were Buck Eppert, of Nappanee; Lester Grover, of Goshen; Vern Schrock, of Goshen; Gene Darr, of Goshen, and Mike Potter. Luckily, no one was injured.

Heat races were won by Olin Friar, of Fort Wayne; Art Johnson, of Warsaw; Don Anderson of Culver; and Gaylord Skyles. A local driver, Ronnie Zimmerman, won the race of the six slowest cars, and Friar captured the checked flag in the race featuring the six fastest cars. Ralph "Cowboy" Likes, of Churubusco, one of the top winners this season, breezed home first in the semi-final event.

KLINGERMAN SENT HOME. Klingerman, one of the heat winners, was slated for the army last week but was sent home for 30 days because he had recently burned his arm in a welding accident.

Another large crowd was on hand for the races, several of which were broadcast over WRSW by Woodie's Service. Another program of stock car racing will be held at the Speedway next Saturday night.

Saturday June 16, 1951
Feature Race At Speedway Won By Fort Wayne Driver

Olin Friar, one of Fort Wayne's better stock car race drivers, won the feature 25-lap event Saturday night before a large crowd at the Warsaw Speedway. The night's festivities were void of any accidents, as all of the races were run off without mishaps to cars or drivers.

Friar, prior to grabbing the checkered flag in the feature, had won the race between the six fastest qualifying cars, so he had a good night in all ways concerned. A Warsaw driver, Gale Smith, had the honor of crossing the finish line first in the semi-feature race of 15 laps, and another Warsaw racer, Mike Klingerman, finished ahead of the field in the third heat race.

Russ Brown, of Fort Wayne, won the race for the six slowest cars and also copped first in the consolation event. Heat winners, in addition to Klingerman, were Rusty Hartman, of Fort Wayne, Don Shively, of Columbia City, and Vernie Schrock, of Goshen.

The races were broadcast over WRSW between 8:45 and 9:15 p.m. by Main Automotive.

There will be another attractive program of stock car racing next Saturday night at the Speedway. Time trials start at 7 o'clock and the first race is held at 8:30. WRSW will also broadcast the races between 8:45 and 9:15 p.m. next Saturday, with H.O. Kring Motors sponsoring the radio show.

Saturday, June 23, 1951
Fort Wayne Stock Car Drivers Wins Top Honors Here

Olin Friar, of Fort Wayne, was in a class all by himself Saturday night at the Warsaw Speedway. A large crowd saw Friar win the race for the six fastest cars and the semi-feature event. Then to cap his brilliant showing, Friar breezed home the winner in the 25-lap feature event. The Fort Wayne stock car standout made this fine showing despite the fact that his car went over the wall in the very first heat race of the night.

Rusty Hartman, of Fort Wayne, captured the first heat race: Paul Hunsberger, of Wakarusa, grabbed the checkered flag in the second heat race; Dick George, of Osceola, the third heat race; and Gene Darr, of Goshen, the fourth heat race. In the race for the six slowest cars, Virgil Keifer, of Nappanee, crossed the finishing line in first place.

BROADCAST OVER WRSW. The stock car races were broadcast over WRSW by H.O. Kring Motors, of Warsaw. Next Saturday night another colorful program of stock car racing will be staged at the local speedway. The time trails will get underway at 7 o'clock with the first race at 8:30. WRSW, broadcasting for Woodie's Service of Warsaw, will be on the air with a description of the races from 8:45 to 9:15 p.m.

Saturday, June 30, 1951
Junior Dear Wins Feature Race Here; Program July 4

There is a new name entered on the list of feature race winners at the Warsaw Speedway. The main event last Saturday night was captured by Junior Dear, of Columbia City, who drove his stock car around the quarter mile oval at such a high speed that the usual favorites could never catch up over the 25-lap distance.

A large crowd witnessed the exciting action, which was void of any accidents. Warsaw Speedway officials expect a capacity crowd this Wednesday night for a special Fourth of July racing program.

The semi-feature Saturday night was won by Olin Friar of Fort Wayne, who earlier had captured the race between the six fastest qualifying cars. Dick Salesman, of Churubusco, won the consolation race, and the race for the six slowest cars was won by Bud Shlater, of Fort Wayne.

KLINGERMAN WINS HEAT. Heat winners were Lester Grover, of Plymouth; Mike Klingerman, of Warsaw; Bob Stonebraker, of Huntington; and Mickey Potter, of Fort Wayne. The races Saturday were broadcast over WRSW by Woodie's Service, of Warsaw.

Time trials Wednesday night will start at 7 o'clock, with the first race slated to get underway at 8:30. WRSW will broadcast the races for Main Automotive, of Warsaw, between 8:45 and 9:15 P.M.

Wednesday, July 4, 1951
Fireworks, Races Attract Huge Crowd; Holland Here Saturday

The Junior Chamber of Commerce and officials of the Warsaw Speedway collaborated in giving a huge crowd a gala evening of Fourth of July entertainment in the form of fireworks and stock car racing, respectively, Wednesday night at the fairgrounds in Warsaw. Despite high winds, weather that was on the chilly side, and threatening rain there were thousands of people on hand for the program. The stock car races were held up while the big fireworks display was in progress at the east end of the fairgrounds.

The display was under the auspices of the J.C.C and under the supervision of James Painter, of the Jaycees. The colorful program which included aerial bombs, salutes, sky rockets, etc., was climaxed with a display of fireworks which formed the American flag in bright colors.

BILL HOLLAND HERE. Speedway officials expect the largest crowd in local race history this Saturday night when Bill Holland, famous Indianapolis 500-mile race driver, appears here for competition against stock car drivers from this area. Holland, former winner of the famed Memorial Day race in Indianapolis, will appear here Saturday night and then will go to New Paris for stock car races on Sunday night.

The 25-mile lap feature race here last night was won by Gene Bowers, of Columbia City, who earlier had grabbed the checkered flag in the third heat race. Russ Brown, of Fort Wayne, captured the semi-feature and Max Hile, of Columbia City, won the race between the six fastest qualifying cars. Heat winners, in addition to Bowers, were John Nisely, of Churubusco; Rollin Smith, of North Manchester and Gene Darr, of Goshen.

Several of the exciting races were broadcast last night over WRSW by Main Automotive of Warsaw. The races on Saturday night, in which Holland will be featured, will be aired over WRSW at 8:45 P.M. by H.O. Kring Motors, of Warsaw.

Saturday, July 7, 1951
4,500 Race Fans See Bill Holland At Local Speedway

Bill Holland, 1949 Indy 500 Winner, visiting the Warsaw Speedway

The largest crowd ever to watch races at the Warsaw Speedway, an estimated 4,500, saw the celebrated Bill Holland compete last Saturday night with outstanding stock car drivers from this area. In fact, the area drivers had the better of the deal as Holland could finish no better than ninth place in the feature event of the evening.

Holland, 1949 winner of the Indianapolis 500-mile race, was also scheduled to appear in stock car races Sunday night at the New Paris Speedway. However, rain last night forced postponement of the races until Monday night. Holland agreed to stay over and officials of the New Paris track said he would be on hand when time trials get underway at 7 o'clock tonight.

Although he finished far back in the feature race, Holland gave Warsaw Speedway fans a thrill by driving his car around the quarter-mile oval in 19.8 seconds in the qualifying trials. This gave him the honor of being the fastest qualifier for the night, although Archie Holle, of Warsaw was only a tenth of a second slower.

LIKES WINS FEATURE. The feature race was won by Ralph "Cowboy" Likes, of Millersburg with Don Shively, of Columbia City, finishing second. Lester Grover, of Plymouth, was third and Gene Darr, of Goshen, fourth. Although Holland finished ninth, it must be considered that he was forced to start in last place due to his faster qualifying time.

Holland didn't leave Warsaw without a victory. He crossed the finish line first in the race between the six fastest qualifying cars. He also competed in the first heat race, but could do no better than third as Rusty Hartman, Fort Wayne favorite, grabbed the checkered flag. Other heat winners were Vernie Shrock, of Goshen; Don Shively, of Columbia City; and Nook Tulley, of Ligonier.

Several cars hit the fence during the festivities, but the greatest thrill of all came in the race between the six slowest qualifying cars. Keith Coldren, of Fort Wayne, escaped injury when his car rolled over on its radiator endways. The car bounced over on its wheels and Coldren was able to drive it off the track. The car was badly wrecked but Coldren received a big hand from the crowd when he was able to right the car and leave the track unharmed. The race was won by Lester Grover, of Plymouth.

TWO DOUBLE WINNERS. Likes, a big favorite at the Warsaw Speedway and other tracks in this area, not only won the feature event but also finished ahead of the field in the semi-feature. Lester Grover, who earlier had won the race for the six slowest cars, was also a double winner. He finished first in the consolation event.

Holland was interviewed over WRSW by Milo Clase, sports director. The famous driver said his son had been injured in a highway accident and thus could not be here for the races. He is recovering in a hospital at Reading, PA., from where Holland drove to Warsaw to compete in the races. The WRSW broadcast of the races, and interview of Holland was sponsored by H.O. Kring Motors.

Saturday, July 14, 1951
Stock Car Races Provide Many Thrills At Warsaw, New Paris

Stock car racing fans were treated to many thrills and spills at the Warsaw and New Paris Speedways over the weekend, but although some of the cars were badly mangled not a single driver was injured.

A large crowd saw Gene Darr, of Goshen, win the feature race Saturday night at the Warsaw Speedway. Darr finished ahead of a large field with Kirk McNagney of Columbia

City, and Junior Dear, of Fort Wayne, not far behind in second and third place respectively.

Warsaw drivers turned in commendable performances as Baldy Himes won the consolation race and Art Johnson grabbed the checkered flag in the semi-feature. Forrest Egner won the race between the six slowest cars, and Mike Lott of New Paris, topped the field of the six fastest qualifying cars. Heat winners at the local track were Mickey Potter, of Fort Wayne, Max Hile of Columbia City, Devon Metzler, of Goshen, and Junior Dear of Fort Wayne.

The races in Warsaw were broadcast over WRSW by Woodie's Service. The stock cars will be running here again next Saturday night with Main Automotive sponsoring the WRSW broadcast at 8:45 p.m.

Saturday, July 21, 1951
Max Hile Wins Feature Race At Warsaw Speedway

Over 2,000 fans were treated to thrills of stock car racing Saturday night at the Warsaw Speedway with Max Hile, of Columbia City, winning the feature event.

There was one event of unusual interest. That was what the race track officials call a "ca-dag-it" race. This is a race of cars to see who gets onto the track first. The first one out of the pit area starts in the poll position. The cars came out so fast after the surprise call that an accident occurred at the pit gate. Eleven cars started this event, with the winner being Don Anderson, of Culver. Heat winners were, Gale Smith, of Warsaw; Gene Darr, Goshen; Ernie Fisher, and Bob Stonebreaker, Bippus.

OTHER WINNERS. The dash of the six slowest cars was won by Bob Stonebreaker, and Don Anderson won the race for the six fastest cars. The semi event of the evening consisting of 15 laps, was captured by Devon Metzler, of Goshen. In the feature event a display of fine driving was put on by Hile to grab the checkered flag. Don Shively, Columbia City, was second, and Gale Smith was third. It was announced at the track that on July 28 the Mermaid Festival queen and her attendants would be presented to the crowd.

WRSW was on hand with Sports Director Milo Chase giving thrill by thrill account of the racing for Main Automotive. Next week the races will be broadcast by H.O. Kring Motors, of Warsaw.

Saturday, July 28, 1951
Large Crowd At Warsaw, New Paris Speedways

Large crowds of stock car racing fans from this area attended the races held over the weekend at the Warsaw and New Paris Speedways. An estimated 2,500 fans were in Warsaw Saturday night to see Miss Betty Bray, 1951 queen of the North Webster Mermaid Festival, and her two attendants, Miss Jonella Miller of Pleasant Lake, and Miss Nancy Cox of Warsaw. The races Sunday night at New Paris also drew over 2,000 spectators.

The three Mermaid Festival beauties were guests of honor at the Warsaw Speedway. They rode around the track in convertibles furnished by the Kring, McKown and Bledsoe dealers, and then viewed the races from a special box. One of the highlights came when Miss Bray awarded a trophy to Russ Brown, of Fort Wayne, who had the fastest qualifying time. The ceremony was broadcast over WRSW.

Gene Darr, of Goshen, won the 25-lap feature race at the local speedway, which welcomed the return of Fred Boggs, of Warsaw, racing here for the first time this year. Boggs won the race between the six fastest qualifiers, but was defeated in a special match race with Russ Brown. The semi-feature was won by Steve Osborn of Warsaw, while Jake Burtsfield, of Syracuse, won the special "Cadagit" race. Jim Elliott, of Warsaw, won the race between the six slowest qualifiers, and Fred Harris, of Warsaw captured the consolation race, which was strictly stock. Heat winners were Gale Smith, of Warsaw; Darr; Max Hile, of Columbia City; and Jerry Ott, also of Columbia City.

Saturday, August 4, 1951
3 Wrecks In Feature Race At Warsaw Speedway

After a thrilling feature race won by Gale Smith, 2,000 fans went away from the Warsaw Speedway practically talking to themselves Saturday night. The feature was stopped three times to allow the track to be cleared of wrecks so that the race could continue.

Among heat winners were Don Anderson, of Culver, and Jim Elliott, of Warsaw, who won his first race in his first year of racing. Freddie Boggs won the third heat after much discussion as to the track rules that requires no passing when there is a wreck on the track. It was finally decided that Boggs was the winner over Jake Burtsfield.

In the fourth race Max Couch, of Columbia City, got the checkered flag. In the race for the six slowest cars, Earl Lotter, Columbia City was the winner. Gale Smith copped the flag for the six fastest cars.

The "strictly stock" cars ran a consolation race of their own and the winner was Noah Blanton, Elkhart. In the consolation event for the modified stocks, Irv Pattonbrook, of Churubusco, came in first with a brand new car that had never been on the track.

The semi-final event of the evening was won by Mickey Potter of Fort Wayne in a race complete with spills. A special Cadagit race was held for the jalopies and Don Wallace, of Warsaw, won it very easily driving a 1938 Plymouth Tudor.

The weirdest feature event ever to be held on the speedway took place with the race being stopped three times. The boys were off to a seemingly good start when in the third lap eight cars smashed up and the track was blocked. On the next restart a car rolled over in front of the grandstand and the race had to be stopped again. After the seventh lap another crash occurred that blocked the track, so again the cars were lined up single file. This time the race was completed, with Gale Smith the winner.

WRSW reported the races, with Milo Clase at the mike. The broadcast was presented by Woodie's Service, Warsaw.

Saturday, August 11, 1951
Gale Smith Wins Feature Races At Warsaw, New Paris

Gale Smith, of Warsaw, spent a very successful weekend of stock car racing, winning feature races at both the Warsaw speedway and the New Paris speedway. Smith topped the field in the 50-lap feature here Saturday night winning the mid-season championship trophy. Mickey Potter, of Fort Wayne, was second and Archie Holle, Warsaw, was third. All three received trophies from Gene Detchemendy, manager of the Warsaw Speedway.

On Sunday night, Smith took his car to New Paris and won the feature race there, finishing ahead of Chuck McKibben, of Columbia City, and Bob Terehek of Goshen.

A capacity crowd witnessed the races in Warsaw Saturday night. Detchemendy, in a special ceremony, presented trophies to Randy Zuck, of Winona Lake, and Dale Millington, of Warsaw, winners last Wednesday of the boys' Koastin-Krates Derby. Randy, Dale and 17 other boys who had competed in the derby were taken around the speedway track in their Koastin-Krates. Devon Metzler, of Goshen, the fastest stock car qualifier of the evening started pulling the small cars around the quarter-mile oval but five of the cars broke loose on the first turn and Irv Pattenbrook of Churubusco then took over and towed the boys the rest of the way around the track.

FAVORITE DRIVER. Another feature of the Saturday night program, a surprise affair, came when Kenny Pollack a four-year old Pierceton boy, walked onto the track with his father and presented a trophy to Steven Osborn, of Warsaw, for being "his favorite stock car driver".

Heat winners at the local speedway were Pattenbrook, Bud Shlater, of Fort Wayne, Don Nusbaum, of Cleveland, Ohio and formerly of Warsaw, and Jim Elliott, of Warsaw. Bill Lotz, of North Manchester, won the race between the six slowest cars. Gale Smith, who later won the feature race and championship trophy, also copped first place in the race between the six fastest qualifiers. Doyle Miller, of Columbia City, won the consolation race, and Gene Darr, of Goshen, grabbed the checkered flag in the semi-feature.

The races in Warsaw were broadcast over WRSW by Main Automotive. Announcer Milo Clase interviewed the two Koastin – Krates champions, Randy Zuck and Dale Millington. It was announced that races will be held here on Thursday and Saturday nights of this week, as a sports feature of the Kosciusko County fair.

Saturday, August 18, 1951
Times Union Article Missing, No Results

Saturday, August 25, 1951
Art Johnson Wins Feature At Warsaw Speedway

A hometown favorite, Art Johnson, won the feature race Saturday night at the Warsaw Speedway. A large crowd saw Johnson, a Warsaw resident, guide his stock car into first place early in the race and then hold off all challengers to grab the checkered flag. Mickey Potter, of Fort Wayne, was second and Archie Holle, of Warsaw, came from far behind to finish third. The feature race had to be stopped and restarted at the end of the first lap after cars driven by Fred Boggs, Max Hile and Jake Burtsfield were involved in a collision.

Hile, of Columbia City, won the semi-feature while Carl Salesman, of Churubusco, copped the consolation event. Don Shively, of Columbia City, was first in the race between the six fastest qualifiers.

HOLD TAG RACE. In a special "tag race", first held here this year, Forrest Egner came in ahead of the field. Heat winners during the evening were Mickey Potter, Fort Wayne; Dean Rans, Culver; Ned Spath, of Michigan; and Jerry Ott, Columbia City. The races were broadcast over WRSW by Main Automotive, of Warsaw. The stock cars will be racing again next Saturday night, with time trials starting at 7 o'clock, and the first race at 8:30 p.m.

Saturday & Monday, September 1 & 3, 1951
Dick Salesman Wins Feature Races Here Saturday, Monday

Dick Salesman, of Churubusco, must have a special liking for the Warsaw Speedway, as well as one of the fastest stock cars in this area. The Labor Day weekend found Salesman winning top honors at the local quarter-mile race track on Saturday night and again on Monday night. By capturing the feature 50-lap race in 16:47.4 last night, he won the special trophy.

Last night's race card was a thriller. In the feature race Archie Holle and Gale Smith, both of Warsaw, finished second and third, respectively, after a series of spectacular accidents, one of which resulted in considerable damage to two new automobiles parked behind the guard fence. This happened during the first lap when a racer driven by Miller, of Churubusco, went over the wall and the guard fence. His car smashed the front ends of the two new automobiles, one owned by Arthur Hanes, of Nappanee, and the other by Walter Williamson, of Route 2, Bourbon.

In the third lap of the feature, cars driven by Art Johnson, of Warsaw, and Chester Hughes hit the wall and a car driven by Bob Stonebraker went through the fence. Johnson and Hughes were able to continue the race.

Mickey Potter, Ft. Wayne

POTTER WINS SEMI. The semi-feature last night was won by Mickey Potter, of Fort Wayne, who also copped the consolation race. Dick Heeter, North Manchester, won the event between the six fastest cars, and Jim Smiley, of Talma, finished first among the six slowest qualifiers. Heat winners were Archie Holle, Warsaw; Gale Smith, Warsaw; Harold Shrock,

Syracuse; and Dick Briggs, Columbia City.

On Saturday night, Salesman finished ahead of Gale Smith, Warsaw, and Gene Darr, Goshen, in the feature. In this race, cars driven by Art Johnson, of Warsaw, and Jerry Ott, Columbia City, became tangled and both crashed into the wall. Again, there were no injuries.

Smith won the semi-feature event and Salesman won the consolation race. Smith also won the race between the six fastest qualifiers. Heat winners Saturday night were Archie Holle, Warsaw; Mickey Potter, Fort Wayne; Dee Johnson, Cromwell; and Dale LeMaster Goshen.

A special "tag" race was also held. With ten cars in the race, the final two cars could not tag each other and it was finally declared a draw between "Mouse" Leak and Joe Cutler, of Warsaw.

Saturday, September 8, 1951
Dick Briggs Fractures Neck in Mishap At Warsaw Speedway

A bad accident, which resulted in a serious injury to Dick Briggs, of Coesse, occurred Saturday night during the semi-feature stock car race at the Warsaw Speedway. Briggs, the 22-year old son of Mr. and Mrs. Robert Briggs, of Coesse, suffered a broken neck when his car rolled completely over. Attendants at the McDonald hospital said Monday that the young man's condition is not critical and that he will recover. However, it is probable that he will have his neck in a cast for a considerable period of time.

LEADING AT TIME. Briggs was leading the semi-feature race when the mishap occurred. He also sustained numerous cuts and bruises. Dick is employed with the International Harvester company in Fort Wayne. The feature race was won by Art Johnson, of Warsaw, with Archie Holle, also of Warsaw, finishing second and Gene Darr, of Goshen, third.

Winners of heat races were Holle, Russ Tracy, of North Manchester, Duck Rowe, of Fort Wayne and Darr. Mouse Leak, of Warsaw, won a special "tag" race, and Mike Lott, of New Paris, won the "Cadagit" race. Lott also finished first in the special "Hot Dog" race, an event in which the six fastest qualifying cars competed. At the end of three laps the drivers stopped for a hot dog and coke, and then completed three more laps.

Saturday, September 15, 1951
Gene Darr Wins Stock Car Feature At Warsaw Speedway

A large field of stock cars, 52 in all—showed up at the Warsaw Speedway Saturday night and gave local and area racing fans one of the most entertaining programs of the year. The 52 cars were qualified in only 35 minutes.

The feature race was won by Gene Darr, Goshen's outstanding driver who had to come from far behind to nose out Jim Hoagland, of Fort Wayne, who was second, and Don Anderson, of Culver, who finished third. Anderson won the semi-feature crossing the finish line ahead of Carl Salesman, of Churubusco, and Lucky Long, of Fort Wayne.

A match race between drivers of the Fort Wayne Racing association and the Tri-States

Racing circuit was one of the feature events on the program. Five drivers competed for each team, and the winner was Mickey Potter, of Fort Wayne. Darr, of the Tri-States circuit was second, and Hoagland, of Fort Wayne, finished third. There were no pile-ups in this race, which proved to be very interesting.

In addition to Potter and Hoagland, and other Fort Wayne drivers were Lucky Long, Elmer Harpe and Archie Holle. Competing for Tri-States, in addition to Darr, were Devon Metzler, Gale Smith, Don Anderson and Art Johnson.

LOCAL DRIVER WINS. Johnson, of Warsaw, won the race between the six fastest qualifiers, covering six laps in the excellent time of 1:54.6. Salesman won the race between the six slowest qualifiers, and also grabbed the checkered flag in the consolation race, which had to be restarted after Leon Depay, of Star City, rolled his car over during the first lap. He was not injured.

Heat winners were Potter, Hoagland, Devon Metzler, of Goshen, and Dick Heeter, of North Manchester. Several of the races were broadcast over WRSW by H.O. Kring Motors.

Saturday, October 13, 1951
Gale Smith Wins 100 Lap Feature At Local Track

Gale Smith, of Warsaw, copped top honors at the Warsaw Speedway Saturday night. He came in for the checkered flag to take first place in the 100-lap feature race. A good crowd was on hand despite the chilly weather. The long race was run off in the fast time of 33 minutes.

Heat winners in the racing were Mickey Potter, of Fort Wayne, Bob Stonebreaker of Bippus, Steve Osbun, of Warsaw, and Jerry Ott, Columbia City. The race for the 6 fastest cars was won by John Nisely, of Goshen.

The semi-feature race of 15 laps was captured by Devon Metzler, of Goshen. Twenty four cars started this race, and it was thrilling event all the way as the drivers were fighting for a spot in the feature event.

The feature race of 100 laps or 25 miles around the oval was won by Smith who started on the pole position and led all the way. Art Johnson, of Warsaw, was well up in front until the halfway mark when he slid in the east curve and collided with Gene Darr's car that had been previously wrecked in a collision with Mickey Potter. The wreck eliminated these three fast cars.

Trophies were awarded the winners, Gale Smith, John Nisely who placed second, and to Steve Osbun, who was third. Main Automotive broadcast the heat races, and the feature was aired by Bledsoe Buick of Warsaw, with Milo Clase at the mike.

Saturday, October 20, 1951
Field Day For Gale Smith In Speedway Races

Gale Smith, of Warsaw, enjoyed a field day at the final races of the season staged Saturday night at the fairgrounds speedway before a small crowd. He won the feature race of 25 laps, finished first in the heat for the six fastest cars and saw his car come in victorious when driven by Joe Fisher, of Warsaw, in the special race for mechanics.

John Nisely, of Goshen, finished first in the opening heat; Phil Gingerich, of Kokomo, won the second heat and Dick Mitchell, of Plymouth, wheeled his mount to a victory in the third heat. Then followed the race for the six fastest cars and this was won by Gale Smith, of Warsaw, who followed by taking the 25-lap feature event. Second place in the feature race went to Lester Groves, of Plymouth, and third place to Phil Geiger, of Churubusco.

In the special race for mechanics, who have not before driven in races, the winners were as follows: Joe Fisher, driving Gale Smith's car, first; Paul Brown, Oswego, second, and Kenny Hawkins, Warsaw, third.

Saturday's races concluded a season of auto events at the speedway. These races have been broadcast over WRSW through courtesy of H.O. Kring Motors, Main Automotive and Woodie's Service.

1952
A Year of Transition & Improvement

The Kosciusko County Fair Association took over the management of the speedway in 1952 with new racing officials and a commitment to improve the racing facilities. The new improvements included a 400 foot link wire fence about 12 feet high in front of the grandstand, a third rail on top of the former two-rail retaining wall, and along the back stretch a third fence to prevent parked cars from getting too close to the track and also to prevent the racing cars from crashing into the passenger cars in case they hurdle the retaining wall. A new attractive weekly racing program was printed and available for fans to fill in time trial times and race winners.

WARSAW Speedway
Kosciusko County Fairgrounds

AUTO RACES
Nº 2036

Every Saturday Night
Time Trials, 7 p.m.   1st Race, 8:30

Operated By
KOSCIUSKO COUNTY FAIR BOARD
Concessions By
WINONA LAKE FIREMEN

RACING OFFICIALS	
President	Nub Wysong
Vice President	Art Hartley
Secretary	Bud Shlater
Treas. & Business Mgr.	Russ Holden
Official Starter	Bud Shlater
Announcer	Wm. (Bill) Lipkey

Thursday, May 1, 1952
WRSW to Broadcast First Night of Racing Saturday

Stock cars will speed around the quarter-mile track of the Warsaw Speedway Saturday night as drivers of the Northeastern Indiana Racing Association converge on the Kosciusko county fairgrounds for the first time this summer.

WRSW will be on hand to broadcast the initial races of the season. The Runyan Dairy Service, of Winona Lake, will sponsor Saturday night's broadcast with Milo Clase at the WRSW microphone from 8:45 to 9:15 p.m. Through the summer, other Saturday night race programs will also be broadcast direct from the track by Bledsoe Buick, Woodie's Sinclair Service, and Rapps Body Shop, all of Warsaw.

The Warsaw Speedway is being operated this summer by the Kosciusko County Fair Association, which has succeeded in making many improvements at the track. The 440-yard oval is in great shape and a woven fence was built in front of the large bleacher section to greatly aid safety of the fans.

Time trials are slated to get underway at 7:30 p.m. with the first race at 8:30 o'clock. This will be the third consecutive year that WRSW will broadcast the races direct from the Speedway.

Saturday, May 3, 1952
Large Crowd Witnesses First Night Of Stock Car Racing

Stock car racing at the Warsaw Speedway got off to a grand start Saturday night at the fairgrounds as a very fast and large number of cars from the Northeastern Indiana Racing Association performed before a near-capacity crowd.

Many spills dotted the evening's entertainment around the quarter-mile track. However, there were no injuries. A car driven by Mil Born, of Fort Wayne, hurtled the fence during the second heat race, the car landing on its side after rolling over the retaining wall. Gale Smith, of Warsaw, ran into tough luck in the feature race. Having worked his way into a bid for first place, Smith saw his motor conk out, and he had to pull out of the race.

The feature race was won by Jerry Ott of Columbia City, who negotiated the 25 laps in the fast time of 8:32.51. Ott also won the second heat race to capture top individual honors for the night. Jim Salesman, of Columbia City, was second, and Bob Stonebraker, of Huntington, was third in the feature.

Other Winners: Other winners were Tom Anderson of Culver, first heat; Lee King, of Corunna, third heat; Forest Egner, of Akron, fourth heat; Chuck Martin, of Fort Wayne, first consolation race; and Jim Salesman, of Columbia City, second consolation race.

Several new safety features added by the Kosciusko County Fair Association, which owns and operates the track, brought approval from the large crowd. The new improvements include a 400 foot link wire fence about 12 feet high in front of the grandstand; a third rail on top of the former two-rail retaining wall; and along the back stretch a third fence to prevent parked cars from getting too close to the track and also to prevent the racing cars from crashing into the passenger cars in case they hurdle the retaining wall.

WRSW, with Milo Clase at the microphone, broadcast 30 minutes of the heat races direct from the track, sponsored by Runyan's Dairy Service.

Saturday, May 10, 1952
Jim Martin wins Main Race Here; Local Drivers Absent

Jim Martin, of Fort Wayne, enjoyed a big night at the Warsaw Speedway Saturday, winning the first heat, the race between the six fastest qualifiers, and then capping his performance by receiving the checkered flag in the 25-lap feature.

Cool weather held the crowd to a minimum, but thrilling races rewarded the braver fans who were present. Race drivers participating in the events Saturday were members of the Northeastern Racing Association. Several local and county drivers who are non-members, failed to appear at the track. They are protesting financial arrangements and had previously announced that they would not compete here while the Northeastern Racing Association is sanctioning the races.

The local drivers announced their withdrawal following the opening card of racing here a week ago, claiming that they were not paid enough prize money. Most of them raced Sunday night at the New Paris Speedway,

Track Unfavorable. Previous rains left the local quarter-mile track quite slippery and treacherous Saturday night, and as a result several cars ran into the retaining wall. The Kosciusko County Fair Association, which operates the track, faced the decision of whether or not to hold the races because of Friday's all day rain. However, it was decided to hold the program after the track was rolled and put into the best shape possible under the circumstances.

Gerry Ott, of Columbia City, who won the feature race a week ago, copped the second heat race. The third heat race was won by Whitey Damaree of Fort Wayne, and Dick Briggs of Columbia City finished first in the fourth heat.

Rollin Smith, popular North Manchester driver who had gone through the retaining wall earlier, won the first consolation race while Forrest Egner, of Columbia City, finished first in the second consolation event. Martin, as previously noted, won the race between the six fastest cars and then came right back to capture the checkered flag in the main event.

Several of the races were broadcast over WRSW, with Milo Clase at the microphone by the Rapp Body Shop, of Warsaw. Each Saturday night, WRSW presents a 30-minute broadcast from 8:45 to 9:15 p.m., direct from the speedway.

Rainout Saturday, May 17, 1952
Rain forced cancellation of the stock car racing program Saturday night at the Warsaw Speedway.

Rainout Saturday, May 24, 1952
There were no races held Saturday night at the Warsaw Speedway due to wet grounds.

Saturday, June 7, 1952
Many Thrills At Local Speedway

Forty-five cars and drivers of the Northeastern Indiana Racing association entertained a capacity crowd to some exciting races Saturday night at the Warsaw Speedway, with several wrecks adding to the thrill-packed program.

Smokey Zent, of Fort Wayne, won the featured 25-lap event after a weird race that saw many crashes and position changes which left even the timers and scorers confused. It was finally determined that Zent was the winner, even though Dick Heeter, of North Manchester, had first been announced to the crowd as having won the race. Twenty-two cars were entered in the feature event. The outcome was finally determined by a recording device, which keeps an accurate count of all positions in each lap. Heeter was given second place.

Heat winners were Leon Meadows of Kokomo, Gerry Ott, of Columbia City, Dick Martin, of North Manchester, and Whitey Damaree, who came from last place to get the checkered flag. Fenton Gingerich, of Kokomo, driving his first race at the Warsaw Speedway, won the event between the six fastest qualifying cars.

No One Injured. The first consolation race was stopped by a wreck on the first turn. However, it was re-started and finally won by Carl Salesman, of Columbia City. A six-car pileup marred the second consolation race, and it also had to have a second start. Several cars collided in this race, but no one was injured. Dick Heeter was the winner, and he received a great ovation as he carried the checkered flag on the victory lap.

Thirty minutes of the racing program were broadcast over WRSW by Woodie's Service of Warsaw, with Milo Clase at the microphone. The races are held here each Saturday night, and WRSW is on the air from the track between 8:45 and 9:15 p.m.

Saturday, June 14, 1952
Gale Smith Wins Stock Car Crown

A local stock car driver, Gale Smith, captured top honors Saturday night in a thrill-packed race program held before some 2,000 fans at the Warsaw Speedway. Smith won the 50-lap feature race fo the early-season championship and was presented a beautiful wrist watch from the Fitch Jewelry store. The watch was presented by Milo Clase, WRSW sports director.

In addition to winning the championship race, Smith made it a "field day" by grabbing the checkered flag in the first heat race and finishing second to Dick Heeter of North Manchester, in the race between the six fastest qualifiers.

The scheduled "surprise race" was postponed until next Saturday night due to the soggy condition of the infield, where the race was to have taken place. A pair of shoes, donated by the Fashion Shoe Store, will go to the winner of this race next Saturday night.

Order of Finish. In winning the feature, Smith finished ahead of Ed Roy, of Fort Wayne, who was second; Junior Dear of Columbia City, third; and Archie Holle, of Warsaw, fourth.

The appearance of Smith and Holle on the Warsaw track gave evidence that some of the local drivers have returned to action here after a month of idleness due to "differences" on certain matters.

Two semi-feature races were held, the first being won by Hal Douglas, of Logansport, and second by Dick Briggs, of Coesse. Heat winners, in addition to Smith, were Jim Salesman, of Churubusco, Bob Chilcote, of Bryan, O., and Bill Brinsley, of Columbia City.

Saturday, June 21, 1952
Stock Car Races Feature Novelty

Bob Stonebrake, of Huntington, won his first feature race Saturday night at the Warsaw Speedway, moving up from his 14th starting position to take the lead early in the race.

The feature shared top billing with a special "novelty race" which saw the cars racing two laps forward, then one lap backward, two laps forward again, and finally one lap backward to the finish line. "Hig" Hillegas, of Fort Wayne, was the winner in this surprise race and thus received a free pair of shoes donated by the Fashion Shoe Store.

Despite rather threatening weather, a large crowd was on hand for the program of stock car racing. There were several collisions during the night's festivities, but no injuries.

Heat Winners. Heat winners were Jim Salesman, of Columbia City; Archie Holle, of Warsaw; Bill Martin, of Huntington; and Red Creech, of Columbia City. Gale Smith, of Warsaw, winner of the early season championship race a week ago, last night finished first in the consolation race.

As an added attraction, boats of the Lakeland Boat club were towed around the track so that spectators could get a glimpse of some of the boats that will be racing in the annual Fourth of July regatta on Winona Lake. Thirty minutes of the stock car racing program were broadcast over WRSW Saturday night by Bledsoe Buick, with Milo Clase at the microphone.

Saturday, June 28, 1952
Carl Salesman Wins Feature At Local Speedway

Carl Salesman, of Columbia City, ran off from the pack Saturday night to win his first feature stock car race at the Warsaw Speedway. Salesman finished far ahead of Hig Hillegas of Fort Wayne, who finished second.

The 25-lap feature was the most interesting event of the evening, due to several spin-outs and collisions. In the first turn six cars became involved in a mix-up, causing a re-start.

A novelty race was won by Smokey Zent. In this race, the drivers race two laps, stopping en-route to leave their shoes with the flagman, then two more laps, stopping to pick up their shoes and finally two more laps to the finish line. Kenny Harmon won the consolation event of 18 laps, while heat winners were Bob Stonebreaker, Carl Salesman, Bill Martin and Paul Snepp.

The stock cars will race here again Friday night as a feature of the Fourth of July program.

There will be a feature race of 75 laps.

Saturday, July 5, 1952
Gale Smith Captures 75-Lap Mid-Season Stock Car Title

Gale Smith, of Warsaw, climaxed a very successful holiday weekend of stock car racing by winning the 75-lap mid-season championship race Saturday night before a capacity crowd of 3,000 fans at the Warsaw Speedway. Smith had won the Fourth of July 25-lap feature on Friday night.

For winning, Smith received a large trophy from the Kosciusko County Fair Association, and a beautiful wrist watch donated by the Fitch Jewelry Store. Trophies also went to Dick Heeter, of North Manchester, who placed second in the feature, and Bob Stonebraker, of Huntington, who was third.

15 Cars Finish. The 75-lap race featured a starting field of 22 cars and 15 managed to finish the grueling pace.

Fenton Gingerich, of Kokomo, won the first heat, while Smith captured the second heat race. The winner of the third heat event was Walt Potter, of Huntertown, while Forest Egner, of Columbia City, copped the checkered flag in the fourth heat.

Smith made it a banner night by also winning the six lap "shoe dash" event. Russ Tracy, of North Manchester, won the first consolation race, while the second consey was taken by Dick Briggs, of Coesse. The races were broadcast over WRSW between 8:45 and 9:15 p.m. for Bledsoe Buick of Warsaw.

Saturday, July 12, 1952
Gale Smith Wins Another Feature

Gale Smith, who has started to make a habit out of winning feature stock car races at the Warsaw Speedway, did it again last Saturday night. Smith, of Warsaw, followed his usual procedure of qualifying fastest out of a field of 48 cars and then piloted his car to the feature race championship, which was a hectic affair that had to be restarted three times due to the spins and collisions.

In the first start, cars were driven by Bob Carpenter, Joe Bair, Bob Stonebraker and Mel Miller got in a jam on the second curve. After the second start, cars driven by Dick Martin, Ike Holderman and Carpenter went through the fence on the same curve. A third start found a clash of fenders, spins and jam-ups four laps later on the far turn with Dick Heeter, Johnny Malott, Ed Roy and Bob Stonebraker in the trouble. Traffic became so heavy, another start was necessary.

Smith takes lead. When the race finally got started, Smith held back and waited his opportunity. He took his lead in the 17th lap and was never headed. Heat winners Saturday night were Bill Frederick, of Sharpsville, Dick Heeter, of North Manchester; Wayne Stewart, and Cliff Setser, of Fort Wayne.

Smith won the special "shoe race", a novelty affair of eight laps, while Bob Stonebraker, of Huntington, won the first consolation race. The second consey was won by Smoky

Zent, of Fort Wayne. Finishing in order behind Smith in the feature were Bill Frederick, of Kokomo; Jim Salesman, of Columbia City, Joe Bair, of St. Joe; and Russ Tracy, of North Manchester.

Saturday, July 19, 1952
Stock Car Races Rained Out Here

Rain caused cancellations of the scheduled stock car races Saturday night at the Warsaw Speedway.

It was announced today **that** the races will not be run on Tuesday night, as previously announced in case of a rainout. Instead, they will be held next Saturday night, with the "demolition race" again scheduled as the feature event.

Saturday, July 26, 1952
Kokomo Driver Wins Feature Race Saturday

Bill Eubank, of Kokomo, won the 25-lap feature race at the fairground speedway Saturday night before a large and enthusiastic crowd of race fans. Eubank took the lead on the tenth lap, nosing out Oscar Knerr, who held the lead, and held top position throughout the race. Leon Meadows and Fenton Gingarich made it a clean sweep for Kokomo, finishing second and third respectively.

Gale Smith, of Warsaw, fastest qualifier of the 45 entries, had traffic trouble and finished fourth. Ray Staley and Carl Salesman, of Columbia City, finished fifth and sixth.

A feature of the evening was a parade of soap box derby cars which were towed around the track by Gale Smith and Max Hile.

Six cars started in the demolition race but only one finished. Ed Smith, in a Fashion Shoe Store car, after taking a roll on the back stretch, got back into the race and finished the winner.

The fastest qualifiers were Gale Smith, 19.34; Max Hile, Columbia City, 19.76; and Bob Stonebraker, Bippus, 19.84.

Heat winners were as follows:

First heat, 10 laps—Fenton Gingarich, first; Gale Smith, Warsaw, second; Jim Salesman, Columbia City, third. Time-3.23.25.

Second heat, 10 laps—Bill Eubank, Kokomo, first; Carl Salesman, Columbia City, second; Leon Meadows, Kokomo, third. Time 2.23.99.

Third heat, 10 laps—Oscar Knerr, Fort Wayne, first; Red Creech, Columbia City, second; Bill Green, Columbia City, third. Time 3:30.47.

Fourth heat, 10 laps—Ray Staley, Columbia City, first; Earl Lotter, Columbia City, second; Shorty Badgett, Wabash, third. Time 3:28.45.

First Consolation, 15 laps—Dick Briggs, Columbia City, first; Max Hile, Columbia City, second; Bob Stonebraker, Bippus, third; Whitie Demaree, Fort Wayne, fourth; Paul Snepp, Columbia City, fifth.

Second Consolation, 15 laps—Dick Gamble, Fort Wayne, first; Charlie Howell, Wabash, second; Cliff Asher, Rome City, third; Dick Heeter, North Manchester, fourth.

Saturday, August 2, 1952
Goshen Driver Wins 25-Lap Feature At Warsaw Speedway

DeVon Metzler of Goshen, won the 25-lap feature stock car race Saturday night at the Warsaw Speedway. A restart was necessary when, in the second lap of competition, two cars went into a spin. Gale Smith,of Warsaw, who has been capturing most of the feature race honors lately, was crowded into the fence late in the race and had to make a pit stop which knocked him out of contention. Dick Heeter, of North Manchester, finished second, while third place went to Dick Briggs, of Columbia City.

The first consolation race was so rough that all of the cars had to be called into the pits for repairs while the second consey was being run. On the far turn of the first lap, Wheaties Smith slid and an eight-car jam-up followed. Dick Heeter won the first consolation race of 15 laps, while Cliff Asher, of Rome City, finished ahead of the field in the second consolation event, also 15 laps.

Wheaties Smith and Crew

Smith Wins Heat. Heat winners were Gale Smith, Warsaw, Jim Salesman, Columbia City, Smokey Zent, Fort Wayne, and Earl Lotter, Columbia City. Metzler, in addition to winning the feature, also won the race between the six fastest qualifiers. Altogether, 43 cars qualified during the evening trials, with Gale Smith posting the best time of 19.12.

Children under 12 years of age were given a special treat when they were driven two laps around the track in the cars entered in the feature race. WRSW broadcast 30 minutes of the racing program for Rapps Body Shop of Warsaw.

Saturday, August 9, 1952
Gale Smith Wins Another Feature

Gale Smith, of Warsaw, copped another feature stock car race at the Warsaw Speedway Saturday night as several cars were eliminated early due to collisions.

During the sixth lap, three cars bumped together with the rest of the field doing some quick swerving in an effort to miss Doc Brewer, of Columbia City, who took a hard roll. Two cars were not able to restart. Later, six other cars became entangled, leaving Whitey Demaree, of Fort Wayne, parked on top of the fence. Six more cars were eliminated. Smith finally took the lead on the 20th lap and was being pushed by Carl Salesman, of Columbia City, and Bob Stonebraker of Bippus, when he crossed the finish line.

Due to a damp track, there were other tense moments of driving. Paul Snepp lost a wheel going into the first turn, but kept his car under control and was able to stop clear of traffic on the back stretch. In the second consolation race, cars driven by Wayne Stewart and Keith Coldren came together in a crash against the fence. At the same time Bill Green's car went into a spin coming out of the far turn and shook a light post.

Novelty Race. A novelty race was sponsored by the Fashion Shoe Store. Cars lined up five abreast to take three laps, stop long enough to have their pit men feed them a pie, and then back to their cars for three more laps. The winner was Red Creech of Columbia City.

Heat winners were Bill Fredericks, of Kokomo, Whitey Demaree of Fort Wayne, Jim Salesman, of Columbia City, and Red Creech of Columbia City. Oscar Knerr, of Fort Wayne, won the first consolation race, while Cliff Asher, of Kendallville, finished first in the second consey.

The stock cars will run again Wednesday night as a Kosciusko County fair feature, with time trials starting at 7:30 p.m. There will also be stock car racing on the final night of the fair next Saturday.

Wednesday, August 13, 1952
2 25-lap Races Staged

Two 25-lap feature races highlighted the stock car program last night before a capacity crowd at the Warsaw Speedway. The first feature was won by Gray Robeling, of Kokomo, while Carl Salesman, of Columbia City, captured the second feature event, which consisted of the 22 fastest qualifiers.

As an added attraction for the fair crowd, six midget cars were on hand to provide a thrilling 10-lap race. Bill Eubanks, of Kokomo, broke the track record with his qualifying lap of 18.99 seconds, only to see Gale Smith, of Warsaw, recapture the record with his qualifying run of 18.96 seconds.

In the first feature race, Robeling took over the lead on the 16th lap and held it to the finish. In the second feature, Salesman overcame an early lead by Cliff Asher and was never headed after the 17th lap. Salesman beat out Gale Smith, who was second, while Eubanks was third, Asher fourth and Bill Frederick, of Kokomo, fifth.

In the first feature, Robeling finished ahead of Jack Reilley, of Huntington, Cliff Setser of Fort Wayne, Earl Lotter, of Columbia City, and Dick Martin, of Rochester, who were second, third, fourth and fifth, respectively.

Russ Tracy, of North Manchester, edged out Wheaties Smith, of Warsaw, in the special "destruction race". The entrants crashed into each other until only Tracey's mount was left in the running. Heat races were won by Russ Tracy, of North Manchester; Bill

Eubanks, of Kokomo; Vern Gerigan, of Huntington; and Oscar Kneer, of Fort Wayne.

Saturday, August 16, 1952
Bob Stonebraker Captures Gold Cup Championship At Speedway

Bob Stonebraker, of Bippus, captured the 50-lap gold cup championship stock car race Saturday night before an overflow crowd at the Warsaw Speedway. Stonebraker received his championship trophy from Russell Smith, chairman of the Kosciusko County fair board. The stock car races featured the final night of the county fair. The second place gold cup went to Jim Salesman of Columbia City, while Max Hile, also of Columbia City, received the third place award.

Stonebraker jumped into an early lead and started lapping cars during the fourth lap. He lost his lead to DeVon Metzler, of Goshen, on the 12th lap. However, on the 24th lap, Metzler, Stonebraker and Salesman clashed just before the first turn. Metzler went into the infield, Stonebraker's car stood on two wheels and Salesman's racer parked against the fence.

Early in the race, Oscar Knerr, of Fort Wayne, made the timbers fly when his car flew through the fence on the far turn, running one of the fence planks into the grill, radiator, and motor of his auto.

There were several other unexpected thrills for the crowd's pleasure. The second heat race saw the four lead cars stack up, and Carl Salesman, who had been in fifth place, came home the winner. The first consey race called for a restart when Russ Tracy, Dick Heeter, Gray Robeling and Lee Grover clashed on the third turn. Bill Green lost a wheel during the second consey. The wheel ran a lap up and down the straightaway before heading for the infield. Highlights of the racing program Saturday night were broadcast over WRSW by Woodie's Sinclair Service, of Warsaw.

Columbia City drivers dominated the heat races. The four heat winners were Max Hile, Carl Salesman, Jim Salesman and Dick Briggs, all of Columbia City. Hile also won the special six-lap "shoe race". Cliff Asher, of Columbia City captured the first consolation event of 15 laps while Doc Brewer, of Huntington, coasted home ahead of the field in the second consey.

Saturday, August 23, 1952
Jim Salesman Wins Feature Race on Fast Track at Warsaw Speedway

Jim Salesman, of Columbia City, won out over 21 other speedsters in the 25-lap stock car feature Saturday night at the Warsaw Speedway. A fast track provided a great deal of "spin action" during the feature. There was one crash. Bill Holle, of Silver Lake, went into a skid on the backstretch of the 11th lap. His car went careening toward the guard rail, where he crashed head-on into a car driven by Bill Martin, of Rochester. Luckily, no one was hurt.

In the second heat race, a car driven by Keith Cole, of Columbia City, jumped the fence in the second turn. Leon Meadows, of Kokomo, was leading when he rode the wall in the main stretch of the sixth lap. He came back to challenge for the lead at the ninth lap, but went into the fence.

A surprise finish in the fourth heat race developed near the finish line as Earl Lotter, of Columbia City, overcame Ivan Ort, of Fort Wayne, who had led all the way. Dick Briggs, of Columbia City, won the race between the six fastest qualifiers, thus receiving a free pair of shoes, from the Fashion Shoe Store.

Heat Winners. Heat winners during the evening were Carl Salesman, E.B. Crowell, Bob Stonebraker and Earl Lotter. Bob Shlater won the first consolation race of 10 laps. This race was re-started at the end of two laps when Ernie Powell, of Wabash, and Bill Holle, of Silver Lake, locked together in the main stretch.

Fifteen cars buzzed around the quarter-mile track in the second consolation event. Jerry Ott, of Columbia City, took the lead in the 12th lap and finished first ahead of fellow townsmen Paul Snepp and Johnny Malott. The racing highlights were broadcast direct from the speedway over WRSW as a public service by Rapp Body Shop, of Warsaw.

Saturday, August 30, 1952
Gale Smith Cops Fifth Feature

Rain washed out the scheduled Labor Day races Monday night at the Warsaw Speedway, but a large crowd was on hand last Saturday night to see Gale Smith, of Warsaw, register his fifth feature race triumph, more than any other one driver this season.

Smith topped the 22-car field in the 25-lap feature event with Bob Stonebraker, of Bippus, a car-length behind in second place. Max Hile, of Columbia City, was third. The feature race was stopped on the 18th lap when Smith, Buck Beasley of Columbia City and Gene Ringle, of Warsaw, were involved in a tangle on the backstretch guard rail. Ringle was out on the restart, but Smith and Beasley re-entered the competition and Smith went on to win. Women were special guests at the speedway Saturday night, being admitted free of charge.

See Parachute Jump. Although the Monday night races were cancelled, fans who were on hand Saturday night saw Lloyd Sproat, of Fort Wayne, make a delayed parachute jump. He bailed out at 2,500 feet and came down in a perfect landing in the parking area between Winona Lake and the backstretch of the speedway.

Winners of the four heat races were Whitey Demaree, Gale Smith, Bob Stonebraker and Steve Osborn. The special "shoe race" sponsored by the Fashion Shoe Store, was declared a dead heat between Gale Smith and Bob Stonebraker. Earl Lotter won the first consolation race, while Dick Martin grabbed the checkered flag in the second consolation event.

The stock cars will run again next Saturday night, with WRSW broadcasting the racing highlights at 8:45 p.m. for Bledsoe Buick.

Saturday, September 6, 1952
New Record At Local Speedway

Dick Heeter, of North Manchester, and Doc Brewer, of Huntington, shared honors Saturday night at the Warsaw Speedway. Heeter set a new track record of 18.94 seconds in his qualifying round, while Brewer won his first feature race.

Heeter had some tough luck in the 25-lap feature, failing to finish due to a flat tire on the 12th lap. Brewer took the lead on the 17th lap and maintained it to the end although followed closely by Lenny Juday, of Goshen.

There were numerous collisions, although no serious injuries resulted. The accidents started early. In the first heat race, Steve Osborne, of Warsaw, went into a skid and struck the judges' stand, putting his car out of action for the balance of the evening.

Another Injury. During the third heat, Keith Cole, of Columbia City, completely jumped the fence on the back stretch. The fourth heat was marked by plenty of spins and an accident which sent Bob France to the hospital after his mount upset when he and Tom Holden, of Peru, tangled. The second consolation event saw another driver, Johnny Malott, going to the hospital for treatment of injuries suffered in a four-car pile-up.

Gale Smith, of Warsaw, won the special "shoe race" sponsored by the Fashion Shoe Store, with Bob Stonebraker finishing second. Heat winners were Gray Robeling, of Fort Wayne, Bob Shlater, of Churubusco, Jack Reilly, of Huntington, and John Pollock. Lenny Juday won the first consey, while Whitey Demaree romped home first in the second consolation event.

Saturday, September 13, 1952
Gale Smith Top Winner Again At Local Speedway

Gale Smith, Warsaw's most consistent stock car race winner, captured the 25-lap feature Saturday night at the Warsaw Speedway. Smith maintained the lead for the full distance, and was followed by Devon Metsler, of Goshen, in second place, and Dick Heeter, of North Manchester, who was third.

Action was fast, but there was very little auto damage. However, Bill Martin and Doc Brewer got together in the first turn and battered down a stretch of fence.

Next Saturday night the Fashion Shoe race will be run by local representatives of the Junior Chamber of Commerce and fire department.

Heat winners last Saturday were Dick Briggs, of Columbia City; Chuck Grover, of Goshen; Whitey Demaree, of Fort Wayne; and Johnny Malott, of Columbia City. Paul Snepp, of Columbia City, won the first consolation race, while Gale Smith, of Warsaw, grabbed the checkered flag in the second contest. The "shoe race" was won by Ray Staley, of Columbia City. WRSW broadcasted 30 minutes of the racing action for the Rapp Body Shop, of Warsaw.

Saturday, September 20, 1952
Gale Smith Adds Another Triumph

The popular Gale Smith, of Warsaw, continued to show his superiority over northern Indiana stock car drivers by copping the feature race Saturday night at the Warsaw

Speedway. In registering his eighth feature race victory, Smith set a new 25-lap record of 8:17.72.

Sharing top billing with the feature event was a special grudge race between members of the Warsaw Jaycee and the Winona Lake fire department. It was Jim Painter, president of the Jaycees, and Bruce Howe, the fire chief, who finished one-two in a red-hot, nip and tuck battle. Other contenders were Bob Bayne, Mike Fawley, Jay Shue, Wayne Graff, and Jerry Lessig, with Russell Smith flagging the eleven-lap heat.

In the feature race of the evening, Smith stepped out in front at the drop of the green flag and was never headed. Dick Briggs, of Columbia City, was second, followed by Bob Shlater, of Churubusco, Bob Stonebraker, of Bippus, and Jake Burtsfield, of Syracuse. There were no accidents to mar the feature, but competition was fast and close.

In addition to copping the feature, Smith also won the third heat race. Other winners were Dick Briggs, Keith Cole, and Ray Staley, all of Columbia City. Jake Burtsfield won the 15-lap consolation event. WRSW broadcast the racing highlights for the Fashion Shoe Store, of Warsaw.

Saturday, September 27, 1952
Dick Briggs In First Feature Race Victory

Dick Briggs, of Columbia City, won his first feature race of the year Saturday night at the Warsaw Speedway. Briggs took the lead early in the 25-lap race and was never headed. Devon Metsler, of Goshen, was second, followed by Bob Shlater, of Churubusco, Doc Brewer, of Huntington, and Earl Lotter, of Columbia City.

Only six cars, out of a starting field of 12, were able to cross the finish line in the third heat race which called for two restarts. Several collisions resulted in six of the cars dropping out of the race.

Herman Ginther, of Etna Green, will have occasion to remember his first time on the Warsaw track. During qualifications, his stock car rolled sideways, flipped in the air with nose down, and over again, finally coming to earth with a loud "bang".

Heat winners during the evening were Dick Briggs, of Columbia City; Keith Cole, of Columbia City; Gale Smith, of Warsaw; and Whitey Demaree, of Fort Wayne. Smith also won the special "Fashion Shoe Race" of six laps.

A preview of the late model stock cars that will run at Fort Wayne was run in the form of a 10-lap race with Jimmy Clark the winner. The 15-lap consolation event was won by Don Nusbaum, of St. Louis, Mo. Highlights of the race program were broadcast over WRSW by Bledsoe Buick.

Saturday, October 4, 1952
Final Stock Car Race Here Won By Bob Shlater

The stock car racing season at the Warsaw Speedway came to a close last Saturday night, with Bob Shlater, of Churubusco, winning the feature 25-lap finale. Shlater took his lead during the fourth lap and held it throughout. Gale Smith, big winner of the year, was forced to pull out of the race while holding fourth position when his car collided with Keith Cole's racer.

In addition to the heat events, consolation race and feature, there was also a special "owners' race", won by Monty Miller, of Bippus, driving the white car in which Bob Stonebraker is usually seen. Miller's win was good for a pair of shoes from the Fashion Shoe Store. A car driven by Ed Barrus was wrecked on the back stretch after hitting a guard rail.

Heat winners Saturday night were Bob Stonebraker, of Bippus, Tom Holden, of Peru, Archie Holle, of Warsaw, and Bob Chilcote, of Kendallville. The consolation race of 10 laps was won by Dick Parker, of Columbia City.

The final night of racing activity was broadcast over WRSW by Sears Roebuck and Company, of Warsaw.

1953
The "Hoot" Gibson Era

In 1953, my great-uncle, Claris "Hoot" Gibson, took over as the Promoter and General Manager for the Warsaw Speedway. Gibson, from Columbia City, lived with very modest means and although he didn't have the flamboyance of initial manager Tyrrell, he dedicated the next 25 years of his life to the week-in and week-out physical and managerial work at the speedway. The stock car racing at the racetrack thrived during the 1950's and produced many popular and talented drivers. The most successful of these was Freddie Boggs, of Warsaw. He won many feature races at Warsaw and throughout the Midwest in both the midget and hot-rod stock classes. His success also took him to the most famous stock car race of all, the Daytona 500 in 1957. He qualified and took the green flag to race against famous Lee Petty and company on what then included racing on the beach as part of the track.

Owner's races, Powder Puff Derbys for female racers, Midget races, and "jalopy" races were also featured during the 1950's era. The greatest change in car types came around 1957 with the emergence of the open wheel modified stock cars to the scene. They proved faster and exciting with many collisions and roll-overs, but yet relatively safe with the built in roll-bar construction. This second "Modified" class was added on a full-time basis along with the "Strictly Stock" class for even more Saturday night races and enjoyment.

Thursday, April 8, 1953
Stock Car Races Begin Saturday

Stock car racing will open Saturday night at the Warsaw Speedway, located at the county fairgrounds in east Warsaw, and a large crowd is expected to witness the inaugural program. Radio stations WRSW AM and FM will broadcast a full 30-minute portion of the race program, direct from the speedway, at 8:30 p.m. with Milo Clase at the microphone.

The races this year are being sponsored by the Hoosier Hot Rods, Inc., of Warsaw and Columbia City. This organization is composed of some of the best-known stock car drivers in the area. Time trials are scheduled to get underway at 7 o'clock tomorrow night, with the first big race at 8:15. Clase, WRSW sports director, will handle the public address system.

Saturday, May 9, 1953
Mishawaka Drivers Win Feature Race At Warsaw Inaugural

A large crowd witnessed the summer season's first program of stock car racing Saturday night at the Warsaw Speedway, with Bill Clemons, of Mishawaka, taking top honors by winning the 30-lap feature race.

Thirty minutes of the racing action were broadcast over Radio Stations WRSW AM and FM for Bledsoe Buick. Milo Clase, WSRW sports director, announced the racing thrills from 8:15 to 8:45 p.m. and will continue to do so every Saturday night, with next week's radio broadcast being sponsored by Dean's Gulf Service.

Clemons was followed across the finish line of the quarter-mile track at the county fairgrounds by Bill Fredericks, of Wabash, who was second, and Archie Holle, of Warsaw, who was third.

There were plenty of thrills for the fans. Several minor accidents happened, but no one was injured. A car driven by Kenny Maggart, of Warsaw, upset and rolled over on the stretch in front of the grandstand.

Clown Act—Added entertainment featured a clown act by Ralph "The Hobo", who will be at the speedway every Saturday night. The races are operated this summer by Hoosier Hot Rods, Inc., a newly-organized group featuring well-known drivers of this part of the state.

John Pollock, of Columbia City, won the first heat race, Bill Clemons the second heat, Bill Fredericks the third, and Ray Staley, of Columbia City, the fourth heat. The race between the six fastest qualifiers was won by Dick Raizi, of Hobart. Bill Guy, of Marion, won the first consolation race and Max Hile, of Columbia City, flashed across the finish line first in the second consolation event.

Saturday, May 23, 1953
Muncie Driver Wins Feature at Local Speedway

Audie Swartz, of Muncie, nosed out Warsaw's Archie Holle Saturday night in one of the most thrilling feature stock car races ever seen at the Warsaw Speedway.

A fair-sized crowd at the fairgrounds saw Swartz and Holle battle it out over the 25-laps, with the lead exchanging hands several times. The race capped a very interesting evening of close finishes.

A half-hour of the racing program was broadcast over Radio Stations WRSW AM and FM by Milo Clase for Dean's Gulf Service. These broadcasts are featured every Saturday night at 8:15 p.m. by various sponsors.

Swartz, in addition to winning the feature event, also won the race between the six fastest qualifiers and thus will receive a pair of shoes from the Fashion Shoe Store. Fred Boggs, of Warsaw, was second in this race, and he finished third in the feature.

Bob Stonebraker, of Bippus, won the consolation race of 20 laps, beating out Ray Staley, of Huntington, who was second. Heat winners were Max Hile, of Columbia City; Roland Smith, of North Manchester; Junior Dear, of Columbia City; and Bill Martin, of Rochester.

Saturday, May 30, 1953
Columbia City Drivers Win Feature Races

The Columbia City drivers, Jerry Ott and Forrest Egner, walked off with top honors in a special Memorial Day stock car racing program which attracted an estimated 3,000 persons to the Warsaw Speedway Saturday night.

Ott won the "A" feature race of 30 laps, finishing ahead of Cowboy Likes, of Millersburg, and Gale Smith, of Warsaw, who were second and third respectively. In the "B" feature race, also of 30 laps, Egner defeated Cecil Grossnickle, of North Manchester, Dick Parker, of Columbia City, and Art Johnson, of Warsaw, who were second, third and fourth, respectively. As a result of their triumphs, both Ott and Egner received trophies.

Likes, second in the "A" feature, crossed the finish line first in the race between the six fastest qualifiers. Ray Staley, of Columbia City, was second and Art Johnson was third. Heat winners were Roland Smith, of North Manchester, first heat; Junior Dear, of Columbia City, second heat; Forrest Egner, Columbia City, third heat; and Art Johnson, Warsaw, fourth heat.

There were no serious crashes, although the speed and daring tactics of the drivers kept the near-capacity crowd in a constant uproar. Thirty minutes of the racing action were broadcast over WRSW AM and FM by the L and L Body Shop, of Warsaw. Each Saturday night WRSW airs the race from 8:15 to 8:45 o'clock.

Saturday, June 13, 1953
Fred Boggs Wins 1st Feature Race

A large crowd saw Fred Boggs, of Warsaw, win his first feature race Saturday night at the Warsaw Speedway, as 20 cars and drivers participated in the 25-lap main event. Boggs finished ahead of Chuck Grover, of Goshen, who was second, and two Columbia City competitors, Jerry Ott and Dick Briggs.

There were many thrills for the racing fans, although no serious accidents happened. In the consolation race, the finish was so close that a wire recording of the event had to be played back in order to determine the winner. It turned out that Jim Rex, of Huntington, finished first, with Dick Parker, Columbia City, second. There were 19 cars in this race.

Thirty minutes of the racing action were broadcast over WRSW AM and FM by Hoffer's

Market, of Warsaw.

Jerry Ott, in addition to finishing third in the feature, captured first place in the race between the six fastest qualifying cars. Jeff Culp was second and Gene Bowers third. Heat winners were Ray Staley, Columbia City, first heat; Chuck Grover, Goshen, second heat; Bob Perrine, South Bend, third heat; and Dick Briggs, Columbia City, fourth heat.

The stock car races are held at the speedway, located on the county fairgrounds, each Saturday night.

Saturday, June 20, 1953
Columbia City Driver Wins Feature Here

A large crowd saw Dick Briggs, of Columbia City, nose out Art Johnson and Freddie Boggs, both of Warsaw, in the 30-lap feature stock car race Saturday night at the Warsaw Speedway. Johnson finished second and Bogs third in the feature race, which was completed just before the rain. Twenty cars took part in the feature event.

The crowd received an added pleasure when race officials had the drivers take youngsters under 12 years of age around the track in the race cars. Many boys took advantage of this treat.

There were two semi-feature races, each of ten laps, with Forrest Egner of Columbia City, winning one and Johnny Pollock, of Columbia City, the other. Dick Heeter, of North Manchester, finished ahead of the field in the race between the six fastest qualifying cars. Heat winners were Art Johnson, of Warsaw, Jerry Ott, of Columbia City, Bob Staley of Warsaw, Buck Beezley of Wolf Lake, and Junior Dear also of Columbia City. In the race won by Johnson, six cars were involved in a collision, but no one was hurt.

A collection was taken for Bob Chilcotte's widow amounting to $130. Chilcotte was killed recently in a race at Fort Wayne.

Saturday, June 27, 1953
(No race results article)

Saturday, July 4, 1953
Fireworks, Stock Car Races, Draw Overflow Crowd

An estimated 8,000 persons celebrated the Fourth of July here Saturday night by attending the stock car races and fireworks display at the Warsaw Speedway located on the county fairgrounds.

Officials of the Kosciusko County Fair Association and Hoosier Hot Rods, Inc., who co-sponsored the program, said it was probably the largest crowd ever to attend the annual holiday program here. The bleachers inside the speedway were filled to overflow capacity, with hundreds of spectators sitting on the hillside and standing around the fence circling the quarter-mile track. Hundreds of others watched the fireworks display from outside the speedway, in parked cars on the fairgrounds and nearby streets.

The fireworks display started promptly at 10 o'clock, just after the semi-feature race was completed. Financed by the fair association and the Hoosier Hot Rods, the fireworks were set off by members of the Junior Chamber of Commerce, headed by Jim Painter.

The racing program featured many thrills, climaxed by the 50-lap mid-season championship event, held immediately after the 30-minute fireworks display had ended. Art Johnson, of Warsaw, was the winner of this feature event, but he turned over his entire purse of $130 to Archie Holle, of Warsaw, who was injured when his car was wrecked in a spectacular collision. Holle was leading the race at the time. Holle was taken to the McDonald hospital, but was dismissed after receiving treatment for cuts and bruises. Four stitches were required to close a cut above his eye.

During the qualifying laps, Duke Crocker, of Garrett, set a new lap record of 18 and 65-hundreth seconds. The former record of 18.88 was held by Gale Smith, of Warsaw. Behind Johnson in the feature 50-lap event were Dick Briggs, of Columbia City; 2nd, Crocker; 3rd, Steve Asbun, of Warsaw, 4th; and Fred Boggs, of Warsaw, 5th. All of these drivers received trophies.

The semi-feature, a 15-lap event, was won by Cecil Huntley, of Columbia City. Dick Heeter, of North Manchester, won the six-lap race between the six fastest qualifiers, and the heat winners in 10-lap races were Osbun, Buck Beezley, of Wolf Lake, Johnson, and Jerry Ott, of Columbia City. Huntley, by winning the semi-feature, was awarded a wrist watch by Everett Hanft, local jeweler.

Highlights of the racing program were broadcast over WRSW AM and FM by Dean's Gulf Service, of Warsaw.

Archie Holle, Warsaw

Wednesday, July 8, 1953
Aftermath of Speedway Wreck – Archie Holle, of Warsaw, is shown inspecting his stock car racer today after the car was badly damaged in a spectacular collision during the feature 50-lap mid-season championship race last Saturday night at the Warsaw Speedway. Holle escaped with body bruises and a gash over his eye that required three stitches. Art Johnson, of Warsaw, who won the race, turned over his entire purse to Holle. (No other results published) (Times Union Staff Photo)

Saturday, July 18, 1953
Gale Smith Wins Feature Race at Fairgrounds

Gale Smith, of Warsaw, won the feature 30-lap race for stock cars at the fairgrounds track in Warsaw Saturday night before a large crowd. Ray Staley, of Columbia City, was second and Duke Krocker, of Garrett, third.

Duke Krocker, of Garrett, won the first 10-lap heat, his time being 3:19.30. The second 10-lap heat went to Mike Klingaman, his time being 3:27.47. It was Klingaman's first race since returning from military service. Archie Holle, of Warsaw, finished first in the third heat, in the good time of 3:14.78. The fourth heat was won by Keith Cole of Columbia City, time 3:26.55. The six-lap sprint for the six fastest qualifiers was won by Art Johnson of Warsaw. His time was 1:55.40.

An interesting feature of the Saturday night program was a demolition team race which was won by the Magazine team over Freddie Boggs' team. Three autos were entered by each team and before the end of the grueling battle, all were almost completely demolished. Another one of these interesting and thrilling races will be held again in two weeks, it was announced by the race management.

Three bicycle races, open to boys from 6 to 15 years of age, were staged during the race program and these races will be repeated next week.

In the race for boys 6,7, and 8 years of age, the winner was Jimmy Gooch, with Skippy Leake, second and Gary Odell third.

In the race for boys 9, 10 and 11 years old, Brock Blosser was the winner, with Garry Knouff, second and Donald Eaton, third.

In the race for boys 12, 13, 14 and 15 years old, first honors went to Merlin Gibson, of Columbia City, with Jerry Fancil, second and Terry Hatfield, third. The WRSW broadcast of the race program was sponsored by Hoffer's Supermarket.

Saturday, July 25, 1953
Gale Smith Wins Feature Race At County Fairgrounds

Gale Smith, of Warsaw, won the 30-lap stock car feature race before a large crowd at the fairgrounds track in East Warsaw Saturday night. Art Johnson, of Warsaw, was second, and third place went to Junior Dear, of Columbia City.

Winners in the four, 10-lap heats were as follows: First heat, Buck Beazley, Wolf Lake, time 3.33.59; second heat, Jack Yaney, Columbia City, time 3.29.55; third heat, Freddie Boggs, Warsaw, time 3:18.18; fourth heat, Jack Ray, Columbia City, 3.22.25. The Fashion Shoe Store 6-lap sprint for the six fastest cars was won by Freddie Boggs, Warsaw. His time was 1:56.75.

Cecil Grossnickle, of North Manchester, was winner of the consolation race during which Dick Martin, of North Manchester, and Bob Staley, of Warsaw, collided on the back stretch and Martin's car broke off a utility pole. He was rendered unconscious and was given first aid treatment but was not hospitalized. An emergency light was provided by the Winona Lake fire department.

Bicycle races resulted as follows:

Boys 7 and 8 years old—first, Jimmy Hootch; second, Skippy Leak; third, Christy Lawshe, all of Warsaw.

Boys 9, 10 and 11 years old—first, Jim Weigold, of Columbia City; second, Brock Blosser; third, Dick Fancil, both of Warsaw.

Boys 12, 13, 14 and 15 years old—first, Jerry Fancil; second, Don Hanft; third, Merlin Gibson, of Columbia City.

The WRSW broadcast of the races was sponsored by the Zimmer Wrecking Co.

Saturday, August 8, 1953
Johnson Wins 40-Lap Feature

Art Johnson, of Warsaw, won the 40-lap feature stock car race Saturday night at the Warsaw Speedway, finishing ahead of Archie Holle, also of Warsaw, and Dick Briggs, of Columbia City, who were second and third respectively. Gale Smith, of Warsaw, was leading the field when, on the 27th lap, his car lost a wheel, forcing him out of the race.

The night's entertainment also featured the third heat of special bicycle races, which will be climaxed on August 29 with the championship races. The fourth heat of these bicycle events will be held next Saturday night.

In the bicycle races for boys and girls aged five to eight years old, the winner was Jimmy Gooch, with Gary Odell second and Sam Davis third. Brock Blosser won the race for nine, ten and 11-year-olds, with Dick Fancil second and Jessie Gibson third. In the race for those between 12 to 15 years of age, Jerry Fancil was the winner while Merlin Gibson took second and Billy Weigold third. All of those mentioned are from Warsaw with the exception of Gibson and Weigold, who are from Columbia City.

WRSW Broadcast. A special "demolition" race was also staged between four of the stock car drivers. The autos were furnished by Bledsoe Buick of Warsaw, which also sponsored the WRSW broadcast of the racing activities. Russ Tracy, of North Manchester, won the demolition event. Others who competed were Bill Holle, of Silver Lake, and Keith Coldren and Donnie Smith, of Warsaw.

Heat winners of the stock car races were Buck Beazley, Wolf Lake, Jim Rex, Dick Briggs and John Pollock, all of Columbia City. These heat races were over a 10-lap course. Gale Smith of Warsaw won the six-lap race between the six fastest qualifiers and the 10-lap consolation event was won by Keith Cole, of Columbia City.

Saturday, August 15, 1953
Gale Smith Wins 30-Lap Feature

One of stock car racing's most consistent winners here during the past few seasons—Gale Smith of Warsaw—did it again last Saturday night at the Warsaw Speedway by capturing the 30-lap feature event, which saw cars driven by Mel Twaits, of Ligonier, and Keith Cole, of Churubusco, colliding on the 14th lap, causing Cole's racer to upset. He wasn't hurt.

During the time trials Bill Green, of Columbia City, was cut about the face and leg when his car went through the guard rail. He was treated at the wreck by Gerald McHatton, stationed at trackside with the Bilby-McHatton ambulance. In the feature race Smith was trailed across the finish line by Roy Staley, Archie Holle and Dick Briggs, in that order.

Co-featured with the stock car racing events were the special bicycle races which have been in progress for the past several weeks. This was the last of the pre-championship heat races, and on Saturday night, August 29, the riders with the most points will compete in the final bicycle races for trophies donated by The Times-Union as well as cash awards.

Bicycle Results. In the bicycle race Saturday night for those aged from six to eight years, the winner was Donald Fraley, of Warsaw. Skippy Lesh and Jackie Fry, both of Warsaw were second and third, respectively. Brock Blosser, a consistent winner, won the race for those aged from nine to eleven. Blosser, a Warsaw boy, finished ahead of Dick Fancil and Bob Johnson, both of Warsaw. Jerry Fancil, of Warsaw, was first in the race for boys aged between 12 and 15 years. Second was Merlin Gibson, of Columbia City, and another Columbia City boy, Bill Weigold, took third.

There was a special race for riders of English "gear" bikes, and Merlin Gibson was the winner, followed by Joe Clingenpeel and Jim Rutherford. Prizes for this special race were donated by Fitch Jewelry Store.

In the stock car racing program, heat winners were Russ Tracy, of North Manchester; Lewis Stull, of Warsaw; Bill Holley, of Warsaw; and Mel Twaits, of Ligonier. Bob Shlater, of Churubusco, won the race between the six fastest qualifiers, and Gale Smith, in addition to copping the feature, also won the 15-lap consolation event. A mechanics race of 15 laps was also held as a special attraction, and the winner was Ronnie Hile of Columbia City.

Saturday, August 22, 1953
Stock Car Races

The stock car races were completed by 10:30 as drivers and officials of the Hoosier Hot Rods, Inc., cooperated in running the various events in good time without much delay between races. The 30-lap feature was the main event and the winner was Art Johnson of Warsaw. Duke Krocker was second, Buck Beazley third, Gale Smith, fourth, and Dick Heeter, fifth.

Heat winners were Ned Spath of Huntington, first heat; Kenny Hawkins, Warsaw, second heat; Gale Smith, Warsaw, third heat; and Bob Staley, Warsaw, fourth heat. Duke Krocher, of Garrett, won the race between the six fastest qualifiers, and Forrest Egner, of Columbia City, drove his car across the finish line ahead of the field in the consolation race. There were many collisions to thrill the capacity crowd, but none of the drivers were injured.

Friday, August 28, 1953
Stock Car Racers Speak at Rotary

Fred Boggs and Bob Staley, guest speakers, gave Warsaw Rotarians a comprehensive account of stock car racing at the club luncheon Friday in the Camel club rooms. Boggs, one of the best known racers in northern Indiana, and Staley, newest addition to the stock car drivers competing at the county fairgrounds, discussed reinforcement of the cars, fuel and tire requirements.

Also participating in the program feature were Russell Smith, vice-president of the Kosciusko County Fair Association, and Milo Clase, who announces the races over the track public address system and on regular broadcasts over Radio Stations WRSW AM and FM. A few Rotarians accepted an invitation to ride around the track in a stock car after the meeting.

Saturday, August 29, 1953
Johnson Wins 30 Lap Feature At Speedway

Art Johnson, of Warsaw, crossed the finish line ahead of a large field in the 30-lap featured stock car race Saturday night at the Warsaw Speedway, beating out Dick Briggs, Junior Dear, Bob Shlater, Keith Cole and Dick Heeter, who were next in order for second to sixth, respectively.

The 30-lap race highlighted the stock car program with a special feature being the championship bicycle races. The Times-Union and WRSW awarded trophies to winners of the three age-group races between riders of regular-make bicycles, and also a trophy to the winner of a race between English-make bicycles.

Race track officials were unable today to locate the score sheets listing the names of the bicycle winners, but hoped to locate them so that they may be published Tuesday in the Times-Union. It is known that Brock Blosser won the championship race in his age group. He finished just in time, too, because soon after crossing the finish line a pedal came off his bicycle.

The feature stock car race had to be re-started due to a collision involving eight cars early in the event. No one was injured.

Bob Staley, of Warsaw, won his first consolation event, a 15-lap race, with Roy Staley second and Red Creech third. Bob Shlater, of Churubusco, won the race between the six fastest qualifiers. Heat winners were Keith Cole, Jim Salesman, and Junior Dear, all of Columbia City, and Bill Morten, of Rochester.

Highlights of the racing action Saturday night were broadcast over WRSW AM and FM by the Zimmer Wrecking Company. Next Saturday night Bledsoe Buick will sponsor the broadcast. The races next Saturday will include a 100-lap feature event.

Saturday, September 5 & Monday, September 7, 1953
Gale Smith Cops 2 Feature Races During Weekend

Stock car racing fans got a double dose of entertainment over the Labor Day weekend at the Warsaw Speedway. Races were held on Saturday night and again on Monday night, with Gale Smith, of Warsaw, capturing the feature event on both nights.

Smith copped the 100-lap feature Saturday night, finishing ahead of Art Johnson, of Warsaw, and Dick Briggs, of Columbia City. A large crowd was on hand for the Saturday night racing program, which was broadcast over WRSW by Bledsoe Buick.

Forrest Egner, of Columbia City, won the consolation 20-lap race, defeating Bill Green, of Columbia City. Ray Staley, of Warsaw, was a heat winner along with Lewis Stull, of

Warsaw, Sparky Spath, of Huntington, and Jack Yohne, of Columbia City.

Cold Monday. Cool weather Monday night kept the crowd down, but Smith didn't miss the noise as he drove his car across the finish line ahead of the field in the 25-lap feature. Dick Briggs, of Columbia City, was second and the Staley boys—Bob and Ray—were third and fourth respectively. Monday's program was broadcast over WRSW by the L and L Body Shop.

Briggs won the race between the six fastest qualifiers, finishing ahead of Smith and Art Johnson. There was no consolation race. Heat winners were Art Johnson, Ray Staley, Bob Staley and Cecil Huntley. It was announced that there will be a racing program at the Speedway next Saturday.

No more results found for the 1953 season.

1954

Monday, May 31, 1954
Holle, Johnson Win Races Here Over Holidays

Archie Holle, veteran Warsaw stock car race driver, used his brand new car to win the feature event yesterday afternoon during the holiday racing program at the Warsaw Speedway. Art Johnson, of Warsaw, who had won the feature race on Saturday night, finished second behind Holle, and Dick Briggs, or Coesse, was third.

Cecil Grossnickle, N. Manchester

During the time trials, Cecil Grossnickle's car hit the wall head-on. Grossnickle, of North Manchester, was not hurt, but the front end of his car was practically demolished.

It was announced that the races will be held on Saturday nights instead of Fridays, starting this week. Highlights of the racing program are broadcast over Radio Stations WRSW AM and FM each week.

The races last Saturday night were held, due to rain on Friday night. Johnson won the feature event, and was followed across the finish line by Bob Staley, of Warsaw, and Ronnie Hile. The first three cars were close all the way. Heat winners Saturday night were Bob France, of Wabash, Bob Staley, Red Creech, of Columbia City, Cecil Grossnickle and Dick Briggs. In the feature race Saturday Gale Smith, of Warsaw, while fighting for second place, hit the wall on the last lap. He was not injured.

Saturday, June 5, 1954
Johnson Wins Feature Race

Three Warsaw drivers finished one-two-three in the feature stock car race Saturday night at the Warsaw Speedway, with Art Johnson crossing the finish line first, ahead of Archie Holle and Gale Smith in the 25-lap event.

The track was in good condition, and the races were excellent. Several of the events found the first two or three cars practically side by side at the finish line. A large field of entries was on hand, including some whose appearances were unexpected. All of the drivers are fighting for points which will determine the winner of a huge trophy at the end of the season. A fine card of racing is anticipated for next Saturday night over WRSW AM and FM.

Heat winners last Saturday were Forest Enger, of Columbia City, Tony Viera of Marion, J. R. Dear, Columbia City, and Jim Salesman, also of Columbia City. Johnson, in addition to winning the feature race, also won the six lap event between the six fastest qualifiers. Art Riley, of Marion, won the race between the six slowest qualifiers, and Cecil Grossnickle, of North Manchester, was first in the 15-lap consolation race.

Saturday, June 12, 1954
Columbia City Driver Wins 50-Lap Feature

A large crowd was on hand at the Warsaw Speedway Saturday night to see this area's best stock car race drivers compete for various trophies donated by merchants.

The big race, of course, was the special 50-lap feature, and the winner was Junior Deer, of Columbia City, who finished ahead of Art Johnson and Gale Smith, who were second and third, respectively. Deer thus captured the first place trophy captured the first place trophy and also received a beautiful wrist watch from Ward's Jewelry store.

The races provided many thrills and the usual amount of collisions, but there were no injuries. The track was "lightning fast," having been baked under 90 degree temperatures during the day.

Winners of 10-lap heat races were Jim Salesman of Churubusco, Mike Klingerman of Warsaw, Art Johnson of Warsaw, and Ned Spaz of Huntington. Bob Staley, of Warsaw, won the six-lap event between the six fastest qualifiers, and Bob Morris, of Wabash, crossed the finish line first in the race for the six slowest qualifiers. The 15-lap consolation race was won by Red Creech, of Columbia City.

Saturday, June 19, 1954
Rain Washes Out Stock Car Races, Baseball Game

The rain storm Saturday night forced cancellation of the scheduled stock car races at the Warsaw Speedway and also the American Legion junior baseball game at the city park diamond between Warsaw and Ligonier.

Saturday, June 26, 1954
Johnson Wins Feature Race At Local Speedway

Art Johnson, of Warsaw, won the featured 25-lap stock car race Saturday night before the largest crowd of the season at the Warsaw Speedway.

Johnson sped across the finish line ahead of Ned Spath, of Huntington, who was second, and Dick Briggs, of Coesse, who placed third. Both Spath and Briggs had won earlier races. Spath placed first in the third heat race, and Briggs won the event between the six fastest qualifiers, nosing out Johnson in that race.

Other heat winners were Bill Morris, of Wabash; Bill Hawley, of Nappanee; and Fats Wyman, of Nappanee. Dave Shroeder, of Wyatt, finished first in the race between the six slowest qualifiers. The consolation event, a 15-lap race, was won by Ronnie Hile, of Columbia City.

As an added feature, a special 10-lap race was held between Freddie Boggs in his midget car and Art Johnson in his stock car. Boggs was the winner. The racing program was broadcast over Radio Stations WRSW AM and FM from 8:45 to 9:15 for Hoffer's Super Market.

Elaborate plans are being made for stock car racing during the coming holiday weekend. There will be the usual program on Saturday night, July 3, but on Monday night, July 5, a colorful fireworks display will be added to the races. It is planned to have the fireworks display at 10 O'clock.

Freddie Boggs, Warsaw

Saturday, July 3 & Monday, July 5, 1954
Stock Car Races Attract Record Crowds Here

Stock car racing fans in this area were given a real treat over the holiday weekend, as programs at the Warsaw Speedway were held on both Saturday and Monday nights.

The racing program Monday was stopped for a giant fireworks display, probably the finest ever seen here. There were big crowds on both nights, but the Monday centennial crowd was tremendous in size. Race officials said it was the largest gathering ever to watch the local races.

On Saturday night, the 25-lap feature was won by Art Johnson, of Warsaw, with Ned Spath, of Huntington, second. Archie Holle, of Warsaw, won the consolation race, and heat winners were Spath, Dave Fordyce, of Wabash, Gale Smith, of Warsaw, and Ike Holderman, of North Manchester. Red Creech, of Columbia City, won the race between the six fastest qualifiers, and Lester Holloway, of Warsaw, was winner of the race between the six slowest qualifying cars.

Mac Brewer, of Wabash, escaped injury twice Saturday night. His car rolled over during the time trials, landing on its top, and then in the feature race his auto hit the retaining wall. Spath won the feature race Monday night, with Bob Staley, of Warsaw, second. Ronnie Hile, of Columbia City, won the consolation event. Heat winners Monday were Staley, Jim Rex, of Columbia City, Gale Smith and Cecil Huntley, of Columbia City. Smith also won the race between the six fastest qualifying cars.

Several cars were "bumped" or rolled over Monday night. Charlie Howell, of Wabash, escaped injury, when his car rolled over in front of the grandstand. The feature race had to be re-started three times because of wrecks. There were 27 cars in the feature race.

The racing program was broadcast over WRSW by the Lewis Shell Oil Company. Next Saturday night's racing program will include the Mid-Season Championships.

Saturday, July 10, 1954
Johnson Cops Mid-Season Stock Car Championship

Art Johnson, high point leader of the Hoosier Hot Rods association, Inc., captured the 50-lapMid-Season Championship race Saturday night before a very large centennial crowd at the Warsaw Speedway.

The races proved to be very exciting, with highlights broadcast over WRSW AM and FM for Bledsoe Buick. There were no injuries during the night, but Gene Clevenger, of Warsaw, was lucky to escape when his car went over the wall. The car landed right side-up in the parking area outside the track.

Two consolation races were held, with Cliff Gibson and Junior Dear, both of Columbia City, the winners. Archie Holle, of Warsaw, won the race between the six fastest qualifiers, and heat winners were Phil Geiger and Ray Staley of Columbia City, Art Smith of Fort Wayne, and Don Riley of Marion.

Saturday, July 17, 1954
Johnson Takes First In Feature Stock Car Race

A large crowd was treated to some exciting stock car races Saturday night at the Warsaw Speedway, with Art Johnson winning the feature 25-lap event.

Junior Dear, Columbia City

Johnson, of Warsaw, is the leading point-winner in the racing activities this summer and recently won the mid-season 50-lap championship stock car race, staged during the centennial. Saturday night he bested Ned Spath and Dick Briggs, who finished second and third, respectively. A special race, called the "jalopies" event, was held for old cars, strictly stock, and the winner was Wendell Fike, of North Manchester. There will be another of these races next Saturday night.

Heat winners were Ronnie Hile, Columbia City; Dale Smith, Warsaw; Jim Rex, Huntington;

and Archie Holle, Warsaw. Holle also won the race between the six fastest qualifying cars. Junior Dear, of Columbia City, flashed home first in the consolation race.

Highlights of the racing program were broadcast over Radio Stations WRSW AM and FM for Hoffer's Super Market.

Saturday, July 24, 1954
Racing Program Provides Many Thrills, Wrecks

A Muncie driver, Audie Swartz, captured the 25-lap feature race Saturday night in a stock car program at the Warsaw Speedway that produced a number of wrecks, some minor injuries, and the most spectacular thrills of the season before a large crowd. Swartz edged out Jim Salesman, of Columbia City, in the feature event, with Gale Smith, of Warsaw, coming in third.

During the feature race two cars lost wheels that sailed into the crowd, but luckily no one was hurt. The race had to be started four times due to the number of wrecks. Ten cars were involved in one collision, six in another, and four in still a third wreck, and two more came together in a fourth mishap.

Jake Burtsfield, of Syracuse, was injured slightly when his car was struck broadside during the feature race. He received treatment at the track. Art Johnson's car spun out causing him to lose his position. Archie Holle's car hit the fence, and Gale Smith was involved in two of the collisions. There were many new cars on the track, including some from Fort Wayne, Crown Point, Muncie and Edgerton, Ohio.

OTHER WINNERS

Heat winners were Ned Spath of Huntington, Art Johnson of Warsaw, Jim Salesman and Cliff Gibson, both of Columbia City. Dick Briggs, of Coesse, won the race between the six fastest qualifiers. There were two consolation races, with Kenny Leiter, of Warsaw, winning the first, and Junior Dear, of Columbia City, the second. The special "jalopy" race was won by Kenneth Hawkins, of Warsaw.

Highlights of the racing program were broadcast over WRSW AM and FM by the Lewis Oil Company.

Saturday, July 31, 1954
Art Johnson Wins Feature At Local Speedway

Art Johnson, of Warsaw, one of the most consistent stock car race winners at the Warsaw Speedway, grabbed another checkered flag last Saturday night in the feature event, as Archie Holle, of Warsaw, placed second ahead of Dick Briggs, of Columbia City, who was third.

Several collisions and other thrills proved interesting to a good-sized crowd. Highlights of the racing program were broadcast over Radio Stations WRSW AM and FM by Bledsoe Buick.

Two consolation races were held, with Jack Yahney, of Huntington, finishing ahead of the field in the first race, and Arden Leiter, of Warsaw, winning the second. Briggs defeated both Johnson and Holle in the six-lap race between the six fastest qualifiers. Winners of the four heat races, each 10 laps in distance, were Holle, Kenny Harmon of Bourbon, Jim Rex of Huntington, and Jake Burtsfield of Syracuse.

Saturday, August 7, 1954
Stock Car Races Provide Thrills Here Saturday

Thrills and excitement were plentiful Saturday night at the Warsaw Speedway, as numerous collisions kept a large crowd of fans on the edges of their seats, with one driver knocked unconscious temporarily and another sent to the hospital.

Bill Morris, of Wabash, was knocked unconscious when his car hit the wall in front of the grandstand during one of the races. However, he was revived at the track and did not request hospital treatment. Jake Burtsfield, of Syracuse, who was injured two weeks ago, was hurt again in a crash on the 13th lap of feature race. He suffered fractured ribs and a fractured shoulder and was taken to the McDonald hospital, from where he was later released.

The feature race was won by Jack Riley, of Huntington. Heat winners were Jim Hullinger, Gale Smith, of Warsaw, Ronnie Hile, of Columbia City, and Burtsfield. Dick Briggs, of Coesse, won the race between the six fastest qualifiers, and Ike Holderman, of North Manchester, and Ned Spath, of Huntington, won the two consolation races.

Thirty minutes of the racing action were broadcast over Radio Stations WRSW AM and FM for the Open Air Fruit Market. The stock car races will be featured on Wednesday and Saturday nights during the county fair this week.

Saturday, August 14, 1954
Gale Smith Wins Feature Event At Local Speedway

Despite a wet and slippery track, the stock car races brought out a big crowd to the Warsaw Speedway Saturday night, as one of the closing night features of the county fair, and thrills and spills were numerous.

The rain delayed the start of the races about an hour, but the program was completed in good time, with Gale Smith, of Warsaw, capturing the 25-lap feature race ahead of Art Johnson, also of Warsaw, and Jack Riley, of Huntington, who were second and third respectively.

Junior Clem, of Fort Wayne, was overcome by gas while circling the track while in his stock car. He brought the car to a halt, staggered out the door of the auto and collapsed on the track. Clem was taken to the McDonald hospital by ambulance, but suffered no after effects and was dismissed.

Two consolation races, each 10 laps, were held with the first being won by Cecil Huntley, of Columbia City, and the second by Jack Riley, of Huntington. Smith, in addition to winning the feature race, also finished ahead of the field in the race between the six fastest qualifiers. Winners of the four heat races were Ronnie Hile, Columbia City; Art

Johnson, Warsaw; Kenny Harmon, of Bourbon, and Ike Holderman, North Manchester.

Saturday, August 21, 1954
Gale Smith Cops Feature Race

Gale Smith, of Warsaw, one of the most consistent winners at the Warsaw Speedway, won another feature race Saturday night, finishing ahead of a large field that included Jack Riley, of Huntington, who was second, and Art Johnson, Warsaw, who placed third.

Archie Holle, of Warsaw, and B. Morris, of Wabash, were winners of the two consolation races, while Art Johnson finished ahead in the race between the six fastest qualifying cars. Heat winners were M. Klingerman, Johnson and Bob Staley, of Warsaw, and S. Huntley, of Columbia City.

Saturday, August 28, 1954
Johnson Wins Feature Race

Art Johnson, of Warsaw, one of the most consistent winners of stock car races at the Warsaw Speedway, captured another feature race Saturday night, finishing ahead of another frequent winner, Gale Smith, of Warsaw, with Ronnie Hile, of Columbia City, placing third.

It was announced that the program next Saturday will feature a special race between the race car owners. They will compete in cars they own. The races last Saturday were broadcast over WRSW AM and FM for Bledsoe Buick.

Heat winners were Junior Clem, of Fort Wayne, Forrest Egner, of Columbia City, Slug Morr, of Albion, and Kenny Leiter, of Warsaw. Johnson and Smith also finished one-two in the six-lap race between the six fastest qualifiers. The 15-lap consolation race was won by Jack Riley, of Huntington. A "jalopy" race was also featured for the fans' entertainment, and it was won by Paul Brown, of Warsaw.

Saturday, Sept. 4 & Monday, Sept. 6, 1954
Racing Season Ends In Warsaw

The stock car racing season ended over the Labor Day weekend, with action at the Warsaw Speedway attracting many fans on both Saturday and Monday nights. In closing the season, officials of the Hoosier Hot Rods, Inc., sponsoring organization, said they were looking forward to even bigger and better races next summer.

The last race Monday night was a 50-lap feature, won by Art Johnson,

Art Johnson, Warsaw, receiving the Fitch Award from Track President, Hoot Gibson

of Warsaw, who finished ahead of Gale Smith, of Warsaw, and Dick Briggs, of Columbia City, who were second and third, respectively.

Johnson won a championship trophy, donated by the Fitch Jewelry store, for being high-point man as the most consistent winner during the season, and also received a trophy for capturing the 50-lap feature race.

The consolation race Monday was won by C. Gibson, of Columbia City, Gale Smith won the race between the six fastest qualifiers, and heat winners were Junior Rex and R. Hile, both of Columbia City, and M. Klingerman and Steve Osbun, both of Warsaw.

A special "jalopy" race last night was won by Dick Smith, of Warsaw. The racing highlights Monday were broadcast over WRSW for the Lewis Oil Company.

Art Johnson, Warsaw, 50-Lap Feature Winner

On Saturday night, Dick Briggs, of Coesse, won the feature event, beating out Dick Heeter and Dick Salesman, who were second and third, respectively.

Red Creech, of Columbia City won the consolation race, and Salesman, of Churubusco, finished first in the race between the six fastest qualifiers. Heat winners were D. Schroeder, of Wyatt, Junior Rex, of Columbia City, Junior Riley, of Huntington, and M. Klingerman, of Warsaw.

An "owners and mechanics race" was also held Saturday night, and the winner was Bob Miner, of Warsaw, who serves as a mechanic for Bob Staley, veteran Warsaw race driver. The "jalopy" race Saturday night was won by Dick Leiter, of Warsaw. The WRSW broadcast Saturday was for Hoffer's Super Market.

1955

Saturday, May 21, 1955
Staley Wins Feature As Race Season Begins

Bob Staley, of Warsaw, won the first feature race of the 1955 stock car racing program at the Warsaw Speedway, flashing home ahead of the field in the 25-lap windup Saturday night.

Jack Riley of Huntington and Arden Leiter of Warsaw finished second and third, respectively, in the feature race as a large crowd turned out for the season opener at the speedway, located at the county fairgrounds. Threatening weather failed to hold down the enthusiasm of the fans, and they were treated to some exciting races.

Staley had a great night. In addition to winning the feature event, he also won the race between the six fastest qualifiers and one of the four 10-lap heat races. Other heat race winners were Leiter, Riley and Ronnie Hile of Columbia City.

Saturday, June 11, 1955
Midgets Attract Big Crowd At Local Speedway

The midget race cars attracted a large crowd to the Warsaw Speedway Saturday night, with Bob McLean, of South Bend, winning the feature race after a close duel with Freddie Boggs, of Warsaw.

The cars driven by McLean and Boggs raced practically bumper to bumper for several laps before McLean finally won. Tom Ward, of Lafayette, finished third.

The heat races were won by George Renfro, of Findley, Ohio; Louie Herrold, of Three Rivers, Mich.; Hank Dumon, of Lafayette; and Jim Deck, of Elwood. Renfro also won the race between the six fastest qualifiers.

There were many thrills, including a collision in which Cowboy Likes, of Millersburg, had his car bumped six or seven times. Likes had to be taken to the hospital due to a head injury, but it proved only minor and he returned to the track before the races were completed. The excitement evidently was too much for his wife, who fainted at her husband's mishap, and she too, had to be taken to the hospital for treatment. Next Saturday night the stock cars will resume at the speedway.

Saturday, June 18, 1955
Johnson Wins Stock Car Feature

Another fine evening of stock car racing was enjoyed by a large crowd Saturday night at the Warsaw Speedway, with a local favorite, Art Johnson, speeding home ahead of the field in the 25-lap feature race. Johnson's car finished ahead of Kenny Leiter, of Warsaw, who was second, and Jim Hullinger, of Bunker Hill, who was third. There were the usual thrills and spills, but no serious mishaps. Many new cars and drivers were on hand.

A Kentucky man, Don Neusbaum, of Newport, won the race between the six fastest qualifiers. There was a special eight-lap race for "jalopies", and this event was won by Paul Brown, of Warsaw. Leiter, in addition to being runner-up in the feature, also won the consolation race. Winners of heat races were Walt Potter of Huntertown, Harry Rhodes of Plymouth, Archie Holle of Warsaw, Jim Hullinger of Bunker Hill.

Thirty minutes of the racing action are broadcast each Saturday night over Radio Stations

WRSW AM and FM by the Lewis Oil company, Perry Shell and Sisk Shell, all of Warsaw, and Burch Shell, of near Silver Lake.

Saturday & Monday, July 2 & 4, 1955
Rain Postpones Races, Fireworks Until Saturday

Yesterday afternoon's cloud burst washed out the scheduled stock car races and fireworks display Monday night at the county fairgrounds, but officials said the fireworks display has been rescheduled for next Saturday night, July 9, at 10 p.m., following the regular stock car program.

Races were held last Saturday night with Archie Holle, of Warsaw, winning the feature 25-lap event. He was followed across the finish line by Jim Hullinger, of Bunker Hill, and Bob Staley, of Warsaw.

Kenny Leiter of Warsaw, won the consolation race, and Dick Leiter, of Pierceton, was winner of the special "jalopies" race. The race between the six fastest qualifiers was won by Holle. Heat winners Saturday were Joe Hamsher, of New Paris, Ike Holderman, of North Manchester, Arden Leiter, of Warsaw, and Holle.

The races were very exciting and there was a big crowd on hand. Bob Staley was injured slightly when a stone came through his side window. He raced in the feature event and then was taken to the hospital for treatment. He sustained a cut under the eyelid.

Saturday, July 9, 1955
Stock Car Races, Fireworks Draw Crowd Saturday

Jim Hullinger, of Bunker Hill, won the 50-lap feature race Saturday night at the Warsaw Speedway, located at the county fairgrounds, as one of the largest crowds of the season was on hand, many of them to see the beautiful fireworks display which came at exactly 10 o'clock.

Hullinger finished ahead of Art Johnson and Bob Staley, both of Warsaw, who were second and third, respectively, in the feature event. Joe Hamsher, of New Paris, won the 15-lap consolation event, and Staley finished first in the six lap race between the six fastest qualifiers. Winners of the four heat races, over 10 laps, were Cliff Gibson of Columbia City, Kenny Leiter of Warsaw, Archie Holle of Warsaw, and Art Johnson, also of Warsaw.

The fireworks display was sponsored by the Kosciusko County Fair association, Hoosier Hot Rods, Inc., and the Junior Chamber of Commerce. Hundreds of spectators went to the fairgrounds shortly before 10 p.m. and parked their cars outside of the speedway to watch the colorful display.

Trophies were awarded to the winners of the 50-lap feature race as a climax to a very fine night of entertainment. Thirty minutes of the racing program were aired over Radio Stations WRSW AM and FM for Lewis Shell Oil, Perry Shell and Sisk Shell, all of Warsaw, and Burch Shell station, of near Silver Lake.

Saturday, July 16, 1955
Jim Hullinger Wins Feature At Local Speedway

A Bunker Hill race driver, Jim Hullinger, flashed home first in the feature stock car race Saturday night at the Warsaw Speedway, finishing ahead of a field that included Gale Smith, Warsaw, who was second, and Charles Howell, Wabash, who was third.

A nice-sized crowd was on hand for the race program, which was completely without any major crashes or injuries. Hullinger, in addition to winning the feature 25-lap event, also crossed the finish line first in the first heat race. Smith also had a big night, finishing second in the feature and winning the second heat race and the event between the six fastest qualifiers.

Howell also won a heat race, and the fourth heat event was won by Ray Staley, of Columbia City. Cliff Gibson, of Columbia City, won the 10-lap consolation race, and the special race for "jalopies" was won by Max Bessinger, of Bourbon.

Saturday, July 30, 1955
Holle Captures Stock Car Trophy

Archie Holle, veteran Warsaw race driver, won the feature 50-lap mid-season championship stock car race Saturday night before a large crowd at the Warsaw Speedway. Holle, by winning, now leads in the point standings among drivers who compete at the speedway each Saturday night. A beautiful trophy was awarded to Holle, and winners of several other events also received trophies.

Bob Staley, of Warsaw, was second and Jim Hullinger, of Bunker Hill, third in the feature race. Each had previously won a heat race, as had Cliff Gibson of Columbia City and Bob Shlater of Churubusco. Staley also won the six-lap race between the six fastest qualifiers, while the special race for jalopies was won by Pealy Heckaman, of Bourbon.

Saturday, August 13, 1955
Holle Finishes First in Feature Race At Fair

Archie Holle, of Warsaw, won the feature stock car race Saturday night at the Warsaw Speedway, as the races drew a very big crowd for the second time during the county fair. Bob Staley, of Warsaw, was second behind Holle and Jim Hullinger, of Bunker Hill, was third. Staley is the current point leader for the summer racing program. Holle is second and Hullinger third.

Arden Leiter, of Warsaw, won the consolation race, and another Warsaw driver, Gale Smith, finished first in the race between the six fastest qualifying cars. Heat winners were Joe Hamsher, New Paris, Cecil Huntley, Columbia City, Smith, and Laverne Morr of Albion.

Thirty minutes of the racing program were aired over Radio Stations WRSW AM and FM from 8:45 to 9:15, by Burch Shell Service, of near Silver Lake, and Perry Shell Service and Kendall Shell Service, both of Warsaw.

Saturday, August 13, 1955
Holle Nears Track Record As He Is Top Winner At Warsaw
from *The Mail Journal*, The Papers, Inc., Milford, IN 46542

Archie Holle, Warsaw, had the fastest qualifying time of 18.83 seconds Saturday night at the Warsaw Speedway as he neared the track record of 18.28 set by Gale Smith, his hometown neighbor. Holle also won top prize money as he took first in the 20-car feature race and second in both the third heat and the race among the six fastest cars. Smith was the winner in both of the latter races. He was forced out of the feature by two flat tires.   Flagman, Phil Geiger; Scorers, Gene and Madaline Gregory

Others receiving prize money were first heat: Joe Hamsher, New Paris; Buck Beazley, Wolf Lake; and Bill Jones; second heat: Cecil Huntley, Columbia City; Steve Osbun, Warsaw; and Gerald Bills, Columbia City; third heat: Smith, Holle, and Bob Staley, Warsaw; fourth heat: "Slug"' Morr, Albion; Charlie Howell and Cliff Gibson, Columbia City; six fastest qualifiers: Smith, Holle, and Jimmy Hullinger; consolation (includes all drivers not winning money in other races): Arden Leiter, Pierceton; Wendell Fike, Dick Parker, Columbia City; Rollin Smith, and Don Riley, Marion; feature: Holle, Staley, Hullinger, Gibson, Huntley, Leiter, "Wheaties" Smith, Riley, Morr, and Fike.

In an added attraction, Bud Gullett, Arkle Yeazel, and Max Bessinger were the first three finishers in the jalopy race, which included 17 cars.

The wins by Holle the last three weeks has brought him to within six points of the leading total of 130 for the season held by Bob Staley. The five drivers finishing the season with the most points will receive trophies from the Hoosier Hot Rods Racing Association, Inc. C. E. "Hoot" Gibson, Columbia City, is president of the association. The drivers are awarded points according to the place in which they finish in the various races. A crowd of about 2,000 persons attended Saturday night's races aided by the attraction of the Kosciusko County fair.

Saturday, August 20, 1955
Columbia City Driver Wins Feature Race

A Columbia City race driver, Junior Dear, had his best night at the Warsaw Speedway last Saturday, winning the 25-lap feature event and also the first heat race on the program.

In the feature, Dear beat out Archie Holle, of Warsaw, and Jim Hullinger, of Bunker Hill. Both Dear and Hullinger had unusual experiences in the feature. The hood of Hullinger's car flew up during the race and then came off. Just before Dear crossed the finish line, the hood of his car flew up into the windshield, cutting off his vision. However, it did not prevent his winning the race.

Other heat winners, in addition to Dear, were Dick Parker, Columbia City; Fred Boggs, Warsaw; Bob Staley, Warsaw. Staley also won the race between the six fastest qualifiers. The consolation race, over 12-laps, was won by Cliff Gibson, Columbia City, and Pealy Heckaman, of Bourbon, finished first in the jalopy race, in which there were 15 cars.

Not including Saturday night's results, Staley leads in the point standings for the championship trophy which will be awarded on Labor Day night. Staley, up until Saturday, had 130 points, and was trailed by Holle, 124; Hullinger, 114; Leiter, 72; Gale Smith, 61; Kenny Leiter, 47; Rollin Smith and Charlie Howell, each 46; Cliff Gibson, 44; Joe Hamsher, 40; and Ronald Hile, 37.

Next Saturday night will be "Kids' Night", as youngsters will be taken around the track by their favorite drivers and in the favorite cars. The races are broadcast from 8:45 to 9:15 each Saturday night by the Kendall and Perry Shell service stations, of Warsaw, and Birch Shell station, of near Silver Lake, in conjunction with the Lewis Shell Oil Company.

Saturday, August 27, 1955
Bunker Hill Race Driver Captures Feature Here

Jim Hullinger, who travels from Bunker Hill to race at the Warsaw Speedway, captured the featured 25-lap stock car event Saturday night. There was considerable action during the evening and many thrills, but no serious crashes or injuries. Hullinger had a very big night, winning the race between the six fastest qualifiers. Archie Holle, of Warsaw, was second and veteran Fred Boggs, of Warsaw, was third.

Heat winners during the night were Rollin Smith, of North Manchester, Art Johnson, of Warsaw, Bob Staley, of Warsaw, and Holle. The consolation event was won by Claude Everingham, while the jalopy race was won by Dick Kindig, of Warsaw.

Flagman, Phil Geiger and Scorers, Gene Gregory and Madaline Weigold (Gregory)

Saturday was "Kids' Night" and many boys and girls were on hand to cheer for their favorite drivers. They were given rides around the track in the race cars. It was announced that a fireworks display will be staged next Saturday night for the fans, in recognition of their patronage. The display will be held just before the feature race.

In the current "point standings" for the championship trophy, the leader is Bob Staley, of Warsaw, with 154 points, followed by Archie Holle, 146, and Jim Hullinger with 145. Those three will probably go right down to the final wire before the winner is decided. The others are too far behind to be in contention.

Saturday, September 3, 1955
2 Tied For Point Leadership At Local Speedway

A 50-lap feature race next Saturday at the Warsaw Speedway could decide the "point" champion of the summer season. By virtue of his victory last Saturday night in the 25-lap feature event, Jim Hollinger, of Bunker Hill, has pulled into a first place tie with Archie Holle, of Warsaw. Each has 159 points. Holle finished second to Hullinger in the feature race Saturday.

Bob Staley, of Warsaw, holds third place in the standings with 157 points. Staley was involved in a pileup Saturday night with Gale Smith of Warsaw during the feature race, and that mishap knocked Staley out of the point leadership. Next Saturday's 50-lap feature will be a championship trophy race.

Heat winners last Saturday were Cliff Gibson and Cecil Huntley, both of Columbia City, Claude Everingham of New Paris, and M. Kissinger, of Bourbon. Everingham also won the race between the six fastest qualifiers. Holle won the consolation event.

Wheaties Smith Crash

Wheaties Smith, of Warsaw, required first aid at the track for a cut over his eye, sustained when his car rolled over during the time trials. Bill Hawley, of Nappanee, escaped injury when his car rolled over during one of the heat races. A Columbia City child was given first aid by ambulance attendants at the track after the child swallowed some object, causing her to choke.

Saturday, September 10, 1955
Schedule Races Here Wednesday

The stock car racing program at the Warsaw Speedway rained out last Saturday night, and has been rescheduled for this coming Wednesday evening, with time trials starting at 7 o'clock and the first race at 8 p.m.

Officials said the program would feature the 50-lap championship race, in which a number of trophies will be awarded. Altogether, there will be 21 trophies presented during the night including trophies for the "jalopy" race. In case of a rain-out Wednesday, the races will be held next Saturday night.

Wednesday, September 14, 1955
Jim Hullinger Wins Stock Car Championship

Jim Hullinger, of Bunker Hill, last night won the 50-lap championship stock car feature race at the Warsaw Speedway, and with his triumph also won a huge trophy donated by Freddie Boggs, of Warsaw, for being the "point champion" of the season. Hullinger finished with 174 points. Archie Holle and Bob Staley, both of Warsaw, tied for second, each with 169 points. Staley finished second and Holle fourth in the feature race last night. Third place was taken by Claude Everingham, of New Paris.

This was the final night of racing here except for an open competition event that may be held in approximately two weeks, depending on the weather. If such a race is held, drivers from all tracks will be invited to compete in one grand finale.

It was a great night all-around for Hullinger. During the time trials, he came within a fraction of tying the quarter mile track record, which is 18.28, set by Gale Smith of Warsaw two years ago. Hullinger's time last night was 18.29 seconds.

Hullinger also won one of the four 10-lap heat races last night. The other winners were Kenny Leiter of Warsaw, Mac Brewer of Fort Wayne, and Joe Michaels of Bourbon. Everingham won the six-lap event between the six fasted qualifiers, and Staley won the consolation race, Lamar Secrist, of Bourbon, finished first in the "jalopy" race.

Saturday, September 24, 1955
Holle Captures Feature In Last Night of Racing

Archie Holle, of Warsaw, won the feature race Saturday night in the final stock car racing program of the 1955 season at the Warsaw Speedway. Jim Hullinger, of Bunker Hill, placed second behind Holle as a rather slim crowd, held down by cool weather, watched the action around the quarter-mile track. Hullinger earlier had defeated Holle in the race between the six fastest qualifiers.

Winners of the four heat races were Holle, Charles Howell of Wabash, Bud Gullett of Goshen, and Dick Leiter of Warsaw. During the time trials, Rex Yazel, of Bourbon, escaped injury when he was thrown from his car, which rolled over.

1956

Saturday, May 19, 1956
Set Track Record on 1st Night of Stock Car Racing

The first night of stock car racing this year at the Warsaw Speedway featured the setting of a new track record by Jim Hullinger, of Bunker Hill, last Saturday night.

Hullinger, in his qualifying lap, completed the quarter-mile course in 18.03 seconds. The old record was 18.28, set in 1954 by Gale Smith, of Warsaw. Forty-two cars qualified for the races Saturday. The feature 25-lap event was won by Archie Holle, of Warsaw, who nosed out Hullinger. Claude Everingham, of New Paris, was third.

Winners of the four heat races were Max Lambert of Columbia City, Bob Staley of Warsaw, Bob Grindle of Warsaw, and Hullinger. Don Holloway, of Warsaw, won the consolation event, and the race between the six fastest time-trial qualifiers was won by Everingham. A second consolation race, over 10 laps, was won by Don Riley, of Huntington.

The races will be held each Saturday night at the Warsaw Speedway, located on the county fairgrounds.

Wednesday, May 30, 1956
Bob Staley Wins Stock Car Feature

Bob Staley, of Warsaw, won the feature stock car race Wednesday night at the Warsaw Speedway, nosing out Archie Holle, also of Warsaw, in the last lap after both had raced side by side for a considerable portion of the race.

Heat winners were Holle, Ellis Hartman and Jim Elliott, all of Warsaw, Bob Grindle, of Leesburg, and Jim Hullinger, of Bunker Hill. Staley, in addition to winning the feature, also placed first in the race between the six fastest qualifiers. Ron Hile, of Columbia City, won the consolation event.

A feature of the evening was a "jalopy race", with 18 cars in the starting field. The race, won by Bob Grindle, of Leesburg, included many crashes and spills. There were no serious injuries during the racing activities, but Pealy Heckaman, of Bourbon, had his car roll over in one of the events. Jim Hullinger had an axle break in his car early in the evening and was not able to participate in the feature race.

Thirty minutes of the racing action were broadcast over WRSW. The races will be held again on Saturday night of this week.

Saturday, June 2, 1956
Staley Captures Stock Car Feature

Bob Staley, of Warsaw, won the 25-lap feature stock car race Saturday night at the Warsaw Speedway, where a large crowd was thrilled by many roll-overs and crashes. Max Lambert, of Warsaw, was taken to the McDonald Hospital after his car rolled over on a guard rail. An examination showed a lacerated and bruised elbow but no fractures.

Winners of the five heat races were Dick Leiter, Archie Holle and Herb Mann, all of Warsaw, Cliff Gibson. of Columbia City, and Claude Everingham, of New Paris. Junior Dear, of Columbia City, won the race between the six fastest qualifiers, and Dick Leiter, Warsaw, finished ahead of the field in the special "jalopy" race. Ronnie Sheets, of Fort Wayne, won the consolation race. Races will be held again next Saturday night. WRSW broadcasts the racing action from 8:45 to 9:15 each Saturday night.

Saturday, June 9, 1956
Bob Staley Again Wins Feature At Local Speedway

The largest crowd of the 1956 season at the Warsaw Speedway saw Bob Staley, of Warsaw, again win the feature stock car race Saturday night.

There were several crashes during the night. In the consolation event, Earl Conklin, of Huntington, suffered minor skin abrasions when his car crashed. He was taken to the McDonald Hospital, but released later that night. Max Lambert, of Warsaw, had his car roll over in front of the grandstand. His door came open. Lambert had no protection beneath his auto, and it was feared he was hurt. However, he was pulled from the car uninjured.

Winners of the five heat races were Pealy Heckaman, of Bourbon, Cecil Huntley, of Columbia City, Bud Gillett, of Goshen, Staley, and Jim Hullinger, of Bunker Hill. Oscar Cook, of Fort Wayne, won the race between the six fastest qualifiers, and Heckaman finished ahead of the field in the stock consolation race, while Buck Beezley, of Cromwell, was first in the modified consolation race.

Thirty minutes of the racing action were broadcast over WRSW AM and FM from 8:45 to 9:15 p.m.

Saturday, June 16, 1956
Hullinger Cops Stock Car Feature

Jim Hullinger, of Bunker Hill, had a great night at the Warsaw Speedway Saturday, winning the 25-lap feature stock car race, as well as capturing the race between the six fastest qualifiers and the fourth heat race.

Bob Staley, of Warsaw, who had been making a habit out of winning the features, ran into trouble Saturday night. His car hit a utility pole in the early part of the race, knocking out several lights on the pole. However, Staley got back in the race and finished strong although the mishap ruined his chance to win.

There was a fine crowd on hand and the races were very entertaining. WRSW broadcast the action between 8:45 and 9:15.

In addition to Hullinger, winners of heat races were Tom McCaulley of Wabash, Cliff Gibson of Columbia City, Herb Mann of Warsaw, and Don Riley of Marion. A 15-lap stock feature was held with Dick Leiter of Warsaw as the winner. In the 10-lap consolation event, the winner was Oscar Cook of Wabash.

Saturday, June 23, 1956
Holle Captures Stock Car Feature In Close Finish

Archie Holle, of Warsaw, won the 25-lap feature stock car race here Saturday night 'in a photo finish' over Bob Staley, also of Warsaw. There was a big crowd on hand for the excellent races, as more than 40 cars qualified in the trials. The racing action was broadcast over WRSW AM and FM from 8:45 to 9:15.

Winners of the five heat races were Gerald Egner, Columbia City; Cecil Huntley, Columbia

City; Dick Leiter, Warsaw; Junior Dear, Columbia City; and Don Riley, Marion. Dear also won the six-lap race between the six fastest qualifying cars, with Holle second and Staley third. A semi-feature of 15 laps was also held, with Leiter winning. The consolation race was won by Buck Beezley, of Cromwell.

Saturday, June 30, 1956
Speedway Scene Of Many Crashes In Auto Races

A "wild" night of racing at the Warsaw Speedway found many cars rolling over and crashing, but luckily no one was injured.

The crowd was thrilled at the number of mishaps and also some very good races. There was a big field of 50 cars qualifying for the races. The feature was won by Jim Hullinger, of Bunker Hill. One car rolled over in front of the grandstand and another was struck by a car while it was rolling over.

Winners of heat races were Gregg Smith of Leesburg, Charlie Howell of Wabash, Lamar Sechrist of Bourbon, Claude Everingham of New Paris, and Bob Shlater of Churubusco. Shlater also won the race between the six fastest qualifiers. The "Jalopy" race was won by Bob Gobel, of Garrett, while Buck Beezley, of Cromwell, won the consolation race.

Bob Shlater, Churubusco

Thirty minutes of the racing action were broadcast over Radio Station WRSW from 8:45 to 9:15.

Saturday, July 14, 1956
Holle Captures Feature Race At Local Speedway

A large crowd saw Archie Holle, of Warsaw, win the 25-lap feature stock car race Saturday night at the Warsaw Speedway. It was a fine night of racing, as 57 cars were qualified in the time trials, and 25 of them started in the stock feature event won by Leonard Bloomfield, of Warsaw.

Jack Riley, of Huntington, re-injured a leg that had just healed from a previous accident when his car rolled over during the time trials. It was a spectacular spill that resulted in the motor still running after the car was upside down and the driver still in the car. However, his leg injury was not serious.

WRSW broadcast the races from 8:45 to 9:15. Next Saturday night will feature the 50-lap mid-season championship race.

Holle won the feature event in a brand new race car, using it in competition for the first time. Heat winners were Bob Crago of Huntington, Bud Gullett of Goshen, Bob Grindle and Fred Boggs, both of Warsaw, and Buck Beezley, of Wolf Lake. Jim Hullinger, of Bunker Hill, won the race between the six fastest qualifying cars, and the consolation event was won by Devon Metzler, of Goshen.

Saturday, July 21, 1956
Holle Has Big Night Of Racing

Archie Holle, of Warsaw, had a big and successful night Saturday in the stock car races at the Warsaw Speedway. Holle won the 25-lap feature race, also the race between the six fastest qualifiers, and added the fifth heat race to his "triple crown" for the night.

An estimated 2,000 fans witnessed the racing program despite threatening weather. It was a very fine racing night, as no less than 60 cars qualified during the time trials. There were many thrills, including a six-car pile-up in the consolation event. Bill Hawley was shaken up and received first aid.

Other heat race winners, in addition to Holle, were Bob Coyle of Kendallville, Cliff Gibson of Columbia City, Dick Leiter of Warsaw, and Dick Nunemaker of Huntington. Leiter also won the 20-lap consolation race, while Dick Parker, of Columbia City finished first in the 10-lap concey.

Saturday, July 28, 1956
Hullinger Wins Stock Car Feature

Jim Hullinger, of Bunker Hill, won the 25-lap feature stock car race Saturday night at the Warsaw Speedway.

A large crowd was treated to an exciting program of races. Gregg Smith, of Leesburg, received only a bump on the head when his car flipped end over end in a three-car pileup. There were other crashes, including one that put Bob Staley out of the feature race.

Winners of the five heat races were Joe Adams, of Warsaw, Gerald Bills and Dick Parker, both of Columbia City, Hullinger, and Bill Herendeen, of Albion. Hullinger made it three wins for the night by also winning the race between the six fastest qualifiers. The 15-lap feature was won by Mike Klingerman, of Warsaw. Buck Beezley, of Wolf Lake, won the 10-lap consolation event. Races were broadcast from 8:45 to 9:15 over WRSW.

Saturday, August 4, 1956
Staley Captures Stock Car Feature

Bob Staley, of Warsaw, won the feature race Saturday night in the stock car program at the Warsaw Speedway. The races will be featured twice during county fair week—on Wednesday and Saturday nights.

More than 2,000 fans were present Saturday and they witnessed some fine races and many thrill-packed crashes and roll-overs. However, none of the drivers were injured. In the consolation race, John Hutchinson, of North Manchester, rolled his car over about six times in a distance of 200 feet. Sixty cars qualified for the races.

Two cars rolled over a guard rail into the pit area, scattering pit men in all directions. A wheel came off Junior Leiter's car and hurtled into the pit area. No one was struck by the wheel, however.

Heat race winners were Joe Adams, of Warsaw, Bill Green, Don Huntley and his brother Cecil, both of Columbia City, and Joe Hamsher of New Paris. Staley won the race between the six fastest qualifiers. The stock feature was won by Don Huntley, while Jake Burtsfield, of Syracuse, won the concey. The races Wednesday night will be broadcast from 8:30 to 9 p.m. and on Saturday from 8:45 to 9:15, over Radio Stations WRSW AM and FM, by announcer Milo Clase.

Saturday, August 25, 1956
Holle Captures Stock Car Feature

Archie Holle, of Warsaw, captured the feature 25-lap event Saturday night at the Warsaw Speedway. A big crowd witnessed the stock car races, which included several collisions and roll-overs. Watches donated by Fitch Jewelry Store were given to Holle for winning the feature race and to Mike Klingerman, of Warsaw, winner of the 15-lap modified stock feature.

Next Saturday night's program will feature an "officials" race. There will also be racing on Labor Day, next Monday night, including a 100-lap feature event.

Heat winners Saturday were Earl Cocklin, of Huntington, Charles Howell, of Wabash, Dean Spicher, of Leesburg, Junior Dear, of Columbia City, and Oscar Cook of Hartford City. Holle also won the race between the six fastest qualifiers, and Joe Hamsher, of New Paris, finished ahead of the field in the 15-lap consolation event.

Monday, September 3, 1956
Unable To Name Winner Of Stock Car Feature Race

The winner of last night's 100-lap stock car championship race at the Warsaw Speedway was still in doubt today. There were so many collisions, restarts, and lappings of the field by faster cars that judges were unable to determine who won the Labor Day feature. Officials said they would have to check all their figures and announce the winner next Saturday night.

More than 2,000 fans witnessed the races last night. Twenty-four cars started the 100-lap feature. Bob Staley, after all kinds of trouble, was forced out in the 95th lap. He received a gold wrist watch for being chosen the "hard luck driver" of the night.

The stock feature, a 20-lap race, was won by John Nisely, of New Paris. The 10-lap consolation event was won by Herb Mann, of Warsaw, while Bud Gullett, of Goshen, won the modified consolation race, also over 10 laps.

Saturday, September 8, 1956
Gale Smith Cops Stock Car Race

Fifty cars and drivers competed Saturday night in stock car races at the Warsaw Speedway with Gale Smith, of Warsaw, winning the feature event.

It was announced that the Labor Day 100-lap race winner was Joe Hamsher, of New Paris, with Buck Beezley second and Jack Nunnemaker third. Officials had been unable to name the winner the night the race was held.

In "point standings" Jim Hullinger of Bunker Hill is first with 164, followed by Archie Holle, Warsaw, with 153, and Bob Staley, Warsaw, 120. In the "strictly stock" point standings, Dick Leiter of Warsaw won with 178, followed by LaMarr Sechrist of Bourbon and Bob Grindle of Warsaw.

TO RECEIVE TROPHY. A large trophy will be awarded to point winner Hullinger at the annual Hoosier Hot Rod banquet later in the fall. It was also announced that there will be racing again this next Saturday night and each succeeding Saturday as long as weather permits. WRSW broadcasts the races from 8:45 to 9:15 each Saturday night.

Heat race winners last Saturday were Tom Beck of Huntington, Bill Green of Columbia City, Jim Lozier of Burket, Charles Howell of Wabash, and Joe Hamsher of New Paris. The race between the six fastest qualifiers was won by Arden Leiter of Warsaw. John Huff of Burket, won the stock car feature, while Junior Leiter, Warsaw, was first in the consolation event.

Saturday, September 15, 1956
Archie Holle Wins Stock Car Feature Here

Archie Holle, of Warsaw, won the feature stock car race Saturday night at the Warsaw Speedway, as cool weather held down the size of the crowd. Winner of the strictly stock feature was Dean Spicher, of Leesburg. Cowboy Likes, of Ligonier, won the race between the six fastest qualifiers.

There were two mechanic races held. Max Hay, of Warsaw, won one, and the other was won by Max Hile of Columbia City. Winners of the four heat races were Al Rude of Plymouth, Charles Howell of Wabash, Spicher, and Gale Smith of Warsaw.

Earl Cocklin, of Huntington, received treatment at the McDonald Hospital for a bruised leg after his car rolled over a fence. There were several other collisions during the racing program but no injuries.

Officials said there would be racing again next Saturday providing warm weather prevails. The races are broadcast over Radio Stations WRSW AM and FM from 8:45 to 9 p.m.

1957

Saturday, May 11, 1957
Main Stock Car Race At Bourbon Halted by Rain

Racing fans who went to Bourbon Sunday afternoon had a thrilling afternoon watching many spills and rolls as the stock cars roared around the half-mile dirt track at the Bourbon fairgrounds. Intermittent rains made the track quite slippery causing the spills and Bob Adams and Bill Green escaped injury in two spectacular roll-overs on the slippery track. The main event of the afternoon was halted after a few laps because of rain. The racing at the Kosciusko County Fairgrounds gets underway next Saturday night on the quarter-mile oval. Radio Station WRSW will air the races from 8:45 to 9:15 with Milo Clase at the mike. Smith and Wuthrich Sinclair Service, Warsaw, will sponsor this year's sportscasts.

Events at Bourbon were won by Don Rogan, of Huntington, first heat; Don Parker, of North Manchester, second heat; Lamarr Sechrist of Bourbon, the third heat; and Archie Holle, of Warsaw, fourth heat. The feature stock car race was won by Chuck Reich of Warsaw, and the modified stock car race was called because of rain. A double feature will be run next week on the half-mile oval.

Saturday, May 30, 1957
Holle Breaks Speed Record

The one-lap speed record was broken last night at the Warsaw Speedway by Archie Holle, of Warsaw, during the stock car racing program. The previous record for the one-quarter mile oval was 18.03 seconds. Last night it was turned by Holle in 17.90. The record was broken during the opening night of the race track with the track in excellent condition.

The large crowd witnessed a spectacular rollover by Glen Owens of Silver Lake that demolished his car. Owens was unhurt except for scratches despite the fact that in the rollover he accidentally released his safety belt. His wife, who was in the stands, was taken to the hospital at the same time as Owens when she fainted during the excitement.

Following are the winners of the events:
1st heat - Dick Tarton of Kendallville
2nd heat-Dick Parker of Columbia City
3rd heat-Don Hartley of South Whitley
4th heat-Gale Smith of Warsaw
5th heat-Junior Dear of Columbia City
Six Fastest-Archie Holle of Warsaw
Main stock event-Jack Hickman of Columbia City
Feature event-Bob Staley of Warsaw

Saturday, June 8, 1957
Hartford City Driver Captures Stock Car Feature

Oscar Cook, of Hartford City, won the 25-lap stock car feature Saturday night at the Warsaw Speedway as a large crowd took in the races. The 15-lap stock feature was won by Whitey Steiner of Huntington. Winners of the 10-lap races, of which there were four, were Bob Bernhard, of South Whitley, Junior Leiter, of Columbia City, Steiner, and Chuck Grover, of Goshen. Grover also won the race between the six fastest qualifiers, while the 10-lap consolation event was captured by Junior Dear.

The races were broadcast over Radio Stations WRSW AM and FM from 8:45 to 9:15 for Smith and Wuthrich, Argonne Road Sinclair service station. There were several thrills and car collisions during the races, and color and excitement were added by the entry of many new cars, including a racing team of brothers, Cliff and Fred Setser, from Fort Wayne.

Saturday, June 15, 1957
Goshen Driver Captures Feature Race

Bob Tucker, Burket

Chuck Grover, of Goshen, won the 25-lap feature stock car race Saturday night before a large crowd on a warm night at the Warsaw Speedway. Grover edged Archie Holle, of Warsaw, who finished second. The stock feature was won by Lamarr Sechrist, of Bourbon, while Joe Hamsher of New Paris, captured the consolation event. Heat winners were Leslie Bills, Junior Dear and Dick Parker, all of Columbia City, Holle and Sechrist. Holle also won the race between the six fastest qualifiers, as Grover came in second.

There were many thrills and spills. Gale Smith, of Warsaw, had his throttle stick while going at full speed and as his car went into a turn, the car flipped end over end into the pit area. He was not injured, although his car caught on fire. Joe Hamsher also escaped unscratched when his car rolled over in front of the grandstand.

The races, as they are every Saturday night, were broadcast over WRSW from 8:45 to 9:15 for Smith and Wuthrich Sinclair service, of Argonne Road.

Saturday, June 22, 1957
Goshen Driver Wins Feature At Local Speedway

Chuck Grover, of Goshen, won the modified stock car feature race Saturday night at the Warsaw Speedway, defeating Junior Dear of Columbia City, who was second. In the strictly stock car feature race, Bob Tucker of Claypool finished ahead of the field. Bill Green, Columbia City, won the "consey" race, and Archie Holle, Warsaw, the event for the six fastest qualifiers.

Heat winners were Cliff Gibson and Leslie Becker, both of Columbia City, Bob Staley of Warsaw, Pealey Heckaman of Bourbon and Grover. Radio Stations WRSW AM and FM broadcast the racing action from 8:45 to 9:15 p.m.

Saturday, June 29, 1957
Large Crowd Sees Stock Car Races

A large crowd enjoyed an exciting evening of racing at the quarter-mile oval at the Kosciusko County fairgrounds Saturday evening. The crowd witnessed a spectacular roll-over by Gale Smith. His car flipped over and tore the front end of the vehicle completely out from under him, but Smith escaped injury.

Thursday, July 4, there will be races starting at 7:30. A fireworks display will be featured near the end of the Program. Results of the heats Saturday were as follows: 1st heat – Bill Hentzler; 2nd heat - Fat Ryman; 3rd heat-Lamarr Sechrist; 4th heat-Joe Hamsher; 5th heat-Archie Holle; Six fastest-Archie Holle; Stock feature-Carl Cocklin; Consolation-Dick Parker; Feature event-Archie Holle.

Saturday, July 6, 1957
Estimate 8,000 See Fireworks

Hoosier Hot Rod and Kosciusko County fair association officials said today that the crowd at the Warsaw Speedway Saturday night for stock car races and a fireworks display was undoubtedly the largest in local history. It was estimated that about 8,000 persons saw the fireworks display, about half of them from the grandstand, inside the speedway grounds and the rest from the fairgrounds area, lake fronts, cottages, etc. The fireworks display was sponsored by the Hoosier Hot Rods, Inc., Kosciusko County Fair Association, and were set off by the Warsaw Junior Chamber of Commerce.

RACE WINNERS. The racing program proved quite interesting, with Archie Holle of Warsaw winning the feature modified stock event. Bob Staley of Warsaw was second.

The strictly stock feature was won by Earl Cocklin, of Huntington. The consolation event was won by Claude Everingham of New Paris, and the race between the six fastest qualifiers by Oscar Cook of Hartford City. Heat winners were Leslie Bills of Columbia City, Joe Hamsher of New Paris, Dan Huntley of Columbia City, Staley and Cook.

The races were broadcast over WRSW from 8:45 to 9:15 for Smith and Wuthrich Argonne service station.

Saturday, July 13, 1957
Archie Holle Wins Stock Car Feature Here

Archie Holle, of Warsaw, who has won many feature stock car races at the Warsaw Speedway, did it again Saturday night. A large crowd saw Holle flash across the finish line in the 25-lap modified stock feature. John Huff, of Burket, won the regular stock feature, and Oscar Cook was winner of the race between the six fastest qualifiers. Cook is from Hartford City. Dick Parker, Columbia City, won the consolation event. Heat winners were Cook, Holle, Victor Nash of Ligonier, Kenneth Leiter of Warsaw, and Earl Conklin of Huntington.

The races were broadcast from 8:45 to 9:15 over WRSW for Collett's Standard Service, and Dick Whitesell's Standard Service, both of Warsaw.

Saturday, July 20, 1957
Hot Oil Burns Stock Car Driver

Fans witnessed a thrilling night of racing at the Warsaw Speedway oval Saturday on the Kosciusko County Fairgrounds. In the 50-lap feature event, Forest Egner, of Columbia City, was sprayed with hot oil when an oil line broke in the car. He was burned about the face, chest, and shoulders and was taken to the Murphy Medical Center. He was released Sunday afternoon, however, and the burns were not serious.

Heat winners for Saturday night's events were Dick Tariton, Kenny Leiter, Leslie Bills, Chuck Grover, and Arden Leiter, and the six fastest by Oscar Cook. The stock feature was won by Dick Leiter, and the Feature race by Oscar Cook.

Saturday, July 27, 1957
52 Stock Cars In Races Here

A total of 52 cars qualified and competed in Saturday night's stock car races at Kosciusko County fairgrounds and produced an evening of thrills and spills. A large crowd witnessed the events. Gale Smith, who has been plagued with misfortune throughout the season, overcame his streak of bad luck and won the feature event of the evening.

Heat winners were Ed Napier, Earl Myer, Dick Leiter, Archie Holle, and Gerald Bills. The six-fastest race was won by Gerald Bills. The stock feature was copped by Dick Lynch, with Kenny Leiter taking the consolation. The main event was won by Gale Smith.

Saturday, August 10, 1957
4,000 See Stock Car Races At Fair

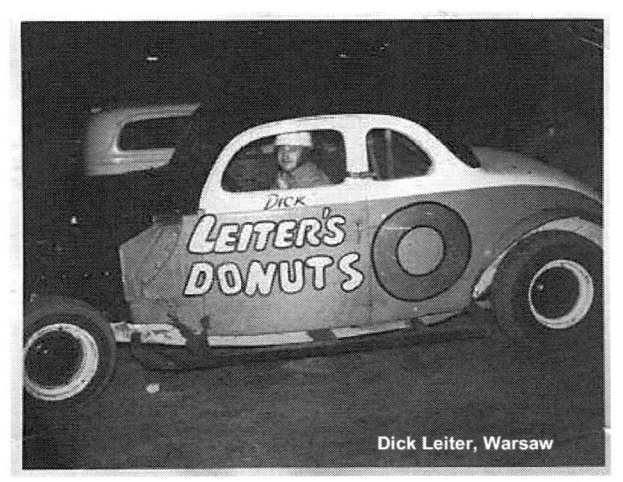

Dick Leiter, Warsaw

A crowd, estimated at more than 4,000, witnessed the stock car races Saturday night at the fairgrounds on the final night of the county fair. The fans were treated to one of the best evenings of racing at the quarter mile track all year. The crowd thrilled to numerous rollovers, smashups and collisions, including a spectacular 14-car pile-up. Archie Holle once again dominated the field in the feature event as he copped top honors in that race.

The heat winners were Mike Klingaman, Jim Alexander, Dick Leiter, Gale Smith, and Gerald Bills for the first five heats in that order. The dash event of the six fastest was copped by Gerald Bills. The strictly stock feature was won by Dick Leiter, the consolation race by Charlie Howell, and the feature race by Archie Holle. The races are broadcast over WRSW every Saturday between 8:45 and 9:15 p.m.

Saturday, August 17, 1957
Goshen Driver Wins Feature At Local Speedway

Chuck Grover of Goshen sped across the finish line as winner of the feature race Saturday night, before a fine crowd at the Warsaw Speedway.

The stock feature was won by Dave Cornish of Elkhart, while Jack Reilley of Marion won the consolation race and Bob Staley of Warsaw the dash event. Heat race winners were Dave Gagnon of Beaver Dam, Junior Dear of Columbia City, Dick Leiter and Archie Holle, both of Warsaw and Oscar Cook of Hartford City.

The races were broadcast for 30 minutes over Radio Station WRSW and WRSW-FM for Ford's Bowling Lanes and Ford's Auto Supply of Warsaw.

Saturday, August 31, 1957
Stock Car Races Draw Crowds Here

Stock car races attracted large crowds Saturday night and again on Monday (Labor Day) night at the Warsaw Speedway. The races were held Monday night despite rain early in the evening. The 40-lap feature race was won by Oscar Cook, of Hartford City.

Heat winners Monday were Mike Klingaman of Warsaw, Dick Parker and Gerald Bills of Columbia City, Oscar Cook of Hartford City, and Bob Bernhard of South Whitley. Cook also won the race between the six fastest qualifiers. Earl Cocklin of Huntington finished first in the feature event between strictly stock cars.

Car Rolls Over. Bob Staley, of Warsaw, escaped with only bruises when his car rolled over during one of the Monday night races.

On Saturday night the feature race was won by Chuck Grover of Goshen. Junior Leiter, of Pierceton, captured the consolation event and Cocklin the stock car feature. Oscar Cook of Hartford City won the dash event and also one of the heat races. Other heat race winners were Bob Grindle of Warsaw, Dick Parker of Columbia City, Cocklin, and Hank Easley of Logansport.

The races were broadcast at 8:45 over WRSW AM and FM for Ford's Auto Supply and Ford's Bowling Lanes. A 100-lap feature race will be the main attraction next Saturday night, Sept. 7, with time trials starting at 7 0'clock, the first race at 8 p.m.

Saturday, September 7, 1957
Chuck Grover Wins Feature At Local Speedway

A large crowd at the quarter-mile Warsaw Speedway last Saturday night thrilled to the usual rollovers, spills, and crashes. Chuck Grover won the feature event. One spectacular roll-over by Dave Gagnon during the strictly stock feature pulled the fans out of their seats as he emerged uninjured.

Next Saturday night at the fairgrounds oval the feature event will include a 40-lap race with an expected bumper to bumper field of 40 or more cars.

The winners for Saturday's evening of racing were: 1st race, Mike Klingaman; 2nd race, Charlie Howell;3rd race, Glen Owens; 4th race, Oscar Cook; 5th race, Arden Leiter; Dash Event, Hank Easley; Strictly Stock Feature, Lamarr Sechrist; Feature event (100 laps) Chuck Grover.

Saturday, September 21, 1957
Honor Youngsters at Race Track

It was kiddie's night Saturday at the Warsaw Speedway and the youngsters were allowed to take a ride in their favorite stock car as the season for racing neared its close.
The local track at the fairgrounds will be the scene of one more night of racing as the season is wrapped up next Saturday.

Heat winners for Saturday were Dave Gagnon, Burket; Don Walker, Kokomo; Frank Muffley, Plymouth; and Archie Holle, Warsaw, for the first, second, third and fourth heats respectively. The dash event featuring the six fastest cars was won by popular local driver Archie Holle.

Dick Leiter, Warsaw, won the "strictly stock" event while Archie Holle, also of Warsaw, drove to victory in the feature to make a sweep of the main events for local drivers. The races are broadcast over Radio Station WRSW each Saturday evening at 8:30, sponsored by Ford's Bowling Lanes and Ford's Auto Supply.

Saturday, September 27, 1957
Wind Up Stock Car Races Here

A large crowd witnessed the final night of stock car racing Saturday at the Warsaw Speedway at the county fairgrounds.

Jack Smith, in the strictly stock feature race, rolled over on the fence and the impact tore one of his shoes completely off and the other was nearly pulled off. He was treated by attendants at the McHatton ambulance at trackside for a badly bruised leg but not taken to the hospital.

Winners were: 1st heat, Tubby Beck; 2nd heat, Gerald Bills, of Columbia City; 3rd heat, Glen Owens, Silver Lake; 4th heat, Don Walker, Kokomo; six fastest dash event, Junior Dear, Columbia City.

Dick Leiter, of Warsaw, collected for winning the strictly stock event while Oscar Cook, a familiar name at the track and hailing from Hartford City, copped the modified stock feature event. The final broadcast over WRSW was sponsored by Ford's Lanes and Ford's Auto Supply.

1958

Bob Staley, Warsaw

Saturday, May 17, 1958
Stock Car Races Under Way Here

More than 2,000 fans witnessed the first night of stock car racing at the Warsaw Speedway Saturday night, climaxed by a three-car smash-up at the finish line of the feature race.

Fifty cars qualified for events at the track as the weatherman co-operated with perfect weather. The five heat events were won by Bob Albright, of Kokomo; Lester Bills, of Columbia City; Hank Easley, of Logansport; Dick Leiter, of Warsaw; and Jim Hullinger, of Bunker Hill. Earl Cocklin won the 18-car "strictly stock" feature while Hullinger won the dash event for the six fastest qualifiers. Oscar Cook, of Hartford City, won the consolation feature.

In the modified stock feature, with 20 cars entered, Oscar Cook won the race when he spun and rolled over at the finish line at the same time. He suffered only safety belt burns. Bobby Burns, of Warsaw, and Cliff Gibson, who placed third in the event, were also involved in the pile-up. Racing on the fast Warsaw quarter-mile track is scheduled again for next Saturday.

Saturday, May 24, 1958
7 Cars Crash In Stock Car Race

One driver was injured as the result of a seven car crack-up in the "strictly stock" feature at the Warsaw Speedway Saturday night. Everett Tarlton, of Kendallville, suffered a laceration of the face in the wreck. He received emergency treatment by the McHatton ambulance crew and was taken to the Murphy Medical Center for stitches. No one else involved in the crash was injured.

Heat winners were Bobby Beck, of Big Lake; Bob Albright, Logansport; Everett Tarlton, Kendallville; Bill Fortune, Kokomo; and Wayne Brockman, of Fort Wayne. Winner of the dash event was Bob Staley, Warsaw. Hank Easley, of Logansport, won the consolation event and the feature, while Dick Lynch, of Claypool, won the stock feature.

Saturday, June 7, 1958
Local Drivers Win Feature Stock Car Races

Warsaw drivers came away with victories in both feature events in Saturday night's racing card at the local speedway. Dick Leiter got the checkered flag in the strictly stock feature while Bob Staley took the checkered banner in the modified feature.

Heat winners were Dick Pierce, of Kokomo, Ronald Gagnon, of Beaver Dam, Jim Hullinger, of Bunker Hill, Leslie Bills, of Columbia City, and Bill Fredrick of Kokomo. Winner of the dash event was Bob Staley of Warsaw. Don Walker of Kokomo won the consolation event. The races were broadcast over WRSW AM and FM from 8:45 to 9:15.

Saturday, June 17, 1958
Kokomo Driver wins Feature Races in Warsaw

Kokomo stock car driver Bill Fredrick won both the consolation and modified stock car feature race at the Warsaw Speedway Saturday night while Max Lambert of Warsaw, won the strictly stock feature.

Heat winners were Junior Dear, of Columbia City; Bob Hostetler, of Goshen; Bob Tucker of Burket; and Bud Stillwell, Kokomo. Winner of the dash event featuring the six fastest cars was Bob Grindle of Warsaw. A large crowd witnessed many spills. The races are broadcast from 8:45 to 9:15 p.m. over Radio Stations WRSW AM and FM.

Saturday, June 21, 1958
Leiter, Staley win Feature Stock Car Races

Dick Leiter and Bob Staley took top stock car racing honors Saturday night at the Warsaw Speedway as they won the stock feature event respectively.

Heat winners were Bud Stillwell, K. Coyle, Chuck Grover, L. Sechrist and Joe Hamsher. G. Owens was the winner of the six fastest dash event and Jack Reilly won the consolation race. The evening of racing featured many spills and pile-ups, but no injuries. The races are broadcast each Saturday at 8:45 p.m. over WRSW FM with Milo Clase at the mike.

Saturday, July 5, 1958
Local Race Driver Loses Winnings In Apparent Theft

Bob Staley, of Route 2, Warsaw,(near the West Wayne School) reported to Sheriff Carl Latta Sunday morning that $125 had been taken from his home Saturday night during a party.

The $125 was Staley's winnings as a stock car race driver at the Kosciusko County fairgrounds Saturday night. Staley told Sheriff Latta the money was in a brown envelope on the television set. He said that after one of his 11 guests went to the TV to get some cigarettes the money came up missing. Latta said those at the party would be questioned today. (No race results article was published)

Saturday, July 19, 1958
4 Race Stewards Slightly Hurt At Local Speedway

Four race stewards sustained minor injuries Saturday at the Warsaw Speedway when a car smashed through the pit rail during one of the races and knocked them off a platform.

A car driven by Leslie Bills crashed through the pit platform, knocking the stewards to the ground. Treated at the track for minor cuts and lacerations were Carl Weigold and Dell Ballard, both of Columbia City, and Jim Smith and Dale Sapp. Bills was uninjured and none of the stewards required hospitalization.

Heat winners were Jack Hickman, of Syracuse; Tom Wyman, Ernie Keefer, Dick Leiter and Bob Staley, all of Warsaw. Staley also won the dash event. The consolation event was won by Kenneth Bowton, of Goshen, and the strictly stock event by Carroll Hostetler, also of Goshen. The mid-season 50-lap championship race was won by Archie Holle of Warsaw.

Saturday, July 26, 1958
Large Crowd Sees 62 Cars Compete At Local Track

Almost a record number of 62 cars qualified for the races at the Warsaw Speedway Saturday night before the second largest crowd of the season.

The consolation and modified stock feature races were won by Jimmy Hullinger of Bunker Hill. Heat winners were Dick Parker, Columbia City; Kenny Huntley, Columbia City; Bob Staley, Warsaw; Tubby

Bob Tucker Trophies

Beck, Big Lake; Beezer Humphries, Logansport. Staley also won the dash event featuring the six fastest cars of the evening. The strictly stock feature was won by Al Gasper of Mishawaka. Next Saturday the 25-lap mid-season strictly stock championship race will be held.

Saturday, August 2, 1958
Kokomo Drivers Win Big Events At Local Speedway

Kokomo drivers played an important role in the regular Saturday night stock car races at the Warsaw Speedway last weekend as they won the consolation and feature races at the fairgrounds.

Don Walker and Beezer Humphries won the consolation and feature event races, respectively, but Jim Loser, of Warsaw, won the strictly stock race to keep the Kokomo drivers from sweeping the feature event field.

Fifty percent of the winnings in the feature event went to Warsaw driver Oscar Cook who is recovering following major surgery recently. The race was dubbed the Oscar Cook benefit race. Bob Grindle, popular Warsaw driver, was presented a wrist watch by fellow drivers. He will leave for military service this week and Saturday was his last day of racing at the speedway.

Heat winners before a large crowd were: Kenny Bodenhaven, of Goshen; Kenny Bowser, of Bourbon; Archie Holle, of Warsaw; Bob Tucker, of Burket; and Beezer Humphries, of Kokomo. Holle copped honors in the dash event for the six fastest qualifiers. Races will be broadcast from the speedway Wednesday and Friday during the county fair at 8:45 p.m. with Milo Clase at the mike.

Saturday, August 9, 1958
Pit Mechanic Killed
Race Track Death Mars Final Night Of Fair
By Danny Lee, *Times-Union Reporter*

The 42nd annual Kosciusko County fair was history today. It ended Saturday night on such happy notes as the crowning of a new queen and the awarding of many valuable prizes, including two new cars. But there was a tragic note too, with the death of a 46-year-old Wakarusa auto mechanic in an unfortunate accident during one of the stock car races.

Walter Schroeder was killed instantly when he fell midway across the track while running from infield to the pit area and was run over by several of the racing cars. It was the first fatal accident since stock car races were made an annual part of the summer sports program in Warsaw several years ago. Due to the possibility that Schroeder might have suffered a heart attack prior to falling, an autopsy was held Sunday morning. However, the autopsy disclosed that he did not have any heart ailment. In fact, doctors said his heart was "better than usual" for a man of his age.

4,000 See Tragedy – The tragic accident at the speedway occurred shortly before the queen crowning ceremony. Some 4,000 fans were in the grandstand when Schroeder and a friend, Walter Weaver, Wakarusa town marshal, ran from the infield toward the pit area, onto the east end of the quarter-mile track.

Weaver told the Times-Union reporters that Schroeder pitched forward and fell midway across the track. With the field of cars bearing down on them, Weaver tried to lift Schroeder. However, it was necessary for Weaver to jump to his own safety. Several of the cars ran over Schroeder. He was dead on arrival at the Murphy Medical Center, where he was rushed by McHatton ambulance.

Son a Driver – Schroeder's son, Don, of Route 3, Goshen, was driving one of the cars in the race. He ran from his car and to his father's side when the race was stopped. The victim's daughter and daughter-in-law witnessed the tragedy from the grandstand. Schroeder and Weaver were both members of Don's pit crew.

Saturday, August 9, 1958
4,000 See Races At County Fair

A crowd of more than 4,000 persons jammed the Warsaw Speedway Saturday night to witness an exciting evening of racing that was marred by the death of Walter Schroeder, a mechanic from Wakarusa, who ran onto the track from the pit area and was struck by some of the stock cars. (See story on Page 1).

Heat winners were Bill Fredricks of Kokomo; Bill Baxter of Columbia City; Cap Arnold of South Bend; Dick Leiter of Warsaw; Bob Staley of Warsaw. Chuck Grover, of Goshen, won the dash event of the six fastest qualifiers in the race.

The consolation event winner was copped by Ray Kenens, of Delphi, with the strictly stock feature won by Jim Frushour, of Wabash. Winner of the modified stock feature was Freddie Boggs of Warsaw. Seventy cars qualified for racing Saturday night.

Saturday, August 16, 1958
Bunker Hill Drivers Win Feature Races

Luther Holloway, of Warsaw, and Jimmy Hullinger, of Bunker Hill, were the top winners Saturday night of stock car races held at the Warsaw Speedway. Holloway won the "strictly stock" feature and Hullinger the "modified" feature race.

A record number of 72 cars qualified for the races. Freddie Boggs, of Warsaw, won the dash event and Ray Kenens, of Delphi the consolation. Heat winners were Earl Conklin, of Huntington; Dean Hamilton, of Leesburg; Gale Smith, of Warsaw; Tubby Beck, of Big Lake; and Bud Stillwell, of Logansport. Next Saturday night time trials will start at 7 o'clock instead of the usual 7:30. Two 50-lap modified feature events will be staged.

Carroll Hostetler, of Goshen, required hospital treatment Saturday after his auto rolled over on the track. Jim Butler of Kokomo was also taken to the hospital for several stitches

Luther Holloway, Warsaw

in his left leg. He injured the leg when his racing car and another collided during the practice runs prior to the start of the races.

Saturday, August 23, 1958
3 Feature Races At Local Speedway

Three feature races topped the stock car racing program Saturday night at the Warsaw Speedway. There were two 50-lap feature races for modified cars. One was for the slowest qualifiers, won by Ray Kenens of Delphi, and the other for the fastest qualifiers, won by Freddie Boggs, of Warsaw. The stock feature was won by Kenneth Huntley, of Columbia City, with Bob Tucker of Beaver Dam second and Tubby Beck of Big Lake third.

Bob Staley of Warsaw, won the race between the six fastest qualifying cars. There were only two heat races, due to the three feature events. Roy Coyle, of Columbia City, won the first heat, and the second was captured by Huntley. There will be racing as usual again next Saturday night, plus a big program on Labor Day night, Monday, Sept. 1. Just before the feature event Monday night (at approximately 10 p.m.) there will be a huge fireworks display.

Saturday, August 30, 1958
Boggs Sets New Qualifying Mark At Local Races

Jim Hullinger Prototype

A new Warsaw Speedway qualifying record topped off a weekend of racing last night as seven cars broke the old mark during qualifications.

Freddie Boggs, of Warsaw, turned the quarter-mile distance in 17.08 seconds to eclipse the old time of 17.45 set by Archie Holle last year. Seven other drivers turned the oval in a faster time than the old mark during the Labor Day racing event.

A big crowd saw the Labor Day night program, which included a display of fireworks at approximately 9 o'clock. The races were stopped while the many colorful aerial rockets were set off. Hundreds of youngsters, and their parents, also witnessed the display from outside the speedway.

Heat winners Saturday night were Bill Albright, of Logansport, Chet Warren, of Talma, Max Lambert, of Winona Lake, and Bob Staley, of Warsaw. Bob Ziegler of South Bend, won the dash event. Bill Fortune, of Kokomo, won the consolation race, while the "strictly stock" feature was copped by Kenny Huntley of Ligonier. The "modified stock" feature event was won by Bob Staley, of Warsaw. Labor Day heat winners were Junior Dear, of Columbia City, Tommy York, of Elkhart, Bob Ziegler of South Bend, Jim Loser of Warsaw. The dash event was won by Ray Kenens, of Delphi. Dick Parker, of Columbia

City won the consolation event and Duane Fox, also of Columbia City, won the strictly stock feature. Jim Hullinger, of Bunker Hill, went home with the winnings for the feature event.

Saturday, September 6, 1958
Holloway, Boggs Win Big Races

The season's championship racing events were held last Saturday night at the Warsaw Speedway with two Warsaw drivers coming away with the titles for modified and strictly stockcars. Luther Holloway won the strictly stock championship race of 25 laps while Freddie Boggs won the modified stock 50-lap race. Boggs also won the dash event for the six fastest cars qualified during the evening. More than 30 trophies were awarded during the evening.

Heat winners were Ted Schroeder, of Gary; Dale Cornish, of Elkhart; Bob Staley, of Warsaw; Tommy York, of Elkhart; and Don Walker, of Kokomo. Chuck Grover, of Goshen, won the consolation event. In the modified stock championship race Bob Sigler of South Bend placed second and Archie Holle, of Warsaw, placed third.

During the evening, Dick Linch, of Claypool, escaped injury when his car flipped over twice in the air and Dale Speicher of Warsaw, was uninjured when his car hit the wall head-on. J. Lindley, of Gary, jumped the retaining wall in his first time on the track and the car smashed into spectators' cars, badly damaging one and causing slight damage to three others. No one was hurt.

Saturday, September 13, 1958
Race Car Hits Fire Truck But No One Injured

Warsaw drivers were blanked from a win Saturday night at the Warsaw Speedway and the Winona Lake fire truck was struck by an out-of-control car.

A car driven by Pealy Heckaman, of Bourbon, spun out in front of the fire truck in the infield. The fire apparatus sustained only a scratched fender while the front of the race car was demolished. Pealy was not injured in the mishap.

Oscar Cook, of Hartford City, won the dash event while Tom York, of Elkhart, took the strictly stock feature. Slug Morr, of Albion, won the consolation event, while Ernie Kiefer, of Nappanee, won the modified stock feature.

Saturday, September 20, 1958
Local Drivers Blanked in Final Night of Racing

Local stock car drivers were unable to pick up a win Saturday night in the last evening of races at the Warsaw Speedway. The feature event was won by Oscar Cook of Hartford City, who was out most of this season due to major surgery. Cook won the first feature event of the season last May when the track opened.

Winner of the strictly stock feature was Tom York, of Elkhart, while the consolation event was won by Dick Salesman, of Churubusco. The dash event for the six fastest qualifiers was won by "Cap" Arnold of South Bend. Heat winners were Junior Dear, Columbia City; Bill Baxter, of Big Lake; Bob Ziegler, of South Bend; Phil Waldo, of Niles, Mich.; and Oscar Cook, of Hartford City.

Stock Car Driver Injured Here

Robert King, Wabash stock car driver, was in good condition today at the Murphy Medical Center after he suffered possible head injuries in a crash at the Warsaw Speedway Saturday night. King walked away from the wreck but other drivers noticed he was wobbly and dazed. He was taken to the hospital for observation.

1959

Saturday, May 2, 1959
2,000 See Stock Car Races Open

About 2,000 fans were on hand last Saturday for the first night of racing at the Warsaw Speedway as local drivers dominated the feature wins on the quarter-mile oval. About 45 cars were entered in the races. Bobby Grindle won the modified stock feature and Tom Wyman won the strictly stock feature. Dean Speicher was the consolation race winner. All three drivers are from Warsaw.

Steve Walker, of Kokomo, won the first heat race; Tommy York, of South Bend, the second; Bill Fortune, of Kokomo, the third; and Jimmy Hullinger, of Bunker Hill, the fourth. Bob Staley, of Warsaw, was winner of the dash event. The races were broadcast over WRSW AM-FM from 9 to 9:30 p.m. sponsored by Ford's Auto Supply of Warsaw.

Saturday, May 9, 1959
2 Drivers Hurt During Stock Car Races Here

Two drivers required treatment for minor injuries as the result of smashups at the Warsaw Speedway Saturday evening.

Dick George, of Route 3, Elkhart, sustained three cracked ribs when his stock racer hit the retaining wall and rolled over. He was treated at the Murphy Medical Center and returned to the track. Bob Smiley, of Warsaw, was treated for lacerations to his face and leg after his car bounced off the retaining wall during a race. Luther Holloway escaped injury when his auto rolled over during time trials.

Bob Grindle, of Warsaw, won the consolation race while Barney Baker, of South Bend, took the stock feature. Chuck Fortune of Kokomo, won the feature race. Heat race winners were Gerald Egner, Columbia City; Junior Dear, Columbia City; Deepey Walker, Hobart; Bob Staley, of Warsaw; Chuck Fortune, of Kokomo; and Archie Holle, of Warsaw.

Saturday, May 16, 1959
Local Drivers Win at Speedway

Warsaw drivers won both feature stock car races at the Warsaw Speedway Saturday night while a South Bend pilot copped the consolation event.

Tom Wyman, of Warsaw, won the strictly stock feature race and Bob Grindle, also of Warsaw, rolled to victory in the modified stock feature race. Cap Arnold, of South Bend, won the consolation race. John Davis, of Warsaw, was rushed to the Murphy Medical Center for examination and later released after rolling his stock car over during a heat race.

Heat race winners were Gerald Egner, Columbia City, Walt Preston, Jr., Kokomo; Tom Wyman, Warsaw; Bob Ziegler, South Bend and Jeff Culp, Hobart. Beezer Humphries, of Kokomo, won the dash event of the six fastest qualifiers.

Saturday, May 23, 1959
Close Finish Features Stock Car Race Here

Freddie Boggs, of Warsaw, won the feature stock car race at the Warsaw Speedway Saturday night just a wheel length ahead of Bob Staley, of Warsaw. The two local drivers fought for the lead through the last few laps of the event. The crowd came to its feet on the final lap and witnessed the thrilling near-photo finish.

Gerald Egner, of Columbia City, was treated and released at the Murphy Medical Center after his racer was struck from the rear in the feature. Bob Sechrist rolled his stock car over but was unhurt and Jimmie Elliott jumped the fence in his car and was not injured.

Art Smith, of Warsaw, won the consolation, and Leslie Bills, of Columbia City, won the stock feature. Oscar Cook, of Hartford City, was winner of the dash event for the six fastest qualifiers. Heat winners were: Leslie Bills, Columbia City; Dean Speicher, Warsaw; Tom Wyman, Warsaw; Oscar Cook, Hartford City; and Bob Staley, Warsaw.

Les Bills, Columbia City

A 50-lap feature for Memorial Day evening is planned at the local speedway. The races are broadcast over WRSW AM-FM from 9 to 9:30 p.m.

Saturday, June 6, 1959
Outside Drivers Win Honors At Local Speedway

Drivers from outside the county won all three of the feature stock car racing events at the Warsaw Speedway Saturday night.

Bob Ziegler of New Carlisle, won the 50-lap feature with Dick George, of South Bend, close behind. Bob Staley, of Warsaw, running second throughout the 50 laps, blew a tire making a bid for the lead in the last lap. The consolation event was won by Jim Cuthbert, of Niles, Mich., and the strictly stock feature by Bill Hare, of Columbia City.

Heat winners before a crowd of near 4,000 were Ronnie Zimmerman, Warsaw; Bob Rebeck, Kokomo; Bob Bernhard, South Whitley; Jack Hickman, Syracuse; Dean Speicher, of Warsaw. The dash event for the six fastest qualifiers was won by Jack Hickman, of Syracuse.

The races were broadcast over WRSW AM-FM for 30 minutes, sponsored by the Mobile gas and oil dealers and distributors of Warsaw.

Saturday, June 13, 1959
Holle Captures Feature Event At Local Speedway

A Warsaw driver won the feature event at the Warsaw Speedway Saturday night while drivers from outside the county won the consolation and stock feature.

Archie Holle, of Warsaw, won the feature event of the evening while Jim Hullinger, of Bunker Hill, won the consolation and Pealy Heckaman, of Bourbon, the stock feature. Only one minor injury was reported as the result of a six car pile-up in the consey race.

Heat winners were Bob Wiles, Nappanee; John Huff, Burket; Charles Fortune, Kokomo; DeWayne Fox, Columbia City; and Bill Fredricks, Kokomo. Bob Staley won the dash event of the six fastest qualifiers.

Saturday, June 20, 1959
Large Crowd Sees Bob Staley Win 50-Lap Race

One of the largest crowds of the season was on hand for the stock car races at the Warsaw Speedway Saturday night as two Warsaw drivers and a Columbia City pilot won the feature and consolation events.

Bob Staley, Warsaw, won the feature 50-lap race at the quarter-mile oval while Bill Hare, of Columbia City, won the stock feature. Art Smith, of Warsaw, won the consolation race.

Two drivers were taken to the Murphy Medical Center for treatment of minor injuries and later released after they were involved in crack-ups at the track. Paul Grim, of Columbia City, suffered a lacerated lip and Roger Wise, of Wakarusa, was treated for abrasions.

Heat race winners were Walt Yoder, of Warsaw; L. C. Drabenstot, Warsaw; Freddie Boggs, Warsaw; Bob Bernhard, South Whitley; Walter Preston, Jr., Kokomo; and the dash event of the six fastest qualifiers was won by Bob Staley of Warsaw.

Saturday, June 27, 1959
Car rolls over 10 times; Race Driver Not Hurt

More than 2,500 persons jammed the Warsaw Speedway Saturday night and witnessed one of the most spectacular crashes of the season as Ervin Papenbrook rolled his car over 10 times but was not injured. Papenbrook, of Churubusco, walked out of the hospital after a checkup for injuries he could have suffered in the awesome crash.

Max Lambert, of Warsaw, won the strictly stock feature while Hank Easley, of Logansport, won the modified feature and Oscar Cook, of Hartford City, the consolation. Heat winners were Carol Hostetler, of Goshen; Ronald Gagnon, of Beaver Dam; Hobe Noel, of Logansport; Pealy Heckaman, of Bourbon; Charles Fortune, Kokomo; and Hank Easley, of Logansport.

Saturday the local track will feature a fireworks display along with the regular card of racing.

Saturday, July 4, 1959
6,000 See Races, Fireworks Here

The largest crowd in the history of the Warsaw Speedway was on hand last Saturday for the races and the fireworks display sponsored by the Kosciusko County Fair association and Hoosier Hot-Rods association. Officials said 6,000 tickets were sold.

The races were filled with many crack-ups and roll-overs although only one driver, Earl Cocklin of Huntington, was taken to the hospital. He sustained only a sprained wrist. The modified car feature race of the evening was rained out and a double feature will be held this Saturday.

Jim Elliott, of Warsaw, won the consolation feature race while Bill Baxter of Columbia City, was the winner of the stock feature. Heat winners were Hal Douglas, of Kokomo; Luther Holloway, of Columbia City; Fred Boggs, of Warsaw; Ben Simmers, of Columbia City; Junior Dear, of Columbia City; and the dash event by Bob Ziegler, of South Bend.

Jimmie Elliott, Warsaw

Saturday, July 11, 1959
Warsaw Drivers Star at Speedway

Two feature races were held at the Warsaw Speedway Saturday night, one a delayed running of the scheduled Fourth of July feature that was rained out on that date.

It was won by Fred Boggs of Warsaw with Archie Holle, also of Warsaw, second, and Bob Ziegler of South Bend, third. The regular feature stock car race was won by Bob Staley of Warsaw. Ziegler was second and Holle third.

Bob Staley, Warsaw

Max Lambert of Warsaw won the stock feature Saturday. Bob Wiles, of Syracuse, won the consolation event. Staley was first in the race between the six fastest qualifiers. Heat winners were Pealy Heckaman of Bourbon, Bob Albright of Noblesville, Bill Hare of Columbia City, Beezer Humphries of Kokomo, and Bud Stillwell of Logansport. It was Albright's first win in one and one-half years of racing here.

Nearly 3,000 fans witnessed the stock car races. There were several spills, with one driver, Ken Bowser of Bourbon, taken to the hospital for examination after a two-car wreck.

Saturday, July 25, 1959
Warsaw, South Bend Drivers Race Winners

Two Warsaw drivers and a South Bend pilot figured in the winnings last Saturday at the Warsaw Speedway in the feature races. Dick Leiter, of Warsaw, won the consolation event while Jim Lozier flashed across the finish line to win the stock feature.

#99, Jim Hullinger, #20 Bill Forture, #25 Bob Ziegler

#99, Jim Hullinger, #113 Ray Kennens

The feature event of the evening was won by Bob Ziegler, of South Bend. Beezer Humphries, of Kokomo, won the dash event of the six fastest qualifiers for the nights racing.

Heat winners were Hal Douglas, of Kokomo; Bill Hare, of Columbia City; Jim Hullinger, of Bunker Hill; Bill Baxter, of Columbia City; and Dean Spicher, of Warsaw. A large field of 63 cars qualified for the racing card before a crowd estimated at 2,500 persons.

Earl Egolf, of North Manchester, sustained a lacerated hand when his car rolled over and Charles Neal, of Wabash, escaped injury when his stock car flipped end-over-end over the fence. Elbert Rider, of Cromwell, received emergency treatment at the Murphy Medical Center when he was burned by steam from a radiator.

Saturday, August 1, 1959
Record 75 Cars Qualify Here For Stock Races

A record number of 75 cars qualified for the stock car races Saturday night at the Warsaw Speedway as 3,000 spectators saw Bob Staley, of Warsaw, capture the feature event.

Les Bills & Archie Holle

The thrills and spills were many during the night. A car driven by Beezer Humphries of Kokomo rolled over several times then went over the wall, but Humphries climbed out uninjured.

Joe Scott, of Bourbon, was not so fortunate. He sustained an injured wrist in a two-car crash and required treatment at the Murphy Medical Center. So did Pealy Heckaman, of Bourbon. Don Schroeder, of Walkerton, was also taken to the hospital after his car rolled over and landed on its top. None of the drivers were seriously hurt.

OTHER WINNERS - The stock feature was won by Jack Clark, of Warsaw. Junior Dear, of Columbia City, won the concey race, and Bob Ziegler, South Bend, finished ahead of the field in the race between the six fastest qualifiers. Heat race winners were Bob Rail and Bill Fredericks, both of Kokomo, Tom Wyman and Bob Staley, both of Warsaw and Paul Bills, of Columbia City. A portion of the racing program was broadcast over WRSW from 9 to 9:30 p.m. by Mobil dealers of the area. There will be races Thursday and Saturday nights this week during the county fair.

Saturday, August 8, 1959
5,000 See Stock Car Races At County Fair

Nearly 5,000 persons witnessed the card of stock car racing at the Warsaw Speedway Saturday night as a highlight of the final night of the county fair. Local drivers were unable to cop a win as over 60 cars qualified for the races.

Among several spectacular smash-ups was one involving the auto of Tom Ward of Kokomo. His car hit a utility pole in front of the grandstand. A wheel flew off, bouncing into the McHatton ambulance and the Winona Lake fire truck standing by at track side. The fender on the ambulance and a spot light on the truck were damaged. One driver, Sleepy Walker, of Kokomo, was taken to the hospital after his car struck a stalled racer on the track and his head struck the steering wheel. He was examined at the hospital but was apparently not seriously injured.

Oscar Cook, of Hartford City, won the consolation race while Glen Kaser, of Gary, and Bob Ziegler, of South Bend, won the stock feature and feature races of the evening. Bob Fortune, of Kokomo, won the dash event of the six fastest cars. Heat winners were Jim Rebeck, of Gary; Tubby Beck, of Big Lake; Charlie Fortune, of Kokomo; Bob Bernhard, of South Whitley; and Bud Stillwell of Kokomo.

Saturday, August 15, 1959
Stock Car Races Attract 2,000

An estimated 2,000 fans saw an exciting night of stock car racing Saturday at the Warsaw Speedway.

Beezer Humphries of Kokomo won the modified feature event while the stock feature was won by Paul Bills of Columbia City. Humphries also won the modified consolation event. Bill Fredricks of Kokomo finished ahead of the field in the race between the six fastest qualifiers.

Heat winners were Jack Hickman of Syracuse, Kenneth McKissick of Fort Wayne, Bill Fortune of Kokomo and Jim Lozier of Warsaw. Several cars rolled over during the night but no one was injured seriously. Sixty-eight cars, many of them brand new, qualified for the races.

Saturday, August 22, 1959
2,000 Brave Rain to See Stock Car Races

An estimated 2,000 fans sat through a flash shower to witness the stock car races Saturday night at the Warsaw Speedway.

Pealy Heckaman, Bourbon

Charlie Fortune of Kokomo finished ahead of the field to win the feature race. Pealy Heckaman of Bourbon captured the stock feature. Fortune also won the consolation event.

After the rain stopped, the crowd stayed through the process of drying the track, making the racing program about an hour late.

Heat winners were Bud Weigold of Columbia City, Bob Bernhard of South Whitley, Oscar Cook of Hartford City,

Bill Fortune of Kokomo, and Jim Elliott of Warsaw. Archie Holle of Warsaw won the race between the six fastest qualifiers.

Saturday, August 22, 1959
Fortune-Schroeder Star at Warsaw, Ind.
By "The Bryants" (Track photographer)

With two cars left to qualify in a field of 59 cars, a sudden downpour soaked most of the crowd. (Some of the people parked in cars on the backstretch got only a light sprinkle). A thousand race fans just sat there in the downpour while their less hardy neighbors ran to get the inside of their cars all wet. I heard Jim Hullinger trying to get his wife out of the car so she wouldn't get the upholstering all wet.

All these crazy people just sat there and wouldn't go home, so what cha gonna do? Race? Right! All available equipment on wheels was called out to dry the track but that was too slow by itself so one hour and forty-five minutes after the heavy dew slackened off, and after 15 bags of cement had been added to the well-stirred surface, the races were finally started at 10:15.

Charlie Fortune was just trying out a new car so didn't do so good and ended up in the consy. From there on it was a different story. He got it handling so good he just won the consy and came right back to do it again in the feature.

Saturday, September 5, 1959
Set Records At Local Speedway

It was a record breaking weekend at the Warsaw Speedway Saturday night and Labor Day (Monday) as records for qualifiers and speeds for one lap were broken.

In Saturday's action a record 76 cars qualified for the evening of racing events at the track. Monday night the standing record of 17 seconds for one lap was smashed by Bob Staley, of Warsaw, with a time of 16.92 seconds. Moments later Ray Kenens ran a qualifying lap in 16.90 to break the Staley mark.

Warsaw's Eldon Burgess escaped injury in a Saturday night race when his car rolled over in front of the grandstand and came to rest upside down with Burgess hanging from his safety belt. Two other autos in the race smashed into the Burgess car and completely demolished the racer.

2 Injured. In the nights of racing only two men suffered injuries. Glen Owens, of Warsaw, hit the wall Monday night and suffered a lacerated nose while Bob Crago, of Huntington, rolled his auto over the fence on the same night and sustained bruises to the shoulder and leg.

Saturday heat winners were Jim Elliott, Warsaw; Donald Gagnon, Beaver Dam; Beezer Humphries, Kokomo; Charles Mann, Claypool; and Hobe Noel, Logansport. Charlie Fortune, Kokomo, won the dash event. Winner of the consolation race was Cap Arnold, of South Bend, while John Davis of Warsaw won the stock feature and Ray Kenens, of Delphi, won the feature race.

Monday Results. Monday heat winners were Earl Cocklin, of Huntington; Luther Holloway, Columbia City; Beezer Humphries, Kokomo; DeWayne Fox, Columbia City, and Dick Lynch of Claypool. Ray Kenens, of Delphi, won the dash event for the six fastest qualifiers. Oscar Cook, of Hartford City, won the consolation event while Ben Simmers, of Columbia City, won the stock feature and Bob Staley, of Warsaw, won the feature.

The races are broadcast from 9 to 9:30 p.m. over WRSW AM-FM, sponsored by three Mobil dealers and Silveus and Bradway, distributors of Kosciusko County.

Saturday, September 5, 1959
Warsaw Feature To Ray Kenens
By "The Bryants" (Track photographer)

After last week's complete rain-out a huge crowd turned out to watch a record field of 76 cars. Some of the heat races had more cars than some tracks can round up to put on an entire show.

Junior Dear had a hard time of it in the Consie. All tangled up in three separate melees and still came through with a second place. Ray Kenens had a good night with a new car, 3rd fastest time – 4th in his heat, 3rd in the dash—then started 18th in a field of 20 in the Feature and came all the way thru to win.

The Summaries:
Fast Time-Jim Hullinger, 17.47.
1st Heat—Jim Elliott, Hal Douglas and K. L. Bowser.
2nd Heat—Ron Gagnon, Dean Hamilton and
Wayne Stahly.
3rd Heat—Beezer Humphries, Archie Holle and Bob Staley.
4th Heat—Chuck Mann, Pealey Heckaman, and Ben Simmers.
5th Heat—Hobe Noel, Bud Stillwell and Bill Fredrick.
Dash—Charlie Fortune, Bob Ziegler and Ray Kenens.
Consi—Cap Arnold, Jr. Dear and Dick Lynch.
Stock Feature—John Davis, Chuck Mann and Ben Simmers.
Modified Feature—Ray Kenens, Bob Ziegler and Cap Arnold.

Saturday, September 12, 1959
Out Of County Drivers Star at Speedway

A total of 64 cars qualified for stock car racing at the Warsaw Speedway Saturday night and county drivers were able to win only two of nine events.

Out of county drivers figured in the win column of two of the three main events. Jack Hickman, of Syracuse, won the consolation race while Ben Simmers of Columbia City and Bob Ziegler, of South Bend, won the stock feature and the feature respectively.

During the evening the crowd was asked to vote, by ballot, for the driver they believed best qualified for the sportsmanship award. The ballots were placed in the ticket box and the results will be announced next Saturday in the championship card of racing at the track.

Paul Grim, Columbia City

One Driver Injured. Earl Cocklin, of Huntington, was the only driver to suffer injuries during the evening. He was treated at the Murphy Medical Center for a lacerated arm suffered when his car and another racer smashed together.

Heat winners were Glen Owens of Warsaw; Charlie Neal, of Wabash; Leslie Bills and Paul Hazen of Columbia City; and Hobe Noel, of Logansport. Ray Kenens, of Delphi, won the dash event for the six fastest qualifiers. The races were broadcast over WRSW AM-FM from 9 to 9:30 p.m. sponsored by Walter's Drug Store.

Paul Hazen, Columbia City

Saturday, September 19, 1959 – No Results Published

John Crum, Roy Norman, Jerry Clase, John Davis, Sam Davis

Saturday, October 3, 1959
End Stock Car Racing Season

The 1959 stock car racing season at the Warsaw Speedway ended Saturday night before approximately 1,000 spectators who braved threatening weather. Ray Kenens of Kokomo won the feature event. Harold Egner of Columbia City won the stock feature. The concey race was won by Bill Fredericks of Kokomo. Bud Stillwell finished first in the race between the six fastest qualifiers. Bud is also from Kokomo.

Heat winners were Hal Douglas of Logansport, Don Holloway of Columbia City, Archie Holle and Eldon Burgess, both of Warsaw. Jim Lozier of Warsaw rolled his car end over end in a spectacular accident. He was taken to Murphy Medical Center by McHatton ambulance, which was involved in a collision with an automobile while en route. Lozier was not seriously injured. It was announced that there will be new bleachers added and the track revamped for the races next season.

Archie Holle & Bob Staley

HOOSIER HAPPENINGS
By The Bryants (Track photographer)
Columbia City, Ind., Oct. 24, 1959

For once, we Bryants were on time. The annual Hoosier Hot Rod Banquet was held at Columbia City in the American Legion Home at 6:30 CST, but we got there on DAYLIGHT SAVING TIME. (That gave us more time in the dugout).

A wonderful steak dinner was served to around 150 couples, followed by a few nice (short) speeches and presentation of the point trophies for both Modified and Stock. We'll have a rundown of the point standings in the near future, but top point honors in the Stock Division went to Max Lambert and Bob Staley walked off with the top point trophy in the Modified Division.

Bob Staley, Glen Longnecker, Ted Ferguson, John Williams, Kenny Hawkins

The Stewart Bros. Orchestra furnished the music for both regular and square dancing after the tables were put away. At that point I would like to mention that as a whole, these drivers are better on the track than they are on the dance floor, otherwise I'd be forced to give up Speedway photography as unsafe. I don't know what time it was when

Hoot Gibson & Paul Bills

they got the place cleared out. We finally left about 1:30, and 120 miles and several coffee breaks later, we finally got to bed at 6 a.m.(DST) that is. The next regular meeting for Hoosier Hot Rod members will be in Columbia City, Saturday night, Nov. 7.

1960
"Wings" & Things

The 1960's brought in even more speed as the modified class continued to improve which added a new concept to dirt track racing......broadsliding. As the 60's continued, so did the transformation of the modified class. For the first time wings were added to the tops of the cars giving them more downforce and control that allowed for even faster speeds and track times. They soon became known as "Super Modifieds" sharing the Saturday racing program with late model stock cars and hobby stocks. All three racing classes provided their own type of entertainment and all three were highly popular. In the late 60's another new high-tec breed of "modified" car had made its way up to Warsaw and by 1969 many of the modifieds had transformed into full-blown sprint cars. Sporting both top wings and front wings, torsion bars, specially-staggered tires, and a more aerodynamic body, these cars ran up to 75mph on the straight-aways and nearly always had 1 to 2 inside tires off the track in the corners.

Saturday, May 14, 1960
2,000 See First Stock Car Races

Over 2,000 fans witnessed a Saturday evening of spills and thrills at the Warsaw

Speedway as over 60 cars qualified for the evening's card of racing, with one from Michigan. It was the opening night of the stock car racing season here.

Ben Ulshafer, of South Whitley, won the stock feature which saw Floyd Cook, of Hartford City, and Jerry Wyman, of Warsaw, roll their cars over and over. No one was injured in either mishap, however.

The modified feature was won by Don Walker, of Kokomo, with Bud Stillwell, also of Kokomo, taking the concey. Warsaw's Bob Staley turned in the fastest time of the six heat winners. The heat winners were Joe Wallace, of Fort Wayne; Larry Bills, of Columbia City; Bill Fortune, of Kokomo; Tom Word, of Kokomo; Dick Lynch, of Claypool; and Staley.

One half-hour of the race was broadcast direct from the speedway over Radio Station WRSW AM and FM, presented by Holland Mobile Homes, of Warsaw.

Saturday, May 28 & Monday, May 30, 1960
Big Crowd At Memorial Day Races In Warsaw

Some 2,000 spectators witnessed one of the fastest feature events in the history of the Warsaw Speedway Monday night as the Memorial Day racing card was complete with spills and thrills from start to finish.

Lanny Scott, 21, of Goshen, was taken unconscious to the Murphy Medical Center with a bump on the head. He was later released to the Goshen hospital where he is reported in satisfactory condition today.

Bob Tucker

Tom Wyman, of Warsaw, also rolled over, but he was uninjured.

Saturday night, despite a last minute rain that made the track muddy and caused the races to start late, 1,700 persons were at the speedway. A total of 66 cars qualified for the events. One half-hour of each race was broadcast over Radio Stations WRSW AM and FM, and sponsored by Holland Mobile Homes.

Saturday Winners. On Saturday night Mike Johnson, of Martinsville, was the winner of the modified feature, while Bob Tucker, of Mentone, copped the stock feature. The consolation race was won by Bill Fortune, of Kokomo, and the dash event was won by Johnson. Heat winners were Bob Albright, of Noblesville; Tom Word, of Kokomo; Hank Easley, of Logansport; DeWayne Fox, of Columbia City; and Ray Kenens, of Lafayette.

Monday Winners. Jim Kerby, of Frankfort, was the Memorial Day victor in the 50-lap modified feature, while Jack Clark, of Syracuse, won the stock feature. Dick Lynch, of Claypool, won the "concey", and Jim Hullinger, of Bunker Hill, had the fastest heat lap. Heat winners were Kipp Bowser, of Warsaw; Leslie Bills, of Columbia City; Cap Arnold, of South Bend; Jack Clark, of Syracuse; and Art Smith, of Warsaw.

Saturday, June 4, 1960
2,500 See Stock Car Races Here

An estimated 2,500 excited rain-threatened fans jammed the Warsaw Speedway Saturday night to see Larry Bills, of Columbia City, cop the stock feature, Dick Lynch, of Claypool, win the modified feature, and Jack Hickman, of Syracuse, come home first in the consolation race.

Warsaw's Bob Staley won the race of the six fastest qualifiers, and heat winners were Bob Albright, of Noblesville; Harold Egner, of Columbia City; Art Smith, of Warsaw; Ben Simmers, of Columbia City; and Don Walker, of Kokomo. Holland Mobile Homes sponsored a one-half hour broadcast of the card over Radio Station WRSW AM and FM.

A car driven by Floyd Cook, of Hartford City, vaulted over the fence to land on its wheels near the spectator cars, and Ben Simmers, of Columbia City, rolled his racer over and over. Neither man was injured.

Saturday, June 18, 1960
2,400 See Stock Car Races Here

An estimated 2,400 fans jammed the Warsaw Speedway Saturday night as 71 Hoosier drivers thrilled the crowd with a terrific card of stock car racing. Ernie Kiefer, of Three Rivers, Mich., copped the feature in one of the hottest duels seen all season, as he outlasted his opponent, Hank Easley, by takin the lead with only six laps to go.

Bill Baxter, of Columbia City, won the stock feature, and Kokomo's Gene Rayne was first in the "concey". Milo Clase was at the WRSW AM and FM mike for one-half hour of racing sponsored by Holland Mobile Homes.

Easley won the event for the six fastest qualifiers, and heat winners were Gerald Bills, of Columbia City; Bill Hare, of Columbia City; Kiefer; Bill Kirk, of Wabash; and Howard Bice, of Anderson.

Saturday, June 25, 1960
Art Smith Wins Feature Race

A large crowd watched an exciting Saturday night of stock car racing at the Warsaw Speedway as Art Smith, of Warsaw, won the feature event for modified stocks by taking the lead in the last lap of the race.

A total of 72 cars qualified for the evening of racing that was sprinkled with accidents and spills. A six-car accident occurred at the start of the feature event, but luckily no one was injured. Twice during the evening, Cap Arnold, of South Bend, had a car driven by Leslie Bills, drive over his wheel and as a result, the wheel came into Arnold's cockpit. Once the tire had to be deflated so it could be removed from the cockpit.

Taken To Hospital. In the stock feature, Paul Grim, of Columbia City, was taken to the Murphy Medical Center following a collision with Carl Sarner, of Wabash. Officials of the hospital reported this morning that Grim is being held for observation, and the he had a quiet night.

Other winners in addition to Smith were Cap Arnold in the "concey", and Harold Egner, of Columbia City, in the stock feature. Winner of the race for the six fastest qualifying cars was Bud Stillwell, of Kokomo. Heat winners were Bill Miller, of Wabash, Bill Hare, of Columbia City, Art Smith, of Warsaw, Paul Hazen, of Columbia City, and Don Walker, of Kokomo.

Saturday, July 2 & Monday, July 4, 1960
Big Crowd Sees Races, Fireworks

In probably what was one of the largest crowds ever to jam the Warsaw Speedway, many spectators Monday night witnessed an exciting fireworks display and a thrilling racing card complete with many accidents. There were boats on Winona Lake, and cars parked in every available spot to see the fireworks.

Paul Bills, of Columbia City, was first in the stock feature, Hank Easley, of Logansport, copped the modified feature, and Warsaw's Jim Elliott won the "concey".

Hal Douglas, Logansport

Heat winners were Dean Spicher, of Nappanee; Harold Egner, of Columbia City; Cap Arnold, of South Bend; Pealey Heckaman, of Bourbon; and Hal Douglas, of Logansport. Ernie Kiefer, of Three Rivers, Mich., won the race for the six fastest qualifiers.

Saturday Results. On Saturday night, Paul Hazen, of Columbia City, won the stock feature, with Don Walker, of Kokomo, taking the modified feature, and Hobe Noel, of Logansport, winning the consolation race.

Beezer Humphries, of Kokomo, was tops for the six fastest qualifiers, and heat races were won by Charlie Fortune, of Kokomo; Pealey Heckaman, of Bourbon; Oscar Cook, of Hartford City; Bill Hare, of Columbia City; and Hank Easley, of Logansport.

Pealy Heckaman, Bourbon

Charlie Neal, of Wabash, rolled over in front of the grandstand, but fortunately was not injured. Both racing cards were aired from 8:30 to 9 p.m. by Milo Clase over Radio Station WRSW AM and FM, sponsored by Holland Mobile Homes.

Saturday, July 9, 1960
Ziegler Wins 50-lap Feature At Speedway

An excited crowd at the Warsaw Speedway Saturday night saw a race in the feature event that had to be restarted after 37 laps due to a three-car wreck.

The 50-lap championship race was won by Bob Ziegler, of South Bend. He won several extra prizes and a large trophy, as this was the big mid-season 50-lap championship feature at the speedway.

Jack Hickman, of Syracuse, was the winner in the modified "concey" race, and Pealey Heckaman, of Bourbon, copped the stock feature. Hobe Noel, of Logansport, won the dash event, and heat winners were Coral Hostettler, of Goshen; "Tubby" Beck, of Fort Wayne; Hank Easley, of Logansport; Harold Egner, of Columbia City; and Tom Wyman, of Warsaw. Next Saturday a championship race for strictly stock cars will be held.

Saturday, July 16, 1960
Bill Baxter Cops Mid-Season Racing Title

A large crowd at the Warsaw Speedway watched 60 qualifying cars in an exciting evening of racing Saturday as Bill Baxter, of Columbia City, won the mid-season championship for the strictly stock cars.

The fast track resulted in numerous accidents. Bill Tincher, of Kokomo, was in a two-car accident and was taken to the Murphy Medical Center when he collapsed in the pit area after he thought he had recovered after the wreck.

Hank Easley and Art Smith, of Warsaw, were both involved in two-car smashups, but neither was injured. Milo Clase broadcast one-half hour of the races over WRSW AM and FM, sponsored by Holland Mobile Homes.

The modified heat winner was Hal Douglas, of Logansport, Joe Hamsher, of New Paris, won the "concey", and Archie Holle, of Warsaw, copped the dash event. Heat winners were Jim Hullinger, Bunker Hill; Jim Frushour, Wabash; Bud Stillwell, Kokomo; Luther Holloway, Warsaw; and Hal Douglas, Logansport.

Saturday, July 23, 1960
Plenty of Action During Saturday Night Race Card

A total of 60 cars qualified for the Saturday night stock car race card which saw an abundance of excited spectators at the Warsaw Speedway.

Oscar Cook, of Hartford City, was in a two-car crackup. His car leaped the retaining wall, lit on its wheels and kept on going, but off the track. Bud Stillwell also went over the retaining wall when a spindle bolt broke and he couldn't steer the car. The car rolled over on its side and back upright. He had leaped the Hal Douglas car in the process.

Max Lambert, of North Manchester, won the stock feature, Claypool's Dick Lynch was winner of the "concey", and Art Smith, of Warsaw, won the modified feature. Heat winners were Joe Hamsher of New Paris; Doug Method of Warsaw; Hank Easley of Logansport; and Archie Holle of Warsaw. Bob Zeigler of South Bend won the dash event.

Saturday, July 30, 1960
Wild Night Of Racing Saturday At Fairgrounds

Paul Hazen was the stock feature winner at the Warsaw Speedway Saturday night in what public address announcer Milo Clase described as the wildest driving he has seen in a long time.

In the race, which was aired over Radio Station WRSW AM and FM from 8:45 to 9:15 and sponsored by Holland Mobile Homes, Bud Stillwell of Logansport won the modified feature, and Bill Fortune of Kokomo won the "concey".

In the first race, Chuck Pollock, of Fort Wayne, driving at the track for the first time, rolled over and over. Then in the second heat, Wayne Stokley rolled over about three times. Joe Hamsher, of New Paris, tangled with another car when his steering mechanism broke and he tore up about a rod of fence in front of the grandstand. Like his predecessors, Joe was not injured. Then in the third heat race, Bud Grossnickle, of North Manchester, was taken to the Murphy Medical Center after being involved in a three-car wreck. He was later released after being examined.

A total of 61 cars qualified and the heat winners were Coral Hostetler, of Goshen; Paul Bills, of Columbia City; Bud Stillwell, of Logansport; Paul Hazen, of Columbia City; Bob Staley, of Warsaw; and Hobe Noel of Logansport.

Thursday, August 4, 1960
Stock Car Races Draw Big Crowd At County Fair

A total of 60 qualifying cars furnished plenty of excitement to a big county fair crowd at the Warsaw Speedway last night in a program of stock car racing complete with wrecks.

Art Smith, of Warsaw, leaped the guard rail in the feature event, but was uninjured as Paul Joyce, of Kokomo, came home first in that race. Charlie Fortune spun out on the west curve and went through the guard rail backwards, and in the third race seven cars piled up, but no one was injured.

Hal Douglas, of Logansport, won the "concey" and Hank Easley was the winner of the modified feature in the evening of racing that was broadcast over WRSW AM and FM with Holland Mobile Homes as the sponsor.

Art Smith, of Warsaw, won the dash event, and heat winners were Bill Miller, Beezer Humphries, and Paul Joyce, of Kokomo, Hank Easley, of Logansport, and Paul Bills, of Columbia City.

Saturday, August 6, 1960
Racing Thrills Fair Crowds

The Saturday night of racing, which was the final attraction at the Kosciusko County Fair, held its share of thrills for the spectators which numbered between 5,500 and 6,000.

Hank Easley, of Logansport, locked wheels with Beezer Humphries, of Kokomo, and as a result, Easley rolled end over end three times before coming to rest on his wheels. The top was torn from the car and the frame was broken in half, and it was an anxious crowd that received word from the Murphy Medical Center that Hank had suffered only cuts and bruises.

Come to the FAIR
Saturday's Grandstand Attraction
STOCK CAR RACES
Time Trials Start at 7:30 p.m.
Coronation Of Fair Queen
FOLLOWING RACES
Kosciusko County FAIRGROUNDS
Indiana's Most Beautiful Fairgrounds On Winona Lake, East Warsaw

Harold Egner, of Columbia City, also had a twirl with fate when his car flipped over a mound of dirt at a light pole and came down on the top flipping high in the air. Egner was also taken to the hospital when he later became ill as a result of the bruises.

Larry Plummer, Larwill

Holland Homes. Holland Mobile Homes sponsored one-half hour of the program over Radio Stations WRSW AM and FM with Milo Clase at the mike.

Bill Tincher, of Kokomo, was the stock feature winner, Howard Bice, of Auburn, captured the "concey", and Jim Kerby, of Frankfort, won the modified feature.

Bud Stillwell, of Logansport, won the dash event, and heat winners were Walt Yoder, of Syracuse; Larry Plummer, of Larwill; Art Smith, of Warsaw; Paul Joyce, of Kokomo, and Oscar Cook, of Logansport.

Memorial Day Mon. May 30, 1960
Warsaw Speedway — Wayne Bryant Omega Photo

Jimmy Hullinger & Ray Kennens

Labor Day, Sept. 5, 1960
Warsaw Speedway — Wayne Bryant Omega-Photo

Larry Plummer, Larwill

Ray Kennens Modified Feature Sat. Sept. 5, 59
Warsaw Speedway — Wayne Bryant Omega Photo

Ray Kennens, Lafayette

Saturday, Sept. 24, 1960
Warsaw Speedway — Wayne Bryant Omega Photo

Paul Hazen, Columbia City

Larry Plummer & John Davis

Jimmy Hullinger, Bunker Hill

Saturday, August 13, 1960
8-Car Crackup Delays Races; No One Injured

In the second heat race at the Warsaw Speedway Saturday night an eight-car crackup created a short delay while the cars were pulled apart by wreckers.

The only other mishap of the night was when Earl Egolf, of North Manchester, had car trouble and his racer was struck from behind by a car that was warming up as the Egolf auto was parked on the track. No one was injured in either accident.

Bill Tincher, of Kokomo, was the winner of the feature event which was threatened by rain on occasions. Beezer Humphries, of Kokomo, was the winner of the "concey", and Oscar Cook, of Hartford City, copped the modified feature.

Hal Douglas, of Logansport, won the dash event. Heat winners were Joe Hamsher, New Paris; Tom Ward, Kokomo; Hobe Noel, Logansport; Lanny Scott, Goshen; and Jim Hullinger, Bunker Hill.

Saturday, August 20, 1960
Race Driver Critically Hurt In Crash At Warsaw Speedway
By Don Derry, Times-Union Sports Editor

Monday, August 22 (Warsaw, In) – Oscar Cook, 39, of Hartford City, lies unconscious and in critical condition at the Murphy Medical Center today as the result of injuries suffered in a collision at the Warsaw Speedway in the Saturday night stock car racing program.

Hospital officials said that he is suffering from head injuries, a severely jammed shoulder, chest injuries, fractured ribs, and possible internal injuries.

Witnesses at the speedway said that coming down the front stretch, Kenny Bowser, of Warsaw, seemed to be having car trouble and suddenly slowed down. In trying to avoid a collision, Cook swerved to miss Bowser and lost control.

His car flipped over sideways, then end over end several times, throwing him from the car when his safety belt broke. He landed on the track and rolled against the retaining wall. The car, which had landed on its wheels, narrowly missed rolling over him, but stopped just as it touched him with the rear wheel.

Hurt 2 Years Ago. Cook was seriously injured in a stock car crash at the Warsaw Speedway two years ago, which resulted in the removal of his spleen at that time.

Bill Tincher, of Kokomo, was the winner of the stock feature, and Bob Zeigler, of South Bend, won the 100-lap modified feature. Bill Fortune, of Kokomo, copped the consolation race. Two of the heat winners were Larry Plummer, of Larwill, and Tom Word, of Kokomo.

Saturday, August 27, 1960
Large Crowd At Stock Car Races

Many close stock car races and scraped fenders thrilled a large crowd at the Warsaw Speedway Saturday night, but the only injury resulted when Duke Long, of Columbia City, suffered burns in the pit area. Attendants at the Murphy Medical Center said Long was later released after being treated for first degree burns on the right forearm and hip. The mishap occurred when the radiator hose came loose on Long's car and sprayed him with hot water.

A total of 60 cars qualified for the events and the track was extremely fast. Next Saturday a 50-lap feature event will be the highlight of the evening and will be strictly stock cars. On Labor Day night a gigantic display of fireworks will be featured.

Bill Tincher, of Kokomo, was the winner of the stock feature. Hal Douglas, of Logansport, won the modified feature, and Dick Lynch, of Claypool, copped the "concey". Heat winners were Fred Boggs, of Warsaw; Larry Plummer, of Larwill; Archie Holle, of Warsaw; DeWayne Fox, of Columbia City; and Jim Elliott, of Warsaw. Jim Hullinger, of Bunker Hill was the winner of the dash event.

The races were broadcast over Radio Stations WRSW AM and FM from 8:45 to 9:15 p.m., sponsored by Holland Mobile Homes.

Freddie Boggs, Warsaw

Saturday, September 3 & Monday, September 5, 1960
Large Crowds At Stock Car Races

Large crowds at the Warsaw Speedway Saturday and Monday nights were pleased with the two nights of racing and the fireworks display on Labor Day. No one was injured although many wrecks occurred both nights.

One-half hour of the races was broadcast over Radio Station WRSW AM and FM by Milo Clase and sponsored by Holland Mobile Homes.

On Saturday night John Davis, of Warsaw, won the 50-lap stock feature as few cars finished. Davis won a 39 inch trophy. Hank Easley was the winner of the modified feature, and Bill Fortune copped the modified consolation event.

John Davis, Warsaw with C.E. "Hoot" Gibson

Heat Winners. Heat winners were Don Walker, of Kokomo; Bob Kirk, of Warsaw; Art Smith, of Warsaw; and Easley. Bob Zeigler, of South Bend, won the dash event for modified cars.

On Monday, Jim Hullinger, of Bunker Hill, won the modified feature. Larry Plummer won the stock feature, and Jim Kirby, of Frankfort, won the "concey". Heat winners on Monday were Dick Lynch, of Claypool; Bill Hare , of Columbia City; Hal Douglas, of Logansport; R. Heckaman, of Bourbon; and Earl Egolf, of North Manchester. Archie Holle, of Warsaw, won the dash event.

Saturday, September 10, 1960
Large Crowd At Stock Car Races

A large crowd watched a big night of stock car racing on a fast track at the Warsaw Speedway Saturday in which 55 cars qualified and ten of them were piled up in a big crash in the third heat, although no one was injured. Bob Zeigler, of South Bend, won the modified feature, his cohort Cap Arnold finished second, and Art Smith, of Warsaw, was third.

Qualifying times were as low as 17.20. The track record is 16.90. An added feature was a powder-puff derby in which 15 ladies raced cars around the track to the delight of the fans. One-half hour of the racing card was aired over Radio Stations WRSW AM and FM and sponsored by Holland Mobile Homes.

Jack Clark, of Syracuse, won the stock feature and Jim Elliott, of Warsaw, captured the consolation event. Heat winners were Bill Miller, of Kokomo; John Godshalk, of Bristol; Bud Stillwell, of Logansport; Jack Clark, of Syracuse; and Ray Kenens, of Lafayette. Hank Easley, of Logansport, won the dash event.

Saturday, September 17, 1960
Zeigler Breaks Track Record At Speedway

A rather small, rain-threatened crowd was thrilled by a lightning fast track at the Warsaw Speedway Saturday night when they watched the track record broken and race starter Clark Graff narrowly escape injury.

A car driven by Jim Backus, of Columbia City, struck the wall at the starter's ramp, causing Graff to leap from the ramp and run up the main grandstand steps to avoid the impact. The ramp and wall were torn up where Clark had been standing.

The track record of 16.90 was broken by Bob Zeigler, of South Bend, with a time of 16.88. The record was formerly held by Ray Kenens who achieved his mark in September of last year. A light shower almost stopped the night of racing, but quit just before the clay track could be spoiled.

A total of 20 cars competed in the strictly stock event which was the championship event for this class of cars and the 25 lap race was won by Jack Clark, of Syracuse.

Other Winners: Hal Douglas, of Logansport, won the modified feature, and Bob Grindle of Warsaw, won the "concey". Heat winners were Jim Elliott, of Warsaw; Hal Douglas, of

Logansport; Paul Bills, of Columbia City; Ray Kenens, of Lafayette; and John Davis, of Warsaw. Hank Easley, of Logansport, won the dash event.

The final standings in points for modified cars were announced for the year. Jim Kirby, of Frankfort, was first with 131 points. Hank Easley, of Logansport, second with 128 points, and Archie Holle, of Warsaw, third, with 117 points.

Speedway officials announced that racing will be held next Saturday. One-half hour of the race was aired over Radio Stations WRSW AM and FM with Milo Clase at the mike and was sponsored by Holland Mobile Homes.

Ray Kennens, Lafayette

Saturday, September 24, 1960
End Season of Stock Car Races

An excited crowd at the Warsaw Speedway Saturday night watched Jimmy Hullinger, of Bunker Hill, nose out Bob Zeigler, of South Bend, in the modified feature race to end one of the most successful seasons of racing at the local track.

Paul Bills, of Columbia City, came home first in the stock feature, and Don Walker, of Kokomo, won the consolation race. Hank Easley, of Logansport, was first in the dash event, and heat winners were Joe Hamsher, of New Paris; Paul Bills, of Columbia City; Art Smith, of Warsaw; Harold Egner, of Columbia City; and Jim Elliott, of Warsaw.

One-half hour of the final program was broadcast over Radio Stations WRSW AM and FM with Holland Mobile Homes as the sponsor.

1961

March 4, 1961
Prepare for Stock Car Racing Season

C. E. "Hoot" Gibson, of Columbia City, president of the Hoosier Hot Rod Association, announced today that stock car races at the Warsaw track will get underway either the last Saturday in April or the first Saturday in May, depending on the weather.

Gibson reports this should be the finest racing season ever as many new drivers plan to race at Warsaw this year and some of their cars are extremely fast. The track at the county fairgrounds will also be faster, Gibson said, after completely re-claying the oval last fall. He added that several more bleacher seats have been constructed for the coming season.

In recalling the popularity of the races last year, "Hoot" said that on one night 80 cars were qualified to race, and that drivers were attracted from places such as Tennessee, Michigan, and the entire state of Indiana. WRSW AM and FM veteran sportscaster Milo Clase will again air one-half hour of the races to area racing enthusiasts.

Saturday, April 29, 1961
Local Driver Wins Feature As Auto Races Begin

Bob Grindle, of Warsaw, won the first feature race of the 1961 stock car racing season at the Warsaw Speedway Saturday night as approximately 1,200 paid spectators enjoyed opening night festivities.

About 45 cars were on hand for the races, and public address announcer Milo Clase said many cars not completed at this time will be on hand for racing next Saturday. Clase broadcast one-half hour of the program over Radio Stations WRSW AM and FM which was sponsored by Holland Mobile Homes.

Tom Ward, of Kokomo, won the stock feature. Grindle also captured the "concey", and Ray Kenens, of Lafayette, won the race of the six fastest qualifiers. Heat winners were Hal Douglas, of Logansport; Bill Hare, of Columbia City; John Davis, of Warsaw; Cap Arnold, of South Bend; and Kenens.

Saturday, May 6, 1961
Columbia City Racer Wins Feature Here

About 1,200 persons braved a rain-threatening night at the Warsaw Speedway Saturday for stock car races and although many accidents dotted the evening, only one man—Paul Scott of Goshen, was taken to the Murphy Medical Center—and he was released without suffering any serious injuries.

Only two Warsaw men won events during the night, with DeWayne Fox of Columbia City winning the feature, Don Walker of Kokomo copping the modified feature, and Bill Fortune of Kokomo winning the "concey".

Warsaw's Art Smith won the race for the six fastest qualifiers, and Bob Grindle captured the third heat race of the evening. Other heat winners were Jack Riley, Huntington; Ron Napkins, Westville; Paul Hazen, Columbia City, and Cap Arnold, South Bend.

Saturday, May 13, 1961
Many Spills But No Injuries At Local Speedway

More than 2,000 fans and 64 cars combined to make Saturday night one of the biggest nights of the racing of the young season at the Warsaw Speedway as the track was dotted with spills, but no one was injured.

Si Marner of Kokomo and Warsaw's Archie Holle were shaken up when involved in a two-car accident that saw Marner flip high in the air and light on his top in front of the grandstand near the starter's ramp. Persons exclaimed it was one of the most vicious spills they had seen. Milo Clase aired one-half hour of the race over WRSW AM and FM, sponsored by Holland Mobile Homes.

Jim Freshour, of Wabash, was the winner of the stock feature with Joe Hamsher, of New Paris, taking the modified feature, and Kokomo's Don Walker copping the "concey". Bud Stillwell, Kokomo, Bill Hare, Columbia City, Hal Douglas, Logansport, Ron Fisher, Lapaz, and Jack Riley, Huntington, were heat winners, with Bill Fortune, of Kokomo, taking the event for the six fastest qualifiers.

Saturday, May 20, 1961
Wheel Comes Off Racer, Injures 2 Spectators At Warsaw Speedway

Two spectators were injured in a freak mishap during a "wild" night at the Warsaw Speedway Saturday, but both were dismissed from the Murphy Medical Center following treatment and observation.

Fifteen-year old Frederick Warner, of Michigan City, was treated for bruises and abrasions after being struck in the back by a "flying" wheel, and Donna Lytell, of Niles, Mich., received an X-ray to her leg after being struck by the same wheel. The wheel came off a car driven by Hank Easley and careened into the spectators along the back stretch, also striking and damaging three parked cars.

Larry Plummer, Columbia City

2,000 Spectators. About 2,000 fans witnessed the night of racing, watching Bob Ziegler, of South Bend, turn the quarter-mile oval in 17.18, for the fastest qualifying time of the night. A new event was inserted in the card of racing, which was a six-lap dash event, won by Larry Plummer of Columbia City. Fred Sibley, of Goshen, was the winner of the stock feature, Bill Fortune, of Kokomo, the modified feature, and Cap Arnold, South Bend, the "concey".

Heat Winners. Heat winners were Fortune and Don Walker of Kokomo, Bill Hawley of Nappanee, Harold Egner of Columbia City, and Art Smith and Bob Grindle, both of

Warsaw. One-half hour of the race was broadcast by Milo Clase over Radio Stations WRSW AM and FM, through the courtesy of Miller's Mens and Boys Wear, and the Piggie Inn Drive-In restaurant.

Saturday, May 27, 1961
Install Fence To Protect Fans At Local Speedway

A new wheel fence was in evidence at the Warsaw Speedway Saturday as some 2,000 fans witnessed a fast night of racing with some 60 cars qualifying. With most fans of the opinion that autos are becoming faster and faster, a 12-foot high fence was installed around the track to protect fans from flying debris. Last week two spectators were struck by a flying wheel that became dislodged from one of the cars.

On Saturday, Jim Frushour, of Wabash, was treated and dismissed from the emergency room of the Murphy Medical Center following a mishap in one of a series of crack-ups. Ernie Kiefer, the fastest qualifier of the night turned the Oval in 16.87. The evening was complete when Warsaw High School pole vaulter, Dick Fancil, was driven around the track on a fire truck after the flying Tiger soared 12 ft. 9 in, to win state pole vault honors earlier Saturday in the state track meet in Indianapolis.

Heat winners of the night were Lanny Scott, Goshen; John Jacobs, Elkhart, in event number two and a race among the six fastest qualifiers; Bill Fortune, Kokomo; Ron Windfall, Mishawaka; Don Walker, Kokomo; and Cap Arnold, South Bend. Luther Holloway, of Warsaw, topped the stock feature race. Fortune won the modified feature, and Jack Reiley, of Huntington, won the "concey".

It was announced that the gates would be open on Memorial Day night at the track with the time trials beginning at 6 p.m. and the first race at 7:30 p.m.

Tuesday, May 30, 1961
2,700 See Track Record Broken At Local Speedway

An estimated 2,700 persons at the Warsaw Speedway saw three drivers miraculously walk away from wrecks almost unscratched, and the track record broken three times in Memorial Day races at the fairgrounds last night.

Hobe Noel, of Logansport, flashed off a tremendous 16.30 for the new track record, surpassing that of 16.88 set by Bob Zeigler of South Bend, last year.

One spectacular crash saw Jim Hullinger, of Bunker Hill, flip end over end and then roll over and over in the

Hobe Noel, Logansport

back stretch and walk away no more than shaken up after the ordeal.

2 Other Crashes. Ron Hopkins, of North Manchester, rolled his auto over in front of the grandstand, and Rick Jones, of Mishawaka, lost his brakes in the east curve after a crack-up, and went roaring into the pit area, finally coming to a stop after running up a hill. Both Hopkins and Jones were also uninjured.

Heat winners Tuesday were Bud Stillwell, of Kokomo; Bob Jones, of Westville; Jim Kurby, of Frankfort; Bill Hare, of Columbia City; and Jack Reiley, of Huntington. Ernie Kiefer, of Three Rivers, Michigan, won the race for the six fastest qualifiers, and Larry Plummer, of Larwill, captured the stock dash event.

John Davis, of Warsaw, was the winner of the 25-lap stock feature, and Bill Fortune, of Kokomo, copped the concey. One-half hour of the race was broadcast by Milo Clase over WRSW AM and FM, sponsored by Millers Men's and Boy's Wear, and the Piggie Inn Drive-In.

Saturday, June 3, 1961
Driver Hurt At Speedway Races Here

Earl Egolf, 27, of North Manchester, was listed in fair condition in the Murphy Medical Center this morning after sustaining a laceration over the left eye and shock in a wreck at the Warsaw Speedway Saturday.

Another wreck saw Walter Preston, Jr., of Kokomo, miraculously escape injury when his racer went out of control and flipped upside down on top of the guard rail, causing a gaping hole in the top of the auto with the rail just missing Preston's head. Preston was moving about 85 miles per hour at the time of the crash.

The ideal night for racing saw 2,800 fans fill the speedway with 64 cars qualifying, including a new entry from Bryan, Ohio.

WINNERS. Event winners Saturday were Jack Reiley, of Huntington; Max Lambert, of North Manchester; Cap Arnold, of South Bend; Lanny Scott, of Goshen; and Ray Kenens, of Lafayette. Art Smith, of Warsaw, was the winner of the six fastest modified race, and Bill Havens, of Goshen, won the race of the six fastest strictly stock cars.

Bill Sarver, of Kokomo, won the stock feature. Bob Grindle, of Warsaw, was the concey winner, and Ray Kenens, Lafayette, was the modified feature winner. Kenens was also the special 40-lap modified winner on Memorial Day which was not included in the report. One-half hour of the race was broadcast by Milo Clase on WRSW AM and FM with Holland Mobile Homes as the sponsor.

Saturday, June 10, 1961
Wet Track Fails To Halt Stock Car Races Here

A rain-threatened crowd enjoyed an interesting if not unusual night of racing at the Warsaw Speedway Saturday, brought on by a dampened track that caused some unusual matchings of contestants.

With the track a quagmire at 7:30 p.m., passenger cars, trucks, and just about anything on wheels moved around the oval in an attempt to dry off the track. Their work was successful and by 9 p.m. the races were being run as scheduled. Due to the mud and water, however, no time trials were held and positions were determined by drawing numbers from a hat with the result that in some races a slower car would be pitted in the same race ahead of a faster vehicle.

There were several crack-ups but no injuries resulted. A portion of the race was broadcast over Radio Stations WRSW AM and FM sponsored by Miller's Mens' and Boys' wear, and Piggie Inn.

John Davis, of Warsaw, was the winner of the stock feature, while Ernie Kiefer, of Three Rivers, Mich., won the modified feature and Bill Fortune, of Kokomo, won the consolation affair. Bill Baxter, of Columbia City, captured the six fastest strictly stock event, and Jack Reilley, of Huntington, won the six fastest modified race. Other event winners during the evening were Don Walker of Kokomo, Pinky Stewart of Kokomo, Bob Grindle and John Davis, of Warsaw, and Hal Douglas, of Logansport.

Saturday, June 17, 1961
8 Cars Crack Up In Feature Race

Tremendous speeds and many wrecks thrilled a large crowd at the Warsaw Speedway Saturday night as a total of 65 cars qualified for the night. The feature race saw eight cars crack-up on the front turn, but no one was injured although it took some time to untangle the autos.

The modified feature attraction went to Bill Fortune, of Kokomo, while Fred Sibley, of Elkhart, won the stock feature, and Don Walker of Kokomo won the consolation race. South Bend's Bob Zeigler was the fastest qualifier of the night.

Other Winners: Bob Jonas, of Westville, won the second event race and the six fastest strictly stock contest, with Ernie Kiefer, of Three Rivers, Mich., winning the race of the six-fastest modified cars. Other event winners were Joe Hamsher of New Paris, Ray Kenens of Lafayette, Bob Bauman of Argos, and Coral Hostetler of Goshen.

Sportscaster Milo Clase broadcast one-half hour of the races over Radio Stations WRSW AM and FM, sponsored by Holland Mobile Homes.

Saturday, June 24, 1961
Rain Cancels Stock Car Races

Everything was perfect but "Mother Nature" failed to cooperate at the Warsaw Speedway Saturday as the night of racing was postponed due to rain.

Track officials had scraped away one layer of mud and the race was ready to begin about 9 p.m. when the racing question was settled for good when rain came once again. All of the tickets for last Saturday's race will be honored next Saturday. Sixty-seven cars were on hand to qualify.

Saturday, July 1, 1961
Fireworks At Fairgrounds Here Tuesday Night

A double feature racing card and giant fireworks display will be in store for fans at the Warsaw Speedway Tuesday as racing officials promise an outstanding "Fourth" at the county fairgrounds. Gates will be open at 5 p.m., time trials will begin at 6 p.m., and the first race will get underway at 7:30.

On Saturday, 72 cars qualified for an exciting night even though rain came in the "concey" and caused the rest of the scheduled events to be cancelled.

In one of the heat races, Kenny Bowser, of Warsaw, and Zickafoose, of Huntington crashed in the back stretch with Zickafoose rolling completely over before landing on his wheels unhurt. Many other wrecks occurred but no one was injured. One driver was taken to the hospital when burned by hot steam from a bursted radiator hose but he was not seriously injured.

2 In Wheel Chairs. Bob Grindle and Bill Gross, Warsaw drivers who were injured in a one-car accident near Leesburg last month, watched the racing card in wheel chairs.

Heat winners for the night were Don Schroeder, of Goshen, Don Rathburn, Roann, Bud Zeigler, South Bend, Dace Wright, Goshen, and Beezer Humphries, Kokomo. Zeigler also won the race of the six-fastest modified cars, and Fisher the six-fastest of the stock cars. The concey, stock feature and modified feature were all cancelled.

Tuesday, July 4, 1961
Rainout

Saturday, July 8, 1961
Record Crowd For Spills, Thrills, Fireworks At Warsaw Speedway

A crowd estimated as one of the largest in Warsaw Speedway racing history, enjoyed thrills galore and an outstanding fireworks display which was co-sponsored by the Hoosier Hot Rod Racing Association, and the Fair Association Saturday night.

No one was seriously injured but wrecks were the byword. In one of the spectacular incidents, Jim Hullinger, of Bunker Hill, poured through a hole in the retaining wall at full speed and came to a halt just inches from a spectator's car in the back stretch, when Jim's accelerator apparently stuck.

Other mishaps saw Dick Sickafoose, of Columbia City, roll over, and Kokomo's Beezer Humphries take two spills, almost rolling over in one entanglement and then hitting the wall at the starter's ramp in the feature. The hole that Hullinger went through was created when three cars crashed into the fence in the turn.

Davis Wins Feature. In the strictly stock feature, winner John Davis, of Warsaw, was presented a wrist watch, and the modified winner, Bob Zeigler, of South Bend, won a big trophy.

Event winners were Bill Fortune, Kokomo; Slug More, Albion; Howard Rice, Auburn; Ron

Ron Fisher, Windfall

Fisher, Windfall; and Charlie Howell, Wabash. Ray Kenens, of Lafayette, won the race of the six fastest modified qualifiers, and Albion's Slug More copped the stock equivalent. Don Walker, of Kokomo, won the consolation race. In two make-up races from the July 4 card, which was rain-shortened, Archie Holle, of Warsaw, won the modified feature, and Al Corpe, of Elkhart, won the stock feature.

Saturday, July 15, 1961
Sargent Wins Feature Race At Local Track

Excitement was king at the Warsaw speedway Saturday as the capacity crowd went home talking to themselves of the many thrills and spills.

For a beginning, a wheel came off a car driven by Larry Bills, of Columbia City, sending it into the pit area and scattering crewmen galore. Another time, the complete rear end assembly of Cap Arnold's old car came "unglued" and both rear wheels went rolling down the track with the "two wheel car" trailing after.

Carlene Upson, of Warsaw, won the "powder-puff" derby as the ladies provided many laughs for the spectators.

FOUTZ HURT. The only injury occurred when Al Foutz, of Lynn, Ind., burned his foot severely as his muffler broke loose and he finished the strictly stock feature with the broken hot pipe resting on his foot.

Next Saturday will be the mid-season championship race for the strictly stock cars. The stock feature winner this Saturday was Floyd Sargent, of Elkhart, while Ray Kenens, of Lafayette, took the modified feature and Beezer Humphries, of Kokomo, copped the "concey".

Walt Shaver, of Kokomo, won the six fastest modified event with Warsaw's John Davis taking the stock equivalent. Event winners were, Ron Schroeder, Goshen; Ron Fisher, Windfall; Cap Arnold, South Bend; Al Foutz, Lynn, Ind., and Art Smith, of Warsaw.

Saturday, July 22, 1961
Rain Stops Part Of Race Program At Speedway

A large crowd was "washed out" at the local speedway Saturday just as the dash event was completed to set the stage for a double-feature next Saturday.

Robert Ruttenouer, of Mishawaka, finished the excitement as he rolled completely over landing on his wheels, sending the starter, Clark Graff, for cover off the starter's ramp to avoid the rolling auto.

John Davis, of Warsaw, won the stock dash event Saturday and Bob Zeigler, South Bend, the modified dash event. Heat winners were Don Schraeder, Goshen; Paul Grim, Columbia City; Bill Fortune, Kokomo; Jim Freshour, Wabash; Joe Hamsher, New Paris; and Ernie Kiefer, Three Rivers, Mich.

Saturday, July 29, 1961
Albion, Elkhart, Drivers Capture Feature Races

The speed was held down due to a wet track at the Warsaw Speedway Saturday but thrills were just as prevalent for the 70 cars that qualified for the night of racing.

Although many races had to be re-started because of accidents, no one was seriously injured. In make-up races from last Saturday's partial washout at the track, "Slug" Moor, of Albion, won the mid-season strictly stock championship feature, and "Cy" Marner, of Kokomo, won the modified "hang-over" feature.

On Saturday's regular program, Ray Wright, of Elkhart, won the stock feature, Art Smith, of Warsaw, won the modified feature, and Dean Speicher, of Warsaw, won honors in the consolation race. Bob Zeigler, of South Bend, won the modified event. Heat winners Saturday were Don Schroeder, Goshen; Owen Rensburger, Elkhart; Charlie Howell, Wabash; Jene Simon, Columbia City, and Cap Arnold, South Bend.

Wednesday, August 9, 1961
Auto Races Thrill Crowd At Fair

A medium-sized crowd was treated to an exciting night of racing Wednesday at the Warsaw Speedway which produced several unusual wrecks but no injuries. The races are among the featured attractions at the county fair.

In one race on separate occasions cars hurtled through the air but landed on their wheels and Hobe Noel, of Logansport, rolled over in the feature race, escaping injury. Bud Grossnickle, of North Manchester, hit the wall in front of the grandstand and rolled over and over and several cars went through the fence in the eventful night.

Again Saturday. It was announced that for Saturday's card the east gate of the fairgrounds would be open at 4 p.m. for spectators wishing to park around the back stretch, with the main gate opening at 6 p.m. One-half hour of Wednesday's card was broadcast by Milo Clase over Radio Station WRSW AM and FM, sponsored by Holland Mobile Homes.

Archie Holle, of Warsaw, was the winner of the modified feature Wednesday with Harold Sargent, of Elkhart, winning the stock feature and Dean Speicher, of Warsaw, taking the consolation race. Cy Marner, of Kokomo, and Jim Lozier, of Claypool, took the modified and stock dash events respectively. Event winners were Jack Reiley, Huntington; Bill Baxter, Columbia City; Charlie Fortune, Kokomo; and Harold Egner, Columbia City.

Saturday, August 12, 1961
4,000 Witness Stock Car Races

Drivers at the Warsaw Speedway couldn't have followed a script better Saturday night as weird accidents thrilled a capacity crowd of 4,000 spectators. Fortunately no one was injured among the 63 cars that qualified for the racing card, a feature of the county fair.

At one time in the race, Owen Rensberger of Elkhart was caught between two other race cars. They slid sideways together with Rensberger's car turning over on its side and another car crashing into his vehicle, knocking the engine completely out of the frame. When the smoke had cleared the motor lay on the track by itself.

Another time, Ray Kenens of Lafayette flipped on top of Coral Hostettler's hood and was riding piggy back in that position while Hostettler spun out and another car came underneath Kenens' car, putting Kenens in the position of riding on the hood of both autos.

Other Crashes. In the warmup trials before the race started one car struck a push truck causing considerable damage to the truck. The car of Wayne Staley, of Syracuse, flipped high in the air and lit on its side after going through the fence at one point, and Earl Egolf, of North Manchester also went through the fence later in the evening. Jo Ellen McClintic, of Milford, was driven around the track by her favorite driver, Bob Zeigler, honoring her for winning state and national honors in majorette competition.

Winners Saturday were Max Lambert, Warsaw, the stock feature; Hal Douglas, Logansport, the modified feature; and Douglas again in the consolation race. John Davis, Warsaw, won the stock dash event, and Kenens won the modified dash event. Heat winners were Don Thomas, of Lafayette; Paul Hazen, of Columbia City; Walt Shaver, of Kokomo; Rorey Hopkins, of North Manchester, and Coral Hostettler, of Goshen.

Saturday, August 19, 1961
Local Driver Wins Feature Stock Car Race

Inclement weather held down the crowd at the Warsaw Speedway Saturday, but thrills were just as prevalent for those in attendance at the stock car races.

Bud Grossnickle, of North Manchester, went through the fence at one point in a race and rolled end over end, with his car being caught in the protective wheel fence on the east curve, where, according to sportscaster Milo Clase, his car looked like a tennis ball trapped in a net. Grossnickle was not injured.

Don Walker, Kokomo

Other mishaps resulted in multi-car spills and Lloyd Lyons, of Milford, was believed to be injured when hitting the retaining wall, but required only first aid treatment.

The Winners. John Davis, of Warsaw, was the stock feature winner with Don Walker, of Kokomo, taking the modified feature, and Bill Fortune, also of Kokomo, winning the "concey". Bill Havens, Goshen, was the stock dash winner and Hal Douglas, Kokomo, came home first in the modified dash event. Heat winners Saturday were Kenneth Bowser, Warsaw; Bill Hare, Columbia City; Don Walker, Kokomo; Dick Sickafoose, Columbia City; and Lanny Scott, Goshen.

Saturday, August 26, 1961
Columbia City, Kokomo Drivers Win Top Races

Paul Hazen, of Columbia City, won the stock feature and Bill Fortune of Kokomo, the modified feature stock car race at the Warsaw Speedway Saturday night.

Sixty-six cars qualified for the night of racing, including several new drivers. Heat winners were Earl Egolf of North Manchester, Ron Fisher of Windfall, Hank Easley of Logansport, Paul Scott of Goshen and Fortune. Hal Douglas of Logansport won the race between the six fastest qualifiers, and Archie Holle of Warsaw crossed the finish line first in the "concey" event.

No one was injured although cars collided in almost every race. Thirty minutes of the racing program were broadcast over WRSW for Miller's Men's and Boy's Wear, and Piggie Inn Drive-In of Warsaw.

Saturday, September 2, 1961
Lafayette Racer Wins 100- Lap Feature Here

Ray Kenens, of Lafayette, was the winner of the 100-lap Monza style feature event at the Warsaw Speedway Saturday with Bob Zeigler finishing second and Warsaw's Archie Holle third.

Si Marner of Kokomo was taken to the Murphy Medical Center for treatment and released on Sunday after his car smashed into a fence when the steering mechanism went out in the back stretch.

John Davis of Warsaw won the 15-lap stock feature, and Jim Lozier of Claypool was the modified concey winner. Heat winners Saturday were Paul Scott of Goshen, Ron Fisher of Windfall, and Davis of Warsaw.

Due to the 100 lap feature there were no heat races for modifieds and next Saturday the "strictly stocks" drivers will have their night as they race for the trophies in the championship feature event.

Saturday, September 9, 1961
Albion Police Chief Wins Feature Race

A warm, "steamy" night of racing was witnessed at the Warsaw Speedway Saturday and serious accidents were few and far between.

"Slug" More, Chief of Police at Albion, was the winner of a strictly stock 50 lap championship feature with 27 cars starting the event but only about 10 finishing. Fifty-two cars qualified in all for the night. John Davis, of Warsaw, was leading the event when he threw a wheel and broke a radius rod, costing him the advantage.

One-half of the racing card was broadcast over Radio Stations WRSW AM and FM for Holland Mobile Homes and Miller's Mens' and Boys' Wear.

Aside from the stock feature, Hal Douglas, of Logansport, won the modified feature and Kenny Bowser, of Bourbon, the consolation race. The winner of the six fastest modified race was Earl Egolf, of North Manchester. Heat winners were Owen Rensberger and Ray Wright, of Elkhart; Howard Bice, of Auburn; Ray Kenens, of Lafayette, and Rush Bradford, of Akron.

Saturday, September 16, 1961
Kenens, Davis Top Stock Car Drivers Here

A large crowd sat through a chilly night at the Warsaw Speedway Saturday as the racing season is fast drawing to a close. There will be no races next Saturday, but there is a possibility races will be held on the 30th.

It was announced that Ray Kenens of Lafayette was the winner of the point standing championship for modified cars and John Davis of Warsaw won the same award for stock cars.

Accidents Saturday saw Joe Woodling of Warsaw flip his car end over end in his debut in a race car and Hank Easley, of Logansport hit the fence head on at full speed when his accelerator stuck. Neither was injured.

Back row L-R: John Davis, Bob Jonas, Bill Baxter?, Ray Wright?
Front Row: Luther Holloway, Fred Sibley, Slug Moore

One-half hour of the race was broadcast over WRSW AM and FM by Miller's Mens and Boys Wear, and Holland Mobile Homes.

Results Of Races. Winners Saturday were Davis in the stock feature, and Don Walker, Kokomo, the modified feature, while Joe Hamsher copped the "concey". The modified dash event went to Walker and the stock dash winner was Bill Havens of Goshen. Heat winners were Dean Speicher, Warsaw; Paul Bills, Columbia City; "Si" Marner, Kokomo; Bob Kirk, Wabash; and Barbara Kenens won the powder puff derby.

Saturday, September 23, 1961 - No Race

Saturday, September 30, 1961 - Rainout

Saturday, October 7, 1961
Small Crowd At Final Race Card

The 1961 stock car racing season at the Warsaw Speedway ended in a blaze of excitement and accidents Saturday night before a small crowd.

One spectacular wreck saw cars driven by Floyd Sargent of Elkhart and Bill Fincher come together, with Sargent's racer flipping on end, hesitate for a second, then fall on top of the rolling Fincher car. Fortunately, neither driver was injured.

The feature race was won by Bill Fortune of Kokomo, who also captured the race between the six fastest qualifiers. Heat winners were Harold Egner of Columbia City, Bill Baxter of Columbia City, and Kenny Bowser of Warsaw. Baxter also won the race between the six slowest qualifiers. Part of the racing program was broadcast over WRSW for Beau-Monde Beauty Salon.

November 8, 1961
Hoosier Happenings
By The Bryants

South Bend, Ind., Nov. 8 – Had another trip to Columbia City Saturday night for Hoosier Hot Rod's election of officers. The old Chevy should know it's way down there pretty soon. "Hoot" Gibson is still the president; Del Ballard, Vice Pres.; Byron Beaber, Sec.-Treas. Serving on the Board of Directors are Oscar Cook, Howard Rex, Jim Lozier, John Huff, and Joe Fisher.

From the spectator standpoint, the rules will be essentially the same. Though there will be a little closer line drawn on the stock equipment. The regular program will still consist of three modified heats, two stock heats, mod. dash, 15 lap mod. concy, 15 lap stock feature and 25 lap mod. feature. That's a lot of racing for one program.

The fans keep coming back for a program like this and word does get around for the purses keep steadily increasing. The average was $1,300 for 22 shows, against the $1,200 average of 1958. No wonder they're getting ready to add more seating capacity on the natural bank that forms the grandstand area.

1962

Saturday, May 5, 1962
2,000 Witness Stock Car Races

Threatening skies failed to dampen the spirits of some 2,000 fans as the Warsaw Speedway enjoyed its best opening night of stock car races in years Saturday at the fairgrounds. A total of 45 cars were on hand to provide the thrills, and racing was wild at times but there were no serious injuries to mar the activity.

With the track being graded last fall and allowed to settle during the winter, the drivers were able to maneuver better in the curves with the result that leads and places changed many times in the various races.

Bob Jones, of Windfall, was the stock feature winner, Bob Zeigler, of South Bend, the modified winner, and Don Walker, of Kokomo, the winner of the race for the six fastest modified cars. Event winners were Hal Douglas, Logansport; Bud Grossnickle, North Manchester; Jim Kirby, Frankfort; Paul Hazen, Columbia City; and Art Smith, of Warsaw.

Saturday, May 12, 1962
50 Cars Compete In Races Here

Threatening skies and a soggy track held down the crowd and speeds at the Warsaw Speedway, but more than 50 cars turned out for an exciting night of racing.

Thrills were plentiful even though the track was wet from the Saturday morning rains which caused the qualifying times to be a little slower than usual with each event becoming faster and wilder as the track dried out. Wheels flew off several cars and there were some collisions but no injuries.

Several new cars were entered in the racing, including ones from Indianapolis, South Bend and Valparaiso. One-half hour of the racing was broadcast over WRSW through the courtesy of Holland Mobile Homes, the Lake-View Drive Inn, of North Webster, and Lake City Industrial, of Warsaw.

Top Winners. Bob Jones, of LaPorte, was the stock feature winner for the night, Art Smith, of Warsaw, took the modified feature, and Smith also copped the "concey". Jones also won the race of the six-fastest stock cars, and Ray Kenens, of Lafayette, the race of the six fastest modified cars. Event winners were Les Bills, of Columbia City; Doug Lawence, of Valparaiso; Hal Douglas, of Logansport; Bill Baxter, of Big Lake; and Bob Ziegler, of South Bend.

Saturday, May 19, 1962
3 Race Drivers Slightly Injured At Local Track

Larry Peterson, of Bremen, Gerald Egner, of Columbia City, and Mike Smith, of Indianapolis, required treatment at the Murphy Medical Center but none was injured seriously as the result of accidents during stock car races at the Warsaw Speedway Saturday night.

Top winners were Bill Baxter, Columbia City, in the stock feature; Archie Holle, Warsaw, in the modified feature; Cap Arnold, South Bend, in the consolation race; Hobe Noel, Logansport, in the modified dash race; and Dick Leiter, Warsaw, in the stock dash race.

Heat event winners were Archie Holle, Warsaw; Jim Backus, Big Lake; Bob Zeigler, South Bend; and Bill Baxter, Columbia City.

Saturday, May 26 – Rainout

Wednesday, May 30, 1962
Race Driver In Hospital After Car Hurdles Fence

Warsaw race driver, Dick Leiter, was taken to the Murphy Medical Center unconscious following a wreck at the Warsaw Speedway on Memorial Day. He is reported as "fair" today with a large lump on the neck and bruises. Leiter was injured when his car went over a fence. Winners at the speedway were John Davis, of Warsaw, in the stock feature, Bob Ziegler, South Bend, in the modified feature, and Hobe Noel, Logansport, in the consolation race.

Leiter won the race of the six fastest stock cars and Art Smith, also of Warsaw, won the six fastest modified race. Event winners were Kenny Bowser, Warsaw; Gerald Egner, Columbia City; Archie Holle, Warsaw; Bill Baxter, Columbia City; and Jim Kerby, of Frankfort.

Saturday, June 2, 1962
2 Local Drivers Cop Feature Stock Car Races Here

Two Warsaw men, John Davis and Jim Elliott, were winners in the stock and modified features, respectively, at the Warsaw Speedway Saturday night, and Don Fisher, of Windfall, and Ernie Kiefer, of Three Rivers, Mich., won the stock and modified dash events, respectively.

Heat winners were Ken Bowser, of Warsaw; Les Bills, of Columbia City; Bob Ziegler, of South Bend; Dave Letfler, of Elkhart; and Ellliott. Ron Gagnon, of Beaver Dam, required treatment at the Murphy Medical Center as the result of a two-car crash. He was not admitted.

Saturday, June 9, 1962 - Rainout

Saturday, June 16, 1962
Winner At Local Speedway

Winners at the Warsaw Speedway in stock car races over the weekend were Bill Baxter, from Big Lake, in the stock feature; Bob Zeigler, South Bend, in the modified feature; Baxter again in the six fastest stock cars, and Cap Arnold, of South Bend, in the six fastest modified cars.

Event winners were Jim Elliott, Warsaw; Paul Bills, Columbia City; Hal Douglas, Logansport; Doyle Bryant, Elkhart; and Ernie Kiefer, Three Rivers, Michigan.

Saturday, June 23, 1962 - Rainout

Saturday, June 30, 1962
Columbia City, South Bend Race Drivers Win

Jene Simon, of Columbia City, won the stock feature, and Bob Zeigler, of South Bend, the modified feature at the Warsaw Speedway last Saturday night.

Dean Speicher, of Warsaw, was the consolation winner, Cap Arnold, South Bend, was the winner of the six fastest modified cars, and Paul Hazen won the race of the six fastest stock cars. Heat winners were Jim Elliott, Warsaw; Paul Grim, Warren; Bob Zeigler, South Bend; and Ron Fisher, Windfall.

Wednesday, July 4, 1962
Thousands See Races, Fireworks At Fairgrounds

Approximately 5,000 persons enjoyed the Fourth of July racing and fireworks at the Warsaw Speedway Wednesday night and several thousand more were in boats and parked in cars around the fairgrounds to watch the fireworks display.

Results at the race track had Bob Jonas, of LaPorte, the stock feature winner, and Cap Arnold, of South Bend, the modified winner, with Howard Bill, of Auburn, copping the consolation race.

Hobe Noel, Logansport, and Max Lambert, North Manchester, won the races for the six fastest modified and stock cars respectively. Heat winners were Beezer Humphries, Kokomo; Paul Grim, Warren; Hal Douglas, Logansport; and Ron Fisher, Windfall.

Saturday, July 7, 1962
Manchester Driver Burned at Races Here

Ron Hopkins, 25, of North Manchester, suffered first and second degree burns to his back, chest, legs and abdomen when a radiator hose on his race car broke at the Warsaw Speedway Saturday night.

Hopkins was taken to the Murphy Medical Center where he is responding satisfactorily to treatment and the burns are not believed to be of a serious nature. Bill Rush, of Kokomo, also was taken to the hospital following a two-car collision, and he was released after treatment for a bruised eye.

Paul Bills, of Columbia City, was the stock feature winner at the Speedway with Jim Kerby, of Frankfort, taking the modified feature. Jene Simon, of Columbia City, and Don Walker, of Kokomo, won the races of the six fastest stock and modified cars respectively. Heat winners in the races were John Huff, of Warsaw, Larry Bills of Columbia City, Walker, Bills, and Bill Baxter, of Big Lake.

Saturday, July 14, 1962 - Rainout

Saturday, July 21, 1962
Columbia City, Kokomo Drivers Win Races Here

Paul Hazen, of Columbia City, was the stock feature winner and Don Walker, of Kokomo, the modified feature winner at the Warsaw Speedway Saturday night.

Bill Baxter, of Big Lake, won the stock "concey", and Cap Arnold, of South Bend, the race of the six fastest modified cars. Event winners were Jim Elliott, Warsaw; Paul Grim, Warren; Hal Douglas, Logansport; Paul Bills, Columbia City; and Ron Fisher, Windfall.

Saturday, July 28, 1962
Columbia City, Kokomo Drivers Win Races Here

DeWayne Fox, of Columbia City, was the 30-lap stock feature winner Saturday night at the Warsaw Speedway as a large crowd saw 51 cars qualify for the night of racing. In the modified feature, which was won by Bill Fortune, of Kokomo, "Cap" Arnold of South Bend, took a bad spill but escaped without serious injury. The car of "Chuck" Plummer, of Larwill, leaped over the fence in the second heat race and he was treated at the Murphy Medical Center for an arm injury.

Heat winners were Don Schfoeder, of Goshen; Bill Havens, also of Goshen; Charles Howell, of Warsaw; Bill Baxter, of Big Lake; and Ron Fisher, of Windfall. Fisher also won the heat race of the six fastest stock cars, and Ernie Kiefer, of Three Rivers, Mich., the race of the six fastest modified cars. Bill Fortune, of Kokomo, won the consolation race.

One-half hour of the race was broadcast over Radio Station WRSW through the courtesy of the Cozy Cottage Restaurant, Lake City Industrial Services, Deluxe Cleaners, and Holland Mobile Homes.

Saturday, August 4, 1962
50 Cars Race Here; John Davis Among Winners

A total of 50 cars qualified in a big night of racing at the Warsaw Speedway Saturday, and although there were many accidents, there were no serious injuries.

One-half hour of the racing was broadcast over Radio Station WRSW, sponsored by the Cozy Cottage Restaurant and the Lake City Industrial Services Inc.

John Davis, of Warsaw, was the stock feature winner, Bob Zeigler, of South Bend, won the modified feature, and Earl Egolf, of North Manchester, won the consolation race. Bill Baxter, of Big Lake, and Hal Douglas, of Logansport, won the events for the six fastest stock and modified cars respectively. Heat winners were Les Bills, Columbia City; Bill Fortune, Kokomo; Kay Coyle, Columbia City; and Davis.

Wednesday, August 8, 1962
Local Driver Wins Feature Race at Fair

John Davis, the son of Mr. and Mrs. Ted Davis, of Warsaw, was the feature winner among strictly stock cars in races held at the County Fair Wednesday night.

The modified cars will be back with the stock cars for the usual Saturday night races. A portion of the race program Wednesday was broadcast over Radio Stations WRSW, sponsored by Miller Mens' and Boys' Wear and Holland Mobile Homes.

Paul Warren was the consolation winner, and heat winners were Charles Gross and Davis, of Warsaw; Harold Egner and Kay Coyle, of Columbia City; and Dale Schrader, of Wabash.

Saturday, August 11, 1962
Fox, Kiefer, Win At Warsaw Speedway

A huge crowd, topped only by that on the 4th of July, watched DeWayne Fox, of Columbia City, and Ernie Kiefer, of Three Rivers, Mich., win the stock and modified features respectively at the Warsaw Speedway Saturday.

Three drivers were taken to the Murphy Medical Center as the result of crack-ups when their cars rolled over. Frank Suich, of Burket, and Bill Baxter, of Big Lake, were released after treatment. Don Walker, of Kokomo, was admitted and he is listed as satisfactory in the hospital today.

John Huft, of Burket, won the consolation race, Bill Havens, of Goshen, won the race of the six fastest stock cars, and Ernie Kiefer, of Three Rivers, won the race of the six fastest modified cars. Event winners were Dale Schraeder, Wabash; Max Lambert, North Manchester; Bill Fortune, Kokomo; Owen Rensberger, South Bend; and Havens, of Goshen.

Saturday, August 18, 1962
Warsaw, Kokomo, Drivers Win Feature Races

John Davis, of Warsaw, was the stock feature winner, and Beezer Humphries, of Kokomo, the modified feature winner at the Warsaw Speedway last weekend.

The races of the six fastest stock and modified cars were won by Bill Fortune, of Kokomo, and Owen Rensberger, of South Bend, respectively, and heat wins were recorded by Larry Bills, Columbia City; Charles Gross, Warsaw; Bob Zeigler, South Bend; Jene Simon, Columbia City; and Earl Egolf, North Manchester.

No one was injured at the races despite the fact that Wayne Sprait, of Elkhart, rolled his car end over end and over a fence, demolishing the auto.

Saturday, August 25, 1962 - Rainout

Wednesday, August 29, 1962
Win Midget Races Here

Cap Arnold, of South Bend, won the feature race and a heat race in midget races at the Warsaw Speedway Wednesday.

Gary Byers, also of South Bend, won the "pursuit" race and other heat races were won by Bob Zomerhuis, Grand Rapids; Byers, and Nick Wilhem, of Hartford City.

Saturday, September 1, 1962
Crowds Enjoy 2 Nights of Racing Over Weekend

No serious injuries resulted during two nights of racing Saturday and Labor Day at the Warsaw Speedway. The Labor Day crowd was treated to a fireworks display.

Jerry Smith, of Columbia City, collided with a second car and both locked together and went through a fence with Smith's car rolling completely over. The mishap occurred on Labor Day and Smith escaped with a cut to the arm and leg.

One-half of the Saturday races was broadcast over Radio Stations WRSW through the courtesy of Lake City Industrials and Holland Mobile Homes.

On Saturday, John Davis, of Warsaw, won the stock feature, Howard Bice, of Auburn, won the 50-lap modified feature, and Charlie Howell, of Wabash, won the consolation race. Hobe Noel, of Logansport, won the race of the six fastest modified cars and heat winners were Ray Kenens, Lafayette; John Davis, Warsaw; Archie Holle, Warsaw; and Paul Bills, Columbia City.

On Labor Day, Bill Havens, of Goshen, won the stock feature, and the race of the six fastest cars, Paul Hazen, Columbia City, won the race of the six slowest cars, and Owen Rensberger, South Bend, won the "concey". Heat winners were Hazen, Dayton Bryant, of Goshen, and Charlie Gross, of Warsaw.

Saturday, September 8, 1962
Rain Halts Races Here

Rain and wet grounds cancelled the Saturday night of racing at the Warsaw Speedway, but not before Bud Grossnickle of North Manchester walked away uninjured from an accident.

In the crash, Grossnickle's car struck the fence, which tore off the front wheels sending his car over the fence with the wheels remaining on the track. Hal Douglas, of Logansport, was the winner of a modified heat race which was the only event held. It was announced at the track that there will be a complete card of racing next Saturday.

Saturday, September 15, 1962
Davis, Holle Big Winners As Races End Here

The 1962 stock car racing season ended last Saturday night at the Warsaw Speedway with John Davis, of Warsaw, winning the stock feature, the race between the six fastest stock qualifiers, and the fifth heat race. Archie Holle, also of Warsaw, finished ahead of the field in the modified feature and the race between the six fastest modified qualifiers.

Forty-eight cars qualified for the races. There were several collisions but no one was injured during the night. Other heat winners, in addition to Davis, were Bob Bernhard, of South Whitley, Bill Baxter, of Big Lake, Jim Elliott, of Warsaw, and Don Rogan, of Argos.

It was announced that racing would be resumed next spring.

1963

Saturday, May 4, 1963 – Rainout

Saturday, May 11, 1963
Everingham, Douglas Win At Warsaw Speedway

A large crowd watched 49 cars in action on a chilly night at the Warsaw Speedway Saturday. Larry Bills, of Columbia City, rolled over in one of the heat races but was uninjured and Ray Kennans, of Logansport, went through the fence in the qualifying run but escaped injury.

Claude Everingham, of New Paris, won the stock feature and Hal Douglas, of Logansport, won the modified feature. Charles Sarver, of Kokomo, won the consolation race and Jim Elliott, of Warsaw, and Jene Simon, Columbia City, won the race of the six fastest modified and stock cars respectively.

Heat winners were Bill Fortune, Kokomo; Ernie Johnson, North Manchester; Elliott; and Everingham. One-half hour of the race was broadcast over Radio Station WRSW by Milo Clase. Sponsors were the Best Cap Tire Co.; Lake City Industries; and Mid-Town Gulf.

Saturday, May 18, 1963
Elliott Wins 3 Events At Local Speedway

A large crowd at the Warsaw Speedway watched many thrills and numerous accidents Saturday night but no one was seriously injured.

Charles Brown, of Leesburg, in his first year of racing, was involved in one accident and sustained a leg injury. However, he was treated and released from the Murphy Medical Center. Ron Hopkins, of North Manchester, also went through the fence when his steering gear broke, but he escaped injury.

Jim Elliott, of Warsaw, had one of his best nights of racing, winning the modified feature, the race for the six fastest modified cars, and the third heat race.

Bill Baxter also copped the stock feature and the fifth heat race. Jene Simon, of Columbia City, won the race of the six fastest stock cars and a heat race, and Bill Havens, of Goshen, was the consolation race winner. Other heat races were won by Jack Hickman, of Syracuse, and Larry Plummer, of Larwill.

One-half hour of the racing was broadcast over Radio Station WRSW by Milo Clase through the courtesy of Lake City Industrial Service; Mid-Town Gulf; and Best Cap Tire Co.

Saturday, May 25, 1963
Car Demolished At Races Here, But Driver Escapes

Gerald Egner, of Columbia City, escaped serious injury at the Warsaw Speedway Saturday night when his stock car was completely demolished after losing a wheel, ramming straight through a guard rail and flipping end over end.

Many spectators in the enthusiastic crowd said the wreck was possibly the worst they had ever witnessed. Egner was taken to the Murphy Medical Center and then released.

Winners at the speedway were Claude Everingham, of New Paris, in the stock feature, Bob "Curley" Zeigler, of South Bend, in the modified feature, and Earl Egolf, of North Manchester, in the consolation race.

OTHER WINNERS. Bill Baxter, of Big Lake, and Jack Hickman, of Milford, were the winners of the races for the six fastest stock and modified cars, respectively.

Heat race winners were John Huff, Warsaw, Paul and Les Bills, of Columbia City, Hobe Noel, of Logansport, and Charles Sarver, of Kokomo.

It was announced at the track that 50 racers have qualified for races on Memorial Day night next Thursday.

One-half hour of the races was broadcast by Sportscaster Milo Clase over Radio Station WRSW through the courtesy of Mid-Town Gulf, Lake City Industrials, and Best Cap Tire Co.

Saturday, June 1, 1963
Many Accidents At Races Here

Bud Grossnickle, of North Manchester, was treated for a broken nose at the Murphy Medical Center Saturday night as the result of an accident in a wild night of racing at the Warsaw Speedway.

A large crowd saw Larry Baker, of Warsaw, and Grossnickle crash with the latter reportedly smashing his nose against the steering wheel. Several cars went through the fence and the stock feature was halted seven times due to accidents in that event in which 20 cars were entered.

Jim Elliott, of Warsaw, after suffering several broken bones in his hand when hit by a flying stone in last Thursday's race, drove his car despite wearing a cast, recording two victories.

THE WINNERS. Paul Bills, of Columbia City, was the stock feature winner, Elliott won the modified feature race, and Paul Warren was the consolation race winner. Paul Hazen, of Columbia City, won the race of the six fastest stock cars and Elliott the race of the six fastest modified cars.

Heat winners were Hobe Noel, Logansport; Claude Everingham, New Paris; Bob Bernard, South Whitley; John Vogely, Columbia City; and Larry Bills, also of Columbia City.

Saturday, June 8, 1963
DeWayne Fox, Art Smith Capture Feature Races

Good racing was the byword at the Warsaw Speedway Saturday with only one minor injury reported. That was when Ernie Johnson, of Laketon, struck the fence and rolled over in the pit area. He suffered a lacerated chin but was released after treatment at the Murphy Medical Center.

The stock feature race was stopped once because of a spectacular seven-car accident which eliminated six of the racers from the race, but there were no injuries.

DeWayne Fox, of Columbia City, was the winner of the stock feature and Art Smith, of Warsaw, copped its modified counterpart. Paul Bills, of Columbia City, won the consolation race.

Jene Simon, of Columbia City, won the race of the six fastest stock cars, and Jim Elliott, of

Warsaw, the modified dash. Heat winners were Fox, Elliott, Bill Rush, of Walton; Ron Hopkins, of North Manchester, and John Huff, of Warsaw.

Next week a big "destruction derby" will highlight the night's entertainment as the racers go until the only car left in the field is declared the winner. One-half hour of Saturday's race was broadcast over Radio Station WRSW by Milo Clase.

Saturday, June 15, 1963
Jalopy Races Prove Popular At Local Speedway

Jalopy races at the Warsaw Speedway proved a huge success Saturday night with many exciting crashes and no injuries as they were held for the first time as a part of the racing program. At one point, the jalopy of Frank Swick, of Rochester, rolled over three times and landed on its side. He emerged from his car shaken but unhurt. And at another time, Bob Smith, of Milford, rolled over and crawled out the back window unscratched.

Winner of the stock feature was Paul Grim, of Warren. Jesse Gibson, of Columbia City, copped the destruction derby title. Charles Gross, of Warsaw, won the consolation race. The winner of the race of the six fastest stock cars was Bob Jonas, of LaPorte. Heat winners were Paul Bills, of Columbia City; Larry Baker and Dick Leiter, of Warsaw; and Larry King, of Roanoke, on two occasions.

It was announced at the track that the jalopy races would again be held next Saturday. One-half hour of the race was broadcast over Radio Station WRSW by Milo Clase through the courtesy of Mid-town Gulf; Best Cap Tire Co., and Lake City Industrials.

Saturday, June 22, 1963
Many Accidents But No Injuries At Races Here

Many cars rolled over and other close calls and collisions occurred as "weird" accidents at the Warsaw Speedway made a thrilling Saturday night for the large crowd at the county fairgrounds.

Although no one was injured, Max Ummel, of Claypool, rolled through the fence, and cars driven by Charles Goodrich, of North Manchester, and Dan Cuellar, of Kokomo, went "topsy-turvy". Cuellar was most unfortunate as he was running fourth in the feature race when his auto rolled in front of the grandstand just before crossing the finish line.

Les Bills, of Columbia City, was the stock feature winner and Glen Owens, of Silver Lake, took the jalopy feature. Charles Gross, of Warsaw, captured the consolation race and the dash of the six fastest stock cars was won by Bob Jonas, of LaPorte.

Heat winners were Gerald Egner, of Columbia City; Don Murphy of South Whitley; Larry Baker, of Warsaw; and Jonas and Owens.

Saturday, June 29
72 Cars Stage Hot Competition In Races Here

A hot night Saturday and the 72 cars that qualified to make the racing competition even hotter, thrilled the large crowd at the Warsaw Speedway. The races were dotted by several accidents, but no serious injuries.

Max Lambert, of North Manchester, tangled with Dick Leiter, of Warsaw, when Leiter lost a wheel, the result being that Lambert flipped end over end in front of the grandstand, escaping with stomach bruises. In another instance, Paul Grim, of Warren, Ind., rolled up on the retaining wall with his car ending up balanced as if it were a teeter-totter. Dave Sheets, of Columbia City, also rolled over the rail, but escaped injury.

THE WINNERS. Bob Jonas, of LaPorte, won the stock feature race; Jerry Egolf, of North Manchester, the jalopy race; Pinky Stewart, of Kokomo, the consolation race; and DeWayne Fox, of Columbia City, the race of the six fastest stock cars. Other heat winners were Don Murphy, of South Whitley, Larry Bills, of Columbia City, and Larry Baker, Chick Engle, and Charlie Gross, all of Warsaw.

One-half of the race was broadcast by sportscaster Milo Clase over Radio Station WRSW through the courtesy of Hile Pure Oil; Lake City Industrials; and Best Cap Tire Co. A fireworks program is planned for the July 4th races.

Thursday, July 4, 1963
Race Car Hits, Kills North Manchester Mechanic, Injures 5 At Local Speedway
By Don Derry, Times-Union Sports Editor
(Personal details of the victim have been omitted)

An estimated 4,000 auto racing enthusiasts were stunned today to learn that the 20-year old North Manchester young man they had seen "run down" by a rampaging race car at the Warsaw Speedway Thursday night, died about two hours after the Fourth of July tragedy in the Murphy Medical Center.

Roy Cleveland, 20, a factory worker who doubled as a race car mechanic, was the victim of the crash which hospitalized five more persons and sent many others scurrying for cover. Cleveland, the son of Mr. and Mrs. Clarence Cleveland, reportedly was standing about 10 feet from his father when he was hit by the wildly veering race car driven by Glen Smith, of Warsaw. The speedway is located at the county fairgrounds in east Warsaw.

All but one dismissed. Those hospitalized were released after treatment with the exception of Wendell Minnix, 29, Warsaw, who is listed as "satisfactory" with a leg injury.

The Manchester youth was rushed to the Murphy Medical Center by a McHatton ambulance stationed at the track. However, officials stated he bled profusely from the back of his head. Smith stated, "As I was coming out of the No. 3 turn, the accelerator stuck. It throwed me wide open. I couldn't get it shut off quickly enough to miss the pit gate. I spun around and went backwards into the crowd."

Over 70 M.P.H. Smith added that the car was traveling in excess of 70 miles per hour at the time, and Cleveland's father stated, "there was such a crowd nobody could get out of the way."

The tragedy occurred on the east end of the speedway. As the accelerator stuck coming out of the straightaway, Smith's car amazingly veered through the pit gate exit-way, crashing into a guard fence along the pit area. This impact spun the car around, hit young Cleveland, and slammed into several "jalopies" parked in the pit area. The accident occurred during the 25-lap feature on the quarter-mile dirt track.

Others Injured. Others treated and released at the hospital were Smith; Duane Oldenauer, of Michigan City; Earl Bowman, of Huntington; and James Huffman.

Fireworks Display. With the exception of Cleveland's death, the large crowd gave full approval to the outstanding Fourth of July fireworks display. Thousands also viewed the display from their cars in nearby areas and boats dotted Winona Lake in a dense fashion.

Don Smith, of Pierceton, also rolled his car over in the stock feature, but escaped injury as did several other autos involved in mishaps during the night. The winner of the stock car feature race was Jean Simons, of Columbia City, Chuck Elder, of Pierceton, won the jalopy race, and Les Bills, of Columbia City, the race of the six fastest stock cars.

Other Winners. John Vogely, of Columbia City, won the consolation race, and heat winners were Paul Hazen and Gerald Egner, both of Columbia City, and Jim Meade, Dick Leiter, and Roger Gross, all of Warsaw. Don Murphy, of South Whitley, won the race of the six fastest jalopies.

Cleveland's death marked the second fatality at the Warsaw Speedway. On the final night of the Kosciusko County Fair in 1958, Walter Schroeder, 46, of Wakarusa, was killed instantly when run over by several cars as he stumbled when running across the track. He was also a part-time race car mechanic.

Saturday, July 6, 1963
Columbia City Drivers Take Local Honors

A total of 67 cars qualified Saturday at the Warsaw Speedway with most of the laurels being taken by Columbia City drivers. Several cars ran through the fence, and Bud Grossnickle, of North Manchester, rolled over the fence, but escaped injury.

Columbia City drivers to win firsts were DeWayne Fox, in the stock feature; Ted Hare in the jalopy feature; Gerald Egner in the consolation race; Jene Simon in the race of the six fastest stock cars; and Larry Bills, John Vogely, Hare, and Fox in heat races. The lone outside winner was Art Smith, of Warsaw, in a heat race.

Saturday, July 20, 1963
80 Cars Compete in Races Here

Exciting action transpired at the Warsaw Speedway Saturday night as 80 cars qualified in one hour and nine minutes. Although there were several accidents, no serious injuries developed. It was announced at the track that the 30-lap strictly stock championship feature race will be held at the speedway next Saturday.

Bob Jonas, of LaPorte, won the stock feature last Saturday with DeWayne Fox, of Columbia City, copping the race of the six fastest stock cars.

Double Winner. Glen Owens, of Silver Lake, sped home first in both the jalopy race and the race of the six fastest jalopies, and Bill Baxter, of Big Lake, was the consolation race winner. Heat winners were Chuck Plumber, of Larwill; Cecil Huntley; Paul Grim, of Warren; Jerry Smith, of Columbia City; and Charles Gross, of Warsaw.

One-half hour of the race was broadcast by sportscaster Milo Clase over Radio Station WRSW through the courtesy of Hile Pure Oil; Lake City Industrials, and Best Cap Tire Co.

Saturday, July 27, 1963
Larry Moore Captures 30-Lap Mid-Season Championship Race Here

A large crowd at the Warsaw Speedway Saturday night watched Larry Moore, of North Manchester, win the 30-lap mid-season championship strictly stock feature in a close finish. The race was momentarily marred when Bud Grossnickle, also of North Manchester, rolled over several times as he was crossing the finish line, but he escaped injury. Charlie Gross, of Warsaw, also rolled over in the consolation race and was uninjured.

Bob Jonas, of LaPorte, was the winner in the flying stock race. Jene Simon, of Columbia City, won the race of the six fastest cars in a similar event, and Don Murphy, of South Whitley, won the consolation race. Heat winners were Larry Baker and Pete Gross, of Warsaw; Roger Grossnickle, of North Manchester, Paul Grim, of Warren; and Paul Hazen, of Columbia City. One-half hour of the race was broadcast over Radio Station WRSW through the courtesy of Hile Pure Oil, Best Cap Tire Co., and Lake City Industrials.

Saturday, August 3, 1963
Akron, Columbia City Drivers Win Races Here

Major accidents and minor injuries typified action at the Warsaw Speedway Saturday night as 80 cars qualified for the night of racing. Judy Tenney, of Pierceton, was slightly injured in one mishap and was taken to the Murphy Medical Center and released after examination. She was competing in the powder puff derby.

In another mishap, Ted Upson, also of Pierceton, received emergency treatment at the McHatton ambulance when his car struck a stalled auto head-on. According to reports the car had stalled facing the traffic in front of the grandstand and although several cars missed the stalled vehicle, Upson's auto smashed into it head-on. He was treated for a cut on the nose and a cut under the eye after his head hit the steering wheel.

Race Winners. Chuck Sauer, of Akron, won the jalopy feature and Jene Simon, of Columbia City, was the stock feature winner.

Earl Egolf, of North Manchester, was the jalopy dash winner; Max Elder, of Pierceton, won the jalopy consolation race; Jene Simon, of Columbia City, took the stock dash; and Bob Jonas, of LaPorte, won the stock concey. Heat winners were Barney Baker, of Hartford City; Don Drudge of Pierceton; Les Bills of Columbia City; Chick Engle of Warsaw; and Chuck Plummer, of Larwill. Races will be held Wednesday and Saturday nights at the County Fair this week.

Wednesday, August 7, 1963
Big Crowd At Fair Enjoys Races

Although there were no injuries, a large County Fair crowd was treated to an exciting and weird night of racing at the Warsaw Speedway Wednesday night.

Jim Meade, of Warsaw, rolled over after he crossed the finish line and won the second jalopy feature of the evening, and Robert Smith, of Milford, went through the same spot on the fence twice, tearing out 30 feet of the retaining wall. Gerald LaRue, of Pierceton, also rolled over but was not injured.

Other winners in addition to Meade were Earl Egolf, of North Manchester, in the jalopy feature; Les Bills, of Columbia City, in the flying stock feature and Chuck Saner, of Akron, in the concey stock race.

Don Murphy, of South Whitley, won the race of the six fastest jalopies, and Bob Jonas, of LaPorte was the winner of the race of the six fastest stock cars. Heat winners were Ron Hopkins, of North Manchester; Len Gregory, of Ligonier; Bob Jonas, of LaPorte; Earl Egolf, of North Manchester; and Bills.

Saturday, August 10, 1963
Big Crowd Enjoys Races at Fair

Roger Grossnickle, N. Manchester

A large crowd came to its feet on several occasions Saturday night during the exciting races at the Warsaw Speedway. The crowd, increased by many persons attending the County Fair, watched 93 cars qualify for the races, a speedway record for the Warsaw track. The only serious accident to occur was when Ken Juillerat, of Larwill, rolled over, however, he escaped injury.

Les Bills, of Columbia City, won the stock feature and Roger Grossnickle, of North Manchester, was the jalopy feature winner.

Richard Anders, of Warsaw, son the jalopy consolation race, Glen Owens, of Silver Lake, won the race of the six fastest jalopies and Duane Fox of Columbia City, won the race of the six fastest stock cars. Heat winners for the night were Dale Shrader, of Wabash;

Pealey Heckaman, of Bourbon; Paul Grim, of Warren; Max Elder, of Pierceton; and Chuck Plummer, of Larwill.

Saturday, August 17, 1963
Columbia City Racer Wins Feature Here

A small but brave group of chilled fans watched an exciting program of racing at the Warsaw Speedway Saturday night with 75 cars qualifying for action.

Although cars rolled over in three separate accidents, there were no injuries. Joining the "roll-over club" were Jack McKenzie, of Pierceton, Don Drudge of Akron, and Dick Campbell, of Bristol.

Les Bills, of Columbia City, won the stock feature, Bill Baxter, of Big Lake, the race of the six fastest stock cars, and Pete Gross, of Warsaw, the stock car concey. Heat winners in addition to Bills were Don Murphy and Bob Bernhard, both of South Whitley, Paul Hazen of Columbia City, Charles Flaugh, and Ulyssis Francis, of Pierceton.

Saturday, August 24, 1963
Rain Fails To Interfere With Races Here

"Mother Nature" did not co-operate again Saturday night at the Warsaw Speedway, but the crowd was treated to an exciting night of racing as the season championships were completed despite several sprinkles of rain.

Several drivers joined the "roll-over club" including Dave Sheets of Columbia City, Doug Method, of Leesburg, and Earl Egolf, of North Manchester, and several cars went either through or over the fence, but no one was seriously injured. A total of 80 cars qualified for competition including Ron Thomas from as far away as Kalamazoo, Mich.

The Winners. Les Bills, of Columbia City, won the stock feature, Pete Gross, of Warsaw, was the jalopy feature winner, and Paul Grim, of Warren, and Paul Bills, of Columbia City, won the races for the six fastest stock cars and jalopies. Heat winners were Grim, John Vogely, of Columbia City; Jim Jackson, of Pierceton; Don Murphy, of South Whitley; Charles Gross, of Warsaw; and Pealey Heckaman, of Bourbon.

One-half of the program was broadcast by sportscaster Milo Clase, over Radio Station WRSW through the courtesy of Hile Pure Oil, Lake City Industries, and Best Cap Tire Co.

Saturday, August 31, 1963
Columbia City Race Drivers In Limelight Here

Columbia City drivers dominated the racing at the Warsaw Speedway Saturday night by winning five of the nine events. The 78 cars that qualified supplied the crowd with numerous thrills with Bill Yeager, of Anderson, rolling over but escaping injury.

It was announced at the speedway that the highlight of the regular race card next Saturday would be that all of the jalopies would start in the feature, no matter how many, and that the last five cars running would be the winners.

Pealey Heckaman, of Bourbon, won the jalopy feature and Paul Grim, of Warren was the stock winner, while DeWayne Fox, of Columbia City, won the race of the six fastest stock cars. Heat winners were John Vogely, Jesse Gibson, Les Bills and Paul Bills, all of Columbia City; Kent Brown, of Warsaw; and Larry Ihnen, of North Manchester.

Saturday, September 7, 1963
Bills, Engle Win Feature Races Here

A large, enthusiastic crowd enjoyed the stock car races Saturday night at the Warsaw Speedway with top honors going to Lester Bills, of Columbia City, in the stock feature, and Chick Engle, of Warsaw, in the jalopy feature.

Fifty-one cars started in the jalopy feature, and Engle was the winner after driving for 43 minutes in a race scheduled for an hour. Five cars were still running after the 43 minutes and drivers of all five were declared "winners" and each received a trophy.

Other Winners. Heat winners were Ron Hopkins, of North Manchester, and Bills. Glen Owens, of Silver Lake, won the race between the six fastest qualifiers, and Paul Grim, of Warren, won the concey. Bills also finished first in the race between the six fastest super-stock qualifiers.

Next Saturday will feature a big "destruction race". The last car running will be the winner. The goal of each driver is to try to knock all the other cars off the track. Thirty minutes of the racing program were broadcast over WRSW by Latta Pure Oil, Best Cap Tire Co., and Lake City Industries.

Saturday, September 14, 1963
60 Cars Provide Excitement At Local Speedway

A chilly crowd was warmed by the excitement of 60 cars qualifying at the Warsaw Speedway Saturday night. Pete Gross, of Warsaw, flipped his car but escaped injury and Ron Thomas, of Vicksburg, Mich., rolled over after his car struck a guard rail. Thomas was treated and dismissed from the Murphy Medical Center following the accident.

The jalopy feature was a demolition race with the last car running declared the winner. Joe Geiger, of Albion, in a little two-door Chevy, had a battle to cross the finish line after his car took a terrific beating in the event.

Other Winners. In addition to Geiger's win, Les Bills, of Columbia City, won the stock car feature race and Paul Hazen, also of Columbia City, the consolation race.

Larry Plummer, of Larwill, was the stock dash winner and Earl Egolf, of North Manchester, won the jalopy dash event. Heat winners were John Vogely, of Columbia City; John Bickle, of Wabash; and Plummer and Egolf.

Big Race Next Saturday. It was announced at the track that a 100-lap feature would highlight next Saturday's program. It will be open competition with super modified race cars returning to the track. One-half hour of the race card was broadcast by sportscaster Milo Clase over WRSW through the courtesy of Latta Pure Oil Service, Lake City Industrials, and Best Cap Tire.

Saturday, September 21, 1963
Warsaw Racing Season Ends

A small crowd witnessed the end of the 1963 racing season at the Warsaw Speedway Saturday night with a 100-lap modified feature climaxing the year's program.

According to WRSW Sportscaster Milo Clase, who broadcast one-half hour of the race, plans will be made this fall and winter for the next racing season, which is expected to begin approximately the first of May. The broadcast was aired through the courtesy of Best Cap Tire Co.; Crystal Industrials Services; and Latta Pure Oil Services.

Hank Easley, of Logansport, won the modified feature and Earl Egolf, of North Manchester, copped the jalopy feature. Don Walker, of Kokomo, won the modified dash event and winners of the two jalopy heat races were Chuck Sainer, of Akron, and Bob Brubaker, of North Manchester.

1964

Saturday, May 2, 1964
45 Cars in First Night Racing Here

A total of 45 "souped up" cars put on quite a show before the many fans who witnessed the opening night of auto races at the Warsaw Speedway on Saturday.

In the most spectacular mishap of the night, Paul Hazen, of Columbia City, escaped injury when his car went end over end and over the rail after his accelerator stuck going into a turn. His car was badly damaged however.

The new rear engine car driven by Les Bills, also of Columbia City, was one of the front runners in a race until the vehicle developed fuel line trouble. It was announced at the track that many new cars are being built and will be ready to run in next Saturday's racing program.

Roger Grossnickle, of North Manchester, won the stock feature, and Jim Elliott, of Warsaw, the modified feature. Max Lambert, also of North Manchester, and Larry Bills, Columbia City, were respective winners in the semi late model and modified dash events. Heat winners were Dick Drudge, Ligonier; Larry Bills, Columbia City; Dan Cueller, Kokomo; and Larry Ihnen, North Manchester. One-half hour of the racing program was broadcast by sportscaster Milo Clase, over Radio Stations WRSW AM-FM.

Saturday, May 9, 1964
Kokomo Driver Wins Feature Race Here

Jim Elliott of Warsaw, was leading in the 20th lap of the feature race at the Warsaw Speedway Saturday night when his wheel blew, causing his car to collide with an auto driven by Charles Miles, of Peru. Miles' car flipped over a fence. He was given emergency treatment, but was not seriously injured.

Jim Boggs, of Warsaw, finished third in that event which was won by Don Walker, of

Kokomo. Boggs is in his rookie year of modified competition. Other winners, in addition to Walker, included Max Lambert, of North Manchester, in the stock feature, and Paul Grim, Warren, and Dick Leiter, of Warsaw, in the stock and modified dash events, respectively. Heat winners were Walker, Les and Paul Bills, and Charles Gibson, all of Columbia City.

Saturday, May 16, 1964
56 Cars Compete in Races Here

A total of 56 cars raced around a quagmire at the Warsaw Speedway Saturday to the delight of a large crowd, considering the weather conditions. The track was heavily drenched by afternoon rains but a grader was used and the time trials eliminated to enable the track to be "raceable".

It was announced at the track that the customary 50 cent charge for children up to 12 years of age will not be charged during the remainder of the season if the youngsters are accompanied by their parents.

Ted Newsome, of Ligonier, was the stock feature winner and Dan Cueller, of Kokomo, won the modified feature. Chick Engle, and Jim Elliott, of Warsaw, were the winners of the stock and modified dash events, respectively. Heat winners were Bob Johnson and D.C. Drabenstatt, of Warsaw, Harold Mouser, of Kokomo, and Bob Jonas of LaPorte.

Saturday, May 23, 1964
60 Drivers Provide Racing Thrills Here

Saturday night at the Warsaw Speedway might well have been termed "binge of speed" as 60 drivers roared around the "fast track" before a large crowd in the best single night of racing of the season.

Two spectacular crashes occurred but fortunately no one was seriously injured. In one instance a car driven by Ted Newsome, of Andrews, scooted under an airborne car which nearly tore the front end out of the "flying auto" when it hit. On another occasion a car driven by John Vogely, of Columbia City, flipped end over end and rolled over three times, only to escape with lacerations. He was treated in the Murphy Medical Center.

2 Top Winners. Max Lambert, of North Manchester, was the winner of the stock feature and Jim Elliott, of Warsaw, won the modified feature. Lambert also won the dash event of the six fastest cars, and Larry Bills, of Columbia City, won its modified counterpart. Heat winners were Elliott, Bob Brubaker, of Ligonier, John Davis, of Warsaw, and Jack Green, whose address was not listed.

It was announced that next Saturday there will be a 40-lap semi-late model feature event along with the regular racing program. The gates will be open at 5 p.m. with the trials beginning at 7 p.m.

Saturday, May 30, 1964
Dick Leiter Wins 40-Lap Race Here

Dick Leiter, of Warsaw, was the winner of the 40-lap stock feature at the Warsaw Speedway Saturday night before a large crowd.

Sixty-one cars qualified for the races with the most exciting race of the night seeing Don Walker, of Kokomo, nosing Bob Jonas, of LaPorte, in the final lap of the modified feature. Walker also won the race for the six fastest modified cars.

Heat winners were Richard Menzie of Pierceton, Paul Hazen of Columbia City, L. C. Drabenstott, of Warsaw, and Walker and Leiter. There will be a 40-lap feature for modified cars at the speedway next week.

Dick Leiter, Warsaw

Saturday, June 6, 1964
Several Crashes But No Serious Injuries At Warsaw Speedway

Larry Plummer, of Larwill, and Gerald Egner, of Columbia City, were treated for injuries at the Warsaw Speedway during a hot night of racing Saturday night. Neither was seriously injured.

Several crashes dotted the evening but there were no other injuries. Tom Paterson, of Bremen, flipped his car over the wall, escaping none the worse for wear.

Sixty-seven cars qualified in 55 minutes with the modified feature highlighting the action as Kokomo's Don Walker won in the last three laps of the 40-lap event after the lead had changed hands several times.

Max Lambert, of North Manchester, won the stock feature, and Walker was the winner of the six fastest dash event. Heat winners were Charles Gibson, Larry Bills and Les Bills, of Columbia City, Ron Rowland, of Burket, and Roger Grossnickle, of North Manchester.

One-half hour of the race was broadcast over Radio Stations WRSW AM-FM by sportscaster Milo Clase.

Saturday, June 13, 1964 - Rainout

Saturday, June 20, 1964
Local Speedway Crowd Thrilled

A large crowd was treated to probably the most thrilling feature events ever witnessed at the Warsaw Speedway Saturday night as a lightning fast track and the 64 cars which qualified in one hour combined to make an excellent night of racing.

The modified feature was in doubt until the very end with the lead changing hands several times. In fact, according to Milo Clase, sportscaster for Radio Stations WRSW AM-

FM a "blanket" could have been thrown over the first five cars lap after lap.

Elliott Third. The feature was spiced with numerous thrills. Jim Elliott, of Warsaw, was forced to the back of the pack because of an accident but still came back to finish third. And, just as the checkered flag dropped, Bob Jonas, of LaPorte, hit the retaining wall in front of the grandstand. His car went airborne but Bob rode it out over about one-half of the straight-away and finished in fifth place. Larry Bills, of Columbia City, won the event.

Bob Johnson, Warsaw

Method Wins. Doug Method, of Warsaw, was the winner of the stock feature and Jack Hickman, of Milford, copped the dash event of the six fastest modified cars. Hickman also finished second in the modified feature. Heat winners were Bob Johnson, of Warsaw, Chuck Sainer, of Akron, Jim Long, of Bourbon, Don Walker, of Kokomo, and DeWayne Fox of Columbia City.

Saturday, June 27, 1964
Big Fireworks Display During Races July 4

A gigantic fireworks display beginning at dusk will highlight a big night of racing at the Warsaw Speedway next Saturday, July 4. Gates will open at 4 p.m., time trials will begin at 6 p.m. and at dusk the sky will be dotted with the first of some 175 aerial fireworks displays.

A good crowd was treated to another thrilling night of racing Saturday which was sparked by the modified feature which had fans standing on their feet throughout the event. Jack Hickman, of Milford, finally won the race, nipping Jim Elliott, of Warsaw, after the lead changed hands several times.

One Driver Burned. Bill Rush, of Logansport, was burned about the arm, chest, and leg when steam engulfed his car after it collided with one driven by Jene Simons, of Columbia City, when the radiator burst. He was given emergency treatment at the track.

Roger Grossnickle, of North Manchester, won the stock feature, and Paul Hazen, of Columbia City, copped the dash event. Heat races were won by Larry Oswalt and Dick Leiter, of Warsaw, Bill Rush, of Logansport, Paul Grim, of Warren, and Max Lambert, of North Manchester.

Saturday, July 4, 1964
$3,500 Purse At Big July 4 Races Here

A tremendous crowd filled every inch of the Warsaw Speedway Saturday to watch 70 drivers battle for a record equaling purse of $3,500.

According to sportscaster Milo Clase the excitement on the track was outshone only by the outstanding 35-minute fireworks display which brought comments of "great, terrific, and best yet", from the pleased crowd.

Two "Jims" copped the feature events of the evening as Jim Long, of Bourbon, won the stock feature and Jim Boggs, of Warsaw, was the modified feature winner.

Paul Hazen, of Columbia City, was the winner of the dash event and heat races were won by L.C. Drabenstott and Chick Engle, of Warsaw, Ellis Shepherd, of Mentone, Bill Rush, of Logansport, and Paul Grim, of Warren.

Saturday, July 11, 1964
50-Lap Feature Next Saturday At Speedway

The annual mid-season 50-lap championship trophy race for semi-late-model cars will be run at the Warsaw Speedway next Saturday.

Although a highlight of the season, the night will be hard pressed if it is to surpass the excitement offered last Saturday when no less than 94 cars qualified for top prizes. Time trials were started early to qualify all cars on scheduled time and two additional heat races were added to accommodate the large number of racers.

Winners. Dick Leiter, of Warsaw, was the stock feature winner. Kokomo's Bill Fortune won the modified feature and the races of the six fastest stock and modified cars were won by Bill Brubaker, North Manchester, and Bob Jonas, LaPorte, respectively. Heat race winners included Jim Meade, Larry Shriver, and Leiter, from Warsaw, Paul Joyce and Fortune, from Kokomo, and Charles Wiles, from Peru.

One-half hour of the race was broadcast by Milo Clase over Radio Stations WRSW AM-FM through the courtesy of the following sponsors: Weirick Sinclair and Smith Tire Service, of Warsaw; Tschupp Sinclair, of Leesburg, and Penn and Strombeck, of North Webster.

Saturday, July 18, 1964
50-Lap Race At Local Speedway Next Saturday:

Jimmie Elliott, Warsaw

The 50-lap mid-season modified feature will be the highlight of racing activity at the Warsaw Speedway next Saturday, coming hot on the heels of the stock feature which thrilled fans last weekend.

Bud Grossnickle, of North Manchester, won the stock feature Saturday as 82 cars qualified for the night. Jim Elliott, of Warsaw, who is passing about everything on the track this year, was the modified feature winner. He turned the track in the time of 17.49 seconds for a record, and won the race of the six fastest modified cars.

7-Car Wreck. A seven-car pileup was part of the action in which Jack Green, of Silver Lake, rolled his car over but escaped without injury. Heat winners in addition to Elliott included Jim Bucher, Earl Egolf, of North Manchester, Charles Gibson, of Columbia City, L.C. Drabenstott, of Warsaw, and Ben Ulshafer, of South Whitley. Luther Holloway, of Warsaw, was also the winner of the stock dash event.

Saturday, July 25, 1964
Crowd Stands For Feature Race At Local Speedway

According to Sportscaster Milo Clase, races at the Warsaw Speedway Saturday have seldom been surpassed for sheer excitement with the 50-lap modified feature highlighting the evening.

Bob Jonas, of LaPorte, was the winner of that event with only one-half car length separating him from Don Walker, of Kokomo, and Jim Elliott, of Warsaw, who ran second and third. Ben Ulshafer, of South Whitley, involved in the most serious crash of the night, escaped uninjured when his car rolled-over twice in front of the grandstand.

Walker was the winner of the six-fastest modified dash race. Luther Holloway, of Warsaw, won its stock car counterpart, and Max Lambert of North Manchester, won the stock feature.

Heat races during the night were won by Phillip Gaunt, of Huntington; Jim Sullivan, of Plymouth; Jim Meade, of Warsaw; and Howard Bice, of Auburn. The first five finishers in the modified feature were awarded huge trophies by the Hoosier Hot Rod Racing Assn. One-half hour of the program was broadcast over Radio Stations WRSW AM-FM by Clase.

Saturday, August 1, 1964
List Winners At Warsaw Speedway

Races at the Warsaw Speedway continued to set an exciting pace Saturday as a large crowd was treated to a big night of racing. Several accidents cropped up during the night but no one was injured. Sportscaster Milo Clase broadcast one-half hour of the races over Radio Stations WRSW AM-FM.

Max Lambert, of North Manchester, was the winner of the stock feature and Bob Jonas, of LaPorte, won the modified feature. The race of the six fastest modified cars was won by Jim Elliott, of Warsaw.

Heat races during the evening were won by Fred Hathaway, of Burket; Bill Rush, of Logansport; Jack Hickman, of Milford; and Larry Shriver and Chick Engle, both of Warsaw. A total of 82 cars qualified during the night.

Saturday, August 8, 1964
Capacity Crowd Attracted To Saturday Races

A chilly evening failed to keep a tremendous crowd away from the Warsaw Speedway

Saturday and fans were rewarded with a balanced diet of racing thrills, complete with speed, spills, and chills.

One of the most vicious wrecks in years brought the huge throng (second only to the Fourth of July mass) to its feet as Larry Bills, of Columbia City, flipped end over end and had the undercarriage torn from his car which landed on its top. Bills escaped uninjured.

84 Qualify. A total of 84 cars qualified with times in the low 17 seconds to climax a week of grandstand attractions at the Kosciusko County Fair. Fans saw Earl Egolf, of North Manchester, win the modified feature, Dick Leiter, of Warsaw, the stock feature, and Howard Bice, of Auburn, the dash event.

Heat races were won by Leiter and L.C. Drabenstott, of Warsaw, Bill Fortune and Don Walker, of Kokomo, and Roger Rowland, of Burket. One-half hour of the race was broadcast over Radio Stations WRSW AM-FM by Sportscaster Milo Clase.

Saturday, August 15, 1964
Jim Elliott Wins Feature At Speedway

A chilly crowd watched 86 cars qualify and put on an exciting night of racing at the Warsaw Speedway Saturday, sparked by two rousing wrecks but no serious injuries.

Bill Rush, of Logansport, rolled over in a fast modified car and other than being shaken up was not injured. Ed Stine, of Etna Green, also rolled his late model stock car four or five times but escaped injury. The lead changed hands in the feature race several times before Jim Elliott, of Warsaw, came from the rear of the pack to win the modified feature event.

L.C. Drabenstott of Warsaw won the stock feature, and Don Walker of Kokomo, won the dash event. Heat winners were Phillip Gaunt, Huntington; Ben Ulshafer, South Whitley; Roger Rowland, Burket; Jerry Baker, Warsaw; and Walker.

A 50-lap event for semi-late models will be featured at the local speedway next Saturday. One-half hour of last Saturday's races was broadcast over Radio Stations WRSW AM-FM.

Saturday, August 22, 1964
50-Lap Race Scheduled Here Next Saturday

A 50-lap championship race for semi-late model cars will be held at the Warsaw Speedway next Saturday, hot on the wheels of an exciting card last weekend. Two drivers joined the "roll-over" club, Roger Grossnickle of North Manchester, and David Shepperd, of Burket, but both luckily escaped injury.

A total of 21 cars participated in a demolition race which ended with debris galore on the track and Ray Kiser from the state of Virginia piloting the lone car remaining.

Jim Elliott, of Warsaw, was the winner of the modified feature, Dick Leiter, also of Warsaw, won the stock feature, and Larry Bills, of Columbia City, won the dash event of the six fastest qualifiers. Heat races were won by Larry and William Powell, both of Silver Lake, Jene Simons and DeWayne Fox, both of Columbia City, and Richard Menzie, of

Pierceton.

Saturday, August 29, 1964
74 Cars Compete In Races Here

Saturday night was no exception to the many thrills at the Warsaw Speedway as 74 cars qualified and several wrecks ensued but no one was injured.

It was announced at the track that a 100-lap season championship feature for modified cars will be held and promised that racing will continue as long as the warm weather prevails.

John Davis, of Warsaw, won the modified feature and Luther Holloway, also of Warsaw, won the 50-lap stock feature. Jim Elliott, a third Warsaw driver, copped the race of the six fastest qualifiers. Heat winners were Jim Boggs and L.C. Drabenstott, of Warsaw; Estil Shepherd, of Mentone; Jene Simons, of Columbia City; and Mike Dickson, of Bourbon.

Saturday, September 5, 1964
Crowd Thrilled At Races Here

A chilled but enthusiastic crowd at the Warsaw Speedway saw all the thrills of racing Saturday as Bob Jonas, of LaPorte, won the 100-lap feature race going away and the remaining were places not decided until the finish. Seventy cars qualified for the races.

Kenton Krieg, of Warsaw, struck the fence in the time trials, causing his head to strike the steering wheel and his teeth to puncture his lip. It required approximately 10 stitches to close the wound. Richard Menzie, of Pierceton, also rolled his car in front of the grandstand but walked away uninjured.

The Winners. Glen Owens, of Silver Lake, won the stock feature and Howard Bice, of Auburn, was the winner of the six fastest qualifiers race. Heat winners included Owens, Harold Carl of Huntington, Ben Ulshafer, of South Whitley, Don Taylor, of Pierceton, and Les Bills, of Columbia City.

There will be a 100-lap "Monza" style race for semi-late models at the Speedway next Saturday. One-half hour of the races was broadcast by sportscaster Milo Clase over Radio Stations WRSW AM-FM through the courtesy of Smith Tire Service and Wierick Sinclair, of Warsaw, Tschupp Sinclair, of Leesburg, and Penn and Strombeck Sinclair, of North Webster.

Saturday, September 12, 1964
Great Feature Race Climax to Warsaw Season

The semi-late-model 100-lap feature was a fitting climax to a great racing season at the Warsaw Speedway Saturday night as Warsaw's Dick Leiter won the event after the first three positions changed hands at least nine times during the race.

The first 70 laps during the last race of the season were run without a stop and consumed only 25 minutes. The race was stopped and after a restart the final 30 laps were completed without interruption. Thirty cars started the event and about 20 finished the long grind with 67 qualifying for the night of racing.

Jim Elliott, of Warsaw, was the winner of the modified feature, and Columbia City's Paul Hazen was victorious in the race of the six fastest qualifiers.

Heat Winners. Heat winners were Mike Dickson, Plymouth; John Vogely, Columbia City; Gerald Meyer, Servia; Joe Deal, North Manchester; and Jim Bucher, Akron.

It was announced at the track that races at the Warsaw Speedway will be resumed in May, 1965. One-half hour of the races was broadcast over Radio Stations WRSW AM-FM by Sportscaster Milo Clase through the courtesy of Sinclair Dealers Penn and Strombeck, of North Webster; Myron Tschupp, Leesburg; and Max and Bill Weirick and Eddie Smith, of Warsaw.

1965

April 1965
Stock Car Races Start at Local Track May 1

The opening night for stock car races at the Warsaw Speedway have been set for Saturday night, May 1, according to an announcement today by C.E. "Hoot" Gibson, president of Hoosier Hot Rod Racing Assn.

Gibson said approximately 75 cars are expected to enter the opening night competition and will include many new cars that have been built during the winter months. The president stated that any drivers who wish to practice on the track may do so this Saturday afternoon, April 24, between the hours of 4 and 6 p.m. He said this will be the only time the track will be opened for practice until the official opening night.

Gibson reported that rules of the association are primarily the same as last year with one exception. He said the semi-late model stock class will include automobiles only between the years of 1955 and 1961. He related that rules for the super modified class remains as before. Gibson said that all cars must undergo a safety check on opening night and any new cars that come to the track that have not been checked must be inspected before they will be able to race. He added that all cars must have a metal top.

The track is expected to be in excellent condition for this year's racing season. Another layer of clay was added last fall and was allowed to settle properly during the winter, Gibson stated. He said all new guard rails and posts have also been installed. Grading work on the track is now in progress and is expected to be completed by Saturday for the two-hour practice session, Gibson concluded.

Saturday, May 1, 1965
55 Cars Enter Races Here On Opening Night

A good crowd on hand at the Warsaw Speedway Saturday night was treated to high speed thrills as 55 cars entered competition to open the 1965 racing season. For the first time in several years, weather conditions were excellent on opening night. Many more cars are expected to be ready for competition next week.

The super modified feature was filled with thrills as the lead in the early laps changed hands several times before Jim Elliott, of Warsaw, was given the checkered flag. Jack Hickman, of Milford, placed second and Bob Jonas, of LaPorte, was third.

Dick Leiter, of Warsaw, won the late model stock feature. The dash event in the stock class was won by Jim Bucher, of Akron, and Hickman won the race for the six fastest qualifiers in the super modified class.

Heat Winners. Heat winners were Hickman, Bud Grossnickle, of North Manchester, Les Bills, of Columbia City, and William Powell of Silver Lake.

Next week one-half hour of the races will be aired over WRSW AM-FM from 8:45 to 9:15 p.m. with Milo Clase describing the action. The broadcast will be sponsored by Gast Fuel and Service, of Warsaw, along with four cooperating Sinclair dealers: Tschupp's Service, of Leesburg, Penn and Strombeck of North Webster, Smith Tire Service, of Warsaw, and Lakeland Service of Warsaw.

Saturday, May 8, 1965
2 Injured In Thrill-Packed Race Card Here

Spectators at the Warsaw Speedway Saturday night were treated to a thrill packed racing card that saw two drivers injured in the semi-late model stock feature that was restarted several times due to pileups.

Chuck Saner, of Akron, was treated at the Murphy Medical Center for a broken nose when his racer rammed a mound of dirt and his head struck the steering wheel. Phil Hill, of Fort Wayne, was rushed to the hospital and x-rayed for a possible arm injury after his race car was involved in a three-car crash. Wayne Miller, of North Webster, added a bit of excitement when his racer ran through the pit gate fence forcing mechanics and drivers to flee but no one was injured.

57 CARS QUALIFY. A total of 57 cars qualified for the racing activity and as many as 18 were entered in some of the heat races. All events were hotly contested with the lead changing hands several times before the checkered flag dropped.

The modified stock feature was won by Jimmie Elliott, of Warsaw, for the second straight week. Paul Hazen, of Columbia City, was second and Bob Jonas, of LaPorte, finished third. Hazen also won the dash event for the six fastest qualifiers. Jerry Egolf, of North Manchester, was the winner of the action packed semi-late model feature race and Doug Method, of Warsaw, copped the dash event.

Heat winners were Chuck Saner, of Akron; DeWayne Fox, of Columbia City; Egolf and Larry Bills of Columbia City. One-half hour of the races was broadcast over Radio Stations WRSW AM-FM from 8:45 to 9:15p.m.

Saturday, May 15, 1965
Kokomo Driver Cops Feature At Races Here

"Speed" was the password Saturday night as a smaller than usual crowd, apparently kept away because of the threatening weather, was treated to one of the best nights of racing ever at the Warsaw Speedway.

Don Walker, of Kokomo, with a brand new car, won the modified feature, but not before a vicious duel with Jimmie Elliott, of Warsaw for the top spot. Howard Bice, of Akron, passed Elliott and moved into second place late in the race.

A total of 64 cars qualified for the event and many new cars were on hand including several new super modified racers.

Paul Hazen, of Columbia City, won the race for the six fastest qualifiers and added another win in a heat race; Larry Baker, of Warsaw, copped the stock feature. Other heat winners include Gerald Meyer, of Servia; Paul Joyce, of Kokomo; Don Drudge, of Burket; and Dick Leiter, of Warsaw.

Saturday, May 22, 1965 - Rainout

Saturday, May 29 & Monday, May 31, 1965
Howard Bice Wins 40-Lap Feature Race

Howard Bice, of Auburn, copped the 40-lap modified feature race at the Warsaw Speedway Monday night in a thrilling climax to a two night racing card in which a total of 162 cars qualified. Bice and Luther Holloway, of Warsaw, were the fastest qualifiers of the night in the modified and semi-late model stock classes respectively.

In the 30-lap late model feature, Holloway joined the roll-over club when his racer lost a wheel in the west turn and flipped two times landing on its top. He was uninjured and said he would return to the track in two weeks with a brand new car. Max Lambert won the late model feature. Lambert also won the dash event and Bob Jonas, of LaPorte, won the modified race for the six fastest qualifiers.

Heat Winners. Other heat winners Monday night were Gerald Meyer, Servia; Bill Rose, Silver Lake; Earl Egolf, North Manchester; Don Adams, Columbia City; and Don Walker, Kokomo.

Saturday night Larry Moore, of North Manchester, and Les Bills, of Columbia City, were the winners of the stock and modified feature races, respectively. Dick Leiter, of Warsaw, and Paul Hazen, of Columbia City, copped the stock and modified dash events respectively.

Other heat winners Saturday night were Jim Bucher, Akron; Larry Bills, Columbia City; Larry Baker, Warsaw; Jim Elliott, Warsaw.

One-half hour of the races each evening were broadcast over Radio Stations WRSW AM-FM.

Saturday, June 5, 1965
Don Walker Cops Modified Feature Here

Threatening skies failed to keep a large crowd from enjoying a thrilling night of stock car races at the Warsaw Speedway Saturday night.

Roger Grossnickle, of North Manchester, was involved in the most spectacular accident of the evening when his semi-late model racer struck the wall, spun around and was hit in both the front and rear simultaneously by other cars. When the smoke and dust had lifted Grossnickle's racer had taken the appearance of an accordion, but due to the many safety features required in the cars, he was uninjured.

The fastest qualifiers were Don Adams, of Columbia City, in the semi-late model stocks and Les Bills, also of Columbia City, who roared around the quarter-mile oval for the fastest time in the modified class. Don Walker, of Kokomo, copped the modified feature with DeWayne Fox, of Warsaw, second and Bob Jonas, of LaPorte, third.

Stock Feature. Larry Powell, of Silver Lake, took the checkered flag of victory in the semi-late model stock feature. Dick Leiter, of Warsaw, finished second and Paul Bills, of Columbia City third place.

All the races were hotly contested throughout and many ended in near photo finishes. Other heat winners were Jim Boggs, Warsaw; Grossnickle; Bill Fortune, Kokomo; Doug Method, Warsaw; Walker; Adams; and Duane Fox, Warsaw.

One-half hour of the races were broadcast over Radio Stations WRSW AM-FM from 8:45 - 9:15p.m. by Milo Clase. The broadcast is sponsored by Gast Fuel and Service, of Warsaw; and four Sinclair dealers, Weirick's Sinclair, and Smith Tire Service, both of Warsaw; Penn and Strombeck, North Webster; and Tschupp's Service, Leesburg.

Saturday, June 12, 1965
Les Bills Sets New Mark at Local Speedway

A capacity crowd was on hand to see Les Bills, of Columbia City, set a new season record in the stock car qualifications at the Warsaw Speedway Saturday night.

Bills, who had previously held the fastest time of the season at 17.03 seconds, bettered his mark when he roared around the quarter mile dirt and clay oval in his modified stock car number 22 in a time of 16.88 seconds. Max Lambert, of North Manchester, in car number zero, turned in the best time in the semi-late model stock car class by touring the race course in 18.51 seconds.

In the late model stock feature, Luther Holloway, of Warsaw, crossed the finish line just inches ahead of Don Taylor, of Columbia City, in a near photo finish. Holloway had taken the lead only one lap previously.

Bill Fortune, of Kokomo, copped the modified feature in a hotly contested race as second place finisher, Bob Jonas, of LaPorte, ran bumper to bumper with the leader for the last half of the race.

A highlight of the racing was the return of Bob Grindle, of Warsaw. Grindle, a longtime favorite who has not raced at the speedway in four years, drove his new car number six to a third place finish in the modified dash event. A total of 60 cars qualified for competition.

The following is the summary of the racing activity listing the first three finishers in each race:

First Heat: Jim Ratliff, Don Drudge, Larry Oswalt.
Second Heat: Jerry Baker, Chuck Sainer, Don Taylor.
Third Heat: Earl Egolf, Les Bills, Bob Jonas.
Fourth Heat: Bob Johnson, Bud Grossnickle, Luther Holloway.
Fifth Heat: John Davis, Paul Hazen, Don Walker.
Six Fastest (Stock): Doug Method, Dick Leiter, Don Adams.
Six Fastest (Modified): Jene Simons, Don Walker, Bob Grindle.
Stock Feature: Luther Holloway, Don Taylor, Max Lambert.
Modified Feature: Bill Fortune, Bob Jonas, Paul Hazen.

Saturday, June 19, 1965
Elliott Wins Dash, Feature in Racing Here

Jimmie Elliott, of Warsaw, captured both the dash and feature events for super modified cars in racing at the Warsaw Speedway Saturday night.

Elliott drove a car owned by the Egner brothers, of Columbia City, while his own racer is in the process of being overhauled. A total of 69 cars qualified for the racing activity.

The following is the summary of first three finishers in each race:

First Heat: Doug Method, William Powell, David Carpenter.
Second Heat: Don Drudge, Larry Powell, Gerald Meyer.
Third Heat: Bill Fortune, Duane Fox, Kenneth Bowser.
Fourth Heat: Roger Grossnickle, Dick Leiter, Bud Grossnickle.
Fifth Heat: John Davis, Larry Bills, Jene Simons.
Six Fastest (Late Model Stocks): Paul Bills, Larry Montel, Dick Leiter.
Six Fastest (Modified): Jimmie Elliott, Paul Hazen, Don Walker.
Stock Feature: Larry Powell, Dick Leiter, Larry Baker.
Modified Feature: Jimmie Elliott, Bill Fortune, Duane Fox.

Saturday, June 26, 1965
Les Bills Cops Feature Race at Local Speedway

Les Bills, of Columbia City, copped the modified feature in an exciting night of stock car racing at the Warsaw Speedway Saturday night.

Next Saturday a 30-car demolition derby has been scheduled during the regular night of racing. A special racing card is on tap for next Monday night, July 5, with a gigantic fireworks display to follow.

The results of Saturday's races are as follows:

First Heat: Charles Masterson, Paul Cox, Junior Stutzman.
Second Heat: Luther Holloway, Al Taylor, Don Drudge.
Third Heat: Jim Elliott, Don Walker, Bob Ruch.
Fourth Heat: Roger Rowland, Dick Leiter, Earl Egolf.

Fifth Heat: Duane Fox, Larry Bills, Bill Fortune.
Dash (Stock): Glen Owens, Ed Stine, Dick Leiter.
Dash (Modified): John Davis, Paul Hazen, Art Smith.
Stock Feature: Max Lambert, Ed Stine, Jim Bucher.
Modified Feature: Les Bills, Duane Fox, Bob Jonas.

Saturday, July 2 & Monday, July 4, 1965
Elliott, Bills Cop Feature At Local Speedway

Les Bills, Columbia City

A total of 155 cars qualified for a combined purse of $5,300 in a gigantic doubleheader racing card at the Warsaw Speedway over the holiday weekend.

Standing room only crowds both nights saw some of the most thrilling action at the speedway this season. The activities were highlighted by a tremendous fireworks display Monday sponsored by the Hoosier Hot Rods Assn. and the County Fair Assn.

Last night Chuck Saner, of Akron, and Doug Method, of Warsaw, were treated at the Murphy Medical Center for injuries in separate crashes at the speedway. Saner suffered bruises and cuts on his right arm when his racer lost a wheel and flipped end over end. Method was shook up and dazed when his late model stock car rammed the fence in the southeast turn.

Demolition Derby. Tom Patterson, of Bremen, was the winner of a 20-car demolition derby Saturday night while Jerry Egolf, of North Manchester, and Les Bills, of Columbia City, were the winners of the stock and modified features respectively. Monday night Dick Leiter, of Warsaw, won the stock feature and Jimmie Elliott, also of Warsaw, won the modified feature.

Racing fans Saturday contributed more than $700 to the widow and family of race car owner Tom Hendrickson, of Columbia City, who died of a heart attack at the speedway one week ago.

The summary of the races each evening are as follows:

Saturday Summary:

First Heat: Larry Montel, Don Taylor, Bob Johnson.
Second Heat: Doug Method, Jerry Baker, Jerry Benson.
Third Heat: Earl Egolf, Bill Fortune, Bill Rush.
Fourth Heat: Jerry Egolf, Roger Rowland, Don Adams.
Fifth Heat: Bob Jonas, Paul Hazen, Les Bills.
Dash (Stock): Ed Stine, Jerry Egolf, Bud Grossnickle.
Dash (Modified): Bob Jonas, Les Bills, Paul Hazen.
Stock Feature: Jerry Egolf, Max Lambert, Don Adams.
Modified Feature: Les Bills, Don Walker, Jim Elliott.

Monday Summary:

First Heat: Don Drudge, Jim Balliff, Jerry Benson.
Second Heat: Doug Method, Jim Bucher, Dick Menzie.
Third Heat: Art Smith, Bob Grindle, John Vogely.
Fourth Heat: Don Taylor, Bob Johnson, Don Adams.
Fifth Heat: Jim Elliott, Les Bills, Bob Jonas.
Dash (Stock): Don Adams, Bud Grossnickle, Roger Grossnickle.
Dash (Modified): Jim Elliott, Les Bills, Jack Hickman.
Stock Feature: Dick Leiter, Roger Grossnickle, Max Lambert.
Modified Feature: Jim Elliott, Don Walker, John Davis.

Saturday, July 9, 1965
Elliott, Bills Set New Record On Local Track

Two drivers shattered the track record in qualification runs at the Warsaw Speedway Saturday night. Jim Elliott, of Warsaw, broke the old mark of 16.80 held by Les Bills, of Columbia City. Bills then met the challenge and roared back to the new time of 16.69 set just seconds earlier by Elliott. A total of 65 cars qualified for the racing activity.

In the modified feature Bills hooked the fence in the main stretch and his car rolled over several times. He was uninjured but his racer was heavily damaged.

Dick Leiter, of Warsaw, captured the stock feature while Bob Jonas, of LaPorte, was the victor in the modified feature event. One-half hour of the races were broadcast over WRSW AM-FM from 8:45 to 9:15 p.m.

The summary of the races follows:

First Heat—Jim Meade, 1st; Bill Rose, 2nd; Junior Stutzman, 3rd.
Second Heat—Les Sroufe, 1st; Paul Bills, 2nd; Charles Prater, 3rd.
Third Heat—Bob Jonas, 1st; Jene Simon, 2nd; Earl Egolf, 3rd.
Fourth Heat—Max Lambert, 1st; Bob Johnson, 2nd; Jim Bucher, 3rd.
Fifth Heat—Paul Grim, 1st; Duane Fox, 2nd; Don Walker, 3rd.
Dash (Stock)—Bud Grossnickle, 1st; Dick Leiter, 2nd; Jerry Baker, 3rd.
Dash (Modified)—Duane Fox, 1st; Paul Grim, 2nd; Paul Hazen, 3rd.
Stock Feature—Dick Leiter, 1st; Don Adams, 2nd; Max Lambert, 3rd.
Modified Feature—Bob Jonas, 1st; John Davis, 2nd; Paul Hazen, 3rd.

Saturday, July 16, 1965
Elliott Cops Championship Feature Here

Jim Elliott, of Warsaw, drove his car number 74 to victory in the 50-lap mid-season super modified championship race held at the Warsaw Speedway Saturday night. Next week a 50-lap mid-season championship feature will be staged for semi late model stock cars.

Fastest qualifiers Saturday were Les Bills, of Columbia City, in modified and Roger Rowland, of Burket, in the late model class as 68 cars entered competition under threatening skies.

The summary of the racing activity is as follows:

First Heat—Don Carpenter, 1st; Jerry Meyer, 2nd; Howard Troup, 3rd.

Second Heat—Don Drudge, 1st; Larry Montel, 2nd; Jim Ratliff, 3rd.
Third Heat—Fred Boggs, 1st; Bill Fortune, 2nd; Jack Hickman, 3rd.
Fourth Heat—Paul Bills, 1st; Roger Grossnickle, 2nd; Glen Owens, 3rd.
Fifth Heat—Paul Hazen, 1st; Bob Jonas, 2nd; Jim Elliott, 3rd.
Dash (Stock)—Max Lambert, 1st; Dick Leiter, 2nd; Roger Rowland, 3rd.
Dash (Modified)—Don Walker, 1st; Bob Jonas, 2nd; Duane Fox, 3rd.
Stock Feature—Dick Leiter, 1st; Luther Holloway, 2nd; Bud Grossnickle, 3rd.
Modified Feature—Jim Elliott, 1st; Don Walker, 2nd; Paul Hazen, 3rd.

Saturday, July 23, 1965
Holloway, Smith Win Events At Local Speedway

Warsaw race drivers Luther Holloway and Art Smith copped the stock and modified feature races respectively in a wreck-filled night of racing at the Warsaw Speedway Saturday.

Although accidents were frequent the only injury to occur was to Larry Powell, of Silver Lake, who was released after treatment at the Murphy Medical Center for a whiplash injury to the neck. His car crashed into the wall.

In the semi-late model event 20 cars started in the field but only nine finished. Les Sroufe, of Huntington, was the winner of the six fastest stock car event and Paul Hazen, of Columbia City, won the modified dash event.

Stock heat winners included Bill Rose and Jerry Baker, of Warsaw, and Jerry Max Lambert, of North Manchester, with the modified heat events going to Art Smith, Warsaw, and Don Walker, of Kokomo. One-half hour of the action was aired over Radio Station WRSW AM-FM by Sportscaster Milo Clase.

Saturday, July 30, 1965
Double Feature Program Set At Local Speedway

A total of 65 cars qualified for activity at the Warsaw Speedway Saturday night that was shortened to four completed races because of rain.

Officials announced that a double feature program will be held this Saturday night to compensate for the rain-out.

Ellis Shepherd, of Mentone, joined the roll-over club in the time trials when his late-model stock car struck the fence and flipped over three times.

The finishers for the four events were as follows:
First Heat—Larry Oswalt, 1st; Bob Johnson, 2nd; Paul Cox, 3rd.
Six Fastest (Stock)—Les Sroufe, 1st; Luther Holloway, 2nd; Roger Rowland, 3rd.
Six Fastest (Modified)—Don Walker, 1st; Paul Grim, 2nd; Jim Elliott, 3rd.
Second Heat—Roger Grossnickle, 1st; Larry Montel, 2nd; Richard Menzie, 3rd.

Saturday, August 7, 1965
Art Smith Cops 2 Feature Races At Local Track

A capacity crowd was treated to an exciting night of racing on the final night of the Kosciusko County Fair Saturday night as Art Smith, of Warsaw, captured both modified feature races.

Two features were staged in both the modified and semi-late model stock classes to compensate for the rain out one week ago. The stock features were won by Roger Grossnickle, of North Manchester, and Luther Holloway of Warsaw.

Tom Egolf, of North Manchester, was treated at the Murphy Medical Center for a whiplash injury to his neck suffered in a wreck and starter Walt Yoder, of Syracuse, sustained a minor knee injury when he was struck by a wheel that had come loose from one of the race cars. Ed Stine, of Etna Green, escaped injury when his semi-late model racer overturned on the southwest turn during the fourth heat race.

It was announced that a demolition race will be held next Saturday night in which about 40 cars are expected to enter.

The summary of the first three finishers in each race is as follows:

Stock Feature—Roger Grossnickle, 1st; Bob Staley, 2nd; Luther Holloway, 3rd.
Modified Feature—Art Smith, 1st; Bob Jonas, 2nd; Paul Hazen, 3rd.
First Heat—Jim Ratliff, 1st; Bob Johnson, 2nd; Jack Green, 3rd.
Six Fastest (Stock)—Don Taylor, 1st; Doug Method, 2nd; Larry Powell, 3rd.
Six Fastest (Modified)—Larry Bills, 1st; Jim Boggs, 2nd; Paul Hazen, 3rd.
Second Heat—Al Taylor, 1st; Don Adams, 2nd; Larry Montel, 3rd.
Third Heat—Bill Ruch, 1st; John Davis, 2nd; Larry Bills, 3rd.
Fourth Heat—Paul Bills, 1st; Jerry Baker, 2nd; Luther Holloway, 3rd.
Fifth Heat—Jene Simon, 1st; Bob Jonas, 2nd; Larry Bills, 3rd.
Stock Feature—Luther Holloway, 1st; Jerry Meyer, 2nd; Roger Grossnickle, 3rd.
Modified Feature—Art Smith, 1st; Bob Jonas, 2nd; Paul Hazen, 3rd.

Saturday, August 14, 1965
Art Smith Wins 4th Straight Feature Here

Art Smith, of Warsaw, captured his fourth modified feature race in a row in action at the Warsaw Speedway Saturday night that was highlighted by a gigantic 34-car demolition derby. Smith was awarded the Buchanan Trophy for winning three consecutive features before he added his fourth to the string of victories.

A total of 70 cars qualified for the activity and a capacity crowd was kept standing during the ever popular demolition derby. When the dust had cleared Jerry Smith, of Columbia City, was given the checkered flag in the event and Larry Baker, of Warsaw, placed second.

Paul Bills, of Columbia City, copped the stock feature. The first three finishers in each race are as follows:

Race Summary:

First Heat—Jim Bucher, 1st; Jerry Meyers, 2nd; Bob Barnett, 3rd.
Six Fastest (Stock)—Jerry Baker, 1st; Dick Leiter, 2nd; Doug Method, 3rd.
Six Fastest (Modified)—Paul Hazen, 1st; Jim Elliott, 2nd; Larry Bills, 3rd.
Second Heat—Don Adams, 1st; Bob Staley, 2nd; Bill Rose, 3rd.
Third Heat—Kenny Bowser, 1st; Duane Fox, 2nd; Sam Davis, 3rd.
Fourth Heat—Larry Heisler, 1st; Paul Bills, 2nd; Larry Baker, 3rd.
Fifth Heat—Jim Elliott, 1st; Paul Hazen, 2nd; Larry Bills, 3rd.
Stock Feature—Paul Bills, 1st; Don Adams, 2nd; Larry Baker, 3rd.
Modified Feature—Art Smith, 1st; Jim Elliott, 2nd; Larry Bills, 3rd.

Saturday, August 21, 1965
Art Smith Wins 5th Straight Feature Race

Art Smith, of Warsaw, who was plagued with minor problems the first half of the season, had his car number 67 "purring like a kitten" and roared to his fifth straight feature win at the Warsaw Speedway Saturday night.

Smith, who was disqualified in one race for racing faster than his qualifying time and was sent to the back of the pack midway in the feature due to a spin, displayed a true form of sportsmanship and came charging back to take the 25 lap feature event.

A total of 76 cars qualified for the activity and included five newcomers from the Lima, O., area. The six lap dash event for modified cars was run in a rapid time of 1:27.10, with Don Walker, of Kokomo, the victor. The stock car was won by Larry Montel, of Columbia City.

It was announced that next week a season championship race for supermodified cars will be staged and trophies awarded. One-half of the races were broadcast over Radio Stations WRSW AM-FM from 8:45 to 9:15 p.m. by Milo Clase.

Race Summary:

First Heat—Jerry Myers, 1st; Jim Ratliff, 2nd; Jerry Benton, 3rd.
Six Fastest (Stock)—Les Sroufe, 1st; Don Adams, 2nd; Don Taylor, 3rd.
Six Fastest (Modified)—Don Walker, 1st; Jim Elliott, 2nd; Jim Boggs, 3rd.
Second Heat—Richard Menzie, 1st; Sunny Carpenter, 2nd; Dick Leiter, 3rd.
Third Heat—Bill Rush, 1st; Kenny Bowser, 2nd; Jene Simon, 3rd.
Fourth Heat—Roger Grossnickle, 1st; Ed Stine, 2nd; Jerry Baker, 3rd.
Fifth Heat—Les Bills, 1st; Paul Hazen, 2nd; Don Walker, 3rd.
Stock Feature—Larry Montel, 1st; Dick Leiter, 2nd; Paul Bills, 3rd.
Modified Feature—Art Smith, 1st; Jim Elliott, 2nd; Paul Hazen, 3rd.

Saturday, August 28, 1965
Bob Jonas Wins Trophy Race Here

Bob Jonas, of LaPorte, copped the big 50-lap modified championship feature race at the Warsaw Speedway in a thrill-packed racing card Saturday night.

In the stock feature a car driven by Don Adams, of Columbia City, rolled over three times but due to protective equipment in the racer, he escaped injury. Bill Parker, of Warsaw, was given emergency treatment at the track when his stock car struck the pit gate exit and acid from the battery spilled on him. Quick treatment prevented serious burns.

A total of 64 cars qualified for the activity before a crowd that was small because of the chilly weather. Next week, a 40-lap semi-late model stock championship feature will be the highlighted event.

Race Summary:

First Heat- Ellis Shepherd, 1st; Fred Hathaway, 2nd; Jim Ratliff, 3rd.
Six Fastest (Stock)—Max Lambert, 1st; Les Sroufe, 2nd; Don Drudge, 3rd.
Six Fastest (Modified)—John Davis, 1st; Duane Fox, 2nd; Les Bills, 3rd.
Second Heat—Larry Oswalt, 1st; Jim Bucher, 2nd; Larry Montel, 3rd.
Third Heat—Jene Simon, 1st; Bill Rush, 2nd; Kenny Bowser, 3rd.
Fourth Heat—Don Taylor, 1st; Junior Stutzman, 2nd; Don Adams, 3rd.
Fifth Heat—Paul Hazen, 1st; Jim Boggs, 2nd; Les Bills, 3rd.
Stock Feature—Roger Rowland, 1st; Dick Leiter, 2nd; Junior Stutzman, 3rd.
Modified Feature—Bob Jonas, 1st; Duane Fox, 2nd; Paul Hazen, 3rd.

Saturday, September 4, 1965—Rainout

Saturday, September 11, 1965
Luther Holloway Wins Trophy Race

Luther Holloway, of Warsaw, captured the semi-late model stock championship feature races in a thrilling card at the Warsaw Speedway Saturday night.

A moderate but loyal crowd saw plenty of thrills on a very fast track which included a new record of 16.49 by Les Bills, of Columbia City, set in the qualifications. Bills previously shared the fastest time of 16.69 with Jimmie Elliott, of Warsaw. The new time means that the race car turned in an average speed of 57.02 miles per hour around the quarter mile dirt and clay oval.

Ted Hare, of Columbia City, was the winner of the demolition derby which is always a thrilling event for race fans.

It was announced that weather permitting races will be held at the track again next Saturday night.

One-half hour of the races were broadcast over Radio Stations WRSW AM-FM by Milo Clase and sponsored by Gast Fuel and Service of Warsaw, and four cooperating Sinclair Dealers: Penn and Strombeck, of North Webster; Tschupp's Service, Leesburg; Smith Tire Service, Warsaw; and Hensley Sinclair, Warsaw.

Race Summary:

Dash (Stock)—Max Lambert, 1st; Ed Stine, 2nd; Luther Holloway, 3rd.
Dash (Modified)—Art Smith, 1st; Duane Fox, 2nd; Paul Hazen, 3rd.
First Heat—Jim Ratliff, 1st; Jim Barnett, 2nd; Jerry Egolf, 3rd.
Second Heat—Larry Bills, 1st; Earl Egolf, 2nd; Bob Jonas, 3rd.

Third Heat—Doug Method, 1st; Roger Grossnickle, 2nd; Jim Bucher, 3rd.
Fourth Heat—Art Smith, 1st; Les Bills, 2nd; John Davis, 3rd.
Stock Feature—Luther Holloway, 1st; Roger Grossnickle, 2nd; Max Lambert, 3rd; Doug Method, 4th; Don Taylor, 5th.
Modified Feature—Bob Jonas, 1st; Art Smith, 2nd; Paul Hazen, 3rd.

Saturday, September 18, 1965
Art Smith Wins Closing Night Feature Here

Fans were treated to a thrilling night of racing at the Warsaw Speedway Saturday to close one of the most successful seasons ever at the track.

A total of 46 cars qualified for the activity as Art Smith of Warsaw captured the final night 25-lap modified feature race, but not before a hotly contested battle from Bob Jonas, of LaPorte, who finished second. Paul Bills, of Columbia City, won the 20 lap late model stock feature event.

One-half hour of the races were broadcast over Radio Stations WRSW AM from 8:45 to 9:15 p.m. The summary of the top finishers in each race follows:

Race Summary:

Dash (Stock)—Ed Stine, 1st; Doug Method, 2nd; Bob Jonas, 3rd.
Dash (Modified)—Paul Hazen, 1st; Jim Boggs, 2nd; Jim Elliott, 3rd.
First Heat—Richard Menzie, 1st; Roger Richards, 2nd; Wayne Miller, 3rd.
Second Heat—Art Smith, 1st; John Vogely, 2nd; Bob Jonas, 3rd.
Third Heat—Orville Taylor, 1st; Jr. Stutzman, 2nd; Max Lambert, 3rd.
Fourth Heat—Les Bills, 1st; Paul Hazen, 2nd; Jim Boggs, 3rd.
Stock Feature—Paul Bills, 1st; Dick Leiter, 2nd; Max Lambert, 3rd; Jr. Stutzman, 4th; Ed Stine, 5th.
Modified Feature—Art Smith, 1st; Bob Jonas, 2nd; Jim Boggs, 3rd; John Vogely, 4th; Jim Elliott, 5th.

Tuesday, November 2, 1965
Point Winners Honored At Racing Banquet

(Photo from the Whitley County Observer, Nov. 2, 1965, page. 15.) Array of Trophies – This shining array of trophies being carefully watched over by Officers Max Cox and Dick Engle were the awards given by the Hoosier Hot Rod Racing Association Saturday night at their annual banquet in the

American Legion Hall. Paul Hazen, of Columbia City, was top point winner and took home the biggest trophy. Over 215 guests were present for the banquet.

More than 20 trophies were awarded to the top point winners at the Hoosier Hot Rod Racing Assn. banquet held the past weekend at Columbia City. Paul Hazen, of Columbia City, was the point standing winner in the modified competition and Dick Leiter and Luther Holloway, both of Warsaw, shared top honors in the semi-late model stock class.

Milo Clase, of Warsaw, acted as the master-of-ceremonies for the evening and introduced drivers, car owners and mechanics. The new board of directors installed at the meeting included Ellis Hartman, Warsaw; Otto Boschett, Columbia City; Don Coleman, Warsaw; Duke Long, Columbia City; Bill Hare, Columbia City; and Dick May, Warsaw, was named as an alternate board member.

GIBSON RE-ELECTED. C. E. (Hoot) Gibson, of Columbia City, was re-elected president of the group and Del Ballard, Columbia City, was re-named vice-president.

At a recent meeting, plans were formulated for the 1966 racing season. There were very few changes in the past policy with the exception that next year the semi-late model stock class will include models from 1955 through 1961.

It was reported at the meeting that 21 races were held this past summer with the largest purse nearly $3,000 for one night and more than $5,000 was awarded drivers during the Fourth of July weekend.

1966

Saturday, May 21, 1966
Bills Capture Feature Races At Local Track

After a two-week weather delay the racing season at the Warsaw Speedway got underway in convincing style Saturday night as several spectacular wrecks highlighted action.

A total of 60 cars qualified during the evening that saw Les Bills, of Columbia City win the modified feature and Paul Bills, of Columbia City, capture the checkered flag in the semi-late model stock feature.

Jim Marvel, of Warsaw, was treated at the Murphy Medical Center for minor injuries following a head-on-crash in which one of the racers caught fire. The impact of another collision was so severe that the rear wheels of a car were completely torn loose.

It was announced that a full racing card will be held on Monday, May 30 in addition to the regular program next Saturday night.

The first three finishers in each race follow:

Six Fastest-(Stock)—Jerry Baker, 1st; Paul Bills, 2nd; Bob Tucker, 3rd.
Six Fastest-(Modified)—Les Bills, 1st; Jim Boggs, 2nd; Bob Jonas, 3rd.
First Heat—Larry Baker, 1st; Sam Taylor, 2nd; Don Drudge, 3rd.
Second Heat—Charles Wiles, 1st; Kenny Bowser, 2nd; Ralph Mumaw, 3rd.

Third Heat—Paul Bills, 1st; Bob Tucker, 2nd; Jr. Stutzman, 3rd.
Fourth Heat—Paul Joyce, 1st; Jim Boggs, 2nd; Doug Method, 3rd.
Consolation—Larry Shriver, 1st; Bob Cozzi, 2nd; Larry Smeltzer, 3rd.
Stock Feature—Paul Bills, 1st; Jim Bucher, 2nd; Bob Maggart, 3rd.
Modified Feature—Les Bills, 1st; Paul Joyce, 2nd; DeWayne Fox, 3rd.

Saturday, May 28 & Monday, May 30, 1966
Joyce, Egolf Cop Modified Feature Races

Racing fans were greeted by two chilly nights at Warsaw Speedway Saturday and again Monday as speed and thrills highlighted the racing card.

During the Saturday night action Mike Dickson, of Etna Green, joined the roll-over club but escaped injury. Several other wrecks occurred during the two evenings but there were no injuries.

Paul Joyce, of Kokomo, and Jerry Egolf, of North Manchester, took the modified and stock features Saturday and Earl Egolf, of North Manchester, and Sunny Carpenter, of Etna Green, caught the checkered flags first in the modified and stock features Monday.

One-half hour of the races were broadcast both nights by Milo Clase over WRSW AM-FM and sponsored by Sumpter Sinclair, Warsaw; Smith Tire Service, Warsaw; Wagoner Sinclair, North Webster; and Hensley Sinclair, Warsaw. The complete summaries of the races follow:

Saturday Summary
Six Fastest Stock—Jerry Baker, 1st; Bob Grindle, 2nd; Paul Bills, 3rd.
Six Fastest Modified—Paul Hazen, 1st; Bob Jonas, 2nd; Les Bills, 3rd.
First Heat—Jr. Stutzman, 1st; Jerry Bucher, 2nd; Dick Smith, 3rd.
Second Heat—Earl Egolf, 1st; Kenny Bowser, 2nd; Jack Vogely, 3rd.
Third Heat—Jerry Egolf, 1st; Bob Tucker, 2nd; Paul Bills, 3rd.
Fourth Heat—John Davis, 1st; Larry Bills, 2nd; Paul Hazen, 3rd.
Consolation—Gerald Mayer, 1st; Larry Montel, 2nd; Chuck Saner, 3rd.
Stock Feature—Jerry Egolf, 1st; Bob Grindle, 2nd; Jerry Baker, 3rd.
Modified Feature—Paul Joyce, 1st; Bob Jonas, 2nd; Paul Hazen, 3rd.

Monday Summary
Six Fastest Stock—Paul Bills, 1st; Bob Grindle, 2nd; Bob Tucker, 3rd.
Six Fastest Modified—John Davis, 1st; Les Bills, 2nd; Paul Hazen, 3rd.
First Heat—Jr. Stutzman, 1st; Ellis Shepherd, 2nd; Larry Montel, 3rd.
Second Heat—Earl Egolf, 1st; Denny Johnson, 2nd; Dick Tyson, 3rd.
Third Heat—Bud Grossnickle, 1st; Paul Bills, 2nd; Jerry Baker, 3rd.
Fourth Heat—John Davis, 1st; Ed Stine, 2nd; Jim Boggs, 3rd.
Consolation—Garry Baker, 1st; Dick Smith, 2nd; Larry Oswalt, 3rd.
Stock Feature—Sunny Carpenter, 1st; Larry Montel, 2nd; Bob Tucker, 3rd.
Modified Feature—Earl Egolf, 1st; Paul Joyce, 2nd; Bob Jonas, 3rd.

Saturday, June 4, 1966
Jim Boggs Cops Feature Race

Fierce competition with some races in doubt until the checkered flag dropped kept fans on the edge of their seats in a thrill packed night of racing at the Warsaw Speedway Saturday.

A large crowd on hand was standing for the finish of the modified feature as Jim Boggs, of Warsaw, took the outside of the track to pass other competitors and receive the checkered flag in a spine tingling finish. Numerous other races were not decided until the final lap. Junior Stutzman, of Silver Lake, took honors in the stock feature.

Several wrecks occurred during the evening but no drivers were injured. It was reported that several new modified cars are expected to be on hand this week. The summary of the first three finishers of each race follow:

Six Fastest (Stock)—Bob Grindle, 1st; Luther Holloway, 2nd; Jerry Baker, 3rd.
Six Fastest (Modified)—Jim Boggs, 1st; Larry Bills, 2nd; John Vogely, 3rd.
First Heat—Junior Stutzman, 1st; Bud Grossnickle, 2nd; Ellis Shepherd, 3rd.
Second Heat—Paul Hazen, 1st; Paul Joyce, 2nd; Kenny Bowser, 3rd.
Third Heat—Dick Leiter, 1st; Bob Grindle, 2nd; Jerry Baker, 3rd.
Fourth Heat—Duane Fox, 1st; Jim Boggs, 2nd; Earl Egolf, 3rd.
Consolation—Gary Baker, 1st; Dick Smith, 2nd; Mark Anderson, 3rd.
Stock Feature—Junior Stutzman, 1st; Jim Bucher, 2nd; Luther Holloway, 3rd.
Modified Feature—Jim Boggs, 1st; Les Bills, 2nd; Ed Stine, 3rd.

Saturday, June 11, 1966
No Times Union microfiche history

Saturday, June 18, 1966
Les Bills Cops 3 Races Here

It is rare that the fastest qualifier wins every race that he enters but Les Bills, of Columbia City, "turned the trick" in action at the Warsaw Speedway Saturday night.

Bills qualified at 16.32 or just .02 slower than the track record as speed was the key word during the evening. The driver with the fastest time starts each race at the "back of the pack" but Bills came through to win the dash event, the fourth heat race and the modified feature.

Each event was hotly contested and many were not decided until the final lap as 65 cars, including racers, qualified for action. The fast driver in the stock class was Jim Bucher, of Akron. Jerry Baker, of Warsaw, gained the checkered flag in the stock feature. The summary of the first three place finishers in each race follows:

Six Fastest (Stock)—Bob Grindle, 1st; Orville Taylor, 2nd; Jim Bucher, 3rd.
Six Fastest (Modified)—Les Bills, 1st; Jim Boggs, 2nd; Paul Joyce, 3rd.
First Heat—Dick Leiter, 1st; Jerry Baker, 2nd; Gary Baker, 3rd.
Second Heat—Paul Grim, 1st; Danny Johnson, 2nd; Charlie Sarver, 3rd.
Third Heat—Junior Stutzman, 1st; Paul Bills, 2nd; Don Drudge, 3rd.
Fourth Heat—Les Bills, 1st; Larry Bills, 2nd; Paul Joyce, 3rd.
Consolation—Dick Smith, 1st; Ellis Shepherd, 2nd; Sunny Carpenter, 3rd.
Stock Feature—Jerry Baker, 1st; Bob Grindle, 2nd; Junior Stutzman, 3rd.

Modified Feature—Les Bills, 1st; Ed Stine, 2nd; Paul Joyce, 3rd.

Saturday, June 25, 1966
Bob Jonas Cops Modified Race At Local Track

Drivers were eager at the Warsaw Speedway Saturday night and as a result numerous pileups occurred and the heavy wooden retaining fence was torn out by the rod but there were no injuries.

Les Bills, of Columbia City, led a field of 68 entries with the fastest qualifying time in the modified class and Bud Grossnickle, of North Manchester, turned in the fastest lap in the stock class. The big modified winner was Ed Stine, of Etna Green, with two firsts in heat races while Bob Jonas, of LaPorte, copped the modified feature. Dick Leiter, of Warsaw, captured the consolation and feature in the stock class.

Summary (Many were unreadable):
Six Fastest (Stock) – Bob Grindle, 1st; Jerry Baker, 2nd; Jim Bucher, 3rd
Six Fastest (Modified) – Ed Stine, 1st; Les Bills, 2nd; DeWayne Fox, 3rd
Stock Feature – Dick Leiter, 1st; Luther Holloway, 2nd; Ellis Shepherd, 3rd
Modified Feature – Bob Jonas, 1st; Paul Hazen, 2nd; Earl Egolf, 3rd

Saturday, July 2, 1966
Fireworks Slated At Speedway Here

Two nights of racing highlighted by a gigantic fireworks display on Monday will be on tap for patrons of the Warsaw Speedway over the Fourth of July weekend, it was announced today.

The regular racing card will be held Saturday night, then Monday a special night of stock car racing will be topped by a colorful fireworks display. Officials said the display will start shortly after dark to allow parents to get children home early. They stated that the fireworks will be more colorful and will be of a greater variety than last year. The fireworks program is expected to last from 30 to 45 minutes.

Saturday, July 2 & Monday, July 4, 1966
Jim Bucher Top Race Winner Here In Holiday Card

A gigantic and colorful fireworks display at the Warsaw Speedway last night capped a big two-night racing card which saw drivers "gunning" for a purse of nearly $5,000.

The fireworks display was said to be the most varied and well organized at the fairgrounds in a number of years. One scene depicted a wrecker actually pushing a replica of a race car complete with number and all.

The big winner during the Saturday and Monday activity in the stock class was hard-charging Jim Bucher, of Silver Lake, who drove his car number 29 to victory in a heat race and the feature each night. The modified purse was divided between Paul Joyce, of Kokomo, who won the feature Saturday while Ed Stine, of Etna Green, copped the event Monday. Joyce also took one other heat race while Bob Jonas, of LaPorte, caught the checkered flag twice in heat events during the two nights.

Large crowds both evenings were treated to the usual thrills and spills with cars going through fences and colliding but no driver was injured. A heavy afternoon rain Monday delayed racing for more than an hour before the track was packed sufficiently to start qualifications. The summary of the first three place winners in each event follows:

Saturday Summary

Six Fastest (Stock)—Bud Grossnickle, 1st; Bob Grindle, 2nd; Junior Stutzman, 3rd.
Six Fastest (Modified)—Jim Elliott, 1st; Larry Bills, 2nd; Bob Bernhard, 3rd.
First Heat—Dick Leiter, 1st; Vernon Krom, 2nd; Gary Baker, 3rd.
Second Heat—Bob Jonas, 1st; Sam Davis, 2nd; Earl Egolf, 3rd.
Third Heat—Jim Bucher, 1st; Luther Holloway, 2nd; Bud Grossnickle, 3rd.
Fourth Heat—John Davis, 1st; Paul Joyce, 2nd; Jim Boggs, 3rd.
Consolation—Bob Cozzi, 1st; Mark Anderson, 2nd; John Stull, 3rd.
Stock Feature—Jim Bucher, 1st; Luther Holloway, 2nd; Dick Leiter, 3rd.
Modified Feature—Paul Joyce, 1st; Jim Elliott, 2nd; Ed Stine, 3rd.

Monday Summary

Six Fastest (Stock)—Max Lambert, 1st; Don Adams, 2nd; Bob Tucker, 3rd.
Six Fastest (Modified)—Les Bills, 1st; Ed Stine, 2nd; Paul Hazen, 3rd.
First Heat—Bud Grossnickle, 1st; Paul Bills, 2nd; Dick Leiter, 3rd.
Second Heat—Bob Jonas, 1st; Charles Sarver, 2nd; Ray Mumaw, 3rd.
Third Heat—Jim Bucher, 1st; Max Lambert, 2nd; Bob Tucker, 3rd.
Fourth Heat—Paul Joyce, 1st; Sam Davis, 2nd; Ed Angle, 3rd.
Consolation—Garry Baker, 1st; Chuck Saner, 2nd; Ellis Shepherd, 3rd.
Stock Feature—Jim Bucher, 1st; Luther Holloway, 2nd; Max Lambert, 3rd.
Modified Feature—Ed Stine, 1st; Paul Hazen, 2nd; Les Bills, 3rd.

Saturday, July 9, 1966 - Rainout

Saturday, July 16, 1966
Mid-Season Race Slated At Local Track Saturday

A 50-lap mid-season championship race for the semi-late model stock racers is planned at the Warsaw Speedway next Saturday following action on the newly clayed oval this weekend.

The track was in excellent shape after several loads of new clay were spread on the surface to fill he large holes that had developed due to rains this season. Modified drivers will be shooting for a $200 purse that has been offered to the one breaking the track record of 16.32 which was set earlier this year by Les Bills, of Columbia City.

Les Bills won the Saturday night modified feature race although Warsaw's John Davis led 22 laps of the event. But due to a number of laps run under the yellow flag due to minor wrecks, Davis' racer ran out of gas and he failed to win the event. Junior Stutzman, of Silver Lake, captured the stock feature as 72 cars qualified for the evening of racing.

Race Summary

Six Fastest (Stock)—Bob Tucker, 1st; Dick Leiter, 2nd; Max Lambert, 3rd.
Six Fastest (Modified)—Sam Davis, 1st; Jim Boggs, 2nd; Ed Stine, 3rd.

First Heat—Don Drudge, 1st; Roger Grossnickle, 2nd; Larry Baker, 3rd.
Second Heat—Jene Simon, 1st; Earl Egolf, 2nd; Lamar Sechrist, 3rd.
Third Heat—Bob Tucker, 1st; Max Lambert, 2nd; Luther Holloway, 3rd.
Fourth Heat—Larry Bills, 1st; Bob Jonas, 2nd; John Davis, 3rd.
Consolation—Bob Cozzi-1st; Jim Barnett, 2nd; Jim Ratliff, 3rd.
Stock Feature- Junior Stutzman, 1st; Bob Tucker, 2nd; Dick Leiter, 3rd.
Modified Feature—Les Bills, 1st; Ed Angle, 2nd; Paul Joyce, 3rd.

Saturday, July 23, 1966
Crash At Local Speedway (Front Page)

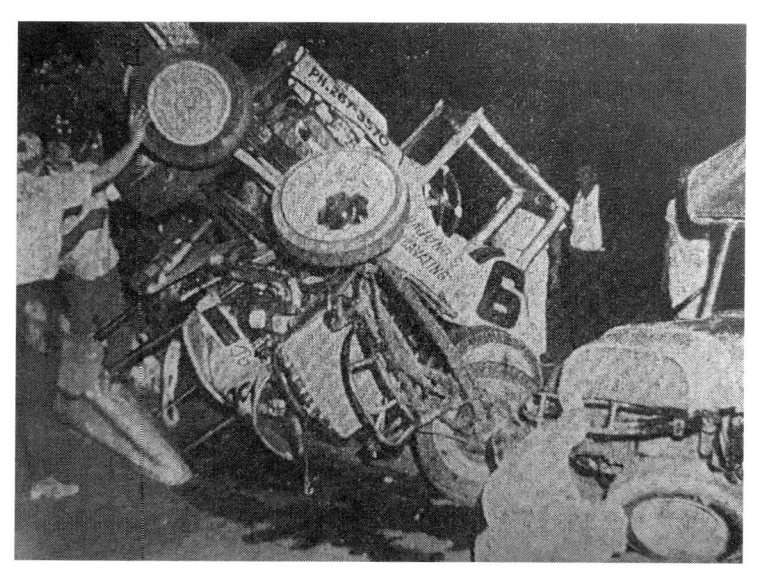

Workers attempt to untangle three race cars following a pileup at the Warsaw Speedway Saturday. However, due to seat belts and other safety devices, all drivers escaped unhurt. The car at the bottom is owned by Sam Davis, of Warsaw, and was being driven by Danny Johnson, of South Bend when the crash occurred. Davis left the track when his father, John W. (Ted) Davis, 2034 East Center St., suffered a fatal heart attack while watching the races. The racer on top was operated by Jim Boggs, of Warsaw, and the vehicle at right was driven by Larry Bills, of Columbia City. See complete story on Sports, Page 9—(Times-Union Photo by Hagg)

Saturday, July 23, 1966
Bucher Cops Mid-Season Stock Race

Jim Bucher, of Burket, captured the 50-lap mid-season championship late-model stock car feature race and set a new track record for stocks in a wild night of racing at the Warsaw Speedway Saturday night. Bucher led the field all the way in the feature after lowering the stock class track record to 17.25 in qualifications.

A series of wrecks and roll-overs prolonged the racing card until nearly 1 a.m. Sunday. Two drivers, Lawrence Hanson, of Wabash, and Frank Hall, of Pierceton, were taken to the Murphy Medical Center following crashes. Hanson was dismissed after treatment but Hall was admitted to the hospital for observation.

Racing fans were saddened by the sudden heart attack and the resulting death of John W. (Ted) Davis, manager of the concession stand and the father of John and Sam Davis, of Warsaw. Ironically, the boys were running one-two respectively in the modified feature when the father suffered his heart attack and the event was stopped while he was taken to the Murphy Medical Center.

When the race was restarted, Danny Johnson, driving Same Davis' car in his absence, was involved in a vicious three-car pileup, but all drivers escaped unhurt. Paul Hazen captured the modified feature.

Point Standings. Next week a mid-season championship race for the modified cars is planned. The current point standings are as follows: Jim Bucher, 1st; Les Bills, 2nd; Paul Joyce, 3rd; Ed Stine, 4th; Jim Boggs, 5th; Paul Hazen, 6th; Jerry Baker, 7th; Bob Grindle, 8th; Junior Stutzman, 9th; Larry Bills, 10th. Bucher has 70 points and only five points separate the first four drivers.

The racing summary follows listing the first three finishers in each race:
Dash (Stock)—Luther Holloway, 1st; Dick Leiter, 2nd; Bob Grindle, 3rd.
Dash (Modified)—John Davis, 1st; Les Bills, 2nd; Larry Bills, 3rd.
First Heat—Larry Baker, 1st; Richard Sheets, 2nd; Chuck Sainer, 3rd.
Second Heat—Hal Apple, 1st; Ed Angle, 2nd; Duane Fox, 3rd.
Third Heat—Paul Bills, 1st; Bud Grossnickle, 2nd; Max Lambert, 3rd.
Fourth Heat—Les Bills, 1st; Jean Simon, 2nd; John Davis, 3rd.
First Consolation—Jim Kuhn-1st; Orville Taylor, 2nd; Larry Hatfield, 3rd.
Second Consolation – Larry Montel, 1st; Don Taylor, 2nd; Vernell Krom, 3rd.
Modified Feature- Paul Hazen, 1st; Les Bills, 2nd; Sam Davis/Danny Johnson, 3rd.
Stock Feature—Jim Bucher, 1st; Paul Bills, 2nd; Luther Holloway, 3rd.

Wins Championship Race – Jim Bucher, of Burket, right, gets a trophy from starter, Walt Yoder, after winning the mid-season championship race for semi-late model stock cars at the Warsaw Speedway Saturday night. The mid-season race for modified cars will be held next Saturday. Bucher also currently leads the driver point standings for the season. (Times-Union, Photo by Hagg)

Saturday, July 30, 1966
Les Bills Cops 50-Lap Feature

Columbia City drivers Saturday dominated the top spots in the 50-lap mid-season championship race in a preview to a two-night card scheduled during the county fair this week at the Warsaw Speedway.

Les Bills took the lead at the start and never relinquished it in winning the feature. He was trailed by Larry Bills and Paul Hazen, in that order, all from Columbia City.

There were 70 cars that qualified for activity and numerous accidents occurred but no drivers were injured. Roger Rowland, of Burket, gained the checkered flag in the stock feature.

Races will be held at the track Wednesday and Saturday nights during the fair this week. The Wednesday activity will get underway with time trials starting at 6:30 p.m. All fans and race crews that will be parking around the track or in the pits are requested to use the west entrance to the fairgrounds as the east drive will be closed.

The summary of the first three finishers in the Saturday races follows:

Six Fastest (stock)—Junior Stutzman, 1st; Dick Leiter, 2nd; Jim Bucher, 3rd.
Six Fastest (Modified)—Ed Stine, 1st; Bob Jonas, 2nd; Les Bills, 3rd.
First Heat—Doug Method, 1st; Jerry Baker, 2nd; Bob Grindle, 3rd.
Second Heat—Jene Simon, 1st; Cap Arnold, 2nd; Bob Bernhard, 3rd.
Third Heat—Roger Rowland, 1st; Dick Leiter, 2nd; Luther Holloway, 3rd.
Fourth Heat—Ed Angle, 1st; Duane Fox, 2nd; Jim Boggs, 3rd.
First Consolation—Vernall Krom, 1st; Jim Barnett, 2nd; Paul Cox, 3rd.
Second Consolation—Bob Cozzi, 1st; Carl Sechrist, 2nd; Carl Hanson, 3rd.
Stock Feature—Roger Rowland, 1st; Dick Leiter, 2nd; Bud Grossnickle, 3rd.
Modified Feature—Les Bills, 1st; Larry Bills, 2nd; Paul Hazen, 3rd.

Wednesday, August 3, 1966
Angle Ties Local Race Track Mark

Ed Angle, of Flora, tied the track record at 16.32 then came back to take the modified feature race in activity at the county fair last night. Angle now shares the track record with Les Bills, of Columbia City, who set the mark earlier this year.

After a long absence, Hank Easley, of Logansport, returned to the local track and grabbed the checkered flag of victory in the first modified heat race. Jim Bucher, of Burket, collected top prize money in the stock feature.

Stock car racing will be held again Saturday night as usual. One-half hour of the races were broadcast over WRSW AM-FM by Milo Clase for Sinclair service stations in this area, Sumpter Sinclair, Warsaw; Waggoner Sinclair, North Webster; Smith Tire Service, Warsaw; and Hensley Sinclair, Warsaw.

Race Summary:

Stock Dash—Roger Rowland, 1st; Dick Leiter, 2nd; Jim Bucher, 3rd.
Modified Dash—Bob Jonas, 1st; Ed Angle, 2nd; Paul Hazen, 3rd.
First Heat—Larry Baker, 1st; Vernell Krom, 2nd; Jerry Baker, 3rd.
Second Heat—Hank Easley, 1st; Sam Davis, 2nd; Ray Mumaw, 3rd.
Third Heat—Junior Stutzman, 1st; Paul Bills, 2nd; Ed Stine, 3rd.
Fourth Heat—Paul Joyce, 1st; Paul Bills, 2nd; Ed Stine, 3rd.
Consolation—Don Parson, 1st; McNeill, 2nd; Mark Anderson, 3rd.
Stock Feature—Jim Bucher, 1st; Dick Leiter, 2nd; Luther Holloway, 3rd.
Modified Feature—Ed Angle, 1st; DeWayne Fox, 2nd; Paul Hazen. 3rd.

Saturday, August 6, 1966
Record Crowd At Fair Views Stock Car Races

The "Bills Boys" of Columbia City were very much in evidence Saturday night as a record

Kosciusko County Fair crowd jammed the Warsaw Speedway grandstand to watch an exciting program of stock car racing. Les Bills won the modified feature and Paul Bills got the checkered flag in the semi-late model feature.

Other event winners were Bob Tucker, Burket, six fastest semi-late dash event; Ed Angle, of Flora, six fastest modified; Carl Sechrist, Bourbon, semi-late model heat race; Bob Jonas, LaPorte, modified heat race; Paul Bills, semi-late model heat race; Jene Simon, Columbia City, modified heat race; Bob Grindle, Warsaw, semi-late model consolation; and Doug Method, Warsaw, second consolation event.

Luther Holloway and Dick Leiter finished second and third, respectively, behind Paul Bills in the semi-late model feature, while Ed Angle and Larry Bills were next behind Les Bills in the modified feature. Five cars were involved in one accident but there were no injuries. County Fair officials commented it was a record-breaking crowd at the races during a fair week.

Saturday, August 13, 1966
Rain Halts Feature At Local Oval

The feature was called off at the 16th lap because of rain in action at the Warsaw Speedway Saturday night. John Davis, of Warsaw, was leading when it was halted. A small crowd watched the abbreviated event. The feature will be the first event on the program next Saturday night.

It was announced there will be another exciting demolition derby next Saturday with it being one of the biggest ever held at the local oval. Paul Grim, of Warren, has returned to the track with a new modified and several other new cars will be racing here soon.

Saturday, August 20, 1966
50-Lap Feature Slated At Local Track Saturday

Don Hartley & Paul Grim

A big 50-lap championship race for late model stock cars is slated at the Warsaw Speedway next Saturday night following a thrill-packed card this weekend which was highlighted by a 20-car demolition derby.

Jim Barnett, of Columbia City, emerged as the winner of the demolition race. In an event carried over from last week, John Davis, of Warsaw, captured the uncompleted modified feature race and came back to take the dash event. In the second modified feature Paul Hazen, of Columbia City, gained the checkered flag.

During the feature a racer driven by Dick Tyson, of Kokomo, went into the fence in the east turn and Tyson was taken to the Murphy Medical Center and admitted for a possible back injury. Chuck Saner, of Akron, was the victor in the stock feature.

Race Summary:

Modified Feature—John Davis, 1st; Paul Hazen, 2nd; Larry Bills, 3rd.
Stock Dash—Junior Stutzman, 1st; Roger Rowland, 2nd; Max Lambert, 3rd.
Modified Dash—John Davis, 1st; Jim Elliott, 2nd; Ed Stine, 3rd.
First Heat—Larry Baker, 1st; Luther Holloway, 2nd; Jerry Baker, 3rd.
Second Heat—Lamar Sechrist, 1st; Paul Grim, 2nd; Jim Sutherland, 3rd.
Third Heat—Roger Rowland, 1st; Paul Bills, 2nd; Junior Stutzman, 3rd.
Fourth Heat—Jim Elliott; DeWayne Fox, 2nd; Art Smith, 3rd.
Consolation—Gary Baker, 1st; Doug Method, 2nd; Carl Sechrist, 3rd.
Stock Feature—Chuck Saner, 1st; Roger Rowland, 2nd; Junior Stutzman, 3rd.
Modified Feature—Paul Hazen, 1st; DeWayne Fox, 2nd; Art Smith, 3rd.

Saturday, August 27, 1966
Paul Bills Cops 50-Lap Feature In Photo-Finish

A photo-finish in the season championship 50-lap stock feature highlighted a thrill-packed racing card at the Warsaw Speedway Saturday night which included plenty of thrills and spills.

Paul Bills, of Columbia City, gained the checkered flag in the championship feature but his margin of victory was no more than a radiator cap over Jerry Baker, of Warsaw. Next week a 50-lap feature race for modified racers is scheduled.

A number of spectacular crashes kept a large crowd on the edge of its seats but only one driver was hurt. Roger Grossnickle, of North Manchester, sustained a bump on the head when his racer rammed the fence in the southeast turn but he returned to the track after being examined at the Murphy Medical Center.

Paul Grim, of Warren, was the only dual winner driving his big red car number seven, commonly known as the "flame-thrower" to victory in both the modified, dash event and the fourth heat. Charlie Sarver, of Kokomo, came away with his first win at this track this season in the modified feature.

Point Standings: In the Hoosier Hot Rods point standings for the season, Les Bills, of Columbia City, is on top with 120 and Jim Bucher, of Burket, is second at 109. Others in the top ten follow: Paul Hazen, Columbia City, 96; Ed Stine, Etna Green, 93; Larry Bills, Columbia City, 78; Jim Boggs, Warsaw, 76; Paul Joyce, Kokomo, 75; Paul Bills, Columbia City, 73; Luther Holloway, Warsaw, 73; and Jerry Baker, Warsaw, 73.

The race summary of the first three finishers in each race follows:

Stock Dash—Larry Montel, 1st; Paul Bills, 2nd; Jim Bucher, 3rd.
Modified Dash—Paul Grim, 1st; John Davis, 2nd; Paul Hazen, 3rd.
First Heat—Don Drudge, 1st; Vernell Krom, 2nd; Jerry Baker, 3rd.
Second Heat—Ray Mumaw, 1st; Ed Angle, 2nd; Les Bills, 3rd.
Third Heat—Max Lambert, 1st; Luther Holloway, 2nd; Larry Montel, 3rd.
Fourth Heat—Paul Grim, 1st; Paul Hazen, 2nd; Jim Elliott, 3rd.
Consolation—Jim Ratliff, 1st; Gary Baker. 2nd; Ted Hudson, 3rd.
Modified Feature—Charlie Sarver, 1st; Earl Egolf, 2nd; Jim Elliott, 3rd.

50-lap Stock Feature—Paul Bills, 1st; Jerry Baker, 2nd; Vernell Krom, 3rd.

Saturday, September 4 & Monday, September 6, 1966
Gigantic Race Card Slated At Speedway

A gigantic racing card is slated at the Warsaw Speedway this Saturday night to make up for events rained out last Saturday including a 50-lap season championship modified feature.

Due to the many added events it was announced that time trials will begin at 5 p.m. Although four races were finished constituting a completed program before the rains came Saturday, officials decided to run the unfinished events this week.

In a Labor Day card at the local speedway, fans on hand saw a vicious seven-car pile-up and also witnessed one of the most spectacular wrecks of the season when a car driven by Charles Sarver, of Kokomo, rolled end over end spinning on the radiator cap before landing on its wheels. But none of the drivers were hurt.

A power failure also developed engulfing the track in total darkness for more than 35 minutes until the problem was found and corrected. The results of the races each evening follow listing the first three finishers and the current season point standings:

Saturday Summary:

Stock Dash—Jim Bucher, 1st; Don Drudge, 2nd; Max Lambert, 3rd.
Modified Dash—Ed Angle, 1st; Larry Bills, 2nd; Les Bills, 3rd.
First Heat—Paul Bills, 1st; Dick Leiter, 2nd; Vernell Krom, 3rd.
Second Heat – Paul Joyce, 1st; Danny Johnson, 2nd; Bob Bernhard, 3rd.

Monday Summary:

Stock Dash—Paul Bills, 1st; Junior Stutzman, 2nd; Luther Holloway, 3rd.
Modified Dash—Jim Elliott, 1st; Art Smith, 2nd; Larry Bills, 3rd.
First Heat—Chuck Saner, 1st; Jim Bucher, 2nd; Pealy Heckaman, 3rd.
Second Heat—John Davis, 1st; Bob Grindle, 2nd; Ray Gilman, 3rd.
Third Heat—Dick Leiter, 1st; Doug Method, 2nd; Larry Bills, 3rd.
Fourth Heat—Danny Johnson, 1st; DeWayne Fox, 2nd; Ed Stine, 3rd.
Consolation—Don Taylor, 1st; Jerry Baker, 2nd; Jim Weirick, 3rd.
Stock Feature—Dick Leiter, 1st; Doug Method, 2nd; Bud Grossnickle, 3rd.
Modified Feature—DeWayne Fox, 1st; Art Smith, 2nd; Les Bills, 3rd.

POINT STANDINGS:

Les Bills	Columbia City	124
Jim Bucher	Akron	118
Paul Hazen	Columbia City	102
Ed Stine	Etna Green	98
Larry Bills	Columbia City	87
Paul Bills	Columbia City	86
Jim Boggs	Warsaw	80
Jerry Baker	Warsaw	80
Paul Joyce	Kokomo	78

Luther Holloway	Warsaw	78
Junior Stutzman	Silver Lake	69
Ed Angle	Flora	69
Bob Grindle	Warsaw	63
Dick Leiter	Warsaw	62

Saturday, September 13, 1966
Racing Season Comes To End At Local Track

Stock car racing at the Warsaw Speedway has ended in a blaze of glory following a 14-race card which produced more than 200 laps of excitement Saturday night.

Paul Grim & the Weenieburner

In addition to the regular racing slate five events that were rained out the previous week were run and the entire program was concluded before 11 o'clock. There were the usual number of minor wrecks but none of the drivers were injured.

In the 50-lap season championship race for modified cars, held over from last week, Paul Grim drove his big red car number seven to victory. It was the first time the Warren, Ind., grandfather has ever gained the checkered flag in a feature race here in his long history at the track. Grim finished second in the regular modified feature behind John Davis, of Warsaw, who also won a heat race and the modified dash.

While the officials of the Hoosier Hot Rods Racing Assn. thank fans for their patronage, already plans are being made for a bigger and better season at the track next year. The summary of the first three finishers in each event follows:

Racing Summary:

Third Heat—Bob Tucker, 1st; Chuck Saner, 2nd; Larry Baker, 3rd.
Fourth Heat—John Davis, 1st; Art Smith, 2nd; Paul Hazen, 3rd.
Consolation—Jim Marvel, 1st; Dick Menzie, 2nd; Ted Hudson, 3rd.
Stock Feature—Larry Bills, 1st; Bob Tucker, 2nd; Glen Owens, 3rd.
50-lap Modified Feature—Paul Grim, 1st; Ed Stine, 2nd; Jim Elliott, 3rd.
Stock Dash—Dick Leiter, 1st; Bob Tucker, 2nd; Chuck Saner, 3rd.
Modified Dash—John Davis, 1st; Art Smith, 2nd; Paul Grim, 3rd.
First Heat—Jerry Baker, 1st; Gary Baker, 2nd; Don Taylor, 3rd.
Second Heat—Danny Johnson, 1st; Charlie Sarver, 2nd; Bob Grindle, 3rd.
Third Heat—Vernell Krom, 1st; Don Drudge, 2nd; Dick Leiter, 3rd.
Fourth Heat—Jim Boggs, 1st; Sam Davis, 2nd; Jim Elliott, 3rd.
Consolation—Ted Hudson, 1st; Dick Menzie, 2nd; Jerry Hull, 3rd.

Stock Feature—Junior Stutzman, 1st; Paul Bills, 2nd; Bob Tucker, 3rd.
Modified Feature—John Davis, 1st; Paul Grim, 2nd; Ed Stine, 3rd.

Tuesday, September 27, 1966
Racing Group Elects Officers

C.E. (Hoot) Gibson, of Columbia City, was re-elected president of Hoosier Hot Rods, Inc., at a recent meeting at Columbia City. Del Ballard, of Columbia City, was elected vice president and Byron Beaber, also of Columbia City, was named treasurer.

Those named to the racing board of directors were Otto Cochett and Bill Bullers, modified; and Harold Mitchell and Don Coleman, semi-late model stock class. John Crum was named a director at large.

More than 100 car owners, mechanics and drivers attended the meeting. It was announced that plans were being made to cover the fairgrounds track with a completely new surface of clay and build a new retaining fence. One rule change was noted in that next season semi-late model racers will be in the 1955 to 1963 classification.

1967

Saturday, May 13, 1967
Smith Wins Opening Race Feature Here

Art Smith, of Warsaw, captured the modified feature to open the racing season at the Warsaw Speedway Saturday night before a good crowd on a chilly evening.

A total of 60 cars were on hand for the initial program and many more are expected this week. Officials said the opening night crowd was probably the best in many years, indicating a great season is in store. The track was in excellent condition and speeds increased in every race.

Danny Johnson, of South Bend, drove his car number 29 to second place in the feature and Ron Fisher of Kokomo, placed third. In the semi-late model stock class, Orville Taylor, of Pierceton, was first and Don Taylor, also of Pierceton, was second. Bob Tucker of Burket, took third place honors.

Saturday, May 20, 1967
Bills' Win Both Feature Races At Local Track

Racing was king for many brave fans Saturday night at the Warsaw Speedway although Mother Nature again brought cool weather. An exciting racing program warmed the atmosphere, however, for about three hours as 64 cars qualified for the events. Jim Sechrist suffered a hip

Larry Bills, Columbia City

injury in the pits when a car broke loose from a wrecker pinning him between the car and wrecker. He was admitted to the Murphy Medical Center for treatment of the injury.

Loses Wheel. Paul Beezley, of Wolf Lake, was unhurt but went through an exciting experience as his super modified racer lost a wheel and careened off the wall two or three times.

Larry Bills, of Columbia City, won the modified feature and Ed Stine, of Etna Green, placed second. Les Bills, of Columbia City, won the stock feature and Larry Baker, took runner up honors. Other heat winners were Charlie Wiles, Don Walker, Paul Bills, Herb Waggle, Les Bills, Larry Bills and Don Drudge.

Races May 30. It was announced that races will be held as usual next Saturday night with a big program planned for Memorial Day night. A 50-lap feature race for semi-late model stocks will be the highlighted attraction of the May 30 program. Time trials will get under way at 6 p.m. One-half hour of the races will be broadcast over Radio Stations WRSW AM-FM from 8:45-9:15 sponsored by Monteith Firestone.

Saturday, May 27, 1967
Big Race Card Here Tuesday; List Winners

Racing fans will be treated to a special Memorial Day card at the Warsaw Speedway and if Saturday's action is any indication of things to come it should be an exciting evening. Gates will open at 4 p.m. Tuesday with the time trials slated to begin at 6 p.m. because of a gigantic 50-lap semi-late model stock feature race.

Two drivers joined the exclusive "roll over club" in a thrill-packed card before a large crowd Saturday night. Larry Bills, of Columbia City, was taken to the Murphy Medical Center for examination after his super modified racer was demolished when it spun and rolled over three times in a vicious crash. Tom Thomas, of Warsaw, was unhurt when his late model stock car skidded sideways and flipped over on its side.

Modified Feature. Les Bills, of Columbia City, drove his Chevy-powered Number 22 racer to victory in hotly contested modified feature event while Don Walker, of Kokomo, finished second and Jene Simon, of Columbia City, took third place. Pete Gross, of Warsaw, was the top winner of the evening in stock class capturing the feature and taking a second in the dash event.

Les Bills, Columbia City

Other winners were Larry Bills, Columbia City, modified dash; Don Taylor, Pierceton, stock heat; Bob Jonas, LaPorte, modified heat; Doug Method, Warsaw, stock heat Don Walker, modified heat; and Arden Leiter, Warsaw, stock consolation.

Wednesday, May 31, 1967
Apple Cops 50-Lap Stock Feature Here

Cold weather limited the crowd for an exciting night of racing Memorial Day which featured a big 50-lap late model stock event won by Hal Apple, of Etna Green.

During a modified race Danny Johnson, of South Bend, was taken to Murphy Medical Center for examination after his car spun out and was rammed by one driven by Bob Bernhard, of South Whitley. Johnson was later released from the hospital. A regular racing card will be held at the speedway this Saturday night.

Race Summary:

Stock Dash—Pete Gross, 1st; Don Taylor, 2nd; Bud Grossnickle, 3rd.
Modified Dash—Dan Johnson, 1st; Art Smith, 2nd; Paul Hazen, 3rd.
Stock Heat—Paul Bills, 1st; Don Drudge, 2nd; Bill Rose, 3rd.
Modified Heat—Charles Sarver, 1st; Bob Bernhard, 2nd; Bob Grindle, 3rd.
Stock Heat—Dick Smith, 1st; Chuck Saner, 2nd; Doug Method, 3rd.
Modified Heat—Jim Elliott, 1st; Ed Stine, 2nd; Dan Johnson, 3rd.
Stock Consolation—Charles Wiles, 1st; Tom Leiter, 2nd; Jerry Baker, 3rd.
Modified Feature—Jim Elliott, 1st; Les Bills, 2nd; John Davis, 3rd.
50-lap Stock Feature—Hal Apple, 1st; Pete Gross, 2nd.

Saturday, June 3, 1967
Art Smith Cops Modified Feature

Mother Nature smiled and the largest crowd of the season turned out for an exciting night of racing at the Warsaw Speedway Saturday as Art Smith, of Warsaw, drove one of his finest races to win the modified feature.

Highlighting the evening was a spectacular roll over by Tom Thomas, of Warsaw, his second trip upside down this year. Emergency workers had to help him from the wreckage but he was uninjured. A total of 66 cars qualified and races were hotly contested with two ending in near "photo finishes" as only inches separated the cars.

Other event winners were Paul Bills, Columbia City, two; Don Walker, Kokomo; Larry Baker, Warsaw; Paul Hazen, Columbia City; John Davis, Warsaw; Jim Coon, Leesburg; Carl Patrick; and Chuck Saner, Akron.

Saturday, June 10, 1967
Elliott, Saner Feature Race Winners Here

A spectacular nine car pileup highlighted racing action at the Warsaw Speedway Saturday night but fortunately all drivers escaped unhurt. Les Bills, of Columbia City, was caught in the middle of the pile and it took wreckers and workers several minutes to untangle the wreckage.

A large crowd on hand saw 68 cars qualify for an exciting race program. Jim Elliott, of Warsaw, took the checkered flag in the modified feature with Warsaw's Art Smith right on his tail. Smith copped the modified dash event. Chuck Saner of Akron drove to victory in the stock feature and also took the checkered flag in a heat race. The complete race summary listing the first three finishers in each race follows:

Race Summary:

Stock Dash—Don Drudge, 1st; Dick Smith, 2nd; Gary Baker, 3rd.
Modified Dash—Art Smith, 1st; Jene Simon, 2nd; Les Bills, 3rd.
Stock Heat—Chuck Saner, 1st; Vernell Krom, 2nd; Paul Bills, 3rd.
Modified Heat—Ron Fisher, 1st; Paul Hazen, 2nd; Charlie Sarver, 3rd.
Stock Heat—Ted Hudson, 1st; Hal Apple, 2nd; Charlie Wiles, 3rd.
Modified Heat—Paul Grim, 1st; Larry Bills, 2nd; Art Smith, 3rd.
Consolation—Dick Leiter, 1st; Gerald Shank, 2nd; Shepherd, 3rd.
Stock Feature—Chuck Saner, 1st; Charlie Wiles, 2nd; Ted Hudson, 3rd.
Modified Feature—Jim Elliott, 1st; Art Smith, 2nd; Paul Hazen, 3rd.

Saturday, June 17, 1967
Baker, Jonas Capture Race Features Here

Two roll overs plus high speed racing thrilled a large crowd on hand at the Warsaw Speedway Saturday night as Jerry Baker, of Warsaw, and Bob Jonas, of LaPorte, captured the stock and modified feature events.

Bob Johnson, of Warsaw, rolled over during the time trials when he lost a wheel and another new comer of the roll over club was Tom Leiter, also of Warsaw. He rolled in the stock consolation event when he struck the fence in front of the grandstand. Neither wreck resulted in injuries, however.

Time trial speeds were high on the smooth track that allowed the drivers to maneuver through the turns with ease. Paul Hazen, of Columbia City, turned the track in 16.38 seconds for the fastest time of the evening which is close to the existing track record.

There were 65 cars qualifying for the evening's racing card and one-hour of the action was broadcast over Radio Stations WRSW AM-FM, sponsored by Monteith Firestone in Warsaw.

Racing Summary:

Stock Dash—Dick Smith, 1st; Chuck Saner, 2nd; Dick Leiter, 3rd.
Modified Dash—Jim Elliott, 1st; Art Smith, 2nd; Les Bills, 3rd.
Stock Heat—Don Taylor, 1st; Roger Grossnickle, 2nd; Don Drudge, 3rd.
Modified Heat—Jim Hines, 1st; John Davis, 2nd; Dave Barnett, 3rd.
Stock Heat—Ted Hudson, 1st; Chuck Saner, 2nd; Charles Wiles, 3rd.
Modified Heat—Paul Grim, 1st; Jim Elliott, 2nd; Les Bills, 3rd.
Stock Consolation—Tom Leiter, 1st; Bob Johnson, 2nd; Krop, 3rd.
Stock Feature—Jerry Baker, 1st; Dick Leiter, 2nd; Chuck Saner, 3rd.
Modified Feature—Bob Jonas, 1st; Art Smith, 2nd; Paul Grim, 3rd.

Saturday, June 24, 1967 - Rainout

Saturday, July 1, 1967
2 Big Nights Of Racing Here Today, Tuesday

Two consecutive nights of auto racing are in store for fans at the Warsaw Speedway tonight and Tuesday with activity to be highlighted by a gigantic Fourth of July fireworks display tomorrow.

Saturday night's program was halted by rain after the running of the demolition derby and that card will be completed tonight starting at approximately 8 p.m. with 75 cars already qualified from Saturday. There will be no time trials tonight. A 50-lap mid-season championship race will be staged tonight. Rain check tickets from Saturday night will be good for tonight only.

Tuesday, the Masons will celebrate their 150th anniversary by adding fireworks to those provided by the Hoosier Hot Rods Racing Assn. and the Kosciusko County Fair Assn. which should make a very colorful program.

Flaming Wreck. Due to the wet track, only the demolition derby was run Saturday with 23 drivers competing. Near the end of the event two cars collided backwards causing gas tanks to rupture sending flaming gasoline in every direction in front of the grandstands. One of the drivers suffered minor burns on his arm when he escaped through the windshield of his flaming car. Firefighters at the track pulled the cars apart and the Warsaw Fire Department was summoned to completely extinguish the wreckage.

Monday, July 3 and Tuesday, July 4, 1967
Capacity Crowd Watches Races, Fireworks Here

A capacity crowd witnessed an exciting racing program and the gigantic fireworks display at the Warsaw Speedway last night in a climax to an otherwise frustrating weekend of rainouts. Saturday night's program was washed out after the demolition derby was run and the make-up night was slated for Monday. Rains, however, came again Monday to shorten activities but not before five races were run constituting a completed program.

Last night, Jim Elliott of Warsaw, turned in the fastest qualifying time of the evening with a 16.94 clocking around the oval. Warsaw's Art Smith copped honors in the modified feature event and another local, Luther Holloway, grabbed the checkered flag in the stock feature. Holloway also won a heat race.

For the two nights of racing the driver's purse totaled nearly $5,500 which eclipsed the record set during the Fourth of July weekend last year. The summary of the first three finishers in each race follows:

Tuesday Results:
Stock Dash—Paul Bills, 1st; Charlie Wiles, 2nd; Don Drudge, 3rd.
Modified Dash—Larry Bills, 1st; Jene Simon, 2nd; Paul Hazen, 3rd.
Stock Heat—Luther Holloway, 1st; Gary Baker, 2nd; Doug Method, 3rd.
Modified Heat—Dave Ragan, 1st; John Davis, 2nd; Bob Jonas, 3rd.
Stock Heat—Dick Leiter, 1st; Bob Cozzi, 2nd; Charles Wiles, 3rd.
Modified Heat—Don Walker, 1st; Art Smith, 2nd; Paul Grim, 3rd.
Stock Consolation—Anderson, 1st; Baker, 2nd; Russell, 3rd.
Stock Consolation—Krop, 1st; Taylor, 2nd; Leiter, 3rd.
Stock Feature—Luther Holloway, 1st; Jerry Baker, 2nd; William Powell, 3rd.
Modified Feature—Art Smith, 1st; Les Bills, 2nd; Paul Grim, 3rd.

Monday Results:

Stock Dash—Chuck Saner, 1st; Jerry Baker, 2nd; Hal Apple, 3rd.
Modified Dash—Larry Bills, 1st; Art Smith, 2nd; Jene Simon, 3rd.
Stock Heat—Charlie Wile, 1st; Gary Baker, 2nd; Don Drudge, 3rd.
Modified Heat—Charlie Sarver, 1st; Bob Jonas, 2nd; Sam Davis, 3rd.

Saturday, July 8, 1967
Big 18-Event Program Held At Speedway

A gigantic 18-event program kept a large contingent of racing fans occupied until nearly midnight in a thrilling evening of action at the Warsaw Speedway Saturday night. The doubled program was the result of rainouts both July 1 and 3 and the races were added to this week's card. There were a total of 83 cars qualified for the races. Excitement reached a peak when a car driven by Jim Barnett, of Columbia City, caught on fire but quick action by fire crews at the track prevented serious injury to the driver.

Don Walker, of Kokomo, won the rescheduled modified feature and Art Smith, of Warsaw, came back to take the checkered flag in the regular feature. Pete Gross, of Warsaw, was the first to cross the finish line in the stock feature. Next Saturday night a 50-lap semi-late model stock mid-season championship race will be featured.

Summary of Carry-Over Events:

Modified Feature - Don Walker, 1st; Paul Grim, 2nd; Jim Elliott, 3rd.
Stock Heat—Dick Leiter, 1st; Chuck Saner, 2nd; Bob Cozzi, 3rd.
Modified Heat—Les Bills, 1st; Don Walker, 2nd; Paul Joyce, 3rd.
Stock Consolation—Larry Shriver, 1st; Krop, 2nd; Jim Coon, 3rd.
2nd Stock Consolation—Carl Patrick, 1st; Charlie Shank, 2nd; Bud Grossnickle, 3rd.
Stock Feature—Jerry Baker, 1st; Pete Gross, 2nd; Chuck Saner, 3rd.

Regular Events Summary:

Stock Dash—Vernell Krom, 1st; Jim Bucher, 2nd; Charlie Wiles, 3rd.
Modified Dash—Don Walker, 1st; Art Smith, 2nd; Larry Bills, 3rd.
Stock Heat—Jerry Baker, 1st; Chuck Saner, 2nd; Don Drudge, 3rd.
Modified Heat—Jene Simon, 1st; Herb Waggle, 2nd; Danny Johnson, 3rd.
Stock Heat—Dick Leiter, 1st; Vernell Krom, 2nd; Jim Bucher, 3rd.
Modified Heat—Bob Grindle, 1st; Jim Elliott, 2nd; Larry Bills, 3rd.
Stock Consolation—Dave Hopper, 1st; Dick Leiter, 2nd; Don Spear, 3rd.
Stock Feature—Pete Gross, 1st; Jim Bucher, 2nd; Charlie Wiles, 3rd.
Modified Feature—Art Smith, 1st; Jim Elliott, 2nd; Paul Grim, 3rd.

Saturday, July 15, 1967
Paul Bills Cops 50-Lap Stock Feature Race

Paul Bills, of Columbia City, captured the 50-lap mid-season late model stock car championship race in a thrill-packed card at the Warsaw Speedway Saturday night.

The event was hotly contested before the checkered flag dropped. Pete Gross, of Warsaw, the point standing leader in the stock class, led the pack for more than half of the race, but a tire blew and he had to retire. The race was restarted several times because of wrecks.

Don Walker, of Kokomo, rolled over in the warmups when an axle broke causing his front wheels to collapse. Walker was uninjured. Art Smith, of Warsaw, drove his car number 67 to victory in the modified feature. The summary of the races follow listing the first three finishers in each event:

Stock Dash—Jim Bucher, 1st; Schering, 2nd; Grossnickle, 3rd.
Modified Dash—Les Bills, 1st; Jim Elliott, 2nd; Art Smith
Stock Heat—Dan Hopper, 1st; Doug Method, 2nd; Chuck Saner, 3rd.
Modified Heat—Larry Bills, 1st; Herb Waggle, 2nd; Danny Johnson, 3rd.
Stock Heat—Ted Hudson, 1st; Charles Wiles, 2nd; Paul Bills, 3rd.
Modified Heat—Paul Grim, 1st; Art Smith, 2nd; Paul Hazen, 3rd.
Consy—Carl Patrick, 1st; G. Shank, 2nd; Tom Leiter, 3rd.
Second Consy—Larry Sroufe, 1st; Larry Montel, 2nd; Dick Smith, 3rd.
Stock Feature—Paul Bills, 1st; Jerry Baker, 2nd; Art Smith, 3rd.
Modified Feature—Art Smith, 1st; Larry Bills, 2nd; Ron Fisher, 3rd.

Saturday, July 22, 1967
Art Smith Wins Third Feature To Gain Trophy

It was another big night at the Warsaw Speedway Saturday night as excitement was "King". Sixty-five cars qualified for the events and a big 25-lap semi-late model race was added to the program. Several wrecks caused restarts, but the most severe accident was Bobby Grindle driving through the fence at full speed. His accelerator apparently stuck sending him into the wall out of control. He was shaken, but not seriously injured.

Art Smith, of Warsaw, driving his white 67 won his third feature event in a row entitling him to the huge Buchanan trophy. It was superb driving on Art's part to pass a charging Jim Elliott who led for several laps.

3 Car Crash. In a semi-late model race, three cars collided and Carl Patrick's vehicle was caved in on the driver's side. He was not injured even though the car was almost demolished. The races, sponsored by Monteith Firestone, were broadcast by Milo Clase for 30 minutes over radio stations WRSW AM-FM.

Saturday, July 29, 1967
Smith Wins Feature At Local Track

Exciting finishes featured races at the Warsaw Speedway Saturday night. A large crowd watched 65 cars qualify and the drivers stage some hotly contested races during the course of the evening. There were several wrecks but no injuries.

Art Smith won the feature for modified cars but not until John Davis in his 44 broke a drive shaft. John led the race for about 15 laps.

It was announced that next week there will be a powder puff derby with about 20 ladies competing for three big trophies. Milo Clase presented a 30-minute broadcast over Radio Stations WRSW AM-FM sponsored by Monteith Firestone.

Clase reminded racing fans that next Saturday night those going into the pits and around the backstretch should use the west drive as the east drive will be blocked due to the Kosciusko County Fair exhibits.

Saturday, August 5, 1967
Powder-Puff Derby Tops Local Race Card

A pre-fair race crowd saw just about everything in racing that could be crammed into one night at the Warsaw Speedway Saturday. The evening was highlighted by a 21-car powder-puff derby. Judy Tenney won the derby going away while Charlene Conley was second and Dora Swick was third.

There were 77 cars qualified for the evening's events and man races were near photo finishes. In the modified feature local drivers John Davis and Art Smith dueled side-by-side and wheel-to-wheel until Davis broke away in his yellow car No. 44 in about the 22nd lap to win.

Stock Winners. The big stock winner of the evening was Pete Gross of Warsaw who drove his car No. 09 to victory in a heat race then took the checkered flag in the stock feature.

The fair week activities will include two nights of racing on Wednesday and Saturday. The summary of the first three finishers in each race follows:

Race Summary:

Stock Dash: Roger Grossnickle, 1st; Jim Bucher, 2nd; Bob Johnson, 3rd.
Modified Dash: Les Bills, 1st; Art Smith, 2nd; Jim Elliott, 3rd.
Stock Heat: Paul Bills, 1st; Ted Hudson, 2nd; Don Taylor, 3rd.
Modified Heat: Tom Beezley, 1st; Ken Miller, 2nd; Bill Bates, 3rd.
Stock Heat: Pete Gross, 1st; Roger Rowland, 2nd; Jim Bucher, 3rd.
Modified Heat: Art Smith, 1st; John Davis, 2nd; Paul Hazen, 3rd.
First Concy: Gary Baker, 1st; E. Nabor, 2nd; Orville Taylor, 3rd.
Second Concy: Bud Grossnickle, 1st; Larry Montel, 2nd; Dick Leiter, 3rd.
Stock Feature: Pete Gross, 1st; Luther Holloway, 2nd; Charles Wiles, 3rd.
Modified Feature: John Davis, 1st; Art Smith, 2nd; Larry Bills, 3rd.

Wednesday, August 9, 1967
Art Smith Cops Feature Race

A moderate Wednesday night fair crowd was treated to an exciting race card on a cool evening at the Warsaw Speedway. Art Smith, of Warsaw, wheeled his car number 67 to victory in the modified feature event and Charlie Wiles, of Syracuse, caught the checkered flag first in the late model stock feature.

During the stock feature, Grover Martin, of Warsaw, spun out and was hit by three other racers. He was taken to the Murphy Medical Center for treatment of a knee injury. A regular night of racing is on tap for the closing of the County Fair Saturday.

Stock Dash—Roger Grossnickle, 1st; Jim Bucher, 2nd; Dan Hopper, 3rd.
Modified Dash—Jim Elliott, 1st; John Davis, 2nd; Jene Simon, 3rd.
Stock Heat—Larry Bills, 1st; Roger Rowland, 2nd; Larry Montel, 3rd.
Modified Heat—Dick Ticen, 1st; Danny Johnson, 2nd; Bob Bernhard, 3rd.
Stock Heat—Luther Holloway, 1st; Charles Wiles, 2nd; Dan Hopper, 3rd.
Modified Heat—Jim Elliott, 1st; Art Smith, 2nd; John Davis, 3rd.
Concy 1—Tom Leiter, 1st; Elbert Russell, 2nd; Acres, 3rd.
Concy 2—Bud Grossnickle, 1st; Don Taylor, 2nd; Gerald Shank, 3rd.
Stock Feature—Charles Wiles, 1st; Jerry Baker, 2nd; Pete Gross, 3rd.
Modified Feature—Art Smith, 1st; Jim Elliott, 2nd; Tom Beezley, 3rd.

Saturday, August 12, 1967
New Driver Challenges At Speedway

Before a huge crowd of excited spectators, the drivers at the Warsaw Speedway proved why stock car racing is such a fast growing sport. The races were some of the best of the season as each driver was out to win some of the big $2000 purse.

A new driver at the track, Buck Cravens of Stillwell, Mich., served notice that he might be a challenger at the speedway as he placed second in the modified feature. Cravens had never raced at the track before. Even though the speeds were high, there were no serious accidents.

Art Smith of Warsaw won the modified feature. Ted Hudson of North Manchester was the winner of the semi-late feature.

Racing Summary:

Stock Dash—Orval Taylor, Pierceton, 1st; Johnson, 2nd; Jim Bucher, 3rd.
Modified Dash—Larry Bills, 1st; Jim Elliott, 2nd; John Davis, 3rd.
Stock Heat—Larry Montel, 1st; Jerry Baker, 2nd; Roger Rowland, 3rd.
Modified Heat—Jene Simon, 1st; Charlie Sarver, 2nd; Tom Beezley, 3rd.
Stock Heat—Ted Hudson, 1st; Dick Leiter, 2nd; Drudge, 3rd.
Modified Heat—Art Smith, 1st; Bob Bernhard, 2nd; Danny Johnson, 3rd.
Concy I—Gerald Shank, 1st; Tom Leiter, 2nd; Lee Ratliff, 3rd.
Concy II—Bud Grossnickle, 1st; Charlie Wiles, 2nd; Doug Method, 3rd.
Stock Feature—Ted Hudson, 1st; Jim Bucher, 2nd; Jerry Baker, 3rd.
Modified Feature—Art Smith, 1st; Buck Cravens, 2nd; Jim Elliott, 3rd.

Saturday, August 19, 1967
Two 100-Lap Features Set Here Saturday

Two big 100-lap feature races will comprise the stock car card at the Warsaw Speedway next Saturday after cold weather held the crowd to a minimum for action over the weekend.

There will be no time trials Saturday and races will be set up on the basis of the current point standings with the first race at 8 p.m. The races will be run Monza style with cars going 50 laps at a time with stops at the midway mark for fuel and mechanical checks. Each winner will receive $300.

There were 70 cars qualifying for the action Saturday on a rain-drenched track. The wet surface held speeds down but allowed drivers to maneuver and created plenty of excitement.

In the modified feature Les Bills of Columbia City, struck the fence in his car number 22 and tore the front of the racer completely apart. The entire event was weird as only seven cars of the original 20 finished the race. Art Smith, of Warsaw, copped the modified event and Paul Bills, of Columbia City, captured the stock feature.

Racing Summary:

Stock Dash—Paul Bills, 1st; Smith, 2nd; Charlie Wiles, 3rd.
Modified Dash—Jim Elliott, 1st; Paul Grim, 2nd; Les Bills, 3rd.
Stock Heat—Don Drudge, 1st; Roger Rowland, 2nd; Jim Bucher, 3rd.
Modified Heat—Danny Johnson, 1st; Bob Bates, 2nd; Chuck Plummer, 3rd.
Stock Heat—Doug Method, 1st; Ted Hudson, 2nd; Paul Bills, 3rd.
Modified Heat—Sam Davis, 1st; Paul Hazen 2nd; Paul Grim, 3rd.
Consy—Gerald Shank, 1st; Luther Holloway, 2nd; Jerry Baker, 3rd.
Stock Feature—Paul Bills, 1st; Larry Baker, 2nd; Jim Bucher, 3rd.
Modified Feature—Art Smith, 1st; Paul Grim, 2nd; Buck Cravens, 3rd.

Saturday, August 26, 1967 - Rainout

Saturday, September 2, 1967
Elliott, Hudson Win Big Features

A big evening with 220 laps of racing highlighted the Saturday card at the Warsaw Speedway as 70 cars competed for large trophies and a large purse. Jim Elliott, of Warsaw, copped the 100-lap modified feature race while Ted Hudson, of North Manchester, drove a steady race to gain the checkered flag in the 100-lap stock feature. The season championship events were run in 50-lap heats.

Tom Beezley, of Wolf Lake, was taken to the Murphy Medical Center for treatment of an injury to his left arm after his car was involved in a pileup during the modified feature. He was not seriously injured and later returned to the speedway. Dick Smith, of Columbia City, escaped injury when his racer overturned along the backstretch during the stock consolation. It was announced that this Saturday's races will be highlighted by another very popular demolition derby.

Race Summary:

Stock Consolation—Ellis Shepherd-1st; Jim Coon, 2nd; Dave Hopper, 3rd.
Stock Feature—Ted Hudson, 1st; Jim Bucher, 2nd; Luther Holloway, 3rd; Paul Bills, 4th.
Modified Feature—Jim Elliott, 1st; Larry Bills, 2nd; Paul Hazen, 3rd; Paul Grim, 4th.

Saturday, September 9, 1967
Destruction Derby Closes Speedway Season

The Warsaw Speedway ended its season in a blaze of excitement with high speed racing and a tremendous demolition derby Saturday night. Dale Larue, of Pierceton, won the destruction derby as 24 cars did their best to destroy each other. Wrecked cars, debris and parts littered the track when the crowd-pleasing event was completed.

High qualifying speeds highlighted the time trials as several cars came very close to the existing track records. Several cars went through the fence and one car in the demolition derby rolled over spilling gasoline over the track causing a hazard but no fire developed.

It was announced that Saturday night's race card was the final one of the season. One-half hour of the track activity was broadcast over Radio Stations WRSW AM-FM by Milo Clase for Monteith Firestone Service, State Rd. 15 North, Warsaw. The summary of the first three finishers of each race follows:

Race Summary:

Stock Dash—Luther Holloway, 1st; Ted Hudson, 2nd; Bud Grossnickle, 3rd.
Modified Dash—Jim Elliott, 1st; Bob Bernhard, 2nd; Paul Grim, 3rd.
Stock Heat—Charlie Wiles, 1st; Gerald Shank, 2nd; Jerry Baker, 3rd.
Modified Heat—Paul Hazen, 1st; Dan Johnson, 2nd; Bob Bates, 3rd.
Stock Heat—Ted Hudson, 1st; Jim Bucher, 2nd; Roger Rowland, 3rd.
Modified Heat—Jim Elliott, 1st; Bob Bernhard, 2nd; Jene Simon, 3rd.
1 Concy—Bill Edmonds, 1st; Orval Taylor, 2nd; Bob Johnson, 3rd.
2 Concy—Don Taylor, 1st; Bill Akers, 2nd; Charlie Shank, 3rd.
Stock Feature—Don Drudge, 1st; Roger Leedy, 2nd; Luther Holloway, 3rd.
Modified Feature—Jene Simon, 1st; Jim Elliott, 2nd; Paul Grim, 3rd.

1968

Saturday, May 18, 1968
Rain Shortens Opening Race Program Here

An abbreviated race card, shortened by rain, ushered in the new season at the Warsaw Speedway Saturday night. From the preview it would appear that racing fans are in for a very interesting summer. Many new cars made their appearances and many more are being built. There were 49 cars on hand for the Saturday opener but threatening skies kept the crowd at a minimum. The dash winners were Luther Hollloway, of Warsaw, in the stock class and Art Smith, of Warsaw, in the modified class.

Race Summary:

Stock Dash—Luther Holloway, 1st; Bob Cozzi, 2nd; Pete Gross, 3rd.
Modified Dash—Art Smith, 1st; Rector, 2nd; Walker, 3rd.
Stock Heat—Jim Bucher, 1st; Gerald Shank, 2nd; Jerry Baker, 3rd.
Modified Heat—Cap Arnold, 1st; Beezley, 2nd; Mouser, 3rd.
Stock Heat—Larry Montel, 1st; Bob Wiles, 2nd; Pete Gross, 3rd.

Saturday, May 25, 1968
Races Planned At Speedway Here Thursday

Ray Chambers, Rochester

A full card of racing is planned at the Warsaw Speedway this Thursday, Memorial Day, with races starting one hour early and gates will open to the track at 4 p.m. Saturday night threatening skies held down the crowd but approximately 1,000 fans turned out to see a full program in addition to four races postponed by rain one week ago.

The evening was highlighted by wrecks, roll-overs and torn down fence in addition to high speeds and plenty of thrills. One driver, Joe Perry, Rt. 2, Noblesville, was taken to Murphy Medical Center for treatment of rib injuries after his racer flipped over in mid-air. He was not admitted to the hospital.

51 Qualify. There were 51 cars qualified for the program, many of which were new racers and were from such towns as Hartford City, Alexandria, and Perkinsville.

Art Smith, Warsaw, captured the make-up modified feature and came back to place second to Warsaw's John Davis in the regular feature. Ray Chambers, of Rochester, took the checkered flag in the first stock feature and Hal Apple, of Etna Green, copped the regular stock feature. One-half hour of the action was broadcast over Radio Stations WRSW AM-FM sponsored by Silveus and Bradway Sunoco service stations.

Race Summary:

Modified Heat—Don Walker, 1st; Smith, 2nd; Joyce, 3rd.
Stock Consey—Dick Leiter, 1st; Spear, 2nd; Shephard, 3rd.
Stock Feature—Ray Chambers, 1st; Wiles, 2nd; Bucher, 3rd.
Modified Feature—Art Smith, 1st; Walker, 2nd; Beezley, 3rd.
Stock Dash—Ted Hudson, 1st; Bucher, 2nd; Rensberger, 3rd.
Modified Dash—John Davis, 1st; Beezley, 2nd; Fisher, 3rd.
Stock Heat—Don Spear, 1st; Taylor, 2nd; Apple, 3rd.
Modified Heat—Paul Joyce, 1st; Loe, 2nd; Holloway, 3rd.
Stock Heat—Jim Bucher, 1st; J. Baker, 2nd; Rensberger, 3rd.
Modified Heat—Art Smith, 1st; Mouser, 2nd; Walker, 3rd.
Stock Consy—John White, 1st; Malott, 2nd; G. Baker, 3rd.
Stock Feature—Hal Apple, 1st; Shank, 2nd; Gross, 3rd.
Modified Feature—John Davis, 1st; Smith, 2nd; Elliott, 3rd.

Thursday, May 30, 1968
Fisher Wins Disputed Race Feature Here

A lull in the May rains brought a large contingent of racers to the Warsaw Speedway in a thrill-packed stock car program Thursday evening. A total of 55 cars qualified for the activity and all races were hotly contested until the checkered flag was waved. The program started at 6 p.m. and all events were concluded by 9:30 p.m.

The modified feature was in doubt for some time after a question arose over the number of laps run under the yellow flag. Art Smith, of Warsaw, was given the checkered flag but it was later ruled that Ron Fisher, of Kokomo, was the winner of the event.

Pete Gross, of Warsaw, drove his car number 09 to victory in the stock feature. A full program of racing will be held at the speedway again Saturday evening.

Race Summary:

Stock Dash—Ted Hudson, 1st; Lowell Krom, 2nd; Bucher, 3rd.
Modified Dash—Ray Mumaw, 1st; Ron Fisher, 2nd; John Davis, 3rd.
Stock Heat—Bob Johnson, 1st; Hal Apple, 2nd; Larry Malott, 3rd.
Modified Heat—Jene Simons, 1st; Ed Stine, 2nd; Bob Bernhard, 3rd.
Stock Heat—Charles Sroufe, 1st; Devon Rensberger, 2nd; Dean Hudson, 3rd.
Modified Heat—Ron Fisher, 1st; Jim Elliott, 2nd; Art Smith, 3rd.
Stock Consy—Doug Method, 1st; Don Taylor, 2nd; Dick Leiter, 3rd.
Stock Feature—Pete Gross, 1st; Larry Malott, 2nd; Hal Apple, 3rd.
Modified Feature—Ron Fisher, 1st; Ed Stine, 2nd; John Davis, 3rd.

Saturday, June 1, 1968
Malott, Fisher Winners At Local Speedway

Larry Malott and Ron Fisher won the stock and modified feature races at the Warsaw Speedway Saturday night.

Malott raced to victory in the stock feature on a treacherous track that had been plagued by rain while Fisher took top honors in the modified feature event.

Race Summary:

Stock Dash—John Davis, 1st; Pete Gross, 2nd; Jim Bucher, 3rd.
Modified Dash—Harold Mauser, 1st; Paul Grim, 2nd; Art Smith, 3rd.
Stock Heat—Hal Apple, 1st; Larry Malott, 2nd; Luther Holloway, 3rd.
Modified Heat—Charlie Sarner, 1st; Jene Simon, 2nd; Ed Stine, 3rd.
Stock Heat—Ted Hudson, 1st; Les Sroufe, 2nd; Pete Gross, 3rd.
Modified Heat—Harold Mauser, 1st; Art Smith, 2nd; Ron Fisher, 3rd.
Stock consolation—Larry Montel, 1st; John White, 2nd; Gerald Sharp, 3rd.
Stock Feature—Larry Malott, 1st; Pete Gross, 2nd; Charles Wiles, 3rd.
Modified Feature—Ron Fisher, 1st; Art Smith, 2nd; Harold Mauser, 3rd.

Saturday, June 8, 1968
Art Smith Big Racing Winner Here

Warsaw's Art Smith, competing in both the stock and modified classes, took three firsts, two seconds and a third to become the big winner before a large crowd of racing fans at the Warsaw Speedway Saturday.

Smith won the modified dash, took the checkered flag in a modified heat race and placed second in the modified feature. He also copped the stock feature and placed second and third in two other stock events. Jim Elliott, of Warsaw, took honors in a modified heat race and came back to nip Smith in the modified feature.

There were 55 cars qualified for the racing and for the first time this season a dry, hard and fast track presented quite a challenge to the drivers. Many spills created some restarts but most of the races were run with a minimum of delay. One-half hour of the races were broadcast over Radio Stations WRSW AM-FM sponsored by Goodyear Service Center, of Warsaw.

Race Summary:

Stock Dash—Pete Gross, 1st; Devon Rensberger, 2nd; Art Smith, 3rd.
Modified Dash—Art Smith, 1st; Ron Fisher, 2nd; Larry Bills, 3rd.
Stock Heat—Luther Holloway, 1st; Dean Hudson, 2nd; Sam Davis, 3rd.
Modified Heat—Jim Elliott, 1st; Ray Loe, 2nd; Tom Beezley, 3rd.
Stock Heat—Les Sroufe, 1st; Art Smith, 2nd; Pete Gross, 3rd.
Modified Heat—Art Smith, 1st; Ron Fisher, 2nd; Ray Mumaw, 3rd.
Stock Consy—Earl Cochran, 1st; Jim Wagoner, 2nd; Tom Leiter, 3rd.
Stock Feature—Art Smith, 1st; Pete Gross, 2nd; Jim Bucher, 3rd.
Modified Feature—Jim Elliott, 1st; Art Smith, 2nd; Tom Beezley, 3rd.

Saturday, June 15, 1968
Rain Cancels Local Races

Three races were completed at the Warsaw Speedway Saturday before the rains came and washed out the remainder of the card.

It was announced that this Saturday night all events would be completed in addition to a Demolition Derby and a Powder Puff Race as added attractions. The Demolition Derby at the local speedway has developed into quite a wild orgy of wrecks through the years and this Saturday should be no exception.

Race Summary:

Stock Dash—Art Smith, 1st; Jim Bucher, 2nd; Ted Hudson, 3rd.
Modified Dash—Paul Joyce, 1st; John Davis, 2nd; Art Smith, 3rd.
Stock Heat—Luther Holloway, 1st; Jim Wagoner, 2nd; Sam Davis, 3rd.

Saturday, June 22, 1968
Destruction, Powder Puff Derbies Spark Race Card

Bob Johnson, Warsaw

A large throng of enthusiastic racing fans was treated to a thrill-packed program which included demolition and powder puff derbies, in addition to regular activity at the Warsaw Speedway Saturday.

Carol Eberly was declared the winner of the 15-car Powder Puff derby for women drivers and Tom Leiter, of Warsaw, emerged as the winner of the demolition derby. Leiter steered his vehicle through the wreckage and debris and was given the checkered flag as the last of 20 cars still running when the destruction classic was completed.

Purse $3,945. Drivers raced for a purse totaling $3,945, according to Hoosier Hot Rods, Inc., President C.E. (Hoot) Gibson, of Columbia City.

Art Smith, of Warsaw, took honors in the stock feature and Wolf Lake's Tom Beezley captured the modified feature event. Warsaw's Bob Johnson and Dick Leiter were the winners of the two stock concy events. Other individual winners were Bud Grossnickle, North Manchester; and Don Walker, Kokomo.

Race Summary:

Powder Puff Derby—Carol Eberly, 1st.
Demolition Derby—Tom Leiter, 1st.
Modified Heat—Jack Hickman, 1st; Bob Murphy, 2nd; Bob Bernhard, 3rd.
Stock Heat—Bud Grossnickle, 1st; Les Sroufe, 2nd; Art Smith, 3rd.
Modified Heat—Don Walker, 1st; Harold Mauser, 2nd; Tom Beezley, 3rd.
Stock Consy 1—Bob Johnson, 1st; McBride, 2nd; Bull Bradley, 3rd.
Stock Consy 2—Dick Leiter, 1st; Gary Baker, 2nd; Don Taylor, 3rd.
Stock Feature—Art Smith, 1st; Don Taylor, 2nd; Luther Holloway, 3rd.
Modified Feature—Tom Beezley, 1st; Harold Mauser, 2nd; Jim Elliott, 3rd.

Saturday, June 29, 1968
Winners At Local Speedway

A good crowd turned out of the Warsaw Speedway Saturday to view another exciting night of racing that adds another in a series of nothing but speed and thrills that local fans have come to expect. Many accidents and near roll-overs brought the crowd to its feet several times during the night. The track was wet due to recent rains, but this allowed drivers to gain traction.

The super modified event was in doubt until the checkered flag was dropped giving the win to Art Smith of Warsaw. The semi-late feature of 20 laps was run in a near record time of just six minutes by Dean Hudson of North Manchester. A total of 65 cars qualified for the various events on the night's program.

One-half of the card was broadcast over Radio Stations WRSW and WRSW-FM by Silveus and Bradway Sunoco Service Stations.

Race Summary:

Stock Dash—Paul Bills, 1st; Hal Apple, 2nd; Pete Gross, 3rd.
Modified Dash—Jim Elliott, 1st; Ron Fisher, 2nd; Art Smith, 3rd.
Stock Heat—Vonell Krom, 1st; Dean Hudson, 2nd; Vogley, 3rd.
Modified Heat—Dave Ragan, 1st; Jack Hickman, 2nd; Ray Loe, 3rd.
Stock Heat—Doug Method, 1st; Pete Gross, 2nd; John Baker, 3rd.
Modified Heat—Harold Mouser, 1st; Paul Joyce, 2nd; Jim Elliott, 3rd.
Stock Consolation—Jack Vocht, 1st; Lyle Butts, 2nd; John Davis, 3rd.
Stock Feature—Dean Hudson, 1st; Vonell Krom, 2nd; Paul Bills, 3rd.
Modified Feature—Art Smith, 1st; Don Walker, 2nd; John Davis, 3rd.

Thursday, July 4, 1968
Elliott Wins Thrill-Packed Feature Race

Jimmie Elliott, Warsaw

A capacity crowd was treated to a mixture of thrill-packed auto races plus a gigantic and colorful fireworks display at the Warsaw Speedway at the county fairgrounds last night.

The modified feature which followed the fireworks was filled with thrills and spills aplenty and was hotly contested throughout and ended in a near photo finish. Jim Elliott, of Warsaw, grabbed the lead and the checkered flag on the very last turn from Don Walker, of Kokomo. Art Smith, of Warsaw, finished third.

During the feature, DeWayne Fox, of Columbia City, miraculously escaped serious injury when his racer flipped over three and one-half times in the number four turn. Fox was treated at the Murphy Medical Center for an ankle injury but later released. On the 19th lap Harold Mouser, of Kokomo, also turned over at the end of the stretch but roll bars and other safety equipment in the stock car again prevented injuries.

Paul Bills, of Columbia City, won the stock feature event and Art Smith was second with Pete Gross, of Warsaw, third. A total of 60 cars qualified for the night's program. This Saturday night two big 50-lap mid-season championship feature events are slated, along with the regular racing card.

Race Summary:

Stock Dash—Jim Bucher, 1st; Les Sroufe, 2nd; Roger Grossnickle, 3rd.
Modified Dash—Jim Elliott, 1st; Art Smith, 2nd; Paul Joyce, 3rd.
Stock Heat—Doug Method, 1st; Jim Wagoner, 2nd; Pete Gross, 3rd.
Modified Heat—DeWayne Fox, 1st; Ray Loe, 2nd; Bob Bernhard, 3rd.
Stock Heat—Roger Rowland, 1st; Hal Apple, 2nd; Jim Bucher, 3rd.
Modified Heat—Danny Howell, 1st; Don Walker, 2nd; Art Smith, 3rd.
Stock Consy—Larry Montel, 1st; Luther Holloway, 2nd; Bill Voght, 3rd.
Stock Feature—Paul Bills, 1st; Art Smith, 2nd; Pete Gross, 3rd.
Modified Feature—Jim Elliott, 1st; Don Walker, 2nd; Art Smith, 3rd.

Saturday, July 6, 1968
Smith, Gross Win 50-Lap Feature Races

Warsaw's Art Smith captured three firsts in the modified competition in addition to nailing down a second place in the stock feature during the racing program at the Warsaw Speedway Saturday. Smith copped the checkered flag of victory in the modified dash and one other heat race before taking the big 50-lap feature. He also placed second behind Pete Gross, of Warsaw, in the 50-lap late model stock feature event.

A large crowd saw the late model stocks roar around the quarter-mile oval for 43 laps in the feature before the yellow flag was displayed and 17 of the original 20-car starting field finished the event. Gross, a hard-charging local driver, chauffeured his Chevy-powered car number 09 to victory in the 50-lap mid-season race and Smith romped home second. Les Sroufe, of Huntington, was third.

Restarts. The modified feature was re-started several times due to spinouts as the drivers set a blistering pace. Smith grabbed the checkered flag of victory with Jim Elliott, of Warsaw, second and Warsawan John Davis third to make a complete sweep for the local pilots. Hoosier Hot Rod, Inc., officials announced that the purse paid to drivers on the past three race nights has totaled $9,246.

Race Summary:

Stock Dash—Dick Leiter, 1st; Roger Grossnickle, 2nd; Les Sroufe, 3rd.
Modified Dash—Art Smith, 1st; Tom Beezley, 2nd; Paul Joyce, 3rd.
Stock Heat—Larry Montel, 1st; Jim Wagoner, 2nd; Hal Apple, 3rd.
Modified Heat—Jim Hickman, 1st; Mike Hanna, 2nd; Bob Bernhard, 3rd.
Stock Heat—Jerry Baker, 1st; Luther Holloway, 2nd; Pete Gross, 3rd.
Modified Heat—Art Smith, 1st; Don Walker, 2nd; Jim Elliott, 3rd.
Stock Consy—Devon Rensberger, 1st; Sam Davis, 2nd; Bud Grossnickle, 3rd.
50-lap Stock Feature—Pete Gross, 1st; Art Smith, 2nd; Les Sroufe, 3rd.
50-lap Modified Feature—Art Smith, 1st; Jim Elliott, 2nd; John Davis, 3rd.

Saturday, July 13, 1968
Thrills, Spills Highlight Local Racing Program

A thrilling race card with wrecks and roll-overs aplenty kept fans on the edge of their seats at the Warsaw Speedway Saturday night.

In the stock feature race Warsaw's Sam Davis rolled over the fence in the backstretch and Don Drudge, of Warsaw, flipped at the same time and his racer landed on top of Davis' car. During the modified feature Mike Hanna, of Warsaw, rolled over the fence and landed back on his wheels when a king pin broke on the front wheel. Several other cars were also demolished in wrecks but no drivers were hurt.

Speeds High. A total of 50 cars qualified for the night's program and speeds were very high during the evening. Art Smith, of Warsaw, and Les Sroufe, of Huntington, were the winners of the modified and stock features respectively but Tom Beezley, of Churubusco, was the big winner with two firsts in modified heats.

Race Summary:

Stock Dash—Paul Bills, 1st; Pete Gross, 2nd; Les Sroufe, 3rd.
Modified Dash—Tom Beezley, 1st; Jim Elliott, 2nd; Don Walker, 3rd.
Stock Heat—Dean Hudson, 1st; Jim Bucher, 2nd; Devon Rensberger, 3rd.
Modified Heat—Dave Ragan, 1st; Jack Hickman, 2nd; DeWayne Fox, 3rd.
Stock Heat—Hal Apple, 1st; Bud Grossnickle, 2nd; Les Sroufe, 3rd.

Modified Heat—Tom Beezley, 1st; Jim Elliott, 2nd; Art Smith, 3rd.
Stock Consy—Don Taylor, 1st; Ellis Shepherd, 2nd; Tom Leiter, 3rd.
Hobby Stock—Montel, 1st; Hare, 2nd; Ronk, 3rd.
Stock Feature—Les Sroufe, 1st; Art Smith, 2nd; Pete Gross, 3rd.
Modified Feature—Art Smith, 1st; Jim Elliott, 2nd; Dave Ragan, 3rd.

Saturday, July 20, 1968
Large Crowd Sees Near Record At Local Speedway

A large crowd was on hand at the Warsaw Speedway Saturday night as 95 cars competed for a purse totaling $1,800 in three classes: super modified, semi-late and hobby stock. Don Walker, of Kokomo, came close to setting a track record with a qualifying time of 16.60 seconds for an average speed of almost 60 mph or 85 mph in the straight-of-ways.

Art Smith of Warsaw won the modified feature event to capture the Big Buchanan Trophy given to any driver who wins three feature events in succession. The stock feature was captured by Jim Bucher. Walker copped a first in a modified heat and dash. Goodyear Service Center of Warsaw presented a one-half hour broadcast of the races over Radio Stations WRSW AM-FM.

Race Summary:

Stock Dash—Doug Method, 1st; Jerry Baker, 2nd; Pete Gross, 3rd.
Modified Dash—Don Walker, 1st; Art Smith, 2nd; Harold Mouser, 3rd.
Stock Heat—Devon Rensbuger, 1st; Dick Vought, 2nd; Jim Bucher, 3rd.
Modified Heat—Jim Cassle, 1st; Paul Joyce, 2nd; Dave Ragan, 3rd.
Stock Heat—Dean Hudson, 1st; Pete Gross, 2nd; Art Smith, 3rd.
Modified Heat—Don Walker, 1st; Jim Elliott, 2nd; Art Smith, 3rd.
Stock Consolation—Roger Rowland, 1st; Steve McClure, 2nd; Luther Holloway, 3rd.
Stock Feature—Jim Bucher, 1st; Paul Bills, 2nd; Pete Gross, 3rd.
Modified Feature—Art Smith, 1st; Don Walker, 2nd; Jim Elliott, 3rd.

Saturday, July 27, 1968 – Rainout

Saturday, August 3, 1968
Caldwell Stars At Local Track

A total of 127 cars were on hand for action at the Warsaw Speedway before a large crowd that braved threatening skies Saturday.

Mark Caldwell of Bunker Hill made his first appearance at the local track and came away with first place in the modified feature, modified heat and modified dash. Les Sroufe of Huntington took the stock feature. Rex Vigar took first place in a hobby stock race with Ray Taylor scoring a win in a second hobby stock race.

It was announced that there will be racing on Wednesday, Friday and Saturday nights this week in conjunction with the Kosciusko County Fair. Several of the events lined up for racing enthusiasts include a demolition race, power puff race and a strut stock race.

Race Summary:

Stock Dash—Roger Rowland, 1st; Pete Gross, 2nd; Jerry Baker, 3rd.
Modified Dash—Mark Caldwell, 1st; Harold Mauser, 2nd; Art Smith, 3rd.
Stock Heat—Jim Bucher, 1st; Hal Apple, 2nd; Devon Rensberger, 3rd.
Modified Heat—Jim Elliott, 1st; Ben Simmers, 2nd; DeWayne Fox, 3rd.
Stock Heat—Jerry Baker, 1st; Pete Gross, 2nd; Vonell Krom, 3rd.
Modified Heat—Mark Caldwell, 1st; Don Walker, 2nd; Larry Bills, 3rd.
Stock Consolation—Roger Grossnickle, 1st; Don Raber, 2nd; Orval Taylor, 3rd.
Modified Consolation—Ellis Shepherd, 1st; Max Eakwright, 2nd; Larry Montel, 3rd.
Modified Feature—Mark Caldwell, 1st; Tom Beezley, 2nd; Don Walker, 3rd.
Stock Feature—Les Sroufe, 1st; Dean Hudson, 2nd; Jerry Egolf, 3rd.

Wednesday, August 7, 1968 – Rainout

Friday, August 9, 1968
Flagman Performs 'Under Fire' At Local Speedway
By Robert Watkins, WRSW Radio Announcer

While marveling at the daring of the race car drivers the spectators at the Warsaw Speedway tend to overlook the cool nerve of the flagman.

To see Walt Yoder, of Syracuse, performing his duties as flagman is to see a genuine display of courage. During the qualifying events he takes a position directly on the track. With his trim athletic physique attired in a black and white uniform he makes an imposing sight while awaiting the approach of the first car.

The speeding car comes closer and closer and the roar is deafeningly loud. He bends his knees, crouches low, and brings the flag down in a swift authoritative motion as the swerving auto thunders past just inches from his body. This ritual is repeated time after time as dozens of cars streak by in frantic attempts to properly qualify.

When the actual racing gets under way, Walt climbs onto a small platform a few feet off the ground. This perch is parallel to the wire fence surrounding the track and serves as an observation post from which he views the race and governs its action.

Openly Exposed. The platform is openly exposed and affords scant protection to its occupant. During one race a car overturned, crashed into the structure and completely demolished it. Walt's alertness and agility enabled him to leap from the platform in time to escape injury. On another occasion, a wheel flew off an auto, made its way to his position and struck him on the knee.

In the course of his job he's frequently covered with dust, spattered with mud, and struck with pieces of rock thrown up by revolving tires. Walt Yoder is a man who loves racing and all that it encompasses. In the six years that he has been a flagman he has never failed to report for work at the speedway.

As a former driver with seven years of experience, he has an excellent insight of the thrills, dangers and rewards of racing. His collection of trophies proves that he is a highly skilled driver in his own right.

Confident. Walt maintains that it's his unwavering confidence in the abilities of the drivers that allows him to venture into the midst of their speeding autos without fearing for his safety.

His wife, Darlene, is also a racing enthusiast. She's always on hand to give her husband moral support and to provide him with the homemade flags that he uses at the track. Last year she drove in the Powder Puff Derby and managed to win a trophy of her own.

Walt's regular occupation is that of a production worker with Sea Nymph Manufacturing Corporation in Syracuse. But each Saturday evening he returns to the activity that he enjoys most of all, the thrilling excitement of the race track.

Saturday, August 10, 1968
Baker, Smith Win Features At Local Track

Jerry Baker and Art Smith, both of Warsaw, won the stock and modified features respectively at the Warsaw Speedway before a large Kosciusko County Fair crowd Saturday night. A total of 95 drivers qualified for the night's racing card as frantic speed was the by-word with drivers set on gaining a share of the large purse.

Smith and Don Walker put on several close duels for the crowd with Smith edging his foe by two feet in one race. Walker finished second behind Smith in the modified feature and a modified heat.

One-half hour of the racing program was broadcast by Silveus and Bradway Sunoco over Radio Stations WRSW AM-FM.

Race Summary:

Stock Dash—Jerry Baker, 1st; Grossnickle, 2nd; Pete Gross, 3rd.
Modified Dash—John Davis, 1st; Paul Grim, 2nd; Jim Elliott, 3rd.
Stock Heat—Bud Grossnickle, 1st; Gerald Shank, 2nd; Orval Taylor, 3rd.
Modified Heat—Jack Hickman, 1st; Tom Holmes, 2nd; Harold Mauser, 3rd.
Stock Heat—Luther Holloway, 1st; Art Smith, 2nd; Dean Hudson, 3rd.
Modified Heat—Art Smith, 1st; Don Walker, 2nd; Ed Stine, 3rd.
Stock Consolation—Paul Bills, 1st; Sam Davis, 2nd; Don Miller, 3rd.
Stock Feature—Jerry Baker, 1st; Dean Hudson, 2nd; Bud Grossnickle, 3rd.
Modified Feature—Art Smith, 1st; Don Walker, 2nd; Ed Stine, 3rd.
Hobby Stock—Sainer Fancil, 1st; Bob Maggart, 2nd; Kiern, 3rd.
Hobby Stock—John Hare, 1st; Chuck Sainer, 2nd; Drabenstott, 3rd.

Saturday, August 17, 1968
Walker Sets New Record At Local Speedway

Don Walker, of Kokomo, set a new track record of 16.12 at the Warsaw Speedway Saturday night, breaking the former record of 16.30 that had stood for two years. The feat was done under almost impossible conditions due to heavy rains Friday. Walker almost twisted his car in two pieces, lifting the left front wheel off the track by about two feet. Walker took the modified feature as well as finished first and second in modified heats. Art Smith of Warsaw won the stock feature.

Dick Terrell of Indianapolis found out that competition was pretty keen at the local speedway as he failed to win in the late Bettenhausen championship car. Three drivers joined the roll-over club as Gary Baker rolled in his modified racer and two hobby stocks driven by Smith and Ted Hare joined the club the hard way.

Ray Kenens was back in action after not racing since 1962, but served notice he hadn't forgotten his way around the local track, finishing second in the dash, fourth in the heat and second in the feature. One-half hour of the races were broadcast over Radio Stations WRSW AM-FM by the Goodyear Service Center.

Race Summary:
Stock Dash—Gross, 1st; Baker, 2nd; Voght, 3rd.
Modified Dash—Walker, 1st; Kenens, 2nd; Smith, 3rd.
Stock Heat—Hudson, 1st; Taylor, 2nd; Drudge, 3rd.
Modified Heat—Sarner, 1st; Simon, 2nd; Murphy, 3rd.
Stock Heat—Bucher, 1st; Baker, 2nd; Gross, 3rd.
Modified Heat—Grim, 1st; Walker, 2nd; Mann, 3rd.
Stock Consolation—Egolf, 1st; Malott, 2nd; Baker, 3rd.
Stock Feature—Smith, 1st; Gross, 2nd; Baker, 3rd.
Modified Feature—Walker, 1st; Kenens, 2nd; Joyce, 3rd.
Hobby Stock (1st race)—Drabenstott, 1st; Cox, 2nd; Fancil, 3rd.
Hobby Stock (2nd race)—Sainer, 1st; Baker, 2nd; Baker, 3rd.

Saturday, August 24, 1968
Art Smith Cops 50-Lap Feature Here

Warsaw's Art Smith drove his car No. 67 to victory Saturday in the 50-lap season championship modified feature race at the Warsaw Speedway. Smith was followed across the finish line in the hotly contested event by Kokomo's Don Walker in second and Jim Elliott of Warsaw, in third.

Dean Hudson, of North Manchester, grabbed the checkered flag in the stock feature. A total of 111 cars qualified for the evening's activities and competed for a purse of $1,550.

Car Flips. Kokomo's Charlie Sarver flipped his modified car No. 5 over three times in the 50-lap feature and was treated at the Murphy Medical Center. His injuries, however, were not serious due to safety equipment required in the racers.

One-half hour of the action was broadcast over Radio Stations WRSW AM-FM sponsored by Silveus and Bradway Sunoco service stations.

Race Summary:
Stock Dash—Les Sroufe, 1st; Pete Gross, 2nd; Jerry Baker, 3rd.
Modified Dash—John Davis, 1st; Tom Beezley, 2nd; Larry Bills, 3rd.
Stock Heat—Venall Krom, 1st; Dean Hudson, 2nd; Ted Hudson, 3rd.
Modified Heat—Ray Kenens, 1st; Charlie Sarver, 2nd; Paul Joyce, 3rd.
Stock Heat—Paul Bills, 1st; Ellis Shepherd, 2nd; Les Sroufe, 3rd.
Modified Heat—Don Walker, 1st; Herb Mann, 2nd; Jene Simon, 3rd.
Consolation—Art Smith, 1st; Dick Leiter, 2nd; Butts, 3rd.
Hobby Stock—Cox, 1st; Montel, 2nd; Maggart, 3rd.
Hobby Stock—Hare, 1st; Baker, 2nd; Hite, 3rd.

Stock Feature—Dean Hudson, 1st; Larry Malott, 2nd; Pete Gross, 3rd.
Modified Feature—Art Smith, 1st; Don Walker, 2nd; Jim Elliott, 3rd.

Saturday, August 31 & Monday, September 2, 1968
50-Lap Race For Stocks Here Saturday

A big double feature program including a 50-lap season championship race for late model stock cars will be held at the Warsaw Speedway this Saturday night following a dual card over the Labor Day weekend. Races were washed out last Saturday night after the seventh event but approximately 90 cars were back at the race course for a full program Monday night.

Mishaps. During the two nights there were plenty of mishaps but no one was injured. Wendall Taylor, of Kokomo, flipped over the fence and was shaken up Saturday but was not hospitalized. Monday's feature winners were Dick Leiter, Warsaw, in the late-model stock class and Warsaw's Art Smith in the modified event.

Monday Summary:

Stock Dash—Paul Bills, 1st; Pete Gross, 2nd; Art Smith, 3rd.
Modified Dash—John Davis, 1st; Art Smith, 2nd; Don Walker, 3rd.
Stock Heat—Dick Leiter, 1st; Roger Rowland, 2nd; Bob Cozzi, 3rd.
Modified Heat—Bob Bernhard, 1st; Don Murphy, 2nd; Jene Simon, 3rd.
Stock Dash—Ted Hudson, 1st; Larry Mallot, 2nd; Bud Shank, 3rd.
Modified Heat—Ray Kenens, 1st; Art Smith, 2nd; Don Walker, 3rd.
Stock consy—Bob Johnson, 1st; Don Taylor, 2nd; Luther Holloway, 3rd.
Stock Feature—Dick Leiter, 1st; Roger Rowland, 2nd; Bob Cozzi, 3rd.
Modified Feature—Art Smith, 1st; Ray Kenens, 2nd; Ed Stine, 3rd.
Hobby Stock—E. Coral, 1st; J. Fancil, 2nd; B. Beezley, 3rd.
Hobby Stock—Wagoner, 1st; Priser, 2nd; Ronk, 3rd.

Saturday Summary:

Stock Dash—Pete Gross, 1st; Jim Bucher, 2nd; Paul Bills, 3rd.
Modified Dash—Larry Bills, 1st; Paul Joyce, 2nd; John Davis, 3rd.
Stock Heat—Bob Cozzi, 1st; Ted Hudson, 2nd; Hal Apple, 3rd.
Modified Heat—Jack Hickman, 1st; Lou Mann, 2nd; Bob Bernhard, 3rd.
Stock Heat—Les Sroufe, 1st; Roger Grossnickle, 2nd; Jerry Baker, 3rd.
Modified Heat—Jim Elliott, 1st; Paul Grim, 2nd; Larry Bills, 3rd.
Stock Consy—Bob Johnson, 1st; Ellis Shepherd, 2nd; Lyle Butts, 3rd.
Officials Race—Don Coleman, 1st; Grover Martin, 2nd; Charles Gibson, 3rd; Bill Bullers, 4th.

Saturday, September 9, 1968
Smith Wins 4 Events In Final Racing Card

Art Smith, of Warsaw, was the big winner at the Warsaw Speedway Saturday as the 1968 racing season bowed out in a thrilling final night blaze of glory. Smith won four events during the evening including two heat races, the modified feature and the

Tom Leiter, Warsaw

50-lap stock championship event held over from the previous week.

The final race was made up of all the street stock cars that were able to run. There were 35 vehicles in the event but the total was reduced to six before the race was stopped and Tom Leiter, of Warsaw, declared the winner. There were four roll-overs during the race which resembled a destruction derby at times.

Race Summary:

Stock Dash—Paul Bills, 1st; Les Sroufe, 2nd; Jerry Baker, 3rd.
Modified Dash—Art Smith, 1st; Jim Elliott, 2nd; Paul Joyce, 3rd.
Stock Heat—Gerald Shank, 1st; Ted Hudson, 2nd; Jim Wagoner, 3rd.
Modified Heat—Jack Hickman, 1st; Charlie Sarver, 2nd; Ed Stine, 3rd.
Stock Heat—Art Smith, 1st; Dean Hudson, 2nd. Roger Grossnickle, 3rd.
Modified Heat—Paul Grim, 1st; Jim Elliott, 2nd; Art Smith, 3rd.
Stock Consy—Sunny Carpenter, 1st; Raker, 2nd; Sands, 3rd.
Stock Feature—Vonell Krom, 1st; Gerald Shank, 2nd; Bob Johnson, 3rd.
Modified Feature—Art Smith, 1st; Jack Hickman, 2nd; Charles Sarver, 3rd.
2nd Modified Feature—Jim Elliott, 1st; Ray Kenens, 2nd.
50-lap Stock Feature—Art Smith, 1st; Pete Gross, 2nd; Paul Bills, 3rd.

1969

Saturday, May 3, 1969
Kenens Big Winner At Local Speedway

The 1969 auto racing season got off to a flying start at the Warsaw Speedway Saturday night as three drivers joined the "roll over club" and Delphi's Ray Kenens was the evening's big winner.

Kenens copped the modified dash, a modified heat race and placed third in the modified feature to go along with his checkered flag victory in the stock consolation event.

Late model stock drivers Tom Stevens and Roger Rowland, of Burket, and modified racer Jerry Priest, Kokomo, were the first drivers initiated into the roll over club this year. None of the drivers were hurt. Several new cars were entered in competition and many more are being built but were not ready for the opening night program. A total of 47 cars qualified.

The modified feature was hotly contested at a brisk pace on the thrilling inaugural night program. Ed Angle, of Flora, took the modified feature and Jim Bucher, of Silver Lake, copped the stock feature event.

Race Summary:

Stock Dash—Jim Wagoner, 1st; Jim Bucher, 2nd; Roger Rowland, 3rd.
Modified Dash—Ray Kenens, 1st; Paul Grim, 2nd; Paul Joyce, 3rd.
Stock Heat—Don Taylor, 1st; Jim White, 2nd; Orval Taylor, 3rd.
Modified Heat—Bob Bernhard, 1st; Don Murphy, 2nd; Harold Mouser, 3rd.
Stock Heat—Less Sroufe, 1st; Jim Bucher, 2nd; Dean Hudson, 3rd.
Modified Heat—Ray Kenens, 1st; Jim Elliott, 2nd; Ed Angle, 3rd.

Stock Consy—Ray Kenens, 1st; Larry Montel, 2nd; Ron Swick, 3rd.
Stock Feature—Jim Bucher, 1st; Less Sroufe, 2nd; Jim Wagoner, 3rd.
Modified Feature—Ed Angle, 1st; Jim Elliott, 2nd; Ray Kenens, 3rd.

Saturday, May 10, 1969 - Rainout

Saturday, May 17, 1969
Egolf, Walker Win Features At Local Track

Jerry Egolf and Don Walker won feature races at the Warsaw Speedway Saturday before a small, but spirited crowd that was held down due to the threatening weather.

Egolf won the stock feature while Walker came back from winning a thrilling modified heat to win the modified feature. In the close heat eight cars were bunched up for eight laps of the 10-lap race until Walker broke around Tom Beezley to hold on for the victory.

A total of 63 cars provided thrills for the brave crowd. Ironically temperatures in Warsaw hovered near the 70 degree mark while in South Bend and Chicago the figure stood near 40 degrees.

Race Summary:

Stock Dash—Les Sroufe, 1st; Dean Hudson, 2nd; Jim Bucher, 3rd.
Modified Dash—Don Walker, 1st; Ray Kenens, 2nd; Paul Grim, 3rd.
Stock Heat—Don Spear, 1st; Art Howard, 2nd; Jim Craig, 3rd.
Modified Heat—Mike Coblentz, 1st; Gary Baker, 2nd; Bob Bernhard, 3rd.
Stock Heat—Ted Hudson, 1st; Ray Kenens, 2nd; Jerry Egolf, 3rd.
Modified Heat—Ray Kenens, 1st; Don Walker, 2nd; John Davis, 3rd.
Stock Consy—Max Lambert, 1st; Bob Johnson, 2nd; Ron Swick, 3rd.
Stock Feature—Jerry Egolf, 1st; Les Sroufe, 2nd; Art Howard, 3rd.
Modified Feature—Don Walker, 1st; Jim Elliott, 2nd; Paul Grim, 3rd.

Saturday, May 24, 1969
Walker Big Winner At Local Speedway

Don Walker of Kokomo was the big winner at the Warsaw Speedway Saturday night, winning three races including the modified feature race.

Walker also captured the modified dash and modified heat events before a good crowd on the clear evening. Sixty cars took part in the night's card that saw a six-car pile-up in the stock feature. However, there were no injuries.

Les Sroufe of Huntington was another big winner Saturday, copping the stock heat and coming back later to take the stock feature. It was announced that there would be racing Friday night with two 30-lap feature events with large trophies going to each winner.

Race Summary:

Stock Dash—Jim Bucher, 1st; Paul Bills, 2nd; Vonell Krom, 3rd.
Modified Dash—Don Walker, 1st; Ray Kenens, 2nd; Ed Stine, 3rd.
Stock Heat—Don Taylor, 1st; Paul Roberts, 2nd; Slug Bradley, 3rd.
Modified Heat—Paul Grim, 1st; Paul Joyce, 2nd; Jack Hickman, 3rd.

Stock Heat—Les Sroufe, 1st; Paul Bills, 2nd; Jim Wagoner, 3rd.
Modified Heat—Don Walker, 1st; Ed Stine, 2nd; Ray Kenens, 3rd.
Stock Consolation—Bob Johnson, 1st; Ed Cotton, 2nd; Higgenbottam, 3rd.
Stock Feature—Les Sroufe, 1st' Ted Hudson, 2nd; Vonell Krom, 3rd.
Modified Feature—Don Walker, 1st; Ray Kenens, 2nd; John Davis, 3rd.

Friday, May 30 & Saturday, May 31, 1969
Large Crowds Witness Local Speedway Races

Art Smith returned to the Warsaw Speedway Saturday and won the feature modified race in a weekend of thrills and spills viewed by a crowd of approximately 5,000 persons.

Threatening skies held down the Saturday night crowd, but a huge throng Friday witnessed the many mishaps. Don Walker of Kokomo, Ed Stine of Warsaw and Paul Grim of Warren tangled in a crash when Walker's car flipped up on two wheels. It was thought that Walker was hurt, but the Kokomo driver came back to win the feature modified race. Grim returned Saturday to win a modified heat race.

Silveus and Bradway Sunoco broadcast one-half hour of the Friday races while the Goodyear Service Store carried a one-half hour broadcast of the Saturday action.

Friday Results:
Stock Dash—R. Grossnickle, 1st; Rowland, 2nd; Bucher, 3rd.
Modified Dash—Grindle, 1st; Grim, 2nd; Walker, 3rd.
Stock Heat—Montel, 1st; Baker, 2nd; White, 3rd.
Modified Heat—Davis, 1st; Hickman, 2nd; Murphy, 3rd.
Stock Heat—Krom, 1st; Hudson, 2nd; R. Grossnickle, 3rd.
Modified Heat—Elliott, 1st; Kenens, 2nd; Mann, 3rd.
Stock Consolation—B. Grossnickle, 1st; Lambert, 2nd; Bradley, 3rd.
Stock Feature—Krom, 1st; Bucher, 2nd; Hudson, 3rd.
Modified Feature—Walker, 1st; Brathwalt, 2nd; Murphy, 3rd.

Saturday Results:
Stock Dash—Sroufe, 1st; Krom, 2nd; White, 3rd.
Modified Dash—Davis, 1st; Grindle, 2nd; Smith, 3rd.
Stock Heat—R. Grossnickle, 1st; Leedy, 2nd; Saner, 3rd.
Modified Heat—Grim, 1st; Beezley, 2nd; Fisher, 3rd.
Stock Heat—Egolf, 1st; Baker, 2nd; Rowland, 3rd.
Modified Heat—Mann, 1st; Elliott, 2nd; Hickman, 3rd.
Stock Consolation—Sroufe, 1st; Bucher, 2nd; Montel, 3rd.
Stock Feature—Krom, 1st; Egolf, 2nd; Bucher, 3rd.
Modified Feature—Smith, 1st; Elliott, 2nd; Stine, 3rd.

Saturday, June 7, 1969
Walker Wins 3 Speedway Events

Despite threatening weather a good crowd was on hand at the Warsaw Speedway Saturday night to see Kokomo's Don Walker win all three races he was in including the modified feature. Walker started the evening by wheeling his modified car number 39 to first place in the dash event. He came back to cop a heat race before grabbing the checkered flag in the modified feature.

Paul Grim supplied the thrills during the evening by getting his modified car number 7 airborne in a heat race, then going airborne again in a late-model stock race. The second mishap involved six cars but no one was hurt. Despite the misfortunes, Grim managed a third place finish in the modified feature.

One-half hour of the activity was broadcast over Radio Stations WRSW AM-FM sponsored by Silveus and Bradway Sunoco.

Race Summary:

Stock Dash—Vonell Krom, 1st; Art Smith, 2nd; Jerry Egolf, 3rd.
Modified Dash—Don Walker, 1st; Art Smith, 2nd; Paul Grim, 3rd.
Stock Heat—Ellis Shepherd, 1st; Roger Rowland, 2nd; Paul Roberts, 3rd.
Modified Heat—Bob Grindle, 1st; Tom Beezley, 2nd; Jack Hickman, 3rd.
Stock Heat—Roger Grossnickle, 1st; Paul Grim, 2nd; Ted Hudson, 3rd.
Modified Heat—Don Walker, 1st; Jim Elliott, 2nd; Art Smith, 3rd.
Stock Consolation—Jim Bucher, 1st; Larry Howard, 2nd; Jim Wagoner, 3rd.
Stock Feature—Dean Hudson, 1st; Vonell Krom, 2nd; Ted Hudson, 3rd.
Modified Feature—Don Walker, 1st; John Davis, 2nd; Paul Grim, 3rd.

Saturday, June 14, 1969
Elliott Wins Feature Here

A small but loyal crowd of fans was on hand at the Warsaw Speedway Saturday night to see Warsaw's Jim Elliott grab the checkered flag in the modified feature.

Kokomo's Don Walker held a comfortable lead in the event when his racer suddenly quit midway through the feature and Elliott took over. Walker, however, won two other events he raced in, the modified dash and a modified heat race.

Rains earlier in the day caused the clay track to be slick and treacherous creating some interesting spins and slides. Jerry Egolf, of Columbia City, was the winner in the stock feature. One-half hour of the races was broadcast over Radio Stations WRSW AM-FM sponsored by Goodyear Service store in Warsaw.

Race Summary:

Stock Dash—Jim Elliott, 1st; Jim Bucher, 2nd; Jerry Egolf, 3rd.
Modified Dash—Don Walker, 1st; John Davis, 2nd; Jim Elliott, 3rd.
Stock Heat—Roger Rowland, 1st; Paul Roberts, 2nd; Ellis Shepherd, 3rd.
Modified Heat—Harold Mauser, 1st; Bob Bernhard, 2nd; Art Braithwaite, 3rd.
Stock Heat—Art Smith, 1st; John White, 2nd; Jerry Egolf, 3rd.
Modified Heat—Don Walker, 1st; John Davis, 2nd; Ray Kenens, 3rd.
Stock Consy—Roger Leedy, 1st; Roger Grossnickle, 2nd; Bob Johnson, 3rd.
Stock Feature—Jerry Egolf, 1st; Ted Hudson, 2nd; Les Sroufe, 3rd.
Modified Feature- -Jim Elliott, 1st; Ray Kenens, 2nd; Paul Grim, 3rd.

Saturday, June 21, 1969
Auto Demolition Derby Attracts Big Crowd Here

The largest crowd of the season turned out at the Warsaw Speedway Saturday night to watch a thrilling auto racing card which was capped off by a gigantic 50-car demolition derby.

When the fender-bending crowd-pleasing event was completed the track was littered with scrap iron and Jim Barnette of Columbia City, was adjudged the winner. Don Rumfelt, of Milford, was awarded the runner-up spot in the derby.

Ed Stine. Etna Green

There was a total of 75 modified and late model stock racers qualifying for the evening's activity and three drivers joined the exclusive "roll-over club". Dave Ragan, of Kokomo, and Don Miller both hit the wall and rolled over and Eldon Burgess, of Etna Green, flipped end over end at the starter's ramp sending flagman Walt Yoder scurrying for safety.

Warsaw's Art Smith was the only modified double winner capturing the dash event then coming back to take the checkered flag in the modified feature. Jerry Baker, of Warsaw, took two stock events, a heat race and the stock feature.

Race Summary:

Stock Dash—Jim Wagoner, 1st; Vonell Krom, 2nd; Art Smith, 3rd.
Modified Dash—Art Smith, 1st; Paul Grim, 2nd; Don Walker, 3rd.
Stock Heat—Jerry Baker, 1st; John White, 2nd; Roger Rowland, 3rd.
Modified Heat—Paul Joyce, 1st; Ed Stine, 2nd; Jack Hickman, 3rd.
Stock Heat—Ted Hudson, 1st; Jim Elliott, 2nd; Dean Hudson, 3rd.
Modified Heat—Bob Grindle, 1st; Ed Angle, 2nd; Ron Fisher, 3rd.
Stock Consolation—Bob Johnson, 1st; John Baker, 2nd; Duane Ronk, 3rd.
Stock Feature—Jerry Baker, 1st; Larry Howard, 2nd; Roger Grossnickle, 3rd.
Modified Feature—Art Smith, 1st; Ed Stine, 2nd; Jim Elliott, 3rd.
Demolition Derby—Jim Barnette, 1st; Don Rumfelt, 2nd.

Saturday, June 28, 1969
Fireworks Set At Speedway On Friday

A gigantic fireworks display is planned during the special July 4 racing card at the Warsaw Speedway this Friday night. Gates will open at 4 p.m., two hours before the time trials, and the first race is slated for 7:30.

In activity Saturday, Warsaw's Art Smith and Jim Elliott were the big winners. Smith captured two third place finishes in the stock competition and copped a second and third in the modified activity. Elliott won the modified dash and feature and placed second in a stock event. Jerry Baker, of Warsaw, took the stock feature.

A large crowd saw plenty of thrills and spills as 65 cars qualified for the evening's program. Many re-starts were necessary because of accidents in the stock consolation and stock features. Bill Taylor, of Elwood, was taken to the hospital with shoulder injuries when his racer flipped over a mound of dirt in front of one of the light poles.

Race Summary:

Stock Dash—Roger Grossnickle, 1st; Jerry Baker, 2nd; Art Smith, 3rd.
Modified Dash—Jim Elliott, 1st; Art Smith, 2nd; Don Walker, 3rd.
Stock Heat—Max Lambert, 1st; Jim Elliott, 2nd; Larry Malott, 3rd.
Modified Heat—Tom Beezley, 1st; John Davis, 2nd; Bob Bernhard, 3rd.
Stock Heat—Dean Hudson, 1st; Vonell Krom, 2nd; Art Smith, 3rd.
Modified Heat—Bob Grindle, 1st; Jim Murphy, 2nd; Art Smith, 3rd.
Stock Consolation—Les Sroufe, 1st; John White, 2nd; Tex Plummer, 3rd.
Stock Feature—Jerry Baker, 1st; Roger Grossnickle, 2nd; Jerry Egolf, 3rd.
Modified Feature—Jim Elliott, 1st; Ed Angle, 2nd; Paul Grim, 3rd.

Friday, July 4, 1969
Huge Crowd Sees Races, Fireworks Here

An overflow crowd jammed the Warsaw Speedway last night to see the annual Fourth of July racing card and to witness the always colorful fireworks display. The racing program went off so smoothly it became necessary to add two special 10-lap races to provide the darkness necessary for the fireworks which were co-sponsored by the Hoosier Hot Rods Racing Assn. and the Kosciusko County Fair Assn.

Les Sroufe, of Huntington, was the big winner in the stock class winning a heat race and the feature while Jim Murphy, of Jackson, Mich., captured his first checkered flag in the modified feature competition. The fast qualifiers for the evening were Jerry Baker, of Pierceton, in the stock class and Don Walker, Kokomo, in the modified competition.

Race Summary:

Stock Dash—Jim Elliott, 1st; Max Lambert, 2nd; Jerry Baker, 3rd.
Modified Dash—John Davis, 1st; Ray Kenens, 2nd; Don Walker, 3rd.
Stock Heat—Larry Montel, 1st; Larry Howard, 2nd; John White, 3rd.
Modified Heat—Paul Joyce, 1st; John Hare, 2nd; Tom Beezley, 3rd.
Stock Heat—Les Sroufe, 1st; Jim Wagoner, 2nd; Jim Elliott, 3rd.
Modified Heat—Don Walker, 1st; Bob Grindle, 2nd; John Davis, 3rd.
Stock Consolation—Swick, 1st; Shephard, 2nd; Heeter, 3rd.
Modified Feature—Jim Murphy, 1st; Don Walker, 2nd; John Davis, 3rd.
Stock Feature—Les Sroufe, 1st; Jim Wagoner, 2nd; Jim Elliott, 3rd.
Special Modified—Harold Mouser, 1st; Ed Stine, 2nd; Sam Davis, 3rd.
Special Stock—Tom Hudson, 1st; L. Roberts, 2nd; Bob Grindle, 3rd.

Saturday, July 5, 1969
50-Lap Feature Here Saturday

A big 50-lap mid-season championship feature race for super modified cars is planned at the Warsaw Speedway this Saturday night following the dual Fourth of July card of activity. Purses paid to drivers for the July 4 and July 5 weekend programs here totaled $5,000. The races Saturday were called off at 4:30 because of the rain, but reinstated at 6 p.m. when the sun dried out the race course and many fans and drivers returned to the track after having left the fairgrounds earlier.

Two cars rolled over during the evening. Bill Taylor, of Elwood, is now a two-time member of the roll over club. Joe Perry, of Perkinsville, went through a slow roll and then returned to competition with only minor damage.

Ray Kenens, of Delphi, won the modified dash and placed second in two other modified events. Bob Grindle, of Warsaw, took the modified feature, Dean Hudson, of Wabash, won the stock feature. The crowd-pleasing powder puff derby was won by Nelda Egolf, of North Manchester, and Charlene Conley, of Pierceton, was second.

Race Summary:

Stock Dash—Jerry Baker, 1st; Jim Wagoner, 2nd; Roger Grossnickle, 3rd.
Modified Dash—Ray Kenens, 1st; Don Walker, 2nd; Jim Murphy, 3rd.
Stock Heat—Vonell Krom, 1st; Larry Malott, 2nd; Mike Cox, 3rd.
Modified Heat—Doug Method, 1st; Joe Perry, 2nd; Jack Hickman, 3rd.
Stock Heat—Roger Grossnickle, 1st; Jim Elliott, 2nd; Jerry Baker, 3rd.
Modified Heat—Ed Stine, 1st; Ray Kenens, 2nd; Jim Elliott, 3rd.
Powder Puff Derby—Nelda Egolf, 1st; Charlene Conley, 2nd.
Stock Feature—Dean Hudson, 1st; Larry Howard, 2nd; Jim Elliott, 3rd.
Modified Feature—Bob Grindle, 1st; Ray Kenens, 2nd; Ed Stine, 3rd.

Saturday, July 12, 1969
Kokomo Driver Wins Big Feature

Don Walker, of Kokomo, wheeled his car number 39 to victory Saturday night in the big 50-lap mid-season championship race for modified racers at the Warsaw Speedway. Ray Kenens, of Delphi, placed second and Ed Stine, of Etna Green, was third. Warsaw's Bob Grindle managed a fourth place finish coasting across the finish line, after his engine failed in the home stretch.

Warsaw's Art Smith was knocked out of competition when his accelerator stuck on his modified number 67 and the racer careened into the fence and rolled over several times. Smith was not injured but the racer was heavily damaged.

Indy Racer. A race car driven to second place in the 1962 Indianapolis 500 by Bud Tinglestead was at the local speedway and was driven by Jim Murphy, of Jackson, Mich. The owner hopes to put the big racer in competition here soon. Murphy is one of several Michigan drivers now competing regularly at the Warsaw Speedway.

Next Saturday night a 50-lap feature for late model stock cars will be highlighted. One-half hour of the races was broadcast over Radio Stations WRSW AM-FM sponsored by Bill Nay Furniture Co., of Warsaw.

Race Summary:

Stock Dash—Dean Hudson, 1st; Art Smith, 2nd; Roger Grossnickle, 3rd.
Modified Dash—Harold Mauser, 1st; Ed Stine, 2nd; Don Walker, 3rd.
Stock Heat—Jim Wagoner, 1st; Sheldon Bowser, 2nd; Vonell Krom, 3rd.
Modified Heat—Paul Joyce, 1st; Gary Baker, 2nd; Sam Davis, 3rd.
Stock Heat—Ted Hudson, 1st; Jim Elliott, 2nd; Art Smith, 3rd.
Modified Heat—Jim Murphy, 1st; Ed Stine, 2nd; Jim Elliott, 3rd.
Stock Consolation—Roger Leedy, 1st; Mike Cox, 2nd; Dick Reed, 3rd.
Stock Feature—Jerry Egolf, 1st; Dean Hudson, 2nd; Art Smith, 3rd.
Modified Feature—Don Walker, 1st; Ray Kenens, 2nd; Ed Stine, 3rd.

Saturday, July 19, 1969
Bucher Captures Stock Feature At Local Track

Jim Bucher of Akron and Don Walker of Kokomo were the feature winners at the Warsaw Speedway Saturday night before a large crowd that turned out despite the threatening weather.

Bucher, in addition to winning the stock dash event and the third heat, won the 50-lap mid-season championship for late model stock cars. Walker, who a week ago won the mid-season championship race for modified racers, won the modified feature. Earlier he captured the dash event for modifieds and the fourth heat.

Fifty-seven cars were on hand when the evening's card got underway. After much discussion it was decided to go ahead with the races as the sun shone through the cloudy skies. After the races started the rains held off to the delight of the hearty crowd.

Qualifying was not held because of the condition of the track. Races were set up by a drawing. One-half hour of the races was broadcast over Radio Stations WRSW AM-FM, sponsored by Silveus and Bradway Sunoco Stations.

Race Summary:

Stock Dash—Jim Bucher, 1st; Jerry Egolf, 2nd; Jim Elliott, 3rd.
Modified Dash—Don Walker, 1st; Harold Mauser, 2nd; Tom Beezley, 3rd.
Stock Heat—Jerry Baker, 1st; Larry Montel, 2nd; Dean Hudson, 3rd.
Modified Heat—Jim Elliott, 1st; Paul Grim, 2nd; Louis Mann, 3rd.
Stock Heat—Jim Bucher, 1st; Art Smith, 2nd; Larry Malott, 3rd.
Modified Heat—Don Walker, 1st; John Davis, 2nd; Bob Grindle, 3rd.
Stock Consolation—Ray Lambert, 1st; Roger Rowland, 2nd; Ted Hudson, 3rd.
Stock Feature—Jim Bucher, 1st; Jim Elliott, 2nd; Vonell Krom, 3rd.
Modified Feature—Don Walker, 1st; John Davis, 2nd; Tom Beezley, 3rd.

Saturday, July 26, 1969
Rains Plague Event At Local Speedway

Heavy rains washed out part of Saturday's card at the Warsaw Speedway, but not before a good crowd watched six events.

Don Walker of Kokomo again supplied thrills with a display of speed that stunned fans as he raced to victory in the modified heat event.

Several other drivers found the track to their liking and put up quite a display of driving skill. It was announced that because of the rain-out prior to the scheduled features, there would be double features this Saturday night.

One-half hour of Saturday's races were broadcast over Radio Stations WRSW AM-FM, sponsored by Bill Nay Furniture Co.

Race Summary:

Stock Dash—Jim Wagoner, 1st; Paul Roberts, 2nd; Dean Hudson, 3rd.
Modified Dash—Jim Elliott, 1st; Paul Joyce, 2nd; Don Walker, 3rd.
Stock Heat—Jerry Baker, 1st; Max Lambert, 2nd; Larry Mallott, 3rd.
Modified Heat—Tom Beezley, 1st; Ed Stine, 2nd; Jack Hickman, 3rd.
Stock Heat—Les Sroufe, 1st; John White, 2nd; Larry Montel, 3rd.
Modified Heat—Don Walker, 1st; Louis Mann, 2nd; John Davis, 3rd.

Saturday, August 2, 1969
Walker Sets Lap Record At Speedway

Don Walker of Kokomo set a new lap record at the Warsaw Speedway before a large turnout Saturday night. Walker had a qualifying time of 15.59 to better his old record of 16.12 before the crowd that saw a double feature as a result of the rainout a week ago.

Walker's time meant that he turned speeds of 90 mph in the short straight-of-ways and 45-50 mph in the curves. The Kokomo driver won the modified heat and the modified feature.

Sam Davis, Bourbon

Jim Elliott of Warsaw shared winning honors by taking the modified feature scheduled a week ago and then coming back to win dash heats in both modified and stock divisions along with the stock heat.

Mother Nature finally cooperated with a warm night and no threat of rain for the first time this season. A one-half hour broadcast of the races was sponsored by Silveus and Bradway Sunoco over Radio Stations WRSW AM-FM. Races will be held Wednesday and Saturday this week in conjunction with the annual Kosciusko County Fair.

Race Results:

Stock Consolation—Hal Taylor, 1st; John Higgenbothen, 2nd; Al Taylor, 3rd.
Stock Feature—Les Sroufe, 1st; Roger Grossnickle, 2nd; Mike Cox, 3rd.
Modified Feature—Jim Elliott, 1st; Don Walker, 2nd; Louis Mann, 3rd.
Stock Dash—Jim Elliott, 1st; Jim Wagoner, 2nd; Roger Grossnickle, 3rd.
Modified Dash—Jim Elliott, 1st; Don Walker, 2nd; Jack Hickman, 3rd.
Stock Heat—Duane Ronk, 1st; Roger Rowland, 2nd; Larry Montel, 3rd.
Modified Heat—Sam Davis, 1st; Bill Green, 2nd; John Hare, 3rd.
Stock Heat—Jim Elliott, 1st; Art Smith, 2nd; John White, 3rd.
Modified Heat—Don Walker, 1st; Harold Mouser, 2nd; Jack Hickman, 3rd.
Stock Consolation—John Higgenbothen, 1st; Miller, 2nd; Al Taylor, 3rd.
Stock Feature—Art Smith, 1st; Jerry Egolf, 2nd; Les Sroufe, 3rd.
Modified Feature—Don Walker, 1st; Jim Elliott, 2nd; Sam Davis, 3rd.

Wednesday, August 6, 1969
Walker, Sroufe Win Features At Local Track

Don Walker continued his recent hot streak at the Warsaw Speedway as he and Les Sroufe won the feature races before a Kosciusko County Fair crowd Wednesday night.

A small, but enthusiastic crowd watched as Walker captured the modified feature and Sroufe took the stock feature. Sroufe, from Huntington, also won a heat race. A Warsaw driver got in on the act as Bob Grindle captured a modified heat.

Racing will resume at the local speedway Saturday, starting at 7 p.m. A one-half hour broadcast of last night's races were broadcast over Radio Stations WRSW AM-FM, sponsored by the Bill Nay Furniture Co.

Race Results:

Stock Dash—Montel, 1st; Shepherd, 2nd, Elliott, 3rd.
Modified Dash—Mann, 1st; Elliott, 2nd; Alker, 3rd.
Stock Heat—Rowland, 1st; Baker, 2nd; Egolf, 3rd.
Modified Heat—Grindle, 1st; Hickman, 2nd; Mann, 3rd.
Stock Heat—Sroufe, 1st; Howard, 2nd; Hudson, 3rd.
Stock Consolation—Blanton, 1st; Swick, 2nd; Higgenbothen, 3rd.
Stock Feature—Sroufe, 1st; Hudson, 2nd; Grossnickle, 3rd.
Modified Feature—Walker, 1st; Davis, 2nd; Mauser, 3rd

Saturday, August 9, 1969
Walker Wins 3rd Straight Race Feature

Despite late afternoon rains and the threat of more, the stock car racing card at the Warsaw Speedway was run without a hitch Saturday night before an enthusiastic county fair crowd.

Time trials were delayed for approximately one hour due to the extremely damp track but the frantic work of drivers and workers enabled the actual racing program to get underway only a few minutes behind schedule.

Kokomo's Don Walker captured his third consecutive modified feature race in a row to win a trophy. He also zipped home first in the modified dash event and won one other modified race. Paul Roberts, of Huntington, took the checkered flag in the stock feature.

Race Summary:

Stock dash—Roger Grossnickle, 1st; Jim Bucher, 2nd; Les Sroufe, 3rd.
Modified dash—Don Walker, 1st; Ed Stine, 2nd; John Davis, 3rd.
Stock heat—Dean Hudson, 1st; Larry Malott, 2nd; Don Taylor, 3rd.
Modified heat—Tom Beezley, 1st; Louie Mann, 2nd; Don Murphy, 3rd.
Stock heat—Paul Roberts, 1st; Ted Hudson, 2nd; Vonell Krom, 3rd.
Modified heat—Don Walker, 1st; Bob Grindle, 2nd; Ed Stine, 3rd.
Stock consolation—Jerry Egolf, 1st; Bob Johnson, 2nd; Ron Swick, 3rd.
Stock feature—Paul Roberts, 1st; Ted Hudson, 2nd; Larry Howard, 3rd.
Modified feature—Don Walker, 1st; Bob Grindle, 2nd; Jim Elliott, 3rd.

Roger Grossnickle, N. Manchester

Saturday, August 16, 1969
Walker, Bucher Feature Winners

Kokomo's Don Walker continued his winning ways by taking the checkered flag in the modified feature race at the Warsaw Speedway Saturday. Akron's Jim Bucher, also a consistent winner, copped the stock feature.

Several new modified cars were on hand for the competition including one driven by Cap Arnold, of South Bend, and one driven by Steve Cannon of Danville, Ill., who has a brother competing on the USAC circuit.

Jim Elliott, of Warsaw, was unable to drive due to a broken wrist and thumb suffered in competition at the local track last week and his racers were chauffeured by Warsaw's Art Smith. The track was in excellent condition and speeds were high. Next Saturday there will be two 50-lap feature races for the modified and late-model stock classes and on Aug. 30 a big demolition derby is planned.

Race Summary:

Stock dash—Larry Montel, 1st' Vonell Krom, 2nd; Les Sroufe, 3rd.
Modified dash—John Davis, 1st; Art Smith, 2nd; Steve Cannon, 3rd.
Stock heat—Larry Malott, 1st; Larry Howard, 2nd; Roger Rowland, 3rd.
Modified heat—Gary Baker, 1st; Bob Bernhard, 2nd; Don Murphy, 3rd.
Stock heat—John White, 1st; Jerry Baker, 2nd; Larry Montel, 3rd.
Modified heat—Louis Mann, 1st; Don Walker, 2nd; Bob Grindle, 3rd.
Stock consolation—Bob Johnson, 1st; Bill Varney, 2nd; Jim Burkett, 3rd.
Stock feature—Jim Bucher, 1st; Roger Grossnickle, 2nd; Dean Hudson, 3rd.
Modified feature—Don Walker, 1st; Bob Grindle, 2nd; Paul Joyce, 3rd.

Saturday, August 23, 1969
Spectacular Crash Viewed At Local Track

A huge crowd watched one of the wildest nights of racing ever held at the Warsaw Speedway Saturday night. Several accidents marred the evening's card, including a nine-car crash in the stock feature.

One of the most spectacular mishaps in the history of the track saw Jerry Priest of Elwood hook wheels with another modified car in the west turn. Priest's car was thrown into the air where it proceeded to spin about eight times before landing on its wheels behind the retaining wall. The area driver walked away with just a few cuts, mute testimony to safety devices employed in modern-day racing.

Don Walker of Kokomo set a new track record of 15.58 to better his former mark of 15.59. Walker won the 50-lap championship in the modified feature. Les Sroufe of Huntington took the championship in the stock feature.

A demolition race will be held at the local track Saturday night. One-half hour of last Saturday's program was broadcast over Radio Stations WRSW AM-FM, sponsored by Bill Nay Furniture Co.

Racing Results:

Stock dash—Art Smith, 1st; Dean Hudson, 2nd; Ted Hudson, 3rd.
Modified dash—Ken Ferrand, 1st; John Davis, 2nd; Louis Mann, 3rd.
Stock heat—Mike Cox, 1st; Jerry Baker, 2nd; Don Burkett, 3rd.
Modified heat—Don Murphy, 1st; Doug Mithel, 2nd; Ed Stine, 3rd.
Stock heat—Paul Roberts, 1st; Larry Montel, 2nd; Larry Malott, 3rd.
Modified heat—Don Walker, 1st; Tom Beezley, 2nd; Louis Mann, 3rd.
Stock consolation—Jim Kiner, 1st; John Higgenbothen, 2nd; Al Taylor, 3rd.
Stock feature—Les Sroufe, 1st; Jerry Egolf, 2nd; Dean Hudson, 3rd.
Modified feature—Don Walker, 1st; Jim Elliott, 2nd; Ed Stine, 3rd.

Saturday, August 30, 1969
Demolition Derby Thrills Speedway Crowd

A large crowd witnessed action at the Warsaw Speedway Saturday night as another driver joined the roll-over club. William Varney of Warsaw flipped on the backstretch after colliding with another stock car. Varney's auto slid on its top for about 30 feet before coming to a halt upside down. Varney crawled out from under the auto unhurt.

A purse of almost $3,000 was divided among the drivers, made possible by the huge audience.

Jim Barnette of Columbia City won the demolition race with Dane Rumfelt of Milford finishing second in the crowd pleaser. All the drivers appeared bent on tearing up any car near them. Two autos caught fire and only quick work by the Warsaw Fire Department prevented serious damage.

Don Walker of Kokomo continued his winning ways at the local track, winning the modified feature. Silver Lake's Don White captured the stock feature.

A one-half hour broadcast of the races over Radio Stations WRSW AM-FM was sponsored by Silveus and Bradway Sunoco stations. A big powder puff derby will highlight Saturday's racing card as lady drivers do their best to keep racers between the fences.

Race Results:

Stock dash—Smith, 1st; Lambert, 2nd; Hudson, 3rd.
Modified dash—Mann, 1st; Joyce, 2nd; Walker, 3rd.
Stock heat—Shepherd, 1st; Taylor, 2nd; Ronk, 3rd.
Modified heat—Method, 1st; Grindle, 2nd; Burnhard, 3rd.
Stock heat—Roberts, 1st; White, 2nd; Wagoner, 3rd.
Modified heat—Walker, 1st; Stine, 2nd; Joyce, 3rd.
Stock consolation—Howard, 1st; Egolf, 2nd; Malott, 3rd.
Stock feature—White, 1st; Roberts, 2nd; Shepherd, 3rd.
Modified feature—Walker, 1st; Elliott, 2nd; Mann, 3rd.

Saturday, September 6, 1969
Walker Takes Spotlight At Local Speedway

Don Walker of Kokomo has found himself with a habit that is hard to break: that of winning in the modified feature event at the Warsaw Speedway. Walker turned the trick again Saturday night after taking a modified dash and heat before another good crowd, which turned out under threatening skies. Paul Joyce, however, gave Walker a scare in the feature race as he was in contention throughout the race and finally finished a close second.

One of the highlights of the evening's card was a powder puff derby won by Judy Tenney. Marilyn Smith was second, followed by Judy Howard. Numerous accidents marred the card, but there were no injuries, although Dick Leiter of Warsaw was shaken up in a spinning spill.

It was announced that there will be one more race this season, scheduled for Saturday night. A one-half hour broadcast of last week's program over Radio Stations WRSW AM-FM was sponsored by the Bill Nay Furniture Co. of Warsaw.

Race Results:

Stock dash—Roberts, 1st; Malott, 2nd; Hudson, 3rd.
Modified dash—Walker, 1st; Joyce, 2nd; Mann, 3rd.
Stock heat—Cox, 1st; Harney, 2nd; Ganu, 3rd.
Modified heat—Murphy, 1st; Burnhard, 2nd; Beezley, 3rd.
Stock heat—Norman, 1st; Howard, 2nd; Sroufe, 3rd.Bb
Modified heat—Walker, 1st; Stine, 2nd; Mann, 3rd.
Stock consolation—Baker, 1st; Rumfelt, 2nd; Taylor, 3rd.
Stock feature—Roberts, 1st; White, 2nd; Hudson, 3rd.
Modified feature—Walker, 1st; Joyce, 2nd; Mann, 3rd.

Saturday, September 13, 1969
Local Drivers Win Features In Race Finale

A good crowd watched the final races of the season at the Warsaw Speedway Saturday night and speed was the password as the track became dry and extremely fast.

Dave Shively, of Claypool, joined the roll-over club as he flipped while driving in the warm-up period but crawled out unhurt. Several new modified cars were on hand for the racing activity including two from the Indianapolis area

Bob Grindle, of Warsaw, won the modified feature event beating Don Walker, of Kokomo and Jerry Baker, of Warsaw, led all the way to win the late model stock feature.

LarrIt was announced that Saturday night was the last race of the 1969 season and plans are being made to modify the track for next year starting the first week of May. One-half hour of the races were broadcast over Radio Stations WRSW AM-FM sponsored by Silveus and Bradway Sunoco service stations.

Race Summary:
Stock dash—Dean Hudson, 1st; Art Smith, 2nd; Les Sroufe, 3rd
Modified dash—Don Walker, 1st; John Davis, 2nd; Paul Joyce, 3rd.
Stock heat—Don Rumfelt, 1st; Mike Cox, 2nd; Charlie Wiles, 3rd.
Modified heat—Tom Hadley, 1st; Tom Beezley, 2nd; Bob Bernhard, 3rd.
Stock heat—Jerry Baker, 1st; Jim Wagoner, 2nd; Paul Roberts, 3rd.
Modified heat—Bob Grindle, 1st; Jim Elliott, 2nd; Don Walker, 3rd.
Stock consolation—Jerry Egolf, 1st; Chuck Sainer, 2nd; Bob Johnson, 3rd.
Stock feature—Jerry Baker, 1st; Jim Wagoner, 2nd; Les Sroufe, 3rd.
Modified feature—Bob Grindle, 1st; Don Walker, 2nd; Jim Elliott, 3rd.

1970
Speed & More Speed

During the 1970's, all three classes of cars became more distinct and separated. The classes now looked totally different and all continued to improve in speed and competition. This speed created a major safety issue and in the early 1970's, a solid concrete wall replaced the wooden retaining wall that had surrounded the speedway since racing started. The biggest car change came in the late model class as they became "not so stock" anymore with enhanced racing engines and specialized tires as well.

Late April, 1970
Local Speedway Sets Initial Practice May 2

The first practice session at the Warsaw Speedway, County Fairgrounds, is scheduled for Saturday, May 2. C.E. (Hoot) Gibson, president of the racing association which sponsors the races, said that the new construction at the track is not complete and so it is impossible to stage the practice any earlier. The first racing night at the track will be May 9.

The track has been enlarged to one-fourth mile on the inside which makes it about one-tenth larger. Gibson said that many new sprint cars along with hobby stock and semi-late models will be in competition at the track this year.

Gibson also said that many questions have arisen since last year on rules and regulations. He emphasized that the management this year will strictly enforce the existing rules and regulations. He also stated that new retaining walls have been installed in both turns and an assistant starter has been added in order to note accidents quicker.

Saturday, May 9, 1970
Local Speedway Opens Before Large Crowd

A large crowd at the Warsaw Speedway Saturday night watched as 55 cars, many of them with new drivers this season, went through their paces in the opening night of racing locally. Veteran sportscaster Milo Clase stated that the first night could go in the record books as one of the best in the history of the speedway.

Don Walker, who got the checkered flag in the three races he was in, received a $100 bonus above the regular purse by winning the modified feature race. Les Sroufe won the semi-late feature race to take home a $75 bonus above the purse.

Racing fans witnessed a six-car pile-up, which occurred in the third heat race. There were no injuries. Bob Snider of Rialto, Calif, rolled over in front of the grandstand when the steering on his auto failed. Snider, however, was not injured.

Race Results:
Stock Dash—Bucher, 1st; Krum, 2nd; Smith, 3rd.
Modified Dash-Walker, 1st; Kenens, 2nd; Murray, 3rd.
Stock Heat—Leiter, 1st; Baker, 2nd; Burket, 3rd.
Modified Heat—Bills, 1st; Hare, 2nd; Fey, 3rd.
Stock Heat—Wagoner, 1st; Roberts, 2nd; Smith, 3rd.
Modified Heat—Walker, 1st; Joyce, 2nd; Stine, 3rd.
Stock Feature—Sroufe, 1st; Smith, 2nd; Egolf, 3rd.
Modified Feature—Walker, 1st; Murphy, 2nd; Joyce, 3rd.
Hobby Stock—Fitzpatrick, 1st; Cox, 2nd; Moore, 3rd.

Saturday, May 16, 1970 - Rainout

Saturday, May 23, 1970
Warsaw Driver Local Stock Feature Winner

Don Walker of Kokomo resumed his torrid racing where he left off two weeks ago, winning the feature modified race at the Warsaw Speedway Saturday after taking the modified dash event earlier in the evening.

Drivers got a break from the weather as the rains held off until the race program was completed. A total of 55 cars qualified before the largest crowd of the season. Very few mishaps marred the action.

Warsaw's Art Smith captured the Stock feature and fellow Warsawan Bob Johnson took the checkered flag in the stock consolation. The hobby feature was won by Jess Gibson of Columbia City.

Race Results:

Stock Dash—Butts, 1st; Sroufe, 2nd; Roberts, 3rd.
Modified Dash—Walker, 1st; Grindle, 2nd; Joyce, 3rd.
Stock Heat—T. Hudson, 1st; Cox, 2nd.
Modified Heat—Beezley, 1st; Arnold, 2nd; Hare, 3rd.
Stock Heat—Egolf, 1st; D. Hudson, 2nd; Paul Roberts, 3rd.
Modified Heat—Bills, 1st; Grindle, 2nd; Walker, 3rd; Elliott, 4th.
Stock Consolation—Johnson, 1st; Leiter, 2nd; Burkett, 3rd.
Stock Feature—Smith, 1st; Sroufe, 2nd; Grossnickle, 3rd; Egolf, 4th.
Modified Feature—Walker, 1st; Elliott, 2nd; Stine, 3rd; Joyce 4th.
Hobby Feature—Gibson, 1st; Cox, 2nd; Fitzpatrick, 3rd.

Saturday, May 30, 1970
Local Drivers Control Action At Speedway

Warsaw drivers dominated action at the Warsaw Speedway over the Memorial Day weekend as the weather cooperated with the large crowd that was on hand to view the popular racing card.

Three local drivers took top honors in the hobby feature, won by Mike Cox. Warsawans John Fitzpatrick and Bob Johnson finished second and third respectively. Another local man, Art Smith, won the stock feature race. Jerry Baker, Jim Wagoner, and Bob Grindle, all of Warsaw, won heat races.

Don Walker of Kokomo, however, was successful as he took the checkered flag in the modified feature and the modified dash. Walker's victory in the feature race was a close decision over Les Bills of Columbia City. Radio Stations WRSW AM-FM broadcast one-half hour of the races, sponsored by Pinky's '76' Service Station, corner of Center and Detroit streets.

Race Results:

Stock Dash—Sroufe, 1st; Smith, 2nd; Krom, 3rd.
Modified Dash—Walker, 1st; Grindle, 2nd; Bills, 3rd.
Stock Heat—Baker, 1st; Gross, 2nd; Egolf, 3rd.
Modified Heat—Burnhart, 1st; Johnson, 2nd; Priest, 3rd.
Stock Heat—Wagoner, 1st; Sroufe, 2nd; Grossnickle, 3rd.
Modified Heat—Grindle, 1st; Walker, 2nd; Bills, 3rd.
Stock Consolation—Grossnickle, 1st; Burkett, 2nd; Leiter, 3rd.
Stock Feature—Smith, 1st; Krom, 2nd; Sroufe, 3rd.
Modified Feature—Walker, 1st; Bills, 2nd; Grindle, 3rd.
Hobby Feature—Cox, 1st; Fitzpatrick, 2nd; Johnson, 3rd.

Saturday, June 6, 1970
Elliott Takes Checkered Flag In Feature

With Don Walker of Kokomo sidelined with mechanical troubles, Jim Elliott of Warsaw took the checkered flag in the modified feature race at the Warsaw Speedway before a large crowd Saturday night. Walker has been a consistent winner at the local track this season and was leading Saturday's feature race when felled by mechanical trouble. Elliott also won the modified dash.

The large crowd watched as 60 cars qualified for the popular racing card. Fans also witnessed a five-car crash on the first lap of the stock heat. Local driver John Davis hit the wall and rolled over during a warm-up session prior to the races.

Numerous other accidents occurred throughout the evening, but no injuries were reported. Several new cars were entered in the card. One-half hour of the evening's program was carried over Radio Stations WRSW AM-FM, sponsored by Schrader's Automotive of Warsaw and Columbia City.

Jerry Baker of Warsaw captured the stock feature. Other area winners were Dean Hudson in the stock heat and Bud Grossnickle in the stock consolation.

Race Results:
Stock Dash—Sroufe, 1st; Grossnickle, 2nd; Allen, 3rd.
Modified Dash—Elliott, 1st; Bills, 2nd; Beezley, 3rd.
Stock Heat—Roberts, 1st; Wagoner, 2nd; Baker, 3rd.
Modified Heat—Johnson, 1st; Bernhard, 2nd; Murphy, 3rd.
Stock Heat—D. Hudson, 1st; T. Hudson, 2nd; Leiter, 3rd.
Modified Heat—Fisher, 1st; Elliott, 2nd; Grindle, 3rd.
Stock Consolation—Grossnickle, 1st; Bradley, 2nd.
Stock Feature—Baker, 1st; Roberts, 2nd; Sroufe, 3rd.
Feature Modified—Elliott, 1st; Bernhard, 2nd; Johnson, 3rd.
Hobby Feature—Grigsby, 1st; Gibson, 2nd; Varnell, 3rd.

Saturday, June 13, 1970 - Rainout

Saturday, June 20, 1970
Local Driver Injured At Warsaw Track

A Rt.3 Warsaw driver, injured in auto races held at the Warsaw Speedway Saturday night, is listed in fair condition at the Murphy Medical Center today. Charles Cotton suffered head injuries when his auto rolled over several times and completely disintegrated. In a separate incident Galen Fugate rolled his car over several times, but escaped injury.

In the feature race for super sprints Don Walker of Kokomo got his car airborne, but managed to control it without an accident.

A large crowd was on hand as 68 cars qualified for the evening's card, which saw six Warsaw drivers take the checkered flag. Local driver Jim Elliott took the modified feature while Gary Baker, also of Warsaw, took the flag in the stock consolation.

Other local winners were Bob Grindle in the modified dash; Larry Baker, stock heat; John Hare, modified heat; and Elliott in a modified heat. A thrilling demolition derby was won by Mick Dallvou of Leesburg. Bob Johnson of Warsaw was 2nd in the 30-car field.

Race Results:

Stock Dash—Roger Grossnickle, 1st; Paul Roberts, 2nd; Vimell Krom, 3rd.
Modified Dash—Bob Grindle, 1st; Paul Joyce, 2nd; Jim Elliott, 3rd.
Stock Heat—Larry Baker, 1st; Larry Howard, 2nd; Ray Norman, 3rd.
Modified Heat—John Hare, 1st; Don Murphy, 2nd; Art Bernhardt, 3rd.
Stock Heat—Ted Hudson, 1st; Roger Grossnickle, 2nd; John White, 3rd.
Modified Heat—Jim Elliott, 1st; Jim Murphy, 2nd; Bob Snyder, 3rd.
Stock Consolation—Gary Baker, 1st; Tom Leiter, 2nd; Tom Fugate, 3rd.
Stock Feature—Paul Roberts, 1st; Art Smith, 2nd; John White, 3rd.
Modified Feature—Jim Elliott, 1st; Jim Murphy, 2nd; Don Walker, 3rd.
Hobby Stock Feature—Jess Gibson ,1st; Mike Cox, 2nd; Bob Griesby, 3rd.

Saturday, June 27, 1970
Warsaw Drivers Dominate Card At Speedway

Local drivers Art Smith and Jim Elliott won the stock and modified feature races respectively in auto racing at the Warsaw Speedway Saturday evening. A total of 75 cars qualified for the evening's card with Smith coming from a third place finish in the stock dash to collect top laurels in the stock feature. Elliott piloted his auto to the checkered flag in the modified heat before coming back to victory in the feature race.

Two other Warsaw drivers won races, Bob Grindle in the modified dash and John Davis in a modified heat. Ted Hudson and Bud Grossnickle, both of North Manchester, won a stock dash and the stock consolation respectively. Dick Tyson, Kokomo, flipped over several times in the modified consolation and was taken to the Murphy Medical Center where he received treatment.

The track's slogan as announced by Milo Clase is: "The world's best racing on the world's best one-quarter mile track with the world's best drivers." Race fans are reminded of the gigantic fireworks display at the local speedway Saturday evening with gates opening at 5 p.m.

Race Results:

Stock Dash—Hudson, 1st; Grossnickle, 2nd; Smith, 3rd.
Modified Dash—Grindle, 1st; Walker, 2nd; Joyce, 3rd.
Stock Heat—Bradley, 1st; Norman, 2nd; Sroufe, 3rd.
Modified Heat—Davis, 1st; Mann, 2nd; Sarber, 3rd.
Stock Heat—Wagoner, 1st; Roberts, 2nd; Hudson, 3rd.
Modified Heat—Elliott, 1st; Murphy, 2nd; Bills, 3rd.
Stock Consolation—Grossnickle, 1st; Larry Baker, 2nd; Garry Baker, 3rd.
Stock Feature—Smith, 1st; Stutzman, 2nd; Jerry Baker, 3rd.
Modified Feature—Elliott, 1st; Murphy, 2nd; Walker, 3rd.
Hobby Feature—Hopper, 1st; Sainer, 2nd; Cox, 3rd.

Saturday, July 4, 1970
Large Speedway Views Fireworks

Bobby Grindle, Warsaw

Bob Grindle highlighted auto racing at the Warsaw Speedway Saturday evening before a large July 4 crowd, labeled the largest of the season.

Grindle, from Warsaw, drove to victory in the modified feature race after earlier winning dash and heat races. Habitual winner Art Smith, also of Warsaw, took the stock heat and came back in the stock feature to take the checkered flag in a race that saw Paul Roberts flip his vehicle in front of the grandstand.

Warsawan John Davis won a modified heat while Larry Baker of Warsaw won in the stock consolation.

The spectators were treated to the finest display of fireworks in the history of the track in addition to the thrilling racing card, which saw 67 cars qualified. A big 50-lap mid-season championship feature for super sprints will be held at the local track Saturday. One-half hour of last week's races were broadcast over Radio Stations WRSW AM-FM, sponsored by Schrader Automotive of Warsaw and Columbia City.

Race Summary:

Stock Dash—Krom, 1st; Roberts, 2nd; Bucher, 3rd.
Modified Dash—Grindle, 1st; Joyce, 2nd; Elliott, 3rd.
Stock Heat—Montel, 1st; Sroufe, 2nd; Baker, 3rd.
Modified Heat—J. Davis, 1st; S. Davis, 2nd; Johnson, 3rd.
Stock Heat—Smith, 1st; Howard, 2nd; Grossnickle, 3rd.
Modified Heat—Grindle, 1st; Elliott, 2nd; Joyce, 3rd.
Stock Consolation—Baker, 1st; Johnson, 2nd; Mallott, 3rd.
Stock Feature—Smith, 1st; Bucher, 2nd; Grossnickle, 3rd.
Modified Feature—Grindle, 1st; Elliott, 2nd; Bills, 3rd.
Hobby Feature—Fitzpatrick, 1st; Cox, 2nd; Sainer, 3rd.

Saturday, July 11, 1970
Warsaw Driver Wins 50-Lap Feature Race

Jim Elliott, of Warsaw, captured a 50-lap mid-season championship race for modified cars during the racing card at

Jimmie Elliott, Warsaw

the Warsaw Speedway Saturday night. Paul Bills, of Columbia City, grabbed second place and Bob Grindle, of Warsaw, took third.

Ted Hudson, of North Manchester, took the checkered flag in the semi-late model stock feature. Next week a 50-lap mid-season championship race for semi-late model stocks will be the highlighted event.

Mike Cox, of Warsaw, was the evening's only dual winner capturing a hobby stock heat race and coming back to claim victory in the hobby stock feature. Milo Clase, track announcer, said that the combined driver's purses for the Fourth of July and Saturday night totaled $6,500 at the track.

Racing Summary:
Stock Dash—Roberts, 1st; Baker, 2nd; Sroufe, 3rd.
Modified Dash—Joyce, 1st; Elliott, 2nd; Burnhard, 3rd.
Stock Heat—Krom, 1st; White, 2nd; Howard, 3rd.
Modified Heat—Bills, 1st; J. Davis, 2nd; Hare, 3rd.
Stock Heat—A. Leiter, 1st; Hudson, 2nd; A. Smith, 3rd.
Modified Heat—Walker, 1st; Joyce, 2nd; Grindle, 3rd.
Stock Consolation—Reid, 1st; Grossnickle, 2nd; Montel, 3rd.
Stock Feature—Hudson, 1st; Wagoner, 2nd; Grossnickle, 3rd.
Modified Feature—Elliott, 1st; Bills, 2nd; Grindle, 3rd.
Hobby Feature—Cox, 1st; Saner, 2nd; Varney, 3rd.

Saturday, July 18, 1970
Warsaw Speedway

Sixty-eight cars qualified for races at the Warsaw Speedway Saturday night, but a heavy downpour washed out the evening's card after three events had been completed.

It was announced that rainchecks would be honored at this week's races, the events starting where they left off when the rains came Saturday. It was also announced that a 50-lap semi-late championship event would be run this Saturday.

Ted Hudson of North Manchester took a stock dash, Paul Joyce of Kokomo won a modified dash and Jess Gibson of Columbia City won a hobby race before rains brought about a premature end to the program.

Saturday, July 25, 1970
Warsaw Speedway

A large crowd at the Warsaw Speedway Saturday night watched in stunned silence as a crash in the 50-lap stock feature injured five persons, none seriously. The incident occurred when a car driven by Leroy Stutzman went out of control and slid into the crowded

Les Bills, Columbia City

infield area, striking a jeep with four track helpers aboard.

The four men were spilled to the ground and rushed to the Murphy Medical Center for treatment. Released later from the local hospital were Richard Jaynes, owner of the Jeep, Warren Rohrer, Dale Allen Jaynes, Don Jaynes and Stutzman. A Warsaw man, Darrell Rovenstine, was also taken to the hospital when he caught his arm in the steering wheel of his auto when it went into a spin following a three-car collision.

Art Smith finally captured the stock feature over Roger Grossnickle. In the 25-lap modified feature race John Davis led for almost 19 laps before Jim Elliott and Les Bills found an opening and zipped past Davis to take first and second respectively. Earlier Davis had won a modified heat.

One-half hour of the race card was heard over Radio Stations WRSW AM-FM, sponsored by Pinkey's "76" service station. Race drivers and spectators are urged to use the west drive this Saturday as the east drive will be closed.

Race Results:

Stock Heat—Bradley, 1st; Gross, 2nd; Leiter, 3rd.
Modified Heat—Sarver, 1st; S. Davis, 2nd; Johnson, 3rd.
Stock Heat—Sroufe, 1st; Krom, 2nd; Smith, 3rd.
Modified Heat—Davis, 1st; Beezley, 2nd; Elliott, 3rd.
Stock Consolation—Norman, 1st; Stutzman, 2nd; Howard, 3rd.
Stock Feature—Smith, 1st; Grossnickle, 2nd; Wagner, 3rd.
Modified Feature—Elliott, 1st; Bills, 2nd; J. Davis, 3rd.

Saturday, August 1, 1970
Warsaw Drivers Cop Features At Local Speedway

Warsaw drivers captured the major feature races at the Warsaw Speedway Saturday night during a program that saw 76 cars qualify for the evening's activities.

Jim Elliott took the modified feature and another heat race while Larry Baker crossed the line first in the stock feature and Mike Cox was given the checkered flag in the hobby stock feature.

The other winners were John White, Wolf Lake; Louie Mann, Kokomo; Jerry Baker, Warsaw; Jim Murphy, Kokomo; Paul Grim, Warren; and Bud Grossnickle, North Manchester.

Racing Summary:

Stock Dash—John White, 1st; Paul Roberts, 2nd; Ted Hudson, 3rd.
Modified Dash—Louie Mann, 1st; Jim Elliott, 2nd; Ed Stine, 3rd.
Stock Heat—Jerry Baker, 1st; Jim Wagoner, 2nd; Larry Howard, 3rd.
Modified Heat—Jim Murphy, 1st; Jerry Baker, 2nd; John Sharp, 3rd.
Stock Heat—Paul Grim, 1st; Vonnel Krom, 2nd; Ted Hudson, 3rd.
Modified Heat—Jim Elliott, 1st; Charlie Sarver, 2nd; Ed Stine, 3rd.
Consolation—Bud Grossnickle, 1st; Tom Leiter, 2nd; Ken Gorman, 3rd.
Stock Feature—Larry Baker, 1st; Vonnel Krom, 2nd; Art Smith, 3rd.
Modified Feature—Jim Elliott, 1st; Charlie Sarver, 2nd; Louis Mann, 3rd.

Wednesday, August 5, 1970
Warsaw Speedway

Warsaw's Bob Grindle breezed by Don Walker of Kokomo on the 20th lap of the modified feature and roared to victory in racing at the Warsaw Speedway Wednesday night before a large Kosciusko County Fair Crowd.

Earlier in the evening the Warsawan had taken the modified dash event. Another Warsaw driver, Jerry Baker, captured the stock feature after winning a stock heat. The stock feature was classified as one of the fastest of the season by track announcer Milo Clase. Grindle and Baker each received a $50 bonus for winning feature races.

Ellis Shepherd of Mentone won the stock consolation as a total of 75 cars qualified for winning feature races. It was announced that gates will open at 4 p.m. for Saturday's card.

Race Summary:

Stock Dash—Wagoner, 1st; Apple, 2nd; Grossnickle, 3rd.
Modified Dash—Grindle, 1st; Walker, 2nd; Davis, 3rd.
Stock Heat—Krom, 1st; Sroufe, 2nd; Howard, 3rd.
Modified Heat—Beezley, 1st; Murphy, 2nd; Mann, 3rd.
Stock Heat—Baker, 1st; Egolf, 2nd; Grim, 3rd.
Modified Heat—Walker, 1st; Barnhardt, 2nd; Stine, 3rd.
Stock Consolation—Shepherd, 1st; Stutzman, 2nd; Johnson, 3rd.
Stock Feature—Baker, 1st; Egolf, 2nd; Grossnickle, 3rd.
Modified Feature—Grindle, 1st; Walker, 2nd; Elliott, 3rd.
Hobby Feature—Gibson, 1st; Grigsby, 2nd; Leiter, 3rd.

Saturday, August 8, 1970
Warsaw Speedway

A capacity Kosciusko County Fair crowd was on hand for auto races at the Warsaw Speedway Saturday night as drivers competed for a $2,500 purse. Fans got plenty of excitement in the modified feature as Jim Elliott raced out to an early lead until his drive shaft broke with Don Walker of Kokomo taking over the lead. Bob Grindle threatened Walker on numerous occasions, but could not pass the Kokomo driver.

Gary Grissom of Anderson flipped his car over several times, but managed to crawl unhurt from the wreckage. During the evening Paul Roberts and Mitch Brown escaped injury when their autos crashed into the cement retaining wall.

Elliott did win a modified heat, one of three Warsaw drivers to take the checkered flag. Art Smith won the stock feature and Tex Plummer won a stock heat. Arden Leiter of Pierceton also captured a stock heat. A demolition derby will be held at the local speedway Saturday with 35-40 cars entered in the competition.

Tex Plummer, Warsaw

Race Summary:

Stock Dash—Hudson, 1st; Stutzman, 2nd; Grossnickle, 3rd.
Modified Dash—Beezley, 1st; Grindle, 2nd; Walker, 3rd.
Stock Heat—Plummer, 1st; Howard, 2nd; White, 3rd.
Modified Heat—Sarver, 1st; Murphy, 2nd; Bernhard, 3rd.
Stock Heat—Leiter, 1st; Baker, 2nd; Hudson, 3rd.
Modified Heat—Elliott, 1st; Davis, 2nd; Bills, 3rd.
Stock Consolation—Nall, 1st; Brumfell, 2nd; Sheppard, 3rd.
Stock Feature—Smith, 1st; Baker, 2nd; Plummer, 3rd.
Modified Feature—Walker, 1st; Grindle, 2nd; Murphy, 2nd.
Hobby Heat—Sheets, 1st; Ireland, 2nd; Womeck, 3rd.
Hobby Heat—Leiter, 1st; Cox, 2nd; Hogue, 3rd.
Hobby Feature—Leiter, 1st; Varney, 2nd; Hogue, 3rd.

Saturday, August 15, 1970
Warsaw Speedway

A demolition derby attracted a capacity crowd at the Warsaw Speedway Saturday evening, creating a purse of $3,200 for drivers. Chuck Sainer of Warsaw and Jim Barnette of Columbia City thrilled the fans in the demolition derby with their intent to knock out the other 44 cars in the field. After the dust had settled Sainer proved to be the winner with Barnette second.

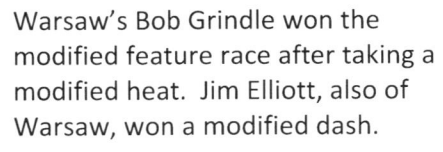

Warsaw's Bob Grindle won the modified feature race after taking a modified heat. Jim Elliott, also of Warsaw, won a modified dash.

In the fastest stock feature of the season at the speedway, Roger Grossnickle finished first in the 30-car field. Tom Leiter of Warsaw earlier had won a stock heat.

Warsaw drivers dominated the hobby feature with Mike Cox leading the

Roger Grossnickle, N. Manchester

pack, followed by Dennis Hopper and William Varney, all of Warsaw. Richard A. Wadley and Ted Morris of the Valentine Boys' Club in Chicago, along with eight members of the club, were guests of the management for the evening's card.

Race Summary:

Stock Dash—Sroufe, 1st; Smith, 2nd; Wagner, 3rd.
Modified Dash—Elliott, 1st; Grindle, 2nd; Bills, 3rd.
Stock Heat—Howard, 1st; Baker, 2nd; Hudson, 3rd.
Modified Heat—Beezley, 1st; Sharp, 2nd; Sarber, 3rd.
Stock Heat—Leiter, 1st; Bradley, 2nd; Smith, 3rd.
Modified Heat—Grindle, 1st; Elliott, 2nd; Murphy, 3rd.
Stock Consolation—White, 1st; Sheppard, 2nd; Sainer, 3rd.
Stock Feature—Grossnickle, 1st; Smith, 2nd; Sroufe, 3rd.
Modified Feature—Grindle, 1st; Elliott, 2nd; Beezley, 3rd.

Saturday, August 22, 1970 - Rainout

Saturday, August 29, 1970
Art Smith Wins 100-lap Feature

Art Smith, of Warsaw, led the entire way in winning the 100-lap feature race for semi-late model stock cars run at the Warsaw Speedway Saturday night. In spite of accidents and a fast pace, 12 of 25 cars finished the grueling grind. Ted Hudson, of North Manchester, finished second taking over for Roger Grossnickle, of North Manchester, who held second place until the 93rd lap when engine failure put him out.

Bruce Hogue joined the "roll-over" club in a hobby stock event when his racer hurdled the retaining wall in the back stretch but Hogue was not injured.

Jim Elliott, of Warsaw, who qualified at a slow speed because of magneto problems, was placed on the pole position in two modified events. However, Elliott insisted on starting on the rear because the magneto had been replaced. And although starting at the back of the field, Elliott won both races he entered. One was the modified feature. Next week there will be a 50-lap championship race for modified cars.

Race Summary:

Modified Dash—Sarber, 1st; Beezley, 2nd; Bills, 3rd.
Hobby—Anders, 1st; Gibson, 2nd; Johnson, 3rd.
Modified Heat—Elliott, 1st; Grindle, 2nd; Stine, 3rd.
Stock Heat—Cox, 1st; Saner, 2nd; Hopper, 3rd.
Modified Heat—Bills, 1st; Priest, 2nd; Sarber, 3rd.
Hobby Feature—Bowerman, 1st; Saner, 2nd; Gibson, 3rd.
Stock Feature—Smith, 1st; Hudson, 2nd; Wagoner, 3rd.
Modified Feature—Elliott, 1st; Grindle, 2nd; Bills, 3rd.

Saturday, September 5, 1970
Grindle Cops 50-Lap Feature

Bob Grindle, of Warsaw, took top honors at the Warsaw Speedway Saturday night when he won the 50-lap championship modified feature and another heat race. Grindle passed Jim Elliott in the 34th lap of the feature and it was his race the rest of the way.

Ed Sharp struck the wall after having steering problems and was knocked unconscious. Sharp was taken to Murphy Medical Center for treatment and was admitted for observation.

Other evening winners were Jerry Baker, Jim Elliott, Vonell Krom, John Davis, Ted Hudson, Dennis Hopper and Prater.

Race Summary:

Stock Dash—Jerry Baker, 1st; Arden Leiter, 2nd; Roger Grossnickle, 3rd.
Modified Dash—Jim Elliott, 1st; John Davis, 2nd; Bob Bernhard, 3rd.
Stock Heat—Vonell Krom, 1st; Sheppard, 2nd; Jim Wagoner, 3rd.
Modified Heat—John Davis, 1st; Bob Bernhard, 2nd; Jerry Priest, 3rd.
Stock Heat—Ted Hudson, 1st; Jim Bucher, 2nd; Don Burkett, 3rd.
Modified Heat—Bob Grindle, 1st; Charley Sarver, 2nd; Jack Hickman, 3rd.
Stock Feature—Vonell Krom, 1st; Jerry Baker, 2nd; Junior Stutzman, 3rd.
Modified Feature—Bob Grindle, 1st; Jim Elliott, 2nd; John Davis, 3rd.
Fast Hobby—Dennis Hopper, 1st; Chuck Saner, 2nd; Jesse Gibson, 3rd.
Slow Hobby—Prater, 1st; Partridge, 2nd; Hite, 3rd.
Hobby Feature—Dennis Hopper, 1st; Mike Cox, 2nd; Carry Pane, 3rd.

Saturday, September 12, 1970
Barnette Wins Final Outing

Last Saturday night was the final evening of racing at the Warsaw Speedway and it went out in style as Jim Barnette, Columbia City, won the hardest hitting demolition derby of the season.

Charlie Sarber, Kokomo, won the modified feature and Arden Leiter of Pierceton captured the semi-late feature. Other winners for the night were Sroufe, Elliott, Johnson, Patterson, Smith, Bills, Saner, Gibson and Hopper. One half-hour of racing was broadcast over WRSW sponsored by Schrader's Automotive.

Race Summary:

Stock Dash—Les Sroufe, 1st; Jr. Stutsman, 2nd; Ted Hudson, 3rd.
Modified Dash—Jim Elliott, 1st; Bob Bernhard, 2nd; Charley Sarber, 3rd.
Stock Heat—Bob Johnson, 1st; Bud Keirn, 2nd; Ellis Sheppard, 3rd.
Modified Heat—Tom Patterson, 1st; Bob Bernhard, 2nd; Dave Ragen, 3rd.
Stock Heat—Art Smith, 1st; Jerry Baker, 2nd; Les Sroufe, 3rd.
Modified Heat—Les Bills, 1st; Bob Trindle, 2nd; Ed Stine, 3rd.
Semi-late Feature—Arden Leiter, 1st; Les Sroufe, 2nd; Vonell Krom, 3rd.
Modified Feature—Charley Sarber, 1st; Bob Grindle, 2nd; Bob Bernard, 3rd.
Slow Hobby—Chuck Saner, 1st; Bob Johnson, 2nd; Larry Dane, 3rd.
Fast Hobby—Jesse Gibson, 1st; Bill Varney, 2nd; Patridge, 3rd.
Hobby Feature—Hopper, 1st; Chuck Saner, 2nd; Jesse Gibson, 3rd.
Demolition Derby—Jim Barnette, 1st; David Duff, 2nd; Jack Cutler, 3rd.

1971

Saturday, May 1, 1971
Bucher, Murphy Speedway Winners

Two Jims—Bucher and Murphy—were the big winners on opening night at the Warsaw Speedway Saturday. Jim Bucher, of Silver Lake, captured a stock heat then came back to win the first stock feature of the season. Jim Murphy, of Jackson, Michigan, also took a modified heat race then zipped across the finish line first in the modified feature.

Other individual winners were Jim Elliott, Warsaw, and Jerry Priest, Elwood, in modified; Larry Baker, Warsaw, and Paul Roberts, Huntington, stock; and Larry Montel, Silver Lake, and Dennis Hopper, Warsaw, in the hobby stock class.

Race Summary:

Stock Dash—Bucher, 1st; Leiter, 2nd; D. Hudson, 3rd.
Modified Dash—Elliott, 1st; French, 2nd; Sarver, 3rd.
Stock Heat—L. Baker, 1st; Sroufe, 2nd; Krom, 3rd.
Modified Heat—Priest, 1st; Mann, 2nd; Hare, 3rd.
Stock Heat—Roberts, 1st; White, 2nd; T. Hudson, 3rd.
Modified Heat—Murphy, 1st; Stine, 2nd; Beezley, 3rd.
Hobby Stock Heat—Montel, 1st; Womach, 2nd; Santer, 3rd.
Stock Feature—Bucher, 1st, Wagner, 2nd; D. Hudson, 3rd.
Modified Feature—Murphy, 1st; Elliott, 2nd; Bernhardt, 3rd.
Hobby Feature—Hopper, 1st.

Saturday, May 8, 1971
Elliott, Baker Win At Speedway

Jim Elliott and Larry Baker took the feature honors Saturday night at the Warsaw Speedway. Baker captured the Stock feature and Elliott took the modified feature race.

Results of the other races follow:

Stock Heat—Jim Wagoner, 1st; Art Leiter, Jr., 2nd; Roger Grossnickle, 3rd.
Modified Heat—Tom Beezley, 1st; Jim Elliott, 2nd; Les Bills, 3rd.
Stock Heat—Tom Leiter, 1st; Max Rumfelt, 2nd; Jerry Baker, 3rd,
Stock Feature—Larry Baker, 1st; (No second) Vanell Krom, 3rd; Max Rumfelt, 4th.
Modified Feature—Jim Elliott, 1st; Jim Murphy, 2nd; Jerry Priest, 3rd.
Hobby Heat—Dennis Hopper, 1st; Larry Montel, 2nd; Larry Daines, 3rd.
Hobby Feature—Dennis Hopper, 1st; Larry Montel, 2nd; Larry Daines, 3rd.

Saturday, May 15, 1971
Elliott, Grossnickle, Fitzpatrick Win At Local Speedway

Jim Elliott, Roger Grossnickle, and John Fitzpatrick were feature winners at the Warsaw Speedway Saturday night. Elliott captured the modified feature with Etna Green's Ed Stine in second and Jim Murphy at the third spot.

Grossnickle took the honors in the stock feature with Jim Bucher in second and Arden

Leiter in third. Fitzpatrick won the feature hobby with Dennis Hopper second and Don Womack in third.

Winners in the other heats were:

Stock Heat—Leiter, 1st; Bucher, 2nd; Grossnickle, 3rd.
Modified Heat—French, 1st; Stine, 2nd; Priest, 3rd.
Stock Heat—Rumfelt, 1st; Johnson, 2nd; Hudson, 3rd.
Modified Heat—Murphy, 1st; Bills, 2nd; Bernhardt, 3rd.
Stock Heat—Smith, 1st; Shepard, 2nd; Wagoner, 3rd.
Modified Heat—Mouser, 1st; Elliott, 2nd; Priest, 3rd.
Hobby Heat—Hopper, 1st; Montel, 2nd; Sarver, 3rd.

Saturday, May 22, 1971
Warsaw Speedway Results

Results at the Warsaw Speedway Saturday night were:

Stock Feature—Roberts, 1st; Crum, 2nd; Luther, 3rd.
Modified Feature—Jim Elliott, 1st; Tom Beezley, 2nd.
Stock Heat—Sroufe, 1st; D. Hudson, 2nd; T. Hudson, 3rd.
Modified Heat—Davis, 1st; Howard, 2nd; Grindle, 3rd.
Stock Heat—Grossnickle, 1st; Roberts, 2nd; Chambers, 3rd.
Modified Heat—Beezley, 1st; Joyce, 2nd; Sam Davis, 3rd.
Stock Heat—Crum, 1st; Hudson, 2nd; Smith, 3rd.
Modified Heat—Priest, 1st; Bills, 2nd; Burnhart, 3rd.
Hobby Heat—Daine, 1st; Johnson, 2nd; Hague, 3rd.
Hobby Feature—Daine, 1st; Varney, 2nd; Sainer, 3rd.

Saturday, May 29, 1971 – No Race Results

Saturday, June 5, 1971
Warsaw Speedway Results

Jim Elliott captured the modified feature along with two modified heats to score big wins at the Warsaw Speedway Saturday night. Dean Hudson took the semi-late feature on the program.

Winners and results of the events were:

Stock Heat—Ted Hudson, 1st; Dean Hudson, 2nd; John Davis, 3rd.
Modified Heat—Jim Elliott, 1st; Tom Beezley, 2nd; John Davis, 3rd.
Stock Heat—Jerry Egolf, 1st; Ellis Shelperd, 2nd; Tom Leiter, 3rd.
Modified Heat—Jim Murphy, 1st; Dick Jones, 2nd; Tom Patterson, 3rd.

Jimmie Elliott, Warsaw

Stock Heat—Vonell Krom, 1st; Paul Roberts, 2nd; Jerry Baker, 3rd.
Modified Heat—Jim Elliott, 1st; Bud Bernhardt, 2nd; John Davis, 3rd.
Stock Feature—Dean Hudson, 1st; Ron Miller, 2nd; Ray Chambers, 3rd; and Wagoner, 4th.
Modified Feature—Jim Elliott, 1st; Jim Murphy, 2nd; Les Bills, 3rd; Priest, 4th.
Hobby (slow) Heat—Larry Montel, 1st; Jim Lagaird, 2nd.
Hobby (fast) Heat—Larry Daine, 1st; Dennis Hopper, 2nd; Bill Uarney, 3rd.
Hobby Feature—Dennis Hopper, 1st; Bob Hague, 2nd; Larry Daine, 3rd.

Saturday, June 12, 1971
Race Winners At Local Track

Victories were evenly distributed in racing at the Warsaw Speedway Saturday night. Feature winners were Roger Grossnickle in the semi-late stock feature; Jim Murphy in the modified feature; and Larry Daine in the hobby stock feature.

The first three finishers in each race were as follows:

Stock Dash—Les Sroufe, 1st; Art Smith, 2nd; Larry Mallot, 3rd.
Modified Dash—Jim Elliott, 1st; Jim Murphy, 2nd; Bob Grindle, 3rd.
Stock Heat—Bud Grossnickle, 1st; Roy Norman, 2nd; Paul Roberts, 3rd.
Modified Heat—Charlie Sarver, 1st; Louie Mann, 2nd; Tom Beezley, 3rd.
Stock Heat—Jim Wagoner, 1st; Art Smith, 2nd; Ron Miller, 3rd.
Modified Heat—Ed Stine, 1st; Ed Angle, 2nd; Jim Murphy, 3rd.
Hobby Heat—Jim LaGarde, 1st; Larry Montel, 2nd; Bill Varney, 3rd.
Hobby Heat—Larry Daine, 1st; Dennis Hopper, 2nd; Chuck Sainer, 3rd.
Hobby Feature—Larry Daine, 1st; Dennis Hopper, 2nd; Tom Wyman, 3rd.
Stock Feature—Roger Grossnickle, 1st; Art Smith, 2nd; Jim Bucher, 3rd.
Modified Feature—Jim Murphy, 1st; Dick Jones, 2nd; Les Bills, 3rd.

Saturday, June 19, 1971
Jim Murphy Cops Modified Feature

Jim Murphy was the big winner at the Warsaw Speedway Saturday night taking the checkered flag in the modified feature to go along with a first place finish in a heat race.

Tom Beezley, who finished second in the modified feature, took a second in a heat race and crossed the line first in the modified dash event. Art Smith won the semi-late model stock feature race. Chuck Sainer captured the hobby stock feature and took one hobby stock heat race.

Race Summary:

Stock Dash—John White, 1st; Robert Grossnickle, 2nd; Ray Chambers, 3rd.
Modified Dash—Tom Beezley, 1st; Larry Howard, 2nd; Bob Grindle, 3rd.
Stock Heat—Bud Grossnickle, 1st; Ellis Shepherd, 2nd; Jerry Baker, 3rd.
Modified Heat—Chuck Mosley, 1st; Tom Patterson, 2nd; Paul Grim, 3rd.
Stock Heat—Jim Wagoner, 1st; Arden Leiter, 2nd; Larry Mallott, 3rd.
Modified Heat—Jim Murphy, 1st; Tom Beezley, 2nd; Jim Elliott, 3rd.
Hobby Stock Heat—Chuck Sainer, 1st; Mike Stevens, 2nd; Elbert Russell, 3rd.
Hobby Stock Heat—Larry Daine, 1st; Phil Hogue, 2nd; Larry Montel, 3rd.
Hobby Feature—Chuck Sainer, 1st; Larry Daine, 2nd; Larry Montel, 3rd.

Stock Feature—Art Smith, 1st; Ted Hudson, 2nd; Arden Leiter, 3rd.
Modified Feature—Jim Murphy, 1st; Tom Beezley, 2nd; Jim Elliott, 3rd.

Saturday, June 26, 1971
Elliott Wins 3 Modified Events

Warsaw's Jim Elliott was the big winner at the Warsaw Speedway Saturday night grabbing the checkered flag in three modified events. Elliott raced home first in the modified dash, captured a heat race and won the modified feature.

The winners in the late-model stock class were evenly distributed with Jene Simon, of Columbia City, taking the feature race. Tom Wyman won the hobby stock feature. Larry Howard, of Akron, joined the roll-over club when he flipped his racer in the modified feature but he escaped injury.

Race Summary:

Stock Dash—Art Smith, 1st; Jim Wagoner, 2nd; Dean Hudson, 3rd.
Modified Dash—Jim Elliott, 1st; John Davis, 2nd; Jim Murphy, 3rd.
Stock Heat—Ellis Shepherd, 1st; Arden Leiter, 2nd; Tom Leiter, 3rd.
Modified Heat—Louie Mann, 1st; Jim Latoz, 2nd; Larry Howard, 3rd.
Stock Heat—Paul Roberts, 1st; Jene Simon, 2nd; Art Smith, 3rd.
Modified Heat—Jim Elliott, 1st; Jim Murphy, 2nd; John Davis, 3rd.
Consolation—Larry Malott, 1st; Les Sroufe, 2nd; Bud Grossnickle, 3rd.
Hobby Feature—Tom Wyman, 1st; Larry Daine, 2nd; Larry Montel, 3rd.
Stock Feature—Jene Simon, 1st; Paul Roberts, 2nd; Art Smith, 3rd.
Modified Feature—Jim Elliott, 1st; Dick Jones, 2nd; Jim Murphy, 3rd.

Saturday, July 2 & Monday, July 4, 1971
Auto Racing Doubleheader

Large crowds were on hand at the Warsaw Speedway over the weekend to witness the fireworks display Saturday night, and the exciting demolition derby Monday. Saturday's huge throng created a purse of $4,914 for the drivers as Jim Murphy, of Coloma, Mich., won the modified feature event while Les Sroufe, of Huntington, took the semi-late model stock feature. Larry Montel captured the hobby stock feature.

Crashes sent three drivers to the Murphy Medical Center for treatment of minor injuries but all were released. They included Philip Partridge, Servia; James LaGarde, Columbia City; and Roger Grossnickle, North Manchester.

In Monday night activity Jim Valentine finished first in the demolition derby and Larry Wolfe was second. Paul Roberts took the checkered flag in the stock feature and Jim Elliott was the modified winner. The hobby stock feature went to Larry Montel. Jim Murphy rolled in the modified feature but escaped injury.

Race Summary:
Saturday
Stock Dash—Larry Malott, 1st; Larry Baker, 2nd; Vonell Krom, 3rd.
Modified Dash—Jim Murphy, 1st; Jim Elliott, 2nd; Jerry Priest, 3rd.

Stock Heat—Ron Miller, 1st; Arden Leiter, 2nd; Ted Hudson, 3rd.
Modified Heat—Ed Stine, 1st; Paul Joyce, 2nd; Don Murphy, 3rd.
Stock Heat—Les Sroufe, 1st; Paul Roberts, 2nd; Jerry Baker, 3rd.
Modified Heat—Jim Elliott, 1st; Bob Grindle, 2nd; Jim Murphy, 3rd.
Stock Consolation—Bud Grossnickle, 1st; Ellis Shepherd, 2nd; Don Purdy, 3rd.
Slow Hobby Stock—Chuck Sainer, 1st; Bob Johnson, 2nd; Mike Stevens.
Fast Hobby Stock—Dennis Hopper, 1st; Tom Wyman, 2nd; Bruce Hogue, 3rd.
Hobby Feature—Larry Montel, 1st; Larry Daine, 2nd; Tom Wyman, 3rd.
Stock Feature—Les Sroufe, 1st; Paul Roberts, 2nd; Larry Malott, 3rd.
Modified Feature—Jim Murphy, 1st; Jim Elliott, 2nd; Dick Jones, 3rd.

Monday
Stock Dash—Larry Malott, 1st; Art Smith, 2nd; Jim Bucher, 3rd.
Modified Dash—Jim Elliott, 1st; Jerry Priest, 2nd; Bob Grindle, 3rd.
Stock Heat—Ray Chambers, 1st; Jerry Baker, 2nd; Jerry Rosburgh, 3rd.
Modified Heat—Dick Jones, 1st; Art Bralthwaite, 2nd; Jim Murphy, 3rd.
Stock Heat—Jim Wagoner, 1st; Paul Roberts, 2nd; Ron Miller, 3rd.
Modified Heat—Tom Beezley, 1st; Jim Murphy, 2nd; Jim Elliott, 3rd.
Fast Hobby Stock—Larry Montel, 1st; Chuck Sainer, 2nd; Dennis Hopper, 3rd.
Hobby Stock Feature—Larry Montel, 1st; Chuck Sainer, 2nd; Bob Johnson, 3rd.
Stock Feature—Paul Roberts, 1st; Ted Hudson, 2nd; Dean Hudson, 3rd.
Modified Feature—Jim Elliott, 1st; Ron Fisher, 2nd; Jerry Priest, 3rd.

Saturday, July 9, 1971
Warsaw Speedway Results

Three winners emerged in the feature events during Saturday night racing at the Warsaw Speedway. Jim Murphy won the modified feature event, Jim Bucher the semi-late stock feature and Dennis Hopper the hobby stock feature.

Race Summary:

Stock Dash—Art Smith, 1st; Jene Simon, 2nd; Don White, 3rd.
Modified Dash—Jim Elliott, 1st; John Davis, 2nd; Jerry Priest, 3rd.
Stock Heat—Ted Hudson, 1st; Ron Miller, 2nd; Jerry Egolf, 3rd.
Modified Heat—Jim Murphy, 1st; Jerry Priest, 2nd; Ed Stine, 3rd.
Stock Heat—Larry Malott, 1st; Les Sroufe, 2nd; Paul Roberts, 3rd.
Modified Heat—Jim Elliott, 1st; Bob Grindle, 2nd; Tom Beezley, 3rd.
Stock Feature—Jim Bucher, 1st; Jerry Egolf, 2nd; Jim Wagner, 3rd.
Modified Feature—Jim Murphy, 1st; Larry Howard, 2nd; Jerry Priest, 3rd.
Hobby Heat—Dennis Hopper, 1st; Chuck Sainer, 2nd; Larry Daine, 3rd.
Hobby Feature—Dennis Hopper, 1st; Larry Daine, 2nd; Chuck Sainer, 3rd.

Larry Howard & Jerry Priest

Saturday, July 16, 1971
Warsaw Speedway Results

Three winners emerged in Saturday night racing at the Warsaw Speedway in an evening marred by numerous accidents. Ron Miller, in a semi-late event, was struck broadside and then taken to the emergency room at Murphy Medical Center. Miller suffered no serious injuries and was later released.

Jimmie Elliott Crash

Jim Elliott, in a qualification attempt, struck the wall and flipped his '57 sprinter over one time. Elliott, always a serious contender, was out of the competition for the evening. In the night's racing, Vonell Krom was the semi-late feature winner. Tom Beezley was first in the feature modified and Dennis Hopper copped top spot in the hobby stock feature.

Race Summary:

Stock Dash—Les Sroufe, 1st; Roger Grossnickle, 2nd; Dean Hudson, 3rd.
Modified Dash—Tom Beezley, 1st; Bob Grindle, 2nd; Jim Murphy, 3rd.
Stock Dash—Jim Wagoner, 1st; Tom Leiter, 2nd; Bob Grossnickle, 3rd.
Modified Heat—Louie Mann, 1st; Don Murphy, 2nd; Larry Howard, 3rd
Stock Heat—Jim Bucher, 1st; Art Smith, 2nd; Vonell Krom, 3rd.
Modified Heat—Jim Murphy, 1st; Tom Beezley, 2nd; Bob Grindle, 3rd.
Hobby Heat—Charles Jefferson, 1st; Russell Elbert, 2nd.
Hobby Heat—Larry Montel, 1st; Bruce Hogue, 2nd; Larry Daine, 3rd.
Consolation—Robert Burdey, 1st; Charlie Prater, 2nd; Larry Baker, 3rd.
Hobby Feature—Dennis Hopper, 1st; Chuck Sainer, 2nd; Larry Daine, 3rd.
Stock Feature—Vonell Krom, 1st; Jim Walmer, 2nd; Jene Simon, 3rd.
Modified Feature—Tom Beezley, 1st; Bob Grindle, 2nd; Jim Murphy, 3rd.

Saturday, July 23, 1971
Warsaw Speedway Results

Saturday night at the Warsaw Speedway was a discouraging time for Roger Grossnickle and a very happy one for Louie Mann.

Grossnickle was the leader for 20 laps of the semi-late model championship race until an ignition wire, which costs about ten cents,

Art Smith, Warsaw

broke dropping him out of the race. Mann meanwhile was a winner in all three races he entered, the modified dash, modified heat and modified feature.

Winning the stock feature was Art Smith and capturing the top spot in the hobby feature was Larry Montel. There were several crashes head on into the wall, but fortunately, no injuries resulted.

Summary:

Stock dash—Les Sroufe, 1st; Vonell Krom, 2nd; Art Smith, 3rd.
Modified dash—Louie Mann, 1st; Jim Elliott, 2nd; Ed Stine, 3rd.
Stock heat—Roy Norman, 1st; Larry Baker, 2nd; Roy Miller, 3rd.
Modified heat—Don Murphy, 1st; Paul Joyce, 2nd; Bob Bernhard, 3rd.
Stock heat—Jerry Baker, 1st; Jene Simon, 2nd; Roy Chambers, 3rd.
Modified heat—Louie Mann, 1st; Tom Beezley, 2nd; Jim Murphy, 3rd.
Stock Feature—Art Smith, 1st; Les Sroufe, 2nd; Paul Bills, 3rd.
Modified feature—Louie Mann, 1st; Tom Beezley, 2nd; John Davis, 3rd.
Hobby heat—Charles Jefferies, 1st; Duane Ronk, 2nd; Mike Stevens, 3rd.
Hobby heat—Larry Montel, 1st; Bill Varney, 2nd; Bruce Hogue, 3rd.
Hobby feature—Larry Montel, 1st; Bruce Hogue, 2nd; Duane Ronk, 3rd.

Saturday, July 31, 1971
Warsaw Speedway Results

A medium sized racing crowd watched one of the best racing cards of the season Saturday night at the Warsaw Speedway.

Several accidents marred the night but no one was injured. Jerry Priest, of Elwood, flipped over in his red and white #33 and Jim Murphy, Jim Elliott, and Tom Beezley were involved in a tangle that badly damaged the cars.

Bruce Hogue, Akron

Winners in the night's top events were Bruce Hogue in the hobby feature, Ellis Shepherd in the stock feature, and Jim Murphy in the modified feature.

Race Summary:

Stock dash—Jean Simon, 1st; Roger Grossnickle, 2nd; Art Smith, 3rd.
Modified dash—Jim Elliott, 1st; Jim Murphy, 2nd; Tom Beezley, 3rd.
Stock heat—Don Rumfelt, 1st; Ellis Shepherd, 2nd; Tom Leiter, 3rd.
Modified heat—Tom Patterson, 1st; Jim Murphy, 2nd; Bob Grindle, 3rd.
Stock heat—Jim Wagoner, 1st; Paul Roberts, 2nd; Jim Bucher, 3rd.
Modified heat—Jim Elliott, 1st; Tom Beezley, 2nd; Jim Murphy, 3rd.
Stock Feature—Ellis Shepherd, 1st; Paul Roberts, 2nd; Roy Neuman, 3rd.
Modified feature—Jim Murphy, 1st; Louie Mann, 2nd.
Hobby heat—Bob Johnson, 1st; John Fitzpatrick, 2nd; David Duff, 3rd.

Hobby heat—Bruce Hogue, 1st; Larry Montel, 2nd; Duane Ronk, 3rd.
Hobby Feature - Bruce Hogue, 1st; Mike Stevens, 2nd; John Fitzpatrick, 3rd.

Thursday, August 5, 1971
Warsaw Speedway Results

Racing fans enjoyed a special night of mid-week competition as the Warsaw Speedway put on a special oval edition for the Kosciusko County Fair. Involved in the night's activities were hobby stocks and semi-late models. It was an evening of numerous accidents, although no injuries were suffered.

Chuck Sainer emerged the night's hobby feature winner and Les Sroufe was the feature winner in the semi-late event. Saturday night the Speedway will feature sprints, modified and semi-late events.

Race Summary:

Stock dash—Jene Simon, 1st; Dean Hudson, 2nd; Art Smith, 3rd.
Semi-late dash—Jerry Baker, 1st; Norman Roy, 2nd; Tom Leiter, 3rd.
Stock heat—Jerry Rosbruck, 1st; Bud Grossnickle, 2nd; Jim Wagoner, 3rd.
Hobby heat—Harry Ayres, 1st; DeLong, 2nd; B. Webster, 3rd.
Stock heat—Ted Hudson, 1st; J. White, 2nd; P. Roberts, 3rd.
Hobby heat—D. Ronk, 1st; G. Harrold, 2nd; Truex, 3rd.
Concy semi-late—R. Grossnickle, 1st; J. Bucher, 2nd; A. Leiter, 3rd.
Stock Feature—Les Sroufe, 1st; Art Smith, 2nd; J. Baker, 3rd.
Hobby Feature—Chuck Sainer, 1st; C. Reiner, 2nd; Daine, 3rd.

Saturday, August 7, 1971
Warsaw Speedway Results

A huge crowd watched the Saturday night races at the Warsaw Speedway which were climaxed by the crowning of this year's Kosciusko County Fair Queen. A number of interesting occurrences happened during the event. After Larry Montel won the Hobby Feature, he experienced serious drive shaft difficulties under the car. Had there been one more lap, Montel would have been unable to finish. Roger Grossnickle was knocked out of the feature event for about the tenth time. He has had some kind of problem every Saturday night and is now tagged by many drivers, "the hard luck driver of the Speedway". Art Smith started last in the Late Model Feature and worked his way into second.

Second District Congressman, Earl F. Landgrege, of Valparaiso, was introduced to the huge crowd and escorted during the event by Mr. William Orr, Kosciusko County Fair President. Saturday night's car race was broadcast in part over radio stations WRSW - AM and FM and sponsored by Warsaw Automotive. One of the main features of next week's Speedway activities will be a Women's Powder Puff Race. Joining Montel as a feature winner were Paul Roberts, Stock Feature winner and Jim Elliott, Modified Feature finalist.

Race Summary:

Stock dash—Jim Wagoner, 1st; Jene Simon, 2nd; Art Smith, 3rd.
Modified dash—Jim Elliott, 1st; Jerry Priest, 2nd; Jim Murphy, 3rd.

Stock heat—Vonell Krom, 1st; Roy Normal, 2nd; Larry Howard, 3rd.
Modified heat—Louie Mann, 1st; Bob Bernhard, 2nd; Gary Baker, 3rd.
Stock heat—Jim Bucher, 1st; Les Sroufe, 2nd; Jim Baker, 3rd.
Modified heat—Jim Elliott, 1st; Jerry Priest, 2nd; Tom Beezley, 3rd.
Stock Feature—Paul Roberts, 1st; Art Smith, 2nd; Les Sroufe, 3rd.
Modified feature—Jim Elliott, 1st; Tom Beezley, 2nd; Jim Murphy, 3rd.
Hobby heat—Terry Ayres, 1st; Duane Ronk, 2nd; Bill Smith, 3rd.
Hobby heat—Larry Montel, 1st; Dennis Hopper, 2nd; Bruce Hogue, 3rd.
Hobby Feature - Larry Montel, 1st; Bruce Hogue, 2nd; Duane Ronk, 3rd.

Saturday, August 14, 1971
Warsaw Speedway Results

A large crowd turned out for Saturday night at the races, Warsaw Speedway style. Highlighting the action were numerous accidents that left the pit area cluttered with twisted metal, and a Powder Puff Derby.

Roger Grossnickle, N. Manchester

Roger Grossnickle extended his right to carry the "hard luck kid" title for another week by becoming involved in another accident. His pit crew had the car back in running condition by the Stock Feature event and Grossnickle finished third.

Winning the Stock Feature race was Jim Bucher. Jim Elliott copped the top spot in the Modified Feature and Larry Montel captured first place laurels in the Hobby Feature event. The race, heard over WRSW AM-FM radio stations was sponsored in part by Warsaw Automotive.

Race Summary:

Stock Dash—Roger Grossnickle, 1st; Jene Simon, 2nd; Ted Hudson, 3rd.
Modified Dash—Louis Mann, 1st; Jim Elliott, 2nd; Tom Beezley, 3rd.
Stock heat—Dave Roberts, 1st; Roy Norman, 2nd; John White, 3rd.
Modified heat—Jerry Priest, 1st; Bob Bernhard, 2nd; Les Bills, 3rd.
Stock heat—Jim Bucher, 1st; Jerry Baker, 2nd; Jerry Egolf, 3rd.
Modified heat—Bob Grindle, 1st; Jim Elliott, 2nd; Louie Mann, 3rd.
Stock feature—Jim Bucher, 1st; Jim Guy, 2nd; Roger Grossnickle, 3rd.
Modified feature—Jim Elliott, 1st; Louie Mann, 2nd; Jim Murphy, 3rd.
Hobby heat—Don Womack, 1st; Bill Smith, 2nd; Bob Webster, 3rd.
Hobby heat—Dick Wiles, 1st; Larry Montel, 2nd; Bruce Hogue, 3rd.

Hobby feature—Larry Montel, 1st; Duane Ronk, 2nd; Bruce Hogue, 3rd.
Powder Puff—B Robin Theme, 1st.

Saturday, August 21, 1971
Warsaw Speedway Results

Close races were numerous in Saturday night action at the Warsaw Speedway. In the semi-late feature, Ted Hudson, the leader, Roger Grossnickle and Art Smith drove bumper to bumper for 20 laps...then finished in that order.

In the modified feature, Don Walker, in a new car, led Jim Elliott for a number of laps until late in the race, when the smaller and lighter car Elliott was driving adapted better to the rapidly drying track, and passed Walker for the win. Les Bills, of Columbia City, looked as if he has finally found the winning formula as he captured fourth place in the super sprint feature.

Next Saturday night, there will be two season championship 50 lap events for modified and semi-late racers. One-half hour of Saturday night's race was sponsored by Warsaw Auto Supply over WRSW AM and FM.

Race Summary:

Stock dash—Ray Chambers, 1st; Jim Wagoner, 2nd; Roger Grossnickle, 3rd.
Modified dash—Don Walker, 1st; Tom Beezley, 2nd; Louie Mann, 3rd.
Stock heat—Larry Daine, 1st; Tom Leiter, 2nd; Don Method, 3rd.
Modified heat—Chuck Garver, 1st; Art Brithwaite, 2nd; Don Murphy, 3rd.
Stock heat—Vonell Krom, 1st; Jim Bucher, 2nd; Jerry Rosebrook, 3rd.
Modified heat—Tom Beezley, 1st; Don Walker, 2nd; Jack Hickman, 3rd.
Stock feature—Ted Hudson, 1st; Roger Grossnickle, 2nd; Art Smith, 3rd.
Modified feature—Jim Elliott, 1st; Louis Mann, 2nd; Don Walker, 3rd.
Hobby heat—Larry Montel, 1st; Bob Johnson, 2nd; Roger Huntley, 3rd.
Hobby heat—Dennis Hopper, 1st; John Fitzpatrick, 2nd; Duane Ronk, 3rd.
Hobby feature—Dennis Hopper, 1st; Chuck Sainer, 2nd.

Saturday, August 30, 1971
Warsaw Speedway Results

A large enthusiastic crowd got their money's worth during the Saturday night races at the Warsaw Speedway.

Jerry Baker lost a wheel in the late model feature and rolled over several times. Slightly shaken, he got into modified 31, normally driven by brother Gary just to make sure he hadn't lost his nerve...he hadn't. Rick Leverton rolled six times in front of the grandstand hitting the track with a crunch each time. He was

Roger Grossnickle & Hoot Gibson

helped out of his car, momentarily stunned, but not seriously hurt.

Both features, semi-late and modified, were 50-lap events and trophies were given to the first three places with a $100 bonus to the winners. Winning the stock car feature was Roger Grossnickle; the modified feature winner was Jim Murphy. Capturing the top spot in the Hobby feature event was Duane Ronk.

On Saturday, September 4, the season's hobby stock championship will be run.

Duane Ronk, Warsaw

Race Summary:

Stock heat—Jerry Rosebrunk, 1st; Ron Miller, 2nd; Paul Roberts, 3rd.
Modified heat—Charlie Sainer, 1st; Art Braithwaite, 2nd; Bob Grindle, 3rd.
Stock heat—Jerry Baker, 1st; John White, 2nd; Ted White, 3rd.
Modified heat—Jack Hickman, 1st; Jim Murphy, 2nd; Tom Beezley, 3rd.
Stock Championship—Roger Grossnickle, 1st; Les Sroufe, 2nd; Jim Bucher, 3rd.
Modified Championship—Jim Murphy, 1st; Jim Elliott, 2nd; Tom Beezley, 3rd.
Hobby Heat—Bob Johnson, 1st; Charles Hyde, 2nd; Gene Demson, 3rd.
Hobby Heat—Chuck Sainer, 1st; Larry Montel, 2nd; Bruce Hogue, 3rd.
Hobby feature—Duane Ronk, 1st; Bruce Hogue, 2nd; Chuck Sainer, 3rd.

Saturday, September 4, 1971
Results At The Warsaw Speedway Saturday Night
Columbia City Post & Mail – Sept. 7, 1971

Dennis Hopper was the winner of the 35-lap Hobby Stock car feature race at the Warsaw Speedway Saturday. Terry Moneal took the lead when the green flag was dropped. He spun in the number one curve when Hopper took the lead. Hopper was the fastest qualifier for the race.

The late model feature was a straight start with the fastest car first. Les Sroufe and Jene Simon battled for the first position from the first lap with the finish of Sroufe, Simon, Ray Chambers and Roger Grossnickle. Jene Simon won the late model dash as he led from the first lap. Simon's car is owned by Kenny Huntley.

Jim Elliott, in a super modified car owned by Paul Hazen won every race he entered, taking the checkered flag in the dash event fast heat and the feature. Tom Beezley won the slow heat and finished third in the feature with Les Bills fourth. Bills also finished third in the fast heat.

Dale Huntley, driving No. 00 in the Hobby Stock had to go to the pits in the fast heat with his front fender dragging and didn't make it back for the feature.

Saturday, September 4, 1971
Warsaw Speedway Results

A large crowd enjoyed late summer Saturday night racing at the Warsaw Speedway. Highlight of the evening was the wheel-to-wheel dual between Jim Murphy and Jim Elliott. Murphy enjoyed a slight lead for 16 laps, then he went into a slide, and Elliott passed for the lead en route to his eventual victory in the super-sprint feature.

Speedway Manager Hoot Gibson has announced one final night of racing, September 11. Featured will be a demolition derby with at least 35 cars entered. One-half hour of Saturday night's radio station WRSW AM-FM race broadcast was sponsored by Warsaw Automotive Supply Co.

Race Summary:

Stock dash—Jene Simon, 1st; Art Smith, 2nd; John White, 3rd.
Modified dash—Jim Elliott, 1st; Ron Fisher, 2nd; Jack Hickman, 3rd.
Stock heat—Ron Miller, 1st; Charlie Sroufe, 2nd; Jerry Baker, 3rd.
Modified heat—Tom Beezley, 1st; Scott Wasljewski, 2nd; Don Murphy, 3rd.
Stock heat—Paul Roberts, 1st; Tom Leiter, 2nd; Jim Wagoner, 3rd.
Modified heat—Jim Elliott, 1st; Jim Murphy, 2nd; Les Bills, 3rd.
Stock feature—Les Sroufe, 1st; Jene Simon, 2nd; Dan Chambers, 3rd.
Modified feature—Jim Elliott, 1st; Jim Murphy, 2nd; Tom Beezley, 3rd.
Hobby heat—John Fitzpatrick, 1st; Duane Ronk, 2nd; Dick Gaby, 3rd.
Hobby heat—Dennis Hopper, 1st; Larry Montel, 2nd; Chuck Sainer, 3rd.
Hobby feature—Dennis Hopper, 1st; Chuck Sainer, 2nd; Bob Johnson, 3rd.

Saturday, September 11, 1971
Warsaw Speedway Results

A large crowd viewed the final race of the season at the Warsaw Speedway Saturday night. A number of wrecks occurred during the night, when the 55 drivers qualified, made an all-out effort to win the season's finales.

Tom Beezley of Wolf Lake was injured when the drive train on his car broke, and the shaft struck his leg as he was trying to leave his car when a potential fire in the cockpit threatened.

Vonell Krom was the stock feature winner. Jerry Priest captured the modified feature event, and Dennis Hopper took the top spot in the hobby feature.

Race Summary:

Stock dash—Jene Simon, 1st; Ted Hudson, 2nd; Roger Grossnickle, 3rd.
Modified dash—Jim Elliott, 1st; Jerry Priest, 2nd; Don Walker, 3rd.
Stock heat—Paul Roberts, 1st; Jay Warner, 2nd; Jerry Baker, 3rd.
Modified heat—Tom Beezley, 1st; Bob Bernhard, 2nd; Eugene Barnes, 3rd.
Stock heat—Vonell Krom, 1st; Les Sroufe, 2nd; Ray Chambers, 3rd.
Modified heat—Jim Elliott, 1st; Les Bills, 2nd; Don Walker, 3rd.
Stock feature—Vonell Krom, 1st; Les Sroufe, 2nd; Paul Roberts, 3rd.
Modified feature—Jerry Priest, 1st; Les Bills, 2nd; Don Walker, 3rd.
Hobby heat—Dennis Hopper, 1st; Paul Kerlin, 2nd; Terry Ayres, 3rd.
Hobby heat—John Fitzpatrick, 1st; Duane Ronk, 2nd; Bruce Hogue, 3rd.
Hobby feature—Dennis Hopper, 1st; Bruce Hogue, 2nd; Roger Huntley, 3rd.
Demolition race—Ron Eads, 1st; Sonny Nellans, 2nd; Todd Grigsby, 3rd.

October 13, 1971
Warsaw Champ Elliott Loses Sight of Eye
by Paul Hazen

Fort Wayne, IN. - As a result of a freak accident at the Bryan, Ohio, Motor Speedway, two-time Warsaw Speedway champion Jim Elliott has lost the sight of his left eye and suffered a facial skull fracture.

Elliott, who holds the lap record at Bryan's half-mile track, was competing in the Sept. 19 supermodified program there when another car churned up a rock, which struck Elliott's facemask, shattering it, and damaged his left eye.

Elliott was first treated at the Bryan Hospital, then transferred to Parkview Hospital in Fort Wayne where three hours of surgery failed to save his eye. Elliott is now recovering at his home, 1503 E. Sheridan St., Warsaw, Ind., and would welcome mail.

October 23, 1971
Warsaw Speedway Holds Annual Banquet

More than 300 persons attended the annual banquet for Warsaw Speedway drivers, mechanics and owners, held at the American Legion in Columbia City recently. C. E. (Hoot) Gibson, track manager, presented awards to point winners in the various classes.

Modified class winners included: Jim Elliott, Warsaw, 1st; Jim Murphy, Michigan, 2nd; Tom Beezley, Wolf Lake, 3rd; Jerry Priest, Kokomo, 4th; Les Bills, Columbia City, 5th. Also, Louie Mann, Kokomo, 6th; Bob Grindle, Warsaw, 7th; Don Murphy, South Whitley, 8th; John Davis, Warsaw, 9th; and Bob Bernhard, South Whitley, 10th.

Hobby stock winners included: Dennis Hopper, Warsaw, 1st; Larry Montel, North Manchester, 2nd; Bruce Hogue, Akron, 3rd; Chuck Sainer, Akron, 4th; and Larry Daine, Akron, 5th.

Winners in the late model class were: Art Smith, Warsaw, 1st; Roger Grossnickle, North Manchester, 2nd; Les Sroufe, Huntington, 3rd; Jim Bucher, Akron, 4th; and Paul Roberts, Huntington, 5th. Also, Ted Hudson, North Manchester, 6th; Vonell Krom, Roann, 7th; Jim Wagoner, Athens, 8th; Jene Simons, Columbia City, 9th; and Jerry Baker, Warsaw, 10th.

Rookie of the year was Ron Miller of the late model class. Sportsmanship trophies, sponsored by Fred and Jim Boggs, went to Tom Wyman, Warsaw, hobby stock; Art Smith,

Claypool, late model; and Tom Beezley, Wolf Lake, Modified.

Already, preparations for the upcoming race season are in progress. Recently, 700 yards of new clay were put on the track and painting and repairing of the track facilities continue as weather permits. Talk is underway concerning a spring slate of racing. The track is officially scheduled to open the first week of May.

Milo Clase, Warsaw Speedway track announcer, has announced that the new 1972 race rules have been printed. They may be obtained by writing to track manager C. E. Gibson, Rt. 3, Columbia City.

1972

Saturday, May 6, 1972
Racing Weekly—Pg.3, May 12 Edition
By Georgia LaFever

Warsaw, May 6, 1972—A large crowd of spectators gathered for the first night of racing at Warsaw Speedway for the 1972 season. Forty-nine cars qualified amidst threatening rain and a few sprinkles. The fastest qualifiers were: Jim Elliott, Super Sprint 57, Vonell Krom in Semi-late models and John Fitzpatrick in Hobby Stock.

Les Sroufe started the racing by taking the lead in the Dash and keeping it all six laps with Jim Bucher second and Jene Simon 47 second and third respectively. Tom Beezley jumped out in front of Super Sprint Dash with Ron Fisher overtaking him in the first lap. It was bumper to bumper the rest of the race for Ron Fisher and Don Walker with Ron Fisher taking the checkered flag. Jim Elliott finished third.

In the First Hobby Heat, Owsley -73, took the lead but spun in the fifth lap and had to go to the pits. Hatfield 44 took the lead and won the race with Mike Stevens and DeLong following.

Tommy Leiter jumped out in front in the first Semi Late Heat and held the lead with Paul Bills hot in pursuit. Midway through the race Paul Bills passed him taking a sizeable lead and checkered flag with Tommy Leiter second and Ronnie Miller third.

Don Walker won the First Super Sprint heat in a brand-new car No. 1. He is presently the track record holder with a time of 15.59. He raced a few times last year but now he is back in his new car.

The second hobby heat started with some excitement as they entered the third turn when one of the lead cars spun and the rest collided. Bob Johnson took the lead with John Fitzpatrick battling him for that checkered flag, but couldn't get around him and finished second.

Jim Wagoner, 21, led the cars in Second Semi-late heat in a close, close race between himself and Jene Simon and Les Sroufe as they were bunched up the entire race, but finished first, second and third respectively.

Jerry Priest had a quarter lap lead in the second Super Sprint heat when he got the checkered flag with Tom Beezley second and Bob Bernhard third. The Late Model Feature offered a bonus of $150 to the winner in a straight start (fastest first). Vonell Krom, sitting in pole position took the lead and kept it for the checkered. In a very fast race with Krom, Sroufe, Smith, Simon, Bills all in contention they began lapping cars when four of the end cars tangled and Krom and Smith just barely missed them and each other. This is one of the many times when we realize that these fellows can really handle their cars. The cars were lining back up and the green was dropped when Jene Simon lost all power on the starting line. When the cars came back around, cars scattered. Paul Bills was running fifth but damaged his car this time and had to go to the pits. Les Sroufe was challenging Vonell Krom in the last few laps but never quite able to pass him and finished second.

Elliott, sitting in pole position for Super Sprint Feature in a straight start, took the lead, checkered flag and also bonus of $150 for winning this race. He had a sizable lead most of the race. It was a great night for racing, as it will be every Saturday with more cars expected next week.

Racing Results:
Late Model Dash: Les Sroufe, 1st; Jim Bucher, 2nd; Jene Simon, 3rd.
First Hobby Heat: Hatfield, 1st; Mike Stevens, 2nd; Fred DeLong, 3rd;
First Super Sprint Heat: Don Walker, 1st; Jim Elliott, 2nd; Ron Fisher, 3rd.
Second Semi-Late Heat: Jim Wagoner, 1st; Jene Simon, 2nd; Les Sroufe, 3rd.
Semi-Late Model Feature: Vonell Krom, 1st; Les Sroufe, 2nd; Jene Simon, 3rd.
Hobby Stock Feature: John Fitzpatrick, 1st; Bob Johnson, 2nd; Mike Stevens, 3rd.
Super Sprint Dash: Ron Fisher, 1st; Don Walker, 2nd; Jim Elliott, 3rd.
First Semi-Late Heat: Paul Bills, 1st; Tom Leiter, 2nd; Ronnie Miller, 3rd.
Second Hobby Heat: Bob Johnson, 1st; John Fitzpatrick, 2nd; Terry Baker, 3rd.
Second Super Sprint: Jerry Priest, 1st; Tom Beezley, 2nd; Bob Bernhard, 3rd.
Super Sprint Feature: Jim Elliott, 1st; Ron Fisher 2nd; Tom Beezley, 3rd.

Saturday, May 13, 1972 - Rainout

Saturday, May 20, 1972
Warsaw Speedway

Perfect weather and a large field—52 cars—welcomed back the first official week of racing back to the Warsaw Speedway Saturday night. The big crowd didn't have to wait long at the season's start for the first spectacular spill. There were several wrecks during the night but the one that caught the crowd's attention took place when Jim Elliott and Don Murphy collided.

According to track reports Elliott's car, out of control, unavoidably ended up on top of Murphy's car almost going into the driver's seat before crashing on its side. It came to a stop at a 45 degree angle still on top of Murphy's car....there were no injuries.

Vonell Krom picked up the victory in the stock feature. Jim Elliott added a triumph in the modified feature and John Kirkpatrick came out on top in the Hobby Feature. Next Saturday night there will be the regular racing card and on Monday night, May 29, there will be a 35 lap super sprint feature with a $200 bonus planned for the feature winner.

Racing Summary:

Stock Dash—Simons, 1st; Bills, 2nd; Baker, 3rd.
Modified Dash—Bernhard, 1st; Priest, 2nd; Beezley, 3rd.
Stock Heat—Hogue, 1st; Chambers, 2nd; Howard, 3rd.
Modified Heat—Elliott, 1st; Beezley, 2nd; Grindle, 3rd.
Stock Heat—Leiter, 1st; Krom, 2nd; Sroufe, 3rd.
Modified Heat—Elliott, 1st; Murphy, 2nd; Grindle, 3rd.
Stock Feature—Krom, 1st; Leiter, 2nd; Roberts, 3rd.
Modified Feature—Elliott, 1st; Grindle, 2nd; Beezley, 3rd.
Hobby Heat—Kain, 1st; Anders, 2nd.
Hobby Heat—Day, 1st; Firzpatrick, 2nd; Hatfield, 3rd.
Hobby Feature—Fitzpatrick, 1st; Hatfield, 2nd; DeLong, 3rd.

Saturday, May 27, 1972
Warsaw Speedway

It was race action both Saturday and Monday night in weekend competition at the Warsaw Speedway.

On Saturday a large crowd watched 66 cars qualify then compete in some of the Speedway's wildest action to date. Warsaw's Tom Leiter captured the top spot in the stock feature, Ron Semelka, Wassion, Ohio, collected top money in the stock feature and Charles Hyde finished on top in the hobby feature.

Paul Bills, Columbia City

Rain kept the attendance down in Monday night's action highlighted by the frantic finish of Paul Bills in the stock feature who crossed the finish line minus the front left wheel which he lost three-fourths of a lap earlier. In action scheduled for this weekend at the Speedway, there will be a 35-lap feature with a $200 bonus going to the winner of the semi-late model feature.

Winners in Monday night's action were: Paul Bills, Columbia City, semi-late dash; Bob Grindle, Warsaw, modified dash; Jene Simon, Columbia City, stock heat; Tom Beezley, Wolf Lake, modified heat; Tom Leiter, Warsaw, stock heat; Louie Mann, Kokomo, modified heat; Dick Day, Warsaw, hobby heat; Bill Kain, Warsaw, hobby heat; Jim Elliott, Warsaw, modified feature; Paul Bills, Columbia City, stock feature; and Jerry Baker, Pierceton, hobby feature.

Top finishers in Saturday night action follow:

Stock Dash—Paul Roberts, 1st; Les Sroufe, 2nd; Paul Bills, 3rd.
Modified Dash—Jerry Priest, 1st; Bob Bernhard, 2nd; Jim Murphy, 3rd.
Stock Heat—Ron Miller, 1st; Roy Chambers, 2nd; Jim Brown, 3rd.

Modified Heat—Bob Grindle, 1st; Ron Semelka, 2nd; Tom Beezley, 3rd; Paul Joyce, 4th.
Stock Heat—Paul Roberts, 1st; Les Sroufe, 2nd; Jim Bucher, 3rd.
Modified Heat—Louie Mann, 1st; Tom York, 2nd; Jim Murphy, 3rd; Don Murphy, 4th.
Stock Feature—Tom Leiter, 1st; Roy Chambers, 2nd; Les Sroufe, 3rd; Vonnell Krom, 4th; Paul Roberts, 5th.
Modified Feature—Ron Semelka, 1st; Louie Mann, 2nd; Jim Murphy, 3rd; Jerry Priest, 4th; Harold Mouser, 5th.
Hobby Heat—Bill Smith, 1st; Bill McKown, 2nd; Bruce Sisk, 3rd.
Hobby Heat—Bill Kain, 1st; Don Rumfelt, 2nd; Don Gaby, 3rd.
Hobby Feature—Charles Hyde, 1st; Don Rumfelt, 2nd; Bill Hull, 3rd.

Saturday, June 3, 1972
Warsaw Speedway

There were 60 cars on hand for Saturday night's racing card at the Warsaw Speedway in an event that was called after the seventh race due to rain.

This Saturday night's action will include a complete schedule of racing, plus the continuation of uncompleted races from last Saturday night. A special purse of $200 will go to the super sprint winner in the 25-lap feature.

Despite the rain, only two accidents marred the night's action. In the last lap of the night Rex Heckaman rolled on his top and Jim Morris lost his gas tank.

Saturday night statistics follow:
Stock Dash—Jene Simon, 1st; Vonnell Krom, 2nd; Ray Chambers, 3rd.
Modified Dash—Lou Mann, 1st; Jim Elliott, 2nd; Don Walker, 3rd.
Stock Heat—Dave Buzzard, 1st; Bud Grossnickle, 2nd; Bruce Hogue, 3rd.
Modified Heat—Jim Murphy, 1st; Tom York, 2nd; Tom Patterson, 3rd.
Stock Heat—Les Sroufe, 1st; Art Smith, 2nd; Jene Simon, 3rd.
Hobby Heat—Dick Day, 1st; Bob Johnson, 2nd; Fred DeLong, 3rd.
Hobby Heat—Larry Montel, 1st; Jim LaGarde, 2nd; Bill Kain, 3rd.

Saturday, June 10, 1972
Warsaw Speedway

Despite the brisk weather, a large crowd turned out to watch Saturday night action at the Warsaw Speedway.

Added to the regular racing card were four additional races carried over from the previous week which were rained out. A $200 bonus was given to Les Sroufe, winner of the June 3 semi-late feature and to the super sprint winner in Saturday night's action.

Winning the top spots in the feature competition were John Fitzpatrick, hobby; Jim Murphy, modified; and Les Sroufe, stock. The four events completed from the weekend of June 3 are listed first followed by Saturday night's winners:

Modified Heat—Mike Johnson, 1st; Bob Bernhard, 2nd; Jim Elliott, 3rd.
Hobby Feature—Larry Montel, 1st; John Fitzpatrick, 2nd; Jerry Baker, 3rd.
Semi-Late Feature—Les Sroufe, 1st; Vonell Krom, 2nd; Hal Grigsby, 3rd.
Super Sprint—Jim Murphy, 1st; Mike Johnson, 2nd; Jim Elliott, 3rd.

Stock Dash—Art Smith, 1st; Jim Bucher, 2nd; Vonnell Krom, 3rd.
Modified Dash—Mike Johnson, 1st; John Elliott, 2nd; Don Walker, 3rd.
Stock Heat—Bud Grossnickle, 1st; Hal Grigsby, 2nd; Bruce Hogue, 3rd.
Modified Heat—Tom York, 1st; Bob Grindle, 2nd; Paul Grim, 3rd.
Stock Heat—Chuck Sainer, 1st; Larry Howard, 2nd; Les Sroufe, 3rd.
Modified Heat—Jim Murphy, 1st; Mike Johnson, 2nd; Bob Bernhard, 3rd.
Stock Feature—Les Sroufe, 1st; Paul Roberts, 2nd; Jim Bucher, 3rd.
Modified Feature—Jim Murphy, 1st; Bob Grindle, 2nd; Don Murphy, 3rd.
Hobby Heat—Fred DeLong, 1st; Bob Johnson, 2nd; Jim Norris, 3rd.
Hobby Heat—Larry Montel, 1st; Louie Adams, 2nd; Jerry Baker, 3rd.
Hobby Feature—John Fitzpatrick, 1st; Dick Day, 2nd; Dave Kerlin, 3rd.

Saturday, June 17, 1972
Warsaw Speedway

One of the smaller crowds of the season watched Saturday night racing at the Warsaw Speedway in action that took place in near record-breaking short time. There were several new super sprints entered, coming from as far as Michigan and Indianapolis.

Ronnie Miller, Huntington, captured the stock feature; Jim Elliott, Warsaw, came in first in the modified feature, and Larry Montel of Manchester captured top honors in the hobby feature.

Jimmie Elliott, Warsaw

Race Summary:

Stock Dash—Vonnell Krom, Wolf Lake, 1st; Arden Leiter, 2nd; Paul Grim, 3rd.
Modified Dash—Jim Elliott, Warsaw, 1st; Bob Grindle, 2nd; Paul Grim, 3rd.
Stock Heat—Paul Roberts, Huntington, 1st; Tom Leiter, 2nd; Don Burkett, 3rd.
Modified Heat—Bob McDaniels, 1st, Indianapolis; Jeff Creason, 2nd; Tom Patterson, 3rd.
Stock Heat—Vonnell Krom, Wolf Lake, 1st; Jene Simon, 2nd; Art Smith, 3rd.
Modified Heat—Jerry Priest, Elwood, 1st; Jim Elliott, 2nd; Don Murphy, 3rd.
Stock Feature—Ronnie Miller, Huntington, 1st; Art Smith, 2nd; Chuck Sainer, 3rd.
Modified Feature—Jim Elliott, Warsaw, 1st; Jerry Priest, 2nd; Bob Grindle, 3rd.
Hobby Heat—Jim LaGarde, Warsaw, 1st; John Fitzpatrick, 2nd; Bob Johnson, 3rd.
Hobby Heat—Dick Wiles, Warsaw, 1st; Terry Hatfield, 2nd; Jerry Baker, 3rd.
Hobby Feature—Larry Montel, 1st, North Manchester; Jim LaGarde, 2nd; Bill Keim, 3rd.

Saturday, June 24, 1972
Warsaw Speedway

Cold weather held the crowd size down in weekend racing action at the Warsaw

Speedway. Despite the cold weather the crowd enjoyed some of the season's finest racing. Jim Elliott, a consistent winner, experienced bad fortune and was forced out of action in the feature. He joined a long list of drivers who experienced mechanical failure.

Saturday night a big demolition race will be held as well as the regular racing card. This past Saturday's action was broadcast directly from the speedway sponsored by Warsaw Automotive Supply. Winners in each event follow:

Stock Dash—Les Sroufe, Huntington, 1st; Arden Leiter, 2nd; Vonnell Krom, 3rd.
Modified Dash—Jim Elliott, Warsaw, 1st; Bob Bernhard, 2nd; Jack French, 3rd.
Stock Heat—Paul Roberts, Huntington, 1st; Jim Bucher, 2nd; Tom Leiter, 3rd.
Modified Heat—Don Murphy, South Whitley, 1st; Tom York, 2nd; Jeff Cresson, 3rd.
Stock Heat—Larry Howard, Roann, 1st; Arden Leiter, 2nd; Chuch Sainer, 3rd.
Modified Heat—Jim Elliott, Warsaw, 1st; Don Walker, 2nd; Jack French, 3rd.
Stock Feature—Paul Roberts, Huntington, 1st; Jon Warner, 2nd; Les Sroufe, 3rd.
Modified Feature—Tom York, Parma, Mich., 1st; Don Walker, 2nd; Jim Murphy, 3rd.
Hobby Heat—Dick Wiles, Peru, 1st; Larry Montel, 2nd; Steve Brown, 3rd.
Hobby Heat—George Conley, Warsaw, 1st; Bryon Witters, 2nd; George Sitts, 3rd.
Hobby Feature—Jerry Baker, Pierceton, 1st; John Fitzpatrick, 2nd; Larry Montel, 3rd.

Saturday, June 24, 1972
Racing Weekly – June 30 Edition
By Georgia LeFever

Fifty-seven cars qualified for racing Saturday night at the Warsaw Speedway with Jim Elliott taking the honors as fastest sprint with a time of 16.47 seconds. Les Sroufe, late model qualifier had a time of 18.30 seconds and Jerry Baker in hobbies with a time of 19.19 seconds.

Paul Roberts led the late model feature from the start to take the checkered flag. Early in the race Roberts' front bumper was dragging and he was sent to the pits. Fast repairs by his pit crew had him back out on the track before the green flag was out again. At this same time Bud Grossnickle and Don Burkett both went to the pits with tire problems. Two laps later, Tom Leiter lost a left front tire coming out of the No. 4 turn while running in third position. Vonell Krom went up over this tire and came down with quite a jolt, jarring his truck deck loose. A quick stop in the infield, off came his truck deck, and he was back racing. Roberts, Jan Warner, Les Sroufe, Larry Howard and Chuck Saner were all bunched together throughout the race with excitement in every turn as they challenged each other but finished as listed.

Tom York shot into the lead in the sprint Feature with Jim Murphy close behind. York and Murphy are team cars both being owned by Art Braithwaite. York led the entire race with Jim Murphy and Paul Grim following. Jim Elliott pulled out early in the race with an axle case sheared. Midway through the race Don Walker and Bob Grindle tangled in the number three turn with Grindle bouncing high off the track. Both cars and drivers were ok.

George Sitts led the first half of the hobby feature. Sitts went high in the corner and Larry Monteal shot into the lead with Jerry Baker and John Fitzpatrick following. Baker took the lead for the checkered flag with John Fitzpatrick, Larry Monteal and George Sitts following.

During qualifications, Bill Swinehart late model 96 from Warsaw, lost his drive shaft on the straight-a-way and went to the pits for the evening. Jerry Priest, Sprint 33, made his qualification laps, but was then sidelined while Jim Elliott ended up with the victory in the Sprint Dash and Fast Sprint Heat with Bob Bernhard and Jack French close behind in the Dash and Don Walker and Jack French following in the heat. Don Murphy was the bossman as the slow sprint heat finished with Tom York and Jeff Creason second and third.

Steve Brown led the pack to start the Fast Hobby heat but lost it coming out of No. 1 when Dick Wiles and Larry Monteal shot around him. In the sixth lap Larry Monteal spun with Steve Brown in his side, Dick Day hitting him head on and Terry Baker in Day's trunk. This took Baker to the pits. Dick Wiles won with Larry Monteal second and Steve Brown third. Larry Howard carried the checkered in the fast late model heat and George Conley in the Slow Hobby heat.

Kenny Huntley, owner of Late Model 47 was driving this '62 Fairlane. He is a veteran driver of the track although he hasn't driven for several years.

Saturday, July 1, 1972
Warsaw Speedway

Ray Fisher, Pierceton, won the demolition derby in Saturday night action at the Warsaw Speedway. In Saturday night competition 64 cars qualified and 40 cars were involved in the derby. In regular action Jim Elliott rolled his car in a modified heat race, got back in and won the event.

Winners in the features were Paul Roberts, Huntington, stock; Tom York, Parma, Mich., modified, and Dick Wiles, Warsaw, hobby.

Race Results:
Stock Dash—Art Smith, Claypool, 1st; Paul Roberts, 2nd; Arden Leiter, 3rd.
Modified Dash—Jim Elliott, Warsaw, 1st; Jack French, 2nd; Bob Grindle, 3rd.
Stock Heat—Ellis Shepherd, Mentone, 1st; Tom Leiter, 2nd; Todd Grigsby, 3rd.
Modified Heat—Tom York, Parma, Mich., 1st; Don Murphy, 2nd; Paul Grim, 3rd.
Stock Heat—Tom Beezley, Wolf Lake, 1st; Larry Howard, 2nd; Paul Roberts, 3rd.
Modified Heat—Jim Elliott, Warsaw, 1st; Jerry Priest, 2nd; Bob Grindle, 3rd.
Stock Feature—Paul Roberts, Huntington, 1st; Les Sroufe, 2nd; Arden Leiter, 3rd.
Modified Feature—Tom York, Parma, Mich., 1st; Jim Murphy, 2nd; Bob Grindle, 3rd.
Hobby Heat—Terry Baker, Pierceton, 1st; John Fitzpatrick, 2nd; Larry Montel, 3rd.
Hobby Heat—Tom Leiter, Warsaw, 1st; George Sitts, 2nd; Larry Sheets, 3rd.
Hobby Feature—Dick Wiles, Warsaw, 1st; Jerry Baker, 2nd; Charles Hyde, 3rd.

Monday, July 3, 1972
Warsaw Speedway

Fireworks and a fast-paced brand of racing helped to overcome the cold Monday night weather which kept the crowd size down at the Warsaw Speedway. Arden Leiter of Pierceton won top honors in the stock feature and Jerry Priest of Elwood came up with a first in the modified feature. Jerry Baker of Pierceton captured top honors in the hobby feature.

This Saturday the feature will be a 50-lap mid-season championship event for super sprints with a $200 bonus for the winner. A quarter hour of Monday night's race was broadcast over Radio Stations WRSW AM-FM, sponsored by Warsaw Automotive Supply.

Race Results:
Stock Dash—Jim Wagoner, Mentone, 1st; Paul Roberts, 2nd; Ron Miller, 3rd.
Modified Dash—Jim Elliott, Warsaw, 1st; Bob Bernhard, 2nd; Bob Grindle, 3rd.
Stock Heat—Dave Bussard, Warsaw, 1st; Tom Leiter, 2nd; Vonell Krom, 3rd.
Modified Heat—Jim Murphy, South Haven, 1st; Don Murphy, 2nd; Tom Beezley, 3rd.
Stock Heat—Art Smith, Claypool, 1st; Chuck Sainer, 2nd; Larry Howard, 3rd.
Modified Heat—Jim Elliott, Warsaw, 1st; Bob Bernhard, 2nd; Bob Grindle, 3rd.
Stock Feature—Arden Leiter, Pierceton, 1st; Les Sroufe, 2nd; Paul Roberts, 3rd.
Modified Feature—Jerry Priest, Elwood, 1st; Jim Elliott, 2nd; Jim Murphy, 3rd.
Hobby Heat—John Fitzpatrick, Warsaw, 1st; Dick Day, 2nd; Jerry Baker, 3rd.
Hobby Heat—Fred DeLong, Warsaw, 1st; Bob Johnson, 2nd; Dick Wiles, 3rd.
Hobby Feature—Jerry Baker, Pierceton, 1st; George Sitts, 2nd; Terry Baker, 3rd.

Saturday, July 8, 1972 - Rainout

Saturday, July 15, 1972
Warsaw Speedway

A young Tony Elliott, Jimmie Elliott, and C.E. "Hoot" Gibson

Art Smith, Jim Elliott, and John Fitzpatrick, three familiar names at the Warsaw Speedway, turned up with feature wins in Saturday night action at the lakeside oval.

There were several mishaps during the night's action. Bob McDaniels of Indianapolis did a slow motion roll and landed on his side after colliding with Don Murphy of South Whitley. There were no injuries.

In the 50-lap mid-season championship event, a five car collision the first time around the track resulted in knocking two cars out of action. The modified feature was won by Elliott who received a $200 bonus. Fitzpatrick came in first in the hobby feature and Smith captured top honors in the stock feature.

This Saturday night there will be a 50-lap feature for semi-late model cars. Winners and top finishers follow:

Stock Dash—Art Smith, Claypool, 1st; Arden Leiter, 2nd; Jene Simon, 3rd; Jim Bucher, 4th; and Larry Howard, 5th.
Modified Dash—Jim Elliott, Warsaw, 1st; Bob McDaniels, 2nd; Jim Murphy, 3rd; Bob Bernhard, 4th; Jerry Priest, 5th.
Stock Heat—John White, Silver Lake, 1st; Rod Sheets, 2nd; Dave Bussard, 3rd; Tom Leiter, 4th; Bruce Hogue, 5th.
Modified Heat—Art Braithwaite, South Haven, Mich., 1st; Tom Patterson, 2nd; Don Murphy, 3rd.
Heat—Paul Roberts, Huntington, 1st; Jim Wagoner, 2nd; Paul Bills, 3rd; Les Sroufe, 4th.
Modified Heat—Jim Elliott, 1st; Don Walker, 2nd; Tom Beezley, 3rd; Jerry Priest, 4th.
Stock Feature—Art Smith, Claypool, 1st; John White, 2nd; Bruce Hogue, 3rd; Les Sroufe, 4th; Arden Leiter, 5th; Paul Bills, 6th; Jene Simon, 7th; Jim Bucher, 8th; Larry Howard, 9th; Jan Warner, 10th; Rod Sheets, 11th.
Modified Feature—Jim Elliott, Warsaw, 1st; Jim Murphy, 2nd; Bob Grindle, 3rd; Jerry Priest, 4th; Tom Beezley, 5th; Tom Patterson, 6th; Herb Waggle, 7th.
Hobby Heat: Tom Leiter, Warsaw, 1st; George Sitts, 2nd; John Fitzpatrick, 3rd; Bob Johnson, 4th; Terry Baker, 5th.
Hobby Heat: Terry Hatfield, Warsaw, 1st; Bill McCollen, 2nd; Rex Heckman, 3rd; Mike Summers, 4th; Fred DeLong, 5th.
Hobby Feature: John Fitzpatrick, Warsaw, 1st; Gerry Baker, 2nd; Dave Kerlin, 3rd.

Saturday, July 22, 1972
Warsaw Speedway

Bobby Grindle, Warsaw

Art Smith, Don Walker and Jerry Baker captured the feature races in Saturday night action at the Warsaw Speedway.

The sprint feature was led by Walker for several laps who held off every effort made by second place Jim Elliott. Then right at the finish line Jim went out a little wide and Tom York took advantage to beat out Elliott for second place.

It was a great night for racing with the temperature near 80 degrees with a slight breeze off Winona Lake cooling the spectators.

George Sitts racing a hobby stock flipped in turn three and rolled twice on the track then rolled over the cement wall. He crawled out of the car uninjured. In the championship 50-lap semi late feature Les Sroufe led for 32 laps before heading out with mechanical trouble.

Top Finishers Follow:

Stock Dash—John White, Silver Lake, 1st; Jene Simon, Les Sroufe, Paul Roberts, Jim Wagoner.
Modified Dash—Don Murphy, South Whitley, 1st; Don Walker; Jim Elliott; Tom York; Harold Mouser.
Stock Heat—Todd Gringsby, Warsaw, 1st; Larry Howard; Dave Bussard; Ray Chambers; Tom Leiter.
Modified Heat—Bob Bernhard, South Whitley, 1st; Harold Renyolds; Jack French; Scot Guadulsoky.
Stock Heat—Art Smith, Claypool, 1st; Paul Bills; Chuck Sainer; Les Sroufe.
Modified Heat—Bob Grindle, Warsaw, 1st; Don Murphy; Tom York; Jim Elliott.
Stock Feature—Art Smith, Claypool, 1st; Paul Roberts; Paul Bills; Bruce Hogue; Todd Gringsley; Bull Bradley; Larry Howard; Ray Chambers; Glen Miller; Dave Bussard.
Modified Feature—Don Walker, Elwood, 1st; Tom York; Jim Elliott; Bob Grindle; Don Murphy; Jack French; Harold Mouser; Tom Beezley; Bob Bernhard; Jeff Creason.
Hobby Heat—Rock Anders, Warsaw, 1st; Bob Johnson; :Lacie Adams; Fred DeLong.
Hobby Heat—Charles Jefferson, Warsaw, 1st; Dave Kerlin; Duane Eckright; Jerry Baker.
Hobby Feature—Jerry Baker, Warsaw, 1st; Dave Kerlin; Steve Brown; John Fitzpatrick.

Saturday, July 22, 1972
Late Model Midseason Champ Is Art Smith
Columbia City Post & Mail – July 27, 1972

Mid-season championship for late models was off to a fast start at the Warsaw Speedway Saturday, with Les Sroufe, as bossman, sitting on the pole and setting a fast early pace. But with only 15 laps to go, Sroufe blew his transmission and clutch plate, forcing him out of the race, and allowing Art Smith to take the checkered flag and become mid-season champ. He received a $200 bonus plus his trophy.

There was a real battle for the second spot, but Paul Roberts kept his position, with Paul Bills, Bruce Hogue and Todd Grigsby following.

Jene Simon pulled out early in the race with a broken radiator hose, his third one for the evening. Chuck Saner stopped dead in the no. 3 turn, with Bull Bradley and Glen Miller putting their cars into a slide to avoid him. It took some quick maneuvering when the pack came around, but everyone missed them. Jim Wagoner lost his left front tire, but Art Smith, following close behind, was able to swerve and miss it.

The sprint feature, straight start, put the fastest qualifier, Don Walker, on the pole. Walker was the bossman throughout the race, warding off every attempt made by Jim Elliott to overtake him. No cautions made this a quick fast race with Tom York finishing second, as Elliott went a little high in the last turn before the checkered flag.

Elliott finished third in the sprint dash, fourth in the fast heat, and third in the feature. Todd Grigsby won the slow late model heat, but Art Smith shot past him, dropping him to second. He received a trophy for finishing third in the feature.

Jene Simon finished second in the trophy dash, but due to broken radiator hoses, he couldn't finish his other races. George Sitts started his evening with some tightrope maneuvers, as he tried to balance his car on the retaining wall in the no. 3 turn. He bounced up and partially over the wall to straddle it. It took the wrecker to remove his car, but he took a couple of laps around the track before he went to the pits for the evening. Roger Huntley finished third in the hobby feature.

Saturday, July 29, 1972
Warsaw Speedway

Don Walker, of Elwood, took first place in the modified dash and heat races with Jim Elliott finishing second but in the feature the trend was reversed at the Warsaw Speedway Saturday night.

Elliott, after taking runner-up honors in the two previous events, grabbed the checkered flag in the feature event as the two drivers continued their fierce duel.

Les Sroufe, of Huntington, was the top semi-late model driver with first, second and third place finishes during the evening's activities.

A good crowd assembled under clear skies to watch 65 cars qualify for the racing card. There were several crashes that resulted in re-starts but fortunately there were no injuries.

Race Results:
Semi-Late Dash—Les Sroufe, Huntington, 1st; Larry Howard, 2nd; Art Smith, 3rd.
Modified Dash—Don Walker, Elwood, 1st; Jim Elliott, 2nd; Jerry Priest, 3rd.
Semi-Late Heat—Ray Chambers, Peru, 1st; Chuck Sainer, 2nd; Paul Bills, 3rd.
Modified Heat—Bob Bernhard, South Whitley, 1st; Jeff Creason, 2nd; Herb Waggle, 3rd.
Semi-Late Heat—Jim Wagoner, Mentone, 1st; Bruce Hogue, 2nd; Les Sroufe, 3rd.
Modified Heat—Don Walker, Elwood, 1st; Jim Elliott, 2nd; Don Murphy, 3rd.
Semi-Late Feature—John White, Silver Lake, 1st; Les Sroufe, 2nd; Chuck Sainer, 3rd.
Modified Feature—Jim Elliott, Warsaw, 1st; Don Walker, 2nd; Bob Grindle, 3rd.
Hobby Slow Heat—Lacie Adams, Warsaw, 1st; Bob Johnson, 2nd; Bill Varney, 3rd.
Hobby Fast Heat—John Fitzpatrick, Warsaw, 1st; Terry Hatfield, 2nd; Charles Hyde, 3rd.
Hobby Feature—Jerry Baker, Warsaw, 1st; Bob Johnson, 2nd; Terry Baker, 3rd.

Saturday, August 5, 1972
Warsaw Speedway

Les Sroufe, of Huntington, won the stock feature and Don Walker, of Elwood, captured the modified feature but the hobby stocks provided some of the exciting moments at the Warsaw Speedway Saturday night.

Larry Montel, of North Manchester, took the checkered flag in the hobby feature. Joe Cutler's hobby stock racer caught on fire following a collision and Reg Clark completed a T-bone crash after his car hurled over a mound of dirt and slammed into a parked racer in the infield. In the modified competition the gear box let go in Jim Elliott's car causing him to be burned by the hot oil and sidelined him from racing.

Race Results:
Stock Dash—Vonell Krom, Wolf Lake, 1st; Paul Roberts, 2nd; Paul Bills, 3rd.
Modified Dash—Tom York, South Haven, Mich., 1st; Jim Murphy, 2nd; Harold Mouser, 3rd.
Stock Heat—Chuck Sainer, Akron, 1st; Bruce Hogue, 2nd; Larry Howard, 3rd.

Modified Heat—Louie Mann, Kokomo, 1st; Jim Elliott, 2nd; Bob Grindle, 3rd.
Stock Heat—John White, Silver Lake, 1st; Jim Bucher, 2nd; Todd Grigsby, 3rd.
Modified Heat—Harold Mouser, Kokomo, 1st; Don Walker, 2nd; Jerry Priest, 3rd.
Stock Feature—Les Sroufe, Huntington, 1st; Arden Leiter, 2nd; Paul Bills, 3rd.
Modified Feature—Don Walker, Elwood, 1st; Louie Mann, 2nd; Tom Beezley, 3rd.
Slow Hobby Heat—Jim LeGarde, Warsaw, 1st; Terry Hatfield, 2nd; Tom Leiter, 3rd.
Fast Hobby Heat—Terry Baker, Warsaw, 1st; John Fitzpatrick, 2nd; Dick Day, 3rd.
Hobby Feature—Larry Montel, North Manchester, 1st; John Fitzpatrick, 2nd; Duane Eckwright, 3rd.

Saturday, August 5, 1972
Walker Wins Sprint Feature At Warsaw Track Saturday
Columbia City Post & Mail – August 7, 1972

Don Walker won the sprint feature at the Warsaw Speedway Saturday night. Jim Elliott moved into the lead midway through the race for one lap but had to pull into the infield with an oil burn to his ankle. Walker held off challenges from Louis Mann and Tom Beezley to move into the winner's circle. Mann finished second with Tom Beezley and Tom York following.

Les Sroufe seized the lead from the drop of the green flag in the late model feature to lead a fast race with the top five cars bumper-to-bumper. Arden Leiter finished second with Paul Bills, Jim Bucher and John White following.

The hobby feature was more like a demolition derby than a regular race. There were numerous restarts and yellow lights but out of the 24 cars starting only nine finished. Larry Monteal took a commanding lead with each drop of the flag and took his victory lap with John Fitzpatrick second. Joe Cutler's engine caught fire at the start of the race.

Jim Elliott was having maneuvering problems. He took the lead in the slow sprint heat but spun out and went to the end. He worked his way back to second before the drop of the checkered flag which found Louie Mann leading.

Tom Beezley had a new engine and ran a fine race finishing third. Jene Simon went to the pits early in the evening with a broken A frame. Paul Bills placed third in the dash and third in the feature. Todd Grigsby had a third in the fast heat and a seventh in the feature.

The fastest qualifiers were Don Walker in the sprints, Arden Leiter in the late models and Dick Wiles in the hobby class.

Wednesday, August 9, 1972
Warsaw Speedway

A small crowd braved the chilly weather to watch the racing card at the Warsaw Speedway during the County Fair last night.

The evening's big winner was Jim Bucher, of Silver Lake, who copped the semi-late model stock feature to go along with victory in one of the heat races. In the hobby division Tom Leiter, of Warsaw, took the checkered flag in the feature.

Racing Summary:
Semi-late Dash—Paul Roberts, Huntington, 1st; Jene Simon, 2nd; Arden Leiter, 3rd.
Hobby Dash—John Fitzpatrick, Warsaw, 1st; Bill Kain, 2nd; Dick Day, 3rd.
Semi-late Heat—Dave Evers, Warsaw, 1st; Ray Chambers, 2nd; Glen Miller, 3rd.
Semi-late Heat—Charlie Prater, Huntington, 1st; Chuck Sainer, 2nd; Larry Howard, 3rd.
Semi-late Heat—Jim Bucher, Silver Lake, 1st; Paul Roberts, 2nd; Arden Leiter, 3rd.
Semi-late Consolation—Vonell Krom, Wolf Lake, 1st; Les Sroufe, 2nd; Bruce Hogue, 3rd.
Semi-late Feature—Jim Bucher, Silver Lake, 1st; Arden Leiter, 2nd; Bruce Hogue 3rd.
Hobby Heat—Terry Hatfield, 1st; Charles Hyde, 2nd; George Setts, 3rd.
Hobby Heat—Jim LaGarde, 1st; Terry Baker, 2nd; Dave Kerlin, 3rd.
Hobby Feature—Tom Leiter, 1st; Dave Kerlin, 2nd; Terry Baker, 3rd.

Saturday, August 12, 1972
Warsaw Speedway

A week of Kosciusko County fair activities was capped by action at the Warsaw Speedway Saturday night in a flurry of races undecided until the final flag.

John Davis, Warsaw

One of the night's top races occurred in the modified feature when Don Walker and Jim Elliott dueled it out in close quarters before the capacity crowd. Walker finally slipped ahead to take the checkered flag.

In the stock feature Art Smith of Claypool captured top honors and Larry Montel of North Manchester added a first in the hobby stock feature.

Jeff Creason of Elwood was slightly injured when a track object came through the windshield and stunned him for a moment. He was treated for the injury and released. There were 62 cars that qualified for Saturday's action. The quarter-hour broadcast was sponsored by Warsaw Automotive Supply.

Race Results:
Stock Dash—John White, Silver Lake, 1st; Jim Bucher, 2nd; Art Smith, 3rd.
Modified Dash—Jeff Creason, Elwood, 1st; Paul Joyce, 2nd; Don Murphy, 3rd.
Stock Heat—John Shepp, South Whitley, 1st; Dave Bussard, 2nd; Ted Hudson, 3rd.

Modified Heat—John Davis, Warsaw, 1st; Gary Baker, 2nd; Skip Smithers, 3rd; Jack Hickman, 4th.
Stock Heat—Les Sroufe, Huntington, 1st; Art Smith, 2nd; Jim Bucher, 3rd; John White, 4th.
Modified Heat—Don Walker, Elwood, 1st; Bob Grindle, 2nd; Tom Beezley, 3rd; Bob Bernhard, 4th.
Stock Feature—Art Smith, Claypool, 1st; Arden Leiter Jr., 2nd; Jene Simon, 3rd; John White, 4th; Jim Bucher, 5th; Paul Bills, 6th, Les Sroufe, 7th; Larry Howard, 8th; Glen Miller, 9th; Bruce Hogue, 10th.
Modified Feature—Don Walker, Elwood, 1st; Jim Elliott, 2nd; Louie Mann, 3rd; Tom Beezley, 4th; Bob Bernhard, 5th; Gary Baker, 6th.
Fast Hobby Heat—Larry Montel, North Manchester, 1st; Genny Hatfield, 2nd; Jim LaGarde, 3rd; Charlie Jefferson, 4th.
Slow Hobby Heat—Terry Baker, Warsaw, 1st; Rock Anders, 2nd; Tom Leiter, 3rd.
Hobby Feature—Larry Montel, 1st; Jim LaGarde, 2nd; Dick Day, 3rd.

Saturday, August 12, 1972
Don Walker Wins Sprint Feature At Warsaw Speedway
Columbia City Post & Mail – August 14, 1972

Don Walker powered into the lead in the sprint feature from his pole position on a rough, tacky track at Warsaw Saturday. He was trailed closely by Bob Grindle with Jim Elliott coming up fast. Grindle was sidelined when he blew a radiator hose on the 23rd lap and Elliott took the lead. Walker shot by Jim Elliott to gain the victory with Elliott second, Louie Mann and Tom Beezley, third and fourth respectively. Don Murphy went to the pits early as did Jeff Creason.

Art Smith and Arden Leiter riding the high groove in the late model feature lapped cars early in the race. Leiter was right on Art Smith's bumper. Smith won with Leiter second followed by Jene Simon, John White and Jim Bucher. Todd Grigsby and Chuck Saner tangled in the second turn.

Larry Monteal cruised out and set his own pace in the hobby feature to cross the finish line as he lost his rear end. Jim LaGarde, Dick Day and Garry Baker finished in that order.

Tom Beezley finished a close third in the fast sprint heat as Bob Grindle squeezed by him on the last lap. He also finished fourth in the feature. Grigsby was sidelined with a broken tie rod in the feature and finished fourth in the feature. Simon was unable to finish the dash due to a spin and the number two turn and finished third in the feature.

Monday, August 14, 1972
Towing Race Car, Auto Goes Out Of Control on U.S. 30
Columbia City Post & Mail – August 14, 1972

A Huntington man towing a race car back home after the Warsaw races Saturday, lost control of the vehicles on U.S. 30 about 2,500 feet west of County Road 550-W on U.S 30 when the trailer wheels dropped off the paved portion of the eastbound lanes and struck new gravel on the berm which followed recent highway resurfacing.

His wife suffered minor injuries and was treated at Whitley County Hospital.

Driver of the car was Paul R. Roberts, 38, of Huntington. Mrs. Rosie Grace Roberts, 36, complained of chest pains and suffered a lower back injury.

Roberts, eastbound, lost control of the vehicle he was driving when the trailer wheels dropped off the resurfaced highway onto new gravel fill on the berm. The car crossed the eastbound lanes into the median strip, rolled over twice in the median strip and came to rest with the right side up. Deputy Sheriff Tom Pugh, who investigated, termed the speed of the driver too great for the vehicle being towed.

Damage to the car was $500 to the top, windshield, left door and rear tire, and to the right rear fender. Damage to the race car and trailer was about $100.

Saturday, August 19, 1972
Don Murphy Wins Sprint Feature At Warsaw Speedway
Columbia City Post & Mail – August 22, 1972

Don Murphy outdueled Harold Mouser to win the sprint feature at the Warsaw Speedway Saturday night. Mouser spun out on the 18th lap, allowing Don Walker to finish second and Tom Beezley third. The most spectacular incident of the evening came when Jim Elliott's car flipped into the air during the sprint dash, and landed on its top. Elliott sustained a bruised elbow, and that getting out of the car. Don Murphy won another duel, this time with Tom Beezley to win the sprint dash by a three foot margin. Louie Mann finished third.

Jimmie Elliott, Warsaw

In the late model feature, Art Smith and Les Sroufe overtook Ray Chambers to finish one-two, while Jim Bucher challenged Sroufe but had to settle for third. Paul Bills placed fourth. Todd Grigsby, Bob Murphy, and Charlie Flaugh went to the pits with wheel or tire problems, while Chuck Saner had to pull into the infield minus the side panel from his car. Jene Simon broke his A frame during qualifications and was unable to race.

During the hobby feature, John Fitzpatrick lost a tire in the backstretch, and it bounced high over the retaining wall and fence. Fortunately, no one was injured. Rocky Anders won the event, with Tom Leiter and Charlie Hyde close behind.

Don Walker covered the 1/4 mile dirt track mark of 15.88, coming close to his track record mark of 15.59 set two years ago. Arden Leiter and Larry Montel were the fastest qualifiers in their divisions. Tom Beezley won the fast sprint heat with ease, while Bob Bernhard and Louie Mann finished second and third respectively.

Les Sroufe captured the fast late model heat, with Paul Bills and John White following behind. During the fast hobby heat, George Sitts rolled his car in front of the grandstand, but was unhurt. Charlie Hyde was the winner, but was unable to take his victory lap because of an accident in the No. 3 turn.

Race Results:

Sprint Feature—Don Murphy, 1st; Don Walker, 2nd; Tom Beezley, 3rd.
Late Model Feature - Art Smith, 1st; Les Sroufe, 2nd; Jim Bucher, 3rd.
Hobby Feature—Rock Anders, 1st; Tom Leiter, 2nd; Charles Hyde, 3rd.
Late Model Dash—Jim Bucher, 1st; Art Smith, 2nd; Paul Bills, 3rd.
Sprint Dash—Don Murphy, 1st; Tom Beezley, 2nd; Louie Mann, 3rd.
Slow Late Model Heat—Ellis Shepherd, 1st; Ray Chambers. 2nd; Paul Cox, 3rd.
Fast Sprint Heat—Tom Beezley, 1st; Bob Bernhard, 2nd; Louie Mann, 3rd.
Fast Late Model Heat—Les Sroufe, 1st; Paul Bills, 2nd; John White, 3rd.
Sprint Heat—Harold Mouser, 1st; John Davis, 2nd; Garry Baker, 3rd.
Fast Hobby Heat—Charles Hyde, 1st; Terry Hatfield, 2nd; Lacie Adams, 3rd.
Slow Hobby Heat—Rex Heckaman, 1st; Tom Leiter, 2nd; Dick Day, 3rd.

Saturday, August 19, 1972
Warsaw Speedway

Cars had a difficult time staying upright in Saturday night action at the Warsaw Speedway. Jerry Baker started things rolling when his car flipped over during the time trials due to a broken bolt in the front end of the frame. Then Jim Elliott kept things going by rolling over in the dash event. Elliott flipped end-over-end then rolled sideways three full turns. He was pulled from the extensively-damaged car uninjured.

George Sitts rolled over in front of the grandstand in a hobby stock race. Sitts was also uninjured. Adding to the excitement were a number of mishaps caused by cars losing wheels. Don Walker, track record holder, was forced out of competition with a broken rear end housing. This Saturday night a Demolition Race will be held along with the regular racing card.

Saturday, August 26, 1972
Warsaw Speedway

There were 64 cars that qualified for Saturday night racing at the Warsaw Speedway. The track was hard and the speeds fast in a night of racing that featured a demolition derby. In the demolition event one of the cars lost a gas tank spilling gas on a large portion of the track.

Don Walker, who was the fastest in the sprint class with a time of 16.08 used the momentum to gun his way into the first place spot in the Modified Feature. Jerry Baker captured top honors in the hobby feature and Les Sroufe nabbed the top spot in the stock feature. Next week championship races for all three classes are planned.

Top finishers in each event:
Stock Dash—Jene Simon, Columbia City; Art Smith; John White; Arden Leiter.
Modified Dash—Don Walker; Don Murphy; Harold Mouser; Tom Beezley.
Stock Heat—Paul Roberts; Roy Norman; Ted Hudson; Charlie Flaghe; Glen Miller.
Modified Heat—Louie Mann; Jerry Priest; Doug Kindred; Bob Conwell.
Stock Heat—Art Smith; Jim Bucher; Larry Howard; Arden Leiter.
Modified Heat—Bob Bernhard; Don Walker; Don Murphy; Harold Mouser.
Stock Feature—Les Sroufe; Art Smith; Arden Leiter; John White; Jene Simon; Jim Bucher; Bruce Hogue; Larry Howard; Tom Leiter; Charlie Flaghe.

Modified Feature—Don Walker; Jim Elliott; Paul Joyce; Don Murphy; Bob Bernhard; Tom Beezley; Jerry Priest.

Saturday, September 2, 1972 - Rainout

Saturday, September 9, 1972
Warsaw Speedway

Jimmie Elliott, Warsaw

The Warsaw Speedway 1972 season ended with wild weekend action that saw numerous cars unable to finish evening racing due to mechanical difficulties.

In the semi-late feature 18 cars started—only six finished. In the event the two lead cars were knocked out in an accident. Also, six cars lost wheels during the evening's action.

The annual Speedway banquet will be held Oct. 27, at the Legion Building at Columbia City. Awards will be given to drivers and owners at that time. A quarter-hour broadcast was sponsored by Warsaw Automotive Supply.

Race Results:
Stock Dash—Les Sroufe, Huntington, 1st; Chuck Sainer, 2nd; Paul Bills, 3rd; Art Smith, 4th; Arden Leiter, 5th.
Modified Dash—Harold Mouser, Huntington, 1st; Jim Elliott, 2nd; Bob Grindle, 3rd; Louie Mann, 4th; Bob Bernhard, 5th.
Stock Heat—Ray Chambers, Peru, 1st; Tom Leiter, 2nd; John Snepp, 3rd; Larry Howard, 4th; Bruce Hogue, 5th.
Modified Heat—Tom Beezley, Wolf Lake, 1st; Dave Ragan, 2nd; Jerry Priest, 3rd; John Davis, 4th.
Stock Heat—Paul Roberts, Huntington, 1st; Les Sroufe, 2nd; Art Smith, 3rd; Jim Bucher, 4th.
Modified Heat—Paul Joyce, Kokomo, 1st; Jim Elliott, 2nd; Bob Grindle, 3rd; Louie Mann, 4th.
Stock Feature—Arden Leiter, North Webster, 1st; Jim Bucher, 2nd; Chuck Sainer, 3rd; Glen Miller, 4th; Todd Grigsby, 5th; Ray Chambers, 6th; John Snepp, 7th; Charlie Flaugh, 8th; Tom Leiter, 9th; Roger Frye, 10th.
Modified Feature—Jim Elliott, Warsaw, 1st; Paul Joyce, 2nd; Tom Beezley, 3rd; Bob Bernhard, 4th; Harold Mouser, 5th; Don Murphy, 6th; Dave Ragan, 7th; Gary Baker, 8th; John Davis, 9th; Doug Kindred, 10th.
Fast Hobby—John Fitzpatrick, Warsaw, 1st; Jerry Hatfield, 2nd; Charles Hyde, 3rd; Larry Montel, 4th.
Slow Hobby—Bill Kain, Warsaw, 1st; Duane Eckwright, 2nd; Rex Heckman, 3rd; Bob Johnson, 4th.
Hobby Feature—Larry Montel, North Manchester, 1st; Jerry Baker, 2nd; John Fitzpatrick, 3rd.

Thursday, October 31, 1972
Race Banquet

The annual race banquet of drivers, mechanics, wives and guests from the Warsaw Speedway was held recently at the American Legion in Columbia City. Nearly 300 persons attended the event that included a dinner, dance and award presentation ceremony.

Trophies were awarded to the following drivers and owners:

Modified and Super Sprint—Jim Elliott, Warsaw, 1st; Don Walker, Elwood, 2nd; Bob Grindle, Warsaw, 3rd; Jerry Priest, Elwood, 4th; Bob Bernhard, South Whitley, 5th; Tom Beezley, Wolf Lake, 6th; Don Murphy, South Whitley, 7th; Harold Mauser, Kokomo, 8th; Louie Mann, Kokomo, 9th; John Davis, Warsaw, 10th. The Sportsmanship Award was also given to Walker of Elwood.
Hobby Stock—Jerry Baker, Pierceton, 1st; John Fitzpatrick, Warsaw, 2nd; Larry Montel, North Manchester, 3rd; Terry Baker, Pierceton, 4th; Terry Hatfield, Warsaw, 5th. The Sportsmanship Award went to Rex Heckaman of Bourbon.
Semi-Late Models—Les Sroufe, Huntington, 1st; Arden Leiter, North Webster, 2nd; Art Smith, Warsaw, 3rd; Paul Roberts, Huntington, 4th; Jim Bucher, Silver Lake, 5th; Vonell Krom, Akron, 6th; Paul Bills, Columbia City, 7th; Jene Simon, Columbia City, 8th; Chuck Sainer, Akron, 9th; John White, Silver Lake, 10th. Sportsmanship Trophy went to Roger Frye, Huntington.

1973

April 24, 1973
Warsaw Speedway Tryouts April 28, Opening Race May 5

Free admittance to the public for the Try Out evening of Saturday, April 28 was announced today by C. E. Gibson. The try-outs will be held from 4 p.m. to 8 p.m.

Many new cars have been built this past winter and are expected to be on hand for the opening race of the 1973 season scheduled for Saturday evening. Super Sprint, Late Model and Hobby Classes will be featured. The Warsaw Speedway is located at the Kosciusko County Fairgrounds.

Thursday, May 3, 1973
Speedway Opens

The first race of the season at the Warsaw Speedway on the fairgrounds is scheduled on Saturday night. C. E. (Hoot) Gibson, track director, said that several new cars have been built during the winter months and there will also be several new drivers.

Time trials begin at 7 p.m. with the first race at 8:30 p.m. The 1973 regulations for the super sprints, late model cars and hobby stock have been adopted. The late model class includes American made cars, 1960 and including 1973. Hobby stock includes the years 1955 to 1969.

Gibson noted that no person under 16 years of age shall receive a pit pass and if not 21 years of age he must furnish a written notarized permit from his parents or guardian. All vehicles must pass safety inspection.

Saturday, May 5, 1973
Warsaw Speedway Results

A classic duel between Art Smith, of Warsaw, and Arden Leiter, of North Webster, highlighted action on the first night of racing at the Warsaw Speedway on the fairgrounds oval Saturday night.

Competing in the semi-late model stock class, Smith took the checkered flag first in the dash event and a heat race with Leiter finishing second. Leiter raced home first in a heat race and the feature with Smith trailing him across the line in both events.

Bob Grindle, of Warsaw, was the top modified driver winning a heat race and the modified feature. Paul Joyce, of Kokomo, finished second in both races. Chuck Sainer, of Akron, won a heat race and the feature in the hobby stock class.

There were 50 cars competing for honors on the opening night of the track and many more are expected next week. Billy Jo Havens was driving the car number 57 that was raced for many years by the late Jimmy Elliott.

Racing Summary:

Stock Dash—Art Smith, Warsaw, 1st; Arden Leiter, 2nd; Jene Simon, 3rd.
Modified Dash—Don Walker, Elwood, 1st; Louie Mann, 2nd; Jim Murphy, 3rd.
Stock Car—Art Smith, Warsaw, 1st; Arden Leiter, 2nd; Todd Grigsby, 3rd.
Modified Heat—Bob Grindle, Warsaw, 1st; Paul Joyce, 2nd; Jerry Priest, 3rd.
Hobby Stock Heat—Dave Kerlin, Silver Lake, 1st; Jim LaGarde, 2nd; Jerry Baker, 3rd.
Stock Heat—Arden Leiter, North Webster, 1st; Art Smith, 2nd; Jim Bucher, 3rd.
Modified Heat—Bob Bernhard, South Whitley, 1st; Don Walker, 2nd; Tom Beezley, 3rd.
Hobby Stock Heat—Chuck Sainer, Akron, 1st; Duane Eakwright, 2nd; Larry Montel, 3rd.
Stock Feature—Arden Leiter, North Webster, 1st; Art Smith, 2nd; Jim Bucher, 3rd.
Modified Feature—Bob Grindle, Warsaw, 1st; Paul Joyce, 2nd; Jim Murphy, 3rd.
Hobby Stock Feature—Chuck Sainer, Akron, 1st; Dave Kerlin, 2nd; Jerry Baker, 3rd.

Saturday, May 12, 1973
Warsaw Speedway Results:

Two drivers were involved in crashes at the Warsaw Speedway Saturday and were hospitalized overnight for observations. Tom Beezley, Albion and Jeff Creason, Kokomo, were the drivers involved in the mishaps.

Arden Leiter, North Webster, was the big winner of the night, winning four races. Leiter won the stock dash, and swept both heats for the stock division. He later won the stock feature. Don Murphy finished first in both modified heats but dropped to second in the modified feature. Paul Joyce, who finished second in both heats, won the feature.

Race Summary:

Stock Dash—Arden Leiter, 1st; Les Sroufe, 2nd; Art Smith, 3rd.
Modified Dash—Bob Grindle, 1st; Bob McDaniels, 2nd; Tom Beezley, 3rd.
Stock Heat—Arden Leiter, 1st; Les Sroufe, 2nd; Jim Bucher, 3rd.
Modified Heat—Don Murphy, 1st; Paul Joyce, 2nd; Bob Bernhard, 3rd.
Stock Heat—Arden Leiter, 1st; Jim Bucher, 2nd; Art Smith, 3rd.
Modified Heat—Don Murphy, 1st; Paul Joyce, 2nd; Billy Jo Haven, 3rd.
Stock Feature—Arden Leiter, 1st; Art Smith, 2nd; Jim Bucher, 3rd.
Modified Feature—Paul Joyce, 1st; Don Murphy, 2nd; Bob Bernhard, 3rd.

Hobby Heat—Bob Johnson 1st; Bill Cain, 2nd; Fred Furis, 3rd.
Hobby Heat—Duane Eckwright, 1st; Chuck Sainer, 2nd; George Sitts, 3rd.
Hobby Feature—Jerry Baker, 1st; Duane Eckwright, 2nd; Chuck Sainer, 3rd.

Saturday, May 19, 1973 - Rainout

Saturday, May 26, 1973
Warsaw Speedway

Threatening weather didn't bother the crowd in Saturday night racing action at the Warsaw Speedway. A total of 55 cars qualified in a night that saw numerous wrecks, although there were no injuries.

Art Smith, one of the top semi-late drivers, had mechanical trouble and was forced out of the feature. Don Walker, a top sprint driver, was forced out of competition due to an accident.

Jim Bucher took a first in the stock heat and followed it up with a win in the stock feature. Ron Miller captured top honors in the modified feature and Sonny Hyde was the top driver in the hobby feature.

Race Summary:

Stock Dash—Jim Bucher, 1st; Les Sroufe, 2nd; Jene Simon, 3rd; Arden Leiter, 4th.
Modified Dash—Bob Bernhard, 1st; Louie Mann, 2nd; Don Walker, 3rd; Paul Joyce, 4th; Mike Kurtz, 5th.
Stock Heat—Jerry DeHaven, 1st; Ray Chambers, 2nd; Jerry Roseburg, 3rd; Terry Hatfield, 4th; Charlie Chopper, 5th.
Modified Heat—Jack French, 1st; Ron Miller, 2nd; Bob Grindle, 3rd; Don Murphy, 4th.
Stock Heat—Jim Bucher, 1st; Les Sroufe, 2nd; Doug Method, 3rd; Arden Leiter, 4th.
Modified Heat—Don Walker, 1st; Tom Beezley, 2nd; Paul Joyce, 3rd; Louie Mann, 4th.
Stock Feature—Jim Bucher, 1st; Ray Chambers, 2nd; Les Sroufe, 3rd; Doug Method, 4th; Jerry Rosbrugh, 5th; Arden Leiter, 6th; Dennis Hopper, 7th; Jene Simon, 8th; Terry Hatfield, 9th; Jerry DeHaven, 10th.
Modified Feature—Ron Miller, 1st; Bob Grindle, 2nd; Don Murphy, 3rd; Tom Beezley, 4th; Jack French, 5th; Bob Bernhard, 6th; Louie Mann, 7th; Paul Joyce, 8th; Mike Kurtz, 9th; Jeff Creason, 10th.
Hobby Heat—Charlie Jefferson, 1st; Bob Johnson, 2nd; Larry Sroufe, 3rd; George Sitts, 5th.
Hobby Heat—Kenneth Thacker, 1st; Mike Jefferson, 2nd; Chuck Sainer, 3rd; Jerry Baker, 4th; Mike Caudill, 5th.
Hobby Feature—Sonny Hyde, 1st; Jerry Baker, 2nd; Dave Kerlin, 3rd; Chuck Sainer, 4th.

Saturday, June 2, 1973
Miller Makes It 2 At Warsaw
Mid-American Auto Racing News, by Jean Simon

It was a very warm and humid evening, with threats of rain, but a very large crowd of fans got to see a full program of races, except for the hobby feature at Warsaw Speedway.

Ronnie Miller, from Huntington, Indiana, driving his new #68 sprinter, won his second feature in a row. Miller is a rookie this year in sprints. Miller led all the way with only one

Ronnie Miller, Huntington

restart. Miller pulled in to a comfortable lead and held it right down to the black and white checkered flag.

The late model division was plagued by accidents and restarts, resulting in blown tires, dented fenders, etc. Arden Leiter hit the wall and rode it several feet, tearing out the fence behind the retainer wall with parts flying everywhere and finally came to rest on all four tires.

Saturday, June 2, 1973
Warsaw Speedway

Sixty-one cars qualified in Saturday night racing at the Warsaw Speedway. A large crowd watched Ron Miller, in his '68 sprint, serve notice he intends to be a factor in local racing circles this summer by posting his second feature in a row.

Louie Mann, in a sprint, was the fastest qualifier of the evening. The hobby stock feature was rained out. Les Sroufe joined Mann as a feature winner. Sroufe came in first in the stock event.

Arden Leiter was involved in a spectacular end-over-end flip along the backstretch that left two adult and two children spectators with minor injuries from flying debris.

Race Summary:

Stock Dash—Jim Bucher, 1st; Arden Leiter, 2nd; Les Sroufe, 3rd; Jene Simon, 4th; Art Smith, 5th.
Modified Dash—Don Walker, 1st; Jim Murphy, 2nd; Paul Joyce, 3rd; Ron Fisher, 4th; Tim Bookmiller, 5th.
Stock Heat—Tom Leiter, 1st; Larry Howard, 2nd; John Fitzpatrick, 3rd; John Snepp, 4th; Jerry Roseburg, 5th.
Modified Heat—Ron Miller, 1st; Don Murphy, 2nd; Jerry Priest, 3rd; Tom Beezley, 4th.
Stock Heat—Arden Leiter, 1st; Doug Method, 2nd; Todd Grisby, 3rd; Jerry DeHaven, 4th.
Modified Heat—Don Walker, 1st; Bob Bernhard, 2nd; Jim Murphy, 3rd; Paul Joyce, 4th.
Stock Feature—Les Sroufe, 1st; Jim Bucher, 2nd; Larry Howard, 3rd; Tom Leiter, 4th; Todd Grisby, 5th; Roy Norman, 6th; Terry Hatfield, 7th; Doug Method, 8th; Arden Leiter, 9th; Art Smith, 10th.
Modified Feature—Ron Miller, 1st; Tom Beezley, 2nd; Don Walker, 3rd; Paul Joyce, 4th; Bob Grindle, 5th; Jerry Priest, 6th; Bob Bernhard, 7th; Jim Murphy, 8th; Jeff Creason, 9th; Don Murphy, 10th.
Slow Hobby—Bud Grossnickle, 1st; Rex Heckaman, 2nd; Bill Cain, 3rd; Mike Caudill, 4th; Earl Collins, 5th.
Fast Hobby—Lacie Adams, 1st; Sonny Hyde, 2nd; Daye Kerlin, 3rd; Ron Luckey, 4th; Tom Leiter, 5th.

Saturday, June 9, 1973
Warsaw Speedway

A large crowd watched as 58 cars qualified in Saturday racing action at the Warsaw

Speedway. There were numerous spins and several major accidents that caused the night's card to run later than usual following the restarts.

Bud Grossnickle and Jerry Priest were the big winners on the first "hot" night fans have experienced this year.

Race Summary:

Stock Dash—Jene Simon, 1st; Arden Leiter, 2nd; Les Sroufe, 3rd; Doug Method, 4th; Jerry DeHaven, 5th.
Modified Dash—Jerry Priest, 1st; Don Murphy, 2nd; Paul Joyce, 3rd; Louie Mann, 4th; Ron Miller, 5th.
Stock Heat—Ray Chambers, 1st; David Howard, 2nd; Jerry Roseburg, 3rd; Rock Anders, 4th; John Snepp, 5th.
Modified Heat—Bob Bernhard, 1st; Bob Grindle, 2nd; Tom Beezley, 3rd; John Davis, 4th.
Stock Heat—Jim Bucher, 1st; Doug Method, 2nd; Chuck Sainer, 3rd; Les Sroufe, 4th.
Modified Heat—Jerry Priest, 1st; Paul Joyce, 2nd; Ron Miller, 3rd; Louie Mann, 4th.
Stock Feature—Jim Bucher, 1st; Arden Leiter, 2nd; Larry Howard, 3rd; Jene Simon, 4th; Chuck Sainer, 5th; D. Flaugh, 6th; John Snepp, 7th; Ray Chambers, 8th; Jerry DeHavens, 9th; Rock Anders, 10th.
Modified Feature—Jerry Priest, 1st; Kurt Mayhew, 2nd; Don Murphy, 3rd; Ron Miller, 4th; Paul Joyce, 5th; Tom Beezley, 6th; Louie Mann, 7th; Bob Bernhard, 8th; Bob Grindle, 9th; Bob Kolacki, 10th.
Hobby Heat—Charlie Jefferson, 1st; Tom Leiter, 2nd; Jim Laguard, 3rd; Fred Furis, 4th.
Hobby Heat—Bud Grossnickle, 1st; Bill Cain, 2nd; Mike Caudill, 3rd; Larry Sroufe, 4th; Larry Montel, 5th.
Hobby Feature (Rainout finals from one week earlier)—Bud Grossnickle, 1st; Jerry Baker, 2nd; Sonny Hyde, 3rd; Tom Leiter, 4th; Mike Caudill, 5th; Ron Luckey, 6th; Dave Kerlin, 7th; John Orr, 8th; Lacie Adams, 9th.
Hobby Feature—Bud Grossnickle, 1st; Ron Luckey, 2nd; Lacie Adams, 3rd; Bill Cain, 4th; and Sonny Hyde, 5th.

Saturday, June 16, 1973
Warsaw Speedway

A near-capacity crowd attended Saturday night's rain-shortened races at the Warsaw Speedway. The track was in excellent condition until 10 p.m. when heavy rains delayed the remainder of the night's racing card. The remaining races will be run this weekend.

There were 60 cars competing in a race that was broadcast for one-half hour over Radio Station WRSW AM.

The broadcast was sponsored by C. S. Myers Ford and Warsaw Automotive.

Race Summary:

Stock Dash—Jim Bucher, 1st; Art Smith, 2nd; Chuck Sainer, 3rd.
Modified Dash—Tom Beezley, 1st; Paul Joyce, 2nd; Don Murphy, 3rd.
Stock Heat—Jerry DeHaven, 1st; Larry Howard, 2nd; Doug Method, 3rd.
Modified Heat—Louie Mann, 1st; Tom Beezley, 2nd; Ron Miller, 3rd.
Stock Heat—Art Smith, 1st; Chuck Sainer, 2nd; Arden Leiter, 3rd.
Modified Heat—Paul Joyce, 1st; Don Murphy, 2nd; Tom Patterson, 3rd.
Stock Feature—Art Smith, 1st; Les Sroufe, 2nd; Chuck Sainer, 3rd

Saturday, June 23, 1973 - Rainout

Saturday, June 30, 1973
Warsaw Speedway

A huge crowd was on hand Saturday night at the Warsaw Speedway in an evening that included the regular racing card plus a makeup on a feature race rained out from last week and a demolition derby.

John Fitzpatrick, Warsaw, rolled his late model during race action and was taken to Murphy Medical Center for treatment, then released. In demolition action 56 cars were entered, the winner 55 cars later was Don Rumfelt. Action continues on the 4th with a fireworks display also planned.

Race Summary:

Stock Dash—Jene Simon, 1st; Art Smith, 2nd; Arden Leiter, 3rd.
Modified Dash—Louis Mann, 1st; Paul Joyce, 2nd; Don Murphy, 3rd.
Stock Heat—Ray Chambers, 1st; Lanny Howard, 2nd; Doug Method, 3rd.
Modified Dash—Paul Joyce, 1st; Ron Miller, 2nd; Bob Bernhard and Tom Beezley, 3rd.
Stock Heat—Arden Leiter, 1st; Art Smith, 2nd; Les Sroufe, 3rd.
Modified Heat—Ed Angle, 1st; Louie Mann, 2nd; Bob Grindle, 3rd.
Stock Feature—Arden Leiter, 1st; Art Smith, 2nd; Jim Bucher, 3rd.
Modified Feature—Louie Mann, 1st; Paul Joyce, 2nd; Ron Miller,
Feature(Rainout)—Ron Luckey, 1st; Sonny Hyde, 2nd; Larry Montel, 3rd.
Hobby Heat—Dick Day, 1st; Charlie Jefferson, 2nd; Henshel Warnock, 3rd
Hobby Heat—Bud Grossnickle, 1st; Jenny Baker, 2nd; Andy Brown, 3rd.
Hobby Feature—Bud Grossnickle, 1st; Andy Brown, 2nd; Charles Hyde, 3rd.
Demolition—Don Rumfelt, 1st; Rick Wolf, 2nd.

Wednesday, July 4, 1973
Big Crowd At Warsaw Speedway For Races And Fireworks, July 4
Columbia City Post & Mail

After the rain early Wednesday, it turned out to be a beautiful night for races at the Warsaw Speedway and for the fireworks display. The fans had many thrills as in the late model dash Jim Bucher driving Larry Dainers No. 2 from Akron hit the wall in front of the grandstand and rode it for a short distance then landed on all four wheels. He tore out several feet of the fence. Then on qualification Bob Grindle tore out more of the same fence. Then Paul Roberts of Huntington hit the same fence and tore out more.

Jerry Priest, from Elwood, driving Rom Lambeston 33 won the Jimmy Elliott Memorial trophy. It was presented by Mrs. Jim Elliott and her son. Louie Mann, driving Paul Hazen's No. 57 sprint, developed problems in the feature.

Steve Brown driving No. 00 owned by Brown and Mike Caudill was leading the Hobby Feature when he got put in the wall and broke a tie rod. George Sitts driving No. 2 owned by Sitts and Bill McKown was warming up his car when an oil line broke and sprayed him with oil. The car was repaired in time for the race.

Todd Grigsby, driving Dale Moser's No. 9 late model was out with engine problems but he hopes to be back Saturday night. Jene Simon driving No. 47 owned by Earl and Nine Cocklin from Huntington took a mud bath as he ran through the mud hole in the infield during the race.

Fastest qualifiers, Sprint - Ronnie Miller 16.36, Late Model - Art Smith, 18.13, Hobby - Jerry Baker 19.36.
Sprint Dash – Paul Joyce, Louie Mann, Don Murphy
Slow Heat – Kirk Mayhew, Tom Beezley, Terry Baker
Fast Heat – Jerry Priest, Paul Joyce, Ron Miller
Feature – Jerry Priest, Paul Joyce, Don Walker, Tom Beezley, Ron Miller
Late Model Dash – Art Smith, Chuck Sauer, Les Sroufe
Slow Heat – Larry Howard, Jerry Rosebreak, Bull Bradley
Fast Heat – Art Smith, Les Sroufe, Arden Leiter
Feature – Art Smith, Les Sroufe, Larry Howard, Ray Chambers, Jene Simon
Hobby Slow Heat – Dan Barker, Charley Jefferson, Bob Johnson
Fast Heat – Dick Day, Larry Montel, Charles Hyde
Feature – Dick Day, Jerry Baker, Bob Johnson, Tom Leiter, Bud Grossnickle.

Saturday, July 7, 1973
Warsaw Speedway Action
Columbia City Post & Mail

It was an exciting night of racing at Warsaw Speedway this week. In the late model feature, Les Sroufe was leading when he lost a tire, then Art Smith was leading when he got knocked into the wall and had to pull out. Arden Leiter took his turn at the lead, but on the white flag he spun into the infield and Chuck Saner took the checkered flag.

In the sprint feature, Don Walker, driving Louie Mann's car, won with Louie Mann, driving Paul Hazen's car, a close second.

In the hobby stockers, Lacie Adams from Warsaw failed to make turn number one and landed on the mound of dirt around the light pole. Bud Grossnickle from North Manchester, Charley Hyde and Tom Leiter were unable to miss him, breaking the huge light pole off even with the ground. The races were held up almost an hour while emergency lights were installed and Lacie Adams and Bud Grossnickle were taken to the hospital for a check-up. They were later released with non serious injuries.

Race Summary:

Sprint – Fastest Qualifier, Jerry Priest 17:18
Dash – Louie Mann, Ron Miller, Jerry Priest
Slow Heat – Tom Beezley, Kirk Mayhew, Paul Grim
Fast Heat – Louie Mann, Paul Joyce, Ron Miller
Feature – Don Walker, Louie Mann, Ron Miller, Jerry Priest, Kirk Mayhew
Late Model – Fastest Qualifier, Art Smith 19:00
Dash – Art Smith, Jene Simon, Arden Leiter
Slow Heat – Chuck Saner, Paul Grim, Larry Howard
Fast Heat – Les Sroufe, Art Smith, Ray Chambers
Feature – Chuck Saner, Larry Howard, Jim Bucher, Jene Simon, Paul Grim
Hobby Stock
Slow Heat – Dan Backus, Charles Jefferson
Fast Heat – Larry Montel, Sonny Hyde, Duane Eckright
Feature – Sonny Hyde, Harold "Buz" Alexander, Larry Montel, Jerry Baker

Saturday, July 14, 1973
Priest Wins At Warsaw Speedway
Columbia City Post & Mail

Jerry Priest came from last place to win the sprint feature over the weekend at the Warsaw Speedway. Louie Mann, who won the dash and the fast heat, was second in a car owned by Paul Hazen. Priest, who was driving Ron Lamberson's auto, received a $100 check for the win.

Scott Wasilewski of Columbia City came in second in the heat and fourth in the feature in a car owned by Art Braithwaite. Bob Bernhard from South Whitley in his super modified was fifth in the feature race.

Don Murphy of South Whitley was third in the dash but he developed car trouble and did not compete in the feature. Art Smith, driving Fred Hudson's car, took almost all the honors in late model winning the dash, placing third in the fast heat, and winning the feature and a $100 bonus. Paul Grim won the slow heat and came in fourth in the feature in a car owned by Dan Ford.

Paul Roberts from Huntinton, driving a new car owned by Doug Bennett, was second in the slow heat. Roger Frye, formerly from Columbia City, came in sixth in the feature.

Several Columbia City drivers experienced some bad luck. Todd Grigsby was out three races with engine trouble, and then, when he was leading the heat race, the engine began to heat up. In the feature race, the engine blew on the third lap. Jene Simon was unable to race because his engine was tore down. Steve Brown had an engine blow, and George Sitts lost his drive shaft twice before the race started and decided to sit out the rest of the night. Walt Rowland and Harold "Buzz" Alexander also had to pull out in the feature.

The Saturday night the mid-season championship races for the sprints and late models are scheduled. Each class will run a 40-lap feature.

Race Summary:
Sprint, Fastest Qualifier – Jerry Priest 16:67
Dash – Louie Mann, Paul Joyce, Don Murphy

Slow Heat – Jim Murphy, Scott Wasiliewski, Joe Perry
Fast Heat – Louie Mann, Paul Joyce, Bob Bernhard
Feature – Jerry Priest, Louie Mann, Paul Joyce, Scott Wasilewski, Bob Bernhard
Late Model, Fastest Qualified – Art Smith 17:79
Dash – Art Smith, Arden Leiter, Jim Bucher
Slow Heat – Paul Grim, Paul Roberts, Larry Howard
Fast Heat – Jim Bucher, Les Sroufe, Art Smith
Feature – Art Smith, Les Sroufe, Arden Leiter, Paul Grim, Ray Chambers, Roger Frye
Hobby, Fastest Qualifier – Dave Kerlin 19:13
Slow Heat – Al Clark, Bob Johnson
Fast Heat – Charles Jefferson, Larry Montel, Duane Eckright
Feature – Bob Johnson, Dave Kerlin, Duane Eckright, Charles Hyde, Paul Sherman

Saturday, July 21, 1973 - Rainout

Saturday, July 28, 1973
Warsaw Speedway

Sixty-four cars qualified for Saturday night racing action at the Warsaw Speedway. Eighteen cars started the semilate feature, only seven finished.

Chuck Sainer took first place honors in the 40-lap championship stock feature. Louie Mann was best in the 40-lap modified feature. Jerry Baker captured the hobby feature. Next week there will be a 30-lap championship race for hobby stocks.

Race Results:
Stock Feature – Chuck Sainer, Paul Grim, Arden Leiter
Modified Feature – Louie Mann, Ron Miller, Jerry Priest
Hobby Feature – Jerry Baker, Bob Johnson, Dan Backus

Saturday, August 4, 1973
Warsaw Speedway

Jerry Baker won the 30-lap Mid-Season Championship race at the Warsaw Speedway Saturday as 70 cars were in action. Finishings in the other races are as follows:

Semi-late Dash – Les Sroufe, Jim Bucher, Arden Leiter
Modified Dash – Don Murphy, Paul Joyce, Don Walker
Semi-late First Heat – Larry Howard, Todd Grigsby, Rod Bailey
Second Heat – Art Smith, John White, Bull Bradley
Modified First Heat – Jerry Priest, Bob Bernhard, Alan Garner
Second Heat – Paul Joyce, Louie Mann, Arden Leiter
Semi-late Feature – Arden Leiter, Paul Grim, Les Sroufe
Modified Feature – Louie Mann, Paul Joyce, Jerry Priest
Hobby First Heat – Steve Knouff, Jim Martin, Dick Day
Second Heat – Larry Montel, Bud Grossnickle, Bob Johnson
Hobby Feature – Jerry Baker, Tom Leiter, Steve Brown

Wednesday, August 8, 1973
Warsaw Speedway

In auto racing action Wednesday at the Warsaw Speedway Oval, Arden Leiter took first place in the semi-late feature and Chuck Roy finished first in the hobby feature. Dash events were won by Paul Grim in the semi-late and Rock Anders in the hobby. Chuck Sainer, Les Sroufe and Terry Hatfield won the three semi-late heats and Larry Montel, Larry Horn and Paul Sherman won the hobby heats. Grim finished second in the semi-late feature and Art Smith was third. Second place in the hobby feature went to Jerry Baker and third to Larry Sroufe.

Saturday, August 11, 1973 - Rainout

Saturday, August 18, 1973 - Rainout

Saturday, August 25, 1973
Warsaw Speedway

Elwood's Don Walker set a new track mark in Saturday night action at the Warsaw Speedway, lowering the existing mark of 15.59 in one lap to 15.25. In posting the new time Walker averaged approximately 60 miles per hour, with a high of 80 in the straights and 45 at the curves. Walker held the previous mark as well.

A total of 63 cars qualified with feature win picked up by Arden Leiter, stock, Don Walker, modified, and Jerry Baker in the hobby.

Race Summary:
Stock Dash—Art Smith, 1st; Ted Hudson, 2nd; Les Sroufe, 3rd.
Modified Dash—Louie Mann, 1st; Don Murphy, 2nd; Don Walker, 3rd.
Stock Heat—Roy Chambers, 1st; Larry Howard, 2nd; John Fitzpatrick, 3rd.
Modified Heat—Ron Miller, 1st; Bob Bernhard, 2nd; Paul Joyce, 3rd.
Stock Heat—Ted Hudson, 1st; Les Sroufe, 2nd; Jim Bucher, 3rd.
Modified Heat—Louie Mann, 1st; Don Walker, 2nd; Jerry Priest, 3rd.
Stock Feature—Arden Leiter, 1st; Les Sroufe, 2nd; Paul Grim, 3rd.
Modified Feature—Don Walker, 1st; Louie Mann, 2nd; Ron Miller, 3rd.
Hobby Heat—Tom Leiter, 1st; Rusty Sunday, 2nd; Dick Day, 3rd.
Hobby Heat—George Sitts, 1st; Jerry Baker, 2nd; Jim Sroufe, 3rd.
Hobby Feature—Jerry Baker, 1st; Dave Kerlin, 2nd; Steve Brown, 3rd.
Demolition—Rick Short, 1st; Rock Anders, 2nd.

Saturday, September 1, 1973
Warsaw Speedway

Saturday night's heat winners at the Warsaw Speedway have been announced as follows:

Stock Dash—Arden Leiter, 1st; Paul Grim, 2nd; John White, 3rd.
Modified Dash—Paul Joyce, 1st; Ron Miller, 2nd; Louie Mann, 3rd.
Stock Heat—Larry Howard, 1st; Roger Frye, 2nd; Doug Method, 3rd.
Modified Heat—Tim Bookmiller, 1st; Alan Garner, 2nd; Arden Leiter, 3rd.
Stock Heat—Art Smith, 1st; Bill Bradley, 2nd; Jim Bucher, 3rd.
Modified Heat—Ron Miller, 1st; Don Walker, 2nd; Bob Bernhard, 3rd.
Stock Feature—Art Smith, 1st; Jim Bucher, 2nd; Paul Grim, 3rd.

Modified Feature—Louie Mann, 1st; Ron Miller, 2nd; Paul Joyce, 3rd.
Hobby Heat—Duane Eckwright, 1st; Joe Cutler, 2nd; Earle Stinger, 3rd.
Hobby Heat—Jerry Baker, 1st; Steven Brown, 2nd; Dan Backus, 3rd.
Hobby Feature—Jerry Baker, 1st; Tom Leiter, 2nd; Dave Kerlin, 3rd.

Saturday, September 1, 1973
Louie Mann Wins Sprints At Warsaw
Columbia City Post & Mail

Louie Mann, No 57, starting on the inside pole, walked away with top points, the season championship, a trophy, and a $100 bonus Saturday night in the sprints at Warsaw Speedway. Ronnie Miller, No. 68, and Paul Joyce finished second and third respectively and also received trophies.

In the Late Models, Art Smith, No. 67, started on the outside of the first row and out-dueled Arden Leiter early in the race before pulling away for an easy win. Jim Bucher, No. 2, and Paul Grim, No. 88, finished second and third respectively. All three received trophies, with Smith getting a $100 bonus.

Jerry Baker, No. 66, Tom Leiter and Dave Kerlin started 1-2-3 and finished the same way in the Hobby Feature. All got trophies, and Baker was awarded a $50 bonus. This Saturday, the Jim Elliott Memorial races will be run at the speedway. Elliott was killed in a motorcycle mishap in March. He was last year's top point standings champion in the sprints.

Saturday, September 8, 1973 – No Results

Saturday, September 15, 1973 – No Results

1974

Saturday, May 11, 1974 - Rainout

Saturday, May 18, 1974
Speedway News

Louie Mann was the top winner in racing action at the Warsaw Speedway here Saturday. Mann captured the modified dash event and took the checkered flag in a heat race during the competition. Mann threatened to add another victory to his record leading the modified feature before a broken hose forced him to the pits.

Jerry Baker raced home first in the hobby stock feature and Jim Bucher outdistanced the field in the stock feature.

Race Results:

Stock Dash—Les Sroufe, 1st; Rod Bailey, 2nd; Jim Bucher, 3rd.
Modified Dash—Louie Mann, 1st; Paul Joyce, 2nd; Mike Caudwell, 3rd.
Stock Heat—Roger Frye, 1st; Tom Leiter, 2nd; Lynn Knisely, 3rd.
Modified Heat—Ron Miller, 1st; Tom Beezley, 2nd; Tom Patterson, 3rd.

Stock Heat—Jim Bucher, 1st; Arden Leiter, 2nd; Rod Bailey, 3rd.
Modified Heat—Louie Mann, 1st; Mike Cauldwell, 2nd; Tom Dixon, 3rd.
Hobby Heat—Mark Hanna, 1st; Earl Steminger, 2nd; John Orr, 3rd.
Hobby Heat—Dan Backus, 1st; Steve Brown, 2nd; Tom Leiter, 3rd.
Hobby Feature—Jerry Baker, 1st.
Stock Feature—Jim Bucher, 1st; Arden Leiter, 2nd; Roger Frye, 3rd.
Modified Feature—Tom Dixon, 1st; Mike Cauldwell, 2nd; Paul Joyce, 3rd.

Saturday, May 25 & Monday, May 27, 1974
Warsaw Speedway

Steve Brown and Jerry Baker took firsts in the hobby feature races at the Warsaw Speedway Saturday and Monday nights respectively.

Ray Chambers placed first in the stock race Saturday with Arden Leiter taking the top slot Monday. Jim Boggs won in the modified division Saturday and Ron Miller was first Memorial Day.

Bob Johnson of Warsaw was taken to the hospital for x-rays Saturday after a four-car pileup. Tom Patterson, of Bremen, rolled his sprint Monday but did not sustain any injuries.

Saturday's Results:
Stock Feature—Ray Chambers, 1st; Jim Bucher, 2nd; Ted Hudson, 3rd; Charles Hyde, 4th.
Modified Feature—Jim Boggs, 1st; Mike Cauldwell, 2nd; Paul Joyce, 3rd; Ron Miller, 4th.
Hobby Feature—Steve Brown, 1st; Jerry Baker, 2nd.

Memorial Day Results:
Stock Feature—Arden Leiter, 1st; Jim Bucher, 2nd; Charles Hyde, 3rd.
Modified Feature—Ron Miller, 1st; Beecher Jackson, 2nd; Tom Beezley, 3rd.
Hobby Feature—Jerry Baker, 1st; Bud Grossnickle, 2nd; Steve Brown, 3rd.

Saturday, June 1, 1974
Race Results

Jerry Baker, Arden Leiter and Jim Boggs all won feature races Saturday night in action at the Warsaw Speedway.

Baker took first in the hobby class, Leiter in the stock event and Boggs in the modified category. Fifty-seven cars and drivers took part in the Saturday events at the Warsaw Race Track.

Other race results are as follows:
Stock Dash—Ray Chambers, 1st; Larry Howard, 2nd; Arden Leiter, 3rd.

Modified Dash—Bob Bernhard, 1st; Ron Miller, 2nd; Don Walker, 3rd.
Stock Heat—Les Sroufe, 1st; Lynn Bradley, 2nd; Paul Sherman, 3rd.
Modified Heat—Richard Jackson, 1st; Jim Murphy, 2nd; Scotty Kaiser, 3rd.
Stock Feature—Arden Leiter, 1st; Ray Chambers, 2nd; Larry Howard, 3rd.
Modified Feature—Jim Boggs, 1st; Ron Miller, 2nd; Richard Jackson, 3rd.
Hobby Heat—Bud Grossnickle, 1st; Bob Johnson, 2nd; Mark Hanna, 3rd.
Hobby Heat—Rex Heckaman, 1st; Alan Drabenstott, 2nd; Dan Baker, 3rd.
Hobby Feature—Jerry Baker, 1st; John Higgenbottom, 2nd; Bob Johnson, 3rd.

Saturday, June 8, 1974 - Rainout

Saturday, June 15, 1974
Speedway Results

Les Sroufe, Jerry Priest and Tom Leiter were victorious in the feature races at Warsaw Speedway over the weekend.

Sroufe copped first in the stock feature, Priest won the modified feature and Leiter took the top spot in the hobby division.

Paul Grim of Warren rolled his new modified racer but sustained only a laceration to one hand which was treated at the track.

Paul Grim, Warren

Race Results:
Stock Dash—Ray Chambers, 1st; Art Smith, 2nd; Larry Howard, 3rd.
Modified Dash—Louie Mann, 1st; Ron Miller, 2nd; Don Walker, 3rd.
Stock Heat—Jerry DeHaven, 1st; Roger Frye, 2nd; Charlie Prater, 3rd.
Modified Heat—Richard Jackson, 1st; Paul Joyce, 2nd; Larry Mayhew, 3rd.
Stock Heat—Les Sroufe, 1st; Art Smith, 2nd; Larry Howard, 3rd.
Modified Heat—Jerry Priest, 1st; Louie Mann, 2nd; Ron Miller, 3rd.
Stock Feature—Les Sroufe, 1st; Arden Leiter, 2nd; Ray Chambers, 3rd.
Modified Feature—Jerry Priest, 1st; Ron Miller, 2nd; Don Walker, 3rd.
Hobby Heat—Steve Brown, 1st; Ron Gagnon, 2nd; Bob Johnson, 3rd.
Hobby Heat—Bud Grossnickle, 1st; Rex Heckaman, 2nd; Tom Leiter, 3rd.
Hobby Heat—Earl Steininger, 1st; Alan Drabinscott, 2nd; Dan Backus, 3rd.
Hobby Feature—Tom Leiter, 1st; Steve Brown, 2nd; John Fitzpatrick, 3rd.

Saturday, June 15, 1974
Jerry Priest Wins The Sprint Feature At Warsaw Speedway Saturday Night
Columbia City Post & Mail – June 17, 1974

Veteran driver Jerry Priest, driving his own car for the first time this year, won the sprint feature Saturday night at Warsaw Speedway, with Ronnie Miller, of Huntington, right behind.

Steve Brown of Columbia City won the No. 1 heat in the hobby division and came in second in the hobby feature. He was driving a blue Ford sponsored by Jim Barnett's Marathon and Ed's Speed Shop.

Les Sroufe of Huntington drove his orange, white and blue Mustang to victory in both the fast heat and the feature race in the late model division.

C. E. Gibson, track supervisor, announced during the evening that races and a fireworks display are being planned for July 4th. A demolition derby is also being scheduled for Saturday, July 13.

Les Sroufe, Huntington

Saturday, June 22, 1974 – Rainout

Saturday, June 29, 1974
Race Results

Chuck Sainer, Don Walker and Jerry Baker walked off with first places in feature races at the Warsaw Speedway Saturday night. Sainer won the stock class, Walker the modified division and Baker the hobby class.

Charles Hyde rolled his semi-late entry in front of the grandstand but got out uninjured.

Other results are as follows:

Stock Dash—Arden Leiter, 1st; Les Sroufe, 2nd; Larry Howard, 3rd.
Stock Heat—Bull Bradley, 1st; Jim Bucher, 2nd; Gary Baker, 3rd.
Stock Heat—Chuck Sainer, 1st; Roy Norman, 2nd; Rod Bailey, 3rd.
Modified Dash—Jerry Priest, 1st; Richard Jackson, 2nd; Don Walker, 3rd.
Modified Heat—Louie Mann, 1st; Paul Joyce, 2nd; Tom Beezley, 3rd.
Modified Heat—Jerry Priest, 1st; Richard Jackson, 2nd; Ron Miller, 3rd.
Stock Feature—Chuck Sainer, 1st; Jim Bucher, 2nd; Ted Hudson, 3rd.
Modified Feature—Don Walker, 1st; Ron Miller, 2nd; John Davis, 3rd.
Hobby Heat—Bob Johnson, 1st; Rex Heckaman, 2nd; Dan Backus, 3rd.
Hobby Heat—Bud Grossnickle, 1st; John Fitzpatrick, 2nd; Jerry Baker, 3rd.
Hobby Feature—Jerry Baker, 1st; Bud Grossnickle, 2nd; John Fitzpatrick, 3rd.

Thursday, July 4, 1974
Warsaw Speedway Results

Arden Leiter, Jerry Priest and Bud Grossnickle paced the pack at the Warsaw Speedway Thursday when they all ended up in the winner's circle in feature race competition. Leiter took the stock feature, Priest the modified and Grossnickle the hobby during a windy and sometimes rainy Fourth of July.

Other results were as follows:

Stock Dash—Ray Chambers, 1st; Larry Howard, 2nd; Todd Grigsley, 3rd.
Modified Dash—John Davis, 1st; Jerry Priest, 2nd; Jim Boggs, 3rd.
Stock Heat—Dave Evers, 1st; Charlie Prater, 2nd; Ellis Shepherd, 3rd.
Modified Heat—John Davis, 1st; Jerry Priest, 2nd; Jim Boggs, 3rd.
Stock Heat—Ray Chambers, 1st; Ted Hudson, 2nd; Arden Leiter, 3rd.
Modified Heat—Ron Miller, 1st; Bob Bernhard, 2nd; Tom Beezley, 3rd.
Stock Feature—Arden Leiter, 1st; Ted Hudson, 2nd; Charles Hyde, 3rd.
Modified Feature—Jerry Priest, 1st; John Davis, 2nd; Ron Miller, 3rd.
Hobby Heat—Russ Blackford, 1st; Gary Stonebraker, 2nd; Bob Johnson, 3rd.
Hobby Heat—L. C. Drabenstott, 1st; Dan Backus, 2nd; Mark Hanna, 3rd.
Hobby Feature—Bud Grossnickle, 1st; Jerry Baker, 2nd; Bob Johnson, 3rd.

Saturday, July 6, 1974 - Rainout

Saturday, July 13, 1974
Race Results

The Warsaw Speedway will host a 40-lap Super Sprint Invitational race Saturday night with top prize being $600. Sprints will run six fastest, two heats and feature. The 20 fastest cars will make the feature.

Arden Leiter, Ron Miller and Tom Leiter won feature races at the track Saturday. Arden Leiter won the stock feature, Miller the modified feature and Tom Leiter the hobby feature. Walter Bailey of Huntington rolled his car but was not injured.

Race Results:

Stock Dash—Chuck Sainer, 1st; Arden Leiter, 2nd; Roger Frye, 3rd.
Modified Dash—Ron Miller, 1st; Ron Fisher, 2nd; Louie Mann, 3rd.
Stock Heat—Ray Norman, 1st; Tom Leiter, 2nd; Chris Chapman, 3rd.
Modified Heat—Jene Simon, 1st; Ozzie Osborn, 2nd; Bob Bernhard, 3rd; Jim Boggs, 4th.
Stock Heat—Bull Bradley, 1st; Ted Hudson, 2nd; Arden Leiter, 3rd.
Modified Heat—Louie Mann, 1st; Tom Beezley, 2nd; Ron Miller, 3rd.
Stock Feature—Arden Leiter, 1st; Roy Norman, 2nd; Ray Chambers, 3rd.
Modified Feature—Ron Miller, 1st; Louie Mann, 2nd; Jene Simon, 3rd.
Hobby Heat—Bill Cork, 1st; Bob Johnson, 2nd; Dave Coil, 3rd.
Hobby Heat—Dean Eckwright, 1st; Tom Leiter, 2nd; Fred Furness, 3rd.
Hobby Feature—Tom Leiter, 1st; Jerry Baker, 2nd; Bob Johnson, 3rd.

Saturday, July 20, 1974
Race Results

Ron Miller won a $600 prize at the Warsaw Speedway Saturday night when he captured first place in the 40-lap sprint feature and the Hormal percentage.

Other feature winners were Ted Hudson in the stock, Ron Miller in the modified and Bud

Grossnickle in the hobby. Ozzie Osborn rolled his modified entry but was not injured

Other Results:

Modified Dash—Louie Mann, 1st; Jim Boggs, 2nd; Ron Miller, 3rd.
Stock Dash—Ted Hudson, 1st; Jim Bucher, 2nd; Todd Grigsby, 3rd.
Stock Heat—Chris Chapman, 1st; Denny Flaugh, 2nd; Charlie Prater, 3rd.
Modified Heat—Bob Bernhard, 1st; Tom Beezley, 2nd; Paul Grim, 3rd.
Stock Heat—Roger Frye, 1st; Jim Bucher, 2nd; Ted Hudson, 3rd.
Modified Heat—Ron Miller, 1st; Louie Mann, 2nd; Ozzie Osborn, 3rd.
Stock Heat—Ted Hudson, 1st; Denny Flaugh, 2nd; Dave Evers, 3rd; Chris Chapman, 4th; Paul Sherman, 5th; Roger Frye, 6th; Roy Norman, 7th; Bull Bradley, 8th; Jim Bucher, 9th; Charlie Prater, 10th.
Modified Feature—Ron Miller, 1st; Louie Mann, 2nd; Ron Fisher, 3rd; Don Fisher, 4th; Jerry DeHaven, 5th; Jim Boggs, 6th; Paul Grim, 7th; Bob Bernhard, 8th; Tom Beezley, 9th; Tom Brewer, 10th.
Hobby Heat—Rex Heckaman, 1st; Ron Gagnon, 2nd; Lacie Adams, 3rd.
Hobby Heat—Jerry Baker, 1st; Al Drabenscott, 2nd; Mark Hanna, 3rd.
Hobby Feature—Bud Grossnickle, 1st; Jerry Baker, 2nd; Steve Brown, 3rd.

Saturday, July 27, 1974
Warsaw Speedway Results

The Warsaw race track Saturday night attracted an entry list of 61 cars. Fastest Qualifiers: Arden Leiter, semi-late, 17.60; Ron Fisher, 16:08, in modified; Jerry Baker, 18.75, in hobby.

The bonus winner of $400 was Bull Bradley, semi-late feature winner. Arden Leiter received a $50 bonus for fastest qualifier in the semi-lates.

Race Results:

Stock Dash—Arden Leiter, 1st; Bull Bradley, 2nd; Chuck Sainer, 3rd.
Modified Dash—Ron Miller, 1st; Jerry Priest, 2nd; Ron Fisher, 3rd.
Stock, first heat—Larry Montel, 1st; Chris Chapman, 2nd; Roy Norman, 3rd.
Modified—Don Fisher, 1st; Bob Bernhard, 2nd; Scott Fisher, 3rd.
Stock—Dave Evers, 1st; Ted Hudson, 2nd; Jim Bucher, 3rd.
Modified—Ron Miller, 1st; Jerry Priest, 2nd; Ron Fisher, 3rd.
Feature-Stock—Bill Bradley, 1st; Larry Montel, 2nd; Jim Bucher, 3rd; Roy Norman, 4th; Arden Leiter, 5th.
Feature-Modified—Louie Mann, 1st; Jerry Priest, 2nd; Ron Fisher, 3rd; Ron Miller, 4th; Don Fisher, 5th.
Hobby Stock-first heat—Rex Heckaman, 1st; Bob Johnson, 2nd; John Orr, 3rd.
Hobby Stock-second heat—Steve Brown, 1st; L.C. Drabenstott, 2nd; Jerry Baker, 3rd.
Feature Hobby—Tom Leiter, 1st; Phil Partridge, 2nd; Jerry Baker, 3rd.

Saturday, August 3, 1974
Racing Results

Two evenings of racing are planned for the Fair this week as the cars hit the track Wednesday and Saturday night. Wednesday's racing will be Hobby Stock only with time trials beginning at 6:30.

Results from Saturday's racing are:

Stock Dash—Larry Montel, 1st; Ted Hudson, 2nd; Jim Bucher, 3rd.

Modified Dash—Jerry Priest, 1st; Louie Mann, 2nd; Jene Simon, 3rd.
Stock Heat—Dick Kirkman, 1st; Chuck Speicher, 2nd; Tom Beezley, 3rd.
Modified Heat—John Davis, 1st; Bob Bernhard, 2nd; Ozzie Osburn, 3rd.
Stock Heat—Jerry Priest, 1st; Ron Miller, 2nd; Jene Simon, 3rd.
Stock Feature—Arden Leiter, 1st; Jim Bucher, 2nd; Larry Howard, 3rd.Jim M
Modified Feature—Ron Miller, 1st; Louie Mann, 2nd; Jerry Priest, 3rd.
Hobby Heat—(First Heat)—Bob Johnson, 1st; John Higgenbottom, 2nd; Walt Rowland, 3rd.
Hobby Heat—(Second Heat)—John Orr, 1st; Rocky Anders, 2nd; Bud Grossnickle, 3rd.
Hobby Feature—Al Drabenstott, 1st; Mark Hanna, 2nd; Dan Backus, 3rd.

Bob Johnson, Warsaw

Wednesday, August 7, 1974
Speedway Racing

Stock car racing returns to the speedway at the County Fair Grounds on Saturday night. In last night's action:

Stock Dash—Chuck Sainer, 1st; Arden Leiter, 2nd; Jim Bucher, 3rd.
Hobby Dash—John Orr, 1st; Mark Hanna, 2nd; Jerry Baker, 3rd.
Stock Heat—Tom Leiter, 1st; Dave Kerlin, 2nd; Charlie Prater, 3rd.
Stock Heat—Larry Howard, 1st; Tom Beezley, 2nd; Arden Leiter, 3rd.
Hobby Heat—Rex Heckaman, 1st; Roger Rowland, 2nd; Bob Johnson, 3rd.
Hobby Heat—Mark Hanna, 1st; Steve Brown, 2nd; Jerry Baker, 3rd; John Orr, 4th.
Stock Feature—Larry Howard, 1st; Chuck Sainer, 2nd; Ted Hudson, 3rd; Dave Kerlin, 4th; Charlie Prater, 5th; Charles Hyde, 6th; Tom Leiter, 7th; Denny Flaugh, 8th; Rod Bailey, 9th; Ray Chambers, 10th.
Hobby Feature—Steve Brown, 1st; Jerry Baker, 2nd; Johnny Orr, 3rd.

Saturday, August 10, 1974 – Rainout

Saturday, August 17, 1974
Hoosier Hot Rods, Inc.

At the recent Hoosier Hot Rods, Inc. meet, Chuck Sainer, Ron Miller and John Fitzpatrick won their specialties; those being Sainer in the Semi-late Feature, Miller the Modified feature and Fitzpatrick the Hobby Feature.

1975

Saturday, May 10, 1975
Warsaw Auto Racing

Ed Angle and Louie Mann were the dominating factors in Hoosier Hot Rods racing at the Kosciusko County fairgrounds over the weekend. Angle won the fast sprints heat and the modified dash, with Mann right on his wheel in both events. Mann came back to win the feature sprint with Angle third.

Keith Smith rolled his No. 13 hobby stock three times before landing on his wheels and walking away unhurt.

Following are the top finishers in each event:

Semi-late Dash Event—Ray Chambers; Jim Bucher; Tom Beezley; Les Sroufe.
Modified Dash Event—Ed Angle; Louie Mann; Jerry DeHaven; Bobby Bernhard.
Semi-Late Slow—Dave Evers; Charles Hyde; Steve Backus; Joe Hock.
Sprint Slow—Tim Bookmiller; Don Rumfelt; Dan Johnson; Jerry DeHaven.
Semi-Late Fast—Bruce Hogue; Dan Backus; Bo Bradley; Steve Brown.
Fast Sprints—Ed Angle; Louie Mann; Tim Bookmiller; Jerry DeHaven.
Hobby Slow Heat—Bob Johnson; Rack Anders; Walt Rowland.
Hobby Fast Heat—John Orr; Jerry Baker; John Fitzpatrick; John Williams.
Feature Semi-Late—John White; Ray Chambers; Bruce Hogue; Bull Bradley.
Feature Sprint—Louie Mann; Dean Rumfelt; Ed Angle; Dan Johnson.
Feature Hobby—John Orr; Terry Baker; John Fitzpatrick.

Saturday, May 17, 1975
Warsaw Racing

Drivers at the Hoosier Hot Rod Inc. races in Warsaw over the weekend were greeted by an enthusiastic crowd and some warm weather.

Ed Angle, for the second week in a row, kept the crowd on its feet, winning a heat race, taking second in another and coming close in the sprint feature, despite losing his regular car in the pre-race warm up. In the feature he was running second when a minor accident put him back to eighth. Sixty cars qualified for the races. Following are the top finishers:

Late Model Dash Event—Ray Chambers; Jim Bucher; Charles Flaugh; Les Sroufe.
Sprint Dash Event—Don Murphy; Ed Angle; Tim Bookmiller; Don Rumfelt.
Late Model Slow—Dave Evers; Ray Norman; Dulane Elwright; Charles Hyde.
Sprints Slow—John Davis; Billie Jo Haven; Ron Miller; Carl Miskotten
Late Model Fast—Larry Howard; Bull Bradley; Bruce Hogue; Roger Fry.
Sprints Fast—Ed Angle; Don Murphy; Tim Bookmiller; Don Rumfelt.
Hobby Slow—Steve Brown; Tim Gay; Bob Johnson; Walt Maley.
Hobby Fast—Terry Baker; Jerry Baker; John Orr; John Fitzpatrick.
Late Model Feature—Bull Bradley; Bruce Hogue; Larry Howard; Roger Fry.
Sprint Feature—Ron Miller; Jerry Priest; John Davis; Scott Waslewckl.
Hobby Feature—Jerry Baker; Terry Baker; John Fitzpatrick, John Orr.

Saturday, May 24, 1975
Warsaw Racing

"Bull" Bradley grabbed the spotlight at the Warsaw Speedway Saturday night when he met the third turn wall head on in the semi-late dash event. Bradley was unhurt, but racing was delayed as repairs had to be made where Bradley knocked off huge chunks of cement from the wall.

In the sprint feature, Jerry Priest passed Louie Mann on the 24th lap to take the lead, but lost it when he spun out just 50-feet from the checkered flag. Mann ended up winning the event with Priest fourth. In that same race, five cars were involved in an accident and knocked out of competition.

Race Results:
Dash Event Semi-Late—Ray Chambers; Larry Howard; Dan Backus; Charlie Prater.
Dash Event Modified—John Davis; Billie Jo Haven; Tim Bookmiller; Jerry Priest.
Slow Semi-Late—Jim Bucher; Denny Flaugh; Dave Evers; Tom Leiter.
Slow Modified—Ron Miller; Carl Miskotten; Tim Boyd; Scott Keiser.
Fast Semi-Late—Tom Beezley; Art Leiter; Les Sroufe; Dan Backus.
Fast Modified—John Davis; Louis Mann; Billie Jo Haven; Tim Bookmiller.
Concey—Semi-Late—Bob Johnson; Walt Maley; Lacey Adams; Scott Bowsman.
Feature—Semi-Late—John Fitzpatrick; Jerry Baker; Steve Brown; Jerry Egolf.
Feature—Modified—Art Leiter; Ray Chambers; Tom Beezley; Roger Fry.
Sprint Feature—Louie Mann; Billie Jo Haven; Ron Miller; Jerry Priest.
Hobby Feature—Jerry Baker; Todd Grigsby; John Orr.

Saturday, May 31, 1975 - Rainout

Saturday, June 7, 1975
Warsaw Racing

A good-sized crowd watched 112 racers battle Saturday night's steamy summer weather at the Warsaw Speedway.

One of the highlights came when Chuck Copeland rolled his late model "29" three times in a vicious spill, but walked away from the wreck. In a season first, a demolition race was held with Todd Grigsby of Columbia City coming home first.

Race Results:
Late Model Dash Event: Arden Leiter; Larry Howard; Chuck Copeland; Ray Chambers.
Sprint Dash Event—Louie Mann, John Davis, Ron Miller, Mark Caldwell.
Late Model Slow—Bruce Hogue; Steve Backus; Tom Leiter; Joe Hock.
Sprint Slow—Chuck Mosley; Scott Keiser; Jerry DeHaven; Denny Garall.
Late Model Fast—Ray Chambers; Jim Bucher; Arden Leiter; Les Sroufe.
Sprint Fast—Ron Miller; John Davis; Jerry Priest; Don Rumfelt.

Bruce Hogue, Akron

Hobby Slow—John Orr; Walter Maley; Dave Foster; Tim Goshert.
Hobby Fast—Jerry Egolf; Jerry Pancock; John Fitzpatrick; Jerry Baker.
Late Model Feature—Arden Leiter; Ray Chambers; Jim Bucher; Les Sroufe.
Sprint Feature—Ron Miller; Paul Joyce; Louie Mann; John Davis.
Hobby Feature—Jerry Baker; Steve Brown; Tim Guy; Jerry Egolf.
Demolition Race—Todd Grigsby; Tim Leek.

Saturday, June 14, 1975 - Rainout

Saturday, June 21, 1975
Warsaw Racing

Sixty-three drivers braved some chilly weather Saturday night to qualify for races at the Warsaw Speedway. Arden Leiter supplied the biggest thrill of the night when he took a ride on about 100 feet of fence, repaired the car and won the late model feature.

For the second time in a row, John Davis in his new No. 3 sprint car served notice he will be a contender for the remainder of the season, winning the feature. The races are broadcast each Saturday night over WRSW.

Race Results:

Dash Event Late Model—Roger Frye; Art Leiter; Les Sroufe; Dan Backus.
Dash Event Sprints—Ron Miller; John Davis; Tim Bookmiller; Don Murphy.
Slow Late Model—Charles Hyde; Tom Leiter; Bruce Hogue; Sam Davis.
Slow Sprints—Bob Bernhard; Scott Keiser; Jene Simon; Mike Blake.
Fast Late Model—Bull Bradley; Roger Frye; Charles Prater; Dan Backus.
Fast Sprints—John Davis; Ron Miller; Tim Bookmiller; Denny Carol.
Slow Hobby Heat—Bob Johnson; Walt Rowland; Walt Maley; Kain.
Fast Hobby Heat—John Orr; Steve Brown; Todd Grigsby; Jim Guy.
Feature Late Model—Arden Leiter; Bruce Hogue; Denny Flaugh; Jim Bucher.
Sprint Feature—John Davis; Ron Miller; Louie Mann; Tim Bookmiller.
Hobby Feature—Jerry Baker; John Fitzpatrick; Terry Baker; Jim Guy.

Saturday, June 28, 1975 - No Results Published

Friday, July 4, 1975
Warsaw Racing

Jerry Baker, Jerry Priest and Arden Leiter were feature winners in the Warsaw Speedway's Fourth of July special Friday night. The evening was highlighted by a fireworks display, as 65 cars qualified for competition.

Jene Simon rolled his No. 47 sprint, but walked safely away to bring the crowd to its feet. Racing will continue tonight with 35-lap sprint and late model features.

Following are Friday's results:

Late Model—Ray Chambers; Jim Bucher; Les Sroufe; Arden Leiter.
Sprint—Ed Angle; John Davis; Rocky Fisher; Danny Johnson.
Hobby Dash—John Fitzpatrick; Dick Day; Steve Brown; Todd Grigsby.
1st Heat Late Model—Bruce Hogue; Larry Montel; Dave Kerlin; Bull Bradley.
2nd Heat Slow Sprint—Scott Keiser; Paul Joyce; Carl Miskotten; Bob Bernhard.
3rd Heat Late Model—Denny Flaugh; Ray Chambers; Bill Northcutt; Dan Backus.
4th Heat Fast Sprint—Ron Miller; Rocky Fisher; Jerry Priest; John Davis.
Slow Hobby Heat—John Orr; Walt Maley; Bob Chambers; Rex Hickman.
Fast Hobby Heat—John Fitzpatrick; Jerry Egolf; Steve Brown; Dick Day.
Late Model Feature—Arden Leiter; Ray Chambers; Bruce Hogue; Larry Montel.
Sprint Feature—Jerry Priest; Rocky Fisher; Ed Angle; John Davis.
Hobby Feature—Jerry Baker; Jerry Egolf; John Fitzpatrick; John Orr.

Saturday, July 5, 1975
Warsaw Racing

Ray Chambers, Rocky Fisher and Jerry Baker were feature winners at Warsaw Racing's regular late model, sprint and hobby competition Saturday night.

John Davis had led the 35-lap sprint feature for 16 laps before getting involved in a three-car accident that damaged his auto enough to force him out of the race. Also in the sprints, Dan Rumfelt, a "rookie", continued his fine showings by placing second.

Race Results:

Late Model Dash Event—Arden Leiter; Bruce Hogue; Roger Frye; Ray Chambers.
Sprints Dash Event—Rocky Fisher; Ed Angle; Don Rumfelt; Louie Mann.
Hobby Heat—Jerry Baker; Walt Maley; Jerry Egolf; Steve Brown.
Late Model Heat—Ray Harp; Ray Norman; Charles Hyde; Rick Knisely.
Sprints Slow—Scott Keiser; Denny Carroll; Carl Miskotten; Larry Howard.
Late Model Heat—Dan Backus; Jim Bucher; Denny Flaugh; Bruce Bradley.
Fast Sprints Heat—John Davis; Rocky Fisher; Billie Jo Haven; Jerry DeHaven.
Slow Hobby Heat—John Fitzpatrick; Lacey Adams; Walt Rowland; Bob Johnson.
Fast Hobby Heat—John Orr; Jerry Egolf; Jerry Baker; Bud Grossnickle.
Late Model Feature—Ray Chambers; Arden Leiter; Devon Rensberger; Tom Leiter.

Rocky Fisher with Jimmy, Tony, & Joni Elliott

Sprint Feature—Rocky Fisher; Jerry DeHaven; Ron Miller.
Hobby Feature—Jerry Baker; John Orr; Jerry Egolf; Steve Brown; Bob Chambers.

Saturday, July 12, 1975 - Rainout

Saturday, July 19, 1975 - Rainout

Saturday, July 26, 1975
Warsaw Racing

Ray Chambers, John Davis and Jerry Baker were feature winners at the Warsaw racing action Saturday night. Some 65 cars entered the competition.

A good crowd was on hand and came to its feet as Baker's Late Model No. 77 caught fire and he wheeled it into the infield. Baker bailed out in a hurry, putting out small blazes on his uniform, but was not injured.

Race Results:
Late Model Dash—Jim Bucher; Ray Chambers; Arden Leiter; Tom Beezley.
Sprint Dash—Rocky Fisher; Louie Mann; Scott Keiser; Ron Miller.
Hobby Dash—John Orr; Jerry Baker; Steve Brown; Todd Grigsby.
Slow Late Model No. 1—Larry Zaring; Tom Leiter; Rock Anders.
Slow Sprints—Don Rumfelt; Bob Bernhard; Denny Caroll; Tom Brewer.
Slow Heat Late Model No. 2—Roy Norman; Charles Hyde; Forest Knisely; Bull Bradley.
Late Model No. 3—Jim Bucher; Steve Backus; Arden Leiter; Tom Beezley.
Fast Sprints—Jerry Priest; Ron Miller; Rocky Fisher; Scott Keiser.
Slow Hobby Heat—Bob Johnson; Jerry Egolf; Dan Cope; Scott Dausman.
Fast Hobby Heat—John Orr; John Fitzpatrick; Walt Maley; Steve Brown.
Late Model Feature—Ray Chambers; Arden Leiter; Devon Rensberger; Tom Leiter.
Sprint Feature—John Davis; Rocky Fisher; Jerry DeHaven; Ron Miller.
Hobby Feature—Jerry Baker; Steve Brown; Jerry Egolf, Bob Chambers.

Saturday, August 2, 1975
Warsaw Racing

Saturday night's racing action at the Warsaw Speedway was halted after six heat races because of rain. The unfinished races will be completed Saturday, August 16.

During the Kosciusko County Fair this week, there will be racing on Wednesday and Saturday night. In Saturday's action, John Fredah was taken to the hospital after a three-car accident and was treated for bruises and lacerations.

Race Results:
Late Model—Tom Beezley; Jim Bucher; Arden Leiter; Roger Frye.
Sprint—Rocky Fisher; John Davis; Louie Mann; Jerry DeHaven.
Hobby—John Fitzpatrick; John Orr; Walt Maley; Steve Brown.
1st Heat Late Model—Larry Zaring; Charley Prater; Rock Anders; Denny Flaugh.
2nd Heat Slow Sprints—Don Rumfelt; Bob Bernhard; Jim Lipkey; Dennis Archer.
3rd Heat Late Model—Sam Davis; Charles Hyde; Tom Beezley; Arden Leiter.

Wednesday, August 6, 1975
A Hot Night Of Fair Racing

The evening may have been cool, but the action was hot as the Kosciusko County Fair patrons were entertained by a night of auto racing for the main grandstand attraction Wednesday.

Late model races and Hobby contests were featured and Rick Krisley in his No. 32 and Jerry Baker in No. 66 were winners in the two events. Baker also won the hobby dash event, edging out John Orr. Krisley was a heat winner prior to taking the main event.

Bob Johnson and John Fitzpatrick were other heat winners in the hobby races, while Bob Grindle and Roger Frye won late model heats.

Tonight's grandstand attraction will shift from the sporting scene slightly as a teen dance is scheduled at 8 p.m. Indiana Chariot Races are featured tomorrow.

Following are Wednesday's results:

Dash Event Semi-Late—Tom Beezley; Bruce Hogue; Ted Hudson.
Dash Event Hobby—Jerry Baker; John Orr; Steve Brown.
Semi-Late Heat 1—Bob Grindle; Sam Davis; Dan Backus; Roger Rowland.
Hobby Heat 2—Bob Johnson; Ray Norman; Charles Hyde.
Semi-Late Heat 2—Roger Frye; Ray Norman; Charles Hyde.
Hobby Heat 4—John Fitzpatrick; Terry Baker; Steve Brown.
Semi-Late Concy—Roger Rowland; Don Luckey.
Semi-Late Heat 3—Rick Knisely; Ray Chambers; Bruce Hogue.
Late Model Feature—Rick Knisely; Sam Davis; Bruce Hogue; Ray Chambers; Arden Leiter; Tom Beezley; Jim Bucher.
Hobby Feature—Jerry Baker; Walt Maley; John Orr; John Fitzpatrick; Jim Guy; Steve Brown; Walt Rowland.

Saturday, August 9, 1975
Fair Comes To End With Auto Racing

A week-long series of top notch Kosciusko County Fair grandstand features came to a close Saturday with local auto racing. A good-sized crowd watched 69 cars battle it out in semi-late, modified and hobby divisions. Ray Chambers, Rusty Perry and Jerry Egolf were winners in those respective classes. In the semi-late feature, 20 cars started, but only nine finished after several accidents on the wet fairgrounds quarter-mile track.

Next week's regular action will contain double features to make up for last week's rain-out. Besides auto racing, fairgrounds fans had a chance to see championship racing, auto thrill drivers and Indiana chariot racing this year.

Race Results:

Late Model Dash—Ray Chambers; Arden Leiter; Tom Beezley; Bruce Hogue.
Sprint Dash—Ron Miller; John Davis; Louie Mann; Don Rumfelt.
Late Model 1st Heat—Joe Rusoco; Steve Backus; Tom Leiter; Bob Grindle.
Modified 2nd Heat—Rusty Perry; Scott Keiser; Tom Brewer; Bob Bernhard.
Late Model 3rd Heat—Charley Prater; Roger Frye; Sam Davis; Ted Hudson.
Modified 4th Heat—Louie Mann; Don Rumfelt; John Davis; Jerry DeHaven.
4th Fastest Hobby—John Fitzpatrick; Todd Grigsby; John Orr; Jerry Baker.
Slow Hobby Heat—Tim Goshert; Jim Guy; Dan Cope; Gary Rayse.
Fast Hobby Heat—John Fitzpatrick; Bob Johnson; Jerry Egolf; Todd Grigsby.
Late Model Feature—Ray Chambers; Ted Hudson; Dan Backus; Tom Leiter; Bruce Hogue.
Modified Feature—Rusty Perry; Ron Miller; Jerry DeHaven; John Davis; Don Rumfelt.
Hobby Feature—Jerry Egolf; John Fitzgerald; Jerry Baker; Jim Guy; Bob Johnson.

Saturday, August 16, 1975
Warsaw Racing

Rusty Perry and Arden Leiter were the big heroes of Saturday night's action at the Warsaw Speedway, taking advantage of a rainout two weeks ago to win two feature races each. Perry took the modified feature in regular racing to go along with his sprints victory from the rainout. Leiter was victorious in both late model features.

John Davis caused a stir when he flipped his No. 3 and landed upside down on top of the cement wall. The car was demolished, but Davis walked away with a bruised arm. Next Saturday, a demolition race will be featured at the track.

Following are results from the two sets of races:

Late Model Dash—Ray Chambers; Ted Hudson; Arden Leiter; Bruce Hogue.
Sprint Dash—Rusty Perry; Ron Fisher; Chuck Mosley; John Davis.
Hobby Dash—John Fitzpatrick; Larry Baker; Jerry Egolf; Jerry Baker.
1st Heat Late Model—Ray Hare; Bob Grindle; Jim Bucher; John Orr.
2nd Heat Slow Sprint—Charlie Sarver; Rich Mickelson; Tom Brewer; Perry.
3rd Heat Late Model—Roger Frye; Ray Chambers; Sam Davis; Arden Leiter.
4th Heat Fast Sprints—Ron Fisher; John Davis; Rusty Perry; Louie Mann.
Late Model Feature—Arden Leiter; Bruce Hogue; Dan Backus; Ray Chambers; Sam Davis.
Modified Feature—Rusty Perry; Ron Fisher; Louie Mann; Chuck Mosley; Scott Keiser.
Slow Hobby—Bob Johnson; Ron Lucky; Rex Heckaman; Lacey Adams.
Fast Hobby—Tom Leiter; Jerry Egolf; Walter Maley; Don Prater.
Hobby Feature—John Fitzpatrick; Jerry Egolf; Jerry Baker; Tom Leiter; Walt Rowland.

Rain Out:

4th Heat Fast Sprints—Rusty Perry; Louie Mann; John Davis; Jerry DeHaven.
Slow Hobby Heat—Terry Baker; Jerry Egolf; Bob Johnson; Willard Sherman.
Fast Hobby Heat—Jerry Baker; John Fitzpatrick; Walt Rowland; John Orr.
Late Model Feature—Arden Leiter; Bruce Hogue; Ray Chambers; Jim Bucher; Jerry Rosenbrook.
Sprint Feature—Rusty Perry; Louie Mann; John Davis; Chuck Mosley; Don Rumfelt.

Hobby Feature—Jerry Egolf; John Orr; Terry Baker; Don Prater; Rex Heckaman.

Saturday, August 23, 1975
Warsaw Racing

Arden Leiter, Louie Mann and Tom Leiter endured a hot evening at the Warsaw Speedway quite well Saturday as they won feature races in late model, sprint, and hobby races respectively. Tom Leiter also won a slow hobby heat.

Bill Green flipped his No. 6 sprinter in an early sprint and was taken to Murphy Medical Center, where it was learned he might have serious back injuries. Next week's racing will feature the season championship with three 30-lap feature races.

Race Results:

Late Model Dash—Denny Flaugh; Ray Chambers; Arden Leiter; Steve Brown.
Modified Dash—Rocky Fisher; Don Rumfelt; Jerry Dehaven; Charlie Sarver.
Hobby Dash—Jerry Egolf; Steve Brown; John Fitzpatrick.
Late Model Slow Heat—Roy Norman; Tom Leiter; Rick Kalsley; Charley Prater.
Late Model Fast Heat—Charles Hyde; Jerry Rosenbrook; Roger Frye; Arden Leiter.
Modified Fast Heat—Rocky Fisher; Ron Miller; Louie Mann; Jerry Dehaven.
Hobby Slow Heat- Tom Leiter; Bob Johnson; Tim Goshert; Rex Heckaman.
Hobby Fast Heat – Jerry Baker, Steve Brown, Walt Rowland, Walt Maley
Late Model Feature – Arden Leiter, Ray Chambers, Denny Flaugh, Charles Hyde, Bruce Hogue
Sprint Feature – Louie Mann, Rocky Fisher, Jerry Dehaven, Don Rumfelt, Ron Miller
Hobby Feature – Tom Leiter, Jerry Baker, Steve Brown, Don Prater, Walt Maley
Demolition Derby – Jim Glassburn, D.L. Ericson, Lonny Cripe

Saturday, August 30, 1975 - Rainout

Saturday, September 6, 1975
Warsaw Racers Finish Season

Arden Leiter, Ron Miller and Jerry Baker completed rather successful seasons of auto racing at the Warsaw Speedway by winning championships in the semi-late, modified and hobby features Saturday night. Leiter also won the semi-late dash event.

Arden Leiter, Warsaw and John Crum

Race Results:

Late Model Dash—Arden Leiter; Ted Hudson; Sam Davis; Larry Montel.
Modified Dash—Don Rumfelt; Rocky Fisher; Don Murphy; Ron Miller.
Hobby 6 Fastest—Walt Rowland; Don Prater; Jerry Egolf; Jerry Baker.
Late Model Slow Heat – Ray Norman; Luckey Luckey; Tom Leiter; Charles Shaw.

Modified Slow Heat – Scott Keiser; Tom Brewer; Walt May; Ron Edington.
Late Model Fast Heat – Dan Backus; Charles Hyde; rick Knisely; Larry Montel.
Modified Fast Heat – Rocky Fisher; Don Rumfelt; Ron Miller; Louie Mann.
Hobby Slow Heat – George Sitts; Bob Johnson; Mark Murray; Ron Lucky.
Hobby Fast Heat – Jerry Baker; Jerry Egolf; John Fitzpatrick; Don Prater.
Semi-Late Season Championship - Arden Leiter (87); Bruce Hogue (25); Jim Bucher (2); Larry Montel (24); Charley Prater (01); Charles Hyde (65).
Modified Season Championship - Ron Miller (68); Louie Mann (14); Rocky Fisher (16); Don Rumfelt (77); Scott Keiser (79); Tom Brewer (81).
Hobby Season Championship - Jerry Baker (66); Jerry Egolf (48); John Fitzpatrick (57); George Sitts (26); Don Prater (46); Bob Johnson (22).

1976

Saturday, May 15, 1976 - Rainout

Saturday, May 22, 1976
Warsaw Racing

Late Model Feature—Arden Leiter; Les Sroufe; Jerry Baker; Dan Backus; Steve Backus; Paul Roberts; Roger Frye; Ted Hudson; Garry Baker; Charles Shall.

Sprint Feature—Ron Miller; Rocky Fisher; Louis Mann; Paul Joyce; Fred Possman; Don Murphy; Scott Keiser; Rod Garn; Jim Lipkey; Denzil Archer.

Hobby Feature—John Fitzpatrick; John Orr; Dave Stevens; Jerry Baker; Tom Leiter; Terry Baker; Bob Johnson; Walt Rowland; Lacie Adams; John Higgenbotham.

Saturday, May 29, 1976
Leiter Wins Two In Warsaw Racing

Arden Leiter captured two firsts in races at the Warsaw Speedway Saturday night, as he won both the semi-late heats and the late model event. Other winners were Rocky Fisher; Paul Roberts; Jerry Priest; Louie Mann; Don Prater; and Dick Day.

Rain prevented completion of three features, and they will be added to the regular card of racing next Saturday.

Race Results:
Semi-Late Heat—Arden Leiter; Bruce Hogue; Dan Backus; Jim Bucher.
Modified—Rocky Fisher; Ron Miller; Louie Mann; Don Fisher.
Slow-Late Model—Paul Roberts; Ray Chambers; Rocky Anders; Rod Bailey.

Slow Sprints—Jerry Priest; Richard Jackson; Jesse Hamm; Denzil Archer.
Fast-Late Model—Arden Leiter; Tom Leiter; Jerry Baker; Steve Backus.
Fast Sprints—Louie Mann; Ron Miller; Jim Lipkey; Don Murphy.
Slow Hobby—Don Prater; Lacie Adams; Rex Heckaman; Tom Danner.
Fast Hobby—Dick Day; Tom Leiter; Terry Baker; Jerry Baker.

Saturday, June 5, 1976
Full Card At Local Speedway

A good crowd at the Warsaw Speedway saw 60 cars compete in both the makeup of the May 29 races and the regular running of the Saturday schedule.

In one of the sprint heats Louie Mann crashed into the wall, jarring loose a huge chunk of concrete and causing a great deal of damage to the sprint, but no injury was reported.

Louie Mann

Race Results:

Late Model Dash Event: Rod Bailey; Bruce Hogue; Dan Backus; Ray Chambers.
Sprint Dash Event: Ron Miller; Don Fisher; Darrell Wines; Don Rumfell.
Slow Late Model—Art Leiter; Roger Frye; Larry Howard; Carl Sherman.
Slow Sprints—Bob Bernhard; Billy Joe Havens; Scott Keiser; Denzil Archer.
Fast Late Model—Les Sroufe; Jerry Baker; Bruce Hogue; Ray Chambers.
Fast Sprints—Ron Miller; Jerry Priest; Don Fisher; Rocky Fisher.
Slow Hobby—John Higginbotham; Walt Rowland; Sam Barrett; Larry Sheetz.
Fast Hobby—Jerry Baker; Dave Stevens; Lacie Adams; Don Prater.
Late Model Feature—Bruce Hogue; Art Leiter; Les Sroufe; Dan Backus; Larry Howard.
Sprints Feature—Jerry Priest; Ron Miller; Scott Keiser; Bob Bernhard; Jesse Hamm.
Hobby Feature—Jerry Baker; John Fitzpatrick; Dave Stevens; Lacie Adams; Terry Baker.

May 29 Makeup Races:

Late Model—Art Leiter; Bruce Hogue; Les Sroufe; Ray Chambers; Garry Baker.
Sprint—Rocky Fisher; Ron Miller; Jerry Priest; Denzil Archer; Jim Lipkey.
Hobby—Jerry Baker; John Fitzpatrick; Terry Baker; Walt Rowland; John Higginbotham.

Saturday, June 12, 1976
Warsaw Racing

In what was described as a wild, exciting evening, Louie Mann, Terry Baker and Bruce Hogue won respective sprint, hobby and late model features at the Warsaw Speedway Saturday evening. John Higginbotham, driving the No. 23 hobby car, caused a lot of "oos and ahs" when his car jumped up on the retaining wall. Fortunately, he was not injured.

For Mann, it was a pretty good evening as he also finished first in a sprint heat race.

Race Results:

Late Model Dash—Les Sroufe; Jim Bucher; Arden Leiter; Bruce Hogue.
Sprint Dash—Ron Miller; Rocky Fisher; Don Rumfelt; Paul Joyce.
Slow Late Model—Rod Bailey; Rocky Anders; Roger Frye; Willard Sherman.
Slow Sprint—Louie Mann; Bob Bernhard; Fred Possman; Bob Shaw.
Fast Late Model—Jim Bucher; Jerry Baker; Dan Backus; Les Sroufe.
Fast Sprint—Paul Joyce; Rocky Fisher; Ron Miller; Billy Joe Havens.
Slow Hobby—Terry Baker; John Higginbotham; Walt Rowland; Gene Floor.
Fast Hobby—Don Prater; John Orr; Dave Stevens; John Fitzpatrick.
Late Model Feature—Bruce Hogue; Roger Frye; Garry Baker; Willard Sherman; Denny Flaugh.
Sprint Feature—Louie Mann; Jerry Priest; Rocky Fisher; Paul Joyce; Bobby Shaw.
Hobby Feature—Terry Baker; John Fitzpatrick; Jerry Baker; Dave Stevens; Walt Rowland.

Saturday, June 19, 1976
Warsaw Racing

A large crowd saw some excellent racing at the Warsaw Speedway Saturday night as Les Sroufe, Ron Miller and Terry Baker won late model, sprint and hobby features respectively, while David Ericson beat out 64 other drivers in a "Demolition Derby". It was an exciting night all together and in one 10 lap race, the lead changed hands five times.

Race Results:

Late Model Dash—Les Sroufe; Arden Leiter; Bruce Hogue, Steve Backus.
Sprint Dash—Rocky Fisher; Paul Joyce; Ron Miller; Ron Fisher.
Slow Late Model—Roger Frye; Larry Howard; Jerry Egolf; Bob Forsyth.
Slow Sprint—Bob Shaw; Steve Ball; Jerry Priest; Bob Bernhard.
Fast Late-Model—Les Sroufe; Bruce Hogue; Arden Leiter; Rod Bailey.
Fast Sprint—Don Rumfelt; Ron Miller; Paul Joyce; Louie Mann.

Slow Hobby—Lacie Adams; Bob Johnson; Clyde Gregory; John Higgenbotham.
Fast Hobby—Terry Baker; John Fitzpatrick; Jerry Baker; Gene Floor.
Late Model Feature—Les Sroufe; Art Leiter; Bruce Hogue; Garry Baker; Paul Roberts.
Sprint Feature—Ron Miller; Louie Mann; Scott Keiser; Rocky Fisher; Paul Joyce.
Demolition—David Ericson; Bernie Smith.

Saturday, June 26, 1976
Warsaw Racing

It was a hot night in Warsaw and it was a hot night for racing at the Warsaw Speedway as a good-sized crowd watched 61 cars compete. In the entrants were two sprints all the way from Truman, Ark., driven by Jack and Cliff McCoy.

Jim Bucher, Louie Mann and John Orr were feature winners in the late model, sprint and hobby classes.

Race Results:

Late Model Dash—Ted Hudson; Jim Bucher; Bob Forsythe; Bruce Hogue.
Sprint Dash—Don Fisher; Paul Joyce; John Davis; Tom Beezley.
Slow Late Model—Ed Martin; Glenn Bradley; Paul Roberts; Kenny Leiter.
Slow Sprint—Scott Keiser; Jack McCoy; Jim Lipkey; Bob Bernhard.
Fast Late Model—Charley Hyde; Les Sroufe; Dan Backus; Ted Hudson.
Fast Sprint—John Davis; Louie Mann; Bobby Shaw; Paul Joyce.
Slow Hobby—Bob Johnson; Jim Lee; Walt Rowland; Rex Heckaman.
Fast Hobby—Lacie Adams; John Orr; Jerry Baker; John Fitzpatrick.
Late Model Feature—Jim Bucher; Ted Hudson; Paul Robert; Bull Bradley; Kenny Leiter.
Sprint Feature—Louis Mann; Scott Keiser; Paul Joyce; Don Rumfelt; Don Fisher.
Hobby Feature—John Orr; Lacie Adams; Jerry Baker; Terry Baker; John Fitzpatrick.

Saturday, July 3, 1976
Warsaw Racing

Jerry Priest, Louie Mann, Ron Miller & Hoot Gibson

Fireworks and automobile racing provided a great combination for an excellent crowd at the Warsaw Speedway Saturday night.

Louie Mann, Bruce Hogue and Lacie Adams also had their combinations right as the trio won sprint, late model and hobby features respectively. For Hogue, there was a big assist in his victory. Kenny Leiter led the 50-lap late model feature for 49 ½ laps before spinning and losing the lead. He still finished sixth though.

Race Results:

Late Model Dash—Jerry Baker; Larry Howard; Dan Backus; Bruce Hogue.
Sprint Dash—Ron Miller; Jerry Priest; Paul Joyce; Dan Rumfelt.
Slow Late Model—Kenny Leiter; Jim Sellers; Charles Hyde; Glenn Bradley.
Slow Sprint—Richard Jackson; Bob Bernhard; Ron Smelka; Scott Keiser.
Fast Late Model—Tom Leiter; Paul Roberts; Bruce Hogue; Jerry Baker.
Fast Sprint—Ron Miller; Bobby Shaw; Tony Ploughe; Jerry Priest.
Slow Hobby—Gene Floor; Bob Johnson; Tom Danner; Paul Sherman.
Fast Hobby—Terry Baker; Lacie Adams; Jerry Baker; John Orr.
Sprint Feature—Louie Mann; Ron Miller; Jerry Priest; Paul Joyce; Ron Smelka.
Late-Model Feature—Bruce Hogue; Jerry Baker; Roger Frye; Paul Roberts; Tom Leiter.
Hobby Feature—Lacie Adams; Terry Baker; John Orr; Jerry Baker; Rex Heckaman.

Saturday, July 10, 1976 – No Results Published

Saturday, July 17, 1976 – No Results Published

Saturday, July 24, 1976
Warsaw Racing

Exciting racing and a good crowd at the Warsaw Speedway Saturday night saw the trio of Larry Howard, Louie Mann and John Fitzpatrick win the late model, sprint and hobby features respectively.

Race Results:

Late Model Dash—Paul Roberts; Bull Bradley; Larry Howard; Ted Hudson.
Sprint Dash—Richard Jackson; Bobby Shaw; Jerry Priest; Don Rumfelt.
Slow Late Model—Willard Sherman; Tom Leiter; Glenn Bradley; Roger Frye.
Slow Sprints—Paul Joyce; Scott Keiser; Steve Alexander; Bob Bernhard.
Fast-Late Model—Charles Hyde; Les Sroufe; Steve Backus; Paul Roberts.
Fast Sprints—Bobby Shaw; Jerry Priest; Larry Shellenbarger; Don Rumfelt.
Slow Hobby—Lacie Adams; Bob Johnson; Tom Beezley; Jon Trerley.
Fast Hobby—Terry Baker; Jerry Baker; John Orr; Rick Hoover.
Late-Model Feature—Larry Howard; Ted Hudson; Kenny Leiter; Garry Baker.
Sprint Feature—Louie Mann; Bobby Shaw; Scott Keiser; Larry Shellenberger.
Hobby Feature—John Fitzpatrick; John Orr; Sam Barrett; Walt Rowland.

Saturday, July 31, 1976
Warsaw Racing

Jim Bucher, Terry Baker and Don Rumfelt all managed to repeat in feature races what they had done in heats—come out in first place during the regular night of racing at the Warsaw Speedway Saturday.

Bucher, in his No. 2 late model, won one heat, came in third in another and then won the feature. Baker took a hobby heat and that respective feature and Rumfelt won a sprint preview, placed fourth in another before winning the feature.

In conjunction with the Kosciusko County Fair, there will be two nights of racing this weekend, Friday and Saturday. Racing both nights will begin at 8:p.m. and trials at 6:30.

Race Results:

Late Model Dash—Jim Bucher; Jerry Baker; Willard Sherman; Les Sroufe.
Sprint Dash—Scott Keiser; Louie Mann; Don Rumfelt; Ron Miller.
Slow Late Model—Ray Chambers; Bruce Hogue; Kenny Leiter; Jerry Egolf.
Slow Sprint—Louie Mann; Ron Miller; Scott Keiser; Don Rumfelt.
Fast Late Model—Denny Flaugh; Terry Baker; Jim Bucher; Steve Backus.
Fast Sprint—Don Rumfelt; Jerry Priest; Don Walker; Bob Bernhard.
Slow Hobby—John Fitzpatrick; William Varney; John Higgenbotham; Gene Floor.
Fast Hobby—Terry Baker; Jerry Baker; John Orr; Tom Barrett.
Late Model Feature—Jim Bucher; Ted Hudson; Bruce Hogue; Kenny Leiter.
Sprint Feature—Don Rumfelt; Jerry Priest; Scott Keiser; Ron Miller.
Hobby Feature—Terry Baker; Jerry Baker; John Orr; Lacie Adams.

Saturday, August 7, 1976
Fair Racing On Tonight After Friday Cancellation

The first night of auto racing action at the Kosciusko County Fair was called off Friday evening, but that's not going to stop promoters from putting on a show tonight. In capping off grandstand events at the fair, time trials will begin at 6:30 p.m. and racing at 8 p.m.

At 3:30 Friday afternoon, there were six-foot puddles all over the track, forcing organizers to cancel the racing. By the time the green flag was to have dropped, many of the puddles had disappeared, but it was still too wet to insure safe competition.

All the regular events scheduled for Friday will not be made up, except for a special "Powder Puff Derby". Twenty-two women—most of them with no racing experience—had submitted entries for the race and will be a part of tonight's card. It will also include sprint, hobby and late model racing.

Saturday, August 7, 1976
Auto Racing Caps Sports at the Fair

Being last among the sporting events at the Kosciusko County Fair certainly didn't mean Saturday's auto racing was last in excitement. Played before a near full house at the Speedway, the three feature races, eight preliminaries, and powder puff derby offered plenty of action for those in attendance.

Sprint car driver Rocky Fisher stole the show in his No. 6 machine, winning the dash event heat, the fast heat and then capping it off by taking the 50-lap feature. Bruce Hogue in the No. 25 late model won his feature, though the best he could finish in a heat was second, while Jerry Baker was the hobby feature winner after taking third in the slow late model heat, but failing to place in the top four in hobby heat competition.

In the powder puff race, Mrs. John Fitzpatrick took over her husband's No. 57 hobby stock machine and drove it to victory over 27 other competitors.

The crowd came to its feet during the warmup period when Charlie Sarver of Kokomo had a rather hot ride in his No.76 sprint. The car caught fire and Charlie was forced to bail out, escaping injury, but receiving a pretty close call as fire engulfed the cockpit area very quickly.

Then in a heat race, Syracuse's Don Rumfelt was shaken up but not seriously injured when his No. 77 sprinter was involved in a collision.

Rocky Fisher, Ft. Wayne

Two new sprinters made their debut in Warsaw. Terry Baer of Sandusky, Ohio and Norm Myers of Deshler, Ohio. Myers finished second in the feature in his No. 12 machine.

Race Results:
Late Model Dash Event—Paul Roberts; Larry Howard; Roger Rowland; Tom Beezley.
Sprint Dash Event—Rocky Fisher; Jerry Priest; Norm Myers; Ron Miller.
Late Model Slow Heat—Willard Sherman; Tom Leiter; Jerry Baker; Dan Backus.
Sprint Slow Heat—Paul Joyce; Scott Keiser; Fred Possman; Jeff Walker.
Late Model Fast Heat—Denny Floyd; Bruce Hogue; Dave Evers; Larry Howard.
Sprint Fast Heat—Rocky Fisher; Jerry Priest; Don Rumfelt; Ron Miller.
Slow Hobby Heat—Sam Cooper; Tom Danner; John Marley; Matt Warren.
Fast Hobby Heat—Lacie Adams; John Fitzpatrick; Walt Rowland; Steve Brown.
Late Model Feature—Bruce Hogue; Larry Howard; Tom Beezley; Ray Chambers; Bull Bradley; Steve Backus; Dave Evers; Mere Shank.
Sprint Feature—Rocky Fisher; Norm Myers; Ron Miller; Paul Joyce; Scott Keiser; Jerry Priest; Terry Baer; Tom Possman.
Hobby Feature—Jerry Baker; Steve Brown; John Fitzpatrick; Terry Baker; Walt Rowland; Lacie Adams; Don Prater; Lori Liez.
Powder Puff—Mrs. John Fitzpatrick; Shelly Pickett; Cris Baker

Saturday, August 14, 1976 – No Results Published

Thursday, August 19, 1976
Speedway Celebrates 26th Anniversary

The Warsaw Speedway will celebrate its 26th year Saturday night with one of the largest and most spectacular fireworks displays ever witnessed at the Kosciusko County

Fairgrounds track.

There will be at least 12 ground pieces, plus a large and beautiful aerial display. All that will be combined with 11 racing events, including a pair of 50-lap features. Rainout will be the following Saturday, August 28.

Saturday, August 21, 1976
Fireworks, Top Racing at Speedway

Saturday night was the 26th anniversary of the Warsaw Speedway and for several drivers it was brought in with a bang—literally. One of the best fireworks displays ever in the Warsaw area had the fans ooing and ahhing all through the 45 minute program.

In the racing portion, some 57 cars thrilled the large crowd to top-notch racing. When it was all over, sprint driver Rocky Fisher repeated his excellent performance of the Kosciusko County Fair, winning two heats and the 25-lap feature. Ted Hudson won the 50-lap late model feature, while John Orr steered his No. 88 to first place in the 50-lap hobby feature.

Lora Lee Sherman, Albion, IN

Race Results:
Late Model Dash—Steve Baker; Ted Hudson; Jerry Baker; Jim Bucher.
Sprint Dash—Rocky Fisher; Jerry Priest; Don Rumfelt; Richard Jackson.
Slow Late Model—Garry Baker; Terry Baker; Chuck Saner; Roger Frye.
Slow Sprint—Joe Perry; Denzil Archer; Jesse Haman; John Davis.
Fast Late Model—Bruce Hogue; Willard Sherman; Rocky Anders; Jerry Baker.
Fast Sprint—Rocky Fisher; Louie Mann; Ron Miller; Don Rumfelt.
Slow Hobby—Don Prater; Bob Johnson; Steve Nightie; Rex Heckaman.
Fast Hobby—Lora Lee Sherman; Ray Brozok; Jerry Baker; John Orr.
Late Model Feature—Ted Hudson; Bruce Hogue; Jim Bucher; Chuck Saner.
Sprint Feature—Rocky Fisher; Ron Miller; Louie Mann; Jerry Priest.
Hobby Feature—John Orr; Terry Baker; Lora Lee Sherman; Dave Stevens.

Saturday, August 28, 1976
Racing Season Ends at Speedway

It was a cool night, but there was plenty of hot racing as yet another year of racing came to an end at the Warsaw Speedway Saturday evening.

Ron Miller in his No. 68 sprint capped off a successful season by beating six other cars in the sprint feature to win the overall season point standings with 164 points, thus taking home two trophies. Meanwhile, Lacie Adams (41) took the hobby feature and Larry

Howard (2) won the late model feature after taking an earlier heat race.

In the final point distribution, owner/driver Kenny Leiter scored 132 points to edge by Jim Bucher's 127 and win the late model division and Terry Baker managed 558 points, compared to John Orr's 521 for the hobby stock crown.

Race Results:

Late Model Dash—Chuck Saner; Larry Howard; Jerry Egolf; Sam Davis.
Sprint Dash—John Davis; Bobby Shaw; Richard Jackson; Louie Mann.
Hobby Dash—Terry Baker; Lacie Adams; John Orr; Rick Hoover.
Slow Late Model—Larry Howard; Charles Hyde; Willard Sherman; Roger Frye.
Slow Sprint—Louie Mann; Ron Miller; Don Rumfelt; Richard Jackson.
Fast Late Model—Steve Backus; Chuck Saner; Ted Hudson; Rocky Anders.
Slow Hobby—Don Prater; John Higgenbotham; Sam Cooper; Larry Sheets.
Fast Hobby—Dave Stevens; John Orr; Gene Floor; Lacie Adams
Late Model Feature – Larry Howard, Chuck Sainer, Charles Hyde, Steve Backus, Willard Sherman, Roger Frye, Jim Sellers, Dee Frye.
Sprint Feature – Ron Miller, John Davis, Louie Mann, Bobby Shaw, Don Rumfelt, Richard Jackson, Ron Green.
Hobby Feature- Lacie Adams, John Orr, Walt Rowland, Dave Stevens, Rick Hoover, Don Prater, Ron Brozoski, Tom Danner.

Lacie Adams, Warsaw

1977

Saturday, May 14, 1977
Season Opens at Warsaw Speedway

Tom Mislich from O'Dell, Ill, served notice he will be a top sprint car racer this season to highlight the opening night of action at the Warsaw Speedway Saturday. Mislich, whose previous experience was in USAC midgets, was competing in a sprint car for the first time and wound up with a victory in both a heat race and feature.

Veteran racers John Fitzpatrick and Ray Chambers showed their status by winning respective hobby and late model features. Jim Bucher won a pair of late model heats, but could do no better than eighth in the feature. Forty cars qualified for the evening's competition. Action will continue next Saturday.

Race Results:

Late Model Dash—Jim Bucher; Ray Chambers; Rock Anders; Les Sroufe.
Sprint Dash—Tom Mislich; Ron Miller; Richard Jackson; Denzil Archer.

Slow Late Model—Terry Baker; Bull Bradley; Jerry Egolf; Roger Harger.
Fast Late Model—Jim Bucher; Willard Sherman; Roger Frye.
Slow Hobby—Scott Dausman; Bob Johnson; Dave Stafford; Tom Danner.
Fast Hobby—Dick Day; Lacie Adams; John Fitzpatrick; Walt Rowland.
Hobby Feature—John Fitzpatrick; Walt Rowland; Dick Day; Lacie Adams.
Late Model Feature—Ray Chambers; Les Sroufe; Charley Prater; Willard Sherman.
Sprint Feature—Tom Mislich; Richard Jackson; Ron Miller; Don Rumfelt.

Saturday, May 21, 1977 - Rainout

Saturday, May 28, 1977
Warsaw Racing

The tragic heart attach death of Lacie Adams marred what would have been an evening of top racing at the Warsaw Speedway last Saturday.

Adams had a heart attack while taking his victory lap after winning the Hobby Stock feature. Earlier, Roger Frye was the other feature winner by driving his No. 6 to victory in the late model action.

Race Results:

Late Model Dash—Jim Bucher; Roger Frye; Ray Chambers; Willard Sherman.
Sprint Dash—Tom Mislich; Denzil Archer; Chuck Monett; Charlie Sarver.
Slow Late Model—Bill Bradley; Terry Baker; Dee Frye.
Slow Sprint—Tom Mislich; Denzil Archer; Chuck Magnett; Charlie Sarver.
Fast Late Model—Roger Frye; Charlie Hyde; Jim Taylor.
Slow Hobby—Jeff Bucher; Don Prater; Arnold Prater; Scott Dausman.
Fast Hobby—John Orr; Paul Sherman; John Fitzpatrick; Bob Johnson.
Late Model Feature—Roger Frye; Ray Chambers; Charley Hyde; Willard Sherman.
Hobby Feature—Lacie Adams; John Fitzpatrick; Gary Baker; Jeff Bucher.

Tuesday, May 31, 1977
Tragedies Mar Holiday For Families of Three.
Times Union, Page 1. (Story edited to only list portion related to the Speedway).

Lacie Adams, 36, of Warsaw, suffered a fatal heart attack while driving his race car on a parade lap following a victory in the hobby stock feature at the Warsaw Speedway Saturday night.

Adams was taking his victory lap around the Warsaw Speedway at the fairgrounds Saturday night when he died of a heart attack and his racer crashed into the (3rd turn) wall in front of spectators.

The driver died of a massive coronary, according to County Coroner Wyman. The race driver was traveling around the track in his hobby-stock car in front of cheering spectators and died before his car crashed into the wall, according to authorities.

Author's Note: This was one of those "I'll never forget" moments! I was in 7th grade sitting up on the 1st turn hill with Troy Martin, our dads were working the ambulance. I can still picture the car running straight into the 3rd turn wall and Lacie dropping the flag on the track. Needless to say, our dads rushed to Lacie, then to the hospital and we were stranded at the track. I called my mom and she came and picked us up, drove up to the hospital where we found out he had passed. It was such a sad night, and yet Lacie won, in more ways than one. The Times Union doesn't record any results for the next Saturday night, June 4. I don't remember if it rained, if we didn't race because of Lacie's death, or just if no results were turned in. If anyone remembers, please let me know.

Saturday, June 4, 1977 – No Results

Saturday, June 11, 1977
Rain Postpones Warsaw Racing

Racing at the Warsaw Speedway never quite got off the ground Saturday night because of a very soggy track so all tickets will be honored this next Saturday. There will be a couple of new wrinkles for spectators and drivers, beginning this week. A "demolition derby" will highlight the night and there will also be a new category added to the regular racing card, street stocks. It adds another class to local racing and provides the opportunity for the new driver to get started in racing at a very low cost.

Saturday, June 18, 1977
Warsaw Racing

One of the biggest crowds of the season witnessed one of the best nights of racing at the Warsaw Speedway this past Saturday.

Excellent competition—especially in the late model division—proved quite exciting to the fans. A demolition derby highlighted the evening as Bernie Smith won and Clarence Adkins was second. The Speedway announced it annual fireworks night is set for July 2 with July 4 as a rain date.

Following are Saturday's results:
Late Model Dash—Jim Bucher; Jim Taylor; Bruce Hogue; Terry Baker.
Hobby Dash—Tom Leiter; Steve Brown; John Orr; Walt Rowland.
Slow Late Model—Willard Sherman; Sam Davis; Terry Sroufe; Charley Prater.
Slow Hobby—Bob Johnson; Gary Baker; Dave Stafford; Tom Danner.
Fast Late Model—Steve Backus; Roger Frye; Chuck Saner; Charles Hyde.
Fast Hobby—John Orr; Jim Springer; Arnold Prater; Tom Leiter.
Street Road Runners—Todd Grigsby; Walt Maley; Paul Sherman.
Late Model Feature—Dave Erickson; Rick Hare; Dave Bouse.
Late Model Feature—Ray Chambers; Willard Sherman; Bruce Hogue; Denny Flaugh.
Hobby Feature—Tom Leiter; John Orr; Steve Brown, Walt Rowland.

Saturday, June 25, 1977
Warsaw Racing

Warm temperatures and exciting racing greeted crowds at the Warsaw Speedway Saturday night. The evening was highlighted by wheel-to-wheel duels in Late Model action between Jim Bucher and Ray Chambers.

Late Model Dash—Ray Chambers; Jim Bucher; Dan Backus; Denny Flaugh.
Hobby Dash—Walt Rowland; Jeff Bucher; John Orr; Tom Leiter.
Slow Late Model—Jerry Baker; Terry Sroufe; Willard Sherman; Bruce Hogue.
Slow Hobby—Dan Prater; Jim Springer; Thames Goon; Sam Barrett.
Fast Late Model—Charles Saner; Jim Bucher; Dan Backus; Les Sroufe.
Fast Hobby—John Orr; Bob Johnson; Tom Leiter; Jeff Bucher.
Street Stock Heat—Terry Baker; Dave Ericson; Tony Elliott; Ben Fitzpatrick.
Late Model Feature—Ray Chambers; Dan Backus; Jim Bucher; Bull Bradley.
Hobby Feature—John Orr; Steve Brown; Tom Leiter; Dean Baker.
Street Stock Feature—Walt Maley; Dave Ericson; Rick Allen; Terry Baker.

Saturday, July 2, 1977
Warsaw Racing

The annual Fourth of July fireworks display at the Warsaw Speedway Saturday evening was as exciting as ever and the good-sized crowd in attendance got some fireworks on the race track, too. Dan Backus, John Orr and Rock Anders were respective feature winners in the late model, hobby and street stock divisions.

Les Sroufe in his No. 11 late model car was the bad luck driver of the night. His car caught fire three different times as the feature was being started before he finally had to head toward the pits.

Late Model Dash—Chuck Saner; Ted Hudson; Roger Frye; Jim Bucher.
Hobby Dash—Jeff Bucher; Steve Brown; Tom Leiter; John Orr.
Slow Late Model—Jerry Baker; Roger Harger; Dave Kerlin; Bull Bradley.
Slow Hobby—Larry Thacker; Sam Barrett; Dave Stafford.
Fast Late Model—Jim Bucher; Les Sroufe; Rod Bailey; Ted Hudson.
Fast Hobby—Bob Johnson; Jeff Bucher; Steve Brown.
Slow Street Stock—Bill Carr; Ron Alexander; Joe Pickens; Dean Green.
Fast Street Stock—Paul Sherman; Rock Anders; Duane Parker; Mark Coleman.
Late Model Feature—Dan Backus; Tom Leiter; Danny Flaugh; Jerry Baker.
Hobby Feature—John Orr; Walt Rowland; Tom Leiter; Jeff Bucher.
Street Stock Feature—Rock Anders.

Saturday, July 9, 1977
Warsaw Racing

The excitement was evident Saturday evening at the Warsaw Speedway as several races weren't decided until the checkered flag was dropped. An enthusiastic crowd stood and cheered as 61 drivers competed for honors in the stock and hobby races.

Tony Elliott, Warsaw

John Orr captured first place in the hobby feature and fast hobby while Tony Elliott raced away with the street stock feature. Other winners were Jim Bucher in the modified feature and semi-dash event; his son Jeff in the slow hobby; Tom Leiter in the semi-fast heat and the second fast hobby race; Jerry Baker in the semi-slow heat; and Dick Acagy and Dave Ericson in the street stocks.

Several father and sons were entered in the race competition. Jim Bucher (from Akron) not only had his Jeff in the events, but also his other son Jim Jr., Roger Frye and his son Dee from Columbia City, and Les Sroufe and son Terry from Huntington were other father-son racing teams.

Race Results:
Late Model Dash—Jim Bucher; Les Sroufe; Larry Howard; Terry Sroufe.
Hobby Dash—John Orr; Steve Brown; Tom Leiter; Walt Rowland.
Slow Late Model—Jerry Baker; Bull Bradley; Jim Sellers; Bill Long.
Slow Hobby—Jeff Bucher; Bob Johnson; Rex Heckaman; Tom Danner.
Fast Late Model—Tom Leiter; Dave Kerlin; Larry Howard; Terry Sroufe.
Fast Hobby—Tom Leiter; Larry Thacker; John Orr; Dave Stafford.
Street Stock—Dick Acagy; Duane Parker; Mark Coleman; Rock Anders.
Street Stock—Dave Ericson; Arnold Prater; Paul Sherman; Joe Pickens.
Late Model Feature—Jim Bucher; Dave Kerlin; Bull Bradley; Roger Frye.
Hobby Feature—John Orr; Bob Johnson; Dave Stafford; Tom Danner.
Street Stock Feature—Tony Elliott; Rock Anders; Paul Sherman; Joe Pickens.

Saturday, July 16, 1977
Warsaw Racing

A good crowd and a warm night greeted 75 racers for an exciting night of racing Saturday at the Warsaw Speedway. Chuck Sainer (No. 8) was leading the late model feature by 20 laps when he developed engine trouble and failed to finish. In another race Tom Leiter (No. 70) spun and hit a huge pole holding a bank of lights. No injuries resulted, but the collision knocked out the lights and caused the remainder of the races to be continued in semi-darkness.

Results:
Late Model Dash—Ray Chambers; Dan Backus; Roger Frye; Denny Flaugh.
Hobby Dash—John Orr; Dean Baker; Dave Stevens.
Slow Late Model—Ron Bailey; Bull Bradley; Terry Sroufe; Tommy Leiter.
Slow Hobby—Walt Rowland; Sonny Hyde; Larry Thacker; Arnold Prater.
Fast Late Model—Chuck Saner; Dave Ellis; Ray Chambers; Charley Prater.
Fast Hobby—Tommy Leiter; Don Prater; Jeff Bucher; Ben Johnson.
Hobby Feature—Dean Baker; Tommy Leiter; Bob Johnson; Walt Rowland.
Late Model Feature—Dan Backus; Ray Chambers; Jim Bucher; Roger Frye.
Street Stock Feature—Dave Erickson; Dean Baker; Bob Grindle.
Slow Street Stock—Bob Johnson; Tony Elliott; Bob Grindle.
Fast Street Stock—Dave Erickson; Rod England; Joe Puckett.

Dan Backus, Warsaw

Saturday, July 23, 1977
Warsaw Racing

The rate of attrition was high during an exciting evening of racing Saturday evening at the Warsaw Speedway. Cars lost wheels and smashed into each other quite often in the events, as witnessed the 20 car late-model feature in which only four of the 20 cars which started actually finished the race.

Probably the highlight race was the late-feature where Bull Bradley (No. 22) led for 24 1/2 laps only to spin out, making the way for Steve Backus to take over the lead and win.

Results:

Late Model Dash—Ray Chambers; Denny Flaugh; Chuck Saner; Bob Forsythe.
Hobby Dash—Steve Brown; Tom Leiter; Jim Bucher; John Orr.
Slow Late Model—Terry Baker; Charley Hyde; Roger Harger; Roger Frye.
Slow Hobby—Larry Thacker; Jeff Bucher; William Varney; Walt Rowland.
Fast Late Model—Bull Bradley; Jerry Baker; Dave Evers; Jerry Egolf.
Fast Hobby—Tom Leiter; John Orr; Steve Brown; Jim Springer.
Slow Street Stock—David Reed; Dick Acagy; Dick Wiehgy; Don Drabenstott.
Fast Street Stock—Paul Sherman; Bob Johnson; Walt Maley; Bud Dausan.
Late Model Feature—Steve Backus; Dave Evers; Denny Flaugh; Roger Frye.
Hobby Feature—John Orr; Steve Brown; Jim Springer; Don Prater.

Steve Backus

Street Stock Feature—Bob Johnson; Paul Sherman; Tom Anders; Walt Maley.

Saturday, July 30, 1977
Warsaw Racing

An unbelievable 83 cars took part in three classes of racing at the Warsaw Speedway Saturday night in the final tune-up for this weekend's double-dose of Friday and Saturday evening racing at the Kosciusko County Fair. Tom Leiter, John Orr and Bob Johnson were respective late model, hobby and street stock winners.

Joe Boleh brought some gasps from the fans as he rolled over during the street stock feature, but luckily was not injured. While upside down, the car continued running and after track helpers righted it, Boleh almost nonchalantly continued driving into the pits. Although his machine was badly damaged, the motor never died.

Tom Leiter, Warsaw – Infield 1977

Race Results:
Late Model Dash—Bill Bradley; Jim Bucher; Don Backus; Ray Chambers.
Hobby Dash—Tom Leiter; Dan Baker; John Orr; Larry Thacker.
Slow Late Model—Jeff Bucher; Jerry Baker; Jerry Egolf; Charley Prater.
Slow Hobby—Thames Goon; Glen Smith; Gary Baker; Dave Stafford.
Fast Late Model—Tom Leiter; Les Sroufe; Roger Frye; Dan Backus.
Fast Hobby—Steve Brown; John Orr; Sonny Hyde; Larry Thacker.
Slow Street Stock—Rock Anders; Sam Barrett; Rick Hare.
Fast Street Stock—Bob Johnson; Paul Sherman; Keith Smith.
Late Model Feature—Tom Leiter; Dan Backus; Danny Flaugh; Jim Bucher.
Hobby Feature—John Orr; Dean Baker; Thames Goon; Glen Smith.
Street Stock Feature—Bob Johnson; DeWayne Barker; Rick Hare; Kim Hare.

Friday, August 5 & Saturday, August, 6, 1977
Rain Soaks Racing

With most of the Kosciusko County Fair racing rained out, the Warsaw Speedway will look forward to regular competition this Saturday, which will be highlighted by a Powder Puff race.

On Friday night, 84 cars qualified and five races were run before the rains came. There were some 80 cars Saturday, but there wasn't any racing—despite hours of drying efforts by track officials.

Saturday, August 13, 1977
Warsaw Racing

It was like a triple header at the Warsaw Speedway Saturday night. There was a logjam of racing after two nights from the week before were rained out. In addition, there was a Powder Puff Derby, won by Sherry Kristner of Warsaw.

So jammed with action was the competition that one heat race drew 26 cars and in the street stock feature, there were 20 cars in the lineup with 20 more listed as "pick-ups".

Race results:

Late Model Dash—Chuck Saner; Jerry Egolf; Jim Bucher; Ray Chambers.
Hobby Dash—Steve Brown; John Orr; Tom Danner; Lora Lee Sherman.
Slow Late Model—Jeff Bucher; Bill Long; Jerry Baker; Tim Goshert.
Slow Hobby—Thames Good; Jim Bucher; William Varney; Dick Achey.
Fast Late Model—Tom Leiter; Roger Frye; Ray Chambers; Jim Bucher.
Fast Hobby—Steve Brown; Gary Baker; Sam Barrett; Walt Rowland.
Street Stock First Team—Keith Smith; Mike Hughes; Rick Hare; Kim Hare.
Street Stock Second Team—Dan Kerlin; Bob Grindle; Bob Johnson; Walt Maley.
Late Model Feature—Ray Chambers; Tom Leiter; Denny Flaugh; Jerry Egolf.
Late Model Consey—Denny Flaugh; Charlie Hyde; Larry Howard; Dan Backus.
Hobby Feature: Steve Brown; John Orr; Walt Rowland; John Higgenbothem.
Street Stock Feature—Walt Maley; Tony Elliott; David Reed; Rick Hare.
Powder Puff—Sherry Kristner; Peg Davis; Deanne Dausman.

Saturday, August 27, 1977
Warsaw Racing

In addition to the regular purse winnings, Ray Chambers walked away $500 richer and John Orr $200 richer to highlight Saturday action at the Warsaw Speedway. The extra prize money was kicked in for the championship 40 lap feature. Next week the street stock championship feature will be run. David Reed was street stock winner Saturday.

Paul Sherman of Merriam, Ind. brought a gasp from the good-sized crowd when he crunched the wall. As a 6-10, 310 pounder, safety units had some trouble getting Sherman from his car. He was taken to the hospital for treatment. Another car, driven by Larry Shepherd, jumped over the high wall but landed on its wheels outside the track and there were no injuries.

Race Results:

John Crum, Ray Chambers, & Hoot Gibson

Late Model Dash: Willard Sherman; Donny Flaugh; Roger Frye; Steve Backus.
Hobby Dash: Terry Leiter; Dean Baker; Curt Danner; Walt Rowland.
Late Model Slow Heat: Bill Long; Dana Kerline; Jerry Baker; Jeff Bucher.
Hobby Slow Heat: Don Prater; Jim Springer; Andy Lee; John Higgenbothem.
Late Model Fast Heat—Tom Leiter; Charles Hyde; Larry Howard; Les Sroufe.
Hobby Fast Heat—Steve Brown; Jim Bucher; Walt Rowland; Gary Baker.
Street Stock Slow Heat—Tom Leiter; Lyle Milburn; Darrelle Warren; Mark Coleman.
Street Stock Fast Heat—Rock Anders; Dan Kerlin; Bob Johnson; Tony Elliott.
Late Model Feature—Ray Chambers; Tom Leiter; Denny Flaugh; Les Sroufe; Jim Bucher; Jerry Baker; Willard Sherman; Bob Forsythe; Terry Sroufe; Dana Kerlin; Chuck Saner; Jerry Egolf.
Hobby Feature—John Orr; Steve Brown; Dean Baker; Curt Danner; Jim Springer; Tom Danner; Gary Baker; Don Prater; Tom Leiter; Walt Rowland; John Higgenbothem.
Street Stock Feature: David Reed; Bob Grindle; Dana Kerlin; Bob Johnson; Walt Maley; DeWayne Parker; Lyle Milburn; Rock Anders; Rod England; Joe Pickett.

Saturday, September 3, 1977
Final Races of Season at Speedway

The Warsaw Speedway closed up shop for the season Saturday night, entertaining a good-sized crowd with some excellent racing.

DeWayne Barker, Steve Backus and John Orr led the charge by winning feature races in the street-stock, late model and hobby divisions respectively. Three of the faster street-stocks raced in the late model feature and did quite well, finishing third, sixth and eighth. Racing will resume next May.

Steve Backus & Rick Gibson

Race Results:
Late Model Dash—Denny Flaugh; Dan Backus; Bill Long; Willard Sherman.
Hobby Dash—Steve Brown; Dean Baker; John Orr; Gary Baker.
Slow Late Model—Terry Sroufe; Steve Backus; Jim Bucher Jr; Jerry Baker.
Slow Hobby—William Varney; Tom Danner; Dave Fitzpatrick; Jim Springer.
Fast Late Model—Denny Flaugh; Willard Sherman; Ted Hudson; Bill Long.
Fast Hobby—Don Prater; Steve Brown; Dean Baker; John Orr.
Street Stock—Jerry Egolf; Terry Leiter; Dean Smith; Lyle Milburn.
Street Stock—Keith Harris; Tony Elliott; Rock Anders; Dan Kerlin.
Street Stock Feature—DeWayne Barker; Walt Maley; Dan Kerlin; Keith Smith.
Late Model Feature—Steve Backus; Jim Bucher Jr., Jerry Baker, Jeff Bucher.
Hobby Feature—John Orr; Walt Maley; Jim Springer; Don Prater.

1978
Time for a Change

In 1978, several racers became frustrated with the management, track operations, and race pay-offs and boycotted the races on July 8, 1978. After a month of discussions and deliberation, the Fairboard gave track manager, Gibson, a vote of confidence less than 12 hours after the striking drivers presented their case. That decision didn't last long though as four drivers went together and bought out the remaining 2 years of Gibson's contract for $4,000 and took over the operations of the speedway on July 24. Racing resumed on July 29 with Jim Bucher, from Akron, as Track President and Manager.

Although Bucher only ran the speedway for 2 1/2 yrs., he added highly entertaining attractions such as Spectator Races, "Hot Dog" races and Watermelon races where the drivers raced 3 laps, stopped to eat a hot dog or slice of watermelon, and then drove backwards around the track for 2 laps. He also had the first $1,000 demolition derby and brought in the world famous World of Outlaws to compete on August 25, 1978. It was the one and only time that they competed in Warsaw with Bobby Allen the feature winner and Steve Kinser finishing second.

Saturday, May 6, 1978
Frigid Opener At Warsaw Speedway

The weather was cold, but the racing was plenty hot in opening night activities Saturday at the Warsaw Speedway. A small crowd of dedicated fans watched some 45 cars compete. The program ended early after several cars were scratched from late races because of early spins. Tom Leiter, Dean Baker, and Terry Hull were respective late model, hobby stock, and street stock feature winners.

Dean Baker

Following are results, with car numbers in parenthesis:

Late Model Dash - Willard Sherman (82), Chuck Saner (8), Jim Bucher (2), Larry Howard (29)
Hobby Dash - John Gilbreath (99), Kurt Danner (00), John Orr (88), Dean Baker (77)
Slow Late Model - Tom Leiter (70), Terry Sroufe (12), Glenn Bradley (22), Steve Backus (3)
Slow Hobby - Kurt Danner (00), Dave Fitzpatrick (57), Bob Keifer (53)
Fast Late Model - Ed Martin (17), Willard Sherman (82), Jim Bucher (2), Chuck Saner (8)
Fast Hobby - Jim Sellers (33), John Orr (88), Dean Baker (77), John Gilbreath (99)
Slow Street Stock - Roger Fitzpatrick (57), Larry Blevins (4), Steve Plotner (12), Mark Coleman (78)
Fast Street Stock - Rod England (83), Bob Johnson (22), Terry Hull (23), Tony Parker (05)
Late Model Feature - Tom Leiter (70), Jim Bucher (2), Glenn Bradley (22), Willard Sherman (82)

Hobby Feature - Dean Baker (77), John Orr (88), Kurt Danner (00), Jim Sellers (33)
Street Stock Feature - Terry Hull (23), Bob Johnson (22), Denny Whippie (18), Barry Lemons (71)

Saturday, May 13, 1978 – Rainout

Saturday, May 20, 1978 - Rainout

Saturday, May 27, 1978
Warsaw Racing

Indianapolis wasn't the only place for automobile racing over the weekend. The Warsaw Speedway drew 65 entries Saturday night for racing in late model, hobby and street stock divisions. A good-sized crowd watched as Jim Bucher won the late model feature, Steve Brown the hobby and Bimbo Atkins the street stock.

Following are results with car numbers in parenthesis:

Late Model Dash - Dan Backus (43), Bob Forsythe (33), Les Sroufe (11), David Green (73)
Hobby Dash - John Orr (88), Dean Baker (77), Scott Dausman (22), Arnold Prater (1)
Slow Late Model - Jim Bucher (2), Jim Bucher, Jr. (27), Rod Bailey (47), Arden Leiter (87)
Slow Hobby - Dave Stafford (5), Dick Aragy (47), Steve Brown (42), Dave Fitzpatrick (57)
Fast Late Model - Steve Backus (3), Dan Backus (43), Les Sroufe (11), Bob Forsythe (33)
Fast Hobby - Bob King (53), John Orr (88), Darrell Prater (44), William Varney (45)
Street Stock Heat - Bob Johnson (22), Rod England (83), Denny Withy (18), Walt Maley (20)
Street Stock Heat - Terry Hull (23), Steve Oswalt (77), Steve Keirn (50), Rocky Anders (14)
Late Model Feature - Jim Bucher, (2), Arden Leiter (87), Glenn Bradley (22), Tom Leiter (70), Jim Bucher, Jr. (27), Rod Bailey (47)

Saturday, June 3, 1978
Warsaw Racing

A two-car collision and subsequent crash into the wall marred activity at the Warsaw Speedway Saturday night, but fortunately, there were no severe injuries.

John Gippenbothem and Tom Danner had an unexpected meeting during one of the races, and both were rushed to Kosciusko Community Hospital by EMS technicians with possible neck and back injuries. But neither was admitted. It left Willard Sherman, Kurt Danner and Bob Johnson to win respective late model, hobby stock and street stock races.

Following are results, with car numbers in parenthesis:

Late Model Dash—Jim Bucher, (2)1st; Arden Leiter (87)2nd; Tom Leiter (70)3rd; Ed Martin(17)4th.
Hobby Dash—John Orr(88)1st; Walt Rowland(62)2nd; Swede Bolander(32)3rd; Don Prater(44)4th.
Slow Late Model—Dan Backus(43)1st; Rod Bailey(41)2nd; Jim Springer(68)3rd; Steve Backus(3)4th.
Slow Hobby—Steve Brown(42)1st; Kurt Danner(00)2nd; Dave Fitzpatrick(57)3rd.
Fast Late Model—Chuck Saner(8)1st; Jim Bucher(2)2nd; Ed Martin(17)3rd; Ray Chambers(67)4th.
Fast Hobby—Jim Sellers(33)1st; John Orr(88)2nd; Bob King(53)3rd; Walt Rowland(62)4th.
Slow Street Stock—Terry Hull(23), 1st; Bill Baumgartner(98),2nd; Bob Johnson(22)3rd; Tom Barrett(19)4th.
Fast Street Stock—Dave Bause(89)1st; Rex Alley(17)2nd; Keith Smith(3)3rd; Jeff Hull(56)4th.

Saturday, June 10, 1978
Warsaw Racing

A fast, safe night of racing highlighted activity at the Warsaw Speedway Saturday night. Ed Martin, Walt Rowland and Bob Johnson stole much of the glory by winning respective feature races in the late model, hobby and street stock divisions.

Following are results with car numbers in parenthesis:

Late Model Dash—Ray Chambers(67)1st; Willard Sherman(82)2nd; Jim Bucher(2)3rd; Ed Martin(17)4th.
Hobby Dash—Jim Sellers(33)1st; John Orr(88)2nd; Dave Fitzpatrick(57)3rd; Andy Lee(48)4th.
Slow Late Model—Steve Backus(3)1st; Dave Stevens, Jim Bucher Jr.(27)4th; Les Sroufe(11)5th.
Slow Hobby—Arnold Prater(1)1st; David Reid(73)2nd; Kurt Danner(00)3rd; Larry Thacker(71)4th.
Fast Late Model—Ray Chambers(67)1st; Ed Martin(17)2nd; Jim Bucher(2)3rd; Denny Flaugh(5)4th.
Fast Hobby—John Orr(88)1st; Bob King(53)2nd;Jim Sellers(33)3rd; Dave Stafford(5)4th.
Slow Street Stock—Walt Maley(20)1st; Rick Zachs(72)2nd; Sam Baumgartner(00)3rd; Scott Dausman(21)4th.
Fast Street Stock—Bob Johnson(22)1st; Jeff Bucher(7)2nd; Larry Hull(23)3rd; Mike Coleman(78)4th.
Late Model Feature—Ed Martin(17)1st; Jim Bucher(2)2nd; Steve Backus(3)3rd; Terry Sroufe(12)4th; Willard Sherman(82)5th; Dan Backus(43)6th; Jim Springer(68)7th; Jim Bucher Jr.(27)8th; Ray Chambers(67)9th. Les Sroufe(11)10th.

Hobby Feature—Walt Rowland(62)1st; John Orr(88)2nd; Tom Leiter(57)3rd; Kurt Danner(00)4th; Dave Stafford, (5)5th; Dave Reid(73)6th; Jerry Baker(14)7th; Andy Lee(48)8th; Bob King(53)9th; William Varney(44)10th.

Street Stock Feature—Bob Johnson(22)1st; Walt Maley(20)2nd; Tim Goshert(80)3rd; Barry Lemmons(71)4th; Tom Barker, (28)5th; Keith Smith(3)6th; Joe Pickett(79)7th; Kevin Plummer(03)8th.

Saturday, June 17, 1978
Warsaw Racing

Warsaw Speedway continued its series of excellent races this past Saturday, hosting eight heat sprints and three features.

Terry Sroufe, John Orr and Bob Johnson

Bob Johnson, Warsaw

were respective late model, hobby and street stock winners.

Following are results, with car numbers in parenthesis:

Late Model Dash—Jim Bucher(2)1st; Ray Chambers(67)2nd; Dean Baker(77)3rd; Ed Martin(17)4th.
Hobby Dash—John Orr(88)1st; Darrell Prater(44)2nd; David Reed(73)3rd; Tom Leiter(57)4th.
Slow Late Model—Willard Sherman(82)1st; Terry Sroufe(12)2nd; Jim Springer(68)3rd; Steve Backus(3)4th.
Slow Hobby—Steve Brown(42)1st; Arnold Prater(1)2nd; Kurt Danner(00)3rd; Bob King(53)4th.
Fast Late Model—Jim Bucher(2)1st; Dean Baker(77)2nd; Ray Chambers(67)3rd; Ed Martin(17)4th.
Fast Hobby—Walt Rowland(62)1st; John Orr(88) 2nd; Tom Leiter(57)3rd; Darrell Prater(44)4th.
Slow Street Stock—Ron Walters(27)1st; Jeff Arnold(04)2nd; Rod Lindgey(30)3rd.
Fast Street Stock—Dave Green(26)1st; Jeff Bucher(7)2nd; Bob Johnson(22)3rd; Barry Lemons(71)4th.
Late Model Feature—Terry Sroufe(12)1st; Ray Chambers(67)2nd; Ed Martin(17)3rd; Chuck Saner(8)4th; Bob Forsythe(33)5th; Steve Backus(3)6th; Jim Springer(68)7th; Jim Bucher(2)8th; Dean Baker(77)9th.
Hobby Feature—John Orr(88)1st; Dave Stafford(5)2nd; Tom Leiter(57)3rd; Kurt Danner(57)4th; Thames Goon(72)5th; Rock Anders(14)6th; Bob King(53)7th; Walt Rowland(62)8th; Dave White(76)9th; Darrell Prater(44)10th.
Street Stock Feature—Bob Johnson(22)1st; Barry Lemons(21)2nd; Keith Smith(3)3rd; Terry Hull(23)4th; Rod England(83)5th; Joe Pickett(79)6th; Jeff Arnold(04)7th; Lyle Milbourne(07)8th.

Saturday, June 24, 1978
Warsaw Racing

Bruce Hogue, Tom Leiter and Bob Johnson won respective late model, hobby and street stock features Saturday evening to highlight action at the Warsaw Speedway.

Bill Whittenberger was the winner in the demolition derby.

Following are results with car numbers in parenthesis:

Late Model Dash—Dean Baker(77)1st; Jim Bucher(2)2nd; Steve Backus(3)3rd; Ed Martin(17)4th.
Hobby Dash—John Orr(88)1st; Darrell Prater(44)2nd; Rock Anders(14)3rd; Tom Leiter(57)4th.
Slow Late Model—Ray Chambers(67)1st; Bruce Hogue(25)2nd; Jim Bucher Jr.(27)3rd; Willard Sherman(82)4th.
Slow Hobby—Bob King(53)1st; Tom Danner(78)2nd; Dave Reed(73)3rd; Dave Stafford(5)4th.
Fast Late Model—Denny Flaugh(5)1st; Steve Backus(3)2nd; Terry Sroufe(12)3rd; Jim Springer(68)4th.
Fast Hobby—Tom Leiter(57)1st; Walt Rowland(62)2nd; Darrell Prater(44)3rd; Jim Sellers(33)4th.

Saturday, July 1, 1978 – Rainout

Monday, July 3, 1978
Warsaw Racing

A spectacular display of fireworks highlighted the show at the Warsaw Speedway Monday night and in between, there was some excellent racing.

Some 76 cars entered and Tom Leiter, Dick Day and Bimbo Atkins came away with respective late model, hobby and street stock 50-lap feature victories.

Following are results, with car numbers in parenthesis:

Kelly & Don Prater, Warsaw

Late Model Dash—Jim Bucher(2)1st; Ray Chambers(67)2nd; Tom Leiter(70)3rd; Willard Sherman(82)4th.
Hobby Dash—Bob King(53)1st; Dick Day(12)2nd; John Orr(88)3rd; Jim Sellers(33)4th.
Slow Late Model—Charley Prater(01)1st; Denny Flaugh(5)2nd; Dave Stevens(08)3rd; Jim Springer(68)4th.
Slow Hobby—Thames Goon(72)1st; Tom Leiter(57)2nd; Bruce Hogue(25)3rd; Kurt Danner(00)4th.
Fast Late Model—Bob Forsythe(33)1st; Ray Chambers(67)2nd; Jim Bucher(2)3rd; Arden Leiter(87)4th.
Fast Hobby—Bob King(53)1st; Jim Sellers(33)2nd; John Orr (88)3rd; Walt Rowland(62)4th.
Slow Street Stock—Greg Egolf(46)1st; Roger Fitzpatrick(57)2nd; Jerry Bucher(92)3rd; Scott Dausman(21)4th.
Fast Street Stock—Barry Lemons(71)1st; Rod England(83)2nd; Bimbo Atkins(34)3rd; Bob Johnson(22)4th.
Concy—Denny Withy—(18)1st; Jeff Bucher(60)2nd; Bob Ness(15)3rd; Tom Maley(20)4th.
Late Model Feature—Tom Leiter(70)1st; Jim Bucher(2)2nd; Dean Baker(77)3rd; Ray Chambers(62)4th; Terry Sroufe(12)5th; Jim Springer(68)5th; Larry Howard(29)6th; Willard Sherman(82)7th; Jim Sellers(33)8th; Ed Martin, (17)9th.
Hobby Feature—Dick Day(12)1st; Walt Rowland(62)2nd; John Orr, (88)3rd; Tom Leiter,(57)4th; Kurt Danner, (00)5th; Jim Sellers(33)6th; Tom Danner, (78)7th; Don Prater(44)8th; William Varney(1)9th; Brian Lolmugh(25)10th.
Street Stock Feature—Bimbo Atkins(36)1st; Joe Pickett(79)2nd; Tim Goshert(80)3rd; Barry Lemons(71)4th; Bob Johnson(22)5th; Rex Alley(17)6th; Keith Smith(3)7th; Terry Gayner(42)8th.

Saturday, July 8, 1978
Drivers And Fans Boycott Warsaw Speedway
By Brian Howey, Sports Writer

Between 75 and 80 drivers, along with nearly 450 supporters, picketed the Kosciusko County Fair Grounds Saturday night as a dispute erupted into public between the drivers and owners and Warsaw Speedway director C. E. "Hoot" Gibson.

Between the two warring sides sits the Kosciusko County Fair Board which is more or less put into a mediator's position. The drivers say they won't race until new management is installed and improvements are made on the track. Gibson still has two years remaining on his contract with the fair board and says he definitely won't step down. The fair board will hear the driver's side of the issue at 8 p.m. Wednesday in the Shrine Building. Groundskeeper Henry Butler said Gibson "definitely would not attend the meeting."

The picketing which began about 4 p.m. Saturday was peaceful according to Chief of Police Jerry A. Johnson. Johnson, Capt. Eugene Brown and several other members of the Warsaw Police Dept. watched the picketing from nearby positions.

We Want No Trouble: "We're not trying to force anybody not to go into the track", said former track flagman Terry Baker, whose wife Linda Baker is the present spokesman for the owners and drivers. "We don't want any trouble or violence."

Baker said he was fired by Gibson last Wednesday after the track director discovered a meeting of drivers was slated for Friday night at the Baker residence. Nearly a third of the drivers attended that meeting while Gibson was denied permission by the Bakers to attend at the urging of other drivers.

The current dispute had been fermenting for quite some time but grew out of last weekend's track action when several drivers were refused entry into a featured event due to a technicality. According to Gibson, a car has to participate in two previous events before it can run in the feature.

Several drivers claim the rule was changed after they had paid their way into the pit area and set up. "They (track officials) told me I could run," said driver Bruce Hogue. "Later they reversed themselves and said that I couldn't run since I hadn't raced here in two previous weeks.

Offered to Run: "I offered to run at the tail end of the feature and not collect any purse money but they wouldn't let me run," he continued. About 8 to 10 cars did run on Saturday night, according to groundskeeper Butler. He also said there weren't many spectators on hand.

Mrs. Baker said three hobby-stocks for the midseason championship ran as well as one late model car and three street stock cars. She claimed no gate admission was charged and only trophies were awarded the drivers. She said most of the cars that did run were from Columbia City, Gibson's hometown.

The drivers and owners have complied a list of "askings" which they will present to the fair board. At the top of the list is the establishment of a committee that would oversee the track's operation. It would consist of drivers and car owners, a fair board member, an accountant and two fans. Also on the list is:

Revision in rules and regulations
Improvements in restroom conditions
A trained fire crew at all events
Better payoffs
Promotion of track events
More driver information
Improvement in racing officials

Improvements in track conditions
Equal rights for all drivers
A new track announcer to replace Milo Clase
Better bleacher conditions
Improvement of lighting
A better public address system

Mrs. Baker and drivers and owners are willing to chip in for the improvement of the bleachers and restrooms, which she said are probably in violation of state regulations. She also showed interest in constructing sound barriers for the benefit of Winona Lake residents.

No Pre-Determined Purse: The driver's purse gripe stems from not knowing exactly what the purse is beforehand. "For instance, say there's 2,000 people that show up at $4 a head", Mrs. Baker began. "That's $8,000 with $400 being the top prize while other prizes go down to $50 making it about $2000 in total prize money. Then they pay the officials, the fair board and the electricity—so where's the other $4,000, she asks.

"There's no way in the world we could cheat on the fair board", Gibson said this morning. "Our accountant will verify that 56.2 percent of the total gate goes into the purse.

No Way I'll Resign: Gibson, whose tenure at the track is around a quarter of a century vowed that he would not resign before the remaining two years on his contract are finished. "There is no way I'll resign. I have a contract and it's good for next year. No way".

Caught in the middle of the squabble is the fair board, which in the words of board member Donald Goon, is kind of the middleman. One of his concerns is that if the strike should continue it will be the fair board that will be losing revenue.

We're one of the few fairs in the state that doesn't receive tax dollars, he added. The fair board does depend on race money for part of the income. Another board member, Myron Metzger, refused comment on the matter. Board President Emra Stookey, was unavailable for comment.

"We've spent hours talking and we've wasted our time", Hogue said. "This is the first time we've done this. Maybe now they'll listen".

Thursday, July 13, 1978
Drivers Have Say, But No Decision
By Brian Howey, Sports Writer

Race drivers who frequent to Warsaw Speedway at the Kosciusko County Fairgrounds essentially had their day in court Wednesday night with the Kosciusko County Fair Board placed in the position of the judge.

No agreement could be reached on the impasse between the drivers and the track management under 'the direction' of C.E. "Hoot" Gibson by the board until the board hears Gibson's side of the story. In the meantime, there will be no racing at the speedway until the board makes a decision. The drivers claim they will not race at the speedway until Gibson and his associates are removed by the board.

Their reasons stem from poor track conditions, a fluctuating undisclosed purse amount before the races and some financial discrepancies concerning the gate and concession figures. Linda Baker, speaking for the drivers, says her group is not on an investigative purge—suggesting the past can be overlooked just as long as current conditions are alleviated. However the fair board was left to mull over some figures that will need explanation.

Revenue Drop: Most prominent on the list of financial figures is the drop in revenue the board received over the period of one year. According to a stock owner's financial statement, the board received $14,709.09 from racing funds and concessions in a one year period ending October 31, 1976.

However, in an equal time period ending Oct. 31, 1977, the board received only $7,917.07

from the same revenue producing sources—a $6,792.02 drop. "I didn't see a big drop in the number of fans", Mrs. Baker said. "And there were about the same number of races. You'd notice it if the fan totals were cut in half. So where's the money gone?"

Another unconfirmed report had the concession stand bringing in some $5,000 alone during 1977, leaving a mere $2,000 from the track. Mrs. Glendora Davis, who runs the concessions, wouldn't confirm the $5,000 figure, saying only that she turned the money into fairgrounds keeper Henry Butler. Butler could not be reached for comment this morning.

Complain About Purse: Drivers complained about the amount of the purse taken from crowds averaging about 1,200 per night and paying $3 a head. "Things have deteriorated", said driver Jack Powell. "There is no listing on the pay envelopes of what the purse was and there is no record kept of the money transaction," which is customary at other tracks.

Payoffs have also fluxuated, a practice different from comparable tracks where a purse is guaranteed. "I was told we were supposed to get $50 for first place and $35 for second", said street stock driver Barry Lemons. "Once I got $10 for second place and the second week I received $15 and a week later it was back to $10. Driver Arden Leiter talked about the bonus for the season's track champion. "The bonus gets guys to come back. It gives us incentive. Last year the Warsaw track champion got $125 and I told him not to spend it all in one place".

Money wasn't the sole concern for the drivers. Driver Jim Bucher told the board that due to the track conditions, it is impossible to break records. "I set a record in 1965 but there's no way I'd break it today", he said. "Racers will race on just about anything but here, more and more won't race because of the track."

Propose Resurfacing: One of the proposals made by the drivers is to resurface the track with clay and calcium. "It's mostly sand now", said Leiter. "And some rocks too." Another problem is lack of a drivers' association. The association dissolved six years ago after an election that elected new leadership in place of Gibson. According to driver Larry Baker, the new president was told by Gibson to go race elsewhere.

Driver Art Smith verified Baker's story. "I raced here for years, but I haven't been back for four years and won't until there's new management." Other complaints include lack of lighting on turn three and the loss of sprint cars from competition here due to track conditions.

I believe you all really want to race or you wouldn't be here", said fair board President Emra Stookey. He said the board wouldn't make any decision until it heard from Gibson, who still has another year on his contract. Gibson was unavailable for comment this morning.

Opposes Picketing: Stookey did take exception to the drivers picketing in front of the fairgrounds, saying "That's something we can do without." Some of the drivers talked of just not showing up although no specific action for Saturday night was determined.

Mike Moore, a newsman for WKJG television in Fort Wayne, departed from his neutral position as a media representative and suggested to the board and the drivers that a benefit race be scheduled for Saturday to help the fair board's expenses. Neither the board nor the drivers acted on that matter Wednesday night. Until the board does act, long-time fan Walter Funk summed it up: "There's no show. These boys aren't going to be here anymore."

Friday, July 14, 1978
No Races Saturday
Gibson Retained; Implies Strike Vandalism
By Brian Howey, Sports Writer

Warsaw Speedway's track manager C.E. "Hoot" Gibson received a vote of confidence Thursday morning from a hastily convened Kosciusko County Fair Board—less than 12 hours after the striking race drivers presented their case.

Gibson, whose contract runs through September, 1979, will serve in the manager's capacity until the contract expires. It is a post he has served for 25 years. The track will remain closed this Saturday night due to what Gibson termed as "vandalism." Gibson didn't come right out and say it, but his implication was the vandalism was a direct result of the drivers' strike.

"They're just a bunch of hotheads," Gibson said Thursday. "The picketing drivers threatened people as they went into the track last Saturday. They told people that anybody who went to would find their car wouldn't look the same.

To Continue Boycott: Terry Baker, the track's former flagman who was fired by Gibson last Wednesday, said his fellow drivers were not responsible for any vandalism and said he felt the drivers would continue their boycott of the speedway.

"Any implication involving us with the vandalism is ridiculous", Baker said. Gibson told me July 3rd that it was young kids who were doing the vandalism. Our members had nothing to do with it". Baker also denied that any threats were made to those who entered the track last Saturday night. Warsaw Chief of Police Jerry Johnson reported Monday the protest had been orderly in all aspects.

Gibson and board member Don Goon said that none of the incidents of vandalism have been reported to the Warsaw Police Department. Baker said he couldn't speak on any other action on the part of the striking drivers until after they meet to decide. However, he did mention the Friday and Saturday night races at the county fair are a possible target.

Baker announced an 8 p.m. driver's meeting for Friday on Thursday afternoon. The meeting will be at his residence on County Roads 200 North and 400 East. "All drivers, owners and other concerned parties are welcome." Baker said the agenda will consist of future actions taken by the drivers for the rest of the current racing season.

The fair board convened, without public notice, at 9 a.m. Thursday to hear Gibson's side of the dispute. However, board member Donald Goon contacted Gibson following the Wednesday meeting and set up the Thursday morning conference. Board President Emra

Stookey was not present at the Thursday meeting, according to Goon, because he attended a cattle show in Franklin. He favored meeting with Gibson on Friday.

Board members who did attend were Eldon Watkins, Myron Metzger, Don Hostetler, William Orr, Helen Albert and Henry Butler. Goon said minutes were taken but there was no official action made by the board.

Goon said there were no financial matters discussed by the board despite what drivers described as discrepancies in purse money and stock owner's financial statements.

Included was a report that total revenue returned to the fair board from racing and concessions funds had decreased by nearly 50 percent between 1976 and 1977 despite comparable crowd and date totals. $14,700.99 was returned to the board in 1976 while only $7,917.07 was returned in 1977.

Board Seems Happy: "We had a definite understanding" Gibson said. "The board seemed happy so things are going to stay as is." Gibson said if the drivers continue to strike, "I'll run a different kind of car." He also said that he would like to meet with the drivers who will race.

Goon also said a move had been made to get Gibson to meet with the drivers. Goon said that there was no move to oust Gibson due to the way his contract was written. "It's valid and it's required that he stay on until September, 1979. We (the fair board) can hardly afford to buy out Hoot's contract.

Goon did say the fair board depends on income from the Saturday night racing but he didn't want to project the effects of a prolonged drivers' strike. "They're striking for nothing", Goon said. And Gibson vowed, "There will be some more races."

Tuesday, July 25, 1978
Warsaw Drivers Buy Out Gibson, to Race Saturday

For the first time in nearly four weeks, race drivers will return in force to the Warsaw Speedway at the Kosciusko County Fairgrounds.

The month-long dispute between Speedway director C.E. "Hoot" Gibson and car owners and drivers was settled Monday afternoon when Jim Bucher—representing owners, drivers and fans, bought out the remaining two years of Gibson's contract with the Fair Board for $4,000.

As a result, the roar of the late model, street stock and hobby racers will once again fill the night this coming Saturday. Bucher, himself a standout driver for several years, is only formally listed on the contract because "it has to be in one name."

Most of the money was raised by four individuals, although Bucher would not release their names. "The contract is in my name now", he said this morning, "but later on, we hope to put it under an association of the drivers. Our deadline on that is by the end of the 1979 season."

Not Upset: Gibson, meanwhile, didn't sound a bit upset by the change of events. The same man who four weeks ago vowed, "There is no way I'll resign", today said, "No, I'm not really disappointed. The way things turned out, these fellas wanted to buy it, so I sold it. It worked out well for me."

"I've been in it a long time," he added. "It's kind of like leaving home. I guess some of the drivers were dissatisfied with the way I was handling things and didn't want to run. They thought they could do a better job, so I let them."

When some 450 drivers, owners and fans first picketed the track July 8, they vehemently complained of the purse situation at the Speedway, claiming there is never prior knowledge just what the winnings will be. They also listed 13 areas where improvements are needed, from track conditions to new rest rooms. Now that there has been a changeover in ownership, Bucher is the first to admit it may take a little time before all the demands are met.

May Take A While: "We'd like to do these things as soon as possible", he said. "But when you're left with nothing but a big mess, it may take a little while. I'm sure Saturday night will be pretty much as is, but we'd like to at least do something about the restrooms.

And of the purse situation?

"We have no idea how much money is there to start with," Bucher said. "He (Gibson) never told us. We're taking the attitude we don't know what happened in the past, we'll just work for tomorrow." Added Linda Baker, who has been spokesman for the racers throughout the walkout, "We know it (the purse) will be honest and different."

Saturday, July 29, 1978
Warsaw Speedway Saturday Results

Seventy-three cars raced at the Warsaw Speedway at the Kosciusko County Fairgrounds last Saturday as racing resumed following a two week drivers' strike. Total purse was $2,771, the biggest purse of the season and best since July 4, 1977.

"It was the largest purse paid back to the drivers this year.", said Terry Baker, track flagman. The overall track take was $4,600 with expenses for the fair board, estimated at about $1,500.

In feature racing highlights, Warsaw's Bob King won the hobby stock, Bruce Hogue of Akron took top honors in the late model and Tim Smith won the street stock feature.

The following are the top three placers in each event:

6 Fastest Hobby Stock—Walt Rowland, Columbia City; Thames Good, Pierceton; Johnny Orr, Columbia City.
6 Fastest Late Model—Bruce Hogue, Akron; Dave Evers, Huntington; Willard Sherman, Marion.
6 Fastest Street Stock—Barry Lemons, Leesburg; Lyle Milburn, Warsaw; Bob Johnson, Warsaw.
Fast Heat Hobby Stock—Rick Sechrist, Warsaw; Dave Stafford, Warsaw; Johnny Orr, Columbia City.
Fast Heat Late Model—Arden Leiter, Barbee lake; Dean Baker, Fort Wayne; Bruce Hogue, Akron.
Fast Heat Street Stock—Mark Coleman, Warsaw; Sam Barrett, Warsaw; Wayne Gibson.
Slow Heat Hobby—Mike Coughenour, Akron; Dennis Day, Roann; Arnold Prater, Warsaw.
Slow Heat Late Model—Denny Flaugh, Huntington; Terry Sroufe, Huntington; Ron Sausaman,

Warsaw.
Slow Heat Street Stock—Rod England, Warsaw; Dean Green, Warsaw; Tim Smith.
Hobby Stock Feature—Bob King, Warsaw; Arnold Prater, Warsaw; Rick Sechrist, Warsaw.
Late Model Feature—Bruce Hogue, Akron; Arden Leiter, Barbee Lake; Willard Sherman, Marion.
Street Stock Feature—Tim Smith, Barry Lemons, Leesburg; Denny White, Lakeville.

Friday, August 4, & Saturday, August 5, 1978
Warsaw Speedway Weekend Results

Saturday night's big attraction at the Warsaw Speedway was the "Hot Dog Race" in which four would race two laps, then eat a hot dog and continue in the opposite direction. This would be repeated. DeWayne Barker won the event followed by Jim Bucher, Jr., Thames Goon and Walt Rowland.

In other Speedway Saturday happenings, Dean Greene rolled his street stock during a fast heat, but escaped with no injuries.

Friday night, Bucher slammed into a retaining wall on the back stretch and was taken to Kosciusko County Hospital but was not admitted. He was back on the track Saturday night. A total of 86 cars raced.

Friday:

Late Model:
Six Fastest—Donald Summers(92); Jim Bucher Jr.(27)Jim Bucher Sr.(2).
Fast Heat—Tom Beezley(69);Dean Baker(77);Willard Sherman(82).
Slow Heat—Ed Martin(17);Roger Frye(06);Larry Howard(10).
Feature—Tom Beezley(69);Donald Summers(92);Jim Bucher Sr.(2).

Hobby Stock:
Six Fastest—Tom Leiter(57);Walt Rowland(62);John Orr(88).
Fast Heat—Steve Brown(42);Tom Leiter(57);Rick Sechrist(4).
Slow Heat—Thames Goon(72);Kurt Danner(00);Don Prater(44).
Feature—Tom Leiter(57);Bob King(53);Walter Rowland(62).

Street Stock:
Fast Heat—Walt Maley Jr.(20)Barry Lemons(71)Bimbo Atkins(36)
Slow Heat—Jeff Bucher(7);Jeff Schilling(81);Tim Goshert(80).
Feature—Barry Lemons(71);Dick Leiter(66);Scott Dausman(21).
Concy—Dick Leiter(60); Kevin Plummer(03);Rex Heckman(77).

Saturday:

Late Model:
Six Fastest—Arden Leiter(87); Willard Sherman(82); Jim Bucher Sr.(2).
Fast Heat—Dean Baker(77); Arden Leiter(87); Bruce Hogue(25).
Slow Heat—Ron Sausman(10); Bull Bradley(22); Roger Frye(06).
Feature—Arden Leiter(87);Jim Bucher Sr.(2); Tom Beezley(69).

Hobby Stock:
Six Fastest—John Orr(88);Jim Sellers(33);Andy Lee(6).
Fast Heat—Tom Leiter(57);Walt Rowland(62);Steve Brown(42).
Slow Heat—Randy Prokop(30);Kurt Danner(00); Thames Goon(72).
Feature—Tom Leiter(57);John Orr(88);Andy Lee(6).

Street Stock:
Fast Heat—Keith Smith(6);Darrell Warren(11);Terry Hull(23).
Slow Heat—Walt Maley Jr.(20); Jeff Bucher(7);Denny Withey(18).
Feature—Jeff Bucher(7);Barry Lemons(71);Walt Maley Jr. (20).
Concy—Tom Anders(16);Rod England(83);Ron McKenzie(24).

Saturday, August 21, 1978
Melons Highlight Speedway Action

Saturday night attracted 16 late models, 21 hobby stocks, and 39 street stockers to the Warsaw Speedway with the Watermelon Race highlighting action.

Jeff Bucher took racing and watermelon-eating honors during the watermelon race. Six drivers drove three laps, stopped and ate melon and then drove backwards two laps. Tom Leiter won the hobby mid-season race although it took him a dozen laps to overcome Bob King. Of the 18 cars that began the race, only 12 finished.

In two track mishaps, Dave Evers ran his late model into a wall during the time trials thus ending his racing for the night. Steve Plotner hit a pole and was taken to Kosciusko County Hospital. He suffered whip-lash but stated he would race next week.

Late Model:
6 Fastest—Bruce Hogue(25); Dean Baker(77); Arden Leiter(87).
Fast Heat—Jim Bucher Sr.(2); Arden Leiter(87); Bruce Hogue(25).
Slow Heat—Jim Bucher Jr.(27); Jerry Baker(10); Roger Frye(04).
Hobby Stock:
6 Fastest—Walt Rowland(62); Tom Leiter(37); Steve Brown(42).
Fast Heat—Thames Goon(72); Walt Rowland(62); John Orr(88).
Slow Heat—Arnold Prater(1); Dave Stafford(5); Brian McFeeter(25).
Feature—Tom Leiter(57); Bob King(53); Andy Lee(6); Thames Goon(72) tied.
Street Stock:
Fast Heat—Lyle Milburn(07); Keith Smith(3); Dave Fitzpatrick(5).
Slow Heat—Barry Lemons(71); Tony Elliott(35); Bob Johnson(22).
Feature—Barry Lemons(71); Walt Maley Jr.(20); Lyle Milburn(07).
Concy—Jeff Bucher(7); Dick Leiter(66); Kevin Plummer(03); Robert Reed(73).

Saturday, August 19, 1978
Wild Street Stock At Speedway

A rather wild and wooly mid-season street stock feature highlighted Saturday night activity at the Warsaw Speedway.

Jeff Bucher ended up winning the event, but only after leader Steve Pickett, driver of car No.91, spun in turn No. 1 with but a few laps to go. Barry Lemons led much of the early part of the race, but ended up settling for second.

Tom Beezley and Tom Leiter were respective late model and hobby stock feature winners. The Speedway also hosted bicycle races for youngsters. Following are both automobile and bicycle race results:

Hobby Stock:
Six Fastest—Tom Danner(78); Darrell Prater(44); Walt Rowland(62).
Fast Heat—Tom Leiter(57); Walt Rowland(62); Steve Brown(42)
Slow Heat—Kurt Danner(00); Dave Stafford(5); John Higgenbotham(46).
Feature—Tom Leiter(57); Walt Rowland(62); John Higgenbotham(46).

Late Model:
Six Fastest—Jim Bucher(2); Robert Forsythe(33); Bruce Hogue(25)
Fast Heat—Tom Beezley (69); Jim Bucher(2); Arden Leiter(89).
Slow Heat—Will Sherman(82); Jerry Baker(10); Les Sroufe(11).
Feature—Tom Beezley(69); Arden Leiter(89); Jim Bucher(2).

Street Stock:
Fast Heat—Tony Elliott(35); Scott Dausman(21); Rod England(83).
Slow Heat—Barry Lemon(71); Joe Pickett(79); Walt Maley Jr.(20).
Feature(Mid-Season Championship)—Jeff Bucher (7); Barry Lemons(71); Terry Hull(23).
Concy—Kevin Plummer(03) Robert Reed(73); Dave Reed(2).

Bicycle Races:
Brent Shepherd (Bremen)8 year old; Brian Townsend (Rochester) 9 year old; Brian Holly (Disko) 10 year old; Robert Johnson (Warsaw) 11 year old; Eddie Cochern (Warsaw) 12 year old; Mark Rowland (Columbia City) 13 year old; Bill Leiter (Pierceton) 14 year old; Bob Heeter (Warsaw) 15 year old.
Drivers' Division—Bruce Hogue and Tony Elliott.

Friday, August 25 & Saturday August 26, 1978
Warsaw Racing
WORLD OF OUTLAWS

Several wheel-to-wheel races highlighted action at the Warsaw Speedway Saturday night in what was very nearly a Leiter sweep. In the street stock division, Dick Leiter started in eighth place in the 10 car field, but came on strong to win. Another Leiter, this one Tom, passed John Orr with six laps to go to capture the hobby feature. But in the late model feature, it was a different story as Arden Leiter and Tom Beezley put on quite a show before Beezley ended up winning.

On Friday, the Speedway sponsored the "Outlaw" sprints for five heat races and a $2,000 feature. In the feature, Danny Smith of Danville, Il., led the first nine laps before Steve Kinser of Bloomington, In., took over. Kinser led until the final 12 laps when Bobby Allen of Hanover, Pa., grabbed - and held - the lead.

Friday Results:

Four Fastest - Steve Smith (19), Bobby Allen (1a), Gary Patterson (3c)
Heat #1 - Dick Liskai (6), Tom Beezley (113), Dean Pedrock (26)
Heat #2 - Bernie Grayheal (93), Ron Fisher (84), John Naida (9)
Heat #3 - Steve Kinser (11), Rick Ferkel (0), Bobby Allen (1a)
Heat #4 - Fred Braronfield (92), Danny Smith (4), Fred Linder (55)
Feature - Bobby Allen (1a), Steve Kinser (11), Gary Patterson (3c)

Saturday Results:

Late Model

Six Fastest—Tom Beezley(69); Bruce Hogue(25); Red Foster(74).
Fast Heat—Tom Beezley(69); Jim Bucher Sr.(2); Red Foster(74).
Slow Heat—Ed Martin(17); Roger Frye(04); Dave Evers(99).
Feature—Tom Beezley(69); Arden Leiter(87); Red Foster(74).

Hobby Stock
Six Fastest—Thames Goon(72); Tom Leiter(57); Don Prater(44).
Fast Heat—John Orr(88); Tom Leiter(57); Bob King(52).
Slow Heat—Walt Rowland(62); Kurt Danner(00); Dennis Day(3).
Feature—Tom Leiter(57); John Orr(88); Don Prater(44).

Street Stock
Fast Heat—Terry Hull(23); Barry Lemons(71); Bimbo Atkins(36).
Slow Heat—Dick Leiter(64); Bob Grindle(61); Don Denny(29).
Feature—Jeff Bucher(7); Randy Woodling(6); Bimbo Atkins(36).
Concy—Jeff Bucher(7); Bob Johnson(22); Darrell Warren(11).

Saturday, September 2 & Monday, September 4, 1978
Warsaw Racing – Hot Dog Race

Late model drivers put on the best show at Warsaw Speedway this past weekend as Bruce Hogue ended up passing Tom Beezley in the last few laps for the feature win. Les Sroufe led the early part of the racing before spinning out.

In the Hobby feature, Thames Goon came from the fourth row to win his race, passing Brian Lomaugh in the final few laps. Barry Lemons was the street stock feature winner, but only after Jeff Bucher rolled his car on the backstretch. He was not hurt.

Barry Lemons, Warsaw

The drivers also had a hot dog race featuring late model racers, and Bruce Hogue ended up the winner.

Saturday:

Late Model:
Six Fastest—Bruce Hogue(25); Tom Beezley(69); David Evers(99).
Fast Heat—Bruce Hogue(25); Tom Beezley(69); Red Foster(74).
Slow Heat—Roger Frye(06); Robert Forsythe(33); Jim Bucher Sr.(2).
Feature—Red Foster(74); Tom Beezley(69); Doug Evers(99).

Hobby Stock:
Six Fastest—Steve Brown(42); Bob Grindle(14); Walt Rowland(62).
Fast Heat—Bob King(33); Tom Leiter(57); John Orr(88).
Slow Heat—Thames Goon(72); Brian Lomaugh(23); Tim Smith(30).
Feature—Steve Brown(42); Tom Leiter(57); Bob Grindle(14).

Street Stock:

Fast Heat—Bimbo Atkins(36); Terry Hull(23); Barry Lemons(71),
Slow Heat—Lyle Milburn(07); Mark Coleman(76);Scott Dausman(21).
Feature—Terry Hull(23); Dick Leiter(64); Mark Coleman(76).
Concy—Tom Leiter(83); Joe Pickett(79); David Bauer(84).

Labor Day:

Late Model:
Six Fastest—Tom Beezley(69); David Evers(99); Bruce Hogue(25).
Fast Heat---Bruce Hogue(25); Tom Beezley(69); Will Sherman(82).
Slow Heat—Terry Sroufe(12); Ed Martin(17); Roger Frye(04).

Hobby Stock:
Six Fastest—Bob Grindle(16); John Orr(88); Walt Rowland(62).
Fast Heat—Tom Leiter(57); John Orr(88); Steve Brown(42).
Slow Heat—David Stafford(5); John Gilreath(99); Denny Day(3).
Feature—Steve Brown(42); Tom Leiter(57); John Orr(88).

Street Stock:
Fast Heat—Barry Lemons(71); Bimbo Atkins(36); Allen Diabenhoff(96).
Slow Heat—Jeff Bronsing(8); Lyle Milburn(67); Tony Parker(15).
Feature—Barry Lemons(71); Terry Hull(23); Dick Leiter(66).

Saturday, September 9, 1978
Rain Wets Speedway

Dave and John Fitzpatrick put on an exciting hobby stock race on the soggy Warsaw Speedway Saturday night, with Dave eventually winning.

In the powder puff race, Joyce Kauffman won the first heat while Tammy Smith powered a win in the second hit. Next week the championship races in all three classes will be run.

Race Results:

Late Model:
Six Fastest—Bruce Hogue(25); Jim Bucher Jr.(37); Red Foster(74).
Fast Heat—Bruce Hogue(25); Red Foster(74); Ron Fowler(76); Dan Backus(29).
Slow Heat—Jim Bucher Jr.(37); Dan Stevens(08); Ed Martin(17).
Feature—Bruce Hogue(25); Tom Beezley(69); Ed Martin(17).

Hobby Stock:
Six Fastest—Johnny Chadwick(6); Darryl Prater(64); Walt Rowland(62).
Fast Heat—Steve Brown(12); John Orr(88); Bob Grindle(16).
Slow Heat—Dave Fitzpatrick(57); John Fitzpatrick(5); Dave Stafford(3).
Feature—John Orr(88); Walt Rowland(62); Bob King(53).

Street Stock:
Fast Heat—Rod England(83); Tony Elliott(35); Bob Johnson(22).
Slow Heat—Terry Hull(23); Tim Goshert(80); Keith Smith(3).
Feature—Rod England(83); Barry Lemons(71); Bimbo Atkins(36).
Concy—Barry Lemons(71); Joe Winteroud(19); Randy Woodling(6).

Saturday, September 16, 1978
Warsaw Racing

Drivers at the Warsaw Speedway put on quite a show Saturday night, highlighted by two 50-lap and one 30-lap feature races. In the late model feature, Bruce Hogue, Jim Bucher Sr. and Arden Leiter had wheel-to-wheel racing throughout until Hogue came out on top.

Steve Brown had to come from the fifth starting position in the 50-lap hobby stock feature before trimming John Orr and Tom Leiter. And in the street stock, Dick Leiter also came up from the pack—starting sixth—to sneak past Barry Lemons and Terry Hull.

Following are results with car numbers in parenthesis:

Late Model:
Six Fastest—Tom Beezley(69); Arden Leiter(67); Terry Sroufe(12).
Feature—Bruce Hogue(25); Jim Bucher Sr. (2); Arden Leiter(67).

Hobby Stock:
Six Fastest—Steve Brown(42); John Orr(88); Tom Leiter(57).
Feature—Steve Brown(42); John Orr(88); Tom Leiter(57);.

Street Stock—
Concy—Joe Winteroud(19); Jeff Hull(56); Danny Brookins(86).
Feature—Dick Leiter(66); Barry Lemons(71); Terry Hull(23).

Saturday, September 23, 1978
Warsaw Racing

Mechanics and owners got a chance to show their worth behind the wheel at Warsaw Speedway Saturday night, as they drove heat races.

In feature races, Tom Beezley took the late model when Jim Bucher Sr. dropped out near the end of the race. Steve Brown took the hobby stock feature, while Tony Elliott won in street stock.

One of the most exciting races came in the hobby stock "six fastest" where Walt Maley passed Brown with one lap to go for the victory. In the owners/sponsors race, Darrell Prater smacked the wall on the white flag lap and lost first place to Roger Richards by two car lengths.

In street stock concy, Bob Johnson and Steve Plotner were fighting for the lead when both spun out, leaving the checkered flag to Zane Gray. In the spectators race, Rick Lowery won with his car and Barry Lemons, with his pickup truck.

Race Results:

Late Model:
Six Fastest—Tom Beezley(69); Jim Bucher Sr.(2); Roger Frye(06).
Slow Heat—Steve Backus(5); Bob Burnsworth(06); D. Baker(77).
Fast Heat—Tom Beezley(69); Roger Frye(06); Bob Walters(17).
Feature—Tom Beezley(69); Dave Evers(99); John White(17).

Hobby Stock:
Six Fastest—Walt Maley(62); Steve Brown(42); Don Prater(44).
Slow Heat—Steve Backus(3); Ron Prater(1); Jerry Parker(16).
Fast Heat—Roger Richards(42); John Chadwick(68); Paul Evers(99).
Feature—Steve Brown(42); Bob Grindle(16); Terry Sroufe(12).

Street Stock:
Slow Heat—Hal Drabenscott(71); Mike O'Rieley(75); Dick Goshert(80).
Fast Heat—Kim Coleman(78); Tony Elliott(35); Terry Hull(23).
Feature—Tony Elliott (35); Duane Ronk (37); Dick Leiter (66).
Concy—Zane Gray (3); Rocky Enders (14); Sam Barrett (49).

1979

Saturday, May 12, 1979 - Rainout

Saturday, May 19, 1979
Warsaw Speedway Opens Season

Warsaw Speedway kicked off its 1979 season in a big way Saturday night as four track records were set on the redone quarter-mile oval.

Don Walker, of Arcadia, made the return of sprint racing a good one as he turned the oval in 16.90 for the track mark in his No. 39 car. In the late model class, Tom Beezley of Churubusco went 17.49 in his No. 69. Bourbon's Tom Danner set a mark in the V-8 Sportsman in No.78 with a record 19.24, while Jeff Bucher, of Akron, had a record in the six-cylinder division with a 20.03. He drove No.7.

However, none of the record-setters could get the checkered flag. In the sprints, that honor went to Ron Miller of Huntington. Dean Baker nipped Ed Martin in the final laps of the late model and Bob Johnson was able to hang on to his comfortable lead to win the V-Sportsman six cylinder combined race.

Race results:

Sprints:
Trophy Dash—Louie Mann.
Fast Heat—Carl Miskatton.
Slow Heat—John Althouse.
Feature—Ron Miller, Rocky Fisher, Louie Mann.

Late Model:
Trophy Dash—Bruce Hogue.
Fast Heat—John White.
Slow Heat—Ed Martin.
Feature—Dean Baker, Ed Martin, Tom Beezley.

Saturday, May 26 & Monday, May 28, 1979
Warsaw Speedway

A wild finish on the late model feature race Monday highlighted a big weekend of action at Warsaw Motor Speedway.

Louie Mann, Kokomo

Bruce Hogue, Akron, and Dean Baker, Bremen, battled for the lead for the final 15 laps of the late model feature and then at the checkered flag, Hogue slipped in front of Baker when the latter's car spun around and crossed the finish line backwards. Hogue and Baker tangled coming out of the fourth turn, causing Baker's car to go out of control.

Other Monday feature winners were Barry Lemons, Warsaw, in the V-8 Sportsman and Rocky Fisher, Fort Wayne, in the sprints.

On Saturday, Don Walker, Arcadia, broke his own track record with a 16.03 clocking in the sprint dash. Louie Mann, Kokomo, won the sprint feature.

Following are two-day results:

Saturday, May 26:

Sprint—Dash—Don Walker, 1st; Heat Race—Don Walker, 1st; Feature, Louie Mann, 1st; Don Walker, 2nd; Ron Miller, 3rd; Whitey Jannssen, 4th; Fred Postman, 5th.

Late Model-Dash-John White, 1st; Slow Heat—Tom Beezley, 1st; Fast Heat—Tony Elliott, 1st; Feature—Bruce Hogue, 1st; Tom Beezley, 2nd; Dean Baker, 3rd; Jim Bucher Jr., 4th; Roger Richards, 5th.

V-8 Sportsman—Dash—Joe Pickett, 1st; Slow Heat—Tony Parker, 1st; Fast Heat—Don Prater, 1st; Feature—Walt Rowland, 1st; Don Prater, 2nd; Joe Pickett, 3rd; Tom Danner, 4th; Bob Johnson, 5th.

6-Cylinder—Heat Race—Dale Bolinger, 1st; Feature—Randy Woodling, 1st; Dale Bolinger, 2nd; George Houck, 3rd.

Monday, May 28:

Sprint—Dash—Rocky Fisher, 1st; Slow Heat—John Bates, 1st; Fast Heat—Rocky Fisher, 1st; Feature—Rocky Fisher, 1st;Dan Smith, 2nd; Don Walker, 3rd; Ron Miller, 4th; John Althouse, 5th.

Late Model—Dash—Tom Beezley, 1st; Slow Heat—Jim Bucher Jr. 1st; Fast Heat—Les Sroufe, 1st; Feature—Bruce Hogue, 1st;Dean Baker, 2nd; Tom Beezley, 3rd; Terry Sroufe, 4th; Ed Martin, 5th.

V-8 Sportsman—Dash—Dick Day, 1st; Slow Heat—Tom Leiter, 1st; Fast Heat—Barry Lemons, 1st; Feature—Barry Lemons, 1st; Arnold Prater, 2nd; Joe Pickett, 3rd; Tom Danner, 4th; Dick Day, 5th.

6-Cylinder—Dash—Randy Woodling, 1st; Heat Race—Jeff Bucher, 1st; Feature—Dale Bolinger, 1st; Jeff Bucher, 2nd.

Saturday, June 2, 1979
Warsaw Speedway

Bruce Hogue, Akron

Bruce Hogue of Akron and Barry Lemons of Warsaw were winners of the late model and V-8 sportsman features, respectively, at the Warsaw Motor Speedway Saturday night.

John White, Warsaw, was second and Tom Beezley, Churubusco, third in the late model feature while Bob Johnson and Bob King, both of Warsaw, were second and third respectively, in the V-8 sportsman feature.

In the late model division, Terry Sroufe, Huntington, was dash and slow heat winner and White was fast heat winner. Dash winner in the V-8 sportsman was Don Prater, Warsaw, while Lemons won the fast heat and Don Denny, Warsaw, the slow heat.

In the sprint division Louie Mann, Kokomo, won the feature with Rocky Fisher, Fort Wayne, second, and Jerry Priest, Warsaw, third. Mann won the fast heat, Fisher the dash and Donny Corwin, Defiance, Ohio, the slow heat.

The six-cylinder feature went to Dale Bolinger, Atwood, with Randy Woodling, Warsaw, second and Jeff Bucher, Akron, third. Woodling won the dash.

Saturday, June 9, 1979 - Rainout

Saturday, June 16, 1979
Warsaw Speedway

Bruce Hogue, Barry Lemons and Don Walker were feature winners Saturday night at the Warsaw Motor Speedway.

Hogue, Akron, won the late model feature; Lemons, Warsaw, was first in the sportsman feature, and Walker, Arcadia, captured the sprint feature.

Race Results:

Late Model—Ed Martin, Dash; Jerry Baker, Slow Heat; Bruce Hogue, Fast Heat; Bruce Hogue, John White, Will Sherman, Jim Bucher Jr. Dave Evers, Feature.

Sportsman—Walt Rowland, Dash; Dale Bolinger, Slow Heat; Bob Johnson, Fast Heat; Barry Lemons, Bob Johnson, Tom Danner, Dan Bradley, Tom Leiter, Feature.

Sprint—Don Walker, Dash; Ron Miller, Slow Heat; Louie Mann, Fast Heat; Don Walker, Louie Mann, Tom Beezley, Jerry Priest, Scott Fisher, Feature.

Saturday, June 23, 1979
White, Bradley, Fisher Speedway Winners

John White, Dan Bradley and Rocky Fisher were feature winners Saturday night at the Warsaw Motor Speedway.

White, Warsaw, and Bruce Hogue, Akron, were locked in a close battle for the late model feature race for the entire 25 laps before White took the checkered flag for the first time this season. Hogue, who has won three late model features, finished second.

Bimbo Atkins, Warsaw

Bradley, Muncie, edged Warsaw's Bob Johnson for the sportsman feature win. Barry Lemons led for most of the 20-lap event before developing suspension problems that forced him to drop out.

Fisher, Fort Wayne, and Louie Mann, Kokomo, were wheel-to-wheel for nearly the entire sprint feature before Fisher, on the inside, came home first. Rich Leming, Topeka, was able to get past Mann just before the finish to grab second place. Mann set a track record for one lap with a time of 15.91 seconds during qualifications.

Race Results:

Sprint—Louie Mann, Dash; Bimbo Atkins, Slow Heat; Louie Mann, Fast Heat; Rocky Fisher, Rich Leming, Louie Mann, Don Walker, Scott Fisher, Feature.

Late Model—Bruce Hogue, Dash; Charlie Hyde, Slow Heat; Dave Ever, Fast Heat; John White, Bruce Hogue, Tom Beezley, Ed Martin, Dean Baker, Feature.

Sportsman—Bob King, Dash; Dick Leiter, Slow Heat; Walt Maley, Fast Heat; Dan Bradley, Bob Johnson, Tom Leiter, Walt Maley, Tom Danner, Feature.

Saturday, June 30, 1979
Leiter, Mann, Foster Claim WMS Features

Tom Leiter, Louie Mann and Red Foster won their feature races Saturday night at the Warsaw Motor Speedway and Scott Fisher survived an end-over-end flip along the backstretch during the sprint feature.

Fisher, Warsaw, lost control of his car during the final laps of the sprint feature, won by Kokomo's Mann, but escaped without serious injuries. It was Mann's second sprint feature win this season as he beat Gary Fisher, Kokomo, and Tom Beezley, Churubusco, second and third respectively, in the 25-lap race.

Making his first appearance of the season, Red Foster, Warsaw, captured the late model feature as Roger Richards, Columbia City, and Beezley finished second and third in the 25-lap event. Tom Leiter, Warsaw, won his first victory of the season in the 20-lap sportsman feature. A bicycle race was held at the speedway Saturday night.

Author's Note: The #84 above was purchased by Denny England from Ron Fisher and became his first sprint car debuting on July 28, 1979!

Race Results:

Sprint—Gary Fisher, Dash; Scott Fisher, Slow Heat; Gary Fisher, Fast Heat; Louie Mann, Gary Fisher, Tom Beezley, Terry Pletch, Tom Patterson, Feature.
Late Model—Ed Martin, Dash; Terry Sroufe, Slow Heat; Red Foster, Fast Heat; Red Foster, Roger Richards, Tom Beezley, Bruce Hogue, Dean Baker, Feature.
Sportsman—Bob Grindle, Dash; Dick Leiter, Slow Heat; Jerry Baker, Fast Heat; Tom Leiter, Tom Danner, Bob King, Bob Johnson, Mike Coughenour, Feature.

Wednesday, July 4, 1979
Speedway Results

Tom Beezley of Churubusco won the late model feature and Rocky Fisher and Bob King were the other feature winners Wednesday night at the Warsaw Motor Speedway. King, of Warsaw, was first in the sportsman feature, besting runner-up Bob Johnson of Warsaw. Bob Maby set a one-lap, sportsman record when he was clocked in 18.98 seconds during qualifying, bettering the previous mark of 19.00 held by Barry Lemons.

Fisher, Fort Wayne, was the sprint feature winner with Ron Miller, Huntington, finishing second. Following Beezley to the finish line in the late model class was Bruce Hogue of Akron.

Race Results:

Sprint—Don Walker, Dash; Bimbo Atkins, Slow Heat; Ron Miller, Fast Heat; Rocky Fisher, Ron Miller, Gary Fisher, Dave Erickson, Jerry Priest, Feature.
Late Model—Roger Richards, Dash; Charlie Hyde, Slow Heat; Tom Beezley, Fast Heat; Tom Beezley, Bruce Hogue, Ed Martin, John White, Little Joe Bennett, Feature.
Sportsman—Bob King, Dash; Dick Leiter, Slow Heat; DeWayne Barker, Fast Heat; Bob King, Bob Johnson, Don Prater, Barry Lemons, Terry Baker, Feature.

Saturday, July 7, 1979
Prater, Walker, Mid-Season Sportsman, Sprint Champions

Don Prater of Warsaw and Don Walker of Arcadia were the sportsman and sprint winners, respectively, at the Mid-Season Championships Saturday night at the Warsaw Speedway.

Roger Richards of Columbia City led all the way in capturing the late model feature, beating Tom Beezley and Bruce Hogue to the finish line. The Mid-Season Championship in the late model division will be Saturday night with a 50-lap race.

Walker steered his sprinter past Louie Mann of Kokomo for his victory. Mark Caldwell started at the rear of the field in the 50-lap race and moved all the way up to third place before the checkered flag fell.

Prater won decisively over Barry Lemons in the 30-lap sportsman race. The lead changed nine times between Lemons, Bob King and Prater. King held a large lead but lost control on the last lap and spun into the infield. Apparently the front fender on King's car was pushed against his tire earlier in the race, making it difficult to steer.

Race Results:

Sprint—Louie Mann, Dash; Gregg Stevens, Slow Heat; Mark Caldwell, Fast Heat; Don Walker, Loue

Mann, Mark Caldwell, Terry Pletch, Rocky Fisher, Feature.

Late Model—Les Sroufe, Dash; Sam Davis, Slow Heat; Terry Sroufe, Fast Heat; Roger Richards, Tom Beezley, Bruce Hogue, John White, Les Sroufe, Feature.

Sportsman—Barry Lemons, Dash; Mike Coughanour, Slow Heat; Dick Day, Fast Heat; Don Prater, Barry Lemons, Tom Leiter, Bob King, Bob Johnson, Feature.

Saturday, July 14, 1979 – Rainout

Saturday, July 21, 1979
Beezley Wins Mid-Season Late Model Title At WMS

Tom Beezley of Churubusco took the lead early and maintained it the rest of the way to win the Mid-Season Late Model Feature Saturday night at the Warsaw Motor Speedway. Beezley finished ahead of Bruce Hogue, Akron, and John White, Warsaw, in the 50-lap event.

John Orr of Columbia City broke the track record in the sportsman division with a one lap time of 18.79 seconds. However, he was unable to even place in the 20-lap race as Bob King of Warsaw came home first. He was followed by Tom Leiter and Don Prater, both of Warsaw, in the sportsman feature.

Ron Miller of Huntington captured the sprint feature, with Louie Mann, Kokomo, second, and Mike Blake, Indianapolis, third. Donny Corwin Jr. of Defiance, Ohio, lost control of his car and it rolled over in the middle of the third turn during the sprint feature. He was unhurt but the car sustained serious damage.

Race Results:

Sprint—Mike Wair, Dash; Rocky Fisher, Fast Heat; Bimbo Atkins, Slow Heat; Ron Miller, Louie Mann, Mike Blake, Don Walker, Rocky Fisher, Feature; Whitey Jannsen, Consy.

Late Model—Dean Baker, Dash; Denny Flaugh, Slow Heat; Tom Beezley, Fast Heat; Tom Beezley, Bruce Hogue, John White, Roger Richards, Dean Baker, Feature.

Sportsman—Bob Grindle, Dash; DeWayne Ronk, Slow Heat; Glenn Bradley, Fast Heat; Bob King, Tom Leiter, Don Prater, Bob Johnson, Glenn Bradley, Feature.

Saturday, July 28, 1979
Beezley Wins Late Model Feature Here

Ron Miller, Tom Beezley and Tom Leiter were respective feature winners Saturday night at the Warsaw Motor Speedway. Leiter, Bob King and Don Prater, all of Warsaw, finished one-two-three in the sportsman feature. Leiter took the lead from Prater late in the race.

Denny Englland, Warsaw

Louie Mann of Kokomo broke his own track record in the sprints, bringing it down to 15.59 seconds from his old mark of 15.91. He was only able to capture the four-lap dash, though, as Miller, of Huntington, won the sprint feature over Don Walker and Tim Bookmiller.

Churubusco's Beezley, John White of Warsaw and Bruce Hogue of Akron were first, second and third in the late model feature. Racing will resume at the speedway Wednesday with a regular program as part of the Kosciusko County Fair. Gates will open at 5 p.m. A demolition derby will be held at the track Friday night.

Race Results:
Sprint—Louie Mann, Dash; Jerry Priest, Slow Heat; Don Walker, Fast Heat; Ron Miller, Don Walker, Tim Bookmiller, Rocky Fisher, Billy Joe Havens, Feature.
Late Model—John White, Dash; Tom Beezley, Fast Heat; Tom Beezley, John White, Bruce Hogue, Roger Grossnickle, Les Sroufe, Feature.
Sportsman—Don Prater, Dash; Terry Hull, Slow Heat; Barry Lemons, Fast Heat; Tom Leiter, Bob King, Don Prater, Bob Johnson, Terry Hull, Feature.

Friday, August 3, 1979
$1,000 Richer

Dick Day of Roann won the demolition derby and the $1,000 first prize Friday night at the Kosciusko County Fair. Second place was Phil Glassburn of Kokomo and third was Joe Cross of Silver Lake. Tonight there will be a full racing program beginning at 7 o'clock at the Warsaw Motor Speedway.

Saturday, August 4, 1979
Races Rained Out

Thunderstorms wiped out the scheduled fair races Saturday night at the Warsaw Motor Speedway but the event has been reset for this Saturday. A Big Wheel race for the children will be held between the regular late model, sprint and sportsman features.

Saturday, August 11, 1979
Lemons, Fisher, White Win Speedway Features

Barry Lemons and John White, both of Warsaw, and Fort Wayne's Rocky Fisher were the feature winners Saturday night at the Warsaw Motor Speedway.

Lemons won his fourth Sportsman feature victory of the season, finishing ahead of Bob Grindle and Tom Leiter, both of Warsaw, who were second and third, respectively. John Orr,

Columbia City, broke the sportsman one-lap track record with a time of 18.73 seconds but a collision with a car driven by Walt Maley during the heats put him out of action.

Fisher captured his fifth sprint victory this season, edging Mike Smith of Lizton, Ohio, in the 25-lap event. White won the 25-lap Late Model feature by working his way to the front from the fourth starting spot. It was his second win of the year.

Race Results:

Sportsman—Walt Rowland, Dash; Jeff Wigent, Slow Heat; Barry Lemons, Fast Heat; Barry Lemons, Bob Grindle, Tom Leiter, Don Prater, Bob Johnson, Feature.
Sprint—Ron Miller, Dash; Mike Smith, Slow Heat; Don Walker, Fast Heat; Rocky Fisher, Mike Smith, Scott Fisher, Don Walker, Don Walker Jr., Feature.
Late Model—Tom Beezley, Dash; Terry Sroufe, Slow Heat; John White, Fast Heat; John White, Steve Brown, Tom Beezley, Jerry Baker, Bruce Hogue, Feature.

Saturday, August, 18, 1979
Barry Lemons Sets Sportsman Record Again at Speedway

Barry Lemons won the Sportsman Class Feature Saturday night at the Warsaw Motor Speedway and in so doing set a one-lap track record, marking the sixth time the Sportsman record has fallen this season.

It is the second time Warsaw's Lemons has rewritten Sportsman record this year. The new mark is 18.70 seconds, bettering the old record by John Orr which was set only last week. Lemons passed Glenn Bradley midway through the 20-lap feature and held on to win by a narrow margin.

Other feature winners were Louie Mann of Kokomo in the sprint and Gene Hall of Fremont in the late model. Mann steered his car to an easy win over Don Walker and Paul Grim, respectively. Hall defeated Jo Bennett of Wolcottville in the 25-lap late model event. John White was making a bid for the lead when he lost control of his car and spun into the infield.

Race Results:

Sprint—Don O'Connor, Dash; Don Walker, Slow Heat; Rocky Fisher, Fast Heat; Louie Mann, Don Walker, Paul Grim, Clarence Atkins, Rocky Fisher, Feature.
Late Model—Jerry Baker, Dash; Jim Jones, Slow Heat; John White, Fast Heat; Gene Hall, Little Jo Bennett, Roger Grossnickle, Bruce Hogue, John White, Feature.
Sportsman—Walt Rowland, Dash; Tim Brown, Slow Heat; Don Prater, Fast Heat; Barry Lemons, Glenn Bradley, Tom Leiter, Bob Grindle, Bob King, Feature.

Saturday, August 25, 1979
White Wins Late Model Feature Here

John White, of Warsaw, won the late model feature while Ron Miller and Barry Lemons won the other features Saturday night at Warsaw Motor Speedway.

White outdueled Tom Beezley, of Churubusco, who finished second and Charlie Hyde in the 25-lap late model feature. White also was the fast heat winner. Ron Miller of Huntington captured the sprint feature, with Ed Stinehouse of Tipton second and Rocky

Roger Grossnickle, N. Manchester

Fisher, Fort Wayne, third.

The sportsman track record was broken again as three drivers dipped below the old mark. Lemons, who won the feature, was first to break the old standard with a time of 18.27 seconds for one lap and then Bob King matched Lemons mark. Tom Leiter later just missed their clocking with an 18.28 time. The old record was 18.70 set by Lemons last week. It was Lemons sixth feature win of the year.

Race Results:

Sprint—Louie Mann, Dash; Charley Sarver, Slow Heat; Ron Miller, Fast Heat; Ron Miller, Ed Stinehouse, Rocky Fisher, Don Walker, Densil Archer, Feature.

Late Model—Roger Grossnickle, Dash; Ed Martin, Slow Heat; John White, Fast Heat; John White, Tom Beezley, Charlie Hyde, Bruce Hogue, Roger Grossnickle, Feature.

Sportsman—John Fitzpatrick, Dash; Arnold Prater, Slow Heat; Tom Leiter, Fast Heat; Barry Lemons, DeWayne Barker, Glenn Bradley, Don Prater, Dewayne Ronk, Feature.

Saturday, September 1, 1979
White, Walker, King Win Season Titles At Speedway

John White won the late model event while Don Walker was the sprint winner and Bob King the sportsman champion in the Warsaw Motor Speedway season championships Saturday night. A 50-lap feature was held in each division with the top 20 drivers in each group competing.

Walker, Arcadia, was involved in a two-car race with Louie Mann of Kokomo when the latter's car developed mechanical problems and was forced to drop out. Walker then breezed to victory.

White, Warsaw, was never challenged in the late model feature, leading from start to finish. Bruce Hogue of Akron was second and Tom Beezley of Churubusco third.

Tom Leiter of Warsaw led for much of the sportsman feature but a flat tire on the 46th lap allowed King, North Manchester, to pass him and go on and capture the victory.

Following are results of Saturday's races and the final point standings:

Sprints—Don Walker, Whitey Jannsen, Ron Miller, Mike Blake, Don Walker Jr.
Late Model—John White, Bruce Hogue, Tom Beezley, Ed Martin, Terry Sroufe.
Sportsman—Bob King, Barry Lemons, Don Prater, Tom Leiter, Randy Woodling.

Season Point Leaders:

Sprints—Louie Mann, 179; Rocky Fisher, 162; Don Walker, 153; Ron Miller, 129; Jerry Priest, 57.
Late Model—John White, 209; Bruce Hogue, 186; Tom Beezley, 179; Ed Martin, 88; Roger Richards, 83.
Sportsman—Barry Lemons, 142; Bob Johnson, 112; Bob King, 89; Tom Leiter, 86; Don Prater, 82.

Above: Driver Jimmie Elliott, kneeling L-R: Car owner Paul Hazen & Phil Heinzman, standing Earl Gaerte
Below: Jimmie Elliott, Warsaw

Above: Paul Grim & Oscar Cook
Below: Jimmie Elliott racing with the broken wing!

Above: Bobby Grindle, Warsaw
Below: Rocky Fisher, Flagman Charles Gibson & John Crum

328

Above: Flagmen Grover Martin & Charles Gibson – 1976
Below: Larry Howard #79 & Don Walker #39

Above: Bob Johnson & Flagman, Charles Gibson
Below: Jim Murphy, 1976

Arden Leiter, Warsaw

1980

Saturday, May 24, 1980 – Rainout/No Results

Monday, May 26, 1980
Warsaw Speedway Results

Bruce Hogue took the checkered flag in the late model feature in Monday night's Memorial Day racing card at the Warsaw Motor Speedway. Ted Hudson was second and Roger Grossnickle third in the late model event.

Louie Mann was the sprint feature winner and Bob King captured the V-8 Sportsman feature. Ron Miller was second and Tom Patterson third in the sprint feature while Glenn Bradley was runner-up and Randy Woodling third in the V-8 feature.

Race Summary:

Sprint:
Dash—Louie Mann, 57, 1st; Al Redman, 9, 2nd; Gregg Stephens, 39, 3rd.
Fast Heat—Louie Mann, 57, 1st; Gregg Stephens, 39, 2nd; Ron Miller, 68, 3rd.
Slow Heat—Denzel Archer, 9, 1st; DeWayne Barker, 24, 2nd; Paul Grim, 43, 3rd.
Feature—Louie Mann, 57, 1st; Ron Miller, 68, 2nd; Tom Patterson, 21, 3rd; Paul Grim, 43, 4th; Bimbo Atkins, 36, 5th.

Late Model:
Dash—Tom Beezley, 69, 1st; Roger Richards, 51, 2nd; Walt Maley, 10, 3rd.
Fast Heat—Walt Maley, 10, 1st; Terry Sroufe, 12, 2nd; Tom Beezley, 69, 3rd.
Slow Heat—Bruce Hogue, 25, 1st; Roger Frye, 6, 2nd; Ted Hudson, 45, 3rd.
Feature—Bruce Hogue, 25, 1st; Ted Hudson, 45, 2nd; Roger Grossnickle, 17, 3rd; Tom Beezley, 69, 4th; Charles Hyde, 65, 5th.

V-8 Sportsman:
Dash—Mike Coughenour, 2, 1st; John Fitzpatrick, 5, 2nd; Jeff Wigent, 30, 3rd.
Fast Heat—Glenn Bradley, 28, 1st; Mike Coughenour, 2, 2nd; Tom Leiter, 57, 3rd.
Slow Heat—Randy Woodling, 75, 1st; Wayne Gibson, 72, 2nd; Tim Smith, 48, 3rd.
Feature—Bob King, 53, 1st; Glenn Bradley, 28, 2nd; Randy Woodling, 75, 3rd; Terry Hall, 23, 4th; Bob Grindle, 6, 5th.

Saturday, May 31, 1980 - Rainout

Saturday, June 7, 1980 - Rainout

Saturday, June 14, 1980
Warsaw Motor Speedway Results

Ron Miller, John White and Jeff Wigent were the feature winners in the sprint, late model and V-8 sportsman classes, respectively, Saturday night at the Warsaw Motor Speedway.

Miller led from start to finish in the sprint feature, with Gregg Stephens finishing second and Denny England third. Van Gurley appeared to have a lock on second when the loss of his wing forced him out with only a few laps remaining.

White won his first feature in a close late model race. He took the lead near the midpoint of the race and kept it. Bruce Hogue was second and Tom Beezley third.

Wigent ended Bob King's reign as the V-8 champion as it was the first sportsman feature of the season that King did not win. He finished second to Wigent, with Walt Roland third.

Sprint:
Dash—Bimbo Atkins, 36, 1st; Van Gurley, 3, 2nd; Gregg Stephens, 39, 3rd.
Slow Heat—Donny Corwin, Jr., 27, 1st; Tom Patterson, 21, 2nd; Jerry Priest, 33, 3rd.
Fast Heat—Van Gurley, 3, 1st; Ron Miller, 68, 2nd; Tony Elliott, 35, 3rd.
Feature—Ron Miller, 68, 1st; Gregg Stephens, 39, 2nd; Denny England, 84, 3rd; Jerry Priest, 33, 4th, John Althouse, 77, 5th.

Late Model:
Dash --John White, 87, 1st; Roger Grossnickle, 17, 2nd; Tom Beezley, 69, 3rd.
Slow Heat—Walt Maley, 10, 1st; Terry Sroufe, 12, 2nd; Roger Richards, 51, 3rd.
Fast Heat—Bruce Hogue, 25, 1st; Roger Grossnickle, 17, 2nd; Tom Beezley, 69, 3rd.
Feature—John White, 87, 1st; Bruce Hogue, 25, 2nd; Tom Beezley, 69, 3rd; Roger Grossnickle, 17, 4th; Roger Richards, 51, 5th.

V-8 Sportsman:
Dash—Jeff Wigent, 30, 1st; Bob King, 53, 2nd; Walt Roland, 62, 3rd.
Slow Heat—Don Prater, 44, 1st; Bob Johnson, 22, 2nd; Dale Bolinger, 35, 3rd.
Fast Heat—Bob Grindle, 6, 1st; Bob King, 53, 2nd; Walt Rowland, 62, 3rd.
Feature—Jeff Wigent, 30, 1st; Bob King, 53, 2nd; Walt Rowland, 62, 3rd; Tom Leiter, 57, 4th; Tim Smith, 48, 5th.

Saturday, June 21, 1980
Mann, Hyde, Lemons Feature Winners

Louie Mann won an accident-marred sprint feature, Charlie Hyde became the latest late model winner and Barry Lemons made a successful debut in the V-8 sportsman's feature Saturday night at Warsaw Motor Speedway.

Mann narrowly won over Van Gurley in the sprint feature after Greg Stephens, running near the front, was forced from the race in a crash that occurred with only a few laps remaining. A crash also eliminated Denzel Archer, whose car lost a tire in a tangle with Van Gurley's sprinter.

Tony Elliott, Warsaw

In an event that has not had the same winner twice this season, Hyde led from start to finish in the late model feature. Still, he was never able to establish a big lead over Bruce Hogue, who was only a half-car length behind in second.

Lemons made his first appearance of the season in the V-8 sportsman's and proved he was ready to resume his winning ways from a year ago. He won the fast heat and the feature, with Wigent second in the latter event.

Sprint:
Dash—Louie Mann, 1st; Van Gurley, 2nd; Gregg Stephens, 3rd.
Slow Heat—Gary Fisher, 1st; Tony Elliott, 2nd; Dick Watson, 3rd.
Fast Heat—Ron Miller, 1st; Gregg Stephens, 2nd; Louie Mann, 3rd; Van Gurley, 4th.
Feature—Louie Mann, 1st; Van Gurley, 2nd; Ron Miller, 3rd; Rocky Fisher, 4th, Donny Corwin Jr., 5th.

Late Model:
Dash --John White, 1st; Ted Hudson, 2nd; Roger Frye, 3rd.
Slow Heat—Charlie Hyde, 1st; Terry Sroufe, 2nd; Roger Richards, 3rd.
Fast Heat—Roger Grossnickle, 1st; Ted Hudson, 2nd; John Orr, 3rd.
Feature—Charlie Hyde, 1st; Bruce Hogue, 2nd; Roger Richards, 3rd; Ted Hudson, 4th; Tom Beezley, 5th.

V-8 Sportsman:
Dash—Bob King, 1st; Randy Woodling, 2nd; John Fitzpatrick, 3rd.
Slow Heat—Dick Day, 1st; Walt Roland, 2nd; Tom Martin, 3rd.
Fast Heat—Barry Lemons, 1st; Randy Woodling, 2nd; Bobby Grindle, 3rd.
Feature—Barry Lemons, 1st; Jeff Wigent, 2nd; Randy Woodling, 3rd; John Fitzpatrick, 4th; Dick Day, 5th.

Saturday, June 28, 1980
Miller, Beezley, Woodling Win

Feature winners at the Warsaw Motor Speedway Saturday night were Ron Miller in the sprint, Tom Beezley in the late model and Randy Woodling in the V-8 sportsman. Miller also won the fast heat in the sprint division, with Rocky Fisher finishing second in both. Miller said the track became "hard and dry with the only good groove being low in the curves."

Beezley's late model win makes him the first two-time winner of that event this season. The victory did not come easy, though, as Ted Hudson finished a close second and nearly passed Beezley a couple times. Charlie Hyde led the feature until a broken axle forced him out.

Woodling defeated runner-up John Fitzpatrick in the V-8 sportsman and also won the fast heat. The auto races were preceded by bicycle races. Winners were Robert Johnson (11-12 age group), Troy Jarvis (9-10), Danny Baker Jr. (7-8), and Kevin Atkins (5-6).

Sprint:
Dash—Gregg Stephens, 39, 1st; Van Gurley, 3, 2nd; John Althouse, 27, 3rd.
Slow Heat—John Davis, 44, 1st; Charlie Sarver, 5, 2nd; Tom Patterson, 21, 3rd.
Fast Heat—Ron Miller, 68, 1st; Rocky Fisher, 21, 2nd; Gregg Stevens, 39, 3rd.
Feature—Ron Miller, 68, 1st; Rocky Fisher, 21, 2nd; Van Gurley, 31, 3rd; Tom Patterson, 21, 4th; DeWayne Barker, 24, 5th.

Late Model:
Dash—Tom Beezley, 69, 1st; Roger Grosssnickle, 17, 2nd; John White, 87, 3rd.
Slow Heat—Ted Hudson, 45, 1st; Bruce Hogue, 25, 2nd; Roger Frye, 6, 3rd.

Fast Heat—Charles Hyde, 65, 1st; Terry Sroufe, 12, 2nd; Tom Beezley, 69, 3rd.
Feature—Tom Beezley, 69, 1st; Ted Hudson, 45, 2nd; Roger Frye, 6, 3rd; John White, 87, 4th; Bruce Hogue, 25, 5th.

Sports:
Dash—Walt Rowland, 62, 1st; Bob King, 53, 2nd; Steve Brown, 42, 3rd.
Slow Heat—Tom Leiter, 70, 1st; Jeff Wigent, 30, 2nd; Bob Johnson, 22, 3rd.
Fast Heat—Randy Woodling, 75, 1st; Barry Lemons, 7, 2nd; Terry Hull, 23, 3rd.
Feature—Randy Woodling, 75, 1st; John Fitzpatrick, 5, 2nd; Walt Rowland, 62, 3rd; Bob King, 53, 4th; Terry Baker, 81, 5th.

Friday, July 4 & Saturday, July 5, 1980
Mid-Season Races Cap Weekend

There was a full weekend of racing activity at the Warsaw Motor Speedway, with a regular card on Friday night and the V-8 sportsman mid-season championship plus racing in the sprints and late models and a demolition derby on Saturday night.

Randy Woodling won the 40-lap V-8 sportsman event on Saturday, edging runner-up John Fitzpatrick. Woodling took the lead when engine problems forced leader Bob King out of the race. Walt Roland was third and Jeff Wigent fourth.

Also, on Saturday, Louie Mann won the dash, fast heat and feature in the sprints. Mann also set a one-lap record of 15.41, only to have Van Gurley erase the mark later in the evening with a lap time of 15.14.

Roger Frye won his first late model feature of the season Saturday, beating second place finisher Tom Beezley by only feet. Beezley won the fast heat, Terry Sroufe the slow heat and Ted Hudson the dash. James Wigent won the demolition derby, outlasting runner-up Jeff Bucher in a five minute battle between the two final cars on the course. Mark Downing was third.

Friday's feature winners were Van Gurley in the sprints, John White in the late model and Bob King in the V-8 sportsman. It was Gurley's first feature win of the season.

Bobby Grindle, Sharon & Roger Frye

Friday, July 4
Sprints:
Dash—Ron Miller, (68), 1st' Van Gurley, (3), 2nd; Jeff Walker (10), 3rd; Don Walker, Jr. (20), 4th.
Slow Heat—Denny England, (84), 1st; Tony Elliott, (35), 2nd; Tom Patterson, (21b), 3rd; Bill Teters, (34), 4th.
Fast Heat—Ron Miller, (68), 1st; Bimbo Atkins, (36), 2nd; Van Gurley, (3), 3rd; John Althouse (77), 4th.

Feature—Van Gurley, (3); 1st; Ron Miller, (68) 2nd; Rocky Fisher (21) 3rd; Jeff Walker (10), 4th; Don Walker, Jr. (20) 5th; DeWayne Barker (24), 6th; Denny England (84), 7th

Late Model:
Dash—John White, (87), 1st; Bruce Hogue (25), 2nd; Roger Frye (6) 3rd; Tom Beezley (69) 4th.
Slow Heat—Charlie Hyde (65), 1st; Terry Sroufe (11) 2nd; Barry Lemons (71) 3rd, Duane Ronk (27) 4th.
Fast Heat—Roger Grossnickle (17), 1st; John White, (87), 2nd; Ted Hudson (45), 3rd; Roger Frye (6), 4th.
Feature—John White (87), 1st; Roger Grossnickle (17), 2nd; Roger Richards (51), 3rd; Roger Frye (6), 4th; Tom Beezley, (69) 5th; Bruce Hogue (25) 6th; Ted Hudson (45) 7th.

Sportsman:
Dash—John Fitzpatrick (5) 1st; Walt Roland (62) 2nd; Jeff Wigent (30) 3rd; Bob Grindle, (6) 4th.
Slow Heat—Tom Martin (00) 1st; Dan Blocker (55) 2nd; Scott Dausman (21) 3rd; Dale Bolinger (33) 4th.
Fast Heat—Bob King (53) 1st; Randy Woodling (75) 2nd; Dick Day (12) 3rd; Terry Baker (81) 4th.
Feature—Bob King (53) 1st; Randy Woodling (75) 2nd; Jeff Wigent (30) 3rd; Dick Day (12) 4th; Tom Leiter (70) 5th; Walt Rowland (62) 6th; Tom Martin (00) 7th.

Saturday, July 5
Sprints:
Dash—Louie Mann (57) 1st; Jeff Walker (10) 2nd; Van Gurley (3) 3rd; Don Walker, Jr. (20) 4th.
Slow Heat—Rocky Fisher (21) 1st; Gary Fisher (37) 2nd; John Althouse (77) 3rd; Denny England (84) 4th.
Fast Heat-Louie Mann (57) 1st; Van Gurley (3) 2nd; Jeff Walker (10) 3rd; Ron Miller (68) 4th.
Feature—Louie Mann (57) 1st; Ron Miller (68) 2nd; Van Gurley (3) 3rd; Denny England (84) 4th; Rocky Fisher (21) 5th; Bimbo Atkins (36) 6th; Jeff Walker (10) 7th.

Late Models:
Dash—Ted Hudson (45) 1st; John White (87) 2nd; Tom Beezley (69) 3rd; Roger Grossnickle (17) 4th.
Slow Heat—Terry Sroufe (12) 1st; Bruce Hogue (25) 2nd; Les Sroufe (11) 3rd; Charlie Hyde (65) 4th
Fast Heat—Tom Beezley (69)1st; Ted Hudson (45) 2nd; John Orr (80) 3rd; Roger Richards (51) 4th.
Feature-Roger Frye (6) 1st; Tom Beezley (69) 2nd; Terry Sroufe (12) 3rd; Les Sroufe (11) 4th; Charlie Hyde (65) 5th; Steve Brown (33) 6th; Duane Ronk (27) 7th.

Sportsman:
Mid-season Championship—Randy Woodling (75) 1st; John Fitzpatrick (5) 2nd; Walt Rowland (62) 3rd; Jeff Wigent (30) 4th; Scott Dausman (21) 5th; Tom Martin (00) 6th; Terry Baker (8) 7th.

Demolition Derby:
Final Standings: James Wigent, 1st; Jeff Bucher, 2nd; Mark Downing, 3rd; Mark Born, 4th.

Saturday, July 12, 1980
Gurley Wins Mid-Season Sprint Title At Speedway

Van Gurley, making his move from second to first late in the race, captured the 40-lap Mid-Season Sprint Championship Saturday night at Warsaw Motor Speedway.

Gurley trailed Ron Miller for most of the race. But with only a few laps remaining, Gurley passed Miller on the outside and held on for the title. Miller settled for second; Mark Caldwell, who started near the back, was third and Bimbo Atkins fourth. Miller was the sprint dash winner. John Althouse won the slow heat and Denny England the fast heat.

In the late model feature, Little Joe Bennett was a winner in only his second appearance of the season. Bennett and Charlie Hyde exchanged the lead twice before Bennett stayed in front. Roger Frye won the dash, Hyde the slow heat, and Ted Hudson the fast heat.

Mike Cochenour was the V-8 sportsman feature winner, finishing ahead of runner-up Walt Rowland.

Sprints:
Dash-Ron Miller, 1st, Bimbo Atkins, 2nd; DeWayne Barker, 3rd.
40 Lap Feature-Van Gurley, 1st; Ron Miller, 2nd; Mark Caldwell, 3rd; Bimbo Atkins, 4th; Rocky Fisher, 5th; DeWayne Barker, 6th; Gary Fisher, 7th.
Slow Heat- -John Althouse, 1st; Rocky Fisher, 2nd; Mark Caldwell, 3rd.
Fast Heat—Denny England, 1st; Van Gurley, 2nd; Ron Miller, 3rd; Bimbo Atkins, 4th.

Late Models:
Dash-Roger Frye, 1st; Tom Beezley, 2nd; Bruce Hogue, 3rd.
Feature—Joe Bennett, 1st; Charlie Hyde, 2nd; Roger Richards, 3rd; Bruce Hogue, 4th; Tom Beezley, 5th; Roger Frye, 6th; John Orr, 7th.
Slow Heat—Charlie Hyde, 1st; Steve Brown, 2nd; Terry Sroufe, 3rd; Duane Ronk, 4th.
Fast Heat—Ted Hudson, 1st; Tom Beezley, 2nd; Joe Bennett, 3rd; Roger Frye, 4th.

V-8 Sportsman:
Dash—John Fitzpatrick, 1st; Mike Cochenour, 2nd; Bob King, 3rd; Randy Woodling, 4th.
Feature-Mike Cochenour, 1st; Walt Rowland, 2nd; Terry Baker, 3rd; Bob Johnson, 4th; Scott Dausman, 5th; Harvey Hayes,6th.
Slow Heat—Harvey Hayes, 1st; Tom Martin, 2nd; Scott Dausman, 3rd.
Fast Heat-Terry Baker, 1st; Mike Cochenour, 2nd; Bob Johnson, 3rd; Randy Woodling, 4th.

Saturday, July 19, 1980
Mid-Season Championship At Warsaw Speedway

The Mid-Season Championships at the Warsaw Speedway are history now and the victors have been crowned the champions in their respective divisions. Saturday night's Mid-Season Championship for Late Models brought to a close the three week series that began with the V-8 Sportsman followed by the Sprints.

Tom Beezley, this year's point leader in the Late Model division started the Mid-Season feature event on the pole position. Tom's consistent running all year gained him the starting position and put just enough space between him and John White that he was able to establish an early lead. This rather sizeable lead was short lived, as White worked his way through the traffic and set his sights on the leader.

This battle continued lap after lap but when the checkered flag was waved, Beezley was the Mid-Season Champ. The trophies were presented by Corey Baker, daughter of Mr. and Mrs. Danny Baker.

Other events in the Late Model Class included Terry Sroufe winning the dash over Ted Hudson. Tom Beezley won the slow heat over Charlie Hyde and Ted Hudson was victorious over Roger Richards in the Fast Heat.

Victorious In Feature. In the Feature, Van Gurley was victorious over Dave Erickson with Denzel Archer, Jeff Walker and Oscar Smith finishing third through fifth respectively. In the Dash, Van Gurley won over second place Don Walker, Jr., followed by John Althouse, third; and Jeff Walker, fourth. The Slow heat was won by Bimbo Atkins with Erickson and Barry Lemons finishing second and third in a repeat of last week's Fast Heat. Denny England was able to take the lead from Archer early in the race and then hold off Gurley for the remaining laps to win back to back events.

In the V-8 Sportsman, Randy Woodling won the Feature and the Fast Heat finishing ahead of Mike Cochenhour and Bob Johnson in the Feature and Fast Heat respectively. Other finishers in the Feature were Walt Rowland (third); Scott Dausman (fourth); with Terry Baker finishing fifth ahead of Tom Martin. The Dash was won by Baker, ahead of second place Woodling and third place Walt Rowland. John Fitzpatrick finished third in the Fast Heat behind Woodling and Johnson, first and second respectively.

Saturday, July 26, 1980 – Rainout

Saturday, August 2, 1980 – Rainout

Wednesday, August 6, 1980
Speedway Results

Van Gurley was three-for-three in the sprint division of the Warsaw Motor Speedway's racing program at the Kosciusko County Fair Wednesday night. Gurley won each of his three races, including the sprint feature.

Other feature winners were Ted Hudson in the late model and Bob King in the V-8 sportsman. Hudson also won the late model dash.

Also on the card was the Penguin Point Big Wheel Race, with Matt Dausman winning the 4-5 year old division and Rodney Naylor the 6-7 age group.

<u>Sprint:</u>
Dash—Van Gurley, 1st; Larry Jordan, 2nd; Oscar Smith, 3rd.
Fast Heat—Van Gurley, 1st; Ron Miller, 2nd; Don Walker, 3rd.

Slow Heat—Louis Mann, 1st; Dennis England, 2nd; Jeff Walker, 3rd.
Feature-Van Gurley, 1st; Louie Mann, 2nd; Ron Miller, 3rd; DeWayne Barker, 4th; Don Walker, 5th.
Late Model:
Dash—Ted Hudson, 1st; Roger Frye, 2nd; Terry Sroufe, 3rd.
Fast Heat—Bruce Hogue, 1st; Roger Frye, 2nd; Ted Hudson, 3rd.
Slow Heat-John Orr, 1st; Joe Bennett, 2nd; Ed Martin, 3rd.
Feature-Ted Hudson, 1st; Tom Beezley, 2nd; Roger Frye, 3rd; Ed Martin, 4th; Bruce Hogue, 5th; Les Sroufe, 6th.
V8 Sportsman:
Dash-Randy Woodling, 1st; Tom Leiter, 2nd; Tom Martin, 3rd.
Fast Heat—John Fitzpatrick, 1st; John Hersha, 2nd; Tom Leiter, 3rd.
Slow Heat-Walt Rowland, 1st; Bob King, 2nd; Mike Coughenour.
Feature-Bob King, 1st; Randy Woodling, 2nd; John Fitzpatrick, 3rd; Tom Leiter, 4th; John Hersha, 5th; Bob Johnson, 6th.
Big Wheel:
4 and 5 Year Olds—Matt Dausman, 1st; Eric Ewert, 2nd; David Kearns, 3rd.
6 and 7 Year Olds-Rodney Naylor, 1st; Christine Tingley, 2nd; Chad O'Reilly, 3rd.

Saturday, August 9, 1980
Van Gurley Wins Sprint Crown

Pole-sitter Van Gurley led from start to finish in capturing the season sprint championship Saturday night at the Warsaw Motor Speedway. Denny England finished second and Ron Miller third in the sprint feature. Ted Hudson won the late model feature and Walt Roland was first in the V-8 sportsman feature.

In the sprint division, England won the dash, DeWayne Barker the slow heat and Miller the fast heat. Hudson won the late model dash, Les Sroufe the late model slow heat and John Orr the fast heat. In the sportsman division, Terry Baker won the dash, and Bob Johnson the fast heat.

Sprint:
Dash—Denny England, 1st; Tony Elliott, 2nd; John Althouse, 3rd.
Slow Heat—DeWayne Barker, 1st; Gary Fisher, 2nd.
Fast Heat—Ron Miller, 1st; Paul Grim, 2nd; Denny England, 3rd; Denzel Archer, 4th.
Feature—Van Gurley, 1st; Denny England, 2nd; Ron Miller, 3rd; Tony Elliott, 4th; DeWayne Barker, 5th; Dave Erickson, 6th; John Althouse, 7th; Gary Fisher, 8th; Paul Grim, 9th.
Late Model:
Dash—Ted Hudson, 1st; Roger Frye, 2nd; Tom Beezley, 3rd; Terry Sroufe, 4th.
Slow Heat—Les Sroufe, 1st; Bruce Hogue, 2nd; Steve Brown, 3rd; Duane Ronk, 4th.
Fast Heat—John Orr, 1st; Roger Richards, 2nd; Roger Frye, 3rd; Charlie Hyde, 4th.
Feature—Ted Hudson, 1st; Tom Beezley, 2nd; Bruce Hogue, 3rd; Roger Frye, 4th; John Orr, 5th; Les Sroufe, 6th; Charlie Hyde, 7th.
V-8 Sportsman:
Dash—Terry Baker, 1st; John Fitzpatrick, 2nd; Tom Leiter, 3rd; Dick Day, 4th.
Slow Heat—Dale Bolinger, 1st; Tom Martin, 2nd; Scott Dausman, 3rd; Joe Pickett, 4th.
Fast Heat—Bob Johnson, 1st; Bob King, 2nd; Walt Roland, 3rd; John Hersha, 4th.
Feature—Walt Roland, 1st; Mike Couchenour, 2nd; John Fitzpatrick, 3rd; Terry Baker, 4th; Bob Johnson, 5th; Randy Woodling, 6th; Alan Marsh, 7th.

Saturday, August 16, 1980 – Rainout

Saturday, August 23, 1980
Speedway Results

Duane Ronk, Warsaw

Season championship winners were crowned in the late model and V-8 sportsman divisions and a blistering one-lap record run was recorded in sprint competition Saturday night at the Warsaw Motor Speedway.

Ted Hudson capitalized on Tom Beezley's engine problems to win the late model season championship while Bob King overcame a strong challenge from Randy Woodling to win the sportsman feature. Beezley, the season point leader and mid-season late model champion, took the feature lead from the pole spot and appeared on the verge of victory when engine trouble forced him out. Hudson, who started beside Beezley, then took over and led the rest of the way as Bruce Hogue finished second. Roger Frye was third.

King, the point leader in the sportsman class, led from the start despite a hard-charging Woodling who wound up second. Walt Roland was third. In the sprints, Louie Mann, the feature winner, set a lap record on the quarter-mile clay oval of 14.98 seconds.

Sprints:
Dash—Van Gurley, 1st; Louis Mann, 2nd; Tim Bookmiller, 3rd; John Althouse, 4th.
Slow Heat—DeWayne Barker, 1st; Tony Elliott, 2nd; Bill Teeters, 3rd; Tom Patterson, 4th.
Fast Heat—Denny England, 1st; Jim Lipkey, 2nd; Louie Mann, 3rd; Don Walker, Jr., 4th.
Feature—Louie Mann, 1st; Rocky Fisher, 2nd; Tim Bookmiller, 3rd; Van Gurley, 4th; Jim Lipkey, 5th; Charlie Sarver, 6th; Daniel Archer, 7th; DeWayne Barker, 8th; Denny England, 9th; Don Walker, Jr., 10th.

Late Model:
Dash—Tom Beezley, 1st; Ed Martin, 2nd; Ted Hudson, 3rd; Terry Sroufe, 4th.
Slow Heat—Charlie Hyde, 1st; Bruce Hogue, 2nd; Roger Richards, 3rd; John Orr, 4th.
Fast Heat—Roger Frye, 1st; Tom Beezley, 2nd; Ed Martin, 3rd; Les Sroufe, 4th.
Feature—Ted Hudson, 1st; Bruce Hogue, 2nd; Roger Frye, 3rd; Charlie Hyde, 4th; Roger Richards, 5th; Terry Sroufe, 6th; John White, 7th; Ed Martin, 8th; Les Sroufe, 9th; Duane Ronk, 10th.

Sportsman:
Dash—Bob King, 1st; Randy Woodling, 2nd; John Fitzpatrick, 3rd; Walt Roland, 4th.
Slow Heat—Tom Martin, 1st; Scott Dausman, 2nd; Alan Marsh, 3rd; Terry Leiter, 4th.
Fast Heat—Terry Baker, 1st; Dick Day, 2nd; Randy Woodling, 3rd; Tim Smith, 4th.
Feature—Bob King, 1st; Randy Woodling, 2nd; Walt Roland, 3rd; John Fitzpatrick, 4th; Terry Baker, 5th; Tom Leiter, 6th; Bob Johnson, 7th; Scott Dausman, 8th; Tom Martin, 9th; Alan Marsh, 10th.

1981
Grindle Gives it a Go

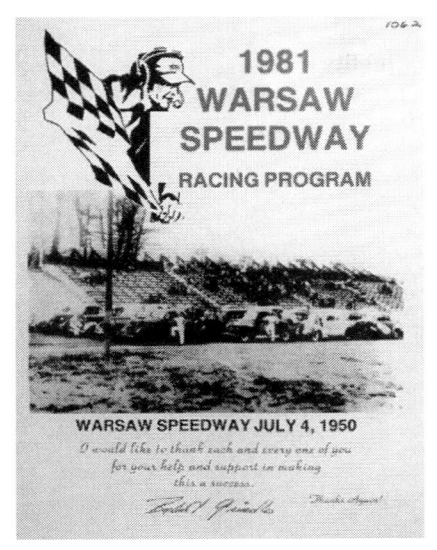

Sprints, late models, and street stock classes all continued into the 1980's with many drivers making a name for themselves as the ones to beat. Bobby Grindle was hired as Speedway Promoter for the 1981 season and continued throughout the end of 1982 bringing in Hoosier Tire's, Irish Saunders, as the track announcer. Bobby brought many interesting happenings to the track including a track clown, city official and school bus driver races, and even a color-lighted pond complete with 3 fountains in the center of the track. The Grindle years were definitely known as highly entertaining and fun for the whole family.

Saturday, May 2, 1981
Warsaw Speedway Opens Season

The Warsaw Motor Speedway opened the season last Saturday night with its regular lineup of races in addition to a special 10-lap event won by a Ringer.

In a special attraction that matched elected county and city officials as well as law enforcement officers, state trooper Dan Ringer edged runner-up Superior Court Judge Robert Burner. However, the latter, convinced he can beat Ringer on the track, will get a rematch with Ringer in a two-car race this Saturday night.

Feature winners on opening night were Louie Mann, sprint; Art Leiter, late model; and Rick Anders, street stock. The runner-up in both the sprint and late model features were winners in their respective fast heats—Ron Miller, sprint, and Tom Beezley, late model. Tom Leiter was the street stock fast heat winner but did not finish among the leaders in the street feature.

Race Results:
Sprint Dash—Ron Miller(68), Rocky Fisher(21), Ron Fisher(17).
Late Model Dash—John Orr(88), Tom Beezley(69), Roger Frye(6).

Street Stock Dash—Tim Goshert(79), Walt Maley(20), Tom Leiter(3), Harvey Hayes(80).
Sprint Slow Heat—Tony Elliott(35), Tom Patterson(21), DeWayne Barker (24), John Althouse(77).
Late Model Slow Heat—John White(87), Scott Dausman(21), Mike Brown(79), D. Owens(8).
Street Stock Slow Heat—Don Prater(1), Dick Day(12), Dean Green(82), Robert Johnson(22).
Sprint Fast Heat—Ron Miller(68), Ron Fisher(17), Rocky Fisher(21), Louie Mann(57).
Late Model Fast Heat—Tom Beezley(69), Art Leiter(78), Terry Sroufe(12), Bob King(53).
Street Stock Fast Heat—Tom Leiter(3), Tim Goshert(79), Walt Maley(20), Rocky Anders(14).
Sprint Feature—Louie Mann(57), Ron Miller(68), Rocky Fisher(21), Tom Patterson (21), DeWayne Barker(24), Terry Shepherd (7), Tony Elliott(35), Ron Fisher(17), Mike Mann(79).
Late Model Feature—Art Leiter(78), Tom Beezley(69), Terry Sroufe(12), John White(87), Roger Richards(51), Mike Brown(79), Roger Frye(61), D. Owens(8).
Street Stock Feature—Rocky Anders(14), Dick Day(12), Walt Maley(20), Don Prater(1), Harvey Hayes(80), Tim Goshert(79), Robert Johnson(22).
Special Event Race—Dan Ringer, State Trooper; Bob Burner, Judge; Mike Miner, Prosecuting Attorney; Mike Hodges, Mayor.

Saturday, May 9, 1981 – Rainout

Saturday, May 16, 1981
Speedway Results

Ron Miller and Tom Beezley dominated the preliminary heats in their respective divisions, but when it came down to the feature races, other drivers took over at the Warsaw Speedway last Saturday.

Miller won the sprint car dash and fast heats but settled for second to Louie Mann in the sprint feature. Likewise, Beezley was first in both the late model dash and fast heat but it was Art Leiter who won the late model feature.

A special race for R.R. Donnelley employees was held, with Dan Hurd finishing first and Larry Needler second.

Race Results:

Sprint Dash – Ron Miller(68), John Althouse(77), Bimbo Atkins(36).
Late Model Dash-Tom Beezley(69), Art Leiter(78), Roger Richards(51).
Street Dash-Tom Leiter(3), Joe Pickett(79), Allen Marsh(75).
Sprint Fast-Ron Miller(68), John Althouse(77), Bimbo Atkins(36), Tom Patterson(21).
Late Model Fast—Tom Beezley(69), Art Leiter(78), Terry Sroufe(12), John White(87).
Street Fast—Dan Blocker(11), Tom Leiter(3), Allen Marsh(75), Dan Bolinger(35).
Late Model Slow—Sam Davis(43), Scott Dausman(21), Thames Goon(73), G. Denman(27).
Sprint Feature—Louie Mann(57), Ron Miller(68), Bimbo Atkins(36), Bob Teters(34), Terry Shepherd(7), Tony Elliott(35), K. Meyers(5), John Althouse(77), Tom Patterson(21).
Late Model Feature—Art Leiter (78), Terry Sroufe(12), Tom Beezley(69), Roger Richards(51), Thames Goon(73), John White(87), Sam Davis(43), Scott Dausman(21), Duane Owens(8), John Fitzpatrick(57), Bob Johnson(22), G. Denman(27).
Street Feature—Allen Marsh(75), Tom Leiter(3), Joe Pickett(79), Dan Blocker(11), Dan Bolinger(35), Rex Alley(17), Harvey Hayes(80), F. Baldridge(71), Robert Johnson(22), Tony Calhoun(27), Dick Day(12).

Saturday, May 23, 1981
Busy Weekend at Speedway

It was a busy holiday weekend at Warsaw Motor Speedway as races were held Saturday and Monday.

On Memorial Day, feature winners were Louie Mann, sprint; John Orr, late model; and Tom Leiter, street stock. Feature winners on Saturday were Bimbo Atkins, sprint; Art Leiter, late model; and Don Prater, street stock.

Terry Leiter, Warsaw

A special grudge race pitting the first two finishers from the opening night's City Officials race was held with the same result: Superior Court Judge Robert Burner beating state trooper Dan Ringer.

Saturday Results
Sprint Dash—Louie Mann (57), John Althouse (77), Bimbo Atkins (36).
Late Model Dash—Art Leiter (78), Randy Woodling (75), John Orr (88).
Street Stock Dash—Allen Marsh(75), Dale Bolinger(35), Don Prater(1).
Sprint Fast Heat—Bimbo Atkins(36), Tony Elliott(35), Louie Mann(57), John Althouse(77).
Late Model Fast Heat—Roger Richards(51), Art Leiter(78), John Orr(88), Bob Johnson(22).
Street Stock Fast Heat—Jeff Arnold(15), Dale Bolinger(35), Don Prater(1), Harvey Hayes(81).
Late Model Slow Heat—Tom Beezley(69), Thames Goon(73), Duane Eckright(18), Dee Frye(13).
Street Stock Slow Heat—Terry Leiter(3), Dewayne May(71), William Varney(47), Dean Green (82).
Street Stock Concey—William Varney(47), Arnold Prater(48), Will Sherman(8), Junior Blocker(4).
Sprint Feature—Bimbo Atkins(36), Louis Mann(57), Denny England(84), Terry Shepherd(7), Jeff Walker(10), John Althouse(77).
Late Model Feature—Art Leiter(78), Bob Johnson(22), John Orr(88), Roger Richards(51), Randy Woodling(75), Roger Frye(6), Sam Davis(43), Thames Goon(73), John Fitzpatrick(57), Duane Owens(8).
Street Stock Feature—Don Prater(1), Jeff Arnold(15), Dale Bolinger(35), Rex Alley(17), Dick Day(12), Dan Blocker(11), Harvey Hayes(81), Dean Green(87), Joe Pickett(79), Robert Johnson(22), Dale Bolinger(35), Arnold Prater(48), Jerry Leiter(3).

Monday Results
Sprint Dash—Jeff Walker(10), Denny England(84), John Althouse(77), Gary Grissom(23).
Late Model Dash—Bob Johnson(22), Terry Sroufe(12), Art Leiter(78), John Orr(88).
Street Stock Dash—Dick Day(12), Tom Leiter(3), Don Prater(1), Allen Marsh(75).
Sprint Heat—Louie Mann(57), Jeff Walker(10), Gary Grissom(23), John Althouse(77).
Late Model Fast Heat—Randy Woodling(75), Terry Sroufe(12), Art Leiter(78), Bob Johnson(22).
Street Stock Fast Heat—Harvey Hayes(81), Dale Bolinger(35), Tom Leiter(3), Dick Day(12).
Late Model Slow Heat—Doug Nusbaum(23), Rocky Anders(14), John Fitzpatrick(57), Dan Richards(37).
Street Stock Slow Heat—Dewayne May(71), Junior Blocker(4), Larry Blevins(01), Dan Blocker(11).
Sprint Feature—Louie Mann(57), Gary Grisssom(23), Jeff Walker(10), Terry Shepherd(7), Tray House(3), DeWayne Barker(24), Rob Roberts(4), John Althouse(77).
Late Model Feature—John Orr(88), Bob Johnson(22), Roger Richards(51), Doug Nusbaum(23), Dee

Frye(13), Gene Denman(27), Dan Richards(37), Rocky Anders(14).
Street Stock Feature—Tom Leiter(3), Dan Blocker(11), William Varney(47), Harvey Hayes(81), Robert Johnson(22), Dale Bolinger(35), Arnold Prater(48), Dewayne May(71).

Saturday, May 30, 1981
Warsaw Speedway Results

Each race, including heats, had a different winner at the Warsaw Motor Speedway program Saturday night. Feature winners were Terry Shepherd, sprint; Art Leiter, late model; and Dick Day, street stock.

In a race matching Warsaw Community Schools bus drivers, Tana Blocker finished first and Betty Engle second.

Greg Jones, Bunker Hill

Race Results:

Sprint Dash—Louie Mann(57), Denny England(84), Tony Elliott(35).
Late Model Dash—John White(87), Bob Johnson(22), Tom Beezley(69).
Street Dash—Walt Maley(20), Allen Marsh(75), Dale Bolinger(35).
Sprint Fast Heat—Bimbo Atkins(36), Louie Mann(57), Tony Elliott(35), Denny England(84).
Late Model Fast Heat—Bob Johnson(22), Tom Beezley(69), Terry Sroufe(12), Art Leiter(78).
Street Fast Heat—Dan Blocker(11), Walt Maley(20), Harvey Hayes(81), Dale Bolinger(35).
Late Model Slow Heat—John Fitzpatrick(57), Gene Denman(27), Thames Goon(73), Mike Brown(70).
Sprint Feature—Terry Shepherd(7), Denny England(84), Steve Kline(12), Rob Roberts(4), Bimbo Atkins(36), Tony Elliott(35), Louie Mann(57).
Late Model Feature—Art Leiter(78), Tom Beezley(69), Roger Frye(6), Bob Johnson(22), John Fitzpatrick(57), Sam Davis(43), Gene Denman(27), Mike Brown(70), Thames Goon(73), Terry Sroufe(12), Dee Frye(13), John Orr(88).
Street Feature—Dick Day(12), Paul Gardner(15), Dewayne May(71), Dan Blocker(11), William Varney(47), Dale Bolinger(35), Arnold Prater(48), Harvey Hayes(81), Dick Bland(3), Robert Johnson(22), Steve Oswalt(77), Jim Brown(28).
Warsaw School Bus Drive—Tana Blocker, Betty Engle, Clelda Harrold, Peggy Keeton, Ellen Green, Beth Stouder, Treva Bowers.

Saturday, June 6, 1981
Track Record Set At Speedway

It was a successful night at the Warsaw Motor Speedway for Tom Beezley Saturday as he won the late model feature as well as the dash. He also was third in the late model fast heat. But another late model driver, John White, got in his licks, too. White set a one-lap track record when he steered his late model vehicle around the oval in 16.68. Still, he finished no better than third in the feature.

Other feature winners were Bimbo Atkins, sprint, and John Fitzpatrick, street stock. Art

Leiter was second in the late model feature, John Althouse second in the sprint and Tom Leiter second in the street stock.

Dash winners were Althouse, sprint; Beezley, late model, and William Varney, street stock. Fast heat winners were Tony Elliott, sprint; Roger Richards, late model; and Dan Blocker, street stock. Randy Woodling (late model) and Kenny Shepherd (street stock) were slow heat winners.

Bimbo Atkins, Warsaw

Race Results:

Sprint Dash—John Althouse(77), Tony Elliott(35), Bob Kolacki(38).
Late Model Dash—Tom Beezley(69), Terry Sroufe(12), Art Leiter(78).
Street Stock Dash—William Varney(47), Rocky Anders(14), Harvey Hayes(81).
Sprint Fast Heat—Tony Elliott(35), Bimbo Atkins(36), Steve Kline(12), Terry Shepherd(7).
Late Model Fast Heat—Roger Richards(51), Terry Sroufe(12), Tom Beezley(69), Roger Frye(6).
Street Stock Fast Heat—Dan Blocker(11), Arnold Prater(48), Dave Fitzpatrick(57), Don Prater(1).
Late Model Slow Heat—Randy Woodling(75), Sam Davis(43), Scott Dausman(21), John Fitzpatrick(57).
Street Stock Slow Heat—Kenny Shepherd(72), Robert Johnson(22), Ron McKenzie(24), Larry Blevins(01).
Sprint Feature—Bimbo Atkins(36), John Althouse(77), Jeff Walker(10), Steve Kline(12), Keith Myers(5), Tony Elliott(35), Terry Shepherd(7).
Late Model Feature—Tom Beezley(69), Art Leiter(78), John White(87), Terry Sroufe(12), Roger Frye(6), Roger Richards(51), Scott Dausman(21), Randy Woodling(75), Bob King(53), Dean Green (27), Mike Brown(70), Bob Johnson(22).
Street Stock Feature—John Fitzpatrick(57), Tom Leiter(70), Arnold Prater(48), Don Prater(1), Dan Blocker(11), Harvey Hayes(81), Tom Schell(5), Robert Johnson(22), Ron McKenzie(24), Dick Day(12), Fred Wiles(25).

Saturday, June 13, 1981 – Rainout

Saturday, June 20, 1981
Warsaw Motor Speedway Results

Louie Mann and Art Leiter won the sprint and late model features, respectively, at the Warsaw Motor Speedway Saturday night. The street stock feature will be held next week.

Van Gurley won the sprint dash and fast heat and Ron Miller was the sprint slow

Joe Pickett, Warsaw

heat winner. John White captured the late model dash and fast heat while Tom Beezley steered to victory in the late model slow heat.

In street stock racing, Joe Pickett won the dash, Arnold Prater the fast heat, Allen Marsh the slow heat and Harvey Hayes the consolation.

Results:

Sprint:
Dash—Van Gurley(3B), Bimbo Atkins(36), Denny England(84).
Fast Heat—Van Gurley(3B), Bimbo Atkins(36), Leon Jordan(8), Steve Kline(12).
Slow Heat—Ron Miller(68), Jeff Walker(10), Louie Mann (57), Terry Shepherd(7).
Feature—Louie Mann(57), Rocky Fisher(21), John Althouse(77), Jeff Walker(10), Ron Miller(68), DeWayne Barker(24), Leon Jordon(8), Steve Kline(12), Charlie Sarver(5), Terry Shepherd(7), Bimbo Atkins(36), Tony Elliott(35).

Late Model:
Dash—John White(87), Roger Richards(51), Bruce Hogue(25).
Fast Heat—John White(87), Bruce Hogue (25), Art Leiter(78), Terry Sroufe(12).
Slow Heat—Tom Beezley(69), Bob Johnson(22), Roger Frye(6), Roger Richards(51), Rocky Anders(14), Dan Richards(37), John White(81), Bob King(53), Sam Davis(43), Dave Sellers(33).

Street Stock:
Dash—Joe Pickett(79), Arnold Prater(48), Rob Reed(37).
Fast Heat—Arnold Prater(48), Rex Alley(17), Dick Day(12), Joe Pickett(29).
Slow Heat—Allen Marsh(75), Harvey Hayes(81), Junior Blocker(4), Ron McKenzie(24).
Consy—Harvey Hayes(81), Ron McKenzie(24), Dan Blocker(11), Junior Blocker(4).

Saturday, June 27, 1981
Mann Sets Sprint Car Pace

Louie Mann's name regularly appears at the top of the list in the sprint car results at the Warsaw Motor Speedway and Saturday night was no exception. With a large crowd on hand, Mann won the sprint car fast heat and feature, making one of two drivers to win two races Saturday night.

Louie Mann, Kokomo

Art Leiter won the late model feature and Tom Leiter was the street stock feature winner.

Van Gurley won the sprint dash and Rocky Fisher the sprint slow heat. Bruce Hogue was the other double winner, taking the late model dash and fast heats while Bob Johnson won the late model slow heat. Dave Fitzpatrick won the street stock dash, Don Prater the fast heat and Joe Pickett the slow heat.

Race Results:

Sprint Dash—Van Gurley(3), Louie Mann(57), John Althouse(77).
Late Model Dash—Bruce Hogue(25), Art Leiter(78), Tom Beezley(69).
Street Stock Dash—Dave Fitzpatrick(57), Dewayne May(71), William Varney(47).
Sprint Fast Heat—Louie Mann(57), Ron Miller(68), Van Gurley(3), John Althouse(77).
Late Model Fast Heat—Bruce Hogue(25), Art Leiter(78), Randy Woodling(75), Tom Beezley(69).
Street Stock Fast Heat—Don Prater(1), Arnold Prater(48), William Varney(47), Dave Fitzpatrick(57).
Sprint Slow Heat—Rocky Fisher(21), Bimbo Atkins(36), Steve Kline(12), Rob Roberts(4).
Late Model Slow Heat—Bob Johnson(22), Rocky Anders(14), Mike Brown(70), Scott Dausman(21).
Street Stock Slow Heat—Joe Pickett(79), Keith Smith(29), Jim Brown(28), Dick Bland(3).
Street Stock Consy—Tony Calhoun(27), Robert Johnson(22), Dan Blocker(11), Joe Pickett(79).
Sprint Feature—Louie Mann(57), Tony Elliott(35), Rocky Fisher(21), John Althouse(77), Ron Miller(68), Van Gurley(3), Steve Kline(12), Tim Bookmiller(5), Bimbo Atkins(36), Jeff Donnelson(20), Rob Roberts(4), DeWayne Barker(24).
Late Model Feature—Art Leiter(78), Bruce Hogue(25), John White(87), Tom Beezley(69), Bob Johnson(22), Roger Richards(51), John Orr(88), Randy Woodling(75), Scott Dausman(21), Dan Richards(37), Mike Brown(70), Bob King(53).
Street Stock Feature—Tom Leiter(57), Allen Marsh(75), Don Prater(1), Dewayne May(71), Rex Alley(17), Harvey Hayes(81), Dave Shaw(80), William Varney(47), Tony Calhoun(27), Robert Johnson(22), Arnold Prater(48), Junior Blocker(4).

Last Week: Street Stock Feature:--Allen Marsh(75), Don Prater(1), William Varney(47), Arnold Prater(48), Danny Kelsey(31), Lance Creamer(69), Jim Brown(28), Rob Reed(37), Joe Pickett(79), Tom Schell(5), Rex Alley(17), Dale Shepherd(6).

Saturday, July 4, 1981
Fireworks On And Above Speedway

Arnold Prater, Warsaw

There were fireworks both on and above the Warsaw Speedway Saturday night. In addition to the annual July 4th fireworks display which takes place at the track, drivers competed in the regular lineup of the late model, sprint and street stock races Saturday.

Louie Mann was the sprint car king once again as he captured the sprint feature and the sprint dash. Jeff Walker won the sprint fast heat, with Mann second, and John Althouse won the slow heat.

Tom Beezley hit the finish line first in the late model feature after John White had captured both the dash and fast heat in the late model racing. Bob King took the late model slow heat.

Street stock feature winner was John Fitzpatrick, with Allen Marsh winning the dash, Arnold Prater the fast heat and Dan Blocker and Rick Shepler taking the slow heat races.

Race Results:

Sprint Dash—Louie Mann(57), Mark Todd(53), Denny England(84).
Late Model Dash—John White(87), Bruce Hogue(25), Tom Beezley(69).
Street Stock Dash—Allen Marsh(75), Harvey Hayes(81), Jeff Arnold(15).
Sprint Fast Heat—Jeff Walker(10), Louie Mann(57), Rocky Fisher(21), Mark Todd(53).
Late Model Fast Heat—John White(87), Bruce Hogue(25), Tom Beezley(69), Art Leiter(78).
Street Stock Fast Heat—Arnold Prater(48), Harvey Hayes(81), Allen Marsh(75), Don Prater(1).
Sprint Slow Heat—John Althouse(77), Tony Elliott(35), DeWayne Barker(24), Terry Shepherd(7).
Late Model Slow Heat—Bob King(53), Dan Richards(37), Sam Davis(43), Mike Brown(70).
Street Stock Slow Heat—Rick Shepler(43), Dewayne May(71), Robert Johnson(22), Kenny Shepherd(72).
Sprint Feature—Louie Mann(57), Bimbo Atkins(36), Tony Elliott(35), Jeff Walker(10), Rocky Fisher(21), John Althouse(77), Mark Todd(53), John Davis(43), Denny England(84).
Late Model Feature—Tom Beezley(69), Bruce Hogue(25), John White(87), Roger Richards(51), Scott Dausman(21), Bob King(53), Roger Frye(6), Dan Richards(37), Mike Brown(70), Randy Woodling(75), Bob Johnson(22), Art Leiter(78).
Street Stock Feature—John Fitzpatrick(57), Dewayne May(71), Harvey Hayes(81), Allen Marsh(75), Joe Pickett(79), Dick Day(12), Dan Blocker(11), Arnold Prater(48), Frank Baldridge(80), Rick Shepler(43), Rex Alley(17), Dale Bolinger(35).

Saturday, July 11, 1981
Gurley, Leiter, Day Win Speedway Features

Winning the dash heat was a good omen for drivers in the sprint and late model divisions at the Warsaw Motor Speedway Saturday night. Van Gurley steered his sprint car to victory in the dash and followed up with a feature win. Art Leiter did exactly the same thing in the late model division.

However, in the street stocks, dash winner Allen Marsh fared no better than fourth in the feature, which was won by Dick Day.

John Althouse

In the sprint feature, Gurley finished one place ahead of Tony Elliott, who won the sprint fast heat. John Althouse captured the sprint slow heat.

Tom Beezley, who was second to Leiter in the late model feature, won that division's fast heat with Roger Frye taking the late model slow heat.

The street stock fast heat was won by John Fitzpatrick while Ron McKenzie won the slow heat and Wayne Gibson the second slow heat race.

In Friday's demolition derby, Mike Geiger of Columbia City was the winner and Jeff Bucher of Rochester finished second.

Race Results:

Sprint:
Sprint Dash—Van Gurley(3), Tim Bookmiller(5), Denny England(84).
Sprint Fast Heat—Tony Elliott(35), Van Gurley(3), Tim Bookmiller(5), Denny England(84).
Sprint Feature—Van Gurley(3), Tony Elliott(35), Tim Bookmiller(5), Leon Jordon(8), Jeff Walker(10), Denny England(84), Terry Shepherd(7), John Althouse(77), Steve Kline(12), Tom Patterson(21), DeWayne Barker(24).

Late Model:
Late Model Dash—Art Leiter(78), Tom Beezley(69), Roger Richards(51).
Late Model Fast Heat—Tom Beezley(69), Terry Sroufe(12), Bob Johnson(22), Bruce Hogue(25).
Late Model Slow Heat—Roger Frye(6), Thames Goon(73), Jeff Ness(16), John Lynn(55).
Late Model Feature—Art Leiter(78), Tom Beezley(69), Bob Johnson(22), Roger Frye(6), Randy Woodling(75), Ted Hudson(88), Bruce Hogue(25), Bob King(53), Terry Sroufe(12), Roger Richards(51), Thames Goon(73), Jeff Ness(16).

Street Stock:
Street Stock Dash—Allen Marsh(75), Dick Day(12), Harvey Hayes(81).
Fast Heat—John Fitzpatrick(57), Dale Bolinger(35), Allen Marsh(75), Joe Pickett(79).
Slow Heat—Ron McKenzie(24), Don Prater(1), Jr. Blocker(4), William Varney(47).
Slow - Slow Heat—Wayne Gibson(19), Robert Johnson(22), Kenny Shepherd(72), Dewayne May(71).
Street Stock Feature—Dick Day(12), Joe Pickett(79), Dale Bolinger(35), Allen Marsh(75), Don Prater(1), Arnold Prater(48), Harvey Hayes(81), Ron McKenzie(24), Dave Shaw(80), Robert Johnson(22), John Fitzpatrick(57), Tony Calhoun(27).

Saturday, July 18, 1981
Mann, Leiter, Marsh Capture Mid-Season Titles At Speedway

It was a good night for Louie Mann at the Warsaw Speedway Saturday night, as he won both the sprint mid-season championship feature and sprint dash, and was the runner-up in the sprint fast heat.

Art Leiter captured the late model mid-season championship and Allen Marsh steered his car to victory in the street stock feature. They were respective runners-up in the late model and street stock dash. The late model dash was won by Tom Beezley and the street stock dash was captured by Ron McKenzie, who was second in the street stock fast heat.

Ron Miller won the sprint fast heat, and Jeff Donnelson finished in first in the sprint slow heat. In the late models, Bruce Hogue and Randy Woodling were victorious in the respective fast and slow heats.

Also in the street stocks, Tony Calhoun drove his car to a first place in the fast heat and Don Prater followed with a win in the slow heat. Frank Baldridge took the consolation event and Jim Brown won the slowest feature.

Results:

Sprint:
Sprint Dash—Louie Mann(57), Tony Elliott(35), Bimbo Atkins(36).
Sprint Fast Heat—Ron Miller(68), Louie Mann(57), Greg Jones(99), Tony Elliott(35).
Sprint Slow Heat—Jeff Donnelson(2), DeWayne Barker(3), Steve Kline(12), John Althouse(77).
Sprint Feature—Louie Mann(57), Tony Elliott(35), DeWayne Barker(3), Terry Shepherd(7), Tom Patterson(21), Bill Teters(34), Steve Butler(98), Greg Jones(99), Denny England(84), Steve Kline(12), Jeff Donnelson(2), Rob Roberts(4).

Late Model:
Late Model Dash—Tom Beezley(69), Art Leiter(78), Bruce Hogue(25).
Late Model Fast Heat—Bruce Hogue(25), Bob Johnson(22), John White(87), Art Leiter(78).
Late Model Slow Heat—Randy Woodling(75), Scott Dausman(21), Jeff Ness(16), Dee Frye(13).
Late Model Feature—Art Leiter(78), Bruce Hogue(25), Bob Johnson(22), Roger Richards(51), Walt Maley(88), Tom Beezley(69), Roger Frye(6), Terry Sroufe(12), Bob King(53), Scott Dausman(21), Jeff Ness(16), Randy Woodling(75).

Street Stock:
Street Stock Dash—Ron McKenzie(24), Allen Marsh(75), Harvey Hayes(81).
Street Stock Fast Heat—Tony Calhoun(27), Ron McKenzie(24), Dave Fitzpatrick(57), Dick Day(12).
Street Stock Slow Heat—Don Prater(1), Arnold Prater(48), Joe Pickett(79), Jr. Blocker(4).
Consolation Street Stock—Frank Baldridge(80), Robert Johnson(22), Randy Brandon(33), Kim Bussard(5).
Street Stock Slowest—Jim Brown(28), Jim Frushour(35), Kim Bussard(5), Jerry Burkett(56).
Street Stock Feature—Allen Marsh(75), Wm Varney(47), Harvey Hayes(81), Don Prater(1), Arnold Prater(48), Keith Smith(29), Jr. Blocker(4), Thurl Kester(83), Dave Fitzpatrick(57), Dan Blocker(11), John Hersha(93), Joe Pickett(79).

Saturday, July 25, 1981
Art Leiter Mid-Season Late Model Champion

Tony Elliott, Warsaw

Art Leiter won his ninth—and biggest—feature race of the Warsaw Motor Speedway season Saturday night when he steered to victory in the late model mid-season championships. He finished the 50-lap event ahead of runner-up Bruce Hogue and third-place finisher John White.

In the other evening features, Van Gurley was the sprint winner and Frank Baldridge was first in the street stock. Gurley also won the sprint dash and Baldridge the street stock dash. Tom Beezley won both the late model dash and fast heat and Scott Dausman took the late model slow heat.

Sprint fast heat winner was Tony Elliott and sprint slow heat winner was Terry Shepherd. Street stock slow heat winner was William Varney and Tony Calhoun won the slow heat. The first street stock consolation went to Sam Barrett and the second to Kim Bussard.

The Big Wheel races were won by Chad McKenzie (4-5 age division) and Jeff Ulshafer(6-7 group).

Race Results:

Sprint Dash—Van Gurley(5), DeWayne Barker(3), Bimbo Atkins(36).
Late Model Dash—Tom Beezley(69), Bob Johnson(22), John White(87).
Street Stock Dash—Frank Baldridge(80), Don Prater(1), Harvey Hayes(81).
Sprint Fast Heat—Tony Elliott(35), Van Gurley(5), Louie Mann(57), Steve Kline(12).
Late Model Fast Heat—Tom Beezley(69), Arden Leiter(78), John White(87), Walt Maley(88).
Street Stock Fast Heat—William Varney(47), Don Prater(1), Terry Baker(37), Rex Alley(17).
Sprint Slow Heat—Terry Shepherd(7), Ron Miller(68), Bill Teters(34), Tom Patterson(21).
Late Model Slow Heat—Scott Dausman(21), Terry Sroufe(12), Sam Davis(43), Bob King(53).
Street Stock Slow Heat—Tony Calhoun(27), Ron Stine(42), John Hersha(93), Joe Pickett(79).
Consy Street Stock—Kim Bussard(5), Sam Barrett(28), Randy Brandon(33), Shane Denny(58).
Sprint Feature—Van Gurley(5), Louie Mann(57), Ron Miller(68), Tony Elliott(35), Steve Kline(12), Terry Shepherd(7), DeWayne Barker(3), Tom Patterson(21), Bill Teters(34), Randy White(44).
Street Stock Feature—Frank Baldridge(80), Tony Calhoun(27), William Varney(47), Harvey Hayes(81), Fred Wiles(25), Arnold Prater(48), Don Prater(1), Rob Reed(37), John Hersha(93), Dewayne May(71), Joe Pickett(79), Rex Alley(17).
Mid-Season Championship Late Model—Art Leiter(78), Bruce Hogue(25), John White(87), Terry Sroufe(12), Randy Woodling(75), Roger Richards(51), Tom Beezley(69), Steve Brown(35), Roger Frye(37), Walt Maley(88), Bob Johnson(22), Rocky Anders(14).
Big Wheel—Age 4-5—Chad McKenzie(5), Sherry Atkins(5), Billy Nadoeski(4).
   Age 6-7—Jeff Ulshafer(6), Chad O'Reeley(7), Brian Althouse(7).

Saturday, August 1, 1981
Mann, Beezley, Marsh Win Speedway Features

Louie Mann, Tom Beezley and Allen Marsh won the respective features of sprint car, late model and street stock features at the Warsaw Speedway Saturday night.

It was a particularly good night for Marsh, who also captured the street stock dash and street stock fast heats. Mann also took home the top prize in the sprint car dash. Art Leiter was a double winner in the late model dash and late model fast heats.

Other top placers were Rocky Fisher in the sprint fast heat (he was second in the sprint feature), Terry Shepherd in the sprint slow heat, Jeff Ness in the late model slow heat and Terry Baker in the street stock slow heat.

Race Results:

Sprint Dash—Louie Mann(57), Bimbo Atkins(36), Tony Elliott(35).
Late Model Dash—Art Leiter(78), Roger Richards(51), Tom Beezley(69).
Street Stock Dash—Allen Marsh(75), Don Prater(1), Harvey Hayes(81).
Sprint Fast Heat—Rocky Fisher(21), Tony Elliott(35), Louie Mann(57), Jeff Walker(10).
Late Model Fast Heat—Art Leiter(78), Walt Maley(88), Bruce Hogue(25), Bob King(53).
Street Stock Fast Heat—Allen Marsh(75), Don Prater(1), William Varney(47), Harvey Hayes(81).

Denny England, Warsaw

Sprint Slow Heat—Terry Shepherd(7), John Althouse(77), Don Walker, Jr.(20).
Late Model Slow Heat—Jeff Ness(16), Sam Davis(43), C. J. Gibbs(52), Gene Denman(27).
Street Stock Slow Heat—Terry Baker(23), Dan Blocker(11), Tony Calhoun(27), Keith Smith(29).
Sprint Feature—Louie Mann(57), Rocky Fisher(21), DeWayne Barker(3), Bimbo Atkins(36), Terry Shepherd(7), Jeff Walker(10), Denny England(84), Don Walker, Jr.(20), Tom Patterson(21b), Leon Jordan(8), Randy White(44), Dick Watson(19), John Althouse(77), Tony Elliott(35), Rob Roberts(4).
Late Model Feature—Tom Beezley(69), Walt Maley(88), Bruce Hogue(25), Bob King(53), C.J.Gibbs(52), Sam Davis(43), Steve Brown(35), Art Leiter(78), Roger Frye(6), Tom Leiter(77), Randy Woodling(75), Thames Goon(73), Jeff Ness(16), Gene Denman(27), D. Howe(2H).
Street Stock Feature—Allen Marsh(75), Arnold Prater(48), Tony Calhoun(27), Dan Blocker(11), Harvey Hayes(81), William Varney(47), Joe Pickett(79), Dewayne May(71), Junior Blocker(4), Tim Gushert(28), Rex Alley(17), Dean Greene(23), Robert Johnson(22), Ron McKenzie(24), John Fitzpatrick(57), Dick Day(12).

Saturday, August 8, 1981
Knorr, Miller, Day Win Speedway Features

Dave Knorr, Ron Miller and Dick Day were feature winners Saturday night at Warsaw Motor Speedway. Knorr won the late model featured event as well as the late model dash. Miller captured the sprint feature and Day the street stock feature.

Louie Mann was first in the sprint dash, Tony Elliott won the sprint fast heat and Rocky Fisher, who was second in sprint feature, was the sprint slow heat winner. In late model racing, Bob King won the fast heat and Walt Maley the slow heat.

Arnold Prater captured the street stock dash, Allen Marsh the fast heat and Dan Blocker the slow heat. Rick Shepler won the street stock consolation.

Race Results:

Sprint Dash—Louie Mann(57), Denny England(84), John Althouse(77).
Late Model Dash—Dave Knorr(99), Bruce Hogue(25), Art Leiter(78).
Street Stock Dash—Arnold Prater(48), Allen Marsh(75), Rex Alley(17).
Sprint Fast Heat—Tony Elliott(35), Terry Shepherd(7), Denny England(84), DeWayne Barker(3).
Late Model Fast Heat—Bob King(53), Joe Bennett(3), Art Leiter(78), Tom Beezley(79B).
Street Stock Fast Heat—Allen Marsh(75), Dewayne May(71), Arnold Prater(48), Frank Baldridge(80).
Sprint Slow Heat—Rocky Fisher(21), Ron Miller(68), Jeff Donelson(20).
Late Model Slow Heat—Walt Maley(88), Terry Sroufe(12), Mike Gerner(45), Sam Davis(43).

Street Stock Slow Heat—Dan Blocker(11), Dick Day(12), Joe Pickett(79), John Hersha(93).
Street Stock Consy—Rick Shepler(43), Shane Denny(58), John Vigar(09), Thurl Kester(83).
Sprint Feature—Ron Miller(68), Rocky Fisher(21), Tony Elliott(35), DeWayne Barker(3), John Althouse(77), Tom Patterson(21B), Jeff Walker(10), Bill Teters(34), Steve Kline(12), Denny England(84), Jeff Donelson(2), Louie Mann(57), John Davis(7A), Terry Shepherd(7).
Late Model Feature—Dave Knorr(99), Terry Sroufe(12), Joe Bennett(3), Mike Gerner(45), Bruce Hogue(25), Tom Leiter(77), Walt Maley(88), Roger Richards(51), Bob King(53), Randy Woodling(75), Bill Ice(62), Gene Denman(27).
Street Stock Feature—Dick Day(12), William Varney(47), DeWayne Eakright(08), Arnold Prater(48), Dewayne May(71), Joe Pickett(79), Roger Fitzpatrick(57), Mark Oswald(69), Ed Eldridge(36), Tony Calhoun(27), Terry Baker(23), Randy Brandon(33), Ron McKenzie(24), Allen Marsh(75), Keith Smith(29), Duane Stout(65).
Demolition Derby—Chuck Ward, Elkhart; Bill Whittenberger, Fort Wayne.

Saturday, August 15, 1981
Late Model Sweep For Beezley

Tom Beezley scored a late model sweep Saturday night at the Warsaw Motor Speedway, winning that division's feature, fast heat and dash.

Louie Mann captured the sprint feature while Allen Marsh drove to victory in the street stock feature. In the sprints, Bimbo Atkins was first in the dash and second to Mann in the feature. Rocky Fisher won the sprint slow heat.

In the street stocks, Marsh also won the dash, Arnold Prater took the slow heat and Dick Day the fast heat. Bruce Hogue was second to Beezley in the late model feature, with Terry Sroufe third and Art Leiter fourth.

Results:

Sprint Cars:
Feature—Louie Mann(57), Bimbo Atkins(36), Denny England(84), Tony Elliott(35), Greg Jones(99), Terry Shepherd(7), Steve Kline(12), Tom Patterson(21), Leon Jordon(8), Dick Watson(19), Rocky Fisher(21), Adam Grissom(7a), John Davis(43), DeWayne Barker(3).
Dash—Bimbo Atkins(36), Terry Shepherd(7), Louie Mann(57).
Slow Heat—Rocky Fisher(21), Dick Watson(19), John Davis(43).
Fast Heat—Louie Mann(57), Tony Elliott(35), Steve Kline(12), Bimbo Atkins(36).

Late Model:
Feature—Tom Beezley(69), Bruce Hogue(25), Terry Sroufe(12), Art Leiter(78), Bob King(53), Sam Davis(43), Steve Brown(35), Jeff Ness(16), Walt Maley(88), Thames Goon(73).
Dash-Tom Beezley(69), Art Leiter(78), Walt Maley(88).
Fast Heat—Tom Beezley(69), Terry Sroufe(12), Bruce Hogue(25), Walt Maley(88).

Street Stock:
Feature—Allen Marsh(75), Tony Calhoun(27), Dewayne May(71), Arnold Prater(48), William

Ernie Cripe

Varney(47), Joe Pickett(79), Shane Denny(58), Keith Smith(29), Junior Blocker(4), Ron McKenzie(24), Larry Blevins(01), Don Prater(18), Rex Alley(17), Kenny Shepherd(72), Tom Martin(00), Wayne Gibson(19).
Dash—Allen Marsh(75), Tom Martin(00), Frank Baldridge(80).
Slow Heat—Arnold Prater(48), Kenny Shepherd(72), Tony Calhoun(27), Joe Pickett(79).
Fast Heat—Dick Day(12), Allen Marsh(75), Arnold Prater(1), Wayne Gibson(19).
Consolation—Ernie Cripe(31), Roger Fitzpatrick(57), Jim Frushour(35), John Vigar(09).

Saturday, August 22, 1981
Mann Wins Two At Speedway

Louie Mann, Art Leiter, and Dave Fitzpatrick won the respective sprint, late model and street stock features at the Warsaw Speedway Saturday night.

Mann won both the fast heat and feature events and placed second in the dash of the sprint events. Rocky Fisher took home the prize in the dash and Jeff Donelson claimed the slow heat title.

Leiter not only won the feature race of the late model class, but was the runner-up in the slow and fast heats. Bob Johnson and Roger Frye were the respective slow and fast heat winners. Walt Maley won the dash event in late model.

In addition to Fitzpatrick's win in street stock feature, other street stock winners were Allen Marsh in the dash, Keith Smith in slow heat, Dan Blocker in fast heat and Rick Sechrist in consolation.

Race Results:
Sprint Dash—Rocky Fisher(21), Louie Mann(57), John Althouse(77).
Late Model Dash—Walt Maley(88), Tom Beezley(69), Art Leiter(78).
Street Stock Dash—Allen Marsh(75), Wayne Gibson(19), Harvey Hayes(81).
Sprint Slow Heat—Jeff Donelson(2), Leon Jordan(8), Charlie Sauer(4).
Late Model Slow Heat—Bob Johnson(22), Tom Leiter(77), Sam Davis(43), Jeff Ness(16).
Street Stock Slow Heat—Keith Smith(29), Dewayne May(71), William Varney(47), Joe Pickett(79).
Sprint Fast Heat—Louie Mann(57), Terry Pletch(14), Greg Jones(99), DeWayne Barker(3).
Late Model Fast Heat—Roger Frye(6), Art Leiter(78), Walt Maley(88), Charlie Hyde(87).
Street Stock Fast Heat—Dan Blocker(11), Ron McKenzie(24), Arnold Prater(48), Randy Brandon(33).
Sprint Feature—Louie Mann(57), Jeff Donelson(2), Tony Elliott(35), Rocky Fisher(21), Steve Kline(12), John Althouse(77), Tom Patterson(21B), Leon Jordan(8), Bill Teters(34), Bob Kolecki(38), DeWayne Barker(3), Charlie Sauer(4), Greg Jones(99), Terry Pletch(14).
Late Model Feature—Art Leiter(78), Tom Beezley(69), Terry Sroufe(12), Walt Maley(88), Rick Kerlin(62), Roger Frye(6), Charlie Hyde(87), Bruce Hogue(25), Tom Leiter(77), Roger Richards(51),

Bob King(53), Terry Hull(23), Randy Woodling(75), Sam Davis(43), Bob Johnson(22), Jeff Ness(14). Street Stock Feature—Dave Fitzpatrick(57), Don Prater(1), Joe Pickett(79), Harvey Hayes(81), Dan Blocker(11), Tony Calhoun(27), Ron McKenzie(24), Keith Smith(29), Randy Brandon(33), Dick Day(12), Allen Marsh(75), Wayne Gibson(19), Rex Alley(17), John Richardson(26), Mark Oswald(69), Robert Johnson(22).

Saturday, August 29, 1981 – Rainout

Saturday, September 5, 1981
Sprint Invitational Ends Season

The Warsaw Motor Speedway season concluded Saturday night with the Sprint Invitational, with several drivers from the well-known "Outlaws" competing.

Tim Green was the 40-lap feature winner, taking home the $2,000 first prize. Mark Caldwell grabbed the $1,000 second place purse and Bill Kammerer took home the third place prize money of $500.

Green also won the sprint dash. Kammerer won the fast heat. Jack Haudenschild took the slow heat and local driver Bimbo Atkins won the slowest heat. Steve Smith was the consolation winner.

Sprint Invitational Results
Dash—Tim Green(20), Ed Angles(9), Mark Caldwell(33), Rick Nichols(17).
Fast Heat—Bill Kammerer(79), Tim Green(20), Louie Mann(57), Hank Lower(37).
Slow Heat—Jac Haudenschild(63), Steve Smith(4J), Ron Miller(68).
Slowest Heat—Bimbo Atkins(36), John Davis(43), Charlie Sarver(4), Randy White(44).
Consy—Steve Smith(4J), Bimbo Atkins(36), Ron Miller(68), Randy White(44), Charlie Sarver(4), Mark Mildenberger(27).
Feature—Tim Green(20), Mark Caldwell(33), Bill Kammerer(79), Allen Bar(66), Steve Smith(4J), Rick Nichols(17), Denny England(84), Ron Miller(68), Steve Kline(12), Randy White(44), DeWayne Barker(3), Charles Sarver(4), Terry Shepherd(7), Jac Haudenschild(63), Bimbo Atkins(36), Mark Mildenberger(27), Louie Mann(57), Donnie O'Conner(00), Ed Angles(9), Hank Lower(37).

1982

Saturday, May 15, 1982
Warsaw Speedway Opens

DeWayne Barker, Tom Beezley and Bill Varney had successful evenings Saturday at the opening night of the Warsaw Speedway, as each captured first places in the feature events. Barker won the sprint feature and sprint dash, Beezley captured the late model feature and late model fast event, and Varney took the top prize in the street stock feature and street stock slow races.

Other winners were Tony Elliott in sprint fast race, Terry Sroufe in late model dash, Rex Alley in street stock dash, Joe Pickett in street stock fast and Monty Lackey in street stock consolation.

Race Results:

Sprint Dash—DeWayne Barker; Tony Elliott; Denny England.
Late Model Dash—Terry Sroufe; Tom Beezley; John Orr.
Street Stock Dash—Rex Alley; Arnold Prater; Ron McKenzie.
Sprint Fast—Tony Elliott; Ron Fisher; DeWayne Barker; Steve Kline.
Late Model Fast—Tom Beezley; John Orr; Randy Woodling; Terry Sroufe.
Street Stock Fast—Joe Pickett; Ron McKenzie; Roger Fitzpatrick; Junior Blocker.
Street Stock Slow—Bill Varney; Robert Johnson; Barry Baker; Jim Owsley.
Street Stock Concy—Monty Lackey; Paul Fitzpatrick; Chuck Tharp; John Vigar.
Sprint Feature—DeWayne Barker; Tony Elliott; Ron Fisher; Denny England; Gary Fisher; Sam Davis; Doug Drudge; Steve Kline.
Late Model Feature—Tom Beezley; Randy Woodling; Tom Leiter; Charlie Hyde; Glenn Bradley; Bennett; Floyd Craig; Roger Richards.
Street Stock Feature—Bill Varney; Randy Brandon; Robert Johnson; Ron McKenzie; Barry Baker; Junior Blocker; Paul Fitzpatrick; Chuck Tharp.

Saturday, May 22, 1982 - Rainout

Saturday, May 29, 1982
Double Wins for Beezley, Mann

It was a night of double victories for Tom Beezley and Louie Mann at the Warsaw Motor Speedway Saturday. In addition to winning the late model feature, Beezley also captured the late model dash. Likewise, Mann won both the sprint feature and sprint dash.

In the street stock division, Ron McKenzie won the feature, Rex Alley the dash, Tony Calhoun the fast heat and Roger Fitzpatrick the slow heat. Dennis Bowers won the consolation.

In the sprints, Van Gurley won the fast heat and Bimbo Atkins the slow heat. Tony Elliott was second to Mann in the feature and Tim Bookmiller was third.

Late model fast heat winner Art Leiter, who also was second to Beezley in the feature. Tim Sabo was third in the feature.

Race Results:

Sprint Dash—Louie Mann; DeWayne Barker; Van Gurley; Terry Shepherd.
Late Model Dash—Tom Beezley; Art Leiter; Charlie Hyde.
Street Stock Dash—Rex Alley; Harvey Hayes; Don Prater; John Fitzpatrick.
Sprint Fast—Van Gurley; Tony Elliott; Terry Shepherd.
Late Model Fast—Art Leiter; Randy Woodling; Charlie Hyde; Dennis Fuchs.
Street Stock Fast—Tony Calhoun; Shane Denny; Don Prater; Joe Pickett.

Sprint Slow—Bimbo Atkins; Ron Miller; Denny England; Rob Roberts.
Street Stock Slow—Roger Fitzpatrick; Randy Brandon; Robert Johnson; Junior Blocker.
Street Stock Concy—Dennis Bowers; Barry Baker; Chuck Tharp; Chuck Leiter.
Sprint Feature—Louie Mann; Tony Elliott; Tim Bookmiller; Van Gurley; Terry Pletch; Terry Shepherd; DeWayne Barker; Kerry Haynes; Denny England; Bimbo Atkins; Ron Miller; Steve Kline; Rob Roberts; Gary Fisher; Doug Drudge; Sam Davis; John Althouse.
Late Model Feature—Tom Beezley; Art Leiter; Tim Sabo; Randy Woodling; Charlie Hyde; Walt Maley; Thames Goon; Glenn Bradley; Dick Day; Terry Sroufe.
Street Stock Feature—Ron McKenzie; Rex Alley; William Varney; John Fitzpatrick; Don Prater; Shane Denny; Randy Brandon; Joe Pickett; Harvey Hayes; Tony Calhoun; Robert Johnson; Dane Ronk; Dennis Bowers; Frank Baldridge.

Saturday, June 5, 1982
England, Beezley Win Dashes, Features at WMS

Winning the dash in their respective divisions was a good omen for both Denny England and Tom Beezley Saturday night at the Warsaw Motor Speedway. England won the sprint dash and then went on to capture the sprint feature while Beezley did likewise in the late model category. Meanwhile, Don Prater drove away with the street stock feature after placing fourth in the fast heat.

Other heat winners were Ron Miller in the sprint fast heat; Randy Woodling, late model fast; John Orr, late model slow; Tony Calhoun, street stock dash; Junior Blocker, street stock fast; Joe Pickett, street stock slow; and Chuck Leiter, street stock consolation.

Pickett finished second in the street stock feature and John Orr was second in the late model feature. Terry Shepherd was second to England in the sprint feature.

Race Results:
Sprint Dash—Denny England; Terry Sroufe; Kerry Haynes.
Late Model Dash—Tom Beezley; Charlie Hyde; Tim Sabo.
Street Stock Dash—Tony Calhoun; Rex Alley; John Fitzpatrick.
Sprint Fast—Ron Miller; Bimbo Atkins; John Althouse; Denny England.
Late Model Fast—Randy Woodling; Tom Beezley; Larry Baker; Tim Sabo.
Street Stock Fast—Junior Blocker; John Fitzpatrick; Allen Marsh; Don Prater.
Late Model Slow—John Orr; Ben Bradway; Thames Goon; Dick Day.
Street Stock Slow—Joe Pickett; Ron McKenzie; Dewayne May; Dane Ronk.
Street Stock Concy—Chuck Leiter; Barry Baker; Robert Johnson; Bill Kane.
Sprint Feature—Denny England; Terry Shepherd; DeWayne Barker; Ron Miller; Bimbo Atkins; Kerry Haynes; John Althouse; John Davis; Doug Drudge.
Late Model Feature—Tom Beezley; John Orr; Ben Bradway; Larry Baker; Charlie Hyde; Thames

Goon; Dick Day; Randy Woodling; Tim Sabo.
Street Stock Feature—Don Prater; Joe Pickett; John Fitzpatrick; Junior Blocker; Frank Baldridge; Rex Alley; Shane Denny; Tony Calhoun; Ron McKenzie.

Saturday, June 12, 1982
England, Bennett, Marsh Win Features At Speedway

Denny England, Joe Bennett, and Allen Marsh were the feature winners Saturday night at the Warsaw Motor Speedway. England won the sprint feature, Bennett the late model and Marsh the street stock. For each feature winner, it was his only win of the night although each was second in a preliminary heat.

England was second in the sprint dash that was won by DeWayne Barker. Rob Roberts won the sprint fast heat and Steve Kline the slow heat.

Randy Woodling, Atwood

In the late model slow heat, Bennett was second to Ben Bradway. The fast heat went to Charlie Hyde and Randy Woodling took the checkered flag in the late model dash.

Marsh was second to Harvey Hayes in the stock fast heat. The stock dash was won by Shane Denny, the slow heat by Robert Johnson and the consolation by William Varney.

Race Results:
Street Stock Concy—William Varney; Robert Johnson; Dane Ronk; Bob Johnson.
Sprint Dash—DeWayne Barker; Denny England; Ron Miller.
Late Model Dash—Randy Woodling; Tom Beezley; Art Leiter.
Street Stock Dash—Shane Denny; John Fitzpatrick; Ron McKenzie.
Sprint Fast—Rob Roberts; DeWayne Barker; Ron Miller; Denny England.
Late Model Fast—Charlie Hyde; Bruce Hogue; John Orr; Tom Beezley.
Street Stock Fast—Harvey Hayes; Allen Marsh; Rex Alley; Randy Brandon.
Sprint Slow—Steve Kline; Rich Leming; John Davis.
Late Model Slow—Ben Bradway; Joe Bennett; Rodger Richards; Dick Day.
Street Stock Slow—Robert Johnson; Bob Johnson; Frank Baldridge.
Sprint Feature—Denny England; Ron Miller; Tony Elliott; Steve Kline; Rob Roberts; Gary Harrold; DeWayne Barker; John Althouse; Rich Leming; John Davis; Doug Drudge.
Late Model Feature—Joe Bennett; Art Leiter; Bruce Hogue; Randy Woodling; John Orr; Ben Bradway; Dick Day; Charlie Hyde; Terry Sroufe; Tom Beezley; Thames Goon; Rodger Richards.
Street Stock Feature—Allen Marsh; Don Prater; Dave Fitzpatrick; Harvey Hayes; Randy Brandon; Jim Frushour; John Fitzpatrick; Dane Ronk; Larry Montel; Frank Baldridge; Tony Calhoun; Rex Alley; Junior Blocker; Joe Pickett; Ron McKenzie; Barry Baker.

Saturday, June 19, 1982
Elliott, Beezley, Marsh Win Speedway Features

Tony Elliott, Tom Beezley and Allen Marsh were the respective winners Saturday night at the Warsaw Speedway in the sprint, late model and street stock events.

Elliott also captured the sprint fast heat. Other first places went to Ron Miller in sprint dash, DeWayne Barker in sprint slow heat, Bruce Hogue in late model dash, Terry Sroufe in late model fast heat, Randy Woodling in late model slow heat, Randy Brandon in street stock dash, William Varney in street stock fast heat, Barry Baker in street stock slow heat, Arnold Prater in feature "B" of street stock and Frank Baldridge in feature "A" of street stock.

Bruce Hogue, Akron

Race Results:

Sprint Dash—Ron Miller; Tony Elliott; Denny England; DeWayne Barker.
Late Model Dash—Bruce Hogue; John White; Tom Beezley; Larry Baker.
Street Stock Dash—Randy Brandon; Rex Alley; Dave Fitzpatrick; Allen Marsh.
Sprint Fast Heat—Tony Elliott; Denny England; Rob Roberts; Gary Fisher.
Late Model Fast Heat—Terry Sroufe; Bruce Hogue; Joe Bennett; Tom Beezley.
Street Stock Fast Heat—William Varney; Allen Marsh; Don Prater; Ron McKenzie.
Sprint Slow Heat—DeWayne Barker; Steve Kline; Ron Miller.
Late Model Slow Heat—Randy Woodling; John White; John Orr; Ben Bradway.
Street Stock Slow Heat—Barry Baker; Shane Denny; Dane Ronk; Matt Warren.
Sprint Feature—Tony Elliott; Denny England; DeWayne Barker; Ron Miller; Steve Kline; Gary Fisher; Bimbo Atkins; Bob Emerton; Rob Roberts.
Late Model Feature—Tom Beezley; Joe Bennett; Ben Bradway; John Orr; Bruce Hogue; Dewayne May; Terry Sroufe; Mike Albertson; John White; Dick Day; Larry Baker; Randy Woodling.
Street Stock Feature A—Allen Marsh; Barry Baker; Shane Denny; Don Prater; Tony Calhoun; Robert Johnson; Joe Pickett; Dave Fitzpatrick; Harvey Hayes; Keith Smith; Matt Warren; Roger Fitzpatrick; Frank Baldridge; Ron McKenzie; Dane Ronk; Larry Blevins.
Street Stock Feature B—Arnold Prater; Don Kelsey; Chuck Leiter.

Saturday, June 26, 1982
Warsaw Speedway Winners

Tony Elliott, Art Leiter and Allen Marsh were winners in feature races Saturday night at Warsaw Speedway. Elliott captured both the sprint feature and the fast heat events. Art Leiter took the late model feature and Marsh won the street stock feature.

Other first places went to Denny England in sprint dash, Bruce Hogue in both late model dash and late model fast heat. Harvey Hayes in street stock dash, Roger Fitzpatrick in street stock fast heat, Dave Erickson in sprint slow heat, Thames Goon in late model fast heat; Terry Baker in street stock slow heat and Rick Cree in feature B of street stock.

Race Results:

Sprint Dash—Denny England; Kerry Haynes; Ron Miller.
Slow Model Dash—Bruce Hogue; Tom Beezley; John White; Art Leiter.
Fast Stock Dash—Harvey Hayes; Shane Denny; Allen Marsh; Randy Brandon.
Sprint Fast Heat—Tony Elliott; Kerry Haynes; Denny England; Bimbo Atkins.
Late Model Fast Heat—Bruce Hogue; Terry Sroufe; Tom Beezley; Art Leiter.
Street Stock Fast Heat—Roger Fitzpatrick; John Fitzpatrick; Randy Brandon; Ron McKenzie.
Sprint Slow Heat—Dave Erickson; Gary Fisher; Dick Watson.
Late Model Slow Heat—Thames Goon; Michael Albertson; Scott Dausman; Ben Bradway.
Street Stock Slow Heat—Terry Baker; Joe Pickett; Don Prater; Arnold Prater.
Sprint Feature—Tony Elliott; Denny England; Steve Kline; Bimbo Atkins; Kerry Haynes; John Davis; Gary Fisher; Dave Erickson; Ron Roberts; Dick Watson; Bob Emerton.
Late Model Feature—Art Leiter; Tom Beezley; Bruce Hogue; John Orr; John White; Randy Woodling; Ben Bradway; Terry Sroufe; Thames Goon; Scott Dausman; Dewayne May.
Street Stock Feature A—Allen Marsh; John Fitzpatrick; Arnold Prater; Joe Pickett; Barry Baker; Terry Baker; a; Harvey Hayes; Randy Brando; Frank Baldridge; Roger Fitzpatrick; Tony Calhoun; Ron McKenzie; Roscoe P. Anders; Dave Fitzpatrick.
Street Stock Feature B—Rick Cree; Robert Johnson; Mike Orr; Chuck Leiter.

Saturday, July 3 & Monday, July 5, 1982
Big Weekend At Speedway

Despite a rainout of the street stock feature event Saturday night, there was still plenty of holiday weekend racing action at the Warsaw Speedway.

DeWayne Barker won the sprint feature and Ben Bradway captured the late model feature in racing action Saturday. Bradway also took home the prize for first place in late model slow heat.

Other winners that night were Denny England, Ron Fisher and Tony Elliott in respective sprint dash, slow and fast heats; Bruce Hogue in late model dash and Joe Bennett in late model fast heat; Randy Brandon, Arnold Prater and John Fitzpatrick in street stock dash, slow and fast heats, and Matt Warren in street stock "B" main event.

Tom Beezley was a feature event winner Monday and Charlie Hyde won in "B" feature. Other first places went to Ron Hekkma in dash, Glenn Bradley in slow heat, Ben Bradway in medium heat and Charlie Sentman in fast heat.

Results: Saturday, July 3

Sprint Dash—Denny England; Bimbo Atkins; Kenny Haynes.
Late Model Dash—Bruce Hogue; Art Leiter; John White.
Street Stock Dash—Randy Brandon; Barry Baker; Dave Fitzpatrick.
Sprint Slow—Ron Fisher; John Davis; Rob Roberts.
Late Model Slow—Ben Bradway; Charlie Hyde; Roger Richards; Floyd Craig.

360

Street Stock Slow—Arnold Prater; Rocky Anders; Shane Denny; Ron McKenzie.
Sprint Fast—Tony Elliott; Dewayne Barker; Steve Kline; Bimbo Atkins.
Late Model Fast—Joe Bennett; Terry Sroufe; Bruce Hogue; Randy Woodling.
Street Stock Fast—John Fitzpatrick; Harvey Hayes; Dave Fitzpatrick; Junior Blocker.
Street Stock B Main—Matt Warren; Rick Cripe; Robert Johnson; Jim Frushour.
Sprint Feature—Dewayne Barker; Denny England; Bimbo Atkins; Tony Elliott; Ron Fisher; Gary Fisher; John Althouse; John Davis; Kenny Haynes; Doug Drudge; Steve Kline; Rob Roberts; Ron Miller.
Late Model Feature—Ben Bradway; Joe Bennett; Randy Woodling; John White; Art Leiter; Terry Sroufe; John Orr; Roger Richards; Mike A. J. Albertson; Thames Goon; Bruce Hogue; Charlie Hyde; Tom Beezley.

Monday, July 5

Dash—Ron Heckaman; Tom Beezley; John White.
Slow Heat—Glenn Bradley; Mike A.J. Albertson; Dewayne May; William Varney.
Medium Heat—Ben Bradway; Thames Goon; Roger Richards; Bill Ice.
Fast Heat—Charlie Sentman; Tom Beezley; Terry Sroufe; John White.
Feature—Tom Beezley; Charlie Sentman; John White; Randy Woodling; Tim Sabo; Ben Bradway; Charlie Hyde; Roger Richards; Terry Sroufe; Mike A.J. Albertson; Shane Denny; Thames Goon; Glenn Bradley; Dewayne May; Bruce Hogue; Tom Ice; Joe Bennett; Harvey Hayes; William Varney; Ron Hekkema.
B Feature—Charlie Hyde; Shane Denny; Harvey Hayes; Don Prater.

Saturday, July 10, 1982 - Rainout

Saturday, July 17, 1982
England, Hogue Capture Two Events Apiece At Speedway

It was a double win night for both Denny England and Bruce Hogue Saturday at the Warsaw Speedway. England was the sprint feature and dash winner while Hogue took the checkered flag in the late model feature as well as the dash. The street stock feature winner was Harvey Hayes.

In the sprint feature, Kenny Haynes, who earlier won the sprint fast heat, finished second and DeWayne Barker was third. John Althouse won the sprint slow heat.

Second to Hogue in the late model feature was John White and third was Joe Bennett. John Orr won the late model slow heat and Bennett the late model fast heat. Barry Baker won a pair of street stock events, the dash and fast heat. Randy Brandon won the slow heat. John Fitzpatrick was second to Hayes in the feature and William Varney was third.

Race Results:

Sprint Feature—Denny England; Kenny Haynes; DeWayne Barker; Bimbo Atkins; John Althouse; John Davis; Rich Leming; Sam Davis; Charles Sarver; Gary Fisher; Bob Cimerton; Ron Fisher; Doug Drudge.

Sprint Dash—Denny England; Kenny Haynes; Bimbo Atkins.
Sprint Slow Heat—John Althouse; Rich Leming; DeWayne Barker; Bimbo Atkins.
Sprint Fast Heat—Kenny Haynes; Denny England; DeWayne Barker; Bimbo Atkins.
Late Model Feature—Bruce Hogue; John White; Joe Bennett; John Orr; Tom Beezley; Thames Goon; Bob Simpson; Mike Schwartz; Ben Bradway; Dewayne May; Randy Woodling; Larry Baker; Max Albertson; Terry Sroufe; Duane Owens; Charles Hyde.
Late Model Dash—Bruce Hogue; Terry Sroufe; Tom Beezley.
Late Model Slow Heat—John Orr; Bob Simpson; Dewayne May; Thames Goon.
Late Model Fast Heat—Joe Bennett; Bruce Hogue; Tom Beezley; John White.
Street Stock Feature—Harvey Hayes; John Fitzpatrick; William Varney; Terry Hull; Dave Fitzpatrick; Arnold Prater; Barry Baker; Ron McKenzie; Randy Brandon; Terry Smith; Bill Kain; Robert Johnson; Roger Fitzpatrick; Dane Ronk; Rex Alley.
Street Stock Dash—Barry Baker; Allen Marsh; John Fitzpatrick.
Street Stock Slow Heat—Randy Brandon; Ron McKenzie; Robert Johnson; Joe Pickett.
Street Stock Fast Heat—Barry Baker; William Varney; Arnold Prater; John Fitzpatrick.

Saturday, July 24, 1982
Big Weekend Of Racing

Ron Miller & DeWayne Barker

It was a big weekend of racing at the Warsaw Speedway with programs on both Friday and Saturday nights. Friday's schedule included the Sprints on Dirt (SOD) Show and there was the regular lineup of races on Saturday.

Feature winners Saturday night were Bruce Hogue, late model; Don Prater, street stock; and Denny England, sprint. In the SOD program, Lee Osborne won the feature event and Ken Mackey took the "B" Main event. Other sprint drivers taking the checkered flag Friday were Osborne, dash; Steve Kline, first heat; Bob Lingang; second heat; Ron Miller, third heat; and Al Hager, fourth heat. In the SOD feature, Al Hager was second and Bimbo Atkins third.

In Saturday's program, Tom Beezley was second and Terry Sroufe third in the late model feature. Randy Woodling took the late model dash, Thames Goon the late model slow heat and John White the late model fast heat.

In the street stock division, John Fitzpatrick was second in the feature and first in both the dash and fast heat. Barry Baker won the slow heat.

In the sprints, Tony Elliott was second and DeWayne Barker third in the feature. Barker was first to the finish line in the fast heat, Kenny Haynes took the slow heat and Terry

Shepherd the dash.

Race Results:

Friday:
Sprint Dash—Lee Osborne; DeWayne Barker; Mike Shaw.
First Heat—Steve Kline; Sam Davis; John Davis.
Second Heat—Bob Lingang; Kurt Kelly; Steve Burch.
Third Heat—Ron Miller; Tony Elliott; John Althouse.
Fourth Heat—Al Hager; Lee Osborne; Mark Caldwell.
"B" Main—Ken Mackey; Troy Chehowski; Steve Kline; Gary Fisher.
Feature—Lee Osborne; Al Hager; Bimbo Atkins; John Naida; Jerry Tierney; Hank Lower; Terry Shepherd; Mark Caldwell; Denny England; DeWayne Barker; Ron Miller; George McCord; Troy Chehowski; Jim Slade; Gary Fisher; Tony Elliott; Ken Mackey; Marv Pifer; John Althouse; Steve Kline.

Saturday:
Sprint Dash—Terry Shepherd; Denny England; Tony Elliott.
Late Model Dash—Randy Woodling; Bruce Hogue; Tom Beezley.
Street Stock Dash—John Fitzpatrick; Ron McKenzie; Rex Alley.
Sprint Slow—Kenny Haynes; Steve Kline; John Althouse.
Late Model Slow—Thames Goon; John Orr; Bob Simpson; Jeff Ness.
Street Stock Slow—Barry Baker; Junior Blocker; William Varney; Roger Fitzpatrick.
Sprint Fast—DeWayne Barker; Bimbo Atkins; Joe Gaerte; Terry Shepherd.
Late Model Fast—John White; Bruce Hogue; Randy Woodling; Terry Sroufe.
Street Stock Fast—John Fitzpatrick; Rex Alley; Ron McKenzie; Harvey Hayes.
Sprint Feature—Denny England; Tony Elliott; DeWayne Barker; Steve Kline; Joe Gaerte; Rich Leming; Doug Drudge; Terry Shepherd; John Althouse; Kenny Haynes; Sam Davis; Bimbo Atkins.
Late Model Feature—Bruce Hogue; Tom Beezley; Terry Sroufe; John Orr; Randy Woodling; Ben Bradway; Charles Hyde; Walt Maley; Bob Simpson; John White; Jeff Ness; Dewayne May; Thames Goon.
Street Stock Feature—Don Prater; John Fitzpatrick; Joe Pickett; Barry Baker; Harvey Hayes; Jerry Baker; Ron McKenzie; Roger Fitzpatrick; Jim Ousley; Rex Alley; Dane Ronk; Frank Baldridge; Shane Denny; Terry Baker; Dennis Bowers; Walt Warren.

Saturday, July 31, 1982
Marsh Wins Street Stock Mid-Season Championship

After finishing second in the street stock dash, Allen Marsh decided to go one better in that division's feature event Saturday night at the Warsaw Speedway as he won the mid-season championships.

Marsh beat runner-up Don Prater and third-place finisher Harvey Hayes, among others, for the mid-season street stock title. Earlier, Marsh was

William Varney, Warsaw

second to Hayes in the dash and second to Terry Sroufe in the late model slow heat. Junior Blocker won the street stock fast heat and William Varney the slow heat.

In the other features, John Althouse won the sprint division and Bruce Hogue the late model. In the sprint feature, Rob Roberts was second and Rich Leming third and in the late model event, John White was second and Art Leiter third.

Denny England won both the sprint dash and fast heat, with Althouse second both times. In late model racing, Tom Beezley took the dash, John Orr the fast heat and Sroufe the slow heat.

Race Results:

Sprint Dash—Denny England; John Althouse; Rich Leming.
Late Model Dash—Tom Beezley; John White; Art Leiter.
Street Stock Dash—Harvey Hayes; Allen Marsh; Jerry Baker.
Sprint Fast Heat—Denny England; John Althouse; Rich Leming; Rob Roberts.
Late Model Fast Heat—John Orr; Roger Richards; Randy Woodling; Bruce Hogue.
Late Model Slow Heat—Terry Sroufe; Allen Marsh; Rick Kerlin; Jeff Ness.
Street Stock Fast Heat—Junior Blocker; Don Prater; Barry Baker; Jerry Baker.
Street Stock Slow Heat—William Varney; Roger Fitzpatrick; Joe Pickett; Frank Baldridge.
"B" Main—Jim Frushour; DeWayne Eakright; Bob Johnson; Frank Baldridge.
"B" Main—Tom Leiter; Ken Shepherd; Jim Frushour; Dan Kelsey.
Late Model Feature—Bruce Hogue; John White; Art Leiter; Tom Beezley; Joe Bennett; Terry Sroufe; John Orr; Roger Richards; Bob Simpson; Jeff Ness; Doug Nusbaum; Ben Bradway; Ron Woodling; Allen Marsh; Rick Kerlin; Jeff Rice.
Mid-Season Street Stock Championship—Allen Marsh; Don Prater; Harvey Hayes; Joe Pickett; Ron McKenzie; Randy Brandon; Shane Denny; Bob Johnson; Dane Ronk; Frank Baldridge; Tony Calhoun; Terry Baker; William Varney; Barry Baker; Terry Hull; Dave Fitzpatrick; John Fitzpatrick; Junior Blocker; Roger Fitzpatrick; Rocky Anders.
Sprint Feature—John Althouse; Ron Roberts; Rich Leming; Sam Davis; Mark Owsley; Denny England; Paul Tetrault.

Saturday, August 7, 1982 - Rainout

Saturday, August 14, 1982
Hogue, Atkins Win Features

Bruce Hogue and Bimbo Atkins were the late model and sprint feature winners respectively, at the Warsaw Motor Speedway Saturday night. There was no street stock feature.

Hogue defeated runner-up Joe Bennett and third place finisher Art Leiter in the late model feature. Hogue also won the late model fast heat while Tom Beezley took the dash and Terry Sroufe the slow heat.

Finishing closest to Atkins in the sprint feature were Denny England, second, and Terry Shepherd, third. Tony Elliott won the sprint dash, Rich Leming the slow heat and Kenny Haynes the fast heat.

Barry Baker captured the street stock dash, Joe Pickett took the fast heat and Shane

Denny the slow heat. In the powder puff, Shandy Dunnuck was first and Sally Stilwell second. Gary Baker won the mechanics race.

Race Results:

Sprint Dash—Tony Elliott; Denny England; Terry Shepherd.
Late Model Dash—Tom Beezley; Ben Bradway; Randy Woodling.
Street Stock Dash—Barry Baker; Jerry Baker; Don Kintzel.
Late Model Slow Heat—Terry Sroufe; John Orr; Allen Marsh; Jeff Ness.
Sprint Slow Heat—Rich Leming; Sam Davis; Paul Tetrault.
Street Stock Slow Heat—Shane Denny; Randy Brandon; Dane Ronk; Bob Johnson.
Late Model Fast Heat—Bruce Hogue; Ben Bradway; Tom Beezley; John White.
Sprint Fast Heat—Kenny Haynes; DeWayne Barker; Steve Kline; Tony Elliott.
Street Stock Fast Heat—Joe Pickett; William Varney; Jerry Baker; Tony Calhoun.
Powder Puff—Sandy Dunnuck; Sally Stilwell; Paula Calhoun; Sally Snyder.
Mechanics Race—Garry Baker.
Late Model Feature—Bruce Hogue; Joe Bennett; Art Leiter; Ben Bradway; John White; Terry Sroufe; John Orr; Roger Richards; Charlie Hyde; Allen Marsh; Jeff Ness; Tom Beezley; Jim Sellers; Doug Nusbaum; Dewayne May; Randy Woodling.
Sprint Feature—Bimbo Atkins; Denny England; Terry Shepherd; Tony Elliott; DeWayne Barker; Ron Fisher; Steve Kline; Kenny Haynes; Mark Mildenberger; Walt Maley; Sam Davis; Rich Leming; Paul Tetrault.

Saturday, August 21, 1982
Marsh Wins Three Races

Allen Marsh pulled off a sweep Saturday night at the Warsaw Speedway, as he won the street stock fast heat, street stock dash and the feature race in the street stock category. Marsh also managed a second place in the late model fast heat.

In the other feature races, Denny England won the feature sprint and Charlie Sentman took first place in the feature late model race.

Other first places went to Robert Johnson in "B" Main event, John White in late model dash, Bimbo Atkins in sprint dash, Terry Sroufe in late model slow heat, John Althouse in sprint slow heat, Randy Brandon in street stock slow heat, Tim Sabo in late model fast heat and Cliff Blundy in sprint fast heat.

Robert Johnson, Warsaw

Race Results:

"B" Main—Robert Johnson; Dick Day; Tom Martin; Bob Johnson.
Late Model Dash—John White; Tom Beezley; Joe Bennett.
Sprint Dash—Bimbo Atkins; Tim Bookmiller; DeWayne Barker.
Street Stock Dash—Allen Marsh; Shane Denny; Harvey Hayes.
Late Model Slow Heat—Terry Sroufe; Bruce Hogue; Charlie Hyde; Walt Waldfogel.

Sprint Slow Heat—John Althouse; Sam Davis; Bob Kolacki.
Street Stock Slow Heat—Randy Brandon; Barry Baker; Roger Fitzpatrick; Robert Johnson.
Late Model Fast Heat—Tim Sabo; Allen Marsh; John Orr; John White.
Sprint Fast Heat—Cliff Blundy; Bimbo Atkins; Tim Bookmiller; Denny England.
Street Stock Fast Heat—Allen Marsh; John Fitzpatrick; Ron McKenzie; Shane Denny.
Sprint Feature—Denny England; Cliff Blundy; Bimbo Atkins; DeWayne Barker; Sam Davis; Dick Watson; Bob Kolacki; Mark Owsley; Tim Bookmiller; John Davis; Charlie Sarver; John Althouse; Bob Emberton; Gary Fisher.
Late Model Feature—Charlie Sentman; Joe Bennett; Tom Beezley; Allen Marsh; John White; John Orr; Art Leiter; Charlie Hyde; Jeff Ness; Doug Nusbaum; Dick Fuchs; Randy Woodling; Dewayne May; Bruce Hogue; Ben Bradway; Jeff Rice; Russel Overmyer; Tim Sabo; Terry Sroufe; Jim Sellers.
Street Stock Feature—Allen Marsh; Tom Beezley; Shane Denny; Jerry Baker; Harvey Hayes; Ron McKenzie; Dick Day; Randy Brandon; Barry Baker; David Fitzpatrick; Junior Blocker; Dane Ronk; Roger Fitzgerald; Mike May; Matt Warren.

Saturday, August 28, 1982
Beezley Takes Checkered Flag Twice in Speedway Program

Tom Beezley was the only double winner at the Warsaw Speedway Saturday night as he captured the late model feature race as well as the street stock fast heat. Other feature winners were Denny England, sprint, and Jerry Baker, street stock.

Finishing behind Beezley in the late model feature were John Orr, second, and Joe Bennett, third. Art Leiter won the late model fast heat, Ben Bradway the slow heat and John White the dash.

Following England to the finish line in the sprint feature were Van Gurley, second, and Terry Shepherd third. The sprint dash was won by Gurley, the fast heat by Tony Elliott, and the slow heat by Steve Kline.

Barry Baker was second in the street stock feature and Allen Marsh third. The stock dash was won by Mike May and the slow heat by John Fitzpatrick. Rex Alley won the street stock Main B event.

Race Results:
Sprint Dash—Van Gurley; Terry Shepherd; Tim Bookmiller.
Late Model Dash—John White; Dave Marks; Tom Beezley.
Street Stock Dash—Mike May; Terry Hull; Shane Denny.
Late Model Slow Heat—Ben Bradway; Joe Bennett; Allen Marsh; Bob Simpson.
Sprint Slow Heat—Steve Kline; Rich Leming; John Althouse.
Street Stock Slow Heat—John Fitzpatrick; Tony Calhoun; William Varney; Ron McKenzie.
Late Model Fast Heat—Art Leiter; Dave Marks; Randy Woodling; John Orr.
Sprint Fast Heat—Tony Elliott; Denny England; Kenny Haynes; Van Gurley.
Street Stock Fast Heat—Tom Beezley; Randy Brandon; Jerry Baker; Joe Pickett.
Street Stock "B" Main—Joe Pickett; William Varney; Robert Johnson; Tom Martin.
Street Stock "B" Main—Rex Alley, Jim Frushour; Dick Day; Bob Johnson.
Sprint Feature—Denny England; Van Gurley; Terry Shepherd; Kenny Haynes; Tony Elliott; Tim Bookmiller; Bimbo Atkins; Steve Kline; John Althouse; John Davis; Mark Owsley; Rich Leming.
Late Model Feature—Tom Beezley; John Orr; Joe Bennett; George Woodling; Art Leiter; Jeff Ness; Tim Sabo; Terry Sroufe; Allen Marsh; Jim Sellers; Bullet Marko; Bruce Hogue.

Street Stock Feature—Jerry Baker; Berry Baker; Allen Marsh; Tom Beezley; Harvey Hayes; Randy Brandon; Dave Fitzpatrick; Shane Denny; John Fitzpatrick; William Varney; Ron McKenzie; Terry Hull; Terry Smith; Tony Calhoun; Don Kintzel; Joe Pickett.

Friday, September 3 & Saturday, September 4, 1982
Hogue, Marsh Win Titles

Bruce Hogue won the late model title and Allen Marsh the street stock crown in the Warsaw Speedway season championship races Saturday night.

Hogue took the checkered flag ahead of runner-up Randy Woodling and third-place finisher Art Leiter in the late model competition. Terry Sroufe was fourth and Charlie Hyde fifth.

In the street stock feature, John Fitzpatrick was second to Marsh, Terry Hull third, Harvey Hayes fourth and Barry Baker fifth. In the street stock "B" main event Keith Smith was first and Jon Ormsby second.

In an SOD program Friday night, George McCord's sprinter won the feature and Hank Lower took the dash. In the heats, Tony Elliott won the first, Mark Caldwell the second and John Naida the third, and in the "B" main event, Elliott was first.

Friday, SOD Program:

Dash—Hank Lower; Chuck Wilson; Mark Slade; Mike Shaw.
Heat No. 1—Tony Elliott; Mike Shaw Jr.; John Davis; Mark Mildenberger; Sam Davis; Dave Bieskie.
Heat No. 2—Mark Caldwell; Steve Kline; Cliff Blundy; Mike Thomas; George McCord; Troy Chehowski; Joe Gaerte; Eric Slade.
Heat No. 3—John Naida; Kenny Haynes; Denny England; Terry Shepherd; Hank Lower; Mark Slade; Chuck Wilson; Mike Shaw.
B Main—Tony Elliott; Mike Shaw Jr.; Dave Bieskie; John Davis; Mark Mildenberger; Jerry Slade.
Feature—George McCord; Mike Thomas; Terry Shepherd; Chuck Wilson; Denny England; John Naida; Tony Elliott; Joe Gaerte; Cliff Blundy; Kenny Haynes; Steve Kline; Dave Bieskie; Mike Shaw; Troy Chehowski; Eric Slade; Mark Caldwell; Mike Shaw; Ken Mackey; Mark Slade.

Saturday:

Street Stock "B" Main—Keith Smith; Jon Ormsby; Roger Pollock; Pat Johnson; Roger Fitzpatrick.
Late Model Feature (Championship)—Bruce Hogue; Randy Woodling; Art Leiter; Terry Sroufe; Charlie Hyde; Allen Marsh; John Orr; Doug Nusbaum; Roger Richards; Dewayne May; Jeff Ness; Jeff Rice.
Street Stock Feature (Championship)—Allen Marsh; John Fitzpatrick; Terry Hull; Harvey Hayes; Barry Baker; Shane Denny; Dave Fitzpatrick; Randy Brandon; William Varney; Rex Alley; Bob Johnson; Frank Baldridge; Dave Ronk; Joe Pickett; Jim Frushour; Arnold Prater; Roger Fitzpatrick; Jerry Baker; Tom Beezley Robert Johnson.

Friday, September 10, 1982 – Late Model Invitational.
No Corresponding Article found in the newspaper.

1983
Monty Miller and a Track to be Reckoned With

Monty Miller, from Huntington, became Speedway Manager/Promoter in 1983 and for the next six years, showed more profit on paper for the speedway than any other time in history. Many track improvements were also made during the 1980 years including moving the scorer's pagoda in the middle of the track to an actual scorer's tower on the grandstand side of the track, moving the speedway lighting from the infield to the outside of the track, adding new and additional grandstand seating, new safety fencing and track clay, and extending the track's 3rd and 4th turns out to make the speedway a true 1/4 mile. The speedway held an Opening Night for the newly improved track on May 17, 1986 with winged sprints, limited late models, and roadrunners. Special events were periodically added including several S.O.D. Sprint, All-Star Circuit of Champions Sprint, Late Model and Winged Sprint Invitationals that brought drivers from as far as Australia and New Zealand to compete.

Mid-May 1983
Warsaw Speedway Offers Something For Everyone

Everyone's got to have some love in life, says Monty Miller, Warsaw Speedway track manager. "My own love happens to be racing." Miller sees the Saturday night sprint and stock car races at the track, located in the Kosciusko Fairgrounds, as being an activity for the whole family. "This is a family thing," he said. "Our family always went, we've been going for 36 years.

Miller says people come from as far away as Illinois to race at the track, "and they're spending money in the city. The track not only generates a place to play, it generates business." A total of about 60-70 cars participate in the races, which started May 14 and will continue until Labor Day. Season tickets are $75 for adults, $25 for children; individual admissions are $5 for adults, $2 for children. Track gates open at 5 p.m., time trials are at 6:30 p.m., and the racing starts at 7:30 p.m.

Saturday, May 14, 1983 – Rainout

Saturday, May 21, 1983
England, Woodling Win Race Features
By Bob Valentine, For the *Times Union*

After last week's rainout, the 1983 racing season officially began at the Warsaw Speedway Saturday night with a large turnout considering the threatening weather. However, the rain held off and the complete program was conducted with Randy Woodling winning the street stock feature and Denny England the sprint feature.

In the street stock feature, Woodling (in car No. 33) was able to work his way from the back of the field to first place in 17 laps. His accomplishment was not without challenge, however, as Arnold Prater (1) kept the pressure on to finish second. Robert Johnson (22) finished third and in doing so served notice that he will be a force to deal with throughout this racing season. Rounding out the top five in the street stock feature was Roger Fitzpatrick (56) fourth and Shane Denny (58) fifth.

The street stock fast heat was won by Woodling to become the night's second double winner. Following him across the finish line was Arnold Prater again. Third was Ron McKenzie (24). The second heat was won by Roger Fitzpatrick (56) with Robert Johnson and Tom Leiter (69) finishing second and third, respectively. In the street stock slow heat, Gene Burchett (6) was able to hold off a challenge from Bob Johnson (80) to finish first. Johnson was second with Steve Holbrook (87) third. The street stock dash was won by Arnold Prater with John Fitzpatrick and Randy Woodling finishing second and third. There was a consolation race in the street stock division, won by Gene Burchett. He was this evening's third double winner. In the consy, Burkett finished ahead of Monte Lackey (8), second, and Steve Rogers (11) third.

Arnold Prater, Warsaw

Denny England (84) was the first double winner, taking the sprint fast heat and the feature. England was the top point leader and season champion in the sprint division at Warsaw last year. In the sprint feature, England started from the third row outside and by the second lap was leading, never to relinquish that lead. This was not an easy victory, though, as Tony Elliott (57) followed him through the field and across the finish line and kept the pressure on through the entire race. At one point Tony managed to overtake England, if only for a brief moment. Even though England broke a jacobs ladder, he was able to control his vehicle and hold on to capture the first feature win of 1983 at Warsaw.

Rounding out the top five places in the sprint feature were Rich Leming (19) third, DeWayne Barker (33), fourth and Terry Shepherd (7) fifth. The sprint fast heat went to England with Bimbo Atkins (36) second and Tray House (9) third. The slow heat for sprints saw Tony Elliott win ahead of Terry Shepherd and DeWayne Barker. The sprint dash was won by DeWayne Barker with Terry Shepherd finishing, second, and Tony Elliott, third.

Saturday, May 28, 1983 – Rainout

Saturday, June 4, 1983
Woodling Again Takes Street Stock Feature
By Bob Valentine, For The *Times-Union*

Randy Woodling captured his second feature win in as many weeks at the Warsaw Speedway Saturday night. Woodling competes in the street stock division and again had to come from the back of the pack to capture the win. He also won the fast heat.

In the sprint feature, a new victor was crowned as Tony Elliott managed to take the lead at the midway point after a battle of several laps with Denny England (the winner of the first feature at Warsaw this year), Bimbo Atkins DeWayne barker and Mark Owsley. Once Elliott was able to take the lead, he was never seriously challenged for the remainder of the race. It was particularly a good win for Elliott who was plagued with minor mechanical problems all evening. Other winners in the sprint division were England both in the fast heat and dash with Barker taking the checkered flag in the slow heat.

In the street stock division, drivers will have another week to think about what it is going to take to beat Woodling in the feature. He was able to take the lead in 15 laps but was under constant pressure from Shane Denny and Ron McKenzie who finished second and third. Woodling also won the fast heat with Roger Fitzpatrick taking the middle heat and Scott Dausman won in the slow heat. In the street stock dash, John Fitzpatrick managed to hold off a hard charge from Allen Marsh and take the checkered flag.

Race Results:

Sprints:
Fast Heat – Denny England, Sam Davis, Rich Lemming
Slow Heat – DeWayne Barker, Mark Owsley, Denny England, Tony Elliott
Dash – Denny England, Bimbo Atkins, Tony Elliott, Mark Owsley
Feature – Tony Elliott, DeWayne Barker, Denny England, Mark Owsley Bimbo Atkins

Street Stocks:
Fast Heat – Randy Woodling, Ron McKenzie, John Fitzpatrick, Shane Denny, Robert Johnson
Middle Heat – Roger Fitzpatrick, Larry Rosenberry, Tom Leiter, Junior Blocher, Joe Pickett
Slow Heat – Scott Dausman, William Varney, Steve Rogers, Mike Orr, Jim Frushour
Dash – John Fitzpatrick, Allen Marsh, Rex Alley, Arnold Prater
Feature – Randy Woodling, Shane Denny, Ron McKenzie, Junior Blocher, Arnold Prater
Consolation – Jim Frushour, Scott Dausman, William Varney, Gene Burkett, Mike Orr

Saturday, June 11, 1983
Elliott Again Dominates Sprinters At Speedway
By Bob Valentine

Two words best describe the action at the Warsaw Speedway Saturday night in the sprint division: "Tony Elliott." Elliott managed to win all three of his races Saturday night, the dash, fast heat, and feature. In fact, Elliott has now won the last four races in as many starts at Warsaw in the sprint class. Elliott is 1983's first double feature winner and the wins come back to back.

In addition to Elliott's accomplishment Saturday, Randy Woodling captured his third street stock feature win in the street stock class to continue his dominance. Finishing second to Woodling in the feature was Jim Freshour with Doug Drudge and Robert Johnson finishing third and fourth respectively. Woodling's win was again from the back of the field, as his previous wins all have been.

For track promoter, Monty Miller, the evening was a strong sign that things are improving for the Warsaw Speedway. There were 19 sprint cars on hand and near twice that many street stocks. The large crowd was treated to the best racing yet this year. This evening, however, was not without problems as Kenny Haynes flipped his sprinter during hot laps and Mark Owsley flipped his during the heat races. DeWayne Barker, a victim of circumstances, severely damaged his sprint in the accident with Owsley.

Miller has announced that, because of the success of the children's promotion Saturday night, the Warsaw Speedway will again offer children, 12 and younger, free admission with a parent this Saturday night.

In the feature for sprints, Elliott received constant pressure and a late charge by Terry Shepherd. Shepherd started running the high groove on the outside and looked at times like he might be able to overtake Elliott for the lead. Bimbo Atkins finished third with Denny England (the evening's fastest qualifier at one-tenth of a second off of the track record) finishing fourth.

Race Results:

Sprints:
Dash – Tony Elliott, Terry Shepherd, Denny England
Fast Heat – Tony Elliott, Steve Kline, Denny England
Feature – Tony Elliott, Terry Shepherd, Bimbo Atkins, Denny England

Street Stocks:
Dash – Dave Fitzpatrick, Scott Dausman, Randy Woodling
Fast Heat – John Fitzpatrick, Scott Dausman, Randy Woodling
Slow Heat – Shane Denny, Robert Johnson, Scott Parker
Feature – Randy Woodling, Jim Frushour, Doug Drudge, Robert Johnson, Ron McKenzie

Saturday, June 18, 1983
Win Streaks Snapped At Speedway
By Bob Valentine

The winning streaks of Randy Woodling in the street stock class and Tony Elliott in sprints came to a close Saturday at the Warsaw Speedway. Woodling had previously won all three features in street stocks this year leading and Elliott had won two consecutive sprint features. Moreover, he had an impressive six wins in as many starts at Warsaw. He won every race that he had been in since winning the feature on June 4.

Saturday's giant killers were Allen Marsh, who shut the door on Woodling in street stocks, and Bimbo Atkins, who ended Elliott's streak in the sprint division. In fact, one look at the sponsor's name (The King & I) on the side of Marsh's car would seem to indicate that he had help with his victory. For Atkins, always a hard charger and previous winner at Warsaw, the help came when Elliott, leading the feature, got a little high in turn one and began to lose it. Denny England and Steve Kline running second and third were so close that all three cars tangled causing a caution.

On the restart, the three drivers were put to the back of the pack allowing Atkins to be first. With only a couple of laps to go after the restart, Atkins managed to hond on for his first feature win of 1983. Finishing second to Atkins was DeWayne Barker and Greg Jones took third. Rounding out the top five in the sprint feature were John Davis, fourth and Rich Lemming, fifth.

Race Results:

Street Stocks:
Dash – Shane Denny, Allen Marsh, John Fitzpatrick, Doug Drudge
Fast Heat – Ron McKenzie, Shane Denny, Arnold Prater, Dane Ronk
Medium Heat – Joe Pickett, Dale Bolinger, Tom Leiter, Harvey Hayes
Slow Heat – Junior Blocher, Sam Pence, Larry Rosenberry, Steve Rogers
Feature – Allen Marsh, Shane Denny, Ron McKenzie, Arnold Prater, Randy Woodling

Sprints:
Dash – Tony Elliott, DeWayne Barker, Steve Kline, Denny England
Fast Heat – DeWayne Barker, Denny England, Bimbo Atkins, Steve Kline
Slow Heat – Dave Darland, John Althouse, Dick Watson, John Davis
Feature – Bimbo Atkins, DeWayne Barker, Greg Jones, John Davis

Saturday, June 25, 1983
Freshour Wins Thrilling Street Stock Feature
By Bob Valentine

In one of the most exciting races to date at the Warsaw Speedway, Jim Freshour managed to hold off all challengers in the street stock feature Saturday night to claim the title for himself. It was his first feature win of the season.

Freshour received constant pressure from drivers Shane Denny, Joe Pickett, Harvey Hayes, John Fitzpatrick and Arnold Prater, but it was Randy Woodling who brought himself through the field to put the most pressure on the leader. The race was so close at times that Woodling was able to overtake Freshour but Freshour never gve up. When the checkered flag fell and the dust settled, Freshour had himself a photo-finish victory over two-time feature winner Woodling.

Other winners in the street stock division were Denny in the dash, Prater in the fast heat, Hayes in the middle heat and Ron McKenzie in the slow heat. The fastest qualifiers in the street stock division were Woodling, Denny, Rex Alley and Dane Ronk.

In the Sprint feature, track conditions played a major role in the outcome. Denny England, starting from the inside of the second row, was able to take advantage of the track conditions early to establish the lead. Because of the dry, hot conditions, the track became hard and slick.

England, a young but veteran driver, used these conditions to his advantage. He needed only to stay out in front and out of trouble while the rest of the field battled themselves to establish their finishing positions. The real battle in the sprint feature came from DeWayne Barker and Steve Kline, who finished second and third, respectively. The fans were treated to some great competition as Barker and Kline battled lap after lap with neither one giving an inch nor gaining any distinct advantage. Late in the race, however, on a restart, Barker did begin to pull away. For the remaining couple of laps, Barker did manage to lengthen his lead over Kline to finish second for his best finish at Warsaw this year.

The fastest qualifiers in the sprint division were Kline fastest followed by Tony Elliott,

Barker and England. England took the trophy dash while Elliott too the fast heat and Bimbo Atkins the slow heat.

Street Stock:
Dash – Shane Denny, Rex Alley, Randy Woodling, Dane Ronk
Fast Heat – Arnold Prater, Joe Pickett, Dave Fitzpatrick, Jim Freshour
Medium Heat – Harvey Hayes, Frank Baldridge, Bob Johnson, Dale Bolinger
Slow Heat – Ron McKenzie, Tom Leiter, Keith Smith, John Ormsby
Feature – Jim Freshour, Randy Woodling, Shane Denny, Joe Pickett, John Fitzpatrick, Harvey Hayes, Arnold Prater, Larry Rosenberry, Tom Leiter, Dale Bolinger

Sprints:
Dash – Denny England, Tony Elliott, DeWayne Barker, Steve Kline
Fast Heat – Tony Elliott, Denny England, Dick Watson, Steve Kline
Slow Heat – Bimbo Atlins, Dave Darland, Sam Davis, Bill Fortune
Feature – Denny England, DeWayne Barker, Steve Kline, Greg Jones, Tony Elliott, Sam Davis, Dave Darland, Leon Jordan, Bimbo Atkins, Bill Fortune

Saturday, July 2, 1983 – Rainout

Monday, July 4, 1983
Elliott, Woodling Win Features

Tony Elliott captured his third feature win of the season at the Warsaw Speedway Monday night. Elliott drives a sprint car for Paul Hazen of Columbia City and also took the fast heat. In addition to the races, the annual fireworks display added to the evening's events.

Randy Woodling won the feature in the street stock division for his fourth win of the year. Finishing second to Woodling was Dane Ronk for his best finish in a feature at Warsaw this year. Rounding out the top five finishers in street stocks were Shane Denny third and Dave Fitzpatrick and Jim Frushour finishing fourth and fifth respectively.

Race Results – Street Stocks
Dash – Rex Alley, Randy Woodling, Shane Denny, Dane Ronk
Slow Heat – Larry Rosenberry, Barry Baker, Mike Orr
Middle Heat – Ron McKenzie, Joe Pickett, William Varney
Fast Heat – Randy Woodling, John Fitzpatrick, Dewayne May
Feature – Randy Woodling, Dane Ronk, Shane Denny, Dave Fitzpatrick, Jim Frushour, Ron McKenzie, Harvey Hayes, John Fitzpatrick, Scott Dausman, Joe Pickett
(Sprint Results are unreadable in the microfilmed copy of the paper)

Saturday, July 9, 1983
Denny, Shepherd Take Speedway Feature Races
By Bob Valentine

Shane Denny was victorious in the street stock feature while Terry Shepherd took the sprint feature Saturday night at the Warsaw Speedway. In both classes, the current season point leaders, Denny England (sprints) and Randy Woodling (street stocks), played the bridesmaids and finished second.

In the street stock feature, Denny took the leady early while Woodling picked his course and one by one put the rest of the field behind him, except for the leader. With the help of a couple caution flags, Woodling eventually got right behind Denny, but despite the constant pressure, Denny was not to be denied a feature win.

The fastest qualifiers in street stocks finished the feature in reverse order from their qualifying positions. Allen Marsh, the fastest qualifier, finished third with Woodling second and third fastest qualifier, Denny, picking up the marbles and taking them home to count until next Saturday. Gene Burkett, who rolled his car last week, was back in action this week, qualifying sixth fastest and placed fourth in the feature. Ron McKenzie, the fifth fastest qualifier, was fifth with Rex Alley sixth.

In the sprint feature, 16 qualifiers battled for the feature title. Whitey Jansen flipped his sprinter between turns one and two, putting him out of the race. Fortunately, Jansen was unhurt and watched the remaining laps from the pits. Those remaining laps were quite hectic with DeWayne Barker taking the high groove and literally flying around the track.

Many racers and fans commented after the races that Barker was really hooking up and possibly could have won this feature if it were not for a broken steering arm that forced him to retire for the evening. Until that point, Barker had passed the leader three times and every time a caution put him back to the position of the last completed lap.

After Barker was forced out, the race was all Shepherd's. England and Kenny Haynes put on a show after Barker retired for the second spot with England edging Haynes by a couple car lengths at the checkered flag. Joe Gaerte finished fourth ahead of Dave Darland and Rob Roberts finished sixth.

Race Summary:

Street Stocks:
Dash – Shane Denny, Allen Marsh, Randy Woodling, Ron McKenzie.
Fast Heat – Rex Alley, Tom Leiter, William Varney, Frank Baldridge.
Middle Heat – Scott Dausman, John Fitzpatrick, Junior Blocker, Scott Parker.
Slow Heat – Dale Bolinger, Dewayne May, Kim Bussard, Steve Keirn.
Feature – Shane Denny, Randy Woodling, Allen Marsh, Gene Burkett, Ron McKenzie, Rex Alley, Jim Frushour, Dave Fitzpatrick, Junior Blocker, William Varney.

Sprints:
Dash – DeWayne Barker, Bimbo Atkins, Joe Gaerte, Kenny Haynes.
Fast Heat – DeWayne Barker, Tony Elliott, Kenny Haynes, Bimbo Atkins.
Slow Heat – Rob Roberts, Rich Leming, Sam Davis.
Feature – Terry Shepherd, Denny England, Kenny Haynes, Joe Gaerte, Dave Darland, Rob Roberts,

Rich Leming, Paul Tetrault, Tony Elliott, Sam Davis.

Saturday, July 16, 1983
Woodling, England Win At Speedway
By Bob Valentine

The mid-season championships at the Warsaw Speedway are now history, with Randy Woodling capturing the street stock title and Denny England taking the sprint title. In both classes the winners received hard competition and constant pressure from the second, third and fourth place finishers.

In the sprint feature, a 40 lap event, the current point leader England started from the front row by virtue of the point standings along with second place point leader Tony Elliott. England led for most of the 40 laps with Elliott leading for the first few.

In a race of this importance, every competitor looks to the man ahead for his mistakes or anything they might capitalize on and gain the advantage. This was the case when England took the lead. Even though England had the lead, it was a position he could not relax with because there were several men just waiting behind for him to make a mistake. Those mistakes never came and the other drivers now found themselves battling with one another for their finishing positions. Steve Kline finished second just ahead of Elliott with DeWayne Barker finishing fourth. Dave Darland, 16 years old, finished fifth.

The street stock feature was a constant battle between the two point leaders, Woodling and Shane Denny with neither giving an inch or claiming any distinct advantage. Denny took the lead early but Woodling spun out on the first turn causing a re-start. This time it was Woodling's turn to take the lead on the restart. This lead would eventually be given up to Denny who took the leader on the back stretch. Denny held this lead for several laps with Woodling right behind. When Denny got involved with lapped traffic, Woodling took the advantage and passed the leader, never to give it up. Denny finished second with Ron McKenzie finishing third and Doug Drudge and Rex Allen finishing fourth and fifth, respectively.

Race Summary:
Street Stock:
Dash—William Varney; Ron McKenzie; Randy Woodling; Allen Marsh.
Fast Heat—Jim Frushour; Doug Drudge; Shane Denny; Dave Fitzpatrick.
Slow Heat—Larry Rosenberry; Steve Keirn; Dave Bolinger; Jim Pickett.
Feature—Randy Woodling; Shane Denny; Ron McKenzie; Doug Drudge; Rex Alley; Harvey Hayes; Roger Fitzpatrick; Larry Rosenberry; Scott Dausman; Steve Holbrook.
Sprint:
Dash—Tony Elliott; Denny England; Kenny Haynes; Steve Kline.
Fast Heat—Kenny Haynes; Dave Darland; Steve Kline; Rich Leming.
Slow Heat—DeWayne Barker; John Althouse; Charlie Sarver; Troy Dunn.
Feature—Denny England; Steve Kline; Tony Elliott; DeWayne Barker; Dave Darland; John Althouse; Paul Tetrault; Troy Dunn; Kenny Haynes; Rich Leming.

Saturday, July 23, 1983 - Rainout

Saturday, July 30, 1983
Barker Sprinter Sets Speedway Record Here
By Bob Valentine

While Randy Woodling continued his winning ways in street stock competition at the Warsaw Speedway Saturday night, DeWayne Barker put on a blistering display of speed and skill in the sprint car division to capture his first feature win of the season here. Barker not only won the sprint feature but also set a track record with a one lap time of 14.76 seconds.

As it turned out, car No. 33 proved to be the number to beat. Woodling powered his No. 33 street stock through the field to capture the feature, continuing his dominance over that class. Barker, meanwhile, carefully controlled his No. 33 sprinter to take the sprint feature. The numbers are not the only similarities between both drivers as they seem to be most comfortable taking the high side and running on the outside groove.

Woodling, also the fastest qualifier in his division, captured the street stock dash and the street stock fast heat. Barker was not as fortunate, however, as Tony Elliott shut the door on Bimbo Atkins and Barker to take the sprint dash. In the fast heat, Barker finished third while Gary Fisher, making his first appearance at Warsaw in 1983, captured the win.

In further action at the Warsaw Speedway, the street stock middle heat was won by John Fitzpatrick and Rick Sechrist took the slow heat. Charlie Sarver won his first race of 1983 at Warsaw by taking the checkered flag in the sprint slow heat.

Race Summary:
Street Stock:
Dash—Randy Woodling; Dewayne May; Jim Freshour; Shane Denny.
Fast Heat—Randy Woodling; Dewayne May; Gene Burkett; Shane Denny.
Middle Heat—John Fitzpatrick; Ron McKenzie; Frank Baldridge; Harvey Hayes.
Slow Heat—Rick Sechrist; Steve Keirn; Rex Alley; Phil Draper.
Feature—Randy Woodling; Ron McKenzie; Bob Johnson; Gene Burkett; Larry Rosenberry; Jim Freshour; Scott Dausman; Joe Pickett; John Fitzpatrick; Robert Johnson.
Sprint:
Dash - Tony Elliott; Bimbo Atkins; DeWayne Barker; Denny England.
Fast Heat—Gary Fisher; Denny England; DeWayne Barker; Bimbo Atkins.
Slow Heat—Charlie Sarver; Leon Jordan; Rich Leming; Tom Jewelll.
Feature—DeWayne Barker; Tony Elliott; Gary Fisher; Bimbo Atkins; Buck Baughan; Leon Jordon; Denny England; Charlie Sarver; Joe Gaerte; Tim Norman.

Saturday, August 6, 1983
Atkins, Woodling Win Races

By Bob Valentine

Bimbo Atkins and Randy Woodling were the feature winners in the Saturday night races at the Warsaw Speedway, which concluded the 1983 Kosciusko County Fair. Eighteen sprint cars took the green flag for qualifying while 34 street stocks made their attempts to be the evening's fastest qualifiers.

DeWayne Barker, the track sprint car top record holder, qualified fastest but was unable to equal last week's record run. Woodling carried the American flag as the evening's fastest qualifier in the street stock class.

Atkins, winner of the sprint dash was victorious in the feature for a long-awaited, well-earned win. Earlier in the evening, Barker survived a spectacular, end-over-end flip between turns one and two, resting with the roll cage on the outside retaining wall. Fortunately, no one was injured.

Continuing with the sprint feature, Atkins worked hard to obtain the lead and even harder to keep it. Early in the race, Atkins was able to overtake the leader after a restart, never to give it up. Tony Elliott finished second with Denny England third.

In the street stock class, Woodling, again the evening's fastest qualifier, won his third feature in a row and seventh feature of the year. Shane Denny does not seem to be able to break the jinks that has befallen him and again had to settle for second best in the feature. Finishing third was Rex Alley, who has run strong all year, but just hasn't quite put it all together for a feature win at Warsaw.

Race Summary:

Street Stocks:
Dash—Randy Woodling; Jim Frushour; Rex Alley; Dewayne May.
Fast Heat—Dewayne May; Shane Denny; Randy Woodling; John Fitzpatrick.
Middle Heat—Rick Sechrist; Scott Dausman; Tom Leiter; Gene Burkett.
Slow Heat—Bob Johnson; Larry Rosenberry; Dan Kelsey; Roger Fitzpatrick.
Feature—Randy Woodling; Shane Denny; Rex Alley; William Varney; Jim Frushour; Tom Leiter; Harvey Hayes; Rick Sechrist; Joe Pickett; Doug Drudge.

Sprints:
Dash—Bimbo Atkins; Gary Fisher; Denny England; DeWayne Barker.
Fast Heat—Tony Elliott; Steve Kline; Bimbo Atkins; Gary Fisher.
Slow Heat—Scott Fisher; Rich Leming; Charlie Sarver; Walt May.
Feature—Bimbo Atkins; Tony Elliott; Denny England; Steve Kline; Buck Baugham; Rich Leming; Tim Norman; Mark Millenberger; Walt May; Rob Roberts.

Saturday, August 13, 1983
Elliott, Woodling Win

By Bob Valentine

Tony Elliott won a tightly-packed sprint feature and Randy Woodling won his eighth street stock feature Saturday night at the Warsaw Speedway.

In the sprint feature, less than a straightaway length separated the first and fourth place finishers. Elliott started from the last row in a completely inverted field. Midway through the race Elliott was able to work his way to first place but received constant pressure from last week's feature winner, Bimbo Atkins, who finished second.

Denny England, Warsaw

Elliott was the evening's second fastest qualifier behind the record-breaking run of Denny England. England managed to break the week-old track lap record set fair week by DeWayne Barker. England's new one lap record was 14.63 seconds, but may not last long given the high level of competition within the sprints. In addition, Elliott also won the sprint fast heat but had problems in the dash and was fourth. Elliott's win in the feature this week ended a drought that followed his early season success when he had three feature wins in a row.

Tom Leiter, Warsaw

In the street stock feature, Woodling was able to set a track record by completing the oval in 18.08 seconds. Woodling also took the street stock fast heat and finished third in the dash. Finishing second to Woodling in the feature was Shane Denny.

Even though Denny could not make his number 58 street stock a winner in the feature, he was able to capture the dash and his car driven by Tracey Heiman won the women's powder puff race.

Street Stocks:
Dash—Shane Denny; Dewayne May; Randy Woodling; Ron McKenzie.
Fast Heat—Randy Woodling; Bob Johnson; Frank Baldridge; Dewayne May.
Middle Heat—Tom Leiter; Robert Johnson Jr.; Harvey Hayes; Dan Kelsey.
Slow Heat—Larry Rosenberry; Kim Bussard; Steve Kiern; Rick Jackson.
Feature—Randy Woodling; Shane Denny; Bob Johnson; Frank Baldridge; Scott Dausman; Joe Pickett; Larry Rosenberry; Dan Kelsey; Jim Frushour; Harvey Hayes.

Sprints:
Dash—Bimbo Atkins; Denny England; Steve Kline; Tony Elliott.
Fast Heat—Tony Elliott; Buck Baugham; Gary Fisher; Dave Darland.
Slow Heat—Charlie Sarver; Sam Davis; Rich Leming; Tim Norman.
Feature—Tony Elliott; Bimbo Atkins; Gary Fisher; Denny England; Charlie Sarver; Rich Leming; Tim Norman; Troy Dunn; Rob Roberts; Sam Davis.

Women's Power Puff—Tracey Heiman; Diane Dausman; Brenda Baldridge; Franky Butler; Linda Backus; Peggy Kern; Shelly Pickett; Edith May.

Saturday, August 20, 1983
Woodling, Elliott Set Pace
By Bob Valentine

With the Pepsi Challenge Traveling Trophy and extra money at stake, the Pepsi Challenge Series Races came to the Warsaw Speedway Saturday night. Randy Woodling won the street stock feature and Tony Elliott captured the sprint feature.

Eighteen sprint cars and 27 street stocks qualified. DeWayne Barker was the fastest qualifier in sprints while Woodling again took the honors in street stocks.

In the street stock feature, Woodling had to come from the middle of the 18-car field to win while Shane Denny had to come from the back of the pack twice after restarts to finish second ahead of third place finisher Gene Burkett.

Tony Elliott established his dominance early by putting his sprinter on the outside and using the cushion was able to move to the number one position within a few laps. After Elliott passed the front runners, they also tried the outside cushion but were unable to get the "bite" that Elliott maintained.

Race Summary:

Street Stocks:
Dash—Ron McKenzie; Shane Denny.
Fast Heat—Shane Denny; Dewayne May; Randy Woodling; Gene Burkett.
Middle Heat—Roger Fitzpatrick; Harvey Hayes; Junior Blocker; Joe Pickett.
Slow Heat—Larry Rosenberry; Keith Smith; Pete Fitzpatrick; Kim Bussard.
Feature—Randy Woodling; Shane Denny; Gene Burkett; Larry Rosenberry; Scott Dausman; Jim Frushour; Steve Holbrook; Robert Johnson Jr.; Roger Fitzpatrick; Dewayne May.

Sprints:
Dash—Denny England; Steve Kline; DeWayne Barker; Buck Baugham.
Fast Heat—Gary Fisher; Bimbo Atkins; Tony Elliott; DeWayne Barker.
Slow Heat—Terry Shepherd; Sam Davis; Rich Leming; Walt May.
Feature—Tony Elliott; Bimbo Atkins; Gary Fisher; Terry Shepherd; Steve Kline; Tray House; Buck Baugham, Rich Leming; Bob Seelman Jr.; Walt May.

Saturday, August 27, 1983
Fitzpatrick Ends Woodling Streak; Atkins Top Sprinter
By Bob Valentine

Dave Fitzpatrick put an end to Randy Woodling's string of five feature wins in a row by taking the feature in street stocks at the Warsaw Speedway Saturday night. Woodling took advantage of caution flags to move up in the field on the restarts but it was Fitzpatrick at the end when the checkered flag fell. Finishing second was Woodling and third through fifth were Jim Frushour, Shane Denny and John Fitzpatrick.

In sprints, Bimbo Atkins proved that the only lap you need to lead in any race is the last one. DeWayne Barker took the lead at the drop of the green flag and led for 24 and three-quarters laps of the 25-lap feature until lapped traffic led to his downfall. At that point, Atkins, who had worked his way to second position from the fourth row, took advantage of the situation and passed Barker coming off of the number four turn. Finishing third through fourth were Gary Fisher, Tony Elliott and Steve Kline.

Race Results:
Street Stocks
Dash – Ron McKenzie, Dave Fitzpatrick, Shane Denny, Randy Woodling.
Fast Heat – Junior Blocher, Dave Fitzpatrick, John Fitzpatrick, Randy Woodling.
Medium Heat – Terry Baker, Rex Alley, Frank Baldridge, Scott Dausman.
Slow Heat – Bob Johnson, Pete Fitzpatrick, Keith Smith, Kim Bussard.
Feature – Dave Fitzpatrick, Randy Woodling, Jim Freshour, Shane Denny, John Fitzpatrick, Harvey Hayes, Joe Pickett, Terry Baker, Mike Orr, Gene Burkett.
Sprints
Dash – Bimbo Atkins, Gary Fisher, Denny England, Dave Darland.
Fast Heat – DeWayne Barker, Gary Fisher, Steve Kline, Denny England.
Slow Heat – Tony Elliott, Tom Jewelll, Scott Fisher, Sam Davis.
Feature – Bimbo Atkins, DeWayne Barker, Gary Fisher, Tony Elliott, Steve Kline, Denny England, Dave Darland, Tom Jewelll, Tim Norman, Sam Davis.

Saturday, September 3, 1983
Woodling, Atkins Win Season Championships
By Bob Valentine, For the *Times-Union*

Closing out the 1983 racing season at the Warsaw Speedway, Randy Woodling finished as he started in street stock competition by taking the 30-lap feature while Bimbo

Randy Woodling, Atwood

Atkins outdistanced everyone to take the sprint feature Saturday night. Both drivers are now season champions by virtue of their season championship feature wins, but only Woodling can claim title to the points championship as well.

Woodling began the feature from the pole position because of his season's points leadership over second place Shane Denny. Denny was able to pressure Woodling for approximately 10 laps but was able to do little beyond that point and had to settle for second place. Finishing third through fifth were Jim Frushour, Doug Drudge and Ron McKenzie.

For Atkins the battle was not so easy. Denny England took the advantage from the green flag to go into turn one ahead of pole sitter Tony Elliott. Both drivers had problems dealing with a lapped car driven by Walt May, but it was Elliott who was forced out early. England broke a Jacobs ladder with the altercation with May, making handling of his car very difficult but he was able to hold off the charges of DeWayne Barker and Atkins for more than half the race.

Bimbo Atkins, Warsaw

Near the midway point, Atkins took over with Barker right behind for the first and second finishing positions. Finishing third through fifth were Steve Kline, Buck Baughan and Tom Jewelll. For Atkins it was a great way to close out a season that had many disappointments.

Earlier in the evening, 16-year old Dave Darland flipped his sprinter end-over-end between turns one and two. Darland was unhurt but was unable to continue.

Race Summary:
Street Stock:
High Points Heat—Allen Marsh; Harvey Hayes; Dave Fitzpatrick; John Fitzpatrick.
Middle Points Heat—Doug Drudge; Dewayne May; Tom Leiter; Bob Johnson.
Low Points Heat—Kim Bussard; Steve Keirn; Keith Smith.
Feature—Randy Woodling; Shane Denny; Jim Frushour; Doug Drudge; Ron McKenzie; Roger Fitzpatrick; Gene Burkett; Bob Johnson; Larry Rosenberry; Dewayne May.
Sprint:
High Points Heat—DeWayne Barker; Steve Kline; Bimbo Atkins; Tony Elliott.
Low Points Heat—Buck Baughan; Lou Mann; Tom Jewelll; Sam Davis.
Feature---Bimbo Atkins; DeWayne Barker; Steve Kline; Buck Baughan; Tom Jewelll; Rich Leming; Scott Fisher; Sam Davis; Denny England; Walt May.

1984

Saturday, May 12, 1984 – No Results Published

Saturday, May 19, 1984 - Rainout

Saturday, May 26, 1984
Elliott, Stone, Fitzpatrick Win Speedway Races

Tony Elliott, Rick Stone and Roger Fitzpatrick won feature races at the Warsaw Motor

Speedway Saturday night. Elliott beat runner-up DeWayne Barker and third-place finisher Tom Jewelll for the sprint feature title. Bimbo Atkins was fourth. Elliott also won the fast heat, while Barker won the sprint dash and Denny England the slow heat.

In the limited late model feature, Stone was first, Hank Hilmer second and Randy Woodling third. Stone won the dash, Woodling the fast heat and John Vigor the slow heat. Fitzpatrick won the road runners feature, ahead of Jon Ormsby and Bob Johnson, who were second and third. Fitzpatrick also took the road runner heat race.

Race Results:

Road Runner's Heat—Roger Fitzpatrick; Bob Johnson; Duane Owens.
Road Runner's Feature—Roger Fitzpatrick; Jon Ormsby; Bob Johnson; Duane Owens.
Qualification—Sprint—Buck Baugham; 15.78
Limited Late Model—Randy Woodling; 18.88.
Sprint Dash—DeWayne Barker; Mark Owsley; Tom Jewelll; Buck Baugham.
Limited Late Dash—Rick Stone; Randy Woodling; Glenn Bradley; Ron McKenzie.
Sprint Slow Heat—Denny England; Louie Mann; Gary Fisher; Dave Darland.
Sprint Fast Heat—Tony Elliott; Bimbo Atkins; DeWayne Barker; Tom Jewelll.
Sprint Feature—Tony Elliott; DeWayne Barker; Tom Jewelll; Bimbo Atkins; Louie Mann; Mark Owsley; Steve Kline; Gary Fisher; Denny England; Dave Darland; Buck Baugham; Jesse Fordyce.
Limited Late Slow Head – John Vigar; Bill Draper; Kim Bussard; Gene Burkett.
Limited Late Fast Heat—Randy Woodling; Glenn Bradley; Ron McKenzie; Hank Hilmer.
Limited Late Model Feature—Rick Stone; Hank Hilmer; Randy Woodling; Glenn Bradley; Dave Fitzpatrick; Ron McKenzie; Gene Burkett; Tim Haupet; John Vigar; Mike Orr; Dewayne May; Kim Bussard; Bill Draper; Scott Dausman; Butch Boggs.

Saturday, June 2, 1984
Barker Wins Feature

DeWayne Barker won the sprint feature and Glenn Bradley the late model feature at the Warsaw Speedway Saturday night.

Chasing Barker to the finish line in the sprint feature were Tony Elliott, who was second, and Bimbo Akins, third. In the limited late model feature, Randy Woodling was second and Dan Christy third.

Glenn Bradley, Marion

Race Results:

Sprint Fast Heat—Van Gurley; Bimbo Atkins; Denny England; DeWayne Barker.
Sprint Slow Heat—Dave Darland; Sam Davis; Rich Leming; Ray Kenans.
Limited Late Fast Heat:--Randy Woodling; Rick Stone; Den Handthorn; Glenn Bradley.
Limited Late Slow Heat—John Fitzpatrick; Kim Bussard; Fred Boggs; Mike Keatting.
Sprint Feature—DeWayne Barker; Tony Elliott; Bimbo Atkins; Steve Kline; Denny England; John Davis; Rich Leming; Louie Mann; Van Gurley; Dave Darland; Sam Davis; Oscar Smith.
Limited Late Model Feature—Glenn Bradley; Randy Woodling; Dan Christy; Hank Hilmer; Rick

Stone; Don Handthorn; Robert Johnson; Dewayne May; Scott Dausman; William Varney; Mike Keatting; John Fitzgerald; Gene Burkett; Kim Bussard.
Road Runners Heat—Fitzpatrick; Johnson; Ormsby.
Road Runners Feature—Johnson; Owsley.

Saturday, June 9, 1984
Hilmer Nips Woodling In Speedway Feature

Hank Hilmer edged Randy Woodling for first place in a controversial limited late model feature race at the Warsaw Speedway Saturday night.

Hilmer and Woodling were locked in a tight battle for the lead on the 20th and final lap of the race. Hilmer was ruled to have had the lead when the 20th lap was completed, but the flagman apparently forgot to drop the checkered flag. Woodling passed Hilmer on the 21st lap, when the checkered flag was finally dropped. However, the final standings were based on the positions after the 20th lap. John Fitzpatrick took third place. Woodling won both the limited late model dash and fast heat.

In the sprint feature, Van Gurley of South Bend was first, Bimbo Atkins second and Buck Baugham third. Baughman took the sprint dash and Tim Norman the fast heat.

Race Results:

Qualifying—Sprint—Van Gurley 15.53.
Limited Late—Randy Woodling 18.18. 1984 record.
Sprint Dash—Buck Baughan; Mark Owsley; Van Gurley; Bimbo Atkins.
Limited Late Dash—Randy Woodling; Ron McKenzie; Scott Dausman; William Varney.
Fast Heat Sprint—Tim Norman; Buck Baugham; Bimbo Atkins; Denny England.
Slow—John Davis; Sam Davis; Tom Jewelll; Rich Leming.
Fast Heat (Limited Late)-Randy Woodling; Dan Handthorn; Dewayne May; Hank Hilmer.
Slow—Glenn Bradley; Kim Bussard; Dave Fitzpatrick; John Fitzpatrick.
Street Stock Heat—Roger Fitzpatrick; Jon Ormsby; Bob Johnson; Jim Long.
Sprint Feature—Van Gurley; Bimbo Atkins; Buck Baugham; Tim Norman; Dave Darland; Rich Leming; Jeff Walker; Sam Davis; Denny England; Oscar Smith; Mark Owsley; Tom Jewelll; John Davis.
Limited Late Feature—Hank Hilmer; Randy Woodling; John Fitzpatrick; Mike Orr: Dewayne May; Kim Bussard; Ron McKenzie; Dan Handthorn; Rich Crashin; William Varney; Scott Dausman; Gene Burkett; Fred Boggs; Robert Johnson.

Saturday, June 16 - Rainout

Saturday, June 23, 1984
Barker, Stone Win Features

DeWayne Barker captured the sprint feature and Rick Stone won the limited late model feature at the Warsaw Speedway Saturday night. In each feature, the previous week's winner finished second as Bimbo Atkins was runner-up in the sprint and Randy Woodling in the late model.

In late model heat races, Stone won the dash, William Varney the fast heat and Scott

Dausman the slow heat. Sprint heat winners were Tony Elliott in the dash, Denny England in the fast heat and Kenny Haynes the slow heat.

Race Results:

Qualifying Time: Sprint—Bimbo Atkins—15.84.
Qualifying Time: Limited Late—Randy Woodling—20.03.
Sprint Dash—Tony Elliott; Steve Kline; DeWayne Barker; Bimbo Atkins.
Limited Late Model Dash—Rick Stone; William Varney; Dewayne May; Allen Marsh.
Sprint Fast Heat—Denny England; DeWayne Barker; Tom Jewelll; Bimbo Atkins.
Limited Late Fast Heat—William Varney; Hank Hilmer; Dewayne May; Allen Marsh.
Street Stock- R. Fitzpatrick; B. Johnson; G. Holloway; D. Cordill.
Sprint Slow Heat—Kenny Haynes; Dave Darland; Paul Tetrault; Sam Davis.
Limited Late Slow Heat—Scott Dausman; Kim Bussard; Phil Draper; Randy Lazian.
Sprint Feature—Barker; Atkins; Haynes; Jewell; Walker; Kline; Darland; Davis; England.
Limited Late Feature—Stone; Woodling; Hilmer; Varney; Burkett; McKenzie; Dausman; Bussard.

Saturday, June 30, 1984
Woodling, Barker Win Features

DeWayne Barker, Warsaw

DeWayne Barker won a close sprint feature that was not decided until the last lap while Randy Woodling went unchallenged in winning the limited late model feature at Warsaw Speedway Saturday.

Barker overtook Denny England on the final lap after running nearly even at the white flag. England wound up second and Tony Elliott third in the sprint feature. Bimbo Atkins won the sprint dash, England the fast heat and Elliott the slow heat.

In the late model feature, Woodling started from the second row and took the lead for good on the fourth lap, passing the leader, Allen Marsh. The race was halted for a brief period after a seven car crash. Hank Hilmer finished second and Marsh third in the feature. Marsh won the dash, Hilmer the fast heat and Kim Bussard the slow heat.

The next racing program will be Wednesday night, following the fireworks program which begins at dusk.

Race Results:

Sprint Cars:
Dash—Bimbo Atkins; DeWayne Barker; Steve Kline; Buck Baugham.
Fast Heat—Denny England; Tim Norman; DeWayne Barker; Steve Kline.
Slow Heat—Tony Elliott; Dave Darland; Troy Dunn; Oscar Smith.

Feature—DeWayne Barker; Denny England; Tony Elliott; Steve Kline; Dave Darland; Oscar Smith; Tim Norman; Buck Baugham; Troy Dunn.
Limited Late Model:
Dash—Allen Marsh; Randy Woodling; Glenn Bradley; Dan Hanthorn.
Fast Heat—Hank Hilmer; Randy Woodling; Allen Marsh; Scott Dausman.
Slow Heat—Kim Bussard; Charles Hyde; Dave Fitzpatrick; Steve Knouff.
Feature—Randy Woodling; Hank Hilmer; Allen Marsh; Doug Drudge; Scott Dausman; Glenn Bradley; Bill Ice; Kim Bussard; B. Cripe.

Wednesday, July 4, 1984
Fireworks Plus Racing Equal Speedway Thrills

An exciting night of racing highlighted the fireworks that were paid for by the Kosciusko County Fair Board, the Warsaw Speedway and the paying spectators. Those who paid to get in were treated with close match racing and a thrilling fireworks display. For the features, the field of cars were totally inverted, meaning the fastest cars started in the back.

In the sprint feature, DeWayne Barker 33B, Tony Elliott 57, and Terry Shepherd 7S were all going for the win, when, with two laps to go, the yellow flag came out. The re-start proved Barker's power as he took the win, followed by Elliott and Shepherd. All three of these cars started the race from the rear of the 11 car field.

The limited late model feature finished with Allen Marsh 75 first followed closely by Hank Hilmer 38 and Randy Woodling 33. Like the sprint feature, all three of these cars started from the rear of the 18 car field.

Race Results:

Qualifying sprint—T. Shepherd 15.31.
Limited Late—Randy Woodling 18.50.
Dash Sprint—T. Shepherd; DeWayne Barker, D. England.
Limited Late—G. Bradley; A. Marsh; Hilmer; Woodling.
Fast Heat Sprint—Elliott; England; Shepherd; Atkins.
Limited Late—Bradley; Hilmer; Marsh; Vigar.
Slow Heat Sprint—Darland; Leming; Walker; Boyer.
Limited Late—Prater; Fitzpatrick; England; Crashin.
Street Stock Heat—Ormsby; Fitzpatrick; Prater; Johnson.
Features—Sprint—DeWayne Barker; Tony Elliott; Terry Shepherd; Dave Darland; Tom Jewelll; John Davis; Rich Leming; Jeff Walker; Denny England; Bimbo Atkins; Brad Boyer.
Limited Late—Allen Marsh; Hank Hilmer; Randy Woodling; Don Prater; Scott Dausman; Butch Boggs; Doug Drudge; Gene Burkett; John Fitzpatrick; Ron McKenzie; Steve Knouff; Tracy Landis; John Vigar; Jim Philpot; Rod England; Rich Crashin; William Varney; Glenn Bradley.
Street Stock—Bob Johnson; Arnold Prater; Gerold Holloway; Jon Ormsby; Roger Fitzpatrick Dan Cordill.

Saturday, July 7, 1984
Woodling Sets Record
Atkins, Bradley Win Speedway Features

With the mid-season championship only a week away, drivers were battling for points Saturday night at the Warsaw Speedway to improve their starting positions for this Saturday's big program.

Feature winners were Bimbo Atkins in the sprints and Glenn Bradley in the limited late model. For the sprints, current point leader DeWayne Barker won both the dash and fast heat and took the early lead in the feature. But with only eight laps left, Barker spun out and was forced out of the race. With Barker out of his way, Atkins moved up a spot from second place and went on to win with Buck Bougham and Steve Kline finishing second and third.

In the limited late model division, Randy Woodling set a one-lap track record, being the first limited late model or hobby stock to break the 18:00 mark. The current points leader, Woodling's record is 17.93. However, Woodling was second to Bradley in the feature, with Rick Stone third. Woodling also took the dash, followed by Allen Marsh. The fast heat was won by Stone with William Varney second.

Race Results:

Dash Sprint—DeWayne Barker; Denny England; Buck Bougham; Steve Kline.
Fast Heat Sprint—Barker; B. Atkins; S. Kline; John Davis.
Slow Heat Sprint—Dave Darland; Rich Leming; Ray Kenans; Jim Payne.
Limited Late—R. Woodling; A. Marsh; G. Bradley; S. Dausman.
Limited Late—J. Vigar; K. Bussard; L. Heintzman; D. Fitzpatrick.
Feature:
Sprint—Bimbo Atkins; Buck Bougham; Steve Kline; Dave Darland; Rich Leming; John Davis; Ray Kenans; Jim Payne; DeWayne Barker; Brad Boyer; Oscar Smith.
Street Stock—Ormsby; Johnson; Draper; Compton; Plotner; Fitzpatrick.
Limited Late—Glenn Bradley; Randy Woodling; Rick Stone; Don Prater; Doug Drudge; Kim Bussard; Dave Fitzpatrick; William Varney; Larry Heintzman; Larry Blevins; Gene Burkett; Allen Marsh; Scott Dausman; Dewayne May; Ron McKenzie; Butch Boggs; Charlie Hyde.

Saturday, July 14, 1984
Kline, Woodling, Ormsby Mid-Season Champions

Steve Kline and Randy Woodling took top honors in the sprint and limited late model mid-season championship races held Saturday night at the Warsaw Speedway, along with Jon Ormsby taking the street stock win.

In the sprint feature, Kline breezed to first, starting from the front row and taking the lead early from Bimbo Atkins in the 40-lap event. Following Kline to the finish line were Buck Bougham, Dave Darland and Rich Leming. Kline also won the first heat race with Bougham taking the second heat and Darland winning the dash.

The limited late model feature was won by Woodling, who started on the poll and led the entire 30 laps. Rick Stone took second place by passing Allen Marsh on the last lap. Hank Hilmer and Scott Dausman rounded out the top five. Like Kline, Woodling also won the fast heat, with Randy Lozier taking the slow heat and Allen Marsh winning the dash.

Jon Ormsby easily won the street stock feature followed by Steve Plotner and Roger Fitzpatrick.

Race Results:

Sprint Dash—Dave Darland; Bimbo Adkins; Buck Bougham; Steve Kline.
Limited Late Dash—Allen Marsh; Randy Woodling; Glenn Bradley; Dewayne May.
Fast Heat Sprint—Steve Kline; John Davis; Ray Kenens; Brad Boyer.
Fast Heat Limited Late—Randy Woodling; Hank Hilmer; Allen Marsh; Scott Dausman.
Slow Heat Sprint—Buck Bougham; Rich Leming; Bimbo Atkins; Dave Darland.
Slow Heat Limited Late—Randy Lozier; Don Prater; Keith Smith; Mike Orr.
Sprint—Steve Kline; Buck Bougham; Dave Darland; Rich Leming; Ray Kenens; John Davis; Bimbo Atkins; Brad Boyer; Jim Payne; Sam Davis.
Limited Late Model—Randy Woodling; Rick Stone; Allen Marsh; Hank Hilmer; Scott Dausman; Doug Drudge; Mike Orr; Glenn Bradley; Don Prater; John Vigar; Bill Ice; Dave Fitzpatrick; Jim Philpot; Butch Boggs; Steve Keans; Kim Bussard; Dewayne May; Gene Burkett.
Street Stock—Jon Ormsby; Steve Plotner; Roger Fitzpatrick; Bob Johnson; Dave Fitzpatrick; Dan Cordill; J.R. Sweet; Phil Shafer; Bill Nickels.

Saturday, July 21, 1984
England Sixth Sprint Champ

Denny England became the sixth different sprint feature winner at Warsaw Speedway and Randy Woodling won his fourth limited late model feature Saturday night.

Aside from winning the features, England took the dash win and Woodling captured the fast heat. Buck Boughan won the sprint fast heat and Ray Kenens the slow heat.

Dewayne May won his first limited late model dash and John Vigar won the slow heat. The street stock feature and heat race were won by Roger Fitzpatrick, followed by Jon Ormsby.

Race Results:

Qualifying: Sprint-Van Gurley 15.60. Limited late: Randy Woodling 19.27.
Dash—Sprint—Denny England; Van Gurley; Steve Kline; Tony Elliott.
Limited Late—Dewayne May; Randy Woodling; Allen Marsh; William Varney.
Fast Heats -Sprint—Buck Bougham; Bimbo Atkins; Dave Darland; Tony Elliott.
Limited Late—Randy Woodling; Allen Marsh; Butch Boggs; Dick Phillips.
Slow Heats-Sprint—Ray Kenens; Rich Leming; Jim Payne; Oscar Smith.
Limited Late—John Vigar; Mike Orr; Keith Smith; Denny Dyson.
Street Stock—Roger Fitzpatrick; Jon Ormsby; Bob Johnson.
Feature-Sprint—Denny England; DeWayne Barker; Steve Kline; Tony Elliott; Buck Bougham; Bimbo Atkins; Dave Darland; Ray Kenens; Jim Payne; Brad Boyer; Oscar Smith; John Davis.
Limited Late—Randy Woodling; Allen Marsh; Dick Phillips; Dan Handthorn; Doug Drudge; John

Vigar; William Varney; Rich Bashem; Tim Goshert; Scott Dausman; Keith Smith; Denny Dyson. Street Stock—Roger Fitzpatrick; Jon Ormsby; Shane Denny, Bob Johnson.

Saturday, July 28, 1984 - Rainout

Saturday, August 4, 1984
Fisher, Woodling Win Features

Even though Saturday was the conclusion of the county fair, there is plenty of action still to come to the fairgrounds, with many weeks of auto racing remaining after action that night.

In the sprint division, Dave Darland took the dash win over Denny England and Gary Fisher while Tony Elliott won the fast heat and DeWayne Barker the slow heat. The sprint feature was won by Gary Fisher, who led the entire race followed by a close second and third of Tony Elliott and Denny England. Bimbo Atkins and Steve Kline rounded out the top five.

The limited late model class had Hank Kilmer the dash winner, Jim Taylor, the fast heat, Glenn Bradley, the middle heat and John Fitzpatrick, the slow heat. The feature was won by Randy Woodling, his fifth of the year, followed by Jim Taylor, Hank Hilmer, Dan Backus, and Glenn Bradley. The street stock heat and feature were won by Jon Ormsby.

Race Results:

Dash Sprint—Dave Darland; Denny England; Gary Fisher; Tom Jewelll.
Limited Late—Hank Hilmer; Randy Woodling; Don Backus; Jim Taylor.
Fast Heat Sprint—Tony Elliott; Denny England; Bimbo
Atkins; Gary Fisher.
Limited Late—Jim Taylor; Dan Backus; Scott Dausman; Allen Marsh.
Middle Heat Limited Late—Glenn Bradley; Bob Forsythe;
Doug Drudge; Gene Burkett.
Sprint—DeWayne Barker; Steve Kline; Jeff Walker; Tim Norman.
Slow Heat Limited Late—John Fitzpatrick; Dan Handthorn; Butch Boggs; Kim Bussard.
Sprint Feature—Gary Fisher; Tony Elliott; Denny England; Bimbo Atkins; Steve Kline; Tom Jewelll; Rich Leming; Jeff Walker; Tim Norman; Brad Boyer; DeWayne Barker; Oscar Smith.
Limited Late Feature—Randy Woodling; Jim Taylor; Hank Hilmer; Dan Backus; Glenn Bradley; Scott Dausman; Bob Forsythe; Ron McKenzie; Doug Drudge; Allen Marsh; Butch Boggs; Terry Duke.
Street Stock—Jon Ormsby; Robert Johnson; Shane Denny; Gerold Holloway; Bill Nichols.

Saturday, August 11, 1984
Newcomer Wins Sprint Feature

Steve Butler, in his first visit to the Warsaw Speedway, drove like a track veteran and won the winged sprint car feature Saturday night. Butler, a three-time USAC feature winner, wheeled it on the high side of the track and worked his way up from his fifth starting position. Steve Kline led 14 of the 25 laps until he spun out, giving Butler the lead. Following the winner was DeWayne Barker, Hank Lower, with Joe Gaerte in the fourth position.

In the three preliminary races, Hank Lower was awarded a trophy for his dash win while the two heats were won by Tony Elliott and Tom Jewelll.

Randy Woodling won his sixth feature in the limited late model division. Although Woodling was involved in a serious crash on the first lap, the car, without much of its sheet metal, was able to make the restart and win the 20-lap feature. Coming in second was Hank Hilmer with Rick Stone in third. Stone also won the fast heat with William Varney winning the slow heat race. The receiver of a trophy in an exciting dash win was Jim Taylor in only his second appearance at the track.

Tom Jewelll, Goshen

In the only roadrunner event, Jon Ormsby took the honors while extending his lead in the track point standings.

Scheduled for this Saturday's show is a special "All Female Demolition Derby" following the regular show of sprints, limited late models, and roadrunners. This is believed to be the only time the speedway has hosted such an event.

Race Results:
Winged Sprints:
Qualifying fast time—DeWayne Barker, 14.72.
Trophy Dash—Hank Lower; Steve Butler; Joe Gaerte; DeWayne Barker.
Slow Heat—Tony Elliott; Don Walker; Paul Tetrault; Oscar Smith; Charlie Sarver; Barry Baker; A.J. Abrums.
Fast Heat—Tom Jewelll; Hank Lower; Steve Butler; Steve Kline; DeWayne Barker; Kenny Haynes; Bimbo Atkins; Joe Gaerte; Denny England.
Feature—Butler, Barker; Lower; Gaerte; Jewell; Atkins; Elliott; Kline; Haynes; Walker; Tetrault; Baker; Abrums; England; Smith: Sarver.

Limited Late Models:
Qualifying Fast Time—Rick Stone, 18.26.
Trophy Dash—Jim Taylor; Rick Stone; Randy Woodling; Gene Burkett.
Slow Heat—William Varney; Kim Bussard; Steve Knoff; Mike Orr; Doug Drudge; Joe Kieg.
Fast Heat—Rick Stone; Randy Woodling; Butch Boggs; Hank Hilmer; Dan Backus; Jim Taylor; Gene Burkett; Scott Dausman; Ron McKenzie.
Feature—Woodling; Hilmer; Stone; Dausman; Rick Bashum; John Vigar; John Fitzpatrick; Kieg; Bussard; Varney; Drudge; Backus; Knoff; Boggs; Charlie Hall; Burkett; McKenzie; Taylor.

Saturday, August 18, 1984
Bimbo Atkins Leads From Start In Sprint Feature

Bimbo Atkins started on the inside of the first row and won his third sprint car feature this year at the Warsaw Speedway Saturday night. Meanwhile, Tony Elliott set a track record and won the dash in sprint competition.

Atkins led all 25 laps but near the end of the feature DeWayne Barker began moving closer to the leader. Barker came within reach of the lead but his car developed problems and slowed. Even with the car troubles, he held off Rusty McClure to finish second. McClure came in third with Denny England and Elliott finishing fourth and fifth.

In qualifying, Elliott set a track one-lap record of 15.03, which broke the old record held by Steve Kline of 15.21. The two preliminary heats were won by Atkins and Barker with Elliott winning the trophy dash.

In limited late model action, Glenn Bradley led all 20 laps to win his third feature of the year. Jim Taylor finished second with Hank Hilmer and Rick Stone placing third and fourth. Bradley also won the trophy dash with heat wins going to Taylor and Doug Drudge.

Jon Ormsby won the street stock feature with Robert Johnson taking the heat win. Cathy Greider won the ladies demolition derby.

This Saturday's program will be the regular show of sprints, limited late models, and street stocks. Back by popular demand, the sprint cars will now be running the wings for the rest of the season.

Scheduled for the rest of the year will be the season championships Sept. 1 with a special Warsaw Invitational on Thursday, Sept. 13, for winged sprint cars. Anyone interested in helping donate prize money, trophies, or ticket drawing prizes for the invitational contact Monty Miller at 356-4410.

Saturday, August 25, 1984
Barker Surprised To Win
By Kim Gregory

With the white flag signaling one lap to go, DeWayne Barker wheeled past Denny England in the first turn and came around to take the checkered flag in the 25-lap, winged sprint feature race at the Warsaw Speedway Saturday. It was Barker's seventh feature win this year in his Barker Auto Sales sponsored sprinter and extends his point leadership over the rest of the field. In other features, Glenn Bradley won the limited late model and Jon Ormsby took the roadrunner.

In the sprint feature, Bimbo Atkins took the early lead but was forced out with mechanical problems, turning the lead over to England. England held a commanding lead until with five laps to go Barker began closing the margin.

It was a surprise win for Barker, who did not realize he had won the race. He headed for the pits after finishing and later admitted that he was unaware Atkins had dropped out and thought he was dueling England for second place. Steve Kline wound up in third place and Dave Darland was fourth. The trophy dash was won by England with heat wins going to Rob Roberts and England. Barker had the fastest time with a 14.78 clocking.

The limited late model feature win by Bradley was his fourth of the season. Jim Taylor was leading with five laps remaining when Bradley moved into first place for good. Taylor settled for second. Third place went to Scott Dausman and Mike McMahan was fourth.

The heat wins went to John Vigar and Randy Loucks, with the trophy dash going to Rick Stone. Randy Woodling broke his own track record with a time of 17.86. Robert Johnson won a roadrunner heat race.

Next week will be the season championships, the last regular show of the year. The Warsaw Invitational will be held Sept. 13 for winged sprint cars. The top prize is $1,000 for the feature.

Saturday, September 1, 1984
Speedway Season Champions Crowned

DeWayne Barker and Randy Woodling were crowned track champions and Denny England, Randy Woodling, and Bill Nichols found themselves taking home first place trophies for their feature victories Saturday night at the Warsaw Speedway,

Randy Woodling, Atwood

England, in his Terry's Automotive - Car Tunes Special sprint car, showed that a wet track is his track as he won his third feature this year. The early leader of the 40-lap feature was Barker, who started from the pole position.

But as the race began to unfold, England started to close the gap between himself and the lead. England's car, which was set up for a wet track, passed Barker and took the lead and maintained it. The track worked in his favor as it stayed moist. Promising driver Dave Darland came in second and Barker, involved in a yellow flag situation near the end of the race, ended up third.

Besides winning the feature, England won his heat race and the trophy dash, making the night a clean sweep. The other heat was won by Barry Baker with Don Walker Jr. having the fastest qualifying time of 16.02.

The 30-lap limited late model feature was won by track champion Randy Woodling in his Gregory Body Shop special. Woodling led the entire race but was dueling near the end with Glenn Bradley for the lead. Bradley came in a close second with Scott Dausman third. The limited late model heats were won by Dausman and Bradley with the trophy dash win going to Dewayne May. Fast time was set by Woodling with a clocking of 20.66.

In the first feature win this season, Bill Nichols came out on top in the l5-lap roadrunner championship race. Second place went to 15-year old David Richard Fitzpatrick.

Fitzpatrick wasn't the youngest driver. The newest and youngest driver ever to drive at Warsaw picked up third place. As his entourage of young fans cheered him on, 12-year old Kevin Atkins outlasted many of the veterans and paced his way carefully through the many wrecks and spins to end up with a third place finish. The heat race was won by Jon Ormsby with a special winners trophy dash going to Robert Johnson. Barker and Woodling won the season point titles for their respective divisions.

The Warsaw Invitational will be held Thursday, September 13, and will conclude the racing this year. The winged sprint car show will match drivers from Michigan, Ohio, Illinois, and Indiana against each other for the top prize of $1,000. For more information, phone 356-4410.

Thursday, September 13, 1984
Hewitt Wins Warsaw Invitational
by Kim Gregory

Ronnie Miller with Jack Hewitt

With a 32 car field competing for the Warsaw Invitational championship, veteran driver Jack "Do-It" Hewitt came to win and did so as he won the 40 lap feature race and the $1,000 prize Thursday night in his Nichols Bros. sprint car. The first 13 laps of the race were led by polesitter, Steve Kline, who had a growing lead until a yellow flag closed the field. On the restart, Fred Linder in second, closed on Kline and passed for the lead. Then just as quickly, Hewitt passed Kline and challenged Linder for the first spot. Midway through the race, Hewitt ducked underneath Linder and took the lead to the finish.

Second place went to Linder, the former All-Star Sprint champion, with DeWayne Barker coming clear up from the 12th starting position to capture the third spot. Kline finished fourth followed by Steve Butler and Tony Elliott to round out the top six. Fast time was set by Joe Gaerte with a time of 14.24. The trophy dash was won by Hewitt with John Scheidelman winning the first of four heat races. Other heat winners were Steve Beitler, from Sedro Woolley, WA., Jeff Donaldson, and Rodney Ritter Jr. winning the fast heat. The 12 lap consolation event was won by Tony Elliott with second going to Bimbo Atkins. Both advanced to the feature.

October 13 will be the track banquet at the legion in Columbia City, IN., for drivers and speedway personnel.

1985

Saturday, May 18, 1985
Speedway Starts Racing

If the season opener Saturday night is to be any indication of what's in store at the Warsaw Speedway this year, the season will be an exciting one for race fans. DeWayne Barker won the sprint car feature with Allen Marsh picking up the limited late model feature and Harvey Hayes taking the road runner main event.

Barker, in his Barker Auto Sales sponsored sprint car, made the night a clean sweep, for besides winning the 25-lap feature, he set a new track record, won his heat and took dash honors as well. The new track record was set with a time of 14.68 which broke the mark of 15.03 held by Tony Elliott. In the first of two sprint heats, Jesse Fordyce took first place with Randy Woodling in the runner-up position. The second sprint heat won by Barker was not just an average heat race, as John Davis, local sprint driver and postal carrier, flipped end-over-end between turns one and two, causing the red flag to fly. Luckily, he emerged from the cockpit uninjured, but the car was unable to compete in the duration of the evening's races. Second place went to Bimbo Atkins. The feature event, again won by Barker, saw Van Gurley, Atkins, and Don Walker Jr. finishing second, third and fourth respectively.

In the Limited Late Model class, the dash went to Jim Bucher Jr. with the heat wins going to Butch Boggs and William Varney. A full field stated the 20-lap feature that ended with Allen Marsh crossing the finish line first, followed by Glenn Bradley, Dan Backus and Boggs. This being only the second year for this class at the speedway, the cars have increased remarkably to put on a terrific show for everyone.

Another class of cars increasing in number is the basically low-dollar Roadrunner division. This class does not qualify with time trials to start the feature, but race in a qualifying heat to determine positions. This race went to Bob Johnson with second place going to Dan Cordill. The feature event was won by Harvey Hayes, followed by Bob Johnson, Garold Holloway and Robert Johnson.

Next week the speedway will again host all three classes with gates opening at 5 p.m. and the first race slated for 8 p.m.

Saturday, May 25, 1985
Barker, Hayes On Streak

A good crowd of fans and race cars were on hand Saturday evening to see DeWayne Barker pick up his second sprint feature win in a row at the Warsaw Speedway. Winners of the other two features were Jim Taylor in the Limited Late Model Class and Harvey Hayes, making it two feature victories in a row for him in the Roadrunner Division.

Barker, in his Barker Auto Sales sprint car, fought a tough battle to a feature win. He dealt with heavy traffic, a dry, slick track, and especially the competition of charging Tony Elliott. The early leader was Dave Darland, who was putting distance between himself and the second place Elliott. By riding up high on the track near the middle of the race, Darland got too close to the third turn wall and flipped end-over-end ending the chance for his first feature victory at Warsaw. With Darland out of the race, second-place Elliott was handed the lead with Barker closing in as the race progressed. Finally, Barker passed Elliott near the end and held on to win the 25-lap event. Elliott placed second as Van Gurley and Bimbo Atkins finished third and fourth.

The first of two sprint car heats went to Jim Lipkey of Kokomo with Tom Jewell in second. Elliott captured the dash win and the other heat win with Darland placing second in the latter of the two races. In time trials, Don Walker Jr., flipped his car before even getting one lap recorded while Barker picked up quick time of 15.60.

In the Limited Late Model division, Jim Taylor of Kokomo, with his P1 numbered Camaro, led the field to his first feature win this year. Second place went to Glenn Bradley with third and fourth going to Ron McKenzie and Hank Hilmer. The first heat was won by Jim Bucher Jr., with Hilmer picking up second and in the second heat the win went to Bradley with Scott Dausman in second. In qualifying, fast time went to Taylor with a mark of 18.68.

Proving to be a dominant leader in the Roadrunner class, Hayes won both the feature qualifying heat and the feature event in his number 49 race car. Other feature places went to Bob Johnson, James Holloway, and Gerold Holloway consecutively. Next Saturday, the speedway will again host the same three classes of cars with each division growing in number as we get further into the racing season.

Saturday, June 1, 1985
Barker, Hayes Keeping Speedway String Alive

DeWayne Barker and Harvey Hayes both made it three in a row in the feature win column Saturday night at the Warsaw Speedway. Barker in the sprint car class and Hayes in the roadrunner division, are proving that they are the cars to beat heading into the fourth week of racing. Hank Hilmer chalked up his first feature victory of the year in the limited late model division.

In the sprint feature, the early leader was Denny England, with Barker slowly closing in. At the same time, a battle was brewing for third and fourth positions between Tony Elliott and John Davis. On lap eight, Barker swung around England on the outside of the track and stayed there to win with England finishing in second spot. Davis, in one of the best races he's driven, drove the outside line and passed Elliott with only a few remaining laps left. Davis held on to take third place with Elliott finishing in fourth. In the sprint preliminary races, it was Barker picking up the dash and one heat win. The other victory went to Tom Jewelll with quick time to Bimbo Atkins with a mark of 15.96.

The limited late model division created a lot of excitement as early in the feature race, fast qualifier Allen Marsh went over the wall in turn three and into a light pole. After the restart, early leader Doug Drudge was overtaken by Hank Hilmer and the race seemed to smooth out when on lap 13 of 20, Butch Boggs car burst into flames. The fire was put out immediately and Boggs escaped with only minor injuries. Hilmer stayed in first to win the race followed by Ron McKenzie, Dan Backus and Jim Bucher Jr., rounding out the top four. The dash event was won by Bucher with heat wins going to Roger Fitzpatrick and Dewayne May.

The roadrunner division also was interesting when, in the feature, Bob Johnson got too far outside in turn three and ended up straddled on top of the wall. The winner of the 15 lap event was Harvey Hayes with Robert Johnson, David Fitzpatrick and Dan Cordill finishing behind the winner. The two heats were won by Jon Ormsby and Bob Johnson.

Bob Johnson, Warsaw

Saturday, June 8, 1985
Newcomers Enter Warsaw Speedway Winners' Circle

A warm summer night and a good field of cars were the setting for another evening of races at the Warsaw Speedway Saturday. DeWayne Barker came out on top for his fourth feature win in a row in the sprint division while in the limited late models feature the win went to Glenn Bradley with Jon Ormsby placing first in the roadrunner class.

In the sprint feature, Tony Ploughe started in the pole position and jumped out to an early lead until the halfway mark when last year's track champion, Barker, shot past Ploughe on the back stretch and led the remaining laps to win and take the checkered flag. In the battle for second place, it went three abreast on the white flag lap with Ploughe pulling out the second place finish, Denny England and Dave Darland ending third and fourth respectively.

The 17-year old Darland won the sprint dash and one of two heat races with John Davis finishing his night of racing upside down in the second turn midway through the race. The other heat was won by Scott Fisher with quick qualifying time going to Barker with a time of 15.32.

In limited late model action, point leader Jim Bucher Jr. led from the start and looked as if the feature was his when on lap 18 of 20 he had a flat tire and had to retire from the race. Acquiring the lead and the win was Glenn Bradley with Hank Hilmer, Allen Marsh, and Ron McKenzie finishing consecutively behind the winner. The winners of the two heats were Bradley and Scott Dausman with the dash win going to Dewayne May and fast time to Jim Taylor.

Jon Ormsby and three-time feature winner Harvey Hayes were racing side-by-side with half a lap to go in the roadrunner feature and in turn three, Ormsby pulled in front to win

Scott Dausman

his first feature of the year. Hayes placed second with a third place photo finish going to Holloway by two inches over fourth place finisher Bob Johnson. In the feature qualifying race, it was Ormsby again over Hayes for the win.

This Saturday night will be the same three classes of cars: coming up is the big July 4th show including a huge fireworks display.

Saturday, June 15, 1985 - Rainout

Saturday, June 22, 1985
Barker Sprints To Warsaw Speedway Feature Victory
By Kim Gregory

DeWayne Barker, for the fifth straight feature in a row, captured the sprint win in his Barker Auto Sales sponsored car, in what turned out to be an accident marred Saturday night at the Warsaw Speedway. The limited late model feature was won by the Budweiser car of Jim Bucher Jr., who is the fifth different winner in a row for this class, keeping the competition tight and the point standings tighter. The roadrunner feature was not run due to the set curfew.

Ian Easton from Shannon, New Zealand, in his newly-purchased sprint car, paid a visit to the track to give the evening's races an international flavor. Easton travelled to the United States, in particular central Indiana, to purchase a sprint car, and came to Warsaw to try out the car before heading back to New Zealand this week.

In the sprint feature, the early leader was Barry Baker, who jumped out on top from the outside of the first row. While a great deal of shuffling was going on in the front half of the pack, Dewayne Barker was steadily making his way up from his 10th starting position. Mid-way through the race, Barker closed in on Baker and passed for the lead. Other challenges for the lead by Dave Darland and Denny England were unsuccessful and then Don Walker Jr., flipped three times end over end between turns one and two causing the red flag to stop the race. After the restart on lap 23, Easton suddenly broke a front axle which dug his car's front end into the dirt track and caused his to flip wildly down the back stretch. His accelerator stuck keeping his momentum up and he went through the back stretch fence, over the wall and was finally caught by the second safety fence. Both Walker and Easton escaped with only minor bumps and bruises. Following Barker to the finish were England, Rich Leming, and Darland, consecutively.

The first of two sprint heats was won by Baker with Walker in the runner-up spot and England took the second heat with Easton following the leader across the finish line. The dash was won by Easton while in qualifying, Baker had fast time with a 15.17 clocking. On his second lap attempt of qualifying, John Davis got out of control in turn three and ended upside down. Again, he had only minor injuries.

The limited late model feature was also eventful as near the end of the race, leader Dewayne May suddenly stopped on the back stretch. With the yellow flag flying, Gene Burchett, apparently unaware of the caution, smashed into the left side of the idle car of May's, causing himself to flip over and land upside down. Neither driver was injured in the mishap. At the finish, it was Jim Burcher Jr., bringing home the win with Doug Drudge, Jim Thor, and John Fitzpatrick finishing second, third and fourth. The dash was won by Allen Marsh while John Fitzpatrick won the first heat race with Roger Fitzpatrick in second. The other heat was won by Bucher with second going to Randy Varney.

In the only roadrunner action of the night, Harvey Hayes and Robert Johnson finished firth and second in the first heat while James Holloway and Dan Cordill were one and two for the second heat race.

Next week will be the same three classes of cars, with the first race starting at 8pm. Thursday, July 4, will be a full program of racing plus the gigantic fireworks display starting at dusk.

Saturday, June 29, 1985
Barker Posts Unbeatable Tag For Warsaw Racing

The bounty is still out on DeWayne Barker as he won his sixth straight sprint car feature in a row Saturday at the Warsaw Speedway. In the limited late model class, Duane Eakright became the sixth different winner in a row while for the roadrunners, last week's feature that was postponed due to the set curfew, was won by Arnold Prater with Gerold Holloway winning for this class.

In the sprint feature, Denny England started on the inside-second row and quickly jumped out into the lead. Barker was making his way up to the front when he spun out and had to start at the back of the field of cars. On the restart, Barker raced high on the track and passed everyone but England. With Barker on his tail, England ran out of gas and slowed on the track. This slowed Barker and Dave Darland grabbed the lead, only to be taken away from him by Barker who then held on to win. Darland finished second with Tony Ploughe rounding out the top three.

Ploughe won the first sprint heat with Barry Baker in second and Barker won the second of two heats. England ended up in the runner-up spot while also picking up the dash win. Fast qualifier was Barker with a time of 15.48.

In the limited late model class, Eakright won his first feature of the year as he battled with Jim Bucher Jr. and Dan Backus for the victory. Bucher was running in first with Eakright second when Bucher hit the wall and dropped back in the field. This gave Eakright the lead and although Backus gave a late challenge, Eakright held on to win with Backus and Glenn Bradley in second and third. Roger Fitzpatrick won the first heat with Robert Forsythe in second and Bradley took the second heat with Eakright following him to the finish line. The dash was won by Dewayne May with Jim Taylor picking up the quick time with a clocking of 18.52.

For the roadrunner class, the make-up feature was undecided until the final lap as Harvey Hayes and Prater were battling side by side on the backstretch for the lead. Prater pulled in front and finished just ahead of Hayes at the checkered flag. Holloway took top honors in the second roadrunner feature of the night. Dave Fitzpatrick won the first heat with Jon Ormsby picking up the second heat win.

This Thursday, July 4, will be a special salute to America as the sprints, limited late models, and roadrunners again invade the speedway along with a large display of fireworks at dusk. The gates open an hour earlier at 4 p.m. and racing at 8 p.m. Next Saturday will be a regular show with the same three classes of racing.

Thursday, July 4, 1985
Leming Finally Breaks Barker's Grip on Sprints
By Kim Gregory

A capacity crowd filled the bleachers and lined the banks for a spectacular evening of racing and fireworks at the Warsaw Speedway Thursday night, and in the process, saw DeWayne Barker's grip on the sprint races loosened a bit.

Rich Leming of Goshen did the honors, collecting a $100 bounty on Barker enroute to the sprint feature victory. Warsaw's Allen Marsh, in his number 75 limited late model, carried the checkered flag to victory for his feature win, while Harvey Hayes took honors in the roadrunner feature for his fourth speedway win of the year.

In the sprint feature, a jubilant Leming in his Mann Enterprises sponsored car started on the outside front row and despite challenges from Barker, led all 25 laps to take home his first win of the year. Barker placed second with Dave Darland finishing a strong third. Coming clear up from the tail to finish fourth was Van Gurley, followed by Denny England and Denny Dyson.

The first of two 10-lap sprint heats was won by Tom Jewell with Dyson in second. In the other heat race, Barry Baker, England, and DeWayne Barker finished one-two-three while crossing the finish line three abreast. The four lap dash was won by DeWayne Barker, while Tony Elliott picked up the quick time with a 15.32 clocking.

A full field of limited late models started the feature that saw William Varney jump to the early lead of the 20 lap race. Fast qualifier Marsh, with a time of 18.62 gradually made his way up to the front. On lap nine he took the lead, never looked back and won his second feature of the year. Dan Backus took the runner-up spot followed by Ron McKenzie and Butch Boggs.

Backus won the first limited late model heat with John Fitzpatrick placing second while Duane Eakright took the other heat victory followed by Doug Drudge. The dash win was also won by Marsh.

The roadrunner feature was led by Jon Ormsby at the green flag until midway through the race, with Hayes closing in for a side by side battle. Hayes picked up the lead and held it to the finish with Ormsby, Gerold Holloway, and Arnold Prater following consecutively.

Hayes also won his heat with Ormsby in second, while Holloway grabbed the second heat with Benny Fitzpatrick in the runner-up spot.

Saturday evening the same three classes of race cars will be back in full force with the first race slated for 8 p.m. Speedway officials also extended a thank you to the Winona Lake Preservation Association and the Winona Lake Park Board for donations and efforts put towards the Speedway's annual fireworks display.

Saturday, July 6, 1985
Elliott, Holloway New Winners At Warsaw
By Kim Gregory

A new name entered the sprint winner's circle as a big 40 lap mid-season championship was the main event of the evening at the Warsaw Speedway Saturday.

Tony Elliott, a regular on the USAC circuit, drove a beautiful race to capture his first win of the year Saturday evening. Meanwhile, Allen Marsh moved into the lead of the point standings with his second feature in a row and third of the year for the limited late model class. The roadrunner feature was won by James Holloway, as he picked up his first win of the season.

In the sprint feature, Elliott, in his Hazen Chevy Sprinter, started in the seventh spot and was in the lead by lap five. While he was extending his lead, a battle was brewing for second between Van Gurley, Dave Darland and Denny England until England bumped the backstretch wall and had to leave the race. Rich Leming then entered the picture and passed Darland and Gurley for the second spot. Although yellow flags tightened the field, Elliott took the checkered flag and the victory, followed by Leming, Gurley, Darland and Barry Baker rounding out the top five.

As the green flag dropped for the first sprint heat, John Johnson got out of shape and flipped end over end in turn two. He escaped uninjured and the car was back in time for the feature. Sam Davis finished as the winner with Denny Dyson in second. The second heat saw Gurley and Darland finish first and second as Gurley also won the dash. Fast time went to England with a time of 15.78.

William Varney took the early lead in the limited late model feature until on lap nine, Marsh passed Varney to lead the race. Challenges came from Jim Taylor and Ron McKenzie, but Marsh held on and won with McKenzie in second, followed by Hank Hilmer, Jim Bucher Jr., and Dewayne May. Doug Drudge and John Fitzpatrick were one-two in the first limited late model heat while Robert Forsythe won the second heat race with Varney crossing the finish line in second. The dash was won by fast qualifier, Taylor.

In the roadrunner division, Holloway led all 15 laps to win his feature. Jon Ormsby came across the runner-up spot followed by Bill Nichols and Brian Head. Ormsby won the first heat with Harvey Hayes in second and Robert Johnson won the second heat with Nichols placing second.

Next week will be the mid-season championships for the limited late model and roadrunner divisions, plus sprints. Other upcoming events will include a demolition derby on Monday, July 29. A big night of sprint, limited late model, and roadrunner action plus a powder puff derby is set for Saturday, August 3, while Saturday, August 10, is Diet Pepsi night. The second annual Warsaw Invitational is scheduled for mid-September.

Saturday, July 13, 1985
Elliott Makes Clean Sweep Of Sprints
By Kim Gregory

A full field of sprints, limited late models, and roadrunners showed up to create an exciting evening of racing at the Warsaw Speedway Saturday night. Tony Elliott, in the Cargo Master-Kercher Engines-Kosins Kustom-Egolf Welding sponsored sprint, raced his car to a clean sweep, winning the 25-lap feature, heat, and dash events. The limited late model mid-season championship was won by Allen Marsh. This was his third feature victory in a row and fourth of the season. The roadrunner mid-season championship was not run this week due to the track curfew. It will be picked up as the first race this Saturday.

The early leader of the sprint feature was Denny England until he was passed by Elliott on lap seven. After Elliott was in the lead, his No. 57 sprint was not to be caught as he pulled away from the field to win his second feature in a row. Fast qualifier DeWayne Barker battled with England for second and succeeded. He then drove high on the cushion in an attempt to catch Elliott but with less than five laps remaining Barker bounced off the second turn wall and was unable to finish the race. Following Elliott to the checkered was England, Rich Leming, Tom Jewell, and Barry Baker, rounding out the top five.

Tony Elliott, Warsaw

The first sprint heat was red-flagged as Dick Watson barrel-rolled violently in turn three. After a quick check-up at the hospital, he was back in time to watch the feature. Newcomer Rick Newsom picked up the win as he held off second place finisher Sam Davis. England followed Elliott to the line for the second sprint heat.

Fast qualifier Marsh led all 20 laps of the limited late model mid-season championship to win and extend his point lead over the rest of the field. Ron McKenzie and Hank Hilmer battled most of the race for second with Hilmer ending up at the finish in the runner-up spot. McKenzie finished third followed by Glenn Bradley, Butch Boggs and Jim Bucher Jr.

Dan Backus and Gene Burchett were one-two in the first of two limited late model heats while McKenzie and Hilmer were likewise in the second heat. Jim Taylor picked up the four-lap dash win.

In the only roadrunner action, Bob Johnson won the first heat with Buddy Compton and Arnold Prater placing second and third. The second heat was won by Jon Ormsby with Scott Woods and Gerold Holloway following Ormsby to the line.

Saturday, July 20, 1985
Marsh Wins Fourth In Row – Gurley New Warsaw Winner
By Kim Gregory

Van Gurley, in his Gurley-Leep Buick sprint car, took the checkered flag to bring home his first feature victory of the year on a warm evening at the Warsaw Speedway Saturday night. Winning his fourth feature in a row and fifth of the year was Allen Marsh in his Camaro-style limited late model. Harvey Hayes was a double feature winner as he won last week's postponed roadrunner mid-season championship and this week's regular feature event.

The sprint feature was led by Randy Woodling in the early stages of the race until Gurley wheeled around on the outside to grab the lead. Gurley was not to be passed as he stayed out in front to win despite many challenges from DeWayne Barker. Barker finished in the second spot followed by Denny England, Barry Baker, and Woodling. In the first sprint heat Sam Davis crossed the line to finish first, with Barker in the runner-up spot. Gurley also won his heat race followed by Barker. The dash was won by Rich Leming with Barker picking up the quick time with a clocking of 15.34.

Dan Backus took the early lead of the limited late model feature event. The first half of the race was dominated by Backus but Marsh was slowly closing in to challenge. The two raced side-by-side for many laps but near the end of the race, Marsh got around Backus to take the victory. Backus was next to finish with Ron McKenzie, Jim Bucher Jr., and Scott Dausman rounding out the top five.

The first of the limited late model heats saw Butch Boggs and John Fitzpatrick finish one and two while Backus picked up the second heat win followed by McKenzie. Fast qualifier, Marsh, also won the four-lap dash.

A fan of smashes and spins would have enjoyed the roadrunner mid-season championship. Only six cars remained at the finish of the 20-lap event that saw Hayes the eventual winner. Holloway was the early leader until lap 16. Scott Woods, in fourth, then smashed into Holloway, taking both cars out of the race. Hayes inherited the lead to the finish followed by David Fitzpatrick, his father, David Lee Fitzpatrick, Arnold Prater and Dan Cordill. The second roadrunner feature of the night again saw Hayes the winner as he led from the early laps of the race. Second and third again went to the father and son team with the younger Fitzpatrick edging out his father for the number two spot. The two roadrunner heats were won by Bill Nichols and David Fitzpatrick.

Upcoming special events include fair night racing with a powder puff derby and an inflated purse on August 3, Diet Pepsi Night on August 10, and the second annual Warsaw Invitational scheduled for Friday, Sept. 13.

Saturday, July 27, 1985
England Gets First Win
By Kim Gregory

Denny England, driving his Geiger Excavating sprint car, battled the weather and the competition to pick up his first feature win of the season Saturday night as racing continued at the Warsaw Speedway. Hank Hilmer took his second major race of the year in the limited late model edition, while Harvey Hayes won his third feature in a row and seventh of the year in the roadrunner division.

In the sprint feature, Randy Woodling jumped out with the early lead, only to be passed by DeWayne Barker. Barker held the lead until lap eight when England took the inside to take the lead for good. Van Gurley battled Barker for second and ended up ahead at the finish, with Barry Baker and Tony Plough rounding out the top five.

The first sprint heat had Rob Roberts winning, with Sam Davis second, while Baker won the second heat, followed by England. Baker also won the dash with Buck Boughn picking up the fast time of 15.02 seconds.

Hilmer passed Jimmy Weir at the halfway mark of the limited late model feature, and stayed in front for the remainder of the 20-lap race. Allen Marsh finished second, followed by Dewayne May, Weir and Ron McKenzie. Butch Boggs and May were one-two in the first limited late model heat, while Dan Backus and DeWayne Eakright took the top two spots in the second heat. Marsh had the fast time of the night.

For the roadrunners, Hayes led from start to finish, while Shane Denny, in his first race of the season, was an impressive second. Gerold Holloway, Dan Cordill and Bob Johnson followed behind the leaders. Denny won the first roadrunner heat, while Rich Hare was second. Arnold Prater took heat two, with James Holloway in the runner-up spot.

Tonight is the annual County Fair demolition derby, starting at 8 p.m. on the track. The last driver surviving the feature event will receive $500.

Saturday, August 3, 1985
Elliott Takes Bonus With Sprint Feature
By Kim Gregory

A dramatic evening of racing topped off the Kosciusko County Fair Saturday night as Tony Elliott sped his way to his third sprint feature victory. Elliott, in addition to the win, picked up bonus money and a nice trophy as did Rick Stone, who got his first victory of the year in the limited late model division. Meanwhile, Harvey Hayes continues to dominate the roadrunner class, winning his eighth feature of the season.

In what many would consider the best sprint feature of the year, DeWayne Barker took the lead from lap one. Barker looked as if he was going to run away with the race but a persistent Elliott slowly gained on the leader. At the halfway point, Elliott had caught up with Barker, and the two dueled until with four laps to go, Elliott wheeled around Barker to take the lead. When the checkered flag fell, the two came across side-by-side in a photo finish with Elliott ahead by inches. Barker took second with Denny England, Dave

Darland and Tony Ploughe rounding out the top five.

The first sprint heat was won by Barry Baker with Sam Davis in second. Barker picked up the other heat win with fast qualifier Van Gurley in the runner-up spot. The dash event was also won by Barker.

In the limited late model division, Jim Bucher and Ron McKenzie were early leaders of the feature, but it was Stone who took command on lap five, leading the rest of the race to pick up the victory. Passing McKenzie on lap nine to pick up the second spot was Dewayne May.

William Varney and Charlie Hyde were one and two in the first limited late model heat while Dan Backus and Butch Boggs finished first and second in the other heat. The dash win went to Stone with Hilmer capturing the quick time.

Hayes led the roadrunner feature from start to finish, but the second spot wasn't decided until the last lap. Shane Denny was holding fast to second place when James Holloway came up on the white flag lap. Denny spun out, leaving Holloway to take second with Gerold Holloway, Robert Johnson and Denny finishing consecutively behind the leader.

The two powder puff races were won by Shelly Goshert and Juanita Fitzpatrick and the two mechanics races were won by Jerry Burkell and Bryan Mappin.

Saturday, August 10, 1985
Second-Time Winners Lead Speedway Field
By Kim Gregory

Second-time winners Denny England, Jim Bucher, Jr., and Jon Ormsby led the way Saturday night as action continued at the Warsaw Speedway.

In the sprints, England, in his Geiger Excavating sponsored-sprint, led from start to finish. Van Gurley, starting in the fourth position, finished second and DeWayne Barker, who started sixth, finished third. Tony Ploughe and Randy Woodling rounded out the top five. The feature was not without incident as with only one lap complete, Dave Darland lost control and violently barrel-rolled his sprint coming out of turn four. He came to rest along the front-stretch wall and climbed from the car uninjured.

Denny England, Warsaw

The first of two sprint heats was won by Sam Davis with Rick Newsom in second, while Randy Woodling won the second heat, followed by Darland. Gurley won the dash event and Barker had quick time with a clocking of 15.23.

Bucher led from the green flag to the checkered flag in the limited late model feature.

Hank Hilmer gave Bucher quite a challenge as with only one lap to go, the two were racing side by side. At the finish it was Bucher ahead by a car length and Hilmer settling for second. Third place went to Scott Dausman while Ron McKenzie and Gene Burchett placed fourth and fifth.

Larry Anglin won the first limited late model heat with John Fitzpatrick in second. Dan Backus took the second heat with Dewayne May in the runner-up spot. The dash went to Butch Boggs and fast time of 18.03 went to May.

Ormsby crossed the finish line first to win the low-dollar but high excitement roadrunner feature. James Holloway finished second followed by Robert Johnson and Shane Denny. The first roadrunner heat was won by Johnson with Ken Schue in second, while Joe Leek and Holloway finished one-two in the second heat race.

Next week the winged sprints are back. They, along with the limited late models and roadrunners, will race for increased purses. August 24 marks the season championship for all three regular classes with August 31 being the rain date. A $1200 purse will be offered to the Warsaw invitational winner for winged sprints September 13.

Saturday, August 17, 1985
Gaerte Joins Marsh And Hayes As Warsaw Winners
By Kim Gregory

Something old and something new went to the winners' circle at the Warsaw Speedway Saturday night. In his first appearance at the track this year, Joe Gaerte in the Gaerte Engines number 3G, captured the sprint feature while Allen Marsh won the limited late model feature making that his sixth win of the year. Harvey Hayes, still dominating the roadrunner class, made it his ninth feature win of the season to round out the awards.

DeWayne Barker took the early lead of the sprint feature while Terry Shepherd was racing in a steady second position. Near the midway point, Gaerte worked around Shepherd and started to reel in Barker. The remainder of the race saw Gaerte trying high, then low, when finally, with the white flag flying, Gaerte got by Barker on the back stretch and went on to win. Barker finished second with Shepherd in third. Coming clear up from the twelfth starting position to finish fourth was Rich Leming. Gary Fedewa, Bimbo Atkins, Jim Lipkey, and Randy Woodling round out the top eight.

The first sprint heat was won by Dave Darland with Leming placing second while Barker won the second heat, followed by Jeff Donaldson. Gaerte won the dash and Fedewa had fast time of 14.47.

In the late model feature it was Rick Stone who led from lap one to lap 10 when Marsh took over the lead. Stone quickly fought back to lead again until he spun in turn two which allowed Marsh to again regain first. Marsh stayed in front to win with Ron McKenzie and Hank Hilmer in second and third. Dewayne May, Scott Dausman, and Butch Boggs followed.

John Fitzpatrick took the first limited late model heat with William Varney in second. Scott Woods won the second heat with John Forsythe in the runner-up spot. Marsh took the dash win and Hilmer had quick time.

Hayes led from start to finish to win the roadrunner feature with David Fitzpatrick, Jon Ormsby, Robert Johnson, and David L. Fitzpatrick following Hayes to the checkered flag. The first heat was won by D. L. Fitzpatrick with Jeff Christner in the second spot while Joe Leek took the second heat race with David Fitzpatrick across the line for second.

Next week are the season championships for all three classes with a big 40-lap feature for the sprints. September 13 concludes the season at the Speedway when the sprints again put the wings on for the Second Annual Warsaw Invitational. The top spot pays $1,600 to win with area donations increasing the purse.

Saturday, August 24, 1985
Rain Stops Speedway Races

Heavy rain Saturday caused action to be stopped at the Warsaw Speedway. The remainder of the program will be run next week with rainchecks good for the three-season championships and remaining heat race that will be completed Saturday night.

Of the races that were run, the results are as follows: The sprint car first heat was won by Bimbo Atkins with John Davis in second. Van Gurley won the second heat with DeWayne Barker following him to the checkered flag. Denny England took the dash event.

Scott Woods won the first limited late model heat with Tim Goshert in the runner-up spot while Gene Burchett captured the second heat with Allen Marsh finishing in the number two spot. Hank Hilmer won the dash.

The first roadrunner heat was won by Shane Denny with Ken Schue in second while Gerold Holloway won the dash. The second heat will be run next week.

Saturday, August 31, 1985
Speedway Closes With Familiar Winners
By Kim Gregory

Track champions were crowned and trophies presented as local drivers closed out the regular season of racing at the Warsaw Speedway Saturday night.

Bruce Clay, Elkhart

Track champions DeWayne Barker, Allen Marsh and Harvey Hayes showed their winning style as each of them won their season championship finale. Sprint champ Barker won his seventh feature of the year in his Barker Auto Sales number 33B, while Marsh took his seventh feature in the No. 75 Camaro in the late model race. Hayes, meanwhile, won for the 10th time in the roadrunner feature.

In the 40-lap sprint feature, Barker led the entire race while Denny England finished a strong second. Rookie sprint driver Randy Woodling finished third followed by Tony Ploughe, John Davis, Greg Jones, Oscar Smith, Bruce Clay, Jesse Fordyce, and Sam Davis, rounding out the top 10. Rich Leming, Van Gurley, Denny Dyson and 13-year old rookie Kevin Atkins completed the field.

Marsh also led from start to finish in winning the limited late model 30-lap feature. In an exciting battle for second, Hank Hilmer and Ron McKenzie dueled side-by-side with the white flag flying signaling one lap to go. At the checkered it was Hilmer while third went to McKenzie. Jim Bucher Jr. took fourth followed by Butch Boggs, Robert Forsythe, Scott Dausman, Dan Backus, Gene Burchett and Charlie Hyde, to finish the top 10.

In the 20-lap roadrunner feature, Hayes crossed the finish line first, followed by Robert Johnson. Shane Denney finished third while Gerold Holloway, Jon Ormsby, 14-year old David Fitzpatrick and James Holloway rounded out the top seven.

The winged sprints will be in action Sept. 13 for their last race of the year in the big $1,600 to win, second annual Warsaw Invitational.

Friday, September 13, 1985
Butler Takes Warsaw Speedway Feature Race
By Kim Gregory

Forty-three cars and drivers from five different states showed up to compete for the second annual Warsaw Invitational Friday evening at the Warsaw Speedway. The event turned out to have the largest field of sprint cars in the recent history of the track.

When the checkered flag dropped and the engines calmed, it was Steve Butler from Kokomo winning the 40-lap feature, $1800 first place prize, and a nice trophy for his driving in the number six winged sprint. Running third in USAC point standings, Butler usually races in the central and lower part of the state but traveled to Warsaw for this special event.

The race was not all Butler's, as Tod Bishop of Bourbonnais, Ill., led for better than half the race. Butler was in second, followed by Warsaw's Bimbo Atkins until lap 24 when Butler shot past Bishop on the backstretch. Atkins then closed on Bishop and got past on lap 28 where they stayed to finish with Butler in first, Atkins second, and Bishop in third. Fourth place went to Hank Lower with Tony Elliott fifth and Terry Shepherd, Rodney Ritter Jr., Jim Lipkey, Tim Norman and Jim Moughan rounding out the top 10.

Bimbo Atkins, Warsaw

In the first of two consolation events, it was DeWayne Barker and Dave Feese finishing first and second with Steve Kline and Moughan first and second in the second consolation run. Ritter won the fast heat with other heat wins going to Barker, Moughan, Rodney Duncan, and Al Schafer. The trophy dash went to Butler and Shepherd won the $300 prize for quick time with a clocking of 14.638.

At the Avilla Nationals, the second half of the Warsaw/Avilla two-day show, Atkins won the 25-lap feature and $2,000 prize. Second place went to John Naida with Terry Shepherd third.

1986

Early May, 1986
Warsaw Opens May 17

Many changes are in the making for the upcoming racing season at the Warsaw Speedway. The ¼ mile clay oval has been renovated and greatly improved as the straightaways have been lengthened by 75 feet. Also, a totally new 3rd and 4th turn has been built including a safer exit from track to the pit area. A new concrete safety wall has been installed and 6 inches of clay added to the track surface. These improvements will make the racing safer and more exciting for everyone.

Opening night is set for May 17 for sprints, limited late models, and road runners. They will compete every Saturday night thru Labor Day. The 1st special event will be on June 14 with a $Grand$ Opening for the winged outlaw sprints paying $1,000 to win.

Saturday, May 17, 1986
Weather Threatens, But Doesn't Stop Speedway Action
By Kim Gregory

Although opening night for the all-new Warsaw Speedway was threatened by thunderstorms, a full evening of racing was completed with Van Gurley winning the sprint feature. The limited late model feature was won by Dewayne May, while Harvey Hayes took the roadrunner feature.

Van Gurley, Mishawaka

In the sprint feature, it was Gurley leading from start to finish in his Gurley-Leep Buick sponsored race car. Barry Baker challenged Gurley for the lead at the start, but could not pass and had to settle for second spot. Third place went to Ray Kenens Jr., with Tony Ploughe and Rob Roberts rounding out the top five. In the first of two sprint heats,

Roberts and Chuck Kryder finished first and second, while Ploughe and Baker finished one-two in the second heat. The sprint dash was won by Randy Woodling and quick time went to DeWayne Barker.

May led the field of limited late model cars across the line to win the 20-lap feature event. He was followed by Ron McKenzie, Butch Boggs and Rick Day. Bob Holloway and Day were first and second in the first limited late model heat, and Dan Backus and Jim Bucher Jr. crossed the line one-two respectively for the second heat. The dash was won by Boggs, who also set the fast time for his class.

The roadrunner feature was won by Harvey Hayes, as he sets out to break his record number of 10 feature wins that he had last year. Jon Ormsby was second, followed by Phil Draper and James Holloway. Next week will be more of the same, with three classes of cars. The gates open at 5pm and the first race is at 8pm. Coming up June 7 will be the winged sprints and a live broadcast from radio station WBTU in Kendallville.

Saturday, May 24, 1986
Barker Takes Sprint Feature At Speedway
By Kim Gregory

Twenty-seven sprint cars showed up for the sprint feature, highlighting activity at the Warsaw Speedway Saturday night. Before a large crowd, DeWayne Barker won the prime race, with Allen Marsh taking the limited late model feature and Robert Johnson the roadrunner feature winner.

Van Gurley led the first 13 laps of the sprint feature with Randy Woodling close behind, but Barker closed on Woodling and slipped by for second spot. Barker then reeled in Gurley and took over the lead to the checkered flag, followed by Gurley, Tim Bookmiller, Denny England, Mark Owsley, and Barry Baker. The event was not without mishap though, as Tony Elliott flipped on lap one in the first turn. He was uninjured but could not continue the race.

The first and second place finishers of the three sprint heat races were: Brett Mann and Tom Patterson, heat one; Louie Mann and Baker, heat two; and Elliott and Owsley, heat three. The consolation race was won by Patterson, the dash event went to Barker, and quick time was set by Bookmiller with a clocking of 16.98.

In the limited late model feature it was Dan Backus taking the early lead with Dewayne May a close second. Marsh closed on May and took second place on lap seven. Five laps later Marsh passed Backus to take the first spot. Marsh held on to win with Backus, Ron McKenzie, Butch Boggs, and Roger Fitzpatrick following.

The first of two limited late model heat races was won by Don Prater with Rick Day in second. Boggs won the second heat with the second spot going to Gene Burkett. The dash was won by McKenzie and quick time was set by Jim Bucher, Jr.

David Fitzpatrick took the lead in the opening laps of the roadrunner feature until Johnson closed in and passed for the lead where he stayed to finish the race. In second spot was Jon Ormsby with Gerold Holloway in third. Jeff Putterbaugh won the first of two roadrunner heats with James Holloway in second. The second heat went to Gerold Holloway with Ormsby next across the finish line. Coming up June 7 will be the limited late models, roadrunners, and for the first time this year, the winged sprints.

Saturday, May 31, 1986
Newcomers Lead List Of Speedway Winners
By Kim Gregory

Record crowds continue to attend the renovated Warsaw Speedway as Tony Elliott became the third different feature winner in as many weeks in the sprint division Saturday night. In similar fashion, Jim Bucher Jr. became the third different winner in the limited late model feature event while Harvey Hayes won his second roadrunner feature of the year.

In the sprint feature, DeWayne Barker jumped out to the early lead with Bimbo Atkins right behind. Elliott, in third, passed Atkins on lap six and started to reel in Barker. With Elliott racing on the high groove and Barker the low road, Elliott shot past on lap 14 and went on to take the checkered flag. Steve Butler finished second with Atkins, Barker, Rodney Duncan, Randy Woodling, Denny England, Rob Roberts, Tony Ploughe, and John Mapes, the top 10.

Brett Mann won the first of three sprint heats in a photo finish over Tom Patterson. Roberts won the second heat over Ploughe and Barker took the final heat win over Elliott. The dash was won by Duncan and a new track record was set by Butler with a time of 16.90.

In the limited late model feature it was Mike Faylor with the early lead until Allen Marsh passed on lap four. Dewayne May got by Faylor and started closing on Marsh until they were bumper to bumper. On the last lap they tangled, putting both cars out of contention for the win. Faylor acquired the lead but on the restart was passed by Bucher, who took the checkered flag for the victory. Faylor was second followed by Butch Boggs, Gene Burkett, Dane Ronk, Bob Holloway, Dan Kelsey, and Roger Fitzpatrick.

Steve Knoff and William Varney placed first and second in the first limited late model heat while Marsh won the second heat with Bucher in second at the finish. The dash went to May with Boggs picking up the fast time of 20.01.

Jeff Putterbaugh took the early lead in the roadrunner feature and looked as if he would win his first feature when on the restart of a caution period he lost a wheel and had to leave the race. Hayes moved up to lead the final laps to win with Gerold Holloway and Jon Ormsby next to cross the finish line. Robert Johnson, last week's roadrunner feature winner, won the roadrunner heat race with Hayes in second. Ormsby set fast time with a clocking of 22.07.

Saturday, June 7, 1986
Weather Halts Speedway

Inclement weather put the scheduled Warsaw Speedway racing program Saturday night on the shelf.

Action with winged sprints, limited late models and roadrunners will continue at the Speedway next Saturday, with more of the special features, including the Grand Opening Celebration with additional prize money for all three classes, still on tap. All tickets sold for the June 7 races will be accepted as rain checks for the June 14 show.

In addition, Speedway officials are promoting June 21 as 4-H Night. Persons buying a 4-H Fish Fry dinner will get $1.00 off on the general admission ticket price. Gates open at 5 p.m. with racing at 8 p.m.

Saturday, June 14, 1986 - Rainout

Saturday, June 21, 1986
Large Crowd At Warsaw Raceway
By Kim Gregory

Racing fans filled the bleachers and banks as the largest crowd ever to attend the Warsaw Speedway witnessed the grand opening event Saturday night. Tony Elliott captured the winged sprint feature in his Kercher Engine, R and B Equipment, Weasner Welding sponsored race car. Hank Hilmer won his first limited late model feature of the year while Harvey Hayes won his third roadrunner feature of the year.

In the winged sprint feature, it was Elliott jumping out to an early lead from his outside front row starting spot. Elliott led the entire race to win his second feature in a row. He did not win easily, though, as DeWayne Barker, Van Gurley, and Denny England all challenged for the lead. England had moved up to second and was on Elliott's tail when he spun and had to start at the rear of the field. At the finish it was Gurley in second place, followed by Barker, England, Tony Ploughe, Randy Woodling, Kurt Danner, and Tom Patterson, the top eight.

Heat wins went to Danner and Gurley, while England won the dash and fast time with a clocking of 15.978.

Hilmer, in a brand new car, jumped out to the lead with Allen Marsh and Jim Bucher Jr., close behind in the limited late model feature. The three stayed this way until the final lap, when Marsh and Bucher spun in turn three, putting Marsh out of the race and Bucher at the end of the field. Hilmer went on to win, with Ron McKenzie next to cross the finish line, followed by Gene Burkett, Rod England, Dan Ronk, Bucher and Steve Knouff.

Heat wins went to Rick Day and Dan Backus, while Bucher won the dash and Butch Boggs set quick time of 19.84.

David Fitzgerald took the early lead in the roadrunner feature with Robert Johnson second. Harvey Hayes closed on Johnson, passed on lap 11 and had Fitzpatrick in sight. With all three close together, Fitzpatrick spun on the final lap in the fourth turn giving the win to Hayes. Johnson, Jon Ormsby, Jay Putterbaugh were among the top seven. Fitzpatrick backed across the line for eighth spot. The roadrunner heat was won by Fitzpatrick while Hayes took fast time of 21.94.

Next week will again be the winged sprints, limited late models, and roadrunners. July 4 and 5 will be a special two-day show with fireworks on July 4 and Mid-Season Championships on July 5.

Saturday, June 28, 1986
New Winners Crowned At Warsaw Speedway
By Kim Gregory

The Warsaw Speedway added three new names to the record book as this was each feature winner's first win of the season Saturday night. Denny England in his Kosins Kustom-Classic Car Centre sprint car, won the 25-lap winged sprint feature, while Rod England and Roger Fitzpatrick won the limited late model and roadrunner features, respectively.

In the winged sprint feature, Randy Woodling took the early lead until Denny England passed on the inside and went on to take the checkered flag for the win. Tony Elliott placed second while DeWayne Barker took third in a pass over Woodling in the final laps. Woodling finished fourth with Tony Ploughe, Dave Darland, Brett Mann, and Barry Baker rounding out the top eight. Winged sprint heat wins went to Chuck Kryder Jr., and Darland with the dash going to Baker. Elliott set a new track record in qualifying with a time of 15.81.

Rod England led all 20 laps to win the limited late model feature. Dewayne May was challenging for the lead when he spun with four laps remaining and had to go to the back of the field of cars. Allen Marsh finished second followed by Butch Boggs, Hank Hilmer, Mike Faylor, May, Ron McKenzie, and Roger Fitzpatrick. William Varney and Marsh won the limited late model heats while Jim Bucher, Jr., won the dash. May set a new track record with a time of 19.64.

In the roadrunner feature it was Gerold Holloway with the early lead. Fitzpatrick took the lead on lap five and went on to win the 15 lap event. Second spot went to Holloway with Jeff Putterbaugh, Robert Johnson, Phil Draper, Harvey Hayes, and Mark Shank among the top eight. The roadrunner heat was won by Hayes with Arnold Prater in second.

July 4 and 5 racing will be for winged sprints, limited late models, and roadrunners as part of a big two-day show. The annual fireworks display will be at intermission on July 4 and mid-season championships will be on July 5.

Friday, July 4 & Saturday, July 5, 1986
England, May Mid-Season Race Champs
By Kim Gregory

Mid-season championships and Kercher Engine night were the scene at the Warsaw Speedway Saturday night, closing off a busy weekend of local racing.

Warsaw's Denny England won the mid-season championship and $1,000 in his Kosins Kustom, Classic Car Centre winged sprint. Dewayne May, of Warsaw, won his second feature win of the year in the limited late model mid-season championship.

In the winged sprint championship race, point leader England jumped out to a commanding lead and led all 30 laps to win. Tony Elliott began closing on England in the final laps but England drove the perfect line and Elliott had to settle for second place. Third went to DeWayne Barker, with Barry Baker, Kurt Danner, Tony Ploughe, Denny Dyson and Oscar Smith following. The winged spring dash and second heat races were won by Elliott, while Sam Davis won the first heat.

Five different lead changes in the limited late model feature made for a close race. Jim Bucher, Jr., was leading when Butch Boggs shot past to lead until lap 10. May then closed and got by to lead through lap 21. Lapped traffic slowed May, allowing Boggs to briefly take the lead before May got it back at the finish. Boggs was a close second, followed by Gene Burkett and Dan Backus. Hank Hilmer came all the way up from the 14th starting position to finish fifth with Ron McKenzie, Dane Ronk and Rod England rounding out the top eight. Limited late model heat wins went to Mike Taylor and Hilmer with the dash going to MaDewy.

The roadrunner heat was won by Scott Dausman with Shane Denny in second. The roadrunner mid-season championship was rescheduled for July 12 because of curfew. There will be two roadrunner features, with the championship race to be run as the first event following qualifying.

Friday, a great crowd saw fireworks and racing action, with Andy Hillenburg of Greenwood taking home his first feature win of the year, plus a six-foot trophy for the 4th of July winged sprint main event. Allen Marsh and Robert Johnson won their second features of the year in the limited late model and roadrunner classes.

In the winged sprint feature, Hillenburg led all 25 laps to win. Terry Shepherd passed Denny England on lap 19 to finish second. England finished third, followed by Steve Kline, John Tierney, Tim Norman, Brad Wickum and Barry Baker. The winners of the four winged sprint heats were John Hajduk, Brad Wickum, DeWayne Barker, and Tony Elliott. The dash was won by Hillenburg with quick time going to England with a time of 16.012.

Gene Burkett took the early lead of the limited late model feature until Marsh closed and raced side by side with Burkett for several laps. Marsh passed on lap 11 and held on to win. At the finish it was Butch Boggs in second, followed by Burkett, Ron McKenzie, Rod England, David Fitzpatrick, Don Prater and Roger Fitzpatrick. Limited late model heat wins went to David Fitzpatrick and McKenzie while Jim Bucher, Jr., won the dash and Dewayne May had quick time.

Johnson led from start to finish to win the roadrunner feature. Harvey Hayes gave Johnson a challenge for the lead in the final laps but had to settle for second spot. Third went to Bob Johnson, followed by Jon Ormsby, Arnold Prater, Phil Draper and Jay Nordman. Prater and Hayes were the winners of the roadrunner heats.

Saturday, July 12, 1986
Johnson Wins Third Straight At Speedway
By Kim Gregory

Although a rainy sky threatened the evening's activities, a full racing program was completed by 11 p.m. at the Warsaw Speedway Saturday night. The popular Tony Elliott, of Warsaw, won his third sprint feature of the year while Jim Bucher Jr. won his second limited late model feature of the season. Robert Johnson won both the roadrunner feature and the rescheduled roadrunner midseason championship feature. This was Johnson's third consecutive feature win and fourth of the year.

Elliott jumped out to the early lead in the 25-lap sprint feature. Denny England closed in to race side-by-side with Elliott for several laps until Elliott pulled away and went on to take the checkered flag for the win. England finished second, with Bimbo Atkins in third. Gary Fisher won out a close battle for fourth over fifth-place finisher Tim Bookmiller. Paul Huntington, Randy Woodling and Barry Baker rounded out the top eight finishers. Kurt Danner and England won the sprint heats and Elliott won the dash event. Bookmiller took fast time of the 22 cars with a 17.14.

In the 20-lap limited late model feature, Hank Hilmer was the early leader until lap 14, when Bucher raced side-by-side with Hilmer and took the lead to the finish. Dewayne May finished second, followed by Allen Marsh, Hilmer, Glenn Bradley, Robert Forsythe, Butch Boggs and Dan Backus. Limited late model heat winners were Rick Day and Forsythe with the dash win going to Marsh. Fast time of 21 cars went to May with a time of 19.95.

Scott Dausman was the early leader of the 15-lap roadrunner feature, but Robert Johnson pulled ahead and led the remaining laps to win. Second spot went to Gerold Holloway, followed by Shane Denny, Jon Ormsby, David Fitzpatrick, Jay Nordman, Dausman and Putterbaugh.

The 20-lap roadrunner mid-season championship was led from start to finish by Johnson. Harvey Hayes finished second with Holloway, Denny, Ormsby, Dausman, Fitzpatrick and Mark Shank next to cross the finish line. The road runner heat went to Holloway, with Johnson in second. Coming up August 16 is Pepsi Night and Labor Day Weekend will include a special show of races and fireworks.

Saturday, July 19, 1986
Speedway Winners Repeat
By Kim Gregory

DeWayne Barker made his way back into victory lane, winning his second sprint feature of the season Saturday at the Warsaw Speedway. Allen Marsh won his third limited late model feature, while Robert Johnson is now four-for-four in roadrunner feature wins.

Mark Owsley was the early leader in the sprint feature while Terry Shepherd and Barker were second and third, respectively. Barker passed Shepherd and on lap 15 did the same to Owsley, and stayed in front the rest of the way. Tony Elliott came from the back of the pack after a spin to finish second. Owsley was third, followed by Tony Ploughe and Barry Baker. Ploughe and Elliott won the two sprint heats and Bimbo Atkins took the four-lap dash. Denny England was the fast qualifier with a time of 17.05.

Marsh led all but one lap to take the limited late model feature. Butch Boggs challenged Marsh on several occasions, but had to settle for second at the finish line. Rick Slone was third, followed by Ron McKenzie and Dan Backus. Marsh won the limited late model dash, as well as his heat race, while Rick Day won the other heat. Jim Taylor had the fast time.

Gerold Holloway was the early leader in the roadrunner feature, until Johnson came on. Harvey Hayes passed Holloway in the final laps for second place, with Holloway, Jon Ormsby, and Shane Denny next to cross the finish line. Roadrunner heat wins went to Johnson and Denny, while Hayes took fast qualifying honors.

Saturday, July 26, 1986
Familiar Faces Romp In Speedway Action
By Kim Gregory

Warsaw's Tony Elliott won his fourth sprint feature of the year Saturday night at the Warsaw Speedway. Also, winning his fourth feature of the season was limited late model driver Allen Marsh, while red hot Robert Johnson won his fifth straight roadrunner feature and sixth for the year.

Elliott jumped out to a commanding lead in the sprint feature and led every lap to win the 25-lap race. Mark Owsley passed Dave Darland on lap four where he stayed the rest of the way to finish second. The third spot went to Tony Ploughe, followed by DeWayne Barker, Mark Alderson and Darland. Kurt Danner was not so fortunate in the finale. Barker had spun early in the race and Danner, in an attempt to dodge him, caught a tire on the inside of the track and flipped end over end. Luckily, he escaped uninjured. Sam Davis and Rob Roberts were heat winners and Owsley was the dash winner. Fast time went to Alderson with a time of 17.11.

Glenn Bradley was the early leader of the limited late model feature until lap eight when Bradley, Butch Boggs, and Marsh ran three abreast for the lead. Bradley's tire went flat and Marsh out-ran Boggs for the lead. At the finish it was Marsh and Boggs one and two, followed by Mike Faylor, Dewayne May, and Ron McKenzie. Dan Backus and Rick Day won the two limited late model heat races, while Bradley won the dash. Faylor set a new track record in qualifying of 19.45 that breaks May's record set back on June 28, with a time of 19.64. Marsh also had a record breaking time of 19.62 before Faylor bettered it for fast time.

Dan Backus, Warsaw

Johnson led every lap of the roadrunner feature to win. Gerold Holloway passed Shane Denny on lap nine to finish second, followed by Jay Nordman, David Fitzpatrick, Harvey Hayes, and Bob Johnson. Nordman and Jon Ormsby won the two roadrunner heats, and Arnold Prater set a new track record in time trials with a time of 21.37. This breaks Hayes' record of 21.62 set on June 21. The feature win for Johnson was the sixth of the season at the speedway.

Saturday, August 2, 1986
England, Marsh, Holloway Warsaw Winners
By Kim Gregory

Denny England won his third sprint feature of the year before a capacity crowd Saturday, closing activities at the Kosciusko County Fair. Allen Marsh, no stranger to the winners' circle, took his third feature in a row and fifth of the season in limited late model action, while Gerold Holloway won his first roadrunner feature, breaking the five-race win streak of Robert Johnson in the process.

England attributed his win in large part to extensive engine work done by his sponsor, Classic Car Centre, before the race, but it wasn't easy. Tony Ploughe led the first ten laps, only to be overtaken by Tony Elliott for the next ten laps. England took the lead for good on lap 21, and was followed to the finish by Elliott, Gary Fisher, Ploughe, Randy Woodling and Kurt Danner. Sprint heat wins went to Woodling and Elliott, while the dash win was Mark Owsley's. Fisher set a track record with a qualifying time of 16.76.

Mike Faylor led in the early stages of the limited late model feature when Marsh took over. Marsh drove his Camaro to the checkered flag, with Dewayne May second. Glenn Bradley was third, followed by Ron McKenzie, Gene Burkett and Rick Stone. Limited late model heat wins went to Dick Day and Bradley, with Butch Boggs winning the dash and quick time honors with a clocking of 20.61.

Jeff Putterbaugh was the early leader in the roadrunner feature, until Johnson took over. Holloway closed on the leader and went side by side with Johnson on the last lap. Both cars collided in the final dash to the flag, with Johnson spinning and Holloway winning. David Fitzpatrick was second, with Johnson, Jay Nordman and Bill Nichols in the top six. Arnold Prater and Fitzpatrick were roadrunner heat winners, while Harvey Hayes had the fast time of 22.84.

Saturday, August 9, 1986
Barker, Marsh, Prater Local Speedway Winners
By Kim Gregory

A beautiful Saturday night at the Warsaw Speedway saw DeWayne Barker of Warsaw drive to his third sprint feature win, while hard-to-beat Allen Marsh made it four in a row and six for the year in limited late model feature wins. Arnold Prater made his way into victory lane to win his first roadrunner feature of the year.

Kurt Danner led early in the sprint feature until Randy Woodling charged by to take the lead on lap six. Woodling fought off a challenge by Denny England to stay out front until lap 23. Barker closed in on Woodling's tail with only two laps to go and got by to take the win. Mark Owsley finished second, followed by Barry Baker, England, Danner, Brett Mann, Denny Dyson, and Woodling. Dyson and Woodling were sprint heat winners and Tony Elliott won the four-lap dash. England flew to a new track record, qualifying with a time of 16.75 that broke the old record of 16.76 held by Gary Fisher.

Marsh started on the outside of the first row and led every lap to win the limited late model feature. Butch Boggs challenged Marsh for the lead but at the finish had to settle for second spot. Glenn Bradley finished third, with Don Prater, Ron McKenzie, Hank Hilmer, Dan Kelsey and Gene Burkett next to cross the finish line. The limited late model heat winners were Rick Day and McKenzie, while Marsh won the dash event. Quick time went to Boggs with a time of 19.55.

In the roadrunner feature, Prater jumped out to the early lead and led every lap to take the victory. Harvey Hayes gave a side-by-side challenge for the lead during the final laps, but at the checkered was second to cross the finish line. Robert Johnson was third, followed by Jay Nordman, Scott Dausman, David Fitzpatrick, Bill Nichols and Jon Ormsby. Nichols and Hayes were roadrunner heat winners, while fast time went to Ormsby with a time of 21.40.

Next Saturday is Pepsi Night and Autograph Night. Coming up August 23 are the season championships while Aug. 30 has a big fireworks display and winged sprints added to the regular show. The third annual Warsaw Invitational for winged sprints is scheduled for Sept. 4 and will pay $2,000 to the feature winner. Sept. 13 is the first ever Stock Car Invitational for limited late models and roadrunners.

Saturday, August 16, 1986
Bradley, Fitzpatrick Warsaw Winners
England Extends Point Lead
By Kim Gregory

Denny England won his fifth feature of the year to extend his point lead in the sprint division Saturday night at the Warsaw Speedway. Winning their second features of the season were Glenn Bradley in his limited late model and David Fitzpatrick in his roadrunner. All three winners received trophies from Pepsi, the sponsor for the evening's event.

The sprint feature pole sitter, John Althouse, led early in the race until Randy Woodling passed on lap 10 to rake over the first position. England got by Althouse for second and started to reel in a tire-troubled Woodling. England passed Woodling and led the last six laps to the checkered flag. Mark Owsley finished second followed by Althouse, Tony Ploughe, Sam Davis, Brett Mann, Woodling, and John Vigar. Rookie driver Kurt Hawkins and Althouse won the sprint heats, while Woodling cashed in on the four-lap dash win. Owsley had the quick time of 16.89.

Denny England, Warsaw

In the limited late model feature, John Fitzpatrick jumped out early to lead the field but Bradley, running a strong race, passed with over ¾ of the race to go and led the remainder of the way for the win. Butch Boggs placed second followed by Hank Hilmer, Rick Stone, Dewayne May, Rick Day, Dan Kelsey and Dane Ronk. Limited late model heat wins went to Ron Norman and Bradley with the dash win going to May. Boggs had fast time of 19.79.

Fitzpatrick led from start to finish in the roadrunner feature, and while Gerold Holloway challenged for the lead, at the finish he had to settle for second spot. Arnold Prater was third followed by Harvey Hayes, Jay Nordman, Robert Johnson, Bill Nichols, and Mark Shank. Fitzpatrick and Holloway won the roadrunner heats and Hayes had fast time of 22.20.

Next week is season championship for all three classes and coming up on August 30 is winged sprints and fireworks plus limited late models and roadrunners.

Saturday, August 23, 1986
England, Boggs, Johnson, Speedway Champs
Trio of Champions Crowned At Warsaw
By Kim Gregory

Track champions were crowned at the Warsaw Speedway Saturday night with only three shows left in the racing season. Denny England, sprint division; Butch Boggs, limited late model division; and Robert Johnson, roadrunner division, are the 1986 speedway champions, having accumulated the most points during the racing season.

England finished the season in style, winning the 30-lap sprint feature while Marsh added another victory to his collection, bringing the total to seven feature wins in his limited late model. Harvey Hayes, meanwhile, won the roadrunner feature.

In the sprint feature, pole-sitter England jumped out front and led every lap to win. Mark Owsley started to challenge for the lead with two laps to go but at the finish had to take second place. Dave Darland finished third followed Barry Baker, Tony Ploughe, Kurt Danner, John Vigar, and John Althouse. Darland and Brett Mann were sprint heat winners while Ploughe won the dash event.

Marsh led all 25 laps of the limited late model feature to take the victory, although he fought off a late challenge by Dewayne May. Second place went to Hank Hilmer, followed by Gene Burkett, Dane Ronk, Dean Baker, May, Roger Fitzpatrick, and Rick Day. Limited late model heat winners were Rick Stone and Ron McKenzie, while Marsh won the dash event.

Hayes jumped out to the early lead in the roadrunner feature and led all the way to the finish to take the checkered flag for the win. Johnson finished second followed by Gerold Holloway, Jeff Putterbaugh, Bill Nichols, Scott Dausman, John Ormsby, and David Fitzpatrick. Shane Denny and Ron Prater were the roadrunner heat winners. Next Saturday will be racing and fireworks with the winged sprints, limited late models and roadrunners. Rain date is Monday, Sept. 1. Friday, Spet. 5 is the Third Annual Warsaw Invitational for Winged Sprints and Saturday, Sept. 13 is the Late Model and Street Stock Invitational, which will close out the racing season.

Saturday, August 30, 1986
England Can't Lose In Speedway Sprints
By Kim Gregory

Winged sprints and fireworks were the added attractions Saturday night at the Warsaw Speedway. Winning his sixth sprint feature of the year and fourth of the last five features was Denny England of Warsaw. Winning their second features of the season were Glenn Bradley, of Marion, in the limited late model and Arnold Prater, of Warsaw, in his roadrunner stock car.

Dave Darland. Lincoln. IN

England jumped out to a commanding lead early in the race and led every lap to win the winged sprint feature. DeWayne Barker passed Jeff Donaldson on lap 10 and was closing on England, but finished in the runner-up position at the checkered. Donaldson was third followed by Tony Elliott, Barry Baker, Randy Hutchinson, Denny Dyson and John Vigar. Sam Davis and Baker were winged sprint heat winners with Donaldson picking up the dash win. Quick time went to Dave Darland with a time of 15.95.

Ron McKenzie was the early leader of the limited late model feature until Bradley closed in for a side-by-side battle. Bradley got by on lap 10 and led to the finish for the win. Allen Marsh, who started in the 18th starting position, fought his way up to finish second. McKenzie finished third, followed by Dick Day, Tom Leiter, Robert Forsythe, Robert Johnson, and Jerry Burkett. Rod England won the first heat in a photo finish over Forsythe and Bradley took the second heat win. William Varney won the dash while Butch Boggs had fast time of 19.45.

In the roadrunner feature, Jeff Putterbaugh grabbed the early lead until Prater closed to race side-by-side and pass Putterbaugh for the lead. Prater led the remainder of the race to take the checkered flag for the win. Harvey Hayes passed Shane Denny on lap nine for second with Denny finishing in third. Putterbaugh finished fourth with Jay Nordman, Bob Johnson, David Fitzpatrick Sr. and David Fitzpatrick Jr.

This Friday is the third annual Warsaw Invitational for winged sprints, paying $2,000 to the winner. Gates open at 5 p.m. with the racing action to begin at 8 p.m. The grandstand will be open all day Friday to reserve seats early. A large crowd is expected.

Friday, September 5, 1986
Jacobs Takes Top Honors In Warsaw Invitational
By Kim Gregory

An impressive field of professional race car drivers awed the fans Friday evening at the Warsaw Speedway. Forty-one winged sprints qualified for the Third Annual Warsaw Invitational and a purse of over $10,000. All-Star Circuit of Champions sprint star Kenny Jacobs raced to the 40 lap feature win and the top prize of $2,000 in his Genesee Beer winged sprint.

Iowa native Rocky Hodges jumped out early in the feature to lead the first 15 laps. Kenny Jacobs closed in to dual side by side with Hodges for nine laps with the advantage for the lead swapping hands with each lap. Lap 24 saw Jacobs pull out in front to lead the 16 remaining laps and take the checkered flag for the win. Hodges finished second with Joe Gaerte, of Rochester, in third. Indy 500 veteran Rich Vogler crossed the finish line in fourth followed by Warsaw's Terry Shepherd, Todd Kane, Johnny Beaber, Randy Kinser, Fred Linder, and Kevin Briscoe.

Heat wins went to Tray House, 15 year old sensation Jeff Gordon, DeWayne Barker, and Rodney Duncan. Jacobs won the four-lap dash and Gaerte had quick time of 15.744. Gaerte also picked up a $200 bonus from Steve Ross Chevrolet for setting a new track record of 15.81 set on June 28 by Tony Elliott.

The C Main consolation event was won by Joe Roush of Indianapolis, with Mark Owsley in second and Tony Ploughe in third. Bloomington's Rodney Ritter Jr. won the B Main consi to advance on to the feature, followed by Linder and Kinser. Also competing with the field was Indy 500 veteran Sheldon Kinser and USAC sprint point leader Steve Butler.

Next Saturday, Sept. 13, is the final show of the year with the First Ever Late Model and Street Stock Invitational, paying over $1,000 to win the 50-lap late model feature.

Saturday, September 13, 1986
Anderson, Denny Win Speedway Invitational
By Kim Gregory

The final show of the season involved the outlaw late models returning to the Warsaw Speedway for the first time in many years for the late model and street stock invitational. Denny Anderson, of Grand Rapids, Mich., won the 50-lap late model feature and $1,100 for his come from behind victory. Shane Denny of Claypool, celebrated his 23rd birthday with a 25-lap street stock win and a prize of over $500. Both winners received a six foot trophy from Kercher Engines.

Terry Sroufe led the first 10 laps of the late model feature when Allen Marsh closed and passed for the lead. Terry Eaglin closed in on Marsh and took over the first spot on lap 16. Eaglin led up until lap 45 when Anderson, who had to come all the way from the back of the pack, dove underneath Eaglin and led the final laps for the win. Eaglin finished second, followed by Marsh, Bill Davis, Randy Woodling, Keith Allen, Sroufe, and Jim Bucher, Jr. Heat wins went to Ron McKenzie and Joe Dorer and the B Main was won by Butch Boggs. Anderson also picked up the quick time of 17.907.

Scott Dausman jumped out to the early lead of the street stock feature until Denny passed on lap six and began to extend his lead. David Fitzpatrick Sr., made his way through the field and began closing on Denny. Fitzpatrick challenged for the lead several times, but at the checkered flag, it was Denny across the line first for the win with Fitzpatrick in the second spot. Arnold Prater finished third, followed by Harvey Hayes, Robert Johnson, David Fitzpatrick Jr., Dausman, and Jay Nordman. Johnson and Mark Shank won the street stock heats and Johnson had fast time of 22.222.

1987

Saturday, May 9, 1987
Familiar Names Start Off Speedway Season Victorious
By Kim Gregory

Opening night brought back familiar faces into the winner's circle Saturday night at the Warsaw Speedway, as a large crowd watched former sprint champ DeWayne Barker start the season off right with a winged sprint feature win. Glenn Bradley won the limited late model feature, while another former speedway champion, Harvey Hayes, took home the roadrunner feature win.

Bimbo Atkins jumped out front to lead the first laps in the winged sprint feature, with Barker closing in. On lap 11, Atkins lost a tire while Barker captured the lead and stayed there to win his first feature of the season. Denny Dyson worked his way through the field of cars to finish second, followed by Kurt Danner, John Hajduk, Sammy Keen, Tony Elliott, Jon Ormsby, and Mark Owsley. Sprint heat wins went to Hajduk and Owsley, with the dash going to Elliott and fast time to Denny England with a time of 16.27

In the limited late model feature, Ed Martin took the early lead until Bradley closed in to race side by side with Martin. Bradley passed on lap six and led to the checkered flag for the win. Martin hung in for a strong second place finish, Doug Drudge, William Varney, and Dick Day.

Drudge and Martin won the limited late model heats with Butch Boggs winning the dash. Roger Grossnickle took fast time and broke the track record with a time of 19.41.

Hayes got out in front and led every lap of the 15-lap event to win the roadrunner feature. Following Hayes to the finish line were David Fitzpatrick, Bob Johnson, Keith Smith, number 70, Tom Graves, John Ong, and Gary Fowler. Roadrunner heat wins went to Phil Draper and Arnold Prater, while Jay Nordman had fast time of 22.24. This Saturday will have the same three classes of racing with all the action beginning at 8 p.m.

Saturday, May 16, 1987
New Winners Highlight Full Speedway Racing
By Kim Gregory

Winged sprints, limited late models, and roadrunners took to the dirt again Saturday night at the Warsaw Speedway. Van Gurley won the winged sprint feature, Ron McKenzie took the limited late model feature, and Shane Denny was the winner of the roadrunner main event. This was each one's first feature win of the year.

Although feature victor Gurley charged out front and led every lap of the winged sprint feature, the remainder of the 20 car field scrambled behind him for position. Denny

Dyson dueled with Gurley for the lead on several occasions but had to settle for second place. Mark Owsley finished third followed by DeWayne Barker, Denny England, Gary Fisher, Rob Roberts, and Kurt Danner. Winged sprint heat wins went to Brett Mann and Roberts while England won the dash. Barker set a new track record of 15.49.

In the limited late model feature, McKenzie and Glenn Bradley battled back and forth for the lead of the 20-lap event. McKenzie led early in the race until Bradley passed to lead on lap eight but McKenzie recovered the first spot and after several challenges, took the checkered flag for the win. Bradley finished second followed by Butch Boggs, Doug Drudge, Ed Martin, Rod England, Dick Day, and Rick Day. McKenzie made it three for three as he also picked up the limited late model dash and first heat win. Dick Day won the second heat while Bradley set a new track record of 19.31.

Tom Graves took the early lead of the roadrunner feature until Denny closed to race side by side and pass Graves on lap six. Denny stayed out front to cross the finish line in first followed by Harvey Hayes, Arnold Prater, Jay Nordman, Brian Fox, Bob Johnson, and Tom Leiter among the top eight. The roadrunner heats were won by Denny and Prater.

This Saturday will be "Night Before the 500 Racing" with winged sprints, limited late models, and roadrunners.

Saturday, May 23, 1987 - Rainout

Saturday, May 30, 1987
Rain Wins Speedway Features

Racing action was halted Saturday night at the Warsaw Speedway as summer thunderstorms claimed the victory over the field of winged sprints, limited late models and roadrunners. Racing will resume next Saturday night with the same three classes of cars competing.

Coming up Friday, June 19, and Saturday, June 20, will be a big double-header racing weekend as the All-Star Circuit of Champions outlaw sprints will invade the speedway in a $3,000 to win feature. Joining them will be the limited late models paying $250 to win the feature. Then back on Saturday night will be the three regular classes of winged sprints, limited late models, and roadrunners with all the action beginning at 8 p.m. both nights.

Saturday, June 6, 1987
Barker Takes Second Warsaw Sprint Feature
By Kim Gregory

DeWayne Barker in his Barker Auto Sales winged sprint won his second feature of the year on a warm Saturday night at the Warsaw Speedway. Ron McKenzie in the D.O.D. Welding limited late model upped his feature winning streak to three in a row and Jay Nordman in his roadrunner stock car won his first feature of the year.

The winged sprint feature was led from start to finish by Barker, as he had command of the lead to the checkered flag. Two car lengths behind Barker was Mark Owsley followed closely by Van Gurley. Fourth went to John Hadjuk with Denny Dyson, Randy Woodling, Brett Mann, and Randy Hutchinson, rounding out the top eight.

The race was not without accident as Brad Boyer on lap two and Denny England on lap 13 ended up with two wheels on top of the wall after making hard contact with the outside retainer. No one was injured. Winged sprint heat wins went to Mann and Woodling while Gurley won the dash. Quick time went to England with clocking of 15.69.

Dick Day jumped out to the early lead of the limited late model feature until lap six when McKenzie passed for first spot. McKenzie led the remaining laps to win by one car length over second place finisher Butch Boggs. Bruce Hogue came across in third followed by Roger Grossnickle, Robert Johnson, Rick Day, Dane Ronk, and Tom Leiter. Thames Goon and Gerold Holloway were LLM heat winners, Hogue claimed the dash win, and Grossnickle the fast qualifier.

The roadrunner feature was being led by Rex Long when he spun and David Fitzpatrick took over the lead. Nordman passed Fitzpatrick on lap five and went on to win. This survival of the fittest race had only four other finishers. Second place went to Shane Denny followed by Fitzpatrick, Harvey Hayes and Arnold Prater. The roadrunner heats were won by Scott Dausman and Prater.

Saturday, June 13, 1987
Newcomers Winners At Warsaw Speedway
By Kim Gregory

The Classic Car Centre sponsored winged sprint made its way into victory lane as driver Denny England powered the car to a near perfect race and his first feature win of the year Saturday night at the Warsaw Speedway. Ed Martin and Arnold Prater were also new faces in the winner's circle as they picked up their first feature wins of the year. Martin drove his Gentry's Corner sponsored limited late model and Prater drove his stock car for the roadrunner win.

Bimbo Atkins, DeWayne Barker, and England were all battling for the lead, but England got the early jump and held off everyone to lead every lap for the win. At the finish, Atkins was second followed by Gary Fisher, Barker, Mark Owsley, John Hajduk, Randy Hutchinson, and Brad Boyer. The first of three heat wins went to John Vigar with Tom Patterson and fast qualifier John Mapes winners of the other two heats. Fisher won the four lap dash.

Robert Johnson, Warsaw

Allen Marsh led the first lap of the limited late model feature, but it was Martin that passed Marsh and took control of the remainder of the race to the checkered flag for the win. Butch Boggs finished second with fast qualifier Roger Grossnickle, Marsh, William Varney, Rod England, Dick Day, and Robert Johnson rounding out the top eight. England and Marsh were limited late model heat winners and Ron McKenzie won the dash event.

Shane Denny was the early leader of the roadrunner feature until Prater closed to race side by side with Denny and pass for the lead on lap five. Prater went on to win followed by Jay Nordman, Phil Draper, Denny, Bob Johnson, Scott Dausman, David Fitzpatrick, and Jeff Christner. The roadrunner heat wins went to Dausman and Prater.

This Friday and Saturday is a double-header weekend of racing with the first-ever appearance of the All Star Circuit of Champions outlaw sprints on Friday and a complete racing program of winged sprints, limited late models, and roadrunners on Saturday.

Friday, June 19 & Saturday, June 20, 1987
Saturday Winners Finish Speedway Weekend Action
(All Star Circuit of Champions)
By Kim Gregory

Denny England of Warsaw pulled off a last lap pass to bring the crowd to its feet and the winged spring feature win home at the Warsaw Speedway Saturday night. Roger Grossnickle put his name in the record book as he won his first limited late model feature of the year and Shane Denny proved he is a tough competitor as he again won the roadrunner feature.

The activity on the local track completed a special weekend of racing, highlighted by the appearance Friday of the All-Star Circuit of Champions winged sprints. Thirty-one sprints were entered for the Friday night racing card, with Bobby Allen of Hanover, Penn., in his No. 1a Allen sprinter, winning the $4,000 first prize. Allen had not been on the Warsaw track in almost a decade before Friday's contest. He survived a wild night of racing on a hard, dusty dirt oval that had two four-car tangles during the feature race. Those accidents eliminated several cars from the 20-car starting field, including Kokomo Klassic winner, Dave Darland. Allen battled side-by-side with Dave

Bobby Allen, Hanover PA

Blaney before taking the lead for good on lap 16. Blaney finished second followed by early feature leader, Rodney Ritter, Jr. Rodney Duncan came across in fourth with Rick

Ferkel, Rick Unger, Joe Gaerte, Rocky Hodges, Jim Moughan and Terry Shepherd finishing out the top 10.

Of the 31 outlaw sprints competing, it was Warsaw's Bimbo Atkins that flew to fast time of 15.922. Atkins also won the B main that advanced him to the feature along with the second, third, and fourth finishers of Todd Kane, Duncan, and Dave Darland. A.J.Wendt, not injured after flipping his car near the end of the feature, won the first of four heats. Other winners were Kelly Kinser, Jack Hewitt, and Moughan.

In Saturday's sprint feature at the Speedway, DeWayne Barker took a commanding lead and was clearly enroute for a victory but England put on the brakes, gradually closing the gap between himself and the first spot before passing on the final lap to win by a car's length. Barker was second followed by Gary Fisher, Jeff Walker, Brad Boyer, Tom Chalk, Randy Woodling, and Brett Mann.

Winged spring heat wins went to Denny Dyson and Mike Mann, the dash went to Boyer, and the fast time was 15.81 set by England.

Grossnickle jumped out to the early lead from his third spot starting position and led every lap of the feature to win in his Sy's Welding limited late model. Second place went to Butch Boggs followed by William Varney, Mike McMahon, Bruce Hogue, Ed Martin, Robert Johnson, and Dane Ronk. Ron McKenzie and McMahon were limited late model heat winners and Grossnickle picked up the dash win.

Rex Long led the first four laps of the roadrunner feature until Denny closed and passed for the lead and at the finish, the win. Second went to Jay Nordman followed by Scott Dausman, Schaffer, Long, Jeff Christner, and Bob Johnson among the top eight. The roadrunner heats went to Denny and Schaffer.

In late model action on Friday's racing card, Martin passed early leader Varney on lap eight and went on to win the limited late model feature. Varney finished second followed by Ron McKenzie, Ronk, Doug Method, Rod England and Hogue. Grossnickle and Hogue battled it out for the two heat wins.

Next Saturday night will be the mid-season championships sponsored by Gaerte's Engines of Rochester. All three classes of cars will be competing for the championship trophies and all the action starts at 8p.m.

Saturday, June 27, 1987
Speedway Point Leaders
Saturday Winners
By Kim Gregory

Saturday night at the Warsaw Speedway was a special night for

Butch Boggs, Warsaw

point leader Butch Boggs, as he drove his Terry's Automotive limited late model to its first feature victory of the year after working around the clock to get the race car ready.

Point leader Denny England, with his Classic Car Centre winged sprint won his third feature race in a row to extend his point lead midway through the season and Jay Nordman won his second roadrunner feature of the year.

DeWayne Barker got the early lead of the winged sprint feature, with England a close second. England raced side by side with Barker and took the lead for good on lap 10 of the 30-lap feature for the win. Barker finished second, despite several late race challenges, and Tony Elliott came all the way up from the 15th starting spot to finish third. Fourth went to Mark Owsley, followed by Randy Woodling, Jeff Walker, John Hadjuk, and Brett Mann. Elliott won the B Main, with Walker and Rob Roberts second and third. Heat winners were Walker, Elliott, and Kurt Danner, while Owsley took the dash win.

Boggs jumped out in front of the limited late model feature and led every lap to the checkered flag for the victory. Ed Martin finished a close second, with Dewayne May coming clear up from the 14th spot to finish third. Dick Day was fourth, followed by Doug Drudge, Gerold Holloway, Dane Ronk, and Doug Method. Martin won both the dash and his heat, while May picked up the other heat win.

The crash-filled roadrunner feature had some unfortunate accidents, as early leader Arnold Prater and competitor Shane Denny were battling for the lead and a slower car spun in front of them. This caused all three cars to collide, and put them all out of the running for the win. At the finish, it was Jay Nordman, who picked up the lead on lap nine, followed by Harvey Hayes, Bob Johnson, David Fitzpatrick, Jeff Christner, and Prater. Phil Schaffer and Denny won the roadrunner heats.

Saturday, July 4, 1987
Speedway Record Crowd Sees Comeback Wins
By Kim Gregory

The largest crowd in the history of the Warsaw Speedway was assembled here Saturday night for a full evening of wheel to wheel racing and fireworks. It marked the fourth win in a row for hard-to-beat Denny England of Warsaw in his Classic Car Centre winged sprint.

Ron McKenzie lifted his feature win total to four also, as he won his way back into the winner's circle in his limited late limited late model. Picking up his second roadrunner feature win of the season was Arnold Prater.

Gary Fisher got the lead of the winged sprint feature until lap nine, when England passed and led to the checkered flag for the

Gary Fisher, Kokomo

win. Fisher stayed up front behind England for second, followed by Tony Elliott, Brad Boyer, DeWayne Barker, Van Gurley, Bimbo Atkins, and Mark Owsley.

McKenzie got a good lead built up from lap one and was never contested as he led all 20 laps of the limited late model feature win. Roger Grossnickle started to close in on the lead on lap 17, but it was too late and he had to settle for second place. Third went to Butch Boggs with Ed Martin, Dick Day, Bruce Hogue, Doug Method, and Rick Day rounding out the top eight.

William Varney, Doug Method, Harvey Hayes, Tom Leiter, Thames Goon, Allen Marsh, Ron McKenzie, Dane Ronk, and Butch Boggs

The 15 lap roadrunner feature was led for two circuits by young David Fitzpatrick, but Shane Denny quickly took the lead away and put some distance between himself and the rest of the field of cars. Not until the end of the race did Denny get challenged, as Prater closed the gap and passed Denny on lap 13 for the win. Prater was followed by Denny, Harvey Hayes, Fitzpatrick, Rex Long, Bob Johnson, Jay Nordman, and Bill Schaffer.

Race summary:

Winged Sprint:
Four lap dash—Denny England.
Heat one—Tony Ploughe, John Vigar.
Heat two—John Althouse, Denny Dyson.
Heat three—DeWayne Barker, Kurt Danner.
B Main—Scott Fisher, Althouse.
Feature—England, Gary Fisher, Tony Elliott.

Limited Late Model:
Four lap dash—Ed Martin
Heat one—Charles Shaw, Rod England.
Heat two—Bruce Hogue, William Varney.
Feature—Ron McKenzie, Roger Grossnickle, Butch Boggs.

Roadrunner:

Heat one—Bill Schaffer, Ron Murphy.
Heat two—Shane Denny, David Fitzpatrick.
Feature—Arnold Prater, Denny, Harvey Hayes.

Saturday, July 11, 1987
Late Charges Give Barker, Grossnickle Speedway Wins
By Kim Gregory

A hot and humid night left the track moist for some tight feature racing Saturday night at the Warsaw Speedway. DeWayne Barker, in his Barker Auto Sales winged sprint, raced to his third feature victory of the year while Roger Grossnickle made his second appearance in the winner's circle by winning the late model feature. Picking up his fourth roadrunner feature of the year was Shane Denny.

The winged spring feature was led by Jerry Carrier until lap 10, when Carrier and Denny Dyson were battling for the lead through lapped traffic and Carrier hit the third turn wall which put him out of the competition. Dyson took the lead until Barker passed Dyson with only five laps remaining in the race for the win. Tom Chalk made a last lap pass over Dyson, Brad Boyer, Jeff Walker, Rob Roberts, Tony Ploughe, and Ray Kenens Jr.

Grossnickle passed Ron McKenzie on lap 18 of the 20 lap race for the limited late model feature win. Butch Boggs led the first 14 laps until his car got a flat tire, and McKenzie acquired the lead for the next four circuits when Grossnickle passed for the win. McKenzie was second, followed by Doug Drudge, William Varney, Bruce Hogue, Dan Kelsey, Rick Day, and Dane Ronk.

Shane Denny, Claypool

Shane Denny passed early leader David Fitzpatrick on lap four and led the remaining laps to win the roadrunner feature. Arnold Prater battled his way up through the field to finish second, followed by Harvey Hayes, Fitzpatrick, Jay Nordman, Scott Dausman, Bob Johnson, and Phil Schaffer.

This Saturday will be Pioneer Days racing, with the same three classes of cars competing on the quarter mile clay oval.

Winged Sprint:
Fast time: Brad Boyer, 16.30.
Four lap dash: Denny Dyson.
Heat one: Rob Roberts, Sammy Keen.
Heat two: Jeff Walker, DeWayne Barker.
Feature: Tom Chalk, Dyson.
Limited Late Model:

Fast time: Roger Grossnickle, 20.54.
Four lap dash: Allen Marsh.
Heat one: William Varney, Charles Shaw.
Heat two: Ed Martin, Dick Day.
Feature: Grossnickle, Ron McKenzie, Doug Drudge.
Roadrunner:
Heat one: Walt Maley, Mark Shank.
Heat two: Shane Denny, Scott Dausman.
Feature: Denny, Arnold Prater, Harvey Hayes.

Saturday, July 18, 1987
Barker Sprints To Win No. 4 At Warsaw Speedway
By Kim Gregory

DeWayne Barker, a not-so-old veteran of the Warsaw Speedway, placed his winged sprint in the winner's circle for the fourth time this season and second week in a row Saturday night. Also winning his second feature in a row was Roger Grossnickle in his limited late model while point leader, Arnold Prater, won his third roadrunner feature of the year.

DeWayne Barker put his experience in action as he held off several close challenges from Mark Owsley to lead every lap of the winged sprint feature for the victory. Owsley came across in second followed by John Hadjuk, Bimbo Atkins, Denny England, Dave Darland, Brad Boyer, and Gary Fisher. Barker's win also tightens the battle for the points championship as point leader, England and Barker have both won four features apiece out of the 11 races completed.

DeWayne Barker, Warsaw

Doug Drudge jumped out to the early lead of the limited late model feature but was soon passed by Dewayne May. Roger Grossnickle raced side by side with May on lap 10 and got by to lead the 20-lap race.

With only five laps remaining, May and Ron McKenzie both closed in on Grossnickle's tail to fight for the first spot. At the finish, though, Grossnickle fought off the challenge to win. May was second followed by McKenzie, Butch Boggs, William Varney, Drudge, Dan Kelsey, and Charlie Shaw.

Jeff Christner was leading the roadrunner feature when a third turn mishap with Rex Long put both out of the competition. Arnold Prater gained the lead and was never challenged as he led to the finish. Jay Nordman was second followed by David Fitzpatrick, Phil Schaffer, Scott Dausman, Rick Essary, Ron Murphy, and Gerald Fowler.

Race Summary:

Winged Sprint:
Fast time—Bimbo Atkins, 15.62.
Four Lap Dash—Van Gurley
Heat One—Larry Hadjuk, John Gurley
Heat Two—Brett Mann, Denny England
Heat Three—DeWayne Barker, John Hadjuk
B Main—Tony Ploughe, Sammy Keen
Feature—Barker, Mark Owsley, John Hadjuk.

Limited Late Model:
Fast Time—Roger Grossnickle, 19.42
Four Lap Dash—Ed Martin
Heat One—Gerold Holloway, Hank Hilmer
Heat Two—Dewayne May, William Varney
Feature—Grossnickle, May, Ron McKenzie

Roadrunner:
Heat One—Ron Murphy, Greg Bell
Heat Two—Phil Shaffer, Jay Nordman
Feature—Arnold Prater, Nordman, Day, Fitzpatrick

Saturday, July 25, 1987
Gurley, McKenzie, Denny Race To Speedway Wins
By Kim Gregory

Mishawaka's Van Gurley raced high on the dirt cushion in his #3B winged sprint to make a repeat visit to victory lane Saturday night at the Warsaw Speedway. Gurley's last feature win was back on May 16. Limited late model winner, Ron McKenzie, and Roadrunner winner, Shane Denny, are boasting the most feature wins in their respective classes as both picked up feature win number five.

Gurley jumped out front on lap one and led every lap to win the winged sprint feature. Point leader, DeWayne Barker, challenged Gurley on lap 19 as he tried both the high groove and the low groove of the track, but Gurley held him off. Then on lap 21, Mark Owsley closed in to pass Barker and finish second at the checkered. Barker finished third, followed by John Hadjuk, Tony Ploughe, Kurt Danner, Randy Hutchinson, and John Vigar. 18 year old, Sammy Keen, picked up his first heat win while Gurley won the other heat, Dave Darland the dash, and Denny England took fast time of 16.12.

McKenzie closed to race side by side with early leader Rick Stone, passed, and led the remainder of the race to win. Stone held on to finish second with Doug Drudge, Allen

Marsh, Fred Click, William Varney, Dan Kelsey, and Robert Johnson next to cross the finish line. McKenzie also picked up the dash win and Varney and Thames Goon were heat winners. Roger Grossnickle had fast time of 19.73.

David Fitzpatrick got the early lead of the roadrunner feature but was passed by Denny in his #58 Camaro more commonly known as the "Green Machine". Denny extended his lead and picked up the uncontested win. The battle for second place started on lap eight between Harvey Hayes and David Fitzpatrick and lasted for six laps as they raced back and forth and side by side until Fitzpatrick got the edge on lap 14 to finish second. Hayes places third, followed by Ron Murphy, Bob Johnson, Jay Nordman, and Scott Dausman among the top eight. Denny and Murphy were heat winners.

Saturday, August 1 - Rainout

Wednesday, August 5, 1987
Gaerte Wins Warsaw Sprints

The Gaerte Engine sprint team could not have been happier as Joe Gaerte in the #3G car and Terry Shepherd in the #3S car took top honors in the open competition winged sprint show Wednesday night at the Warsaw Speedway.

Gaerte battled side-by-side with Kelly Kinser for the first quarter of the 40-lap feature when Kinser took charge to lead with Gaerte right behind. With only 11 laps remaining, Gaerte closed the gap and dove under Kinser to lead, and at the checkered flag, to win. Kinser placed second with Fred Linder in third. Rick Ferkel and Dave Darland came across in a photo finish for fourth and fifth followed by Tim Norman, Mark Owsley, Kevin Huntley, Kurt Hawkins, and Jack Hewitt, who drove young Brett Mann's #19 after blowing one engine and overheating another earlier in the Nichol's brothers #31 car.

Rick Ferkel, Tiffon OH

Terry Shepherd blew away the old track record in qualifying and picked up a $100 bonus for his fast time. Shepherd's time of 15.326 broke the record held by DeWayne Barker of 15.49 which was set in May. Heat winners were Jeff Walker, Barker, A. J. Wendt, and Gaerte. Fred Linder won the dash and Huntley took the B Main.

President of the All Star series, Bert Emick, was also in attendance and scheduled another All Star Circuit of Champions sprint race for Friday, August 21, as well as lending his support to the Fourth Annual Warsaw Invitational, to be held Sept. 11.

This Saturday marks the conclusion of fair week racing, with the return of the winged sprints, limited late models, and roadrunners. Gates open at 5 p.m. with action starting at 8 p.m.

Saturday, August 8, 1987
Rain Dampens Speedway Action

For the second Saturday night in a row rain has halted the racing action at the Warsaw Speedway. Racing will resume this Saturday night with winged sprints, limited late models, and roadrunners.

Only six weeks are left in the Warsaw Speedway racing season and some of the special shows remaining are the All Star Circuit of Champions winged sprints on Aug. 21, season championships on Aug. 29, the Fourth Annual Warsaw Invitational on Sept. 11, and the Limited Late Model/Roadrunner Invitational on Sept. 19.

Saturday, August 15, 1987
England & McKenzie Winners at Warsaw
Track Facts, Volume 2, Issue 22, Page 1
By Kim Gregory

Denny England passed Brett Mann for the lead with only six laps remaining to win the winged sprint feature Saturday night at the Warsaw Speedway.

Ron McKenzie made a clean sweep by taking fast time, winning the dash, heat, and feature in the limited late model class and upped his feature win total to six victories. Point leader Arnold Prater lifted his feature win total to six victories. Point leader Arnold Prater lifted his feature win total to four in the roadrunner class. The three have a combined total of 15 feature wins this season.

Jeff Walker jumped from his pole starting spot to lead until Mann gained the lead on lap nine. DeWayne Barker and England closed in on Mann to make it a three-way battle for first but it was England who went from fourth to first in four laps to win at the checkered. Barker finished second while Mann spun on the last lap. Bimbo Atkins finished third followed by Walker, Mark Owsley, Randy Woodling, Tom Chalk, and Hank Lower. Heat winners were Rob Roberts and Mann while Chalk won the dash and Atkins had fast time of 15.79.

Dick Day passed early race leader, Gerold Holloway, to lead the limited late model feature on lap seven. Shortly after, McKenzie closed in on Day and made a strong move to pass and lead to the finish. Day finished second followed by Bruce Hogue, Charlie Shaw, Doug Drudge, William Varney, Dane Ronk, and other heat winner, Rick Day.

In the roadrunner feature, Rex Long grabbed the lead until lap five when Prater passed and extended his lead every lap to win at the checkered. Jay Nordman came across in second with David Fitzpatrick, Terry Gagnon, Rod Grim, Rex Alley, Danner, and Long rounding out the top eight. Bryan Fox and Jeff Oswalt were heat winners.

This Saturday will be the Season Championships for all three classes of cars and the Fourth Annual Warsaw Sprint Invitational is set for September 11th.

Saturday, August 22, 1987
Barker, Martin, Denny Take Feature Wins
By Kim Gregory, Sports Writer

DeWayne Barker of Warsaw made his fifth appearance in the winged sprint winner's circle during a chilly Saturday night of racing at the Warsaw Speedway. Ed Martin in his #17 limited late model and Shane Denny in his #58 roadrunner also made repeat victories by winning their feature events.

Barker, in his #33b winged sprint, fought off challenges

Ed Martin

from Denny England and Van Gurley near the end of the 25 lap race, but held them off for the feature win. England finished second followed by Gurley, Brett Mann, Mark Owsley, Jeff Walker, Tom Jewelll, and Kurt Danner.

Heat race winners were John Johnson, John Althouse, and Mann while Dave Darland took the dash, and England had quick time of 15.38. The B Main win went to Sam Davis, with Tom Patterson second.

William Varney jumped out to the early lead of the 20 lap limited late model feature event, but was soon passed by Martin. Butch Boggs challenged Martin with only three laps to go, but Martin held on for the win. Boggs was second with fast qualifier, Roger Grossnickle, Varney, Doug Drudge, Bruce Hogue, Gerold Holloway and Dick Day next to cross the finish line. Heat winners were Doug Method and Day, while Martin took the dash.

Denny put forth an incredible effort as he came from the back of the pack of cars twice to win the roadrunner feature. Arnold Prater led the first four laps until he was passed by Jay Nordman, who found himself being passed by Scott Dausman. With eight laps remaining, Denny took the lead for good for the victory. Dausman finished second, followed by David Fitzpatrick, Terry Gagnon, #17, Rick Essary, Nordman, and Bob Johnson. Nordman was a heat winner.

Saturday, August 29, 1987
Winners Announced At Warsaw Speedway
By Kim Gregory

After the checkered flag fell and the dust settled, Warsaw Speedway had its season champions and feature winners for the last points race of the 1987 racing season.

Denny England, of Warsaw, in his own Classic Car Centre #84 winged sprint came into the night only one point down to DeWayne Barker, but ended up winning the feature and picking up the needed points to take his second track title in a row and third overall.

North Manchester's Roger Grossnickle had the limited late model championship wrapped up before the Saturday races began to earn his first title at the track while Ron McKenzie, of Claypool, picked up his seventh feature win of the season. Jay Nordman, of Columbia City, in his #56 roadrunner won his first track championship while David Fitzpatrick, of Silver Lake, led the last two laps of the roadrunner feature to win his first feature of the season.

England led every lap of the winged sprint feature to win his sixth feature of the year. Mark Owsley passed Barker on lap 15 of the 20-lap feature to finish second followed by Barker, Bimbo Atkins, Jeff Walker, John Hajduk, Scott Fisher, and Kurt Danner. Tom Jewell and Brad Boyer were sprint heat winners with Denny Dyson picking up the 4-lap dash win.

Grossnickle jumped out to an early lead of the limited late model feature, but was passed by McKenzie on the 14th lap who went on to win. Grossnickle picked up second place with Butch Boggs, Allen Marsh, William Varney, Bruce Hogue, Doug Drudge, and Dick Day rounding out the top eight. Limited late heat winners were Dewayne May and Ed Martin with McKenzie picking up the win in the dash event.

The early leader of the roadrunner feature was Jay Nordman, but with only two laps remaining, he had mechanical trouble and David Fitzpatrick picked up the win. Arnold Prater finished second followed by Harvey Hayes, Gerry Baker, Phil Draper, Terry Gagnon, Rex Alley, and Nordman. Baker and Prater were winners of the roadrunner heats.

Saturday concludes the regular season of racing with the winged sprints, limited late models and roadrunners. Sept. 11 is the Fourth Annual Warsaw Fall Classic for winged sprints and pays $2,500 to win. Sept. 19 finishes out the season with the Second Annual Stock Car Invitational for limited late models and roadrunners.

Winged Sprints:
4-lap feature—Denny Dyson
First heat—Tom Jewell, John Hajduk, Bimbo Atkins
Feature—Denny England, Mark Owsley, DeWayne Barker, Bimbo Atkins

Limited Late Models:
4-lap feature—Ron McKenzie
First heat—Dewayne May, Charlie Shaw, Allen Marsh
Second heat—Ed Martin, Dick Day, Robert Johnson
Feature—Ron McKenzie, Roger Grossnickle, Butch Boggs

Roadrunners:
First Heat—Gerry Baker, Paul Draper, Bryan Fox
Second heat—Arnold Prater, Scott Dausman, Jay Nordman
Feature—David Fitzpatrick, Arnold Prater, Harvey Hayes

Denny England. Mark Owsley. DeWayne Barker. Bimbo Atkins

Friday, September 11, 1987
Warsaw Raceway Winners

Joe Gaerte, in his No. 3G winged sprint, raced the high groove and low groove to swing by Kenny Norris on the 18th lap to win the Warsaw Fall Classic Friday at the Warsaw Speedway.

Forty-one cars showed up for the $2,500 to win show that ended up earning Gaerte $3,500 as Hoosier Tire put up an extra $1,000 bonus to the winner if he was racing with all four Hoosier Tires at the checkered flag. Gaerte got the extra money.

The Fall Classic had an international flavor as World of Outlaw driver, Tim Gee, of Whitehorse, Yukon, Canada, and Joe Madsen, of Sidney, Australia, made an exciting appearance at the speedway. Gee shot down the track record in qualifying with a blistering 15.240 lap which broke Terry Shepherd's record of 15.326 set August 5th.

In the 40-lap feature, Norris jumped out to an early lead but Warsaw's Bimbo Atkins charged by to lead until the 17th lap when Atkins jumped the cushion and flipped his machine to red flag the race.

Norris regained the lead only to be passed by Gaerte who took the checkered flag for his second feature win at the track this season. Kelly Kinser, of Bloomington, finished second and was followed by Dave Fleese, of Saybroo, Ill. Rounding out the top finishers were Rick Unger of Indianapolis; Norris of Columbus; Tim Norman of Warsaw; Ricky Hood of Evansville; Kevin Huntley of Bloomington; Gee of Canada; and Randy Kinser of Bloomington.

Joe Gaerte, Rochester

USAC sprint champion, Steve Butler, won the B Main with Robbie Stanley, Troy Chehowski and Steve Kline rounding out the top four spots. Heat winners were D.W. Keller, Kenny Haynes, Butler, Randy Kinser, and Gaerte. Kelly Kinser won the four-lap dash. Only one show remains as the limited late models and roadrunners conclude the year's racing during the Second Annual Stock Car Invitational this Saturday evening.

Saturday, September 19, 1987
Warsaw Speedway Results

Ron McKenzie, in his No. 24 D.O.D. welding sponsored limited late model, took home a four-foot trophy and his eighth feature win this year during the Stock Car Invitational Saturday night at the Warsaw Speedway. Making his fifth appearance in the winner's circle was Arnold Prater who captured the roadrunner feature win and a nice trophy on the last night of racing for the season.

McKenzie was challenged on the 15th lap by hard-charging Jim Bucher, Jr., but he held them off. Bruce Hogue finished second followed by Jim Mulkey, William Varney, Gerold Holloway, Bucher and Mike McMan. Holloway and Tim Goshert were heat winners, while Butch Boggs won the dash and Bucher had fast time of 18.62.

Prater was the early leader of the roadrunner feature until Shane Denny closed in and passed. Prater stayed close, and when Denny fell out of the race, took the lead back for the win. Harvey Hayes was second and was followed by Jay Nordman, Jeff Oswalt, Gerry Baker, Terry Gagnon, Tom Leiter and Ron Murphy. Heat winners were Murphy and Prater with Denny running the fastest time with a 21.83.

Sam Davis, Bpurbon

Saturday, 19 June, 1982
Warsaw Speedway   Wayne Bryant Omega-Photo

Ron Miller, Huntington

Above: Allen Marsh, Tommy Leiter, and Tommy's daughters Lisa & Tammy
Below: Bob Johnson – 1988

Above: Denny England, Warsaw
Below: Steve Kline, Warsaw

Tony Elliott, Warsaw

Denny England, Warsaw

1988

Late April 1988
Speedway Plans Busy Summer

Warsaw, IN—The Warsaw Speedway will provide racing entertainment all summer long for the entire family.

The newly refurbished grandstand and lawn chair area seats up to 3,000 people plus back stretch parking is also available. The track is a quarter mile flat clay oval that hosts a variety of different racing classes including winged sprints, non-winged sprints, limited late models, roadrunners, and demolition derbys. The speedway races every Saturday night with two mid-week specials.

Many special shows are scheduled for the 1988 season including the All Star Circuit of Champion winged sprints on June 18, fireworks racing celebration on July 2, Hurryin' Hoosier winged sprints on July 23, August 20 and Sept. 9 during the Warsaw Fall Classic. Two demolition derbys will be run with the first on July 25, and the other on August 3 during fair week.

Admission for all regular shows is $6.00 for adults, $2.00 for children ages 6 to 12 and free for all children under 6. Gates open at 5 pm with the first race at 8 pm and all races completed by 11 pm. Further information can be obtained by calling the speedway at 269-6153.

Early May 1988
Speedway To Open

Kevin Atkins, Warsaw

The Warsaw Speedway, in its fourth decade of racing, has made some major changes and additions to its summer racing schedule. The skilled driving ability and close competitive racing of the non-winged sprints are returning for the 1988 season. This decision was made by the speedway management that determined that the amount of dust raised by the winged cars caused crowd size to diminish. The increased sprint count should not diminish as the purse has been raised and the opportunity for drivers to show their true skills is a benefactor.

In an effort to continually improve the track, new clay was added to the entire racing surface. Also, the main grandstand has been totally refurbished with new boards and the fourth turn lawn chair area has been reconstructed. Back stretch parking will also be available for the entire season.

Denny England, 1987 sprint champion, will be defending his track title along with Limited Late champ, Roger Grossnickle, and Roadrunner champ, Jay Nordman, as the season opens on Sunday with a Mother's Day special and a $1 off all ladies' admissions. Racing will continue every Saturday night throughout the summer.

Many special attractions are being featured throughout the season with the return of the All Star Circuit of Champions winged sprints on June 18 and four appearances of the newly formed Hurryin' Hoosier Winged Sprint Series on May 21, July 23, Aug. 20, and Sept. 9 during the fifth annual Warsaw Fall Classic.

Saturday, May 7, 1988
England Starts Strong In Opener At Warsaw Speedway

Saturday night at the Warsaw Speedway saw Denny England of Warsaw, starting the racing season the same way he finished last fall, with a sprint feature win in a competitive field of cars. The opening night also had Butch Boggs of South Whitley, and Claypool's Shane Denny in the winner's circle as they won the limited late model feature and roadrunner feature respectively.

Butch Boggs, Warsaw

Kurt Danner led the early laps of the sprint feature until England slipped around on lap seven to take command of the race and finish first at the checkered. Rob Roberts challenged England on several of the late laps, but couldn't get by and finished second followed by Danner, Tony Pilthauer, Denny Dyson, Mark Owsley, Randy Hutchinson, and Rod Bailey. John Althouse and Bailey were sprint heat winners with Jeff Walker winning the dash and fast time of 16.79.

The limited late model feature was led early by Ron McKenzie until lap 10, when challenging Boggs gained the lead and led to the finish for the victory. McKenzie claimed second spot followed by Gerold Holloway, Jay Nordman, Harvey Hayes, Allen Marsh, and Dewayne May. McKenzie won both the heat and dash with Boggs picking up quick time of 19.01.

Shane Denny passed early leaders Mike Orr and Bill Morris to take the lead and the win at the finish. Second place went to Bob Johnson with Richard McLeary, Doug Draper, Keith Smith, Bryan Fox, Morris, and Orr following. Roadrunner heats were won by Denny and Morris.

Race Results:

(17 total sprints / 7 limited late models / 9 roadrunners)

Fast Qualifiers - Sprints, #39 Jeff Walker 16.79; Limited Lates, #14 Butch Boggs 19.01
Sprint Dash - #39 Jeff Walker; #36D Dave Darland, #84 Denny England, #4 Rob Roberts
Sprint Heat #1 - #77 John Althouse, #00 Kurt Danner, #84 Denny England, #17D Denny Dyson
Sprint Heat #2 - #09 Rod Bailey (first win ever), #2 Tony Pilthauer, #11 Sammy Keen, #33F Tony Messinger
Sprint Feature - #84 Denny England, #4 Rob Roberts, #00 Kurt Danner, #2 Tony Pilthauer, #17D Denny Dyson, #6x Mark Owsley, #31 Randy Hutchinson, #09 Rod Bailey
Limited Late Dash - #24 Ron McKenzie, #14 Butch Boggs, #75 Allen Marsh, #7H Gerold Holloway
Limited Late Heat - #24 Ron McKenzie, #75 Allen Marsh, #14 Butch Boggs, #7H Gerold Holloway
Limited Late Feature - #14 Butch Boggs, #24 Ron McKenzie, #7H Gerold Holloway, #56 Jay Nordman, #49 Harvey Hayes, #75 Allen Marsh, #00 Dewayne May
Roadrunner Heat #1 - #58 Shane Denny, #22 Bob Johnson, #83 Shawn Morton
Roadrunner Heat #2 - #00 Bill Morris, #7 Bryan Fox, #3 Mike Orr
Roadrunner Feature - #58 Shane Denny, #22 Bob Johnson, #27 Richard McCleary, #11 Doug Draper, #3 Keith Smith, #7 Bryan Fox, #00 Bill Morris, #3 Mike Orr

Saturday, May 14, 1988
Walker, Boggs, Denny Win Races At Warsaw

Jeff Walker, of Kokomo, picked up his first feature victory of the year at the Warsaw Speedway Saturday night in his #39 sprint car. With two wins under their belt are Butch Boggs taking the limited late model feature and Shane Denny, the roadrunner feature winner.

Jeff Walker took the checkered flag for the sprint feature win after he challenged early leader, Kurt Danner, on lap 14, passed him on the high side of the track, and led the rest of the race to the finish. Randy Woodling battled back and forth with Danner for second with Woodling finishing second and Danner in third at the finish. Fourth went to Denny Dyson followed by Bimbo Atkins, Mark Owsley, Brett Mann, and Tony Pilthauer. Pilthauer and Mann were sprint heat winners while Denny England won the dash and Atkins took quick time of 17.22.

The limited late model feature early leader, Thames Goon, was challenged on lap five by Butch Boggs, who went on to pass and cross the finish line in first spot. Allen Marsh finished second followed by Ron McKenzie, Jay Nordman, Goon, Jeff Christner, Gerold Holloway, and William Varney. Limited late heat wins went to Varney and McKenzie with Dewayne May the dash winner and Boggs getting fast time of 19.05.

Heat winner, Shane Denny, pulled out in front on lap four and dominated the race to win the roadrunner feature. Second went to Phil Shafer with David Fitzpatrick, Robert Johnson, David Baker, Ray Dennis, Richard McLeary, and Steve Holbrook next to cross the finish line. Bill Morris won the second roadrunner heat.

This Saturday, the winged sprints return to the speedway as the Hurryin' Hoosier Sprint Series invades the track to compete for the $2,000 to win feature prize. Sprint stars from all over Indiana will be on hand for the first in a series of special shows. Gates open at 5 p.m. with all the action of racing starting at 8 p.m.

Friday, May 20, 1988
Warsaw Plans Winged Sprints
The Fort Wayne Journal Gazette

The Hurryin' Hoosiers Series for winged sprint cars begins Saturday night at Warsaw Speedway's ¼ mile dirt track. Tony Elliott, of Warsaw, leads the field. Elliott won the Hurryin' Hoosiers opening feature May 7 at Avilla and leads in points.

Elliott was the winner of the nationally televised United States Auto Club race in Springfield, Ill., last year on ESPN and also won four Crown Nationals at Eldora Speedway in the fall.

Some of the drivers expected to join Elliott from the Hurryin' Hoosiers series include Bloomington's Robbie Stanley and Kevin Briscoe, Kokomo's Tom Chalk and Mishawaka's Van Gurley. They will be joined by the Warsaw sprint regulars, including this year's feature winners, Denny England, of Warsaw, and Jeff Walker, of Arcadia.

Also Saturday at Warsaw is the Limited Late Model Division, featuring 1986 champion Butch Boggs, who will try for his third straight feature victory in his 1988 Chevrolet Camaro. Time trials begin at 6:30 p.m. with racing at 8 p.m. Warsaw Speedway is located on the Kosciusko County Fairgrounds in Warsaw.

Saturday, May 21, 1988
Kinser Wins At Warsaw
By Kim Gregory, Sports Writer

Randy Kinser, of Bloomington, topped the field of sprinters to pick up the 40 lap feature win in the Hurryin' Hoosier Sprint Series show at the Warsaw Speedway Saturday night. Thirty-six drivers from five different states showed up to compete in this first in a series of four shows. Allen Marsh grabbed his first feature of the year in his number 75 limited late model.

Kelly Kinser, Bloomington — DAVID

Although Kinser started on the inside second row, it was not an easy run to the front as he had to contend with Pete Abel and early leader Terry Shepherd. Shepherd led until lap 29 when challenging Kinser got by to lead to the checkered for the victory. Tony Elliott battled his way up to finish second followed by Shepherd, Kelly Kinser, Jeff Gordon, Andy Hillerud, Abel, and Tom Chalk.

Elliott and Kevin Briscoe advanced to the feature out of the B-Main with Elliott the victor and Briscoe in second while Chalk, K. Kinser, Gordon, and Kurt Danner took the heat wins. Elliott recorded the quick time of the night with a 15.361 clocking.

In limited late model action, Allen Marsh challenged and passed early leader, Dewayne May, on lap five to take the checkered flag for the win. Dane Ronk finished a strong second followed by William Varney, Thames Goon, Jay Nordman, Sam Shaw, Harvey Hayes, and Robert Johnson. Goon and Marsh picked up the wins in the limited late model heats.

This Saturday's racing action continues with the sprints, limited late models, and double points and pay for the roadrunner class.

Race Results:
(36 sprints / 13 limited late models)
Sprint Fast Qualifier - #57 Tony Elliott, 15.361
Sprint Heat #1 - #4c Tom Chalk, #5w Kevin Spease, #22 Tony Engels or John Sargent, #04 Pete Abel
Sprint Heat #2 - #4K Kelly Kinser, #52 Mark Alderson, #15 Bobby Nichols, #40 Terry Shepherd
Sprint Heat #3 - #6 Jeff Gordon, #51 Andy Hillerud, #4 Joe Miller, #6x Mark Owsley
Sprint Heat #4 - #00 Kurt Danner, #24 Rick Keller, #22 Tony Engels or John Sargent, #1x Randy Kinser
Sprint B Main - #57 Tony Elliott, #5 Kevin Briscoe, #21 D.W. Miller, #75 Randy Woodling, #5J Tim Norman, #39 Jeff Walker, #21 John Hadjuk, #09 Rod Bailey
Sprint Feature (40 laps) - #1x Randy Kinser, #57 Tony Elliott, #40 Terry Shepherd, #4K Kelly Kinser, #6 Jeff Gordon, #51 Andy Hillerud, #04 Pete Abel, #4c Tom Chalk, #22 John Sargent, #4 Joe Miller, #24 Rick Keller, #5 Kevin Briscoe, #52 Mark Alderson, #5w Kevin Spease, #22 Tony Engels, #6x Mark Owsley

Limited Late Heat #1 - #72 Thames Goon, #51 William Varney, #4 Sam Shaw, #22 Robert Johnson
Limited Late Heat #2 - #75 Allen Marsh, #14 Butch Boggs, #00 Dewayne May, #24 Dane Ronk
Limited Late Feature - #75 Allen Marsh, #24 Dane Ronk, #51 William Varney, #72 Thames Goon, #56 Jay Nordman, #4 Sam Shaw, #49 Bob Johnson, #22 Robert Johnson, #00 Dewayne May, #7H Gerold Holloway, #81 Gerry Wiles

Saturday, May 28, 1988
Gurley Wins Feature Race
By Kim Gregory, Sports Writer

Van Gurley, of Mishawaka, became the fourth different sprint feature winner in four shows Saturday night at the Warsaw Speedway. Dewayne May captured his first limited late model feature win of the year while Shane Denny made it three in a row in the roadrunner win column.

In the sprint feature, Steve Imel passed Rob Roberts to take the lead on lap 10 but that lead was short-lived. On lap 14, Van Gurley swung by challenging Mark Owsley and leader Imel to capture the front spot and the victory in his Gurley Leep Buick sprint. Owsley finished second, followed by Roberts, Denny England, Bimbo Atkins, Jeff Walker, Randy Woodling, and Tony Pilthauer.

The race was red flagged twice as Kurt Danner, on lap 13, flipped in mid-air and landed the car on its side in turn three and Brett Mann barrel-rolled his sprint five times down the backstretch as he came out of turn two. Fortunately, both drivers were uninjured. Pilthauer, Woodling, and Gurley were sprint heat winners while Walker won the dash event. Gurley had fast time of 16.94.

Dewayne May led every lap but one to take the limited late model feature win in his Dick Woods Builders sponsored number 00. After a four lap challenge, Butch Boggs made a last lap pass over Dane Ronk to cross the finish line in second with Ronk a car length behind in third. Dash winner, Allen Marsh, finished fourth with heat winner, William Varney, Sam Shaw, and Harvey Hayes among the top eight. Boggs had fast time with a 19.17 clocking.

David Baker led the first nine laps of the roadrunner feature until Shane Denny powered his way past Bill Morris and Baker to lead to the checkered. Morris finished second followed by Bob Johnson, Jay Nordman, Shawn Morton, Troy Wolfe, Doug Draper, and Ray Dennis. Roadrunner heat wins went to John Fitzpatrick and Denny.

This Saturday is the first ever Old Timer's Night featuring the three regular racing classes of sprints, limited late models, and roadrunners.

Race Results:
(24 sprints / 10 limited late models / 14 roadrunners)

Fast Qualifiers - Sprints, #3B Van Gurley 16.94; Limited Lates, #14 Butch Boggs 19.17
Sprint Dash - #39 Jeff Walker, #3B Van Gurley, #36a Bimbo Atkins, #19 Brett Mann
Sprint Heat #1 - #2 Tony Pilthauer, #35 Dennis Hopper, #33F Tony Messinger, #34a Kevin Atkins
Sprint Heat #2 - #75 Randy Woodling, #6x Mark Owsley, #77 John Althouse, #7 Rob Roberts
Sprint Heat #3 - #3B Van Gurley, #84 Denny England, #43 Sam Davis, #39 Jeff Walker
Sprint Feature - #3B Van Gurley, #6x Mark Owsley, #7 Rob Roberts, #84 Denny England, #36a Bimbo Atkins, #39 Jeff Walker, #75 Randy Woodling, #2 Tony Pilthauer

Limited Late Dash - #75 Allen Marsh, #14 Butch Boggs, #24 Dane Ronk, #00 Dewayne May
Limited Late Heat - #51 William Varney, #75 Allen Marsh, #00 Dewayne May, #14 Butch Boggs
Limited Late Feature - #00 Dewayne May, #14 Butch Boggs, #24 Dane Ronk, #75 Allen Marsh, #51 William Varney, #4 Sam Shaw

Roadrunner Heat #1 - #56 John Fitzpatrick, #3 Steve Holbrook, #22 Bob Johnson
Roadrunner Heat #2 - #58 Shane Denny, #00 Bill Morris, #11 Doug Draper
Roadrunner Feature - #58 Shane Denny, #00 Bill Morris, #22 Bob Johnson, #56 John Fitzpatrick, #83 Shawn Morton, #27 Troy Wolfe

Saturday, June 4, 1988
England Picks Up 2nd Win
By Kim Gregory, Sports Writer

Hometown, Denny England, became the first repeat sprint winner out of five races Saturday night at the Warsaw Speedway.

The sprint feature was a heated battle between three drivers from the drop of the green flag. Mark Owsley, England, and Van Gurley were all in the hunt as England and Gurley battled with early leader, Owsley, for the first 18 laps. Suddenly, Owsley spun into the infield leaving the lead wide open. England got the advantage over Gurley and took the checkered flag for the win. Gurley finished second followed by Gary Fisher, Randy Woodling, Jeff Walker, Denny Dyson, John Althouse, and John Mapes. Sprint heat winners were Joe Davis and Woodling while Gurley won the dash and Dave Darland had fast time of 17.43.

Allen Marsh picked up his second limited late model feature win of the year after he passed early leader, William Varney, on lap 14 to lead the last six laps for the win. Butch Boggs, running in second, slowed on the last lap leaving the second place finish to Varney with Thames Goon, Dane Ronk, Boggs, Harvey Hayes, Tom Leiter, and Dave Bratten next to cross the finish line. Jon Ormsby and Ronk were limited late model heat winners while Marsh took the dash and Dewayne May had fast time of 19.86.

Bryan Fox led the first seven laps of the roadrunner feature until Shane Denny flew by on a restart and led the remaining laps to win his fourth feature in a row and take a commanding lead in the roadrunner point race. Fox finished second, followed by Bill Morris, #72, Bob Johnson, David Baker, Chad Marsh and Mark Sult. Denny and Shawn Morton were roadrunner heat winners.

Over 30 former drivers showed up for the first-ever Old Timer's Night that was slated as an addition to the regular show. An amazing 350 years of racing was accumulated by these racers with one driver, Bud "Grandpappy" Shlater, going back to 1938 as the year he drove in his first race.

Last Row L-R: Gene Gregory, ??, ??, Paul Grim, ??, Jene Simon, Bobby Grindle, Max Lambert, ??
Middle Row: Bob Shlater, ??, ??, Bud Shlater, ??, ??, ??, ??
Front Row: ??, Terry Sroufe, Bruce Hogue, Sam Davis

Race Results:
(17 sprints / 12 limited late models / 11 roadrunners)

Fast Qualifiers - Sprints, #36D Dave Darland 17.43; Limited Lates, #00 Dewayne May 19.86
Sprint Dash - #3B Van Gurley, #7 Gary Fisher, #39 Jeff Walker, #36D Dave Darland
Sprint Heat #1 - #70 Joe Davis, #5 John Mapes, #7 Rob Roberts, #17 Denny Dyson
Sprint Heat #2 - #75 Randy Woodling, #3B Van Gurley, #84 Denny England, #6x Mark Owsley
Sprint Feature - #84 Denny England, #3B Van Gurley, #7 Gary Fisher, #75 Randy Woodling, #39 Jeff Walker, #17 Denny Dyson, #77 John Althouse, #5 John Mapes, #70 Joe Davis, #31 Randy Hutchinson
Limited Late Dash - #75 Allen Marsh, #00 Dewayne May, #24 Dane Ronk, #14 Butch Boggs
Limited Late Heat #1 - #99 Jon Ormsby, #51 William Varney, #19 Dave Bratten
Limited Late Heat #2 - #24 Dane Ronk, #75 Allen Marsh, #14 Butch Boggs, #49 Harvey Hayes
Limited Late Feature - #75 Allen Marsh, #51 William Varney, #72 Thames Goon, #24 Dane Ronk,

#14 Butch Boggs, #49 Harvey Hayes, #70 Tom Leiter, #19 Dave Bratten

Roadrunner Heat #1 - #83 Shawn Morton, #66 David Baker
Roadrunner Heat #2 - #58 Shane Denny, #00 Bill Morris
Roadrunner Feature - #58 Shane Denny, #7 Bryan Fox, #00 Bill Morris, #72 Phil Shafer, #22 Bob Johnson, #66 David Baker, #75 Chad Marsh, #72s Mark Sult

Saturday, June 11, 1988
Two First-Time Winners At Speedway

Saturday night was HARF Night at the Warsaw Speedway where many Hoosier Auto Racing Fans witnessed two new faces in the winner's circle.

Dave Darland became the fifth different sprint winner in six races and rookie driver Bill Morris picked up his first-ever feature win in the roadrunner division to break the domination of four-time winner, Shane Denny. Butch Boggs ended his three-week dry spell and claimed his third limited late model feature win.

Pole sitter Darland fought off several mid-race challenges from Denny England to lead every lap for the victory. England, Jeff Walker, and John Althouse all scurried back and forth for positions for the first 17 laps, with England finishing second followed by Walker, Gary Fisher, Randy Woodling, Tim Bookmiller, Althouse, and Kurt Hawkins.

On lap 12, Mark Owsley barrel-rolled his sprint several times going into turn one, causing an immediate red flag. Fortunately, Owsley walked back to the pits uninjured. Joe Davis, Kurt Danner and Fisher were the three sprint heat winners with Walker the dash winner and Bookmiller the quick qualifier with a 16.96 clocking.

Boggs and Allen Marsh diced side by side, taking turns leading each lap, and even raced in the infield during the limited late model feature. Boggs pulled away with only five laps remaining to take the checkered flag for the win. Marsh finished second with Dane Ronk, early leader Thames Goon, Harvey Hayes, Tom Leiter, Jon Ormsby, and Dan Kelsey rounding out the top eight. William Varney and Marsh were limited late model heat winners while Ronk took the dash and Dewayne May had fast time.

Morris battled for nearly 2/3 of the roadrunner race with undefeated Shane Denny and out-muscled his side by side challenge to dethrone Denny and pick up the feature win. Denny finished second followed by David Baker, Bryan Fox, Shawn Morton, Phil Shafer, Everett Carroll, and Mark Sult. Roadrunner heat wins went to Arnold Prater and David Fitzpatrick.

Saturday, June 18, 1988
Hood Wins Biggest Prize
By Kim Gregory, Sports Writer

Rick Hood, Memphis, Tenn., aboard the Campbell Performance Machines Nance #1n, bagged $4,000 for his premier performance in the All Star Circuit of Champions 40 lap feature June 18 at the Warsaw Speedway.

Hood started the evening out right as he flew to a 15.201 clocking and set a new track record in qualifying, breaking the record set last September by Canadian, Tim Gee.

In the feature, Hood battled with Rochester's Joe Gaerte and early leader Kenny Jacobs of Holmesville, Ohio. On lap 14, he won the side by side battle with Gaerte, captured the lead and rode the high side cushion to the checkered flag for the win.

Gaerte raced to second place with Rodney Duncan, Columbus, Ohio, making a late race dash for third place. Joey Allen, Hanover, Penn., finished in fourth place, followed by Jacobs, Warsaw's Terry Shepherd, Tim Gee of Whitehorse, Yukon, Canada, and Todd Kane of Powell, Ohio.

Bimbo Atkins won the B Main as he led every lap from his pole position start. Dave Darland finished second with John Hadjuk and Terry Pletch in third and fourth place. Hood was the first of four heats with other heat winners being Rocky Hodges, Allen and Gee. Gaerte won the 4-lap Las Vegas dash.

Butch Boggs captured his fourth feature win of the season in his #14 limited late model. Boggs, racing on the low side of the track, battled three abreast with Dane Ronk in the middle groove and Dewayne May on the high groove and took the lead for good on lap 13 for the win. May finished second followed by Ronk, Harvey Hayes, Doug Method, William Varney, Sam Shaw and Jay Nordman. Varney won the limited late model heat race and Boggs took the Australian Pursuit win.

June 25 will be the Hardee's Jamboree, paying $1,000 for sprints plus limited late models, roadrunners and a big demolition derby.

Saturday, June 25, 1988
Darland Wins Hardee's Jamboree Sprint
By Kim Gregory, Sports Writer

Dave Darland of Lincoln, Ind., picked up his second win of the year during the Hardee's Jamboree sprint feature Saturday night at the Warsaw Speedway. Also making a return visit to victory lane was Allen Marsh

Allen Marsh, Warsaw

taking the limited late model feature and five-time roadrunner winner Shane Denny.

Denny Dyson took the early lead of the sprint feature until he got out of shape on Lap 8 and Terry Shepherd swung by to gain the front spot. Shepherd cut a tire on Lap 18 which left the lead wide-open for a battle between frontrunner Dave Darland and runner-up Denny England. England tried a last lap move, but Darland held him off and took the checkered flag for the victory. England finished second, followed by Bimbo Atkins, Mark Owsley, Van Gurley, Randy Hutchinson, Dyson and Kurt Danner.

Sam Davis and Shepherd were sprint heat winners while Atkins took the dash and Kevin Thomas clinched the fast time of the night with a 16.82 clocking. Both sprint and limited late model fast qualifiers and dash winners were awarded $50 from Schue's Landscaping for their racing talents.

In limited late model action, the night spelled Allen Marsh as he cleaned house by winning the dash, heat, and feature finale. On Lap 5 of the feature, Marsh closed in on early leader Thames Goon, and powered by to take the lead and the win at the finish. This win puts Marsh and fast qualifier Butch Boggs neck in neck for the all-important points lead. Tom Leiter finished second with Dane Ronk, Goon, William Varney, heat winner Harvey Hayes, Gene Burkett and David Fitzpatrick next across the finish line.

Arnold Prater took a commanding lead in the Roadrunner feature with Gary Fowler holding a steady second. Near mid-race Shane Denny passed Fowler for second and then started to reel in Prater. On the last lap with the checkered flag waving, Denny pulled alongside Prater and won by a car-length at the finish line. Prater finished second followed by Fowler, Doug Draper, Bob Johnson, David Baker, Keith Smith and Shawn Martin. Jeff Oswalt and Denny were the two Roadrunner heat winners.

Dave Jenks won the Demolition Derby with Dean DeWitt and Ricky Daniels in second and third places.

Saturday, July 2, 1988
Plenty of Action at the Track
By Kim Gregory, Sports Writer

Tony Elliott & Dewayne May – Fast Times

There were fireworks exploding in the air, as well as on the racetrack Saturday, in front of a capacity crowd. Denny England rocketed for his third sprint feature win of the year in his D.J.'s Bar, Kercher Engines No. 84. Butch Boggs, driving Terry's Automotive No. 14, picked up his fifth limited late model feature. And Shane Denny thrilled the crowd as he spun and won for his sixth roadrunner feature win of the season in his No. 58 Green Machine.

England passed Bimbo Atkins on lap seven and held off several challenges from Dave Darland to take the checkered flag for the victory. Darland finished second, followed by Terry Shepherd, Van Gurley, Jeff Walker, Mark Owsley, Kurt Hawkins and Tony Elliott, who re-started on the tail with only five laps to go, passing seven cars to finish eighth.

Elliott started the night out with a bang as he set a new track record for sprints with a 16.72 clocking. Sprint heat winners were Denny Dyson and Elliott with Darland taking the dash win.

Butch Boggs and Allen Marsh started out the limited late model feature fighting side-by-side with Marsh having the early edge. Boggs blasted into the lead on lap five and led the remainder of the race for the win. Dane Ronk finished second with Marsh, Thames Goon, William Varney, Tom Leiter, Harvey Hayes and Doug Method next across the finish line. Boggs and Leiter were limited late model heat winners, while Ronk won the dash and Dewayne May had fast time.

Shawn Morton took the early lead of the roadrunner feature until Bill Morris closed in and grabbed the front spot on lap six. Morris led until the final lap when he lost a tire and second-running Shane Denny attempted to pass the wounded Morris car. The result was Denny spinning and continuing on for a mad dash to the finish. Denny claimed the win with Morris, one tire short, in second place. They were followed by Morton, Charlie Shaw, Dave Fitzpatrick, Ken Nine, Rex Long and Arnold Prater. Prater and Andy Holderman took the roadrunner heat wins.

Saturday, July 9 will be the mid-season championships for all three classes of racing with an early 7:30 p.m. start and no qualifications.

Saturday, July 9, 1988
Darland Wins Third Race
By Kim Gregory, Sports Writer

Dave Darland, of Lincoln, Ind., won his third sprint feature of the season during Mid-season Championships Saturday at the Warsaw Speedway. A new face made its way into the winner's circle as Dane Ronk, in the #24 McKenzie limited late model, won his first ever feature at Warsaw and Bill Morris returned to victory lane for his second roadrunner feature win.

Dane Ronk, Warsaw

Denny England led the early laps of the sprint feature with a challenging Dave Darland right behind. Darland continued his pursuit until lap nine when he drove the high side of the racetrack and overcame England for the first spot and the checkered flag at the finish. Terry Shepherd, who started way back in the 11th position, battled his sprint up to the third spot by lap 20 and captured second place at the line. Jeff Walker placed third followed by Bimbo Atkins, Denny Dyson, Kurt Danner, England, and Randy Hutchinson.

The race was red flagged on lap four when Randy Woodling flipped his sprint end over end in turn one and hit the outside light pole possibly saving him from continuing into the turn one spectators. Fortunately, Woodling walked away from his wrecked car uninjured. Brad Boyer and Randy Woodling won the sprint heats while Dyson took the dash win.

Dane Ronk passed early leader, Allen Marsh, and continued in the lead to win the limited late model feature in strong fashion. Marsh finished second, William Varney in third, and Bruce Hogue coming all the way up from his last place starting position to finish fourth. Harvey Hayes placed fifth with Thames Goon, Doug Method, and Roger Fitzpatrick rounding out the top eight. Limited late model preliminaries went to Dewayne May in the heat and Marsh in the dash.

Shane Denny led the first four laps of the roadrunner feature until his car lost a wheel handing the lead over to Bill Morris who stayed out front to win. Charlie Shaw battled his way up to second in the concluding laps of the race followed by Phil Schaffer, Bob Johnson, Shawn Morton, Mark Sult, Arnold Prater, and Andy Holderman. Roadrunner heat winners were won by Shaw and Prater.

Saturday, July 16, 1988 - Rainout

Saturday, July 23, 1988
Darland, Ronk Win Races At Warsaw Speedway
By Kim Gregory, Sports Writer

The usually calm Dave Darland of Lincoln, Ind. raised his hand in triumph as he started the feature on the outside of the last row and conquered an entire field of winged sprints to win the Hurryin' Hoosier lap feature Saturday at the Warsaw Speedway.

The race was led by Todd Vance from the drop of the green flag until unexpectedly his car ran out of fuel with only four laps remaining. Darland, who took third place on Lap 27 and second on Lap 33, gained the lead when Vance was sidelined, and took the checkered flag for the $2,000 win. Randy Kinser made a late charge for second place, followed by Joe Miller, Van Gurley, Denny England, Larry Bland, Jeff Walker and Bimbo Atkins.

Heat winners were Mark Christman, Kinser, Miller and Darland with Terry Shepherd picking up the quick time of 15.411. Dave Feese won the B-Main with Tim Norman coming in at a close second.

Dane Ronk won his heat and his second limited late-model feature in a row as he passed early leader William Varney and remained in front for the victory. Dewayne May and Butch Boggs battled back and forth for second place with May in front at the finish line for second and Boggs taking third place. Varney placed fourth followed by heat winner Jon Ormsby, Gerold Holloway, Tom Leiter and Roger Fitzpatrick.

This Saturday is Pit Night. All children and adults are allowed to visit the pits and visit their favorite drivers and cars, starting at 6:15 p.m. Sprints, limited late models and roadrunners will be on hand to compete, with the race winners receiving double points and pay.

Saturday, July 30, 1988 - Rainout

Tuesday, August 2, 1988
Warsaw Speedway Busy This Week

The Warsaw Speedway is proud to host two special events this week in conjunction with the Kosciusko County Fair. The first is the annual Demolition Derby which will take place Wednesday night. The popular derby is the hit of the fair week grandstand attraction that brings in over 40 wildly painted demolition cars ready to crash for the $600 first prize.

Fair Week racing continues Saturday night with the sprints, limited late models and roadrunners taking over the track. Trophies will be awarded for the sprints by Video World and the limited late model and roadrunner trophies will be provided by Lake City Service Center and Dirt Tracker Chassis.

Admission is the regular price of $6 for adults ($2 for admission to the fair and $4 at the gate) and $2 for children ages 6-12. The gates will open at 5 p.m. with all racing action starting at 8 p.m. at the fairgrounds in Warsaw.

Saturday, August 6, 1988
Exciting Action At Speedway
By Jim Amstutz, Sports Writer

It was a case of the "rich getting richer" Saturday night at the Warsaw Speedway. The top feature winner in each division this season chalked up another victory.

In Non-Winged Sprint Cars, Dave Darland of Lincoln scored his fifth victory of the season, his third in a row and fifth in the last seven events. Darland, starting on the pole, was outraced into the first corner by outside front-row starter Gary Fisher of Kokomo. Fisher opened up a lead as much as five car lengths early in the 25-lap race, but as the track dried out, Darland closed in. He began to challenge Fisher by the 10th lap, and finally took the lead on the 14th lap, speeding away for the win. A caution closed up the field with six laps to go, but it was no problem for Darland, who pulled away for a five-car length win. Fisher was second, with point leader Denny England third. Randy Woodling nipped Jeff Walker in a close race for fourth and fifth.

In Limited Late Models, Butch Boggs won his sixth feature of the season. He dueled with polesitter Ed Martin for the first part of the race, but took the lead for good on lap 10. He stayed in front the rest of the 20-lap distance, with Martin eventually dropping out in an accident. Bruce Hogue, in only his second Warsaw race this year, was second, with Ron McKenzie, in his first race since an accident injured him early this season, taking third, followed by William Varney and Harvey Hayes.

gln Roadrunners, Shane Denny won his seventh feature of the season, tops at the Warsaw track, in the 15-lapper. He passed Gary Fowler for the lead on the seventh lap and led the rest of the way. Fowler, Bill Morris, Arnold Prater and Andy Holderman completed the top five.

Racing continues at Warsaw this Saturday, with Ladies Night, featuring Non-Winged Sprints, Limited Lates and Roadrunners, plus free gifts for all women in attendance.

Tuesday, August 9, 1988
Warsaw Speedway To Have Races Saturday

The three point races are moving into the "home stretch" at Warsaw Speedway. Only four point events remain on the 1988 schedule at the quarter-mile dirt track, and one of those is this Saturday.

Non-Winged Sprint Cars, Limited Late Models and Roadrunners will be in action Saturday, on "Ladies Night". Free gifts will be given to all women in attendance.

In sprint cars, Denny England continues to lead the point standings going for his third straight championship. England, of Warsaw, leads with 235 points, followed by Jeff Walker of Arcadia, with 222 points. Dave Darland, of Lincoln, is third in points with 183 points. Darland has won the last three Sprint features at Warsaw, and five of the last seven. Prior to this season, Darland had never won a feature at Warsaw.

In Limited Late Models, the team of Ron McKenzie and Dane Ronk leads the points race. At Warsaw, points actually go to the car. McKenzie, driver of the #24 Camaro, was injured early in the season, and Ronk filled in, winning three features. Last Saturday, McKenzie returned, finished third in the feature and took the point lead with 335. Allen Marsh is in second with 331, followed by top feature winner Butch Boggs with 329.

In Roadrunners, Shane Denny has taken seven of the nine features, and leads with 300 points. Bill Morris, winner of the other two features, is second with 269. Time trials begin at 7 p.m., Saturday, with racing action starting at 8 p.m.

Saturday, August 13, 1988
Darland Takes Fourth In A Row At Speedway
By Kim Gregory, Sports Writer

Saturday night at the Warsaw Speedway put Dave Darland back in victory lane as he made it four wins in a row and six wins for the season in sprint feature wins.

Shane Denny picked up a $100 bonus from Dennie Electric for his eighth roadrunner feature win, while Butch Boggs made his limited late model feature victory the win of the year as he started out the evening by blowing an engine while qualifying. Boggs and his crew immediately left the speedway, dropped in a new engine, returned to the speedway and battled their way back for an emotional win.

Kurt Danner led early on in the sprint feature along with Jeff Walker who took over the lead on Lap 4. Darland quickly made his way up to second place and started to challenge Walker on Lap 7 with several side-by-side moves, but did not take the lead until Lap 14. Darland continued on for the win followed by Walker, Denny England, Randy Woodling, Danner, John Althouse, Randy Hutchinson and Kevin Atkins.

Sprint heat winners were England and rookie driver Tony Messinger, who won his first race ever. Woodling took the dash while Darland nearly broke the track record with a 16.77 time in qualifications.

In the limited late model feature, Butch Boggs closed in on early leader Ed Martin and gained the lead on Lap 7 in route to his seventh feature win of the year. Ron McKenzie placed second followed by Bruce Hogue, Allen Marsh, Martin, Dan Backus, Dewayne May and Doug Method. William Varney and fast qualifier May were limited late model heat winners, while Hogue took the four-lap dash.

Butch Boggs, Warsaw

In his strongest showing of the year, Gary Fowler held off dominating Shane Denny for 10 full laps of the roadrunner feature until Denny passed Fowler for the lead and the win at the checkered flag. Arnold Prater finished second, followed by Andy Holderman, Mark Sult, Phil Shafer, Mike Orr, Ray Dennis and Fowler with car trouble. Roadrunner heat winners were Denny and Prater.

The same three classes of racing will return to the Warsaw Speedway Saturday as the point races move into the final three weeks of competition.

Author's Note: Fortunately for Butch, Terry's Automotive was just down the road from the speedway! This was Butch's favorite win ever at Warsaw and one of his favorite stories to tell, of which I've heard at least 3-4 times, ha. I'll never forget watching them load up and pull out down behind the backstretch, then watching them fly back in with the car and the crowd cheering!

Saturday, August 20, 1988
May, Walker End Drought At Warsaw Speedway
By Kim Gregory, Sports Writer

Two three month dry spells were broken Saturday night as Jeff Walker of Arcadia, Ind., placed his No. 39 Jet Star, Walker Racing Fuel sprinter into victory lane and Dewayne May of Warsaw, put his Dick Woods Builders limited late model back in the winner's circle. For both, this was their second feature win of the season. Shane Denny continued to increase his point lead as he won his ninth roadrunner feature of the year in his Denny and Sons Trucking stock car.

In the sprint feature, Jeff Walker closed in on early leader, Brett Mann, and had the lead by lap four. Denny England gained on Walker and made several inside moves near the end of the 25 lap race, but Walker held him off for the win at the checkered flag. England with a smoking engine, finished second followed by Randy Hutchinson, Kurt Danner, Randy Woodling, Tony Metzinger, Alan Brown, and Kevin Atkins.

Jeff Walker, Arcadia

During sprint preliminaries, veteran driver, John Althouse, took the quick time during qualifying with a 17.16 clocking but in his heat flipped his sprint car several times on the front stretch causing the entire tail section to fly off of the car. Fortunately, Althouse walked back to the pits uninjured. Jon Ormsby barrel-rolled his sprinter during qualifying in turn one and wasn't as fortunate as Althouse, as he broke his collar bone but returned as a bandaged spectator after being released from the hospital. Heat winners were Rod Bailey and Rob Roberts while Kurt Danner picked up his first dash victory.

In limited late model action, Dewayne May closed in and ran side by side with Ed Martin until a spin on lap four by Martin put May in the lead. Ron McKenzie gave May several late race challenges and battled with May on the last lap, but May gained the edge in the fourth turn for the win. McKenzie was second with Doug Drudge, Bruce Hogue, Martin, Harvey Hayes, Charlie Shaw, next across the finish line. Limited late heats went to Gerold Holloway and May while McKenzie took the dash win and Butch Boggs had fast time.

Sixteen year old, Andy Holderman, led 2/3 of the roadrunner feature until Shane Denny reeled him in and passed for the lead to the finish. Holderman finished second followed by Arnold Prater, Ray Dennis, Gary Fowler, Scott Fitzpatrick, Robert Johnson, and David Coleman. Roadrunner heat winners were Denny and Dennis.

This Saturday is "Fan Appreciation Night" with the same three classes of cars in the next to the last week of points racing.

Saturday, August 27, 1988
Rain Wins At Speedway Once Again

For the third time this season the racing program at the Warsaw Speedway has been rained out as continuous showers fell on the track Saturday. This leaves only one more regular points race to determine the track champions which will be this Saturday during season championships.

Trophies will be given by Kercher Engines for all three championship features including the sprints, limited late models, and roadrunners.

Denny England is leading the sprint class with 294 points over Jeff Walker who has 281. If England holds on he would win his third track title and his second in a row. Ron McKenzie, the leader of the limited late model points, is 17 points ahead of Butch Boggs. Both England and McKenzie will have to make the show on Saturday to secure their championship.

Point standings as of August 29:

Sprints—Denny England, 294; Jeff Walker, 281; Randy Woodling, 234; Dave Darland, 231; Kurt Danner, 218.

Limited Late Models—Ron McKenzie, 395; Butch Boggs, 378; Doug Drudge, 355; Dewayne May, 343; William Varney, 299.

Roadrunners—Shane Denny, 358; Bill Morris, 307; Robert Johnson, 270; Gary Fowler, 250; and Arnold Prater, 231.

Saturday, September 3, 1988
Rains Wash Out Warsaw Racing

When it rains it pours on the Warsaw Speedway as drenching rains and thunderstorms flooded the infield into a large lake Saturday to rain out the races for the fourth time this season and for the second week in a row.

This time, it was the season championships that got washed out, but have been rescheduled for Sept. 17, with longer features and trophies for the top three feature finishers in each class. The season point champions will also be crowned that night with the top 10 in points receiving beautiful trophies in the sprint, limited late model, and roadrunner classes.

Friday is the fifth annual Warsaw Fall Classic for winged sprints paying $2,000 to the 40 lap feature winner and $200 to start.

Friday, September 9, 1988
Kinser Wins
By Kim Gregory, *Times-Union* Sports Writer

Another name was added to the prestigious list of winners of the Warsaw Fall Classic as Bloomington's Randy Kinser topped the 40 car field to win the winged sprint feature last Friday night at the Warsaw Speedway.

Kinser, driving the #7C Competition Engines sprint, started out the evening by winning the four-lap dash. His winning ways continued into the 40-lap feature as he battled back and forth with early leader, Tony Elliott, for several laps until a low line pass on lap 10 put Kinser in the lead to the checkered flag.

The most incredible showing was from Steve Kline as he started 15th and charged past 12 competitors by lap 26 to finish third in his best race ever at Warsaw. Elliott led every lap of the B Main to pick up the win. The C Main winner was Randy Hutchinson. Heat winners were Kevin Thomas, Kline, Joey Saldana, and Jerry Carrier while Atkins had fast time of the night with a 15.595 clocking during qualifications.

Only one show remains in the 1988 racing season which will be ran tonight. The Season Championships, previously rained out, will be attempted again with longer features for the sprints, late models, and roadrunners plus the crowning of the Season Points Champions.

Race Summary:

Qualifications, Fastest Six—Bimbo Atkins; Terry Shepherd; Rick Ferkel; Randy Kinser; Jeff Walker; Tony Elliott.
Four Lap Dash—Kinser; Ferkel; Shepherd; Atkins.
Heat One—Kevin Thomas; Tim Norman; Gary Fisher.
Heat Two—Steve Kline; Kinser; Rodney Duncan.
Heat Three—Joey Saldana; Dave Darland; Ferkel.
Heat Four—Jerry Carrier; Denny England; Troy Chahowski.
C Main—Randy Hutchinson; Kurt Danner; Brad Deveraux; Kevin Atkins.
B Main-Elliott; Brett Mann; Van Gurley; Walker; Todd Hutchinson.
Feature-Top 14—Kinser; Elliott; Kline; Ferkel; B. Atkins; Duncan; Fisher; Gurley; Shepherd; Thomas; England; Darland; Norman; Chahowski.

Saturday, September 17, 1988
Speedway Crowns Points Champions

Season champions were crowned and feature winners honored as the dust settled Saturday night at the Warsaw Speedway for the final race of the season.

Dave Darland, of Lincoln, Ind., in his #36D Darland sprint, picked up another feature win to become the winningest sprint driver this year. The season championship was won by Denny England of Warsaw, who led the points race for most of the year. England became one of the few drivers to ever win three championships in a row and this was his fourth title overall.

Limited late model season champion Ron McKenzie won his first feature of the season but his car won its fourth as McKenzie shared his title with young Dane Ronk who filled in to win three features in the car.

Arnold Prater won his first roadrunner feature of the year and Shane Denny won the roadrunner season championship as he dominated the class the entire year by winning nine feature events.

In the sprint feature, Darland started fourth but quickly made his way past Randy Woodling and England to lead all 30 laps to the checkered flag. England fought off several late race challenges from Tony Elliott to finish second followed by Elliott who started back in the 11th position, Woodling, John Althouse, rookie driver Tony Metzinger, Randy Hutchinson, and Kevin Atkins. The B Main went to Ed Kenens with Jesse Fordyce and Atkins winning the heats. Woodling won the dash event while Elliott nearly broke the track record with a fast time of 16.75 in qualifying.

McKenzie fought off several pass attempts from Butch Boggs in the limited late model feature but led all 25 laps for the win. Boggs finished second followed by Thames Goon, Doug Drudge, Bruce Hogue, Harvey Hayes, Allen Marsh and William Varney. Hogue and Varney won the limited late model heats with Drudge the dash victor.

In the roadrunner feature, Denny led the first seven laps when his car then broke and retired to the infield. Prater gained the lead and led the remaining laps for the win. Rookie driver, David Coleman, finished in second with Ray Dennis, Bob Johnson, Larry Staats, Gary Fowler Phil Shafer, and Mark Sult next across the finish line. Andy Holderman and Prater were the roadrunner heat winners.

Race Summary:
Sprints—Dash (four laps): Randy Woodling; Jeff Walker; Dave Darland
Heat one: Jesse Fordyce, Ed Kenens; Steve Imel
Heat two: Kevin Atkins; Darland; Walker
B Main: Kenens, Tom Patterson; Fordyce; Oscar Smith
Feature: Darland; Denny England; Tony Elliott; Woodling; John Althouse; Tony Metzinger; Randy Hutchinson, Atkins, Imel, Cary House.
Limited Late Models-Dash: Doug Drudge; Ron McKenzie; William Varney
Heat one: Bruce Hogue; Allen Marsh; Dewayne May
Heat two: Varney; Thames Goon; McKenzie
Feature: McKenzie; Butch Boggs; Goon; Drudge; Hogue; Harvey Hayes; Marsh; Varney; Gerold Holloway; Doug Method.
Roadrunners—Heat One: Andy Holderman; Phil Shafer; David Coleman
Heat two: Arnold Prater; Bill Morris; Shane Denny
Feature: Prater; Coleman; Ray Dennis; Bob Johnson; Larry Staats; Gary Fowler; Shafer; Mark Sult; Denny, Holderman.

Final Season Standings:
Sprint Car Points—Denny England, 319; Jeff Walker, 301; Dave Darland, 261; Randy Woodling, 260; Kurt Danner, 234; Randy Hutchinson, 205; Kevin Atkins, 191; John Althouse, 186; Rod Bailey, 175; Denny Dyson, 171.
Limited Late Model Points—Ron McKenzie/Dane Ronk, 425; Butch Boggs, 403; Doug Drudge/Allen Marsh, 382; Dewayne May, 343; William Varney, 323; Harvey Hayes, 315; Thames Goon, 206; Northern Indiana Paint Supply Car, 193; Gene Burkett, 177; Doug Method, 173.
Roadrunner Points-Shane Denny, 377; Bill Morris, 326; Bob Johnson, 292; Gary Fowler, 271; Arnold Prater, 260; David Baker, 225; Shawn Morton, 219; Ray Dennis, 209; Phil Shafer, 205; Mike Orr, 201.

Late-Fall, 1988
Warsaw Race Track Leases To 2 Private Individuals
By Julie Kelsey – Times Union Staff Writer, Pgs 1-2

The Kosciusko County Fair Association has leased the race track to two private individuals hoping the change will generate more funds and give board members more time to concentrate on other matters.

The track has been leased to Earl Gaerte and Dee Chapman. Gaerte, of Rochester, has been building racing engines for the past 20 years at his business, Gaerte Engines. Chapman, of Warsaw, is employed with Northern Indiana Paint Supply and said he has been a racing fan for several years.

Although the actual dollar amount of the lease was not disclosed, fair association president, John Hall, said it was at least twice the total amount of profit generated in 1988. According to the fair officials, the track netted approximately $10,000 profit last year. "The board does not have a lot of knowledge in racing or running the race track," said Hall. "By getting somebody in there with interest and experience, we hope it will eliminate problems and be more profitable." In addition, Hall said the lease agreement would give members of the fair association more time to concentrate on other matters. "We've got some real serious financial problems we need to deal with," said Hall.

Gaerte and Chapman said they would like to promote the Warsaw race track as a place for the entire family. "We need to get the community involved more," said Chapman. "We want to promote this as a community activity – a place where you can bring the whole family." A previous policy of no alcohol at the tracks will still be enforced, according to the lessees. And an agreement with the city to finish racing by 11p.m. will also be kept. "We see no reason why it (the 11p.m. curfew) cannot be met almost all the time," said Chapman. "Barring problems with the track, there's no reason why we can't be done by 11." The curfew is an agreement with the city that the noise will be quieted by that hour for the benefit of the track's neighbors.

Even though some things will remain the same, the lessees said they would like to make several changes and improvements. Clay added to the track is one of the first improvements Chapman said would have to be made. "In general we just want to give the whole place a facelift and make it look a lot nicer," he said. Those eye-appealing changes will include reseeding the grassy area in the infield to help eliminate dust; landscaping the ground just outside the track wall; and fix-up of the concession stands and bleachers. Private caterers will probably be used for concessions, according to Chapman.

"We are talking about several thousand dollars expense," said Chapman. He also said the work would not all be done at once, but would depend on the success of the gate sales. The classes and types of racing will not be changed and Gaerte said there would probably be only minor rule changes for the drivers. Gaerte and Chapman said they will be trying to schedule about 21 shows, up from the previous 18 and will also include rain dates for makeup shows. "There's no reason why this can't be the nicest racing facility in Indiana," said Chapman.

Author's Note: This is the article ran on the front page of the Times-Union that put a few Winona Lake residents over the edge and started legal proceedings that became public on June 28, 1989. I have a copy of their paperwork listed "Not for Publication" from the Winona Lake Preservation Association with comments written all over this article along with 13 "Points to note". Although many of the points are true, unfortunately, several of the 13 points listed and comments written are incorrect or totally false.

1989
Gaerte, Chapman, and Too Much of a Good Thing

At the end of the 1988 season, the Fairgrounds was offered and accepted a lease agreement for the 1989 season. Prominent engine builder, Earl Gaerte, and local businessman, Dee Chapman, went together to lease, manage, and promote the speedway with high hopes and big plans. To the fair board the deal sounded great giving them more than twice the profit generated for the entire '88 racing season.

In hindsight, this was the wave that broke the pontoon's back as Winona lakeside residents read the front page article in late fall 1988 promising more race shows, special events, and improvements to the track and racing facilities. Although in reality the season was very much the same as '88, the article was what put the disgruntled lake residents over the edge and suit was filed to discontinue all racing in June 1989, only one month into the racing season.

Warsaw racers in all classes were known around the Midwest as the guys to beat and racing went on as normal, full of excitement that included weekly racing of winged sprints, late models, and street stocks with special event visits from the All Star Circuit of Champions Sprints, Hurryin' Hoosier Sprint Series, and the 6th Annual Warsaw Fall Classic. No one thought with the 40-year history and vast majority of local residents supporting the speedway that there was any way the track could be shut down.

Saturday, May 13, 1989
Warsaw Speedway Gets Season Underway

Robert Johnson & John Althouse

Although wet and muddy conditions were prevalent across the Midwest, 33 winged sprint cars showed up Saturday night for the 1989 opening of the Warsaw Speedway. Terry Starks drove his winged sprint to his first feature win at Warsaw while Ron McKenzie started out the season in champion style with his first Late Model feature win.

In the winged sprint feature, Starks started on the pole and led to the finish as he fought off challenges from Mike Mann and Terry Shepherd in route to the checkered flag. Shepherd passed Jeff Walker with only two laps remaining for the second spot followed by Walker, Mann, Tony Elliott, Van Gurley, Tom Chalk and John Althouse. Starks, Mann and Gurley picked up wins in the winged sprint heats and Dane Ronk captured the B Main win.

In late model action, Glenn Bradley took the early lead of the feature event until lap four when Butch Boggs gained the first spot. Ron McKenzie and Bradley each then led several laps apiece until a flat tire side-lined Bradley and McKenzie paved the way to the finish for the win. Allen Marsh finished second with Terry Sroufe, Dave Fitzpatrick, Rick Spangler, Bradley and Randy Woodling next across the finish line. Boggs and Bruce Hogue were winners in the late model heats.

Saturday, May 20, 1989
Illinois Drivers Winning
By Kim Gregory, *Times Union* Correspondent

For the second week in a row, an Illinois driver has taken the winged sprint feature win. This week Kenny Haynes of Bourbonnais, Ill., won his first feature of the year. Glenn Bradley captured the late model victory, and last year's street stock champion, Shane Denny, won his first feature of the year.

In the winged sprint $1,000 feature, Van Gurley jumped in the early lead with Haynes right behind for the first 10 laps. As the two approached lapped traffic, Haynes shot by on the low side of the track and led to the checkered flag. Gurley finished second followed by Tom Chalk, A.J. Wendt and Randy Woodling. Haynes and fast qualifier Gurley won winged sprint heats while Chalk took the dash win.

Glenn Bradley got the early lead of the late model feature and led every lap for the win while Butch Boggs challenged for the lead several times, but finished second. Ed Martin was third with Allen Marsh and Ron McKenzie rounding out the top five. Late model fast qualifier, Bradley, and Boggs were heat winners and Marsh grabbed the four-lap dash.

Denny passed early leader Arnold Prater on lap six and led the remaining laps en route to the street stock feature win. Prater held on for second followed by Harvey Hayes, Scott Fitzpatrick and Larry Staats. Denny and Long were street stock heat winners.

This coming Memorial weekend will be a special two-day racing program. Saturday kicks off the weekend with the winged sprints, late models and street stocks as they fight for the oval track wins. On Monday, one of the largest demolition derbies in history will be featuring drivers from all over the Midwest as they compete for $5,000.

Saturday, May 27, 1989
Local Race Track Has Busy Weekend
By Kim Gregory, for the *Times-Union*

Van Gurley, of Mishawaka, became the third different winged sprint feature winner in three weeks Saturday night at the Warsaw Speedway. Winning his second late model feature in a row was Glenn Bradley of Marion, while Bryon Fox won his first street stock feature of the year.

Kenny Haynes took a commanding lead of the winged sprint feature and led for 17 laps until Gurley closed in a battle side-by-side with Haynes for five laps. Gurley continued to challenge and swung by to take the lead and the win. Haynes finished a close second and was followed by Joe Saldana, Randy Woodling, Brett Mann, Bimbo Atkins, John Althouse and John Mapes. Haynes and Gurley took the winged sprint heats while Atkins won the four-lap dash and Saldana had the quick time.

Bimbo Atkins Dash Win, photo by David Hamrick

The late model feature was also a two-car battle for first as leader, Chris Patterson, and Bradley raced nose-to-tail and side by side for the first 22 laps. Bradley finally took over command of the race on the 23rd lap to take the checkered flag. Patterson finished second with Butch Boggs, Terry Sroufe, Allen Marsh, Andy Piercefield, Gary Baker and Ed Martin rounding out the top eight. Patterson took the late model dash win and the first of two heat races. Ron McKenzie won the second heat race and Bradley was clocked with the fastest time.

In the street stock action, Fox fought off a chase for the lead from Jeff Bucher and led every lap for the feature win. Bucher came across the line in second, followed by Harvey Hayes, William Varney, Larry Staats, Joe Leek, Jay Nordman and Russ Lowry. The street stock heats were won by Hayes and Shane Denny.

Saturday, June 3, 1989 - Rainout

Saturday, June 10, 1989
Elliott Sprint Winner
By Kim Gregory, for the *Times-Union*

Warsaw's Tony Elliott became the fourth different winged sprint feature winner in four races Saturday night at the Warsaw Speedway over a field of 33 cars. Glenn Bradley continued his winning streak by making it three late model feature wins in a row and Joe Leek won his first street stock feature ever.

Elliott took a commanding lead in the winged sprint feature and never looked back as he led every lap and took the checkered flag for the $1,000 win. The battle in the race was for the second spot as Bimbo Atkins and Terry Shepherd went wheel to wheel on nearly every circuit. Shepherd on the low side of the track, finished second, and Atkins placed third. Fourth went to Van Gurley, followed by Joe Saldana, Mike Mann, Steve Kline and Tom Chalk.

Winged sprint heats went to Kenny Haynes, Kevin Atkins, Denny England and Hank Lower, who also won the B-Main followed by Haynes. Shepherd took the 4-lap dash and Gurley had a quick time of 14.76.

In late model action, Bryan Dunaway went from fourth to second in one lap and ran side by side with Glenn Bradley for the lead near the end of the 25-lap contest, but he came up short as Bradley came out the victor in the feature. Dunaway finished second with Butch Boggs, Tom Beezley and Bruce Hogue in the top five. Hogue and Ed Martin were late model heat winners, while Boggs took the dash. Dunaway had the fast time of 16.88.

In his first win ever, got the early lead in the street stock feature and stayed out front to win over a full track. Harvey Hayes passed Jeff Bucher on lap 8 for second place, followed by Arnold Prater and Mike Orr in the top five. Street stock heats went to Hayes and Leek.

Saturday is Family Night, with all children under 12 years of age admitted free and many prizes given away, including two bicycles.

Saturday, June 17, 1989
Kline Steals Sprint Win
By Kim Gregory, for the *Times-Union*

Steve Kline & Flagman, Dale Bolinger

Saturday night action at the Warsaw Speedway saw Warsaw's Steve Kline become the fifth new face in the winged sprint winner's circle this year in his Video World No. 12. In contrast, Glenn Bradley is proving to be the dominant force in late model competition, winning his fourth feature in a row, while Shane Denny got back on the winning track by picking up his second street stock feature win of the year.

Although it was Van Gurley taking the early lead in the winged sprint feature with Tom Chalk comfortably behind, a battle was brewing between Kline and Terry Shepherd in third and fourth. By lap 10, Kline and Shepherd were side by side, had passed Chalk in second, and were closing in on the leader.

All three were neck to neck by lap 15, but it was Kline who powered by on the low side of the track to take the lead and the checkered flag. Shepherd finished second, followed by

Gurley, Brett Mann and Chalk. Sprint heat winners were Gurley, Tony Elliott and Randy Woodling. Mann won the 4-lap dash. Woodling picked up the B main win, and Shepherd set a new track record in qualifying with a 14.38 clocking.

The late model feature was all Bradley, as he jumped out in front from his second row starting position and led every lap for the win. Butch Boggs closed in on Bradley several times to challenge for the lead but had to settle for the second place finish. Dewayne May placed third with Frank Sedar and Terry Sroufe rounding out the top five. Boggs and Sedar took the heat wins, while Bradley won the dash. Dick Potts broke the late model track record with a 16.27 time.

Heat winner Chuck Maley took the early lead in the street stock feature, but then Denny and Harvey Hayes closed in. Both passed Maley with Denny out front and Hayes nose to tail behind. Hayes closed to race side by side with Denny for several laps, but at the finish it was Denny, with Hayes placing second. William Varney finished third, followed by heat winner Andy Holderman and Jeff Bucher.

Included in Saturday's "Family Night" was the giveaway of two ten-speed bicycles. The winners of the bicycles were Amy Carr and Lucus Monnier. Promotions continue this Saturday with "4-H Night" at which all 4-H members with identification will receive free admission. Also, 10 percent of all grandstand receipts will be donated to 4-H for achievement trip awards.

Saturday, June 24, 1989
Elliott Repeat Winner
By Kim Gregory, for the *Times-Union*

Warsaw's Tony Elliott became the first repeat winged sprint feature winner on 4-H Night Saturday at the Warsaw Speedway in his silver No. 57. Winning their first features of the year were Tom Beezley of Churubusco in his No. 69 late model and Akron's Jeff Bucher in his No. 37 street stock.

Elliott jumped out front in the 25-lap winged sprint feature and paved the way on every circuit to receive the checkered flag for the win. Bimbo Atkins and Terry Shepherd battled side by side for the second spot, with Atkins edging out the runner-up position at the finish. Shepherd placed third, followed by Brett Mann, Randy Woodling and Jeff Walker. Heat winners were Atkins, Denny England and Sam Davis, while Mann took the 4-lap dash and Steve Kline had the quick time of 14.87.

In late model feature action, Terry Sroufe grabbed the early lead with Butch Boggs right behind. On lap 11, Boggs pulled alongside Sroufe and the two continued to battle for the lead for several laps. Just as Boggs pulled ahead to gain control of the race, he spun in turn one and left the lead open for a last lap battle between Sroufe and Tom Beezley. Beezley swung by on the low side in turn four and took the win at the finish. Glenn Bradley was next, followed by Sroufe, Ray Chambers and Bruce Hogue. Beezley and J. Roberts were late model heat winners, and Dick Potts took the dash while C. Roberts had the fast time.

Chuck Maley took the early lead of the street stock feature until Jeff Bucher closed in and took the lead to the finish for the win. Shane Denny moved up from the last starting position to fight for the lead, but had to settle for second, followed by Andy Holderman, William Varney and Russ Lowry. Street stock heat winners were Varney and Bryan Fox.

This Saturday is Hoosier Tire Night. Monday, July 3, the U.M.P. late models will invade the track for the annual Fourth of July Celebration. The program will also include street stocks and a gigantic fireworks display over the shores of Winona Lake.

Wednesday, June 28, 1989
Fair Board Sued - Suit seeks speedway closure, plus $500,000
By Gary Gerard, Times Union Managing Editor, pages 1-2

A suit seeking $500,000 in damages and the permanent closure of the Warsaw Speedway has been filed in Kosciusko Circuit Court. The suit, filed Tuesday afternoon names the Kosciusko County Fair Association, Inc., Earl Gaerte and Dee Chapman as defendants. Chapman, of Rt. 2, Pierceton, and Gaerte, of Rochester, are the promoters who operate the racetrack. The Fair Association owns the racetrack and leases it to Chapman and Gaerte.

The suit was filed by a group of nine Winona Lake property owners including James A. Cummins, 2012 N. Bay Drive; Robert L. Fuson, 1013 Country Club Lane, Michael G. Hall, 1031 Country Club Lane; R. John Handel, 1230 Country Club Drive, George M. Haymond, 945 Country Club Lane, J. Joseph Shellabarger, 1105 Country Club Lane; Frederic T. Stephens, 54 Fairlane Dr., Kenneth O. Truman, 606 S. Colfax St., and H. Rex Wildman, 506 S. Colfax St.

The suit states the plaintiffs all reside within a one-half mile radius of Warsaw Speedway and that the area is "densely settled and predominantly residential." The suit claims that the races conducted at the speedway "constitute a nuisance to the plaintiffs."

The suit, in part, claims:
- ✓ "noise, dust and air pollution produced by the ...racing...interferes with plaintiffs' quiet and reasonable use of their homes.
- ✓ "noise from the race track makes it impossible for the plaintiffs...to carry on a conversation in a normal tone of voice, prevents the enjoyment of outdoor activities, prevents listening to television programs without turning the sound at high volume and causes windows to rattle.
- ✓ "a loud speaker or public address system operates continually at the racetrack...before the races end. Although the races are scheduled to end at 11 p.m. they usually extend past that time. The loud speaker then operates again for approximately one hour after the races.
- ✓ "most of the ...races have been held on weekends and holidays, which is the normal leisure time for plaintiffs, and the noise...has made it impossible for plaintiffs to enjoy the undisturbed use of their homes.
- ✓ "the...races cause the release of exhaust fumes and dust clouds to be released into the air and to contaminate the homes of plaintiffs.
- ✓ "the clouds of dust and smoke permeate the area and residences of the plaintiffs

(causing) a continuing nuisance ... These noises, smells and contamination cause irreparable damages to plantiffs' health and property, and prevent the full enjoyment of plaintiffs' property."

Also, the suit claims the Fair Association has been asked by the plaintiffs on numerous occasions since 1977 to eliminate the races without success. The plaintiffs are asking that the Fair Association, Gaerte and Chapman, be permanently enjoined from operating any type of motor vehicle racing at the fairgrounds. The suit also seeks a judgment of $500,000 against the defendants for "costs and for all other just and proper relief."

Saturday, July 1, 1989
Atkins, Boggs Win At Local Track
By Kim Gregory, for the *Times Union*

Bimbo Atkins, Crew, & Irish Saunders

Two new winners made their debut in victory lane on Hoosier Tire Night Saturday at the Warsaw Speedway. Bimbo Atkins took the winged sprint feature event in his No. 36 Milford Motors car and Butch Boggs, in the Northern Indiana Paint Supply-Smith Machine Shop No. 4, grabbed the late model feature.

In winged sprint competition, Jeff Walker led from the start, but after only 5 laps, his car broke and Steve Kline assumed the lead. Brian Tyler moved in to challenge Kline and Atkins closed in on the leaders to make the race a three-car battle. Atkins went back and forth with Kline near the end and pulled out front for the win at the checkered. Kline took 2nd followed by Tyler, Brett Mann (who rolled his car earlier in the race), Randy Woodling, Dane Ronk, Sam Davis and Jim Bradford. Sprint heat winners were Denny England and Mann, while Tyler took the 4-lap dash and Atkins had a quick time at 15.28.

Glenn Bradley had a commanding lead of the late model feature when on lap 15 his car slowed and the lead was left open for Dewayne May. Butch Boggs started to close in on May and on the

Dee Chapman & Butch Boggs

final lap, they were side by side. As the two approached lapped traffic in turn four, Boggs dipped down low to get the edge and nose out May in a near photo finish. May finished second, followed by Bruce Hogue, Ray Chambers, Bradley, Tom Beezley, Dave Gray, Gary Baker and Doug Method. Beezley and Hogue were late model heat winners, while Bradley was the dash winner and May was the fast qualifier.

Street Stock heat winners were Arnold Prater and Shane Denny, but the feature was delayed due to curfew.

Saturday, July 1, 1989
Race Track Case Could Hinge On Precedent Case
By Dan Spalding, Times-Union Staff Writer, Pages 1-2

Warsaw and Waterloo, N.Y., may be miles apart, but plaintiffs in the pending Warsaw Race Track suit feel the two towns have something in common.

A group of nine Warsaw property owners living within a half-mile of the race track filed suit in Kosciusko Circuit Court Tuesday seeking $500,000 in damages and a permanent closing of the Kosciusko County Fairgrounds Race Track. Earl Gaerte and Dee Chapman, who are operating the track, along with the Kosciusko County Fair Association, have been named as defendants.

While plenty of evidence will be prepared on behalf of the plaintiffs documenting noise levels and dust samples that result from the race track operations, plaintiffs may also point to comparisons of a similar case in Waterloo, N.Y. In that case, a group of residents living near the Seneca County Fairgrounds filed suit to close the racetrack. After an 18-month court case that included death threats and a counter suit, the race track was closed by the courts. However, the judge ruled the track could be used on one night during the annual county fair, said Bruce Ike, a resident of the central New York state village who sought to have the track closed. "God bless them. If they're really going to go for it, they're in for a long hard battle."

The Waterloo case, which began about 1980, was soon taken over by the New York State Attorney General's office. Ike said noise ordinances of that type were difficult to enforce at that time, but because of the neighbors' proximity to the track, "they jumped at it," Ike said. Ike said noise from the track often shook picture windows, "The area of the track – where it was to the homes was not conducive to a family atmosphere," he said.

Like some of the Warsaw plaintiffs, Ike said he received harassing phone calls threatening to cause damage to his home and family. In an attempt to silence Ike, defendants filed a counter suit alleging malicious harassment against him, he said. The counter suit was eventually dropped. "The scars have healed…but it was a real long battle," Ike said.

Like the Waterloo case, Warsaw plaintiffs are expected to argue that the race track is a public nuisance that obstructs area resident's quiet enjoyment of their property. And like Waterloo, the race track is a long-standing fixture of the community. "We wouldn't have filed the lawsuit if we didn't believe there was a significant chance of being successful," Snyder said.

Counter arguments by race track representatives suggesting that property owners knowingly purchased land near the existing track may not carry substantial weight in court, Snyder said. "When the logical course of development is around the particular nuisance center the fact that the nuisance was pre-existing is a factor, but not a major factor to be considered," he said.

Snyder said he doubts an out-of-court settlement will occur. "All attempts at compromise before have been unsuccessful. I'm not sure why it would be any different at this point," he said. Max Reed, an attorney for the fair association, declined comment on the case earlier this week. Chapman had no comment Wednesday.

Saturday, July 8, 1989
Denny Wins Third
By Kim Gregory, for the *Times Union*

Michigan driver Brian Tyler became the seventh different winged sprint feature winner in eight races Saturday night as the competition remains close at the Warsaw Speedway. Terry Sroufe of Huntington won his first late model feature of the year while Shane Denny of Claypool became the first driver to win three street stock features this year.

In winged sprint action, the evening was all Brian Tyler as he made the night a clean sweep by winning the dash, heat and feature events. In the feature, Tyler jumped out front and led the field to the checkered flag for the win. Steve Kline placed second, followed by Bimbo Atkins, Rob Roberts and Brett Mann, who earlier flipped his car.

Terry Sroufe paved the way of the late model feature to lead every lap for the victory. Glenn Bradley made his way up from the sixth starting position to finish second with Dewayne May, Butch Boggs and Ron McKenzie next across the finish line.

In the street stock feature, Arnold Prater grabbed the lead and looked like he would stay out front, but with only a few laps remaining, Shane Denny closed in and passed for the lead and the win. Second place went to William Varney, followed by Harvey Hayes, Andy Holderman and Joe Leek. Prater was sixth.

Saturday, July 15, 1989
Hood Wins Outlaw
By Kim Gregory, for the *Times-Union*

After the dust settled over the Warsaw Speedway Saturday night, it was Ricky Hood of Indianapolis taking the 40-lap All-Star Outlaw Sprint feature in front of a packed house. It was Hood's second straight All-Star win at Warsaw, in which he pocketed over $4,000 for his efforts.

Van Gurley, Mishawaka

The 20-car field was led by Van Gurley from the drop of the green flag, with Terry Pletch and Dave Blaney close behind. Blaney made a move for second on the fourth lap and got by only to red flag the event when he rolled the car in turn three. On the restart, Hood was in third and closing in on Pletch for second. By lap 12, he had passed Pletch. Gurley was next on his list as Hood took the high side of the track and reeled him in by the 15th circuit. The two battled side-by-side for nearly ten laps when Hood took the lead for good. Pletch passed Gurley with only five laps remaining for second, followed by Gurley, Danny Smith, Robbie Stanley, Rocky Hodges, Bimbo Atkins and Steve Kline.

Blaney took the Dash for Cash heat, and had a quick time of 14.584. Other heat winners were Steve Seigel and Steve Butler, while Stanley grabbed the B-main win with Tony Elliott second. Brett Mann flipped his sprint in turn 3 to land the car totally suspended on top of the wall in the B-Main, but he was uninjured.

Brett Mann, Goshen

The street stock also took to the track but saw very limited action as the pit area and half of the track suddenly went dark on lap 5 of the feature. The conclusion of the event will be held Saturday with 16-year-old Rusty Lowry in the lead. He had led from the start. Street stock heat winners were Arnold Prater and Shane Denny.

This Saturday the winged sprints, late models and street stocks will be back in action, with the first race beginning at 7 p.m.

Saturday, July 22, 1989
Hayes Wins Two
By Kim Gregory, for the *Times-Union*

For the third time this year, the winged sprint feature event was captured by Warsaw's Tony Elliott Saturday night in his Kercher Engines-sponsored No. 57. Glenn Bradley made his way back into victory lane by picking up the late model feature, while Harvey Hayes made a sweep of the street stock events as he took both the make-up and regular feature wins.

Bimbo Atkins jumped out front in the sprint feature, with Elliott close behind. Elliott pulled up to challenge Atkins in a side-by-side battle for the lead by lap six and got by to take command. He led the rest of the contest, with Atkins and Joey Saldana picking up second and third. The final lap was a red flag as a three-car pileup in turn three and four blocked the track. Finishing in fourth was Jeff Walker, followed by Dane Ronk, Brett Mann and John Hadjuk.

In late model action, Glenn Bradley took advantage of his front row start, leading the race flag to flag to pick up the win. Butch Boggs powered by Dewayne May on the final lap for a second place finish, followed by May on the final lap for a second-place finish, followed by May, Terry Hull and Terry Sroufe.

Although Rusty Lowry was the leader of the street stock feature when the electricity went out July 15, Harvey Hayes came across the finish line first in the conclusion of the event Saturday. Joe Leek took second, followed by Shane Denny, William Varney and Lowery. In the 15-lap street stock scheduled feature, Charles Maley got the early lead until lap five, when Hayes closed in and passed for the lead and the win. Denny came up from the back of the pack to take second, with Varney, Leek and Prater in the top five.

Saturday, July 29, 1989
Kline Wins Second
By Kim Gregory, for the *Times-Union*

Warsaw native Steve Kline found the low side of the track to his liking Saturday night as he powered by the field en route to his second winged sprint feature victory this season at the Warsaw Speedway. Glenn Bradley continues to lead the late model class, picking up his sixth feature win, and 17-year-old Andy Holderman won his first street stock feature.

Brad Boyer took the early lead in the winged sprint feature, with Van Gurley and Kline next in line. Gurley and Kline started to close in on Boyer, and by lap 11 they were in a three-way battle for the lead. Kline chose the low groove and pulled ahead to gain the first spot and take the checkered flag. Bimbo Atkins placed second as he used the high side cushion to take over the position in lap 15, while Randy Woodling finished third. Fourth went to Gurley, followed by Boyer and Brian Tyler. Sprint heat winners were Boyer and Kevin Atkins, with Bimbo Atkins taking the 4-lap dash and Kline having the quick time of 14.41.

In late model action, Glenn Bradley jumped out in the lead from the drop of the green flag and led every lap to pick up the win. Terry Sroufe and Dewayne May swapped positions on lap 5 and again on lap 7, but at the finish it was May in second and Sroufe finishing third. Terry Hull was fourth with Bill Morris, Ron McKenzie and Ray Chambers next to cross the finish line. Sroufe and Chambers were late model heat winners, while Bradley took the dash and Tom Beezley had the fast time.

Harvery Hayes, Warsaw

Heat winner Andy Holderman took advantage of the front row starting position to gain the early lead of the street stock feature and stay out in front for the win. Shane Denny battled his way up from the back of the pack to challenge for the lead near the end of the race, but had to settle for second place at the finish. Charles Maley placed third, followed by David Baker, Rusty Lowry, William Varney and Harvey Hayes.

This Saturday night will be Fair Night Racing, with the first appearance of TQ Midgets on the ¼ mile clay oval. The late model class will be racing for $800 to win, and the street stocks will complete the program.

Saturday, August 5, 1989
Bradley Dominating
By Kim Gregory for the Times-Union

The United Midget Racing Association (UMRA) made its first appearance at the Warsaw Speedway Saturday night with points leader Ronnie Combs of Greensburg, IN, picking up his third UMRA feature win of the year. Glenn Bradley continues to dominate the late model class as he won his third feature in a row for the second time this season, and William Varney took home his first street stock feature of the year.

Larry Martz took the early lead of the UMRA midget feature until Ronnie Combs closed in to pass for the lead on lap 4. Combs held off Terry Goff near the half-way mark to win. Goff placed second, followed by Tony Stewart, Mark Rutter and John Linville. Midget heat wins went to Combs and Jerry Melloncamp, while Rutter took the dash win and Lynn Ambrose had the fast time.

In late model action, Bruce Hogue passed first-lap leader Ed Martin with Terry Sroufe and Glenn Bradley close behind. By lap 6, Hogue, Sroufe and Bradley were three abreast for the lead, but it was Bradley who pulled ahead of the pack and away from the field to capture the win. Tom Beezley moved up to finish second with Dewayne May, Terry Hull, Sroufe and Terry Shepherd in the top six. Martin and Dave Fitzpatrick were the late model heat winners, with the dash going to Bradley and the quick time to May.

Although Harvey Hayes started on the pole of the street stock feature and led every lap to come across the finish line in the first position, an after-race rule infraction disqualified Hayes, and William Varney, who came across in second, was declared the winner. Shane Denny started the race in the 18th position, but battled his way through the field to place second, followed by Charles Maley, Scott Fitzpatrick, David Baker, David Coleman and Max Goldwood. The street stock heat wins went to Denny and Fitzpatrick.

This Saturday the winged sprints will be back in action for the $1,000 first prize, along with the late models and street stocks. This will also be a special discount night with all W.A.S.P. members receiving $2 off the regular gate admission.

Saturday, August 12, 1989 – Rainout

Saturday, August 19, 1989
Kline Battles For Win

In racing action Saturday night at the Warsaw Speedway, Steve Kline of Warsaw battled through the field to pick up his third winged sprint feature of the season in his No. 12 Video World car. Terry Sroufe of Huntington took the UMP late model feature win in his No. 12 car while Andy Holderman captured his second street stock feature of the year.

Steve Kline used all 25 laps of the winged sprint feature to claim the win as he passed for third on lap 17, was in second by lap 20 and sneaked by early leader Chuck Wilson with only three laps remaining to take the win. Randy Woodling stayed near the front the entire race to place second, followed by Bob Teeple, Bill Tyler, Dane Ronk and Wilson.

The event was red-flagged as Sam Davis got high on the race surface in turn three and snap-rolled his sprint end over end and landed over the wall. Davis was taken to the hospital, but fortunately, was later released uninjured.

In late model action, former sprint car driver Terry Shepherd paved the way the entire race until his car slowed with only two laps to go. Second place runner Terry Sroufe took over the lead and the win. Tom Beezley placed second with Bruce Hogue, Dave Gray and

Art Leiter following.

Street stock racing was led by the youngest drivers on the track as 16-year-old Rusty Lowry picked up his first win ever in the heat and led the early laps until 17-year-old Andy Holderman closed in. Holderman captured the lead on lap 8 and went on for the checkered flag. Heat winner Shane Denny moved through the field to second, followed by Lowery, Jeff Bucher, William Varney, Larry Staats and Kelly Prater.

This Saturday night will be the late model season championship, and $1500 for the winged spring feature. The street stocks will complete the program slated for 7 p.m.

Saturday, August 26, 1989
Elliott Takes Sprint Race
By Sharon Lowry, *Times Union* Sports Writer

Bimbo Atkins led the sprints with points this season, but Tony Elliott took the feature title followed by Randy Woodling, Jeff Walker, Steve Kline, and Atkins. Glenn Bradley led the late model points for the season and topped that honor with a championship win Saturday night.

Tony Elliott & young fans

Bradley led every lap with Terry Shepherd in hot pursuit and Steve Pastua, Terry Hull and Mike Bechelli close behind. The sprint winners Saturday were: Elliott, Joe Saldana, Denny England and Robert Johnson. The late model sprints were won by Bechelli, Dennis Erb and Ron Kekkema.

Shane Denny led the street stock division in points and added another victory to his total Saturday with a feature win. Arnold Prater was a close second and Dave Barker, Andy Holderman and Joe Meek all gave chase. The sprint dash trophy went to Kenny Haynes, while Tom Beezley won the late model trophy dash. Salvana won the B-main race with Butch Boggs close behind. Brett Mann was third.

Trophies were awarded to the top five point leaders in each division. Winning in the sprints were: Atkins, Kline, Woodling, Dane Ronk and Mann. In the late model classs the winners were: Bradley, Terry Sroufe, Boggs, Dewayne May and Ron McKenzie. The street stock winners were: Denny, Prater, Bill Varney, Joe Leek and Holderman.

Drivers and officials voted on new awards which were presented at the first Awards

Night. The rookie of the year went to Russ Lowry, who was 16 years old and the youngest driver at the track. He raced in the street stock division. The Driver Sportsmanship Award went to Boggs in the late model division; Van Gurley in the sprint division; and Prater and Denny in the street stock. The Broken Wrench Award went to Scott Fitzpatrick.

Author's Note: Some of the information and names are odd in this race, but unfortunately I wasn't there that night. One of the only races I missed since being a kid. This was my wedding day and it killed me to have my reception at the Fairground's Shrine Building watching the race cars pull in. If I had to do it all over again, I would have gone to the races after the reception, wedding dress and all!

Monday, August 28, 1989
WASPs' request swatted away
By Dan Spalding, *Times-Union* Staff Writer

WASPers were abuzz at Monday's adoption of the 1990 Warsaw City budget. For a second time, representatives of Warsaw Auto Speedway Patrons (WASP) voiced their displeasure with plans by the city to provide Winona Lake Preservation Association with $1,500 in 1990. About 10 members of WASP - a group organized to fight attempts to close the race track - attended the meeting at city council chambers.

WASP president Lloyd Smith said his group objects to the funding because the money could be used to close the track. Winona Lake Preservation Association (WLPA), has led attempts in a court battle to close the track because of noise from the track during races. Although WLPA is not listed as a plaintiff in the court case, it is seeking donations to support its legal efforts, and members of the group are named in the suit, which includes nine plaintiffs.

"Please do not insult taxpayer's intelligence by giving us the old yarn that the tax money given to the WLPA will be kept separated and not used to support the "Wealthy Nine's lawsuit," said Smith. "Our tax dollars could replace money for some other Winona Lake Preservation activities, freeing their money to be given in support of closing the track.

Council members approved the budget nonetheless. Despite the council's action, further cuts are expected later because of delays in determining property reassessment. Plank defended the $1,500 proposal, saying that those funds are to be used strictly for water conservation activities. Other council members objected to the group's protest. Councilman Bob Gast said he believed WASP was "making a mountain out of a molehill."

Warsaw also provides money to Pike Lake and Center Lake for environmental uses. Plank suggested the city could give WLPA money for specific uses, but the proposal was not acted upon.

Friday, September 1, 1989
Smith Takes First In Classic
By Kim Gregory Baney, Times Union Staff Writer

For the second time in the six-year history of the Warsaw Fall Classic, the Gohr Racing Team has taken home the winner's trophy, as Danny Smith of Danville rode the high side of the track en route to his first victory at Warsaw.

After a multi-car crash occurred on lap 1 of the 30-lap winged sprint feature, the race resumed. Terry Shepherd took the lead, with Joey Saldana right behind. Smith closed in to pass Saldana on the 6th circuit and put his sights on Shepherd as he started to reel in the first place car. With Shepherd down low and Smith racing on the high side, Smith had closed in to race side by side with Shepherd by lap 12, and was in the lead by lap 13. Smith stayed out front for the victory with Shepherd in second and Bimbo Atkins placing third. Saldana was fourth, followed by Randy Kinser, Steve Kline, Chuck Wilson and Rodney Ritter Jr.

Shepherd took the B-Main win with Jim Bradford and Kline in second and third, while Smith also won his heat and had fast time of 14.97. Other heat winners were Tony Elliott, Brian Tyler, Kinser, and Tom Chalk, while Bradford took the 4-lap dash win.

In street stock action, the two heat winners were the two top contenders in the feature as Shane Denny made his way up from the tail of the field to pass early leader William Varney on lap 9 and continue out front for the win at the drop of the checkered flag. Varney finished in second, with Dewayne May, Arnold Prater, Scott Fitzpatrick, Chuck Maley, Kelly Prater and Rusty Lowry rounding out the top eight.

1990
The Black Flag Falls

After the suit was filed during the 1989 season, the fairgrounds took back the management of the speedway for the final year of racing with Don Prater as the promoter and manager. W.A.S.P. (Warsaw Auto Speedway Patrons), a group of Warsaw race fans and supporters of the track, attempted to raise funds along with several private individuals who ended up with extensive monetary support to fight the lawsuit, but despite all efforts, the fair board decided to sign an agreement with the Winona Lake plaintiffs to stop racing and the lawsuit was dropped. Although the vast majority of the community supported the speedway and hundreds of "Letters to the Editor" were written, the signed agreement called for racing to come to an end on Saturday night, August 11, 1990 during the last night of the county fair. Even with the decision to close looming, the racing for the shortened season was full of excitement and great competition. The final night was filled with emotion, drawing an estimated 4,000 fans including television news crews, local media and national racing reporters. Racing went into the early morning with all mufflers being removed as the racers form of protest. The light signals from each turn were removed as souvenirs and drivers and fans visited in the pits until nearly 4am. Many drivers went on to race at other speedways and some never raced again. Many never stepped foot on the fairgrounds again after that day no matter what the event.

Saturday, May 12, 1990 - Rainout

Saturday, May 19, 1990
Warsaw Wet Again

For the second straight week, the season opener of the Warsaw Speedway was cancelled Saturday night due to inclement weather. The track will try to race its opening show this Saturday, May 26th, in one of the latest openings in the speedway's 4 decade history. Featured will be the winged sprints, hobby stocks, and street stocks in a Memorial Weekend Racing Program. Gates will open at 4 p.m. with time trials at 6 and racing at 7 p.m.

Saturday, May 26, 1990
Warsaw Speedway Kicks Off Season
By Kim Baney, *Times-Union* Correspondent

After two weeks of rain, the season opener of the Warsaw Speedway finally got underway Saturday with Kenny Haynes of Boubonnais, Ill., taking the long-awaited winged sprint feature. Rusty Lowry won his first feature ever in the hobby stock class, while Joe Leek took the street stock feature.

In winged sprint action, Bimbo Atkins jumped out front of the feature field to a commanding lead until lap 15 when Jeff Walker and Haynes started to close the gap. Haynes, in the third spot, swung by both frontrunners to take the lead on the 18th circuit and went on to take the checkered flag. Atkins finished second, followed by Walker, Van Gurley, Blake Hollingsworth, Randy Woodling, Tony Ploughe and Ray Starks.

Andy Holderman gained the early lead of the hobby stock feature, but was quickly overcome by strong-runner Ron McKenzie. McKenzie pulled away from the field in what looked to be an easy win. But with only six laps remaining in the contest, the driveshaft dropped off the car, leaving him stranded. Lowry picked up the lead and continued on for the win with Rick Day placing second and Tom Leiter third. Scott Fitzpatrick, Dewayne May, McKenzie, Doug Method and Holderman completed the top eight. Fast qualifier McKenzie picked up the dash win, while Holderman won the hobby stock heat.

The street stock feature was a battle of the red cars as Leek, William Varney and John Oliver held the first three positions the entire race. Heat winner Leek got by early leader Varney and led to the finish for the win, while Oliver took over the second spot on lap 7 and held on. Varney was third, followed by Larry Staats, Carl Kendricks and Arnold Prater. This Saturday will be the first visit this season by the All Star Circuit of Champions winged sprints with the first race starting at 7 p.m.

Saturday, June 2, 1990
Rain Washes Out Speedway Action

For the third time in four weeks, racing action at the Warsaw Speedway had to be called off due to poor weather conditions.

Saturday night was scheduled to be All Star Circuit of Champions action when rain doused the end of the qualifying. A rain date has been set for June 29 when the group will return for a full evening of racing and the $4,000 to win feature prize. All tickets and pit passes for the All-Star show will be redeemable for the raindate. Saturday will have a full line-up of winged sprint, hobby stocks and street stocks beginning at 7 p.m.

Saturday, June 9, 1990
Haynes, McKenzie, Leek Race Winners
By Kim Baney, *Times-Union* Correspondent

Ron McKenzie, Claypool

Kenny Haynes, Bourbonnais, Ill., powered his black #3k to its second winged sprint feature win in two shows Saturday night at Warsaw Speedway. Ron McKenzie picked up the hobby stock feature win, while Joe Leek won his second street stock feature of the season.

In a winged sprint feature where the yellow flag never flew, it was Tony Ploughe flying out to the early lead. Randy Woodling and Kenny Haynes were running second and third when they both closed in on the leader. Haynes swung by both frontrunners on lap 5 to take over the top spot. Haynes extended his lead to take the checkered flag for the win. He was followed by Woodling, Steve Kline, Bimbo Atkins, Brett Mann, John Hadjuk, Russ Gamester and Ploughe.

Winged sprint heats were won by Denny England, Ken Weiland and Haynes, with the dash going to Hadjuk and Atkins taking a quick time of 14.45. England jumped out front of the B-Main to lead every lap for the win with Jesse Fordyce and Joe Davis next across the finish line.

David Baker took the early lead of the hobby stock feature until a charging Ron McKenzie quickly closed in for the pass with only three laps complete. McKenzie held off Andy Holderman to take the victory at the finish. Holderman was second, with Shane Denny, Larry Howard, Steve Holloway, Dick Day, Rusty Lowry and Dan Backus next across the finish line. Day and Holderman were hobby stock heat winners with McKenzie taking the dash win and fast time of 17.98.

In the street stock feature, William Varney passed leader Rex Long as he went from fourth to first on a restart early in the race. Joe Leek closed in on Varney near the end of the race, and the two ran side by side for several laps until Leek got by and took the win at the finish. Jon Ormsby placed second, followed by Arnold Prater, Randy Hines, Everett Caroll, Brian Hyden, Varney and Carl Kendricks. Long and Varney won the street stock heats.

Tuesday, June 12, 1990
Speedway To Close
Auto racing in Warsaw screeches to halt Aug. 11
By Dan Spalding, *Times-Union* Staff Writer

Racing at the Warsaw Speedway will end August 11, according to a tentative agreement between the Kosciusko County Fair Board and plaintiffs in a court suit who have sought to close the race track. The agreement calls for racing to discontinue after August 11—midway through the current racing season.

A statement from Don Goon, president of the fair board, explains that the agreement will prohibit any motorized racing on the dirt track. Representatives for the two sides are working on a final legal document. As a result of the tentative agreement, plans for a June 29 makeup race have been cancelled. Anyone who bought tickets for the rained-out All Star sprint car race of June 2 can have their money refunded, according to the statement.

Members of the fair association met Monday night, and the legal battle was discussed. The plaintiffs, nine homeowners along Winona Lake, filed suit in June, 1989. The case was moved to Fulton Circuit Court. A 10-day trial was set to begin in October, said Steve Snyder, attorney for the plaintiffs.

The plaintiffs contend that noise and dust from the Saturday night races interferes with their right to peace and quiet. The track is located at the Kosciusko County Fairgrounds on the north side of Winona Lake. Most of the plaintiffs live on the southwest side of the lake. Plaintiffs in the suit are James Cummins, Robert Fuson, Michael Hall, John Handel, George Haymond, Joe Shellabarger, Fred Stephens, Ken Truman and Rex Wildman.

According to several people close to the issue, the fair association initiated discussion of a possible agreement because attorney fees were draining the association's available funds. Already, the cost of retaining an attorney for preparation of the court suit has reached about $30,000, according to several sources. The attorney for the fair board is Ted Miller, Huntington. The association reportedly was told by their attorney that another $30,000 to $40,000 would be needed to complete the case.

Saturday, June 16, 1990
Atkins Wins Feature
By Kim Baney, For the *Times-Union*

In racing action Saturday night at the Warsaw Speedway it was Bimbo Atkins in car No. 36a taking a winged sprint feature win in a mad dash to the finish. Ron McKenzie won his second hobby stock feature of the season, while William Varney took home his first street stock feature of the season.

Kim Mock took off from his pole position start to grab the early lead in the winged sprint feature with Dennis Spitz and Atkins close behind. Jeff Walker, in fourth, closed in on the frontrunners, and both he and Atkins swung past Spitz and started to reel in on Mock for the lead. Suddenly, Mock lost power and pulled to the infield, leaving the lead up for grabs. Atkins and Walker raced side by side until the final lap when Atkins gained the edge in the fourth turn and went on to take the checkered flag for the victory. Walker came across the line in second and was followed by Steve Kline, Spitz, Dane Ronk, Tony Ploughe, Sam Davis and Rob Roberts.

Kenny Hayne, Roberts and Jesse Fordyce were winged sprint heat winners, with Haynes taking the dash and Fordyce the B-Main. Kline qualified with a 14.84 for the fastest time of the night.

McKenzie was not to be denied as he made his way up from the 10th starting position to the lead in only five laps. McKenzie passed early leader Scott Fitzpatrick and never looked back as he went on to take the win. Andy Holderman fought off Shane Denny for second with Denny, Steve Holloway, David Baker, Russ Lowry, Dick Day and Dan Backus rounding out the top eight. Winning the hobby stock heats was Rick Day, and the dash winner was Denny.

Varney made a clean sweep of the street stock events as he took the heat win and passed Jay Nordman on the sixth lap of the feature for the lead and the win at the finish. Jon Ormsby took second and was followed by Nordman, John Oliver, Carl Kendricks, Terry Elliott, Larry Howard and Joe Leek. This Saturday will be HARF Night for all Hoosier Auto Racing Fans with winged sprints, hobby stocks and street stocks.

Saturday, June 23, 1990
Racing Rained Out Again

For the fourth time in seven weeks, the Saturday night racing activities at the Warsaw Speedway were canceled due to the rainy weather. This leaves just one more qualifying race, this weekend, for the drivers to race for valuable points before the Mid-Season Championships July 7.

Kenny Haynes has a 55-point lead over Bimbo Atkins in the winged sprint class, while Ron McKenzie has a commanding lead over the field of hobby stocks. Joe Leek needs only 10 points to catch William Varney of the point lead in the street stocks.

Saturday will be the Fireworks and Racing Celebration and Warsaw Transmission Trophy Night. Racing action will begin at 7 p.m. and the fireworks will take place at intermission.

Saturday, June 30, 1990 - Rainout

Saturday, July 7, 1990
Plenty of Action at Warsaw Speedway

After the fireworks lit up the sky, the race cars lit up the track with Bimbo Atkins at the helm of the winged sprint feature winning car Saturday night at the Warsaw Speedway.

The 25-lap winged sprint feature was red flagged twice as multi-car pile-ups on the frontstretch occurred one after another when the field took the green for the start of the race. On the third attempt, the race started and Atkins pulled ahead of the pack. Kenny Haynes and Terry Starks battled for second and third spots but could not catch Atkins as he went on to win his second winged sprint feature in a row. Haynes finished second and was followed by Starks, Tony Ploughe, Sam Davis, Joe Davis, Van Gurley, Jr., and Brian Althouse.

Steve Imel was running in fourth position when, on the 19th lap, he swung too high in turn three and caught the wall just right propelling the car right up the track pole in between the third and fourth turns. Fortunately, all the drivers involved in the evening's incidents were uninjured. Winged sprint heat winners were Kevin Atkins and Starks while Bimbo Atkins took the dash and Steve Kline had the fast time of 14.93.

In hobby stock action, it was a battle between Dick Day and Dewayne May throughout the entire competition. Day grabbed the early lead and then, after several side-by-side laps, lost the lead to May on the ninth lap. Day regained the top spot three laps later and went on to win for the first time this season. May finished second and was followed by Shane Denny, Andy Holderman, David Baker, Doug Method, Rick Day and Russ Lowry. Method and Ron McKenzie were the hobby stock heat winners with Denny the dash winners and May with the quickest time of 18.20.

Don & Kelly Prater, Warsaw

William Varney was the early leader of the street stock feature until Arnold Prater closed in and took the lead on the third lap. Prater was in full control of the race when a tire came off leaving Prater in the infield the lead wide open. Joe Leek took advantage of the situation to take over the lead and the win at the finish. Harvey Hayes was second and was followed by Varney, Kelly Prater,

Larry Hayden, Ron Smith, Arnold Prater and Jon Ormsby. Street stock heat winners were Kelly Prater and Leek, while the dash went to Varney and the fastest time was turned in by Arnold Prater.

This Saturday will be the Mid-Season Championships for all three classes of cars and all the racing action begins at 7 p.m.

Saturday, July 14, 1990
Atkins Wins Again At Speedway
By Kim Baney, *Times-Union* Sports Writer

Bimbo Atkins proved that he was deserving of the trophy as he won his third winged sprint feature in a row and took over the points lead Saturday night during the Mid-Season Championship at the Warsaw Speedway.

Kenny Haynes jumped out front of the 40-lap feature, with Atkins and Tony Ploughe next in line. The three continued in their positions until misfortune struck Haynes on the 15th lap, leaving him in the infield with a broken line. Atkins took over the lead and held on for his third win in a row. Ploughe held off several late charges from Brett Mann to place second. Other finishers were Ron Roberts, Blake Hollingsworth, Kevin Atkins, Denny England and Art Wendt. Randy Woodling, Holllingsworth and Wendt were winged sprint heat winners, while Terry Starks grabbed the four-lap dash.

The early leader syndrome struck again in the hobby stock feature as Ron McKenzie suddenly lost his lead to a flat tire on the eighth lap. Shane Denny, running a close second, picked up the lead and held off Andy Holderman to win his first feature of the season. Holderman took second and was followed by Dick Day, Larry Howard, Scott Fitzpatrick, Doug Method, Rick Day and Tom Leiter.

Flagman, Dale Bolinger & William Varney

The hobby stock heat wins went to David Baker and McKenzie. McKenzie also was the dash winner.

William Varney jumped out front of the street stock feature from the drop of the green flag and led every lap en route to his second feature race of the year. Arnold Prater challenged the leader near the end of the race, but had to settle for second place. Kelly Prater placed third and was followed by heat and dash winner Joe Leek, Harvey Hayes, Jay Nordman, Terry Elliott and Larry Hyden.

Thursday, July 19, 1990
Warsaw Speedway To Close
Fairboard Approves out-of-court pact; racing ends Aug. 11.
By Dan Spalding, *Times-Union* Staff Writer

An agreement to close the Warsaw speedway has been approved, according to a source who asked not to be identified. Members of the Kosciusko County Fair Association approved the agreement Wednesday night. The vote was 8 to 3, the source said. The source could not confirm whether the agreement had been signed. The three no votes came from fair association members Don Hostetler, Ann Schaefer and Larry Yeiter.

Under terms of the agreement, Saturday night racing at the Kosciusko County Fairgrounds—a tradition that has lasted almost 35 years—will conclude August 11. The agreement to close the track ends the threat of a court battle between nine Winona Lake residents and the fair association. Fair board president Don Goon this morning refused to comment on the agreement. A prepared statement from the fair association was not available at press time.

The plaintiffs agreed Monday to the proposal, and then awaited the fair association's approval, said attorney Steve Snyder. Snyder said early today he was unaware the agreement had been approved by the fair board.

The agreement did not include a stipulation prohibiting activities that exceed a 55-decibel noise level. A preliminary agreement had been reached in mid-June, but negotiations hit a snag when the plaintiffs sought the decibel limit. Certain types of activities will be permitted during fair week, Snyder said. He did not elaborate, and a copy of the agreement was not available late this morning.

The Winona Lake area residents filed suit a year ago in an attempt to close the track because of noise and dust that results from racing. They had sought to close the track permanently and asked for damages totaling $500,000. The case was scheduled to go to trial in October in Fulton Circuit Court. Plaintiffs in the suit are James Cummins, Robert Fuson, Michael Hall, John Handel, George Haymond, Joe Shellabarger, Fred Stephens, Ken Truman and Rex Wildman.

Friday, July 20, 1990
Race Fans Frustrated By Decision
By Dan Spalding—*Times-Union* Staff writer

One week ago, Gene Gregory was eager about getting involved in a court battle to keep the Warsaw speedway open. On Thursday his hopes ended after learning the fair association agreed to discontinue motorized racing as part of an out-of-court settlement with a group of residents who sought to close the track.

"There was support galore," Gregory said. It didn't make any difference. They were ready to hang it up no matter what. It's just a frustrating situation."

Gregory, who has been involved in racing for almost 41 years, had gathered about $6,000 in pledges in a matter of hours last week. He told the fair association he could raise more if they would kill plans for a tentative settlement and test the case in court.

But on Wednesday, the fair board approved an agreement with nine plaintiffs to end motorized racing at the fairgrounds race track Aug. 11. Nine Winona Lake residents filed suit a year ago seeking to close the track. The plaintiffs also sought $500,000 in damages.

Gregory's offer was an indication of growing local support for the track and animosity toward those who sought to close it. Pledges were made from a local restaurant company, a retail business and several residents. More was on the way, he said.

"The people were mad. They were willing to do anything, Gregory said. I'm confident we could have raised a lot of money."

Gregory talked with fair association members prior to their decision and said he believed they did not understand the issue, and that some did not care if the track remained open. Despite the pledges, long time fair association member John Hall said it was too little, too late. Hall said they were told that $20,000 to $100,000 would be needed for attorney fees. The Association already had paid about $30,000. The case was scheduled to go to court in October. "Financially, we just couldn't continue. It's difficult for non-profit organizations to enter into litigation", Hall said.

Fair members will try to organize events at the fairgrounds that are permitted under the agreement. Tractor and truck pulls are allowed under the agreement during fair week. Rodeos and concerts may be scheduled for other parts of the year, Hall said. With the court case out of the way, the fair association is now expected to concentrate on asking the county to establish a tax levy to support the fairgrounds.

Author's Note: Although Dad couldn't publically say who was willing to foot the bill for the Speedway attorney fees, the main three more than willing to fight for the track didn't bat an eye at the possibility of contributing $100,000 to legal fees and the fair board knew this. There was also an offer to contact a prominent racing lawyer that they turned down.

Saturday, July 21, 1990
As The Dust Settles On Warsaw Speedway
Potpourri – By The *Times-Union* Staff

Racing Noises - The engines of race cars aren't the only things whining around Winona Lake these days. At least three of the nine plaintiffs in the Warsaw Speedway suit are upset with coverage of the issue by the Times-Union. We won't use their names because we're sure they'd rather have their "names withheld by request." One of them refused an opportunity to comment Thursday when our reporter called. Another was later heard to say our coverage was unfair and that he was going to talk to TV 22 and the Journal-Gazette, which he did. Interesting. The Journal-Gazette ran the story a day later—on page two of the second section. The TV station didn't carry the subject until Friday night. If this individual would have talked to us, he would have made page 1—a whole day earlier.

Another of the plaintiffs claims they were "tried in the newspaper." Apparently, he expects us not to publish letters to the editor that don't support his position. Or maybe he thinks we should just ignore an important community issue. Can anyone honestly remember a more talked about issue in Warsaw in recent memory?

The Times-Union was obligated to its readers to publish the letters to the editor and to cover the issue comprehensively, which is exactly what we did. You'd think these guys would be happy. They won.

The fair association wasn't eager to talk either. It seemed as if no one involved wanted to see anything in the newspaper, and both sides were upset with our coverage. This brings to mind an old theory in the newspaper business. If you've got both sides mad at you, you must be doing your job.

Where is Winona, anyway? The Times-Union received a call Thursday from Winona Lake resident and state legislator Dave Wolkins. He said Winona Lake residents are upset by the fact that the nine plaintiffs in the speedway suit were referred to as Winona Lake residents. Apparently they (Winona Lake residents) don't want to be associated with them (Winona Lake residents). For the record, none of the plaintiffs has a Winona Lake address, but they all live on or near a body of water by the same name. This appears to be a case of Winona Lake residents disowning Winona Lake residents. Can't anybody out there be nice to these nine guys?

WASP Money - WASP spokesman Lloyd Smith said remaining funds from money collected by the race track support group will be donated to the points fund, which is distributed to the top race drivers. Some fair officials have questioned what happened to the money collected during the past year. Smith said the funds were used for newsletters, a candy chase and two picnics. And yes, the group will be disbanded, he said.

Picnic - In a related note, a fan picnic is planned by the Warsaw Speedway at the county fairgrounds on July 28. The picnic will begin at 2:30 p.m. and fans are asked to bring a covered dish and blankets or lawn chairs. Meat, buns, tableware and drink will be furnished.

Saturday, July 21, 1990
Atkins Wins Again
By Kim Baney, *Times-Union* Correspondent

Bimbo Atkins did it again as he powered his 36a winged sprint into victory lane for his fourth straight feature win in a row Saturday night at the Warsaw Speedway.

In the winged sprint feature action, Atkins took advantage of his pole position start to gain the lead from the drop of the green flag. Brett Mann started to reel in on Atkins on the eighth lap and closed in for a side-by-side battle on the 17th lap, but Atkins held off Mann and took the checkered flag for the win. Mann took second and was followed by Jeff Walker, Kenny Haynes, Rob Roberts, Kevin

Atkins, Tony Ploughe and Van Gurley.

Sam Davis, Bimbo Atkins and Terry Sroufe in his first sprint win ever were winged sprint heat winners, with Mann being the dash winner. Gurley was the quickest qualifier with a 14.80 clocking.

Dewayne May jumped out front of the hobby stock feature but was quickly overcome by a charging Ron McKenzie. McKenzie extended his lead until near the halfway mark of the race, when May started a comeback and closed in on the leader. With one lap to go the two were side-by-side, but McKenzie pulled ahead in the final turn to take his third win of the season. May took second and was followed by Dick Day, Rick Day, Roger Fitzpatrick, David Baker, Russ Lowry, and Doug Method. McKenzie ended the night with a clean sweep as he also took the dash, heat and fast time (18.17) honors. Ron Norman won the second of the hobby stock heats.

In the street stock feature, Arnold Prater pulled ahead for the early lead and held off early race challenges by William Prater en route to his first feature win of the season. Joe Leek took second and was followed by Larry Hyden, Scott Shaske, Jim Varney, Terry Elliott and Randy Himes. Ron Brandenburg and Arnold Prater were the street stock heat winners and Harvey Hayes was the fastest qualifier.

Saturday, July 28, 1990
Woodling, McKenzie Get Feature Wins
By Kim Baney, *Times-Union* Correspondent

Randy Woodling in his No. 75 winged sprint and Ron McKenzie in the No. 24 hobby stock, were joyous but exhausted feature winners Saturday night at the Warsaw Speedway in some of the closest racing of the season.

The winged sprint feature saw Bimbo Atkins jump out front from his front row start and lead the early laps of the 25-lap race. Woodling and Jeff Walker were close behind. On lap nine, Atkins got up on two wheels in the fourth turn and landed hard on the dirt surface, putting his car out of the competition. Woodling and Walker took over the top spots and battled nose to tail and side by side for the duration of the contest, but Woodling continued to lead lap after lap and took the checkered flag for his first feature win of the season. Walker took third and following him were: Brett Mann, Van Gurley, Kevin Atkins, Joe Davis, Tony Ploughe and Sam Davis. Davis, Jesse Fordyce and Kevin Atkins were winged sprint heat winners, with Woodling being the dash winner. Davis was the B-Main winner and Mann took the fastest time of the night with a 15.41 clocking.

In hobby stock action, Ron Norman got the early lead until Dewayne May closed in and passed Norman with only three laps completed. McKenzie made his way through the pack of frontrunners to close in on May and race side by side with the leader for several laps. McKenzie finally found some added speed and pulled ahead near the end of the race to take the lead and win at the finish. May took second and was followed by Kyle Howard, Tom Leiter, Roger Fitzpatrick, Norman, Doug Method, and Shane Denny. May took the first of two hobby stock heat wins, the dash and had the fastest time of 19.59. Scott Fitzpatrick won the second hobby stock heat.

Street stock heat winners were Arnold Prater and Ron Brandenburg. The street stock feature was called due to the curfew, but it will be run as the first event this Saturday. This week will also be the Season Championship for all three classes of cars with all the racing action beginning at 7 p.m.

Saturday, August 4, 1990
Warsaw Speedway Notes

For the sixth time this season the racing action at the Warsaw Speedway was rained out Saturday. The season championships that were scheduled for last week will be run this Saturday during the final racing event at the 42-year-old track. This event will conclude the fair week attractions and will feature winged sprints, mini sprints, hobby stocks and street stocks for one last unforgettable night of racing.

The point standings going into the championships have Bimbo Atkins with a 120-point lead over Kenny Haynes in the winged sprint division. Ron McKenzie has a comfortable 295-point lead over Shane Denny in the hobby stock division, and Joe Leek has a slim 40-point lead over William Varney in the street stock class. The top 10-point leaders will receive awards for their accomplishments after the final race Saturday night. Gates will open at 4 p.m. with the first race slated to begin at 8 p.m.

Saturday, August 11, 1990
Final Weekend Provided Action
By Kim Baney, *Times-Union* Correspondent

The last race ever at the Warsaw Speedway came and went in fitting fashion as Jeff Walker took his winged sprint to victory lane for the first time this season in front of the largest crowd in years.

Season points champion, Bimbo Atkins, started on the pole of the 40-lap championship race, and led from the drop of the green

Dale "Termite" Bolinger, Jeff Walker, Max Lambert

Photo by Gary Neiter, Times Union

flag with Kenny Haynes and Jeff Walker close behind. Walker passed Haynes for second on the 18th lap and by the halfway mark, was side-by-side with Atkins for the lead. Haynes got by Atkins on the last lap for second spot followed by Atkins, Van Gurley, Brett Mann, Todd Kelly, Randy Woodling, and Kevin Atkins. The race was halted twice as Scott Hull brought out the red flag on the opening The last race ever at the Warsaw Speedway came and went in fitting fashion as Jeff Walker took his winged sprint to victory lane for the first time this season in front of the largest crowd in years.

Season points champion, Bimbo Atkins, started on the pole of the 40-lap championship race, and led from the drop of the green flag with Kenny Haynes and Jeff Walker close behind. Walker passed Haynes for second on the 18th lap and by the halfway mark, was side-by-side with Atkins for the lead. Haynes got by Atkins on the last lap for second spot followed by Atkins, Van Gurley, Brett Mann, Todd Kelly, Randy Woodling, and Kevin Atkins.

The race was halted twice as Scott Hull brought out the red flag on the opening lap when he barrel-rolled his sprint down the backstretch. Kevin Atkins was running in the fourth position when he flipped his sprint on its side in the third turn to bring out the second red flag of the race. Neither driver was injured and Atkins was able to continue racing. Kelly, Steve Kline, and Ken Weiland were winged sprint heat winners, while Mann took the dash.

In hobby stock feature action, Ron McKenzie grabbed the early lead of the 30-lap contest and led until mid-race when Dewayne May closed in to run nose to tail, then side by side with McKenzie. May gained the lead, but ran out of fuel nine laps later putting him and a pitting McKenzie on the tail. McKenzie fought his way through the field to regain the lead and finish with his fifth feature win of the season and the season championship. Dick Day placed second with Larry Howard, May, Alan Day, David Baker, and Shane Denny rounding out the top finishers. May and Ron Norman were hobby stock heat winners

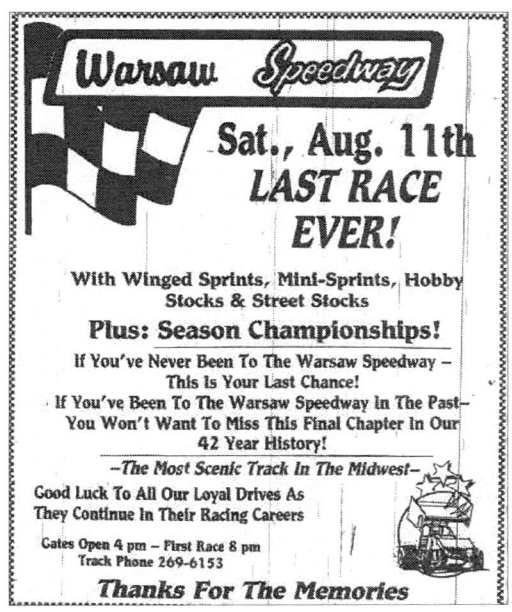

> **Warsaw Speedway**
>
> **Sat., Aug. 11th**
> **LAST RACE EVER!**
>
> With Winged Sprints, Mini-Sprints, Hobby Stocks & Street Stocks
>
> **Plus: Season Championships!**
>
> If You've Never Been To The Warsaw Speedway – This Is Your Last Chance!
> If You've Been To The Warsaw Speedway In The Past – You Won't Want To Miss This Final Chapter In Our 42 Year History!
>
> –The Most Scenic Track In The Midwest–
>
> Good Luck To All Our Loyal Drives As They Continue In Their Racing Careers
>
> Gates Open 4 pm – First Race 8 pm
> Track Phone 269-6153
>
> **Thanks For The Memories**

with McKenzie being the dash winner.

In the survival of the fittest street stock feature, Harvey Hayes made his way through the field from the back of the pack to finish on top for his first feature win of the season. Early race leaders, Joe Leek and Arnold Prater, ended up watching the finish of the race from the infield. Jim Nutter placed second followed by William Varney, Terry Elliott, Scott Shaske, Leek, Mike Fouts and Prater. Season champion, Leek, took the rained-out street stock feature after a long battle with Prater. Randy Himes took second and Jay Nordman was third. Nutter and Varney were street stock heat winners with the dash going to Prater. Jim Hughes won the mini-sprint feature with Ken Hughes and Randy Yates taking second and third.

Good luck to all the loyal drivers as they continue their racing careers at other racing homes. A special thanks goes out to all of the fans who supported family racing for 42 years.

Monday, August 11, 1990
Black Flag Falls On Warsaw Auto Racing
By Jim Walker, *Times-Union* Staff Intern, Pgs. 1-2

At about 1:30 a.m. Sunday, engines roared for the last time at the Warsaw Speedway. More than 4,000 fans packed the speedway Saturday evening to enjoy the final race in the speedway's 42-year history. There wasn't a hint of the rain showers that canceled seven race nights earlier this season.

"There's never a good night for the races to go out," said Warsaw Speedway race promoter Don Prater, "But the weather isn't bad and we've got a great crowd. Everybody's enjoying themselves."

Prater said the crowd is usually large during the week, but Saturday's crowd was one of the biggest in recent years. "Even the back-stretch parking was full," he said. The track has been averaging around 1,800 fans each week this season.

Race fans were given a special treat Saturday night, as a midget sprint class was added. Fans and area residents may have also noticed that the cars were louder than usual, as race drivers removed mufflers as a form of protest.

And as a symbolic gesture, race officials refused to use the traditional checkered flag, instead opting for a black and a white flag. Prater said that the night marked the end of a family tradition. He has driven at the track in the past and his son Kelly ran a car this year. The closing of the track is going to leave a hollow spot in our lives. And in the lives of a lot of people here, Prater said.

Tom Leiter has been driving at the speedway for 25 years. His father, grandfather, cousins, uncle and brothers all drove at the speedway over the years. "I used to sit up in the grandstand and watch my dad drive. It's something that my family has always been involved in," Leiter said. "People have been coming here for generations."

Howard Woodward brought his children and grandchildren to the races during the 42 years he's been a fan at Warsaw Speedway. "It's something we've enjoyed as a family. This is a family track. You don't see drinking or fighting here like you do at other tracks. It's good family fun," Woodward said. "All the kids are race fans now. This was a great place to bring them. It's going to be something we'll miss," Woodward said.

Woodward said he and his family will go to other tracks to enjoy racing on the weekends next summer. Warsaw Speedway race drivers also said they will also find a new place to run Saturdays next year. "We'll keep going somewhere next year," noted Sam Davis, a driver at Warsaw for 26 years." "It will be different because Saturday was always the night we came to Warsaw during the summer." "Everybody who comes a-ways to race here has made the long trip on Saturday. They've done it for years, now it's our turn," Davis said.

Race drivers and fans are hoping that a new track will be built in Warsaw someday. "I think the racers and the fans could get together to build a new racetrack here, Leiter said. "There's terrific fan support here. Somebody who wanted to invest a little could end up making a lot of money."

The decision to close the track was made in an out-of-court settlement between the county fair board and a group of nine Winona Lake area residents who sought to close the track through litigation. The nine plaintiffs—James Cummins, Robert Fuson, Michael Hall, John Handel, George Haymond, Joe Shellabarger, Fred Stephens, Ken Truman and Rex Wildman—sued the fair board in June of 1989. They asked that the track be permanently closed and sought $500,000 damages. The out-of-court settlement was reached last month. It did not include payment of any damages by the fair board.

Twelve-year-old race fan Ben Meyers said he's going to miss the races in Warsaw, but he still has hope for a new speedway. "My dad said if we win a million dollars in the lottery we are going to build a new track in Warsaw."

But for now, racing in Warsaw is just a memory.

Saturday, August 18, 1990
Speedway Memories

One week after the closing of the Warsaw Speedway, and all the remains are memories. Some 4,000 fans turned out for the final night of racing on August 11 for the laps around the dirt track.

"Nights of Thunder" would most likely fit the description by Winona Lake residents of the traditional races that had continued for 42 years. The group of nine residents successfully shut down the track by way of an out of court settlement last month. They had complained about noise, dust and an uncooperative race track management.

Racing brought to Warsaw a form of entertainment, visitors and money. For the drivers, fans and family, there are only memories now. For the lake residents, there is a new-found level of peace and quiet on Saturday nights.

After 30 years, the closing of the track is still felt in the community and a sore subject for many that loved the track and called it home. It was a rare venue where no alcohol was served giving the track a family atmosphere and yet, the stands were packed week in and week out. All classes of racing were family and genuinely cared about each other. Although several attempts to revive racing in Warsaw have been pursued, they've always ended up in controversy or additional lawsuits from local lake residents, so to date, the most scenic speedway in the Midwest sits quietly along the north shore of Winona Lake full of memories and stories that can never be taken away.

Monday, August 13, 1990
Race Track
Editor, *Times-Union*:

The faint smell of exhaust fumes, the dirt sticking to your face on a warm summer night, and the checkered flag waving in victory are gone now as we say goodbye to our dear friend, the Warsaw Speedway.

For the speedway her smell will still remain, her memories will linger over the dirt surface they now plan to use for other "fund-raising" activities. For many, there will never be another experience like she has given us. If only the concrete walls and bleachers could talk.

I feel sorry for the nine lakeside residents and the 15 or so fair board members involved in the closing of our speedway. Men and women who would not compromise nor communicate for more than 10 years. Now we, the ones who love this place and what it stands for, must now suffer the consequences. This situation was not inevitable. It could have been settled years ago to where everyone would benefit from the existence. Now we're all losers, from the nine "Bad Boys of Boomtown" to the fair board trying to keep their head above "Winona" water.

I grew up with Saturday nights at the racetrack and for the past seven years, I have been fortunate enough to have a closer involvement with the racing activity at the track. My thanks to the promoters, Monty Miller, Dee Chapman and Don Prater for this opportunity to work at a job that was a joy and to meet hundreds of fans, drivers, and media personalities.

So as the dust settles over the most scenic track in the Midwest, I will feel a deep sickness in the pit of my stomach for what this city has allowed to happen. I am sure that somehow, somewhere, the dirty dealings that closed this wonderful institution will be justly rendered.

They can take our facility and our fun away from us, but they can never take the friendships that have developed over the last 42 years.

I wish good luck to all the drivers as they continue their racing careers elsewhere and to all the fans as they try to find another racing home.

Kim Gregory Baney
Warsaw Speedway
Public Relations Director

Warsaw Speedway
Season Points Champions

1949	N/A		
1950	N/A		
1951	N/A		
1952	N/A		
1953			
1954	Art Johnson, Stock Cars #81		
1955	Jim Hullinger, Stock Cars #99		
1956	Jim Hullinger, Stock Cars #99	Dick Leiter, Strickly Stock #0	
1957			
1958			
1959	Bob Staley, Modified #80	Max Lambert, Stock #0	
1960	Jim Kirby, Modified		
1961	Ray Kenens, Modified #4	John Davis, Stock #44	
1962			
1963			
1964			
1965	Paul Hazen, Modified #57	Dick Leiter #66 Luther Holloway #51 Tie - Semi-Late Stock	
1966	Les Bills, Modified #22		
1967			
1968			
1969	Jimmie Elliott, Modified #57		
1970	Jimmie Elliott, Sprint #57		
1971	Jimmie Elliott, Sprint #57	Art Smith, Late Model #67	Dennis Hopper, Hobby Stock
1972	Jimmie Elliott, Sprint #57	Les Sroufe, Semi-Late Model #11	Jerry Baker, Hobby Stock #66
1973	Lou Mann, Sprint #57	Art Smith, Late Model #67	Jerry Baker, Hobby Stock #66
1974	Ron Miller, Sprint #68		
1975	Rocky Fisher, Sprint #6	Arden Leiter, Late Model #87	Jerry Baker, Hobby Stock #66
1976	Ron Miller, Sprint #68	Kenny Leiter, Late Model	Terry Baker, Hobby Stock #31
1977	No Sprints		
1978	No Sprints		

1979	Lou Mann, Sprint #57	John White, Late Model #87	Barry Lemons, Sportsman #71
1980	Van Gurley, Sprint #3B	Tom Beezley, Late Model #69	Bob King, Sportsman #53
1981	Lou Mann, Sprint #57		
1982	Denny England, Sprint #84		
1983	Tony Elliott, Sprint #57	Randy Woodling, Street Stock #33	
1984	DeWayne Barker, Sprint #33B	Randy Woodling, Limited Late Model #33	
1985	DeWayne Barker, Sprint #33B	Allen Marsh, Limited Late Model #75	Harvey Hayes, Roadrunner #49
1986	Denny England, Sprint #84	Butch Boggs, Limited Late Model #14	Robert Johnson, Roadrunner #22
1987	Denny England, Sprint #84	Roger Grossnickle, Limited Late Model #17	Jay Nordman, Roadrunner #56
1988	Denny England, Sprint #84	Ron McKenzie / Dane Ronk, Limited Late Model #24	Shane Denny, Roadrunner #58
1989	Bimbo Atkins, Sprint #36a	Glenn Bradley, Late Model #22	Shane Denny, Street Stock #58
1990	Bimbo Atkins, Sprint #36a	Ron McKenzie, Hobby Stock #24	Joe Leek, Street Stock

Special Thanks To Photo And Program Contributors

Vickie Adams-Carter
Bret & Jeanna Backus
Steve Backus
Brian Barger
Rodney Bills
Teresa Bills
Doris Boggs
Travis Boggs
Ron Creech & Linda Creech Stayer
John Crum
Tony Elliott
Carol Engel
Ary Gibson
Madaline & Gene Gregory
Paul Grim
Roger Grossnickle
John Gurley
Lynn Hart Rose
Larry Hawkins
Robert Noel Head
Steven & Bruce Hogue
Davey Howe
Robert Johnson, Jr.
Greg Jones
Juni Krontz
Dick and Tom Leiter
Kevin Oldham
Ginnie & John Ong, John Ong Jr.
Susan Pierce & her dad, Don Walker
Larry Plummer
Kelly Prater
Roger Rowland II

Back cover photo taken on August 11, 1990
Used by permission ~ Oswalt Aeriel Photo

Wayne Bryant photos are used by permission
from the Ted Rockwell Collection

1987-1988 G&J Photos used by permission

1989-1990 photos used by permission
Contact David Hamrick at: david@thepartyshop.com for photo
copies or enlargements from those years.

Acknowledgements

This book represents the work and support of more people than I could hope to thank, but I feel special mention needs to go to:

My mom, Madaline Gregory, and my daughter, Ashley, who jumped on board with hours of retyping race articles into computer format. They truly made this a three-generation work of love. It was a joy to listen to my mom re-live those nights and hear her memories from her 1950's/60's race scoring & timing years as she typed up the stories.

My dad...who gave me the passion for motorsports and taught me that you can do anything you want if you have the courage to start and are smart enough to ask questions ~ his quote.

My husband, Kevin, for listening to me talk about this for 25 years, driving with me across the state to meet race drivers and fans for photos and stories, and putting up with all of my enthusiastic energy.

My son, Taylor, for listening to me talk about this forever as well, giving his insight and ideas, and providing his technical assistance fixing my mom's computer over and over again so she could keep typing away.

My dear friend and kindred spirit Bob, who shares my passion for adventure and creativity. You saw my dream and cheered me along the way ~ thank you.

The Times Union and Gary Gerard, General Manager for his guidance and positive encouragement.

The Warsaw Community Public Library for graciously letting me camp-out with their microfiche machine.

Paul Smith, The Times Union; Kip Schumm, The Papers; The Beebe Family, Marc Times Racing News; and Chris Economaki, National Speed Sport News; for the hundreds of hours I spent on the phone with all of you years ago week in and week out promoting this special place. You were all such a joy and I never tired of working with you.

Milo Clase, for without Milo's dedication to the speedway and anonymous writing of results articles every week for dozens of years, there would be no history to read.

Kim works full-time in the medical device industry, and during the summer you can find her at the Plymouth Speedway, in Plymouth, Indiana helping with their weekly timing & scoring.

She also stays busy with her hobbies which include drawing & painting, trumpet playing in her local symphony and wind ensembles, Jeep trail driving, traveling, and experiencing racing adventures.

Kim lives in Warsaw with her husband, Kevin, and 3 dogs. She has two grown children and one granddaughter.

Powder Puff Flagging, 1983 Warsaw Speedway

Muscle Car Challenge, Las Vegas

Dirt Racing Experience, Plymouth

Made in the USA
Middletown, DE
28 October 2022